10th Edition

MANAGEMENT
A Competency-Based Approach

Don Hellriegel
Mays Business School
Texas A&M University

Susan E. Jackson
School of Management and Labor Relations
Rutgers University

John W. Slocum, Jr.
Edwin L. Cox School of Business
Southern Methodist University

THOMSON
™
SOUTH-WESTERN

Australia · Canada · Mexico · Singapore · Spain · United Kingdom · United States

THOMSON

SOUTH-WESTERN

Management: A Competency-Based Approach, 10/e

Don Hellriegel, Susan E. Jackson, and John W. Slocum, Jr.

VP/Editorial Director:
Jack W. Calhoun

VP/Editor-in-Chief:
Michael P. Roche

Acquisitions Editor:
Joseph A. Sabatino

Developmental Editor:
Leslie Kauffman, Litten Editing
and Production, Inc.

Marketing Manager:
Jacque Carrillo

Production Editor:
Margaret M. Bril

Media Developmental Editor:
Kristen Meere

Media Production Editor:
Karen Schaffer

Manufacturing Coordinator:
Rhonda Utley

Production House:
Cover to Cover Publishing, Inc.

Compositor:
Janet Sprowls,
Cover to Cover Publishing, Inc.

Printer:
Transcontinental Interglobe
Beauceville-Quebec, Canada G5X 3P3

Design Project Manager:
Tippy McIntosh

Cover and Internal Designer:
Tippy McIntosh

Cover Images:
Photodisc

Photography Manager:
John Hill

Photo Researcher:
Sam Marshall

COPYRIGHT © 2005
by South-Western, a division of
Thomson Learning. Thomson
Learning™ is a trademark used
herein under license.

Printed in Canada
1 2 3 4 5 07 06 05 04

ISBN: 0-324-25994-8 (Pkg)
       0-324-28228-1 (text only)

Library of Congress
Control Number:
2003109600

For permission to use material from
this text or product, contact us by
Tel (800) 730-2214
Fax (800) 730-2215
http://www.thomsonrights.com

For more information contact
South-Western,
5191 Natorp Boulevard,
Mason, Ohio 45040.

Or you can visit our Internet site at:
http://www.swlearning.com

To Lois (DH)
To Randall (SEJ)
To Gail and Billie (JWS)

Brief Contents

Contents

Part 2   Managing the Environment 67

Chapter 3

Chapter 4

Chapter
5

Chapter

10

Chapter

13

Chapter
16

Photo Credits

Preface

OUR VISION

Our vision for the tenth edition of *Management: A Competency-Based Approach* is to present a current and comprehensive management text that guides the professional development of students. One way we do this is through a set of six core managerial competencies. Through *competencies*, students develop understanding, skills, insights, knowledge, judgment, and intuition that enable them to become effective managers. This vision required us to identify and present the competencies needed by both employees and managers in 21st-century organizations. Our vision of nourishing *competencies* guided every aspect of this edition—from text content, to special features, to design, to the supplemental enrichment materials. Throughout this preface, we convey the many ways this book implements our vision.

The text is packed with updated and new competency-building features, interesting cases, and intriguing insights. They enable students to experience the excitement of contemporary organizational and managerial concepts, methods, and practices. Real-world examples are brought into the classroom throughout the text. We include fresh, relevant coverage of managers and organizations that will be meaningful to students. In keeping with this reality-based perspective, we focus on *telling it like it is as well as telling it like it should be.* Students will learn from the many applications of methods, practices, and concepts.

In addition, we go beyond text presentations by challenging students to develop deeper insights and a portfolio of competencies. That way, students who study this text should come away equipped with enriched competencies, insights that they can use to develop their own competencies, and the confidence they need to develop their own professional potential.

Our editorial team at South-Western/Thomson Learning has continued and improved upon the vision of creating and implementing an *integrated learning system.* This system supports the process by which students may acquire the competencies they will need upon graduation as professionals and team members, and eventually as team leaders or managers. These two visions are mutually supportive. It was a continuing challenge and learning experience in implementing our vision through the student-oriented *integrated learning system.* This required close coordination with the ancillaries' authors. The results are well worth the added demands along the way. The harmonious merging of our *competency vision with the integrated learning system* vision will delight students and instructors.

We offer a wide variety of support materials for both instructors and students. Our support package assists instructors in their teaching and engages students in learning about management. Information about these materials is presented in this preface and at the book's home page (http://hellriegel.swlearning.com), and is also available from your South-Western/Thomson sales representative.

OUR STRATEGY

Management: A Competency-Based Approach and its support package are tailored for use in introductory management classes taught at any level in the university as well as in junior colleges. Our strategy and the reasons for considering the adoption of *Management: A Competency-Based Approach* are set forth in the following sections.

Student Learning

Students will engage with this book. It's very current and will capture their interest through a variety of methods, including competency features, cases, and self-evaluation questionnaires. It presents an inviting internal design and useful graphics. Examples used throughout the book assist in making discussions in and out of the classroom lively. In addition, the examples help to spark independent exploration. Students need to be challenged to think actively and creatively about real-life issues. *Management: A Competency-Based Approach* achieves that goal.

Management fundamentals are provided and examined in informative, concise, and engaging language appropriate for today's managers. We are not evasive, and we do not hesitate to challenge conventional management practices. This book provides a stimulating experience for students. It guides them well as they learn about management and build their management competencies.

Our commitment to student learning and development is evident throughout the text. The Questions for Discussion and Competency Development section at the end of each chapter calls upon students' thoughtful analysis rather than mere restatement of the material read. The Cases for Competency Development presented at the end of each chapter enable students to take more away from the course than simply a new and improved vocabulary and a general understanding of various management theories. These cases demand that students diagnose problems facing managers and organizations and present thoughtful analyses and reflections. The Exercises for Competency Development presented at the end of most chapters invite students to diagnose various issues in relation to their own experiences, observations, and self-assessments. Active learning requires students to approach problems and issues intelligently and to use self-insight to gauge their responses to management issues. This is a powerful tool. Our text compels students to actively learn and to engage in acquiring managerial competencies.

Our use of *learning objectives* is a pedagogy that adds value, guides students, and reinforces active learning. Every chapter in *Management: A Competency-Based Approach* begins with a statement of *Learning Objectives* and is organized to allow students to meet each objective. Repetition of each objective in the text where content specific to that objective is covered provides opportunities for self-testing and review. Every chapter ends with a Summary that distills the chapter's main points. This summary is organized around the chapter's *Learning Objectives* so that students can easily assess their mastery of the topics presented.

Managerial Competencies

We merge the concerns of managers with the managerial competencies that foster excellence. To appreciate the role of managers today and in the years ahead, a solid understanding of the competencies needed to manage is essential. There are a number of managerial competencies. We focus on six core and vital managerial competencies, including:

- self-management,
- strategic action,
- global awareness,
- teamwork,
- planning and administration, and
- communication.

These competencies can be learned through study, practice, and feedback. Of course, feedback often comes in bits and pieces. In *Management: A Competency-Based Approach*, we create a meaningful whole out of the pieces of information that are seldom related to students' performance or to a team's performance. Students benefit by having the competencies defined and clarified to foster early success in their careers. Throughout the book in a series of specially designed competency boxes, we present students with a variety of ways that they can assess their competencies now and begin to develop their potential as effective managers. We have developed an assessment instrument—provided on a CD-ROM that accompanies this text—for students to use. After completing this instrument, students can compare their development stages with those of hundreds of other students and practicing managers.

Self-Management Competency. Competent managers know that self-awareness is a crucial vantage point from which to view the operation of an organization and his or her role in that organization. Self-identification of strengths and developmental needs is an important first step in the process of learning to manage others. Our presentation of the self-management competency assists students in identifying their own strengths and developmental needs in leadership, motivation, ethics, and other areas. We achieve this through the text material, experiential exercises, and cases. Besides learning about their current strengths and developmental needs, students gain an appreciation for the importance of continual self-assessment throughout their careers.

Strategic Action Competency. Competent managers craft creative strategies to guide an organization. Strategies are the major courses of action selected and implemented to achieve goals. Risk accompanies all strategic decisions, but the competent manager acts to devise contingency plans to minimize those risks. Our discussion of the strategic action competency demonstrates how managers of many types of organizations actually develop and apply unique strategies to achieve a competitive advantage.

Global Awareness Competency. Competent managers stay abreast of important trends among and across nations that have potential impacts on their organizations. They diagnose how well their organizations are faring in global markets. This competency challenges students to recognize the impact of global trends on an organization's plans and growth. The challenges of global expansion and operating in foreign countries demand that students question their own leadership styles, values, and management practices within their own countries. The main factors for successfully doing business internationally are being sensitive to key cultural, political, and economic differences in countries in which an organization operates and assessing the consequences of those differences for the organization.

Teamwork Competency. Competent managers are able to cultivate an active network of relationships and to work well in diverse teams. The teamwork competency involves creating a healthy environment by forming give-and-take relationships, striving to enhance mutual understanding and respect, acknowledging the needs and feelings of others, and managing conflict productively. Competent managers rely on others to help them achieve organizational goals. Managers are forming and staffing teams and monitoring team performance. The right combination of talents is essential for teams to acquire the resources they need in order to be effective and to achieve their goals. Teamwork requires close collaboration and constant information sharing.

Planning and Administration Competency. Competent managers understand that what worked well in the past may no longer serve the needs of an organization or its customers. This competency involves the regular review and adjustment of organizations to meet shifting internal and external needs and the changing competencies of employees. Work gets done when it is well planned, well coordinated, and well monitored. Competent managers help to set clear and challenging goals, and, when problems arise, they step in to help solve them. However, tasks may be neglected when managers spend too much time dealing with trivial problems. Similarly, employees may waste time because of inadequate controls, poor guidance, and slow decision making. Through a series of examples, students learn how effective managers use the planning and administration competency to create organizations that are responsive to customer demands and needs.

Communication Competency. Competent managers lead others—they can't do so without being able to listen and share their ideas well. The communication competency involves listening, informing others, fostering open channels, and negotiating with others. The flow of information in an organization is its lifeblood. To maintain and improve the performance of an organization, information must freely flow upward, laterally, and downward. The communication competency strengthens the foundation for successful management. Communication is so fundamental that managers sometimes forget its significance to managing relationships. Through a series of cases and experiential exercises, students discover the importance of sharing information with others and of developing a culture in which they and others openly share information. Mastering the communication competency greatly expands a manager's influence and effectiveness.

Guided Learning

Every chapter of *Management: A Competency-Based Approach* includes features that make it teachable, readable, and learnable.

Learning Objectives and a Fully Integrated Learning System. The text and all major support materials are organized around *Learning Objectives* that form the basis of our easy-to-use integrated learning system. Along with the text, the *Study Guide*, *Test Bank*, and *Instructor's Manual* provide instructors and students with a fully integrated set of learning objectives and content from which to teach and study.

Opening Preview Cases. Every chapter opens with a current, real-world account that sets the stage for the topics to be presented in that chapter. These cases reinforce chapter concepts, lead into the discussion, and whet students' appetites for what is to come. In the Preview for Chapter 1, for example, students learn about some of the competencies of Allen Questrom at J.C. Penney. In Chapter 15, students learn about the strong leadership abilities of Carly Fiorina at Hewlett-Packard (HP). All of the Preview Cases are **NEW** to this edition.

Graphics. Instructors and students want a management textbook with graphics that are colorful, that reinforce chapter content, and that are inviting to read. We suggest that you quickly page through *Management: A Competency-Based Approach*. You will discover that this book more than measures up to the desired standards. Each figure and table is cited in the narrative and tied to the topic under discussion.

Competency Inserts. Every chapter in *Management: A Competency-Based Approach* contains box inserts that relate the managerial competencies to chapter content. These box inserts are directly related in the text. They provide information that is fully integrated with the text and can be easily introduced into classroom lectures and discussions. In many instances, students are challenged to analyze and evaluate the competency being presented. The boxes aid teaching, learning, and reinforcing chapter content. Questions in the *Test Bank* are provided for instructors who want to test material from these boxed features. There are seventy-three competency inserts, sixty-one of which are **NEW** to this edition.

The Competent Manager. **NEW** to the tenth edition, each chapter presents four margin inserts—seventy-two in total—that provide brief quotes from competent managers, or descriptions of their management examples. This feature presents astute insights, suggestions, and comments that are directly related to the text material where they appear.

Key Terms and Concepts. Key terms and concepts appear in boldface in the text, making it easy for students to check their understanding. The definition of each term and concept is in italic to enhance clarity and student learning. A complete glossary is included on the product support Web site at http://hellriegel.swlearning.com.

Chapter Summaries. Every chapter ends with a Summary that distills the chapter's main points. These summaries are organized around the chapter's *Learning Objectives.* Thus, students can readily assess their mastery of the material presented for those objectives.

Questions for Discussion and Competency Development. Every chapter includes discussion and competency development questions. They require students to apply, analyze, discover, and think about important chapter concepts and related competencies. In addition, these questions build students' communication competencies because they ask for well-thought-out, clearly presented responses. The majority of the questions are **NEW** to this edition.

Cases for Competency Development. There is a substantive case study at the end of 16 of the 18 chapters. Each case enables students to apply chapter concepts to an actual organization's problems—to analyze, evaluate, and make recommendations. These cases cover a wide variety of organizations (Starbucks, Estée Lauder, Kinko's, and American Express, among others). They assist students in developing their competencies. Fourteen of the seventeen cases are **NEW** to this edition.

Exercises for Competency Development. Integrated into the end of 12 chapters, there is a questionnaire or exercise that enables students to diagnose and reflect upon their own attitudes, tendencies, and preferences with respect to such topics as: managerial competencies, cultural orientation, personal creativity, ethical behaviors, emotional intelligence, and personal decision making. Seven of these exercises are **NEW** to this edition.

Videos. All **NEW** videos are available for adopters of the tenth edition. There is a video (or segment) for use with each chapter. These videos provide useful benchmarks against which students can measure their understanding of what managers and organizations actually do. The videos feature a wide variety of organizations. The range of issues addressed in the videos stimulates interesting and challenging analyses. Short cases for these videos, along with discussion questions written by the authors of this text, are available in the Instructor's Manual.

ENRICHMENT MATERIALS

A comprehensive set of enrichment materials is available to instructors and students. We provide an overview of these materials in this section.

Xtra! (http://hellriegelxtra.swlearning.com)

If an X-tra passport is bundled with your NEW textbook you will receive access to our on-line study assistant (access code included in Passport), which includes interactive quizzes, videos, and much more. If an Xtra! Passport is not bundled with your text and you are interested in purchasing one to further enhance your learning, you can purchase one on-line at http://hellriegelxtra.swlearning.com.

InfoTrac College Edition

InfoTrac College Edition is packaged with every new copy of the textbook. It is a fully searchable online university library containing complete articles and their images. Its database allows access to hundreds of scholarly and popular publications—all reliable sources, including magazines, journals, encyclopedias, and newsletters.

Study Guide (ISBN 0-324-28220-6)

Prepared by André L. Honoree of Spring Hill College. Designed from a student's perspective, the value-rich *Study Guide* includes the features needed to improve performance in class and on exams. Chapter outlines and exam preparation questions are organized around the text's *Learning Objectives*. This enables students to isolate the material that is most challenging to them and focus on it. Answers to the questions, along with the rationales for the answers, are provided for all self-tests.

Instructor's Manual (ISBN 0-324-28221-4)

Prepared by David A. Foote of Middle Tennessee State University. Available in print and on CD-ROM, the *Instructor's Manual* emphasizes the integrated learning system. Each chapter includes: (1) *Learning Objectives*, (2) lecture outlines that are annotated with additional examples, (3) lecture-enhancing enrichment modules, (4) cross-references to text figures (also available as transparencies) and PowerPoint slides, and (5) answers to all end-of-chapter questions, cases, and exercises. The instructor's manual also includes short cases related to the tenth edition videos, with suggested answers to the case discussion questions.

Test Bank (ISBN 0-324-28223-0)

Prepared by F. Robert Buchanan of the University of Texas–Arlington. Also organized around the text's *Learning Objectives*, the *Test Bank* is available to instructors in print and on CD-ROM. Tables at the beginning of each chapter classify each question according to type, difficulty level, and learning objective. This classification enables the instructor to create exams at the appropriate level with the desired mix of question types. Special questions aimed at the content of the text's opening preview cases and competency box inserts are designated throughout the *Test Bank*. The *Test Bank* contains more than 2,000 true/false, multiple-choice, and essay questions.

ExamView (ISBN 0-324-28224-9)

ExamView Computerized Testing Software contains all of the questions in the printed test bank. This program is an easy-to-use test creation software compatible with Microsoft Windows. Instructors can add or edit questions, instructions, and answers, and select questions by previewing them on the screen, selecting them randomly, or selecting them by number. Instructors can also create and administer quizzes online, whether over the Internet, a local area network (LAN), or a wide area network (WAN). Contact your South-Western/Thomson sales representative for ordering information.

PowerPoint™ Presentation Slides

Prepared by R. Bryan Kethley of Middle Tennessee State University. PowerPoint slides are available online at http://hellriegel.swlearning.com for use by students as an aid to note taking and by instructors for enhancing their lectures. Prepared in conjunction with the Instructor's Manual, more than 250 PowerPoint slides are available to supplement course content, adding structure and visual dimension to lectures.

Instructor's Resource CD-ROM (ISBN 0-324-28227-3)

This CD-ROM includes the key instructor support materials—*Instructor's Manual, Test Bank, ExamView* and *PowerPoint Slides*—and provides instructors with a comprehensive capability for customizing lectures and presentations.

Transparencies (ISBN 0-324-28226-5)

A full set of acetate transparencies is available to adopters of the tenth edition of *Management: A Competency-Based Approach* to enhance classroom presentations. All text figures included in the transparencies are tied to lecture outlines presented in the *Instructor's Manual.*

Videos

Our package includes a tape of *Video Cases* (**ISBN 0-324-28217-6**) related to each chapter that brings action-based insights right into the classroom. These videos frame management issues in such a way that students must apply some aspect of chapter content to their analyses of the issues. All video cases are **NEW** to this edition. A comprehensive video guide appears in the *Instructor's Manual,* with supporting cases and discussion questions for each video segment. In addition, *CNN Video: Management and Organizations* (**ISBN 0-324-13495-9**) is available. It features 45 minutes of short segments from CNN, the world's first 24-hour all-news network, available on VHS cassette to use as lecture launchers, discussion starters, topical introductions, or directed inquiries.

Product Support Web Site (http://hellriegel.swlearning.com)

An enriching Web site at http://hellriegel.swlearning.com complements the text, providing many extras for students and instructors. The informative resources include: (1) interactive quizzes, (2) downloadable support materials, (3) video clips with a related comprehensive video case, (4) text glossary and management dictionary, and (5) material that was removed from the ninth edition text.

RELATED RESOURCES

Experiencing Management (ISBN 0-324-01598-4)

Prepared by R. Dennis Middlemist of Colorado State University. An innovative product, *Experiencing Management,* is a totally online collection of Web-based modules that uses the latest Flash technology in its animated scenarios, graphs, and models. Designed to reinforce key management principles in a dynamic learning environment, *Experiencing Management* maintains high motivation through the use of challenging problems. Try it by visiting http://www.experiencingmanagement.com. *Experiencing Management* is available for purchase online by each individual module, or as a collection of all 14 modules. For more information, contact your South-Western/Thomson sales representative.

Management Power! PowerPoint Slides (ISBN 0-324-13380-4)

Management Power! is a CD-ROM of PowerPoint slides covering 14 major management and organizational behavior topics: communication, control, decision making, designing organizations, ethics and social responsibility, foundations of management, global management, human resources, innovation and change, leadership, motivation, planning, strategy, and teams. These easy-to-use, multimedia slides can easily be modified and customized to suit individual preferences. Contact your South-Western/Thomson sales representative for more information.

TextChoice

TextChoice is the home of Thomson Learning's online digital content. TextChoice provides the fastest, easiest way for you to create your own learning materials. You may select content from hundreds of our best-selling titles, choose material from one of our databases, and add your own material. Contact your South-Western/Thomson sales representative for more information.

HITS on the Web: Management

This resource booklet supports students' research efforts on the World Wide Web. This manual covers materials such as: an introduction to the World Wide Web, browsing the Web, finding information on the World Wide Web, email, email discussion groups and newsgroups, and documenting Internet sources for research. It also provides a list of the hottest management sites on the Web. Contact your South-Western/Thomson sales representative for package pricing and ordering information.

eCoursepacks

Create a tailor fit, easy to use and online companion for any course with eCoursepacks, from Thomson companies South-Western and Gale. eCoursepacks gives educators access to content from thousands of current popular, professional, and academic periodicals, NACRA and Darden cases, business and industry information from Gale, and the ability to easily add your own material—even collecting a royalty if you choose. Permissions for all eCoursepack content are already secured, saving you the time and worry from securing rights. eCoursepacks online publishing tools also save you time and energy allowing you to quickly search the databases and make selections, organize all your content, and publish the final online product in a clean, uniform, and full color format. eCoursepacks is the best way to provide your audience with current information easily, quickly, and inexpensively. To learn more, visit http://ecoursepacks.swlearning.com.

Management Interactive Self-Assessments

Management Interactive Self-Assessments is an interactive online tool that provides students the real value of what they have learned, from their textbook, by measuring how effectively they apply this knowledge. The self-assessments offer content on decision making, leadership styles, motivation, managing conflict, problem solving, innovative approaches, and solutions. This product is available to bundle with any South-Western Management textbook. To learn more, link to the Management Interactive Self-Assessment Web site at http://selfassessments.swlearning.com or contact your South-Western/Thomson sales representative.

ACKNOWLEDGEMENTS

We give special thanks to: Jerry R. Strawser, Dean of Mays Business School and Angelo S. DeNisi, Head of the Department of Management of Texas A&M University; Al Niemi, Dean of the Cox School of Business of Southern Methodist University; and Barbara A. Lee, Dean of the School of Management and Labor Relations of Rutgers University. They have fostered an environment that made possible the completion of the tenth edition of *Management: A Competency-Based Approach.*

For their outstanding assistance with many of the essential tasks involved in manuscript preparation and review, we express our deep gratitude to Argie Butler of Texas A&M University and Billie Boyd of Southern Methodist University. Their continuing dedication, professionalism, and ability to laugh made this journey easier.

Many individuals at South-Western applied their ample professional competencies in developing this text and the related enrichment materials. Because of them and others, we feel this is an outstanding text with superb enrichment materials—all of which are networked through an *integrated learning system.* Those most directly involved at South-Western include: Joe Sabatino, the thoughtful sponsoring editor for this book; Jacque Carrillo, the creative marketing manager for the tenth edition; Leslie Kauffman, the developmental editor whose splendid suggestions are reflected in every chapter and the enrichment materials; Marge Bril, the production editor who handled so superbly the many issues in the production process; Lorretta Palagi, the copyeditor whose expertise improved the flow and readability of the manuscript; Cover-to-Cover, who is chiefly responsible for the attractive and supportive art program; Sam Marshall, who obtained the effective photos to enrich the written words; and Tippy McIntosh, who led the development of the inviting design.

Thanks also go to our excellent team of enrichment materials authors. Their many competencies and hard work are evident in the outstanding enrichment materials that foster student learning. These authors include:

David A. Foote
Middle Tennessee State University
Instructor's Manual

F. Robert Buchanan
University of Texas–Arlington
Test Bank

André L. Honoree
Spring Hill College
Study Guide

R. Bryan Kethley
Middle Tennessee State University
PowerPoint Presentation Slides

Our colleagues and friends at Texas A&M University, Rutgers University, and Southern Methodist University create environments that nurture our professional development. We thank them. We are grateful to our families for their support and understanding in letting us devote evenings and weekends to our authors' islands in preparing this edition. With the completion of this edition, we look forward to spending more time with families and friends.

Many reviewers made insightful comments as we prepared the tenth edition. As to be expected, there were some differences among them as to what to include, modify, or delete. Regardless, their comments and suggestions resulted in substantial improvements. We are grateful to the following individuals for sharing their professional insights and suggestions.

Adam Berry
Utah State University

Rita Drieghe Kosnik
Trinity University

Gunther S. Boroschek
University of Massachusetts–Boston

David Lei
Southern Methodist University

Cecily Cooper
University of Miami

Robert Roller
LeTourneau University

William Cron
Texas Christian University

James Smith
Rocky Mountain College

Terrell Falk
Cinemark Theaters

Ben Welch
Texas A&M University

Robert W. Hanna
California State University–Northridge

Laura Wolfe
Louisiana State University

Michael Harvey
University of Mississippi

Don Hellriegel
Texas A&M University

Susan E. Jackson
Rutgers University

John W. Slocum ,Jr.
Southern Methodist University

About the Authors

Don Hellriegel

Don Hellriegel is Professor of Management and holds the Bennett Chair in Business within Mays Business School at Texas A&M University. He received his B.S. and M.B.A. from Kent State University and his Ph.D. from the University of Washington. Dr. Hellriegel has been a member of the faculty at Texas A&M since 1975 and has served on the faculties of the Pennsylvania State University and the University of Colorado.

His research interests include corporate entrepreneurship, effect of organizational environments, and organizational innovation and strategic management processes. His research has been published in a number of leading journals.

Professor Hellriegel served as Vice President and Program Chair of the Academy of Management (1986), President Elect (1987), President (1988), and Past President (1989). In September 1999, he was elected to a three-year term as Dean of the Fellows Group of the Academy of Management. He served a term as Editor of the *Academy of Management Review* and served as a member of the Board of Governors of the Academy of Management (1979–1981); (1982–1989). Dr. Hellriegel has occupied many other leadership roles, among which include President, Eastern Academy of Management; Division Chair, Organization and Management Theory Division; President, Brazos County United Way; Co-Consulting Editor, West Series in Management; Head (1976–1980 and 1989–1994), Department of Management (TAMU); Executive Associate Dean and Interim Dean, Mays Business School (TAMU); and Interim Executive Vice Chancellor (TAMUS).

He has consulted with a variety of groups and organizations, including—among others—3DI, Sun Ship Building, Penn Mutual Life Insurance, Texas A&M University System, Ministry of Industry and Commerce (Nation of Kuwait), Ministry of Agriculture (Nation of Dominican Republic), American Assembly of Collegiate Schools of Business, and Texas Innovation Group.

Susan E. Jackson

Susan E. Jackson is Professor of Human Resource Management in the School of Management and Labor Relations at Rutgers University, where she also serves as Graduate Director for the Doctoral Program in Industrial Relations and Human Resources. Prior to joining Rutgers, she taught on the faculties of New York University, the University of Michigan, and the University of Maryland. She received her B.A. in psychology and sociology from the University of Minnesota and her Master's and Ph.D. in organizational psychology from the University of California, Berkeley.

Her primary area of expertise is the strategic management of human resources, and her special interests include managing team effectiveness, workforce diversity, stress and burnout, and the design of human resource management systems to support knowledge-based organizations' business imperatives. She has authored or co-authored over 100 articles on these and related topics. In addition, she has published several books, including *Managing Knowledge for Sustained Competitive Advantage: Designing Strategies for Effective Human Resource Management* (with M. A. Hitt and A. S. DeNisi), *Managing Human Resources in Cross-border Alliances* (with R. S. Schuler and Y. Luo), *Human Resources: A Partnership Perspective* (with R.S. Schuler), *Strategic Human Resource Management* (with R. S. Schuler), *Diversity in the Workplace: Human Resource Initiatives*, and *Creating Tomorrow's Organizations: A Handbook for Future Research in Organizational Behavior* (with C. L. Cooper). She currently serves as a member of the editorial boards for *Academy of Management Journal, Organizational Dynamics, Human Resource Management Journal,* and *International Journal of Manpower.*

Professor Jackson has held numerous positions in professional societies. In the Academy of Management, she is actively involved and currently serves as Representative-at-Large for the Human Resources Division. She also has served as Consulting Editor and Editor of the *Academy of Management Review*, President of the Division of Organizational Behavior, and as a member of the Board of Governors. She is a Fellow in the Society for Industrial and Organizational Psychology, where she has served as Program Chair, and has served as a member of the editorial board of the *Frontiers of Industrial & Organizational Psychology*, the Scientific Affairs Committee, Member-at-Large/Long Range Planning Committee, and the Education and Training Committee. She also is a member of the International Association of Applied Psychology, where she has served as Program Co-Chair. In addition, she has served as a consultant to organizations such as General Electric, American Express, Merrill Lynch, Xerox, and the American Assembly of Collegiate Schools of Business.

John W. Slocum, Jr.

John Slocum is the Chairperson of the Management and Organizations Department, Co-Director of SMU's Corporate Director Institute, and holds the O. Paul Corley Professorship in Organizational Behavior at the Edwin L. Cox School of Business, Southern Methodist University. He has also taught on the faculties of the University of Washington, the Fisher School of Business at the Ohio State University, the Smeal School of Business at the Pennsylvania State University, the International University of Japan, and the Amos Tuck College at Dartmouth. He holds a B.B.A. from Westminster College, an M.B.A. from Kent State University, and a Ph.D. in organizational behavior from the University of Washington.

Professor Slocum has held a number of positions in professional societies. He was elected as a Fellow to the Academy of Management in 1976 for his outstanding contributions to the profession of management and as a Fellow to the Decision Sciences Institute in 1984 for his research in behavioral decision theory. He was awarded the Alumni Citation for Professional Accomplishment by Westminster College; the Nicolas Salgo, Rotunda Outstanding, and Executive MBA Teaching Awards from SMU; SMU Alumni Award for Outstanding Service to Alumni; and the inaugural Carl Sewell Distinguished Service Award. He is a charter member of the *Academy of Management Journal's* Hall of Fame. He served as President of the Eastern Academy of Management in 1973. From 1975–1986, he served as a member of the Board of Governors, Academy of Management. From 1979–1981, he served as Editor of the *Academy of Management Journal*. In 1983–1984, he served as 39th President of the 12,500-member Academy. Currently, he serves as Co-Editor of the *Journal of World Business, Organizational Dynamics*, and *Journal of Leadership and Organizational Studies*.

Professor Slocum has served as a consultant to such organizations as OxyChem, ARAMARK, Fort Worth Museum of Science and History, Pier 1, Celanese, NASA, Lockheed Martin Corporation, Transnational Trucks, and Key Span Energy. Currently, he is a member of the Board of Directors for KISCO Senior Living Communities, the Winston School, and Go-to-Learn.

©Index Stock Imagery

An Overview of Management

©Corbis Inc.

Managing in a Dynamic Environment

Learning Objectives

After studying this chapter, you should be able to:

1. Define managers and management.

2. Explain what managers do.

3. Describe the competencies used in managerial work and assess your current competency levels.

Chapter Outline

In September 2000, when Allen Questrom began his first day as J.C. Penney's new CEO, things didn't look good. The company's valuation was down to about $3 billion, from a peak of $70 billion; its stock was at $13 per share, down from $70 in 1997. The one-time retailing giant, which celebrated its 100th anniversary in April 2002, was in dire financial difficulty. When times were good, customers upgraded to stores such as Lord & Taylor, Nieman Marcus, and Abercrombie and Fitch. When times were economically tight, shoppers sought better values in discount stores, such as Wal-Mart, Target, and Costco, that undercut Penney's prices. To make matters worse, Eckerd, the drugstore chain that Penney's operates, was turning in one disappointing financial quarter after another.

To turn Penney's around, Questrom and his top management team needed to get liabilities off the balance sheet. Penney's closed more than 200 unprofitable stores, sold off its direct insurance service to Aegon, and dismissed 5,000 people. Questrom also sold off Penney's credit card division to GE Capital, which is now responsible for managing all activities related to J.C. Penney credit card holders. He told employees and the financial analysts on Wall Street that Penney's was "putting a renewed emphasis on expense control." To rein in expenses, the policy of centralizing all merchandising started in 1999 by Vanessa Castagna, Penney's chief operating officer, was continued. Castagna came from Wal-Mart, which has a highly centralized distribution system. She believed that decentralization was one of the reasons for low productivity and unprofitability. Store managers could choose the types of merchandise they wanted to carry in their stores. As a result, a Penney's store in Frisco, Texas, might carry different brands than a store in Burlington, Vermont. This was expensive because Penney's was not offered discounts for buying large amounts from a single supplier, such as Hanes, Levi's, etc.—discounts that its competitors, such as Kohl's and Dillard's, enjoyed as a result of centralized purchasing practices.

With a centralized distribution system, all stores would carry the same name brands, such as Levi's. This enabled Penney's to create national television ads that featured lines of clothing that could be purchased in any of the more than 1,060 Penney's stores. Questrom also created a business relationship with Avon cosmetics to carry a line of makeup designed exclusively for Penney's. Unfortunately, after two years, Penney's decided to abandon this relationship because customers didn't buy the product, and its display cases weren't user friendly. It refocused its strategy to emphasize jewelry, belts, and other women's accessories.

Instead of selling Eckerd, as many financial experts on Wall Street suggested, existing stores were remodeled and new stores were opened. Questrom believes that pharmaceuticals are a growth industry. People are living longer and when they do, they typically need more prescription and over-the-counter drugs. Top managers also believed that drugstores were no longer merely drugstores, but were instead convenience stores that happened to sell pharmaceuticals. To be a convenience drugstore, Eckerd's opened drive-through pharmacies, made extensive investments in information systems that linked pharmacies to doctors' offices, automated the prescription refill process, and accepted the J.C. Penney credit card. Questrom also expanded Eckerd's offering to include toys, one-hour photo processing, small gifts, cards, and other convenience items that people buy. Since that decision, Eckerd has become number three in the drugstore market with more than 2,600 drugstores, trailing only Walgreen's and CVS. Now 43 percent of Penney's sales come from Eckerds.[1]

MANAGERS AND MANAGEMENT

1. Define managers and management.

Effective managers such as Allen Questrom are essential to any organization's overall success, regardless of whether it is a global giant or a small start-up enterprise. Indeed, having talented people is so important to the success of a business that *Fortune* magazine includes "the ability to attract, develop, and keep talented people" as one of the key factors used to establish its list of most admired companies. Questrom has several competencies that have enabled him to perform effectively in his company's top managerial job. A **competency** *is a combination of knowledge, skills, behaviors, and attitudes that contribute to personal effectiveness.*[2]

Managerial competencies *are sets of knowledge, skills, behaviors, and attitudes that a person needs to be effective in a wide range of positions and various types of organizations.* Before reading further, please take time to complete the Exercise for Competency Development: Self-Assessment Inventory on pages 28–33. We have grouped into categories the scores of hundreds of students and practicing managers against which you can compare your competency scores. Later in this chapter, we describe these competencies in detail.

People use many types of competencies in their everyday lives, including those needed to be effective in leisure activities, in personal relationships, at work, and at school. In this book we focus on managerial competencies. Throughout, we emphasize the competencies that you will need for jobs having managerial responsibility. Specifically, our goal is to help you develop six key managerial competencies:

- communication,
- planning and administration,
- teamwork,
- strategic action,
- global awareness, and
- self-management.[3]

Figure 1.1 indicates how these six competencies are all interrelated. For now, an overview of what is involved in applying them is sufficient. Table 1.1 identifies several important aspects of each key managerial competency. In practice, knowing where one competency begins and another ends is difficult. You would seldom rely on just one at a time, so drawing sharp distinctions between them is valuable only for purposes of identification and description. Keeping these six managerial competencies firmly in mind will help you think about how the material you are studying can improve your performance in jobs that require you to use them.

What Is an Organization?

Effective managers must pay attention to what goes on both inside and outside of their organizations. Regardless of where their attention might be focused at any particular time, managers are part and parcel of organizational settings. Profit-oriented businesses are one type of organization in which managers are found, but they aren't the only one. Undoubtedly, you could write your autobiography as a series of experiences with organizations such as hospitals, schools, museums, sports teams, stores, amusement parks, restaurants, orchestras, community groups and clubs, government agencies, and others. Some of these organizations were small, and others were large. Some were for-profit

| Figure 1.1 | A Model of Managerial Competencies |

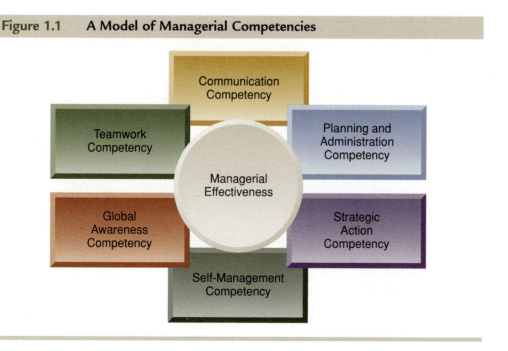

Table 1.1	Six Key Managerial Competencies

Communication Competency

- Informal communication
- Formal communication
- Negotiation

Planning and Administration Competency

- Information gathering, analysis, and problem solving
- Planning and organizing projects
- Time management
- Budgeting and financial management

Teamwork Competency

- Designing teams
- Creating a supportive environment
- Managing team dynamics

Strategic Action Competency

- Understanding the industry
- Understanding the organization
- Taking strategic actions

Global Awareness Competency

- Cultural knowledge and understanding
- Cultural openness and sensitivity

Self-Management Competency

- Integrity and ethical conduct
- Personal drive and resilience
- Balancing work and life demands
- Self-awareness and development

companies, and others were nonprofit organizations. Some offered products, some offered both products and services, and others offered only services. Some were well managed, and others struggled merely to survive.

An **organization** *is a coordinated group of people who function to achieve a particular goal.* Every organization has a structure and strives to achieve goals that individuals acting alone could not reach. All organizations strive to achieve specific goals, but they don't all have the same goals. For example, a goal at FedEx is to offer on-time package delivery service at the lowest prevailing price. A goal at Sony is to create innovative cameras, whereas at Dell Computer a goal is to produce reliable, low-cost PCs and related computer products. All of these goals, however, are related to the overall goals of serving customers and earning profits.

Regardless of an organization's specific goals, the job of managers is to help the organization achieve those goals. In this book, we look at managers in organizations of all types and sizes that have many different goals and many different ways of achieving their goals. Our primary purposes are to help you understand how managers accomplish their goals and to help you develop some of the managerial competencies that you will need to be effective in whatever type of organization you find yourself. Many—indeed, most—of these competencies will be useful to you even if you never have a job with the word *manager* in the title.

The Competent Manager

"You have got to have people who believe in the organization and who do whatever is necessary to make the organization work."

Bill Rivas
CEO
Circuit City

What Is a Manager?

We've been talking about managers for several pages, so it's time to clarify exactly what the term means. A **manager** *is a person who plans, organizes, leads, and controls the allocation of human, material, financial, and information resources in pursuit of the organization's goals.* The many different types of managers include department managers, product managers, account managers, plant managers, division managers, district managers, and task force managers. What they all have in common is responsibility for the efforts of a group of people who share a goal and access to resources that the group can use in pursuing its goal.

You don't have to be called a manager to be a manager. Some managers have unique and creative titles, such as chief information officer (a person in charge of information systems) or team leader. People with the job titles of chief executive officer (CEO), president, managing director, supervisor, and coach also are responsible for helping groups of people achieve a common goal, so they too are managers.

Most employees contribute to organizations through their own work, not by directing other employees. Journalists, computer programmers, insurance agents, machine operators, newscasters, graphic designers, sales associates, stockbrokers, accountants, and lawyers are essential to helping organizations achieve their goals, but many people with these job titles aren't managers.

What sets managers apart, if not their job titles? Simply put, the difference between managers and individual contributors is that managers are evaluated on how well the people they direct do their jobs. Allen Questrom doesn't wait on customers at Penney's Ridgeview mall store in Lewisville, Texas. He hires, trains, and motivates others to manage people who do that job. Carly Fiorina, Hewlett-Packard's CEO, doesn't design or produce HP products. Her job is to position HP in the marketplace by restructuring HP to compete more effectively in the marketplace. She's accomplishing this by working with her management team to smoothly integrate Compaq's employees into HP's system after the merger between those two companies and by creating a work environment in which all employees can grow and prosper.[4]

What Is Management?

If managers are the people responsible for making sure that an organization achieves its goals, what does the term *management* mean? In everyday usage, people often refer to management as a group of managers in an organization. For example, the CEO and other high-level executives often are referred to as top management. The managers under them may be referred to as middle management, and so on.

The term can also be used to refer to the tasks that managers do. These tasks include planning, organizing, leading, and controlling the work of an organization. Recently General Electric (GE) divided GE Capital into four divisions—Commercial Finance, Equipment Management, Consumer Finance, and Insurance—to ensure more clarity about what each manager's job within GE Capital entails. According to Jeff Immelt, CEO of GE, he wanted these businesses to operate separately for faster decision making and execution. Now, managers in GE Consumer Finance focus on credit card services, such as J.C. Penney, and global consumer financing, whereas managers in the GE Equipment Management division focus on aviation services, commercial equipment financing, among others.

Management *refers to the tasks and activities involved in directing an organization or one of its units: planning, organizing, leading, and controlling.* As you will see, people in many different jobs may be expected to do some management tasks, even if that isn't their main focus. For example, quality control programs such as the one at GE involve employees throughout the entire organization in developing plans for improving quality. When GE Consumer Finance looks for ways to reduce errors in the bills it sends to credit card customers, managers enlist the help of billing clerks and data processors. They will be empowered to reorganize some of their work and be expected to continue to look for new ways to control quality. In other words, they will be doing some management tasks, but they won't become managers. We reserve the use of manager to refer to people in jobs that primarily involve management tasks.

Types of Managers

There are many types of managers and many ways in which managerial jobs differ from each other. One difference is the scope of activities involved. The scope of activities performed by functional managers is relatively narrow, whereas the scope of activities performed by general managers is quite broad.

Functional managers *supervise employees having expertise in one area, such as accounting, human resources, sales, finance, marketing, or production.* For example, the head of a payroll department is a functional manager. That person doesn't determine employee salaries, as a general manager might, but makes sure that payroll checks are issued on time and in the correct amounts. Usually, functional managers have a great deal of experience and technical expertise in the areas of operation they supervise. Their success as managers is due in part to the detailed knowledge they have about the work being done by the people they supervise, the problems those people are likely to face, and the resources they need to perform effectively. They rely on the communication, planning and administration, teamwork, and self-management competencies to accomplish their jobs.

General managers *are responsible for the operations of more complex units—for example, a company or a division.* Vanessa Castagna, chief operating officer at J.C. Penney's, is a general manager who oversees the work of functional managers. General managers must have a broader range of well-developed managerial competencies than functional managers to do their jobs well. They also need to acquire global awareness and strategic action competencies. These competencies can be learned through a combination of formal training and various job assignments, or they can be learned simply in the course of trying to adapt and survive in their job. Being adaptable enough to solve whatever problems he ran into has been critical for Tim Green, chief information officer for Reliance Aeroproducts. He tries to bring freethinkers—the rebels and flakes—into his group to get more diversity in thinking. To increase their effectiveness, he doesn't require them to follow normal operating procedures as long as they do not violate ethical, legal, and safety requirements.

WHAT MANAGERS DO

2. Explain what managers do.

As we've described the various types of managers, we've given you some idea of what managers do. But these few examples don't show the whole picture by any means. Let's now consider systematically what managers do—the functions they perform and the specific tasks included in these functions.

General Managerial Functions

The successful manager capably performs four basic managerial functions: planning, organizing, leading, and controlling. However, as you will see, the amount of time a manager spends on each function depends on the level of the particular job. After further describing each of the four general managerial functions, we highlight the differences among managers at various levels in organizations.

Regardless of their level in an organization, most managers perform the four general functions more or less simultaneously—rather than in a rigid, preset order—to achieve organizational goals. Figure 1.2 illustrates this point graphically. In this section we briefly

Figure 1.2   Basic Managerial Functions

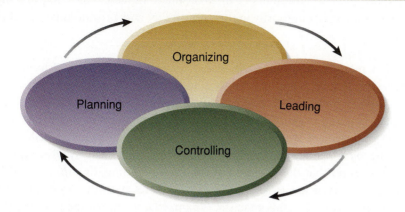

examine the four functions without looking specifically at their interrelationships. However, throughout this book we refer to those interrelationships to help explain exactly how managers do their jobs.

Planning. **Planning** *involves determining organizational goals and means to reach them.* Managers plan for three reasons: (1) to establish an overall direction for the organization's future, such as increased profit, expanded market share, and social responsibility; (2) to identify and commit the organization's resources to achieving its goals; and (3) to decide which tasks must be done to reach those goals. Allen Questrom is a good example of a manager who plans. Through knowledge of the retailing industry, he understood how important the pharmaceutical industry was to the overall profitability of Penney's. He also knew who to recruit to integrate the catalog and Web sites for Penney's Internet, what channels of distribution would be needed to deliver products to customers, and the importance of motivated employees. In other words, he had a good understanding of what planning involves. Questrom also used his planning ability to sell the Penney's credit card operation to GE Capital. Why? Because Penney's didn't have the managerial competencies and/or state-of-the-art technology to operate this business profitably.

The Competent Manager

"There is nothing wrong with pursuing a vision for greatness, but successful companies continually redefine the path to greatness with brutal facts of reality."

Carl Reichardt
CEO
Wells Fargo Bank

Organizing. After managers have prepared plans, they must translate those relatively abstract ideas into reality. Sound organization is essential to this effort. **Organizing** *is the process of deciding where decisions will be made, who will perform what jobs and tasks, and who will report to whom in the company.* At Penney's, having all purchasing managers report to Castagna was a major decision. By centralizing the purchasing decision into one function, Penney's saved million of dollars. By organizing effectively, managers can better coordinate human, material, and information resources. An organization's success depends largely on management's ability to utilize those resources efficiently and effectively.

Organizing involves creating a structure by setting up departments and job descriptions. For example, the U.S. Postal Service uses a structure that helps them deliver mail. At the U.S. Postal Service, most employees think of themselves as production workers, and the degree of job specialization is high. Relatively little attention is paid to the marketing function. Most of the decisions are made by top managers, with mail carriers and postal clerks having little to do with decision making. Carriers and clerks are promoted to other jobs as they gain seniority.

In contrast, GE Capital is organized into four distinct businesses. Employees in each business attempt to serve customers in their business. Immelt hopes that this structure will create clearer lines of authority and responsibility and provide financial clarity for GE's investors.

Leading. After management has made plans, created a structure, and hired the right personnel, someone must lead the organization. **Leading** *involves getting others to perform the necessary tasks by motivating them to achieve the organization's goals.* Leading isn't done only after planning and organizing end; it is a crucial element of those functions. Lois Dimpfel, vice president of Worldwide Olympic Technology Systems for IBM, was given the assignment to coordinate IBM's technology for the Salt Lake City Olympic Games in 2002. She understood that this assignment required planning, organizing, and leading simultaneously. The goal was to bring the games flawlessly to hundreds of millions of people via TV. To accomplish this goal, she organized a team that included hundreds of managers from the United States and around the world. Dimpfel and her team collaboratively planned how to proceed and she led in executing the plan.[5]

Controlling. *The process by which a person, group, or organization consciously monitors performance and takes corrective action* is **controlling**. Just as a thermostat sends signals to a heating system that the room temperature is too high or too low, so a management control system sends signals to managers that things aren't working out as planned and that corrective action is needed. Howard Schultz is CEO of Starbucks, the coffee company based in Seattle, with annual sales of more than $2.7 billion.[6] Schultz believes that Starbucks' success is due to its competitive spirit, ability to respond to customers' needs with diverse and genuine products, ability to attract and retain employees, and its control procedures. The control procedures at Starbucks start with the criteria used to hire people, the type of beans used, the physical layout of each store, and the like. In the control process at Starbucks, Amazon.com, Nike, and other organizations, managers

- set standards of performance,
- measure current performance against those standards,
- take action to correct any deviations, and
- adjust the standards if necessary.

The control system that makes FedEx unique is its central sorting facilities in Dallas, Memphis, and Indianapolis. All packages arrive at a location for sorting by midnight. A DC-10 with more than 50,000 pounds of packages (approximately 131,000 packages) is unloaded within 30 minutes. The packages are unloaded directly into a giant warehouse containing an elaborate system of conveyor belts. All packages must be sorted so that planes can leave for their destinations at 3:00 A.M. From the time a package is placed on one of the intake ramps, the conveyor system takes 6 minutes to scan, sort, and redirect the package to a container to be loaded onto an outgoing plane.

The following Planning & Administration Competency feature illustrates how Cliff Hudson performed these four basic managerial functions daily on his job as CEO of Sonic Drive-Ins. We have indicated these functions in parentheses. Sonic has more than 2,400 drive-in restaurants, mostly in the Sunbelt. For the last five years, its sales have grown by 17 percent and its profits by 28 percent. The average drive-in sells more than $870,000 worth of Ex-Long Cheese Coney hot dogs, Ched 'R' Peppers, Banana Cream Pie shakes, hamburgers, fries, and the like. Sonic competes against McDonald's, Burger King, Taco Bell, and other chains in the fast-food restaurant industry. Some interesting facts about this industry are that Americans eat more than 44 billion hamburgers a year, spend more than $115 billion on fast food, and eat an average of 55 pounds of French fries.[7]

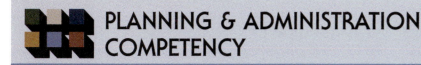

PLANNING & ADMINISTRATION COMPETENCY

Cliff Hudson of Sonic Drive-Ins

When Cliff Hudson took over as CEO in 1995, Sonic had major problems. Each drive-in offered a different menu. Even within the same city, drive-ins offered different menus because each store bought ingredients from different suppliers. In one instance, 500 store managers got together and signed on with Pepsi, when headquarters was in the final stages of signing a nationwide deal with Coca-Cola. Many of the drive-ins hadn't been remodeled since they opened in 1953. Paint was peeling off stores, microphones weren't working, and parking spaces had potholes and lines weren't painted, among other things. Accounting records were still done manually and financial statements from some stores weren't available until four months after the closing date and were filled with errors. The company pitchman, Frankie Avalon, a teen idol in the 1950s and 1960s, wasn't recognized by the 1990s teens. More than 300 unprofitable drive-ins had to be closed, and franchisees were demanding new and better financial contracts. Franchisees also wanted exclusive contracts to build in certain markets

and more decision-making authority (*leading function*).

Hudson met with all stores and franchisee owners and met them half way. In return for giving them exclusive rights and authority to make decisions in their territory, he got consistency in the menu and centralized decisions in advertising and purchasing (*control function*). For example, instead of selling five hamburger sizes, Sonic would offer two. This helped reduce operating expenses. At the same time, he hired experienced fast-food executives from competitors and cut costs. He did not renew Frankie Avalon's contract; instead, he replaced him with skating carhops in Sonic's advertisements. He created a new department (*organizing function*) to oversee the company's image and establish national advertising campaigns. Sonic spent more than $80 million on advertising in 2002, triple what Sonic spent in 1997. For the first time, Sonic began to use market research and focus groups to analyze customer tastes (*planning function*). Sonic spent million of dollars on point-of-sale terminals that track customer trends. When Sonic learned that ice cream sundaes accounted for as much as 30 percent of sales in Texas, the

company offered a national program for sundaes (*control function*). Today Hudson is focusing on ways to attract breakfast customers, which account for only 3 percent of Sonic's business compared to an industry average of 11 percent. He is also looking for ways to cut down the average service time (350 seconds) to match the industry best of 127 seconds held by Wendy's (*control function*).

Hudson plans to focus his attention on building up the breakfast business and wants to keep the company's signature carhops. This means his growth plans focus on the southwestern and southeastern regions of the United States and not on the Midwest or New England, where snow and cold weather would prevent carhops from working during the winter (*planning function*).

Levels of Management

Now that we've told you about the general functions performed by managers in organizations, let's back up and talk about work settings. So far, we've mostly cited examples of managers in large corporations. But managers and the need for effective management are just as important in small organizations. When Tim Koogle founded Yahoo! in a small basement room in Palo Alto, California, he started with a stack of three flat boxes to which he attached a sign reading: DO NOT TOUCH. From this small beginning, Yahoo! now enables millions of customers to view Web pages each month. Yahoo! still doesn't own the servers; it rents them. Koogle knows that, in an intangible world, keeping Yahoo! focused is crucial. At Yahoo! the primary resource is brainpower. Employees can start pursuing radically different tactics in the blink of an eye. The company's assets can become quickly and utterly uncoordinated unless Koogle constantly reinforces its strategic focus.[8]

A small organization usually has only one level of management—often the founder or the owner or an executive director. However, large organizations usually have more than one level of management, with varying goals, tasks, responsibilities, and authority. Thus a company's first-line store manager operates very differently than its CEO.[9] Figure 1.3 shows the three basic management levels. We define them with a broad brush here, returning to add detail later in the chapter and throughout the book.

Figure 1.3   Basic Levels of Management

First-Line Managers. **First-line managers** *are directly responsible for the production of goods or services.* They may be called sales managers, section heads, production supervisors, or team leaders depending on the organization. Employees who report to them do the organization's basic production work—whether of goods or of services. For example, a first-line manager at a steel production plant supervises employees who make steel, operate and maintain machines, and write shipping orders. A sales manager at a U.S. automobile dealership supervises salespeople who sell cars to customers in the showroom. An automobile sales manager in Japan works in an office that has computers and telephones similar to a telemarketing center and supervises salespeople who go to people's homes to sell them cars.

This level of management is the link between the operations of each department and the rest of the organization. First-line managers in most companies spend little time with higher management or with people from other organizations. Most of their time is spent with the people they supervise and with other first-line managers.

First-line managers often lead hectic work lives full of pressure and having little glamour, as Bahadur Singh Katare discovered.[10] Katare manages 36 PC operators in the central district of Madhaya, India. More than half the population consists of illiterate tribal farmers who live in thatched-roof huts and subsist on an average of $270 a year. Thanks to a government program, Katare was able to purchase 39 PCs and install them in kiosks around the village. For the equivalent of one cent, his staff can help farmers use a PC in a kiosk that allows them to check current prices for produce. For a few more cents, his staff also helps farmers obtain land records, get driver's licenses, or look up disease-prevention tips for livestock. One of his farmers was able to find $4.20 more per pound for his soybean crop in a town one hour away. One of his staff drove the farmer to the market where the farmer was able to boost his net income by 18 percent. He also was able to help a pensioner who had not received his $3.12 monthly pension for four months by e-mailing the government and solving the problem. Since the area has unreliable utilities, Katare is working with people to install solar panels and local wireless networks. He spends relatively little time planning and organizing.

First-line managers usually need strong technical expertise to teach subordinates and supervise their day-to-day tasks. Workers usually develop technical expertise before becoming managers. Sometimes, though, a first-line manager is a recent college graduate who is responsible for the work of both hourly employees and professionals. Such a first-line manager is likely to have little hands-on experience. That lack of experience, however, isn't a problem if the new manager is willing to learn and has the competency to communicate with diverse types of people, to coach and counsel subordinates, and to provide constructive feedback.

Middle Managers. Some managers at larger organizations must focus on coordinating employee activities, determining which products or services to provide, and deciding how to market these products or services to customers. **Middle managers** *are responsible for setting objectives that are consistent with top management's goals and translating them into specific goals and plans for first-line managers to implement.*[11] Middle managers typically have titles such as department head, plant manager, and director of finance. They are responsible for directing and coordinating the activities of first-line managers and, at times, such nonmanagerial personnel as clerks, receptionists, and staff assistants. Oftentimes middle managers try to resolve contradictions between what top management hopes to achieve and what first-line managers can actually do. As regional sales manager for Alcatel USA, Audrey Van Drew supervises salespeople who sell equipment to U.S.-based telecommunication companies, such as Southwestern Bell and Atlantic Bell. As a middle manager for Alcatel, Van Drew must translate top management's strategy for growing Alcatel's telecommunications equipment into tangible quotas for first-line managers at Alcatel's production plant.[12]

Many middle managers began their careers and spent several years as first-line managers. Even so, promotion from the first level of management to middle management is often difficult and sometimes traumatic. The heavier emphases on managing group performance and allocating resources represent the most important differences between first-line and middle managers. The middle manager often is involved in reviewing the work plans of various groups, helping these groups set priorities, and negotiating and coordinating their activities. Middle managers are involved in establishing target dates for products or services to be completed; developing evaluation criteria for performance; deciding which projects should be given money, personnel, and materials; and translating top management's general goals into specific operational plans, schedules, and procedures.

Middle managers carry out top management's directives primarily by delegating authority and responsibility to their subordinates and by coordinating schedules and resources with other managers. They often spend much of their day talking on the phone, attending committee meetings, and preparing and reviewing reports. Middle managers tend to be removed from the technical aspects of work, so whatever technical expertise they may have is of less direct help to them now. In many organizations today, developing subordinates and helping them move up in the organization is essential to being viewed as a successful manager. When middle managers fail to develop their people, low morale and high turnover are likely to follow.

Top Managers. *The overall direction of an organization is the responsibility of* **top managers**. Michael Dell, CEO of Dell Computer, and Meg Whitman, CEO of eBay, are two such managers who have built hugely successful Internet companies. Typical titles of top managers are chief executive officer, president, chairman, division president, and executive vice president. Top managers develop goals, policies, and strategies for the entire organization.[13] The goals they set are handed down through the hierarchy, eventually reaching each worker.

CEOs and presidents often represent their organizations in community affairs, business deals, and government negotiations. When Ray Anderson founded his company Interface in 1973, one of his goals was to eliminate waste, use alternative sources of energy, and cut down on harmful fossil fuel emissions. The company annually saves $43 million by eliminating waste. He created a billion-dollar-a-year floor-covering company that introduced biodegradable carpeting products made from corn. Interface also leases its carpet tiles instead of selling them, replacing a customer's worn tiles and keeping the used carpet tiles out of landfills by taking them back and recycling them into new carpet tiles. When Anderson stepped down as CEO in 2001, the new CEO, Dan Hendix, pledged to continue Anderson's stand on environmentalism.[14]

Top managers spend most of their day (over 75 percent) planning and leading. They spend most of their leading time with key people in organizations other than their own. Top managers—like middle managers—spend little time directly controlling the work of others.

Pressures and demands on top managers can be intense. Tightly scheduled workdays, heavy travel requirements, and workweeks of 50 or more hours are common. A true break is a luxury. Coffee is swallowed on the run, and lunch often is eaten during meetings with other managers, business associates, community representatives, or government officials. When there is some free time, eager subordinates vie for a piece of it.

Top managers also face expanding public relations duties. They must be able to respond quickly to crises that may create image problems for their organizations. Imagine that you are Albert Stroucken, president of H. B. Fuller. Headquartered in St. Paul, Minnesota, Fuller manufactures industrial glues, coatings, and paints. Among its products is Resistol, glue used for making shoes. For many years children in Central America have sniffed Resistol because it provides a temporary euphoria that relieves hunger and hopelessness. The Federal Drug Administration (FDA) has evidence that Resistol's fumes are addictive and can cause brain damage. Fuller has tried to stop Resistol's use as a drug by reducing the toxicity of the glue and restricting its sales in Honduras and Guatemala. It has not added mustard oil, which causes vomiting, to the glue because its sales will decline. Stroucken is faced with the issue of whether Fuller should do more to prevent abuse of its product, including withdrawing it from the market, or continue to make this highly profitable glue.[15]

MANAGERIAL COMPETENCIES

3. Describe the competencies used in managerial work and assess your current competency levels.

We've talked about the various levels of management and what managers do, but you may still be wondering about what it takes to be an effective (or even a great) manager. So, let's look more closely at the competencies that managers need in order to succeed.

What It Takes to Be a Great Manager

At the beginning of this chapter, we defined *managerial competencies* as sets of knowledge, skills, behaviors, and attitudes that a manager needs in order to be effective in a wide range of managerial jobs and various organizational settings. We identified six specific competencies as being particularly important: communication, planning and administration, teamwork, strategic action, global awareness, and self-management. These competencies are transferable from one organization to the next.[16] Managerial competencies useful to Jimmy McGill, State Farm Insurance Company sales manager responsible for southern Oklahoma, also would be useful if he took a job at Government Employees

Insurance Company (GEICO). They would be useful to the manager of a local coffee shop who is interested in increasing sales during the breakfast hour and to a project manager in Paris charged with developing a new multimedia game for children. Whether you supervise the work of a small team on the shop floor or serve as CEO of a global company, honing the managerial competencies that we've identified can only enhance your performance.

Regardless of when, where, or how you develop these competencies, you should be able to use them in the future in jobs that you can't yet even imagine holding—or that may not even exist today. One way to enhance your managerial competencies is by studying this book and completing the activities presented at the end of each chapter. By participating in extracurricular activities, you can develop competencies such as communication and teamwork that often can be transferred to a variety of jobs. By taking the appropriate courses and participating in international clubs and associations, you can broaden your knowledge of other countries and build your global awareness competency. By holding an office or taking responsibility for organizing a community event, such as spring cleanup day in the park, you can build your planning and administration competency. Because managerial competencies can be learned through such activities, in addition to on the job, campus recruiters pay a great deal of attention to students' involvement in them, instead of just looking at grade point averages.

Communication Competency

Communication competency *is your ability to effectively transfer and exchange information that leads to understanding between yourself and others.* Because managing involves getting work done through other people, communication competency is essential to effective managerial performance. It includes

■ informal communication,
■ formal communication, and
■ negotiation.

Communication competency transcends the use of a particular communication medium. That is, good communication may involve having a face-to-face conversation, preparing a formal written document, participating in a global meeting via teleconferencing, giving a speech to an audience of several hundred people, or using e-mail to coordinate a project team whose members work in different regions of the country or the world.

Communication isn't something that you do *to* other people; it is something that you do *with* them. It is both informal and formal. Usually, it is a dynamic, give-and-take process that involves both receiving messages from others and sending messages to others. Besides speaking and writing, it involves listening, observing body language, and picking up on the subtle cues that people sometimes use to modify the meaning of their words. Cliff Hudson, CEO of Sonic, pays attention to all of these communication cues as he visits with employees on the job and with customers. As a member of numerous restaurant associations, he also applies his communication skills to network with other managers from other restaurants.

Of the six managerial competencies that we've identified, communication is perhaps the most fundamental. Unless you can express yourself and understand others in written, oral, and nonverbal (e.g., facial expression and body posture) communication, you can't use the other competencies effectively to accomplish tasks through other people. Nor can you effectively manage the vast network of relationships that link you to other people inside and outside of your organization.

The productive employment of workers of all ages, with varying types of work experience and expertise, of both genders and varied cultural and ethnic backgrounds, means that a basic level of communication competency is seldom enough these days. Managing effectively means getting all workers to contribute their best ideas and efforts to the goals of their organization. At J.C. Penney's, Vanessa Castagna knows that this effort requires plenty of spontaneous, informal communication that is sensitive to the different backgrounds and perspectives of employees and customers alike. Moreover, to be sure that you are understood, you need to become comfortable soliciting and accepting feedback.

Through *informal communication*, managers build a social network of contacts. In China, these connections are known as *guanxi*.[17] In Japan, they're called *kankei*, and in Korea they're called *kwankye*. Whatever language you say it in, maintaining social networks is especially important to managerial work. But in a Confucian society, the web of social contacts maintained through informal communication is central to success. In fact, when business leaders in China were asked to identify the factors most important to long-term business success, *guanxi* was the only factor chosen consistently—ahead of choosing the right business location, selecting the right business strategy, and competitive pricing. Through frequent informal communication, managers in all countries lay the groundwork for collaboration within and outside their organizations.

Being able to communicate in more formal situations also is important to managerial effectiveness. *Formal communication*, such as a newsletter, often is used to inform people of relevant events and activities and to keep people up to date on the status of ongoing projects. Public speeches are another example of formal communication. Whether the audience is company executives, professional peers, shareholders, or members of the community, high-impact public presentations can be used to address stakeholder concerns and enhance the firm's reputation.

Formal communication can also take place at a more personal level, such as during conversations with suppliers and clients. Among bankers, for example, formal communication is essential to managing client relationships. Rachel Cheeks, a manager at PepsiCo, is in charge of diversity programs for PepsiCo. Her role as a diversity manager requires her to work with managers at Frito-Lay, Tropicana, and Quaker Oats in creating programs that stimulate and reward diversity programs within their divisions. Although she has traveled to more than 15 countries during the past five years, she isn't expected to be fluent in the language of every country she visits. But she must be able to communicate, often through an interpreter, in all of these countries. In other words, for Rachel Cheeks, effective communication goes hand in hand with a global perspective. Cheeks' job also involves *negotiating*—sometimes at great distances. One negotiation with a bottling plant in South Africa was particularly intense, with down-to-the-wire discussions stretching over days. Working from her hotel room, she needed to build consensus on goals and commitment to achieving them. Good negotiators learn to seek contrary opinions and find ways to respond to the divergent views they uncover. Building consensus and commitment is useful for negotiations with bosses, peers, and subordinates, as well as with clients. Managers also must be able to negotiate to obtain resources for their subordinates and to settle disputes that arise among various stakeholders.[18]

The following Communication Competency feature highlights how The Container Store communicates with its employees. Recognized in 2002 by *Fortune* magazine as America's second best place to work for the second year in a row, the Container Store managers know how important it is to build trust and solid working relationships with employees. They also know that it's important for all managers to be seen as people who are committed to sharing information with others and developing a climate in which they and their employees have open information exchanges. Notice the various forms of communications that the Container Store uses to communicate with its employees.[19]

COMMUNICATION COMPETENCY

The Container Store

With employee turnover of greater than 100 percent in most retail stores but only 15 to 25 percent at the Container Store, how do its managers attract new employees and retain employees?

In 2002, sales exceeded $273 million for its 22 stores. How did it get this ranking? First, it practices what it preaches. Every first-year full-time employee gets about 235 hours of training. It is provided both formally and informally by ongoing communication with managers, who not only ask what their people need to do their jobs well, but also regularly assess how to provide necessary assistance. Each store has a back room where new products are housed prior to display. Employees receive formal training on how to display these new products and how to communicate their benefits. According to Garrett Boone and Kip Tindell, the Container Store's CEOs, "Nothing goes out on the sales floor until our people are ready for it." This program is coupled with extensive training programs designed to meet individual skills and job functions and team-based incentive programs. Moreover, a "super sales trainer" serves each store. These trainers are top sales performers who know how to sell the hard stuff and who have an aptitude for leadership and strong communication and presentation skills. These people give on-the-spot help to employees who ask, but employees are encouraged to take responsibility for their own development.

Guided by what Boone and Tindell call a "do-unto-others" philosophy, the Container Store's more than 2,000 employees, of whom 27 percent are minority and 60 percent are women, work in an environment that ensures open communication throughout the company, including regular discussions of store sales, company goals, and expansion plans. Another guiding principle is to offer the best selection and the best service at the best price. All employees are encouraged to treat customers like they would treat visitors in their homes. Boone and Tindell empathize with those who must cope with multiple demands on their time and energy and need to bring some order to their lives. Balancing both work and motherhood symbolizes their clientele—90 percent of whom are professional women earning more than $75,000.

Because managers spend so much of their time communicating, management recruiters look for people who can communicate effectively. In fact, we can't stress enough the importance of good communication. At a time when organizations increasingly expect employees to work with minimal supervision and show more initiative, competent oral, written, and electronic communication is essential. For more details about communication competency, refer to Table 1.2.

Planning and Administration Competency

Planning and administration competency *involves deciding what tasks need to be done, determining how they can be done, allocating resources to enable them to be done, and then monitoring progress to ensure that they are done.* For many people, planning and administration competency comes to mind first when they think about managers and managing. Included in this competency are

- information gathering, analysis, and problem solving;
- planning and organizing projects;
- time management; and
- budgeting and financial management.

When Cliff Hudson, CEO of Sonic, describes what his workday is like, he puts it this way: "Basically, the whole day comes down to a series of choices." To help him hone his planning and administration competency, Hudson and his staff analyzed his day, and his staff helped him reshape his management approach. Hudson instinctively knew that *information gathering, analysis,* and *problem solving* are important. He also recognized that customers are a rich source of useful information but that they can easily eat up a whole

Table 1.2   Dimensions of Communication Competency

Informal Communication

- Promotes two-way communication by asking for feedback, listening, and creating a give-and-take conversation.
- Has awareness of others' feelings.
- Builds strong interpersonal relationships with people.

Formal Communication

- Informs people of relevant events and activities and keeps them up to date.
- Makes persuasive, high-impact public presentations and handles questions well.
- Writes clearly, concisely, and effectively, using a variety of computer-based resources.

Negotiation

- Negotiates effectively on behalf of a team over roles and resources.
- Is skilled at developing relationships and exercising influence upward with superiors.
- Takes decisive and fair actions when handling problem subordinates.

day. His staff helped him understand that he could delegate the handling of some types of customer phone calls in order to free up 25 percent of his time for meeting directly with customers.

Planning and organizing projects usually means working with employees to clarify broad objectives, discuss resource allocation, and agree to completion dates. Thus Hudson spends 40 percent of his day with employees and customers, 25 percent on the Internet, 10 percent on the telephone, and the rest on paperwork. Because there are more problems and opportunities than he possibly can attend to, Hudson needs to *manage his time and delegate effectively*.

Managers also are accountable for *budgeting and managing financial* resources. Boards of directors and shareholders of public corporations hold CEOs, such as Carly Fiorina at Hewlett-Packard and Michael Jordan at EDS, fiscally accountable. In nonprofit and government organizations, trustees, various regulatory bodies, and elected officials oversee fiscal management.

In Table 1.3, we highlight the various dimensions that make up planning and administration competency.

Teamwork Competency

Accomplishing tasks through small groups of people who are collectively responsible and whose job requires coordination is **teamwork competency**. Managers in companies that utilize teams can become more effective by

- designing teams properly,
- creating a supportive team environment, and
- managing team dynamics appropriately.

In a study of more than 400 organizations and 80,000 managers, the Gallup Organization, a public opinion poll-taking company, found that the best managed companies used employees in teams.[20] Improving customer service was the main reason given for their use, followed by decreasing absenteeism and improving productivity. At Southwest Airlines, effective teamwork makes it possible for ground crews to turn around a plane

Table 1.3 Dimensions of Planning and Administration Competency

Information Gathering, Analysis, and Problem Solving

- Monitors information and uses it to identify symptoms, problems, and alternative solutions.
- Makes timely decisions.
- Takes calculated risks and anticipates the consequences.

Planning and Organizing Projects

- Develops plans and schedules to achieve goals efficiently.
- Assigns priorities to tasks and delegates responsibility.
- Determines, obtains, and organizes necessary resources to accomplish the task.

Time Management

- Handles several issues and projects at one time but doesn't spread self too thin.
- Monitors and keeps to a schedule or changes schedule if needed.
- Works effectively under time pressure.

Budgeting and Financial Management

- Understands budgets, cash flows, financial reports, and annual reports and regularly uses such information to make decisions.
- Keeps accurate and complete financial records.
- Creates budgetary guidelines for others and works within the guidelines given by others.

at the gate in less than 17 minutes. Regardless of their job titles, all employees work together to get passengers unloaded and loaded. When necessary, pilots, flight attendants, and whoever else is available pitch in to ensure that a flight leaves the boarding gate on schedule.

When people think of teamwork, they often make a distinction between the team members and a team leader. We don't hold this view of teamwork. Instead, we view teamwork as a competency that involves taking the lead at times, supporting others who are taking the lead at other times, and collaborating with others in the organization on projects that don't even have a designated team leader. We hold this view of teamwork competency because most managerial work involves doing all of these activities simultaneously.

Designing the team is the first step for any team project and usually is the responsibility of a manager or team leader. But in self-managed teams, the entire team participates in the design. Team design involves formulating goals to be achieved, defining tasks to be done, and identifying the staffing needed to accomplish those tasks. Team members should identify with the team's goals and feel committed to accomplishing them. Members of a well-designed team understand its tasks and how its performance will be measured; they aren't confused about which tasks are theirs and which tasks are some other team's. A well-designed team has just the right number of members. Too many members leave room for free riders; too few create too much stress and leave the team feeling incapable of successfully achieving its goals.

A well-designed team is capable of high performance, but it needs a *supportive environment* to achieve its full potential.[21] All team members should have the competencies needed to create a supportive environment. In a supportive environment, team members are empowered to take actions based on their best judgment, without always seeking approval first from the team leader or project manager. Support also involves eliciting contributions from members whose unique competencies are important for the team and recognizing, praising, and rewarding both minor victories and major successes. A manager having good teamwork competency respects other people and is respected and even liked by them in return. Managers who lack teamwork competency often are viewed as being rude, abrupt, and unsympathetic, making others feel inadequate and resentful. Fundamentally, creating a supportive environment involves coaching, counseling, and mentoring team members to improve their performance in the near term and prepare them for future challenges.

How an organization fosters teamwork is often just as important as teamwork itself. Managers with the greatest likelihood of developing their employees' teamwork competency are those who have input from all levels of the organization, including members of the team, employees who support the team, those who will administer the plan, and even customers. Managers need to pay attention to *managing team dynamics*. If team members remain ignorant about a process, they are more likely to reject it out of hand. People want to be involved. The Teamwork Competency feature highlights how teams work at Whole Foods.[22]

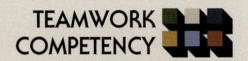

TEAMWORK COMPETENCY

Teams at Whole Foods

The Whole Foods Market culture is based on decentralized teamwork. Each of the stores is a profit center that typically has 10 self-managed teams—produce, grocery, prepared foods, and so on—with designated leaders and clear performance targets. The team leaders in each store are a team, store leaders in each region are a team, and the company's six regional presidents are a team. Three principles define how the company operates.

The first principle is *all work is teamwork*. Everyone who joins Whole Foods quickly grasps the importance of teamwork. That's because teams—and only teams—have the power to approve new hires for full-time jobs.

Store leaders screen candidates and recommend them for a job on a specific team. But it takes a two-thirds vote of the team, after what is usually a 30-day trial period, for the candidate to become a full-time employee. Team members are tough on new hires for another reason: money. The company's gain-sharing program ties bonuses directly to team performance—specifically, to sales per labor hour, the most important productivity measurement at Whole Foods.

The second principle is *anything worth doing is worth measuring*. Whole Foods takes that simple principle to extremes—and then shares what it measures with everyone in the company. John Mackey, the CEO, calls it

a "no-secrets" management philosophy. He states, "In most companies, management controls information and therefore controls people. By sharing information, we stay alighted to the vision of shared fate." The reports are indispensable to the teams, which make the decisions about labor spending, ordering, and pricing—the factors that determine profitability.

The third principle is *be your own toughest competitor*. "All-for-one" doesn't imply complacency. Whole Foods is serious about accountability. Teams are expected to set ambitious goals and achieve them. Teams compete against their own goals for sales, growth, and productivity.

Because more and more organizations are relying on teams to improve quality, productivity, and customer service, it becomes increasingly important for you to develop your teamwork competency and become a productive team member. For more detail about teamwork competency, refer to Table 1.4.

Strategic Action Competency

Understanding the overall mission and values of the organization and ensuring that employees' actions match with them defines **strategic action competency**. Strategic action competency includes

◾ understanding the industry,

Table 1.4   **Dimensions of Teamwork Competency**

Designing Teams

- Formulates clear objectives that inspire team members to perform.
- Appropriately staffs the team, taking into account the value of diverse ideas and technical skills needed.
- Defines responsibilities for the team as a whole and assigns tasks and responsibilities to individual team members as appropriate.

Creating a Supportive Environment

- Creates an environment in which effective teamwork is expected, recognized, praised, and rewarded.
- Assists the team in identifying and acquiring the resources it needs to accomplish its goals.
- Acts as a coach, counselor, and mentor, being patient with team members as they learn.

Managing Team Dynamics

- Understands the strengths and weaknesses of team members and uses their strengths to accomplish tasks as a team.
- Brings conflict and dissent into the open and uses it to enhance performance.
- Shares credit with others.

- understanding the organization, and
- taking strategic actions.

Today, employees at all levels and in all functional areas are being challenged to think strategically in order to perform their jobs better. They are expected to recognize that shifts in a company's strategic direction are to be expected—even anticipated. Managers and employees who understand the industry can accurately anticipate strategic trends and prepare for the future needs of the organization, and they are less likely to find themselves looking for new jobs when the organization changes direction.

One manager who has proved that she is extremely good at *understanding the industry* in which she operates is Susan Kennedy, president of Penguin Putnam, Inc., a publisher of paperback books. In less than three years, Kennedy assembled a team of editors who could recognize author talent and excelled at bringing author manuscripts from the idea stage to the final product. She created Penguin Classics, a division that publishes books that have a long life and a classic meaning to them. Under her leadership, the classic division has quadrupled its profitability and increased its sales fivefold in the past three years. She also managed the acquisition of Fawcett Books and House Collectibles by Penguin.[23]

This competency also involves *understanding the organization*—not just the particular unit in which a manager works—as a system of interrelated parts. It includes comprehending how departments, functions, and divisions relate to one another and how a change in one can affect others. A manager with well-developed strategic action competency can diagnose and assess different types of management problems and issues that might arise. Such a manager thinks in terms of relative priorities rather than iron-clad goals and criteria. All managers, but especially top managers, need strategic action competency. Top managers, such as John Mackey of Whole Foods or Allen Questrom of J.C. Penney's, must perceive changes in the organization's environment and be prepared to *take strategic actions*. For more detail about strategic action competency, refer to Table 1.5.

Table 1.5   Dimensions of Strategic Action Competency

Understanding the Industry

- Understands the industry and quickly recognizes when changes in the industry create significant threats and opportunities.
- Stays informed of the actions of competitors and strategic partners.
- Can analyze general trends in the industry and their implications for the future.

Understanding the Organization

- Understands the concerns of stakeholders.
- Understands the strengths and limitations of various business strategies.
- Understands the distinctive competencies of the organization.

Taking Strategic Actions

- Assigns priorities and makes decisions that are consistent with the firm's mission and strategic goals.
- Recognizes the management challenges of alternative strategies and addresses them.
- Establishes tactical and operational goals that facilitate strategy implementation.

Global Awareness Competency

Carrying out an organization's managerial work by drawing on the human, financial, information, and material resources from multiple countries and serving markets that span multiple cultures refers to a manager's **global awareness competency**. Not all organizations have global markets for their products and services. Nor do all organizations need to set up operations in other countries to take advantage of tax laws and labor that is cheaper or better trained. Nevertheless, over the course of your career, you probably will work for an organization that has an international component. To be prepared for such opportunities, you should begin to develop your global awareness competency, which is reflected in

- cultural knowledge and understanding, and
- cultural openness and sensitivity.

In the course of growing up and being educated in a particular country or region, people naturally develop cultural knowledge and understanding of forces that shape their lives and the conduct of business.[24] These forces include geography and climate, political processes and orientations, economic systems and trends, history, religion, values, beliefs, and local customs. By the time you become a manager in your home country, your own culture has become second nature to you, so you don't need to devote much time developing further a general knowledge and awareness of it. However, unless you have traveled extensively, or have specifically studied other cultures as part of your education, you probably have much less general knowledge and understanding of other countries, except perhaps those that share a border with your own country. Yet because business is becoming global, many managers are now expected to develop *a knowledge and an understanding* of at least a few other cultures, such as those where suppliers are located or those with newly emerging markets that can help sustain their companies' future growth.

The Competent Manager

"I wonder if we can compete profitably in the French market with old-fashioned regulations and generous labor benefits. Coffee served in Styrofoam cups to the French seems ludicrous."

Howard Schultz
CEO
Starbucks

Simply knowing about other cultures isn't sufficient; appropriate attitudes and skills are needed to translate this knowledge into effective performance. An open attitude about cultural differences and sensitivity to them are especially important for anyone who must operate across cultural boundaries. *Openness and sensitivity* involve, first and foremost, recognizing that culture makes a difference in how people think and act. You can't assume that everyone will think and act as you do, nor that everyone will automatically understand your point of view. Second, openness and sensitivity mean actively considering how another culture might differ from your own and examining how your own culture affects your behavior.

Knowledge about other cultures and an open attitude and sensitivity about cultural differences set the stage for working with people from other backgrounds.[25] In any culture, appropriate language, social etiquette, and negotiation skills help in developing effective work relationships. Depending on your job, you may also need to learn country-specific laws, accounting methods, hiring techniques, and so on. Because there are so many cultures and because predicting which cultures will be most important to you in the future is so difficult, you shouldn't expect to develop global awareness competency relevant to many of the world's cultures. But neither can you put off beginning to build a good foundation.

Because of language and cultural differences, organizations must consider product names when selling in international markets. Inadequate translation can result in a negative image for the product and company. Global markets are complex and often difficult to understand. The following Global Awareness Competency feature highlights some problems that Procter & Gamble (P&G) had in its global operations.[26] It employs more than 102,000 people in 80 countries and had sales of $40.2 billion and profits of $4.4 billion last year. What could be the problem?

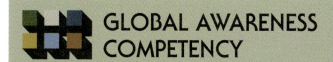

GLOBAL AWARENESS COMPETENCY

Procter & Gamble

It's late afternoon and a dozen of P&G's top managers are meeting in European headquarters in Geneva, Switzerland. Plastered on the conference room walls are poster-sized photos of competitors' brands with direct quotes from shoppers, such as "I buy store brands and not advertised brands. There is really no difference." "Can't see value in brands. Why pay more."

Europe is a billion-dollar battleground for P&G that lost it market share under the prior CEO, Dirk Jager. The managers gathered around the table note that Aldi, a German discounter, has huge success in selling its private brands. Sitting in the back of the room and lis-

tening was A. G. Lafley, P&G's CEO. After listening for several hours, he indicated that the global strategy of trying to find the next billion-dollar product, like Tide or Pampers, was wishful thinking. In an effort to globalize its products, in 2000 P&G decided its products should be sold under the same name around the globe. Unfortunately in Germany, for example, P&G dishwashing liquid changed its name from Fairy to Dawn and sales dropped since no one in Germany knew what Dawn was.

Lafley suggested that perhaps P&G should refocus the company around its 10 big core brands that each generated more than $1 billion in sales. He argued that selling Tide in France

©Diaphor Agency/Index Stock Imagery

was easier than trying to invent the new Tide. More importantly, P&G had known how to ingeniously sell Tide since 1946. Lafley also wanted all managers to spend time in the stores and work as hands-on managers with P&G salespeople. For example, while visiting Greece, he chatted with customers and the store

Managers do not share the same cultural knowledge and understanding around the world. Global managers must understand other societies' religions, languages, values, laws, and ethics. Knowing the behaviors fostered by other cultures can help determine which course of action is most appropriate. In the preceding Global Awareness Competency feature, obvious mistakes were made that cost P&G market share and profits. For more detail about global awareness competency, refer to Table 1.6.

Table 1.6	Dimensions of Global Awareness Competency

Cultural Knowledge and Understanding

- Stays informed of political, social, and economic trends and events around the world.
- Recognizes the impact of global events on the organization.
- Understands, reads, and speaks more than one language fluently.

Cultural Openness and Sensitivity

- Understands the nature of national, ethnic, and cultural differences and is open to examining these differences honestly and objectively.
- Is sensitive to cultural cues and is able to adapt quickly in novel situations.
- Appropriately adjusts own behavior when interacting with people from various national, ethnic, and cultural backgrounds.

Self-Management Competency

Taking responsibility for your life at work and beyond is a manager's **self-management competency**. Often, when things don't go well, people tend to blame their difficulties on the situations in which they find themselves or on others. Effective managers don't fall into this trap. Self-management competency includes

- integrity and ethical conduct,
- personal drive and resilience,
- balancing work and life issues, and
- self-awareness and development.

You may be thinking that self-management really doesn't require much time and effort. Dee Hock would disagree. More than 1 billion people use Visa card, but did you know that Dee Hock is the man who built this worldwide powerhouse? Since 1970, when Hock founded Visa, the company has grown from an idea to a service that operates in more than 24 million locations in 130 countries and has an annual volume of roughly $3.6 trillion. Dee Hock, the man behind this phenomenal success story, isn't a household name, but his success as a manager is unquestioned—which is why he is such a popular speaker at CEO gatherings even though he has retired from Visa.[27]

Just as customers expect companies to behave ethically, organizations expect their employees to *show integrity and act ethically*. When recruiting entry-level employees—who don't yet have a long record of employment or much technical expertise—these qualities may be the most important ones that employers look for. According to a recent

Gallup poll, when companies hire young employees, they are far more concerned with the employees' integrity and interest in the job than with their specific technical skills and aptitudes.

Personal drive and resilience are especially important when someone sets out to do something no one else has done and when that person faces setbacks and failures. As its founder, Jeff Bezos needed personal drive and resilience when he decided to start Amazon.com. Because there were no other online companies, banks and venture capital firms were not interested in funding him. It was his parents who originally gave him the $300,000 to start the company.

According to a Catalyst Organization survey of 1,725 women of color managers and *Fortune* magazine's study of 1,735 MBA students, building a family is a top priority for the majority of the respondents. Hoping to have it all, 75 percent gave developing a career a top rating also.[28] Clearly, these future managers won't succeed unless they can find a way to *balance work and life issues.* These demands, which often conflict, and other family concerns led Congress to pass and the president to sign the Family and Medical Leave Act in 1993. In addition, many of the best companies to work for, including Southwest Airlines, Cisco Systems, SAS Institute, and Edward Jones, have family-friendly policies. The self-management competency is needed to decide when and how best to take advantage of such policies. New mothers and fathers alike may feel pressure to return to work soon after the arrival of a new family member, rather than take the entire leave allowed them. Having succumbed to work pressures, many parents experience pangs of guilt or anxiety when they look at the family photo sitting on the corner of the desk. Knowing your own work and life priorities, and finding a way to juggle them all, may be the most difficult management challenge many of you will face.

The dynamic work environment calls for *self-awareness and development* (as well as the ability continually to unlearn and relearn!). That includes both task-related learning and learning about you. On the one hand, task-related learning can directly improve your performance in your current job and prepare you to take on new jobs. Learning about yourself, on the other hand, can help you make wiser choices about which types of jobs you are likely to enjoy. With fewer opportunities for promotions and upward advancement, finding work that you enjoy doing is even more important today than in the past. Taking responsibility for your own career development—by understanding the type of work you find satisfying and developing the competencies that you will need—may be the best route to long-term success.

Research shows that people who take advantage of the development and training opportunities that employers offer learn much from them and advance more quickly than those who don't take advantage of them. Derailment awaits managers who fail to develop their competencies. A derailed manager is one who has moved into a position of managerial responsibility but has little chance of future advancement or gaining new responsibilities. The most common reasons for derailment are (1) problems with interpersonal relationships and inability to lead a team (weak in teamwork competency); (2) inability to learn, develop, and adapt (weak in self-management competency); (3) performance problems (weak in planning and administration competency); and (4) having a narrow functional perspective (lacking strong strategic action and global awareness competencies).[29] Table 1.7 provides more detail about self-management competency.

Exploring Your Managerial Competencies

Throughout this book, both in the text and in the exercises and cases at the end of each chapter, we present material to help you develop the six managerial competencies that we've just described. For example, you've already read about how managers at The Container Store use their communication competency to help develop employees' passion for customer service. You've also seen how Cliff Hudson's planning and administration

Table 1.7   Dimensions of Self-Management Competency

Integrity and Ethical Conduct

- Has clear personal standards that serve as a foundation for maintaining a sense of integrity and ethical conduct.
- Is willing to admit mistakes.
- Accepts responsibility for own actions.

Personal Drive and Resilience

- Seeks responsibility and is ambitious and motivated to achieve objectives.
- Works hard to get things done.
- Shows perseverance in the face of obstacles and bounces back from failure.

Balancing Work and Life Issues

- Strikes a reasonable balance between work and other life activities so that neither aspect of living is neglected.
- Takes good care of self, mentally and physically, and uses constructive outlets to vent frustration and reduce tension.
- Assesses and establishes own life- and work-related goals.

Self-Awareness and Development

- Has clear personal and career goals.
- Uses strengths to advantage while seeking to improve or compensate for weaknesses.
- Analyzes and learns from work and life experiences.

and self-management competencies helped him develop Sonic into a successful drive-in restaurant business. And you've learned how Lafley at P&G used his global awareness competencies to improve P&G's performance. Examples such as these will help you develop an understanding of how all six competencies contribute to performance in jobs that involve managerial work.

We believe that continual development of your managerial competencies is essential because the challenges you will face on the job are constantly changing. In addition, fundamental changes in the business environment will continue to occur. To ensure that your organization keeps pace with these changes, you will want to improve its performance. Identifying your strengths and development needs is the first important step in the process of improving your managerial performance. To help you assess your strengths and weaknesses, we have included a self-assessment competency questionnaire on pages 28–33. We asked you to complete it earlier, but if you have not done so, please do so now.

CHAPTER SUMMARY

In this chapter we introduced several concepts that you need to understand in order to be a successful manager in the years ahead. Because the nature and scope of management are changing so rapidly, no simple prescription can be given for how to manage. Rather, managers today and in the future need to develop six important competencies to enable them to lead dynamic organizations and tackle a variety of emerging organizational issues. You now should be able to do the following.

1. Define managers and management.

Managers establish organizational goals and then direct the work of subordinates, on whom they depend to achieve those goals. Managers acquire and allocate the human and material resources without which organizations couldn't exist. Effective management is essential to the success of an organization.

2. Explain what managers do.

The managerial functions—planning, organizing, leading, and controlling—are what managers do. Managers at different levels in an organization spend their time differently, but they all spend at least some time performing each function. The three basic levels of management are first line, middle, and top. First-line managers are directly responsible for the production of goods and services. They supervise workers and solve specific problems. Middle managers coordinate the work of several first-line managers or direct the operations of a functional department. They translate top management's goals into specific goals and programs for implementation. Top managers establish overall organizational goals and direct the activities of an entire organization or a major segment of an organization.

Managers at different levels divide their time among the managerial functions quite differently. First-line managers spend most of their time leading and controlling and the rest planning and organizing. Middle managers spend most of their time organizing and leading and the rest planning and controlling. Top managers spend most of their time planning and leading and very little time directly organizing and controlling. Managerial work also varies in scope, broadening at each higher level.

3. Describe the competencies used in managerial work and assess your current competency levels.

To be an effective manager in a dynamic environment requires six managerial competencies: communication, teamwork, planning and administration, strategic action, global awareness, and self-management. You can develop these competencies through study, training, and experience. By doing so, you can prepare yourself for a variety of jobs in various industries and countries. You can continue practicing your managerial competencies by completing the exercises at the end of this chapter.

KEY TERMS and CONCEPTS

Communication competency
Competency
Controlling
First-line managers
Functional managers
General managers
Global awareness competency
Leading
Management
Manager

Managerial competencies
Middle managers
Organization
Organizing
Planning
Planning and administration competency
Self-management competency
Strategic action competency
Teamwork competency
Top managers

QUESTIONS FOR DISCUSSION and COMPETENCY DEVELOPMENT

1. What management functions does Allen Questrom perform as CEO of J.C. Penney's?

2. What competencies do you need to work at the Container Store?

3. What teamwork competencies are needed for a person to work at Whole Foods?

4. Cynthia Bland, a manager for Marriott International, says, "The Internet and e-mail are making it easier to communicate with people across cultures." Do you agree or disagree? Why?

5. Think of a team of which you are a member. Using the Teamwork Competency section of the Exercise for Competency Development Self-Assessment Inventory on pages 30–31, evaluate the team's effectiveness.

6. Why is it so difficult to become an effective middle manager?

7. What combination of competencies did Lafley use to turn Procter & Gamble around?

8. How does a person's background affect the development of his or her managerial competencies?

SELF-ASSESSMENT INVENTORY

Instructions (for self-administration)

Each of the five following statements describes a level of attainment on a dimension of a managerial competency. How well do you think each statement describes you? Following these statements is a list of 95 characteristics that are representative of effective, experienced managers. Next to each characteristic, fill in the number corresponding to the level-of-attainment statement that applies best to you. Presenting an accurate self-appraisal is important to understanding your current competencies and what you need to do to develop them further.

Level of Attainment

1. I have very little relevant experience. I have not yet begun to develop this characteristic.
2. I think that I am weak in this characteristic. I have had relevant experience, but I have not performed well.
3. I think that I am about average on this characteristic. It will take a good deal of focused effort for me to be consistently effective.
4. I think that I am above average on this characteristic. I need to develop this characteristic further in order to be highly effective.
5. I think that I am outstanding on this characteristic. I need to maintain my strong effectiveness on this characteristic.

Characteristic

1. Seeks out and listens to others who have contrary opinions.
2. In speaking with others, is able to make people feel comfortable in different situations.
3. Varies communication approach when dealing with others from different backgrounds.
4. Builds strong interpersonal relationships with a diverse range of people.
5. Shows genuine sensitivity to the feelings of others.
6. Informs people of events that are relevant to them.
7. Makes persuasive, high-impact presentations before groups.
8. When making formal presentations, handles questions from the audience well.
9. Writes clearly and concisely.
10. Communicates effectively using electronic media.

11. Is comfortable using power associated with leadership roles.
12. Skilled at influencing superiors.
13. Skilled at influencing peers.
14. When addressing problems, finds solutions that others perceive as fair.
15. In conflict situations, helps parties move toward win–win situations.
16. Monitors information that is relevant to ongoing projects and activities.
17. Obtains and uses relevant information to identify symptoms and underlying problems.
18. Makes decisions on time.
19. When taking risks, is able to anticipate negative and positive consequences.
20. Knows when expert knowledge is needed and seeks it out to solve problems.
21. Develops plans and schedules to achieve specific goals efficiently.
22. Prioritizes tasks in order to stay focused on those that are most important.
23. Can organize people around specific tasks to help them work together toward a common objective.
24. Is comfortable delegating responsibility for tasks to others.
25. Anticipates possible problems and develops plans for how to deal with them.
26. Handles several issues and projects at the same time but doesn't spread self too thin.
27. Monitors and keeps to a schedule or negotiates changes in the schedule if needed.
28. Works effectively under time pressure.
29. Knows when to permit interruptions and when to screen them out.
30. Knows when to renegotiate established deadlines in order to deliver satisfactory results.
31. Understands budgets, cash flow, financial reports, and annual reports.
32. Regularly uses budgets and financial reports to make decisions.
33. Keeps accurate and complete financial records.
34. Creates budgetary guidelines for others.

_____ 35. Works well within the budgetary guidelines given by others.

_____ 36. Formulates clear goals that inspire team members' commitment.

_____ 37. Appropriately selects team members, taking into account diversity of viewpoints and technical skills.

_____ 38. Provides team members with a clear vision of what is to be accomplished by the team as a whole.

_____ 39. Assigns tasks and responsibilities to individual team members consistent with their competencies and interests.

_____ 40. Creates a process for monitoring team performance.

_____ 41. Creates a team setting in which team members feel that their suggestions make a difference.

_____ 42. Recognizes, praises, and rewards team members for their contributions.

_____ 43. Assists the team in acquiring the resources and support it needs to accomplish its goals.

_____ 44. Acts as a coach, counselor, and mentor for team members.

_____ 45. Is patient with team members as they learn new roles and develop their competencies.

_____ 46. Is aware of team members' feelings.

_____ 47. Understands the strengths and limitations of team members.

_____ 48. Brings conflict and dissent within the team into the open and uses them to improve quality of decisions.

_____ 49. Facilitates cooperative behavior among team members.

_____ 50. Keeps the team moving toward its goals.

_____ 51. Understands the history of the industry of which the organization is a part.

_____ 52. Stays informed of the actions of competitors and strategic partners in the industry of which the organization is a part.

_____ 53. Can analyze general industry trends and understand their implications for the future.

_____ 54. Quickly recognizes when significant changes occur in the industry.

_____ 55. Knows how organizations compete in the industry.

_____ 56. Understands the concerns of all major stakeholders of the organization.

_____ 57. Understands the strengths and limitations of various business strategies.

_____ 58. Knows the distinctive strengths of the organization.

_____ 59. Understands the organizational structure and how work really gets done.

_____ 60. Is able to fit into the unique culture of the organization.

_____ 61. Assigns priorities that are consistent with the organization's mission and strategic goals.

_____ 62. Recognizes and resists pressures to behave in ways that are not consistent with the organization's mission and strategic goals.

_____ 63. Considers the long-term implications of decisions on the organization.

_____ 64. Establishes tactical and operational goals to implement strategies.

_____ 65. Keeps the unit focused on its goals.

_____ 66. Stays informed of political events around the world.

_____ 67. Stays informed of economic events around the world.

_____ 68. Recognizes the impact of global events on the organization.

_____ 69. Travels to gain first-hand knowledge of other countries.

_____ 70. Understands and speaks more than one language.

_____ 71. Is sensitive to cultural cues and is able to adapt quickly in novel situations.

_____ 72. Recognizes that there is great variation within any culture and avoids stereotyping.

_____ 73. Appropriately adjusts behavior when interacting with people from various national, ethnic, and cultural backgrounds.

_____ 74. Understands how own cultural background affects own attitudes and behaviors.

_____ 75. Can empathize with those from different cultural backgrounds.

_____ 76. Has clear personal standards that serve as a foundation for maintaining a sense of integrity and ethical conduct.

_____ 77. Maintains personal ethical standards under fire.

_____ 78. Is sincere and projects self-assurance; doesn't just tell people what they want to hear.

_____ 79. Recognizes own mistakes and admits to having made them.

_____ 80. Accepts responsibility for own actions.

_____ 81. Seeks responsibility beyond what is required by the job.

_____ **82.** Is willing to innovate and take personal risks.

_____ **83.** Ambitious and motivated to achieve goals.

_____ **84.** Works hard to get things done.

_____ **85.** Shows perseverance in the face of obstacles.

_____ **86.** Strikes a reasonable balance between work and other life activities.

_____ **87.** Takes good care of self mentally and emotionally.

_____ **88.** Uses constructive outlets to vent frustration and reduce tension.

_____ **89.** Exercises and eats properly.

_____ **90.** Knows how to enjoy leisure time.

_____ **91.** Has clear personal and career goals.

_____ **92.** Knows own values, feelings, and areas of strengths and limitations.

_____ **93.** Accepts responsibility for continuous self-development.

_____ **94.** Develops plans and seeks opportunities for personal long-term growth.

_____ **95.** Analyzes and learns from work and life experiences.

Scoring and Interpretation

The Exercise for Competency Development Self-Assessment Inventory measures characteristics that are representative of the core dimensions of the six basic managerial competencies. These managerial competencies are discussed on pages 14–25.

Transfer the number that you recorded next to each characteristic in the inventory to the corresponding competency dimension in the following list.

Communication Competency. Effective transfer and exchange of information that leads to understanding between yourself and others.

■ *Informal Communication Dimension:*

1_____ 2_____ 3_____ 4_____ 5_____

Add numbers recorded = _____ / 5 =_____, which equals your average self-assessment on this dimension.

■ *Formal Communication Dimension:*

6_____ 7_____ 8_____ 9_____ 10_____

Add numbers recorded = _____ / 5 = _____, which equals your average self-assessment on this dimension.

■ *Negotiation Dimension:*

11_____ 12_____ 13_____ 14_____ 15_____

Add numbers recorded = _____ / 5 = _____, which equals your average self-assessment on this dimension.

■ *Summary:*

Add the average scores for the three dimensions of this competency =_____ / 3 = _____, which is your overall average self-assessment for communication competency.

Planning and Administration Competency. Deciding what tasks need to be done, determining how they can be done, allocating resources to enable them to be done, and then monitoring progress to ensure that they are done.

■ *Information Gathering, Analysis, and Problem-Solving Dimension:*

16_____ 17_____ 18_____ 19_____ 20_____

Add numbers recorded = _____ / 5 = _____, which equals your average self-assessment on this dimension.

■ *Planning and Organizing Projects Dimension:*

21_____ 22_____ 23_____ 24_____ 25_____

Add numbers recorded = _____ / 5 = _____, which equals your average self-assessment on this dimension.

■ *Time Management Dimension:*

26_____ 27_____ 28_____ 29_____ 30_____

Add numbers recorded = _____ / 5 = _____, which equals your average self-assessment on this dimension.

■ *Budgeting and Financial Management Dimension:*

31_____ 32_____ 33_____ 34_____ 35_____

Add numbers recorded = _____ / 5 = _____, which equals your average self-assessment on this dimension.

■ *Summary:*

Add the average scores for the three dimensions of this competency = _____ / 4 = _____, which is your overall average self-assessment for planning and administration competency.

Teamwork Competency. Accomplishing tasks through small groups of people who are collectively responsible and whose work is interdependent.

- *Designing Teams Dimension:*

  36_____ 37_____ 38_____ 39_____ 40_____

  Add numbers recorded = _____ / 5 = _____, which equals your average self-assessment on this dimension.

- *Creating a Supportive Environment Dimension:*

  41_____ 42_____ 43_____ 44_____ 45_____

  Add numbers recorded = _____ / 5 = _____, which equals your average self-assessment on this dimension.

- *Managing a Team Dynamics Dimension:*

  46_____ 47_____ 48_____ 49_____ 50_____

  Add numbers recorded = _____ / 5 = _____, which equals your average self-assessment on this dimension.

- *Summary:*

  Add the average scores for the three dimensions of this competency = _____ / 3 = _____, which is your overall average self-assessment for teamwork competency.

Strategic Action Competency. Understanding the overall mission(s) and values of the organization and ensuring that your actions and those of the people you manage are aligned with them.

- *Understanding the Industry Dimension:*

  51_____ 52_____ 53_____ 54_____ 55_____

  Add numbers recorded = _____ / 5 = _____, which equals your average self-assessment on this dimension.

- *Understanding the Organization Dimension:*

  56_____ 57_____ 58_____ 59_____ 60_____

  Add numbers recorded = _____ / 5 = _____, which equals your average self-assessment on this dimension.

- *Taking Strategic Actions Dimension:*

  61_____ 62_____ 63_____ 64_____ 65_____

  Add numbers recorded = _____ / 5 = _____, which equals your average self-assessment on this dimension.

- *Summary:*

  Add the average scores for the three dimensions of this competency = _____ / 3 = _____, which is your overall average self-assessment for strategic action competency.

Global Awareness Competency. Carrying out an organization's managerial work by drawing on the human, financial, information, and material resources from multiple countries and serving markets that span multiple cultures.

- *Cultural Knowledge and Understanding Dimension:*

  66_____ 67_____ 68_____ 69_____ 70_____

  Add numbers recorded = _____ / 5 = _____, which equals your average self-assessment on this dimension.

- *Cultural Openness and Sensitivity Dimension:*

  71_____ 72_____ 73_____ 74_____ 75_____

  Add numbers recorded = _____ / 5 = _____, which equals your average self-assessment on this dimension.

- *Summary:*

  Add the average scores for the three dimensions of this competency = _____ / 2 = _____, which is your overall average self-assessment for global awareness competency.

Self-Management Competency. Taking responsibility for your life at work and beyond.

- *Integrity and Ethical Conduct Dimension:*

  76_____ 77_____ 78_____ 79_____ 80_____

  Add numbers recorded = _____ / 5 = _____, which equals your average self-assessment on this dimension.

- *Personal Drive and Resilience Dimension:*

  81_____ 82_____ 83_____ 84_____ 85_____

  Add numbers recorded = _____ / 5 = _____, which equals your average self-assessment on this dimension.

- *Balancing Work and Life Issues Dimension:*

  86_____ 87_____ 88_____ 89_____ 90_____

  Add numbers recorded = _____ / 5 = _____, which equals your average self-assessment on this dimension.

- *Self-Awareness and Development Dimension:*

  91_____ 92_____ 93_____ 94_____ 95_____

  Add numbers recorded = _____ / 5 = _____, which equals your average self-assessment on this dimension.

- *Summary:*

  Add the average scores for the three dimensions of this competency = _____ / 4 = _____, which is your overall average self-assessment for self-management competency.

Overall Profile

Instructions. Plot your overall profile of managerial competencies on the following grid, using the *summary average score* for each competency and multiplying the average score for each competency by 20. For example, if your average score on a competency is 3.2, you would multiply it by 20 to obtain a total score of 64 out of 100 possible points on that competency and mark that point on the grid. Then connect the points marked on each vertical line.

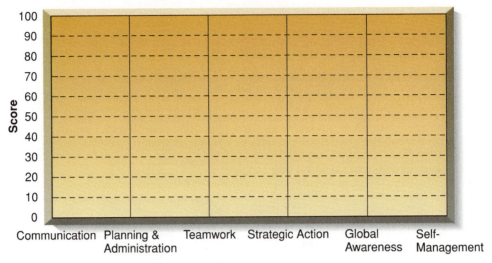

Competency

Overall Interpretations

Score	Meaning
20–39	You have little relevant experience and are quite weak in this competency.
40–59	You are generally weak in this competency but are performing satisfactorily or better on a few characteristics.
60–74	You are generally about average in this competency and above average or better on some characteristics.
75–89	You are generally above average in this competency and outstanding on a number of characteristics.
90–100	You are generally outstanding in this competency.

Questions

1. What does this profile suggest in relation to needed development in areas of your professional and personal life?

2. Based on the managerial competency in most need of development, identify three possible actions that you might take to reduce the gap between your current and desired level for that competency.

3. Would others who work with you closely or who otherwise know you well agree with your self-assessment profile? On what dimensions might their and your assessments be similar? Different?

4. How do your scores compare to those of hundreds of students and seasoned managers, as shown in the graph on page 33?

Scores of Managerial Competencies for Managers and Students

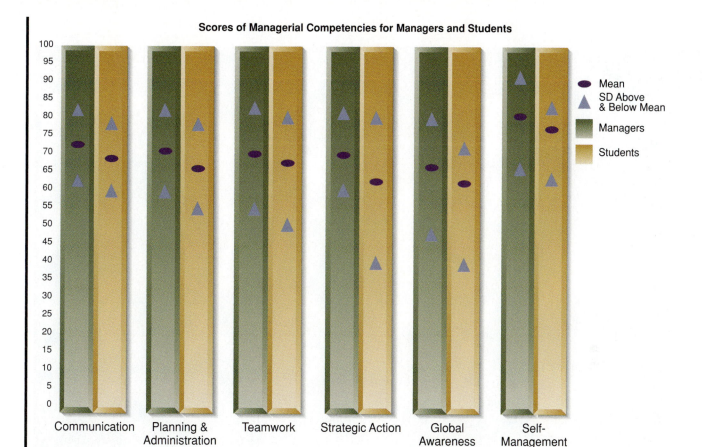

©Index Stock Imagery

The Evolution of Management

Learning Objectives

After studying this chapter, you should be able to:

1. Describe the three branches of the traditional viewpoint of management: bureaucratic, scientific, and administrative.

2. Explain the behavioral viewpoint's contribution to management.

3. Describe how managers can use systems and quantitative techniques to improve employee performance.

4. State the two major components of the contingency viewpoint.

5. Explain the impact of the need for quality on management practices.

Chapter Outline

Jim Casey and Claude Ryan started American Messenger Company, a phone message service, in Seattle in 1907. They soon started making small-parcel deliveries for local department stores and changed the name to Merchants Parcel Delivery. In 1930, the company changed its name to United Parcel Service (UPS) and served residents in the New York City area. In 2001, UPS bought Mail Boxes Etc., a franchiser of stores that offer mailing, packing, and shipping services. Today, UPS has facilities in more than 200 countries and territories. Recently it earned $2.4 billion on revenues of more than $31 billion. How?

The answer is automation and bureaucracy. Mechanized centers sort 51,650 packages per hour. Jobs at UPS centers reflect clearly defined divisions of labor, drivers, and property maintenance employees. There are eight management levels from washer

to president. Property maintenance employees are responsible for washing, fueling, and maintaining more than 160,000 fleet delivery vehicles and 600 aircraft. Employees who operate sorting machines handle more than 2,000 packages an hour and are allowed no more than one mistake per 2,500 packages handled. During the holiday rush, a package is handled every two seconds. The more than 371,000 employees handle 14 million packages daily exactly the same way because of the rules and regulations. Each manager is given several bound policy manuals detailing company rules. For example, drivers are told to walk to a customer's door at a brisk pace of 3 feet per second, carrying the package in their right hand and clipboard in the left. They should knock so as not to lose valuable seconds searching for the doorbell.

Technical qualifications are UPS's criteria for hiring and promotion. The company's manual reads, "A leader does not need to remind others of authority by use of title. Knowledge, performance, and capacity should be adequate evidence of position and leadership." Special favors are forbidden. Employees set objective performance targets with their managers. Promotions and salary increases are based on objective performance criteria.

UPS relies on extensive written records and computer systems to store data. Operating costs and production figures are compared to competitors, such as FedEx, DHL Worldwide Express, and Airborne. Daily worksheets specifying performance quotas are kept on every employee and department. Employee production records are accumulated weekly and monthly.[1]

TRADITIONAL VIEWPOINT OF MANAGEMENT

1. Describe the three branches of the traditional viewpoint of management: bureaucratic, scientific, and administrative.

Working for a global company with plants scattered throughout the world is getting to be commonplace. In the past 10 years or so, companies such as Citigroup, Procter & Gamble (P&G), Marriott, and General Electric, have challenged their managers to manage on a global scale. Managers now lead employees whom they seldom, if ever, see and who may know more about solving a problem than they do. Although new methods of managing employees are needed to keep pace with changes in today's organizations and technology, let's not discard what happened in management before the arrival of the Information Superhighway. The reason is that management today reflects the evolution of concepts, viewpoints, and experience gained over many decades.

During the 30 years following the Civil War, the United States emerged as a leading industrial nation. The shift from an agrarian to an urban society was abrupt and, for many Americans, meant drastic adjustment. By the end of the century a new corporate capitalism ruled by a prosperous professional class had arisen. Captains of industry freely wielded mergers and acquisitions and engaged in cutthroat competition as they created huge monopolies in the oil, meat, steel, sugar, and tobacco industries. The federal government did nothing to interfere with these monopolies. On the one hand, new technology born of the war effort offered the promise of progress and growth. On the other hand, rapid social change and a growing disparity between rich and poor caused increasing conflict and instability.

In 1886, several important turning points in business and management history occurred. Henry R. Towne (1844–1924), an engineer and cofounder of the Yale Lock Company, presented a paper titled "The Engineer as an Economist" to the American Society of Mechanical Engineers (ASME). In that paper Towne proposed that the ASME create an economic section to act as a clearinghouse and forum for "shop management" and "shop accounting." Shop management would deal with the subjects of organization, responsibility, reports, and the "executive management" of industrial works, mills, and factories. Shop accounting would treat the nuts and bolts of time and wage systems, cost determination and allocation, bookkeeping methods, and manufacturing accounting.

Other events in 1886 influenced the development of modern management thought and practice. During this boom period in U.S. business history, employers generally regarded labor as a commodity to be purchased as cheaply as possible and maintained at minimal expense. Thus it was also a peak period of labor unrest—during 1886 more than 600,000 employees were out of work because of strikes and lockouts. On May 4, 1886, a group of labor leaders led a demonstration in Chicago's Haymarket Square in support of an eight-hour workday. During the demonstration someone threw a bomb, killing seven bystanders. The Haymarket Affair was a setback for organized labor, because many people began to equate unionism with anarchy. In his pioneering study of labor history in 1886, *The Labor Movement in America*, Richard T. Ely advocated a less radical approach to labor–management relations. Ely cautioned labor to work within the existing economic and political system. One union that followed Ely's advice was the American Federation of Labor (AFL), organized in 1886 by Samuel Gompers and Adolph Strasser. A conservative, "bread and butter" union, the AFL avoided politics and industrial unionism and organized skilled workers along craft lines (carpenters, plumbers, bricklayers, and other trades). Like other early unions, the AFL protected its members from unfair management practices. Gompers' goal was to increase labor's bargaining power within the existing capitalistic framework. Under his leadership, the AFL dominated the American labor scene for almost half a century.

Chicago in 1886 also was the birthplace of an aspiring mail-order business called Sears, Roebuck and Company. From its beginning Sears, founded by railroad station agent Richard W. Sears, who sold watches to farmers in his area, characterized the mass distribution system that promoted the country's economic growth. For the first time, affordable fine goods were available to both rural and urban consumers. Also in 1886, the first Coca-Cola was served in Atlanta. This scarcely noticed event launched an enterprise that grew into a gigantic multinational corporation. Other companies that began in 1886 and remain in operation today include Avon Products, *Cosmopolitan* magazine, Johnson & Johnson, Munsingwear, and Westinghouse. Thus 1886 marked the origins of several well-known, large-scale enterprises, modern management thought and practice, and major labor unions.

Why are we recounting such old events in a book that presents modern management concepts? One reason is that many of the concepts and practices established in the early days of management are still used today. Many of the rules and regulations found in organizations today were originally created to protect managers from undue pressures to favor certain groups of people. Today FedEx, Wal-Mart, and Amazon.com, to name but a few, use rules and regulations for the same reason. A second reason is that the past is a good teacher, identifying practices that have been successful and practices that have failed. Recognizing that employees join organizations for social as well as economic reasons has led many organizations, such as Toyota, Dell, and General Motors, to use teams to solve problems and base employee pay on team results. A third reason is that history gives us a feel for the types of problems for which managers long have struggled to find solutions. Many of these problems, such as low morale, high absenteeism, and poor quality, still exist in many organizations and continue to plague managers.

Looking back also underscores the fact that professional management hasn't been around all that long. In earlier, preindustrial societies, men and women paced their work according to the sun, the seasons, and the demand for what they produced. Small communities encouraged personal, often familial, relationships between employers and employees. The explosive growth of urban industry—and the factory system in particular—changed the face of the workplace forever. Workers in cities were forced to adapt to the factory's formal structure and rules and to labor long hours for employers they never saw. Many were poorly educated and needed considerable oral instruction and hands-on training in unfamiliar tasks.

The emergence of large-scale business enterprises in Canada, the United States, Asia, and Western Europe raised issues and created challenges that previously had applied only to governments. Businesses needed the equivalent of government leaders—managers—to hire and train employees and then to lead and motivate them. Managers also were needed to develop plans and design work units and, while doing so, make a profit, never a requirement for governments! In this chapter we briefly review how management viewpoints have evolved since 1886 to meet those needs.

During the past century, theorists have developed numerous responses to the same basic management question: What is the best way to manage an organization? We continue to study those responses because they still apply to the manager's job. In the following sections we discuss the five most widely accepted viewpoints of management that have evolved since about 1886: traditional (or classical), behavioral, systems, contingency, and quality. These viewpoints are based on different assumptions about the behavior of people in organizations, the key goals of an organization, the types of problems faced, and the methods that should be used to solve those problems. Figure 2.1 shows when each viewpoint emerged and began to gain popularity. As you can see, all five still influence managers' thinking. In fact, one important source of disagreement among today's managers is the emphasis that should be given to each of them. Thus a major purpose of this chapter is to show you not only how each has contributed to the historical evolution of modern management thought, but also how each can be used effectively in different circumstances now and in the future.

The oldest and perhaps most widely accepted view of management is the **traditional** (or classical) **viewpoint**. It is split into three main branches: bureaucratic management, scientific management, and administrative management. All three emerged during roughly the same time period, the late 1890s through the early 1900s, when engineers were trying to make organizations run like well-oiled machines. The founders of these three branches came from Germany, the United States, and France, respectively.

Figure 2.1   History of Management Thought

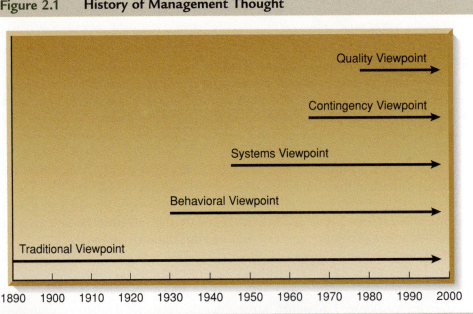

Bureaucratic Management

Bureaucratic management *refers to the use of rules, a set hierarchy, a clear division of labor, and detailed procedures.* Max Weber (1864–1920), a German social historian, is most closely associated with bureaucratic management (so named because Weber based his work on studies of Germany's government bureaucracy). Although Weber was one of the first theorists to deal with the problems of organizations, he wasn't widely recognized by managers and scholars in the United States until his work was translated into English in 1947. He was concerned primarily with the broad social and economic issues facing society; his writings on bureaucracy represent only part of his total contribution to social theory.[2]

Bureaucratic management provides a blueprint of how an entire organization should operate. It prescribes seven desirable characteristics: a formal system of rules, impersonality, division of labor, hierarchical structure, a detailed authority structure, lifelong career commitment, and rationality. Together these characteristics represent a formal, somewhat rigid method of managing. Let's take a look at this method, setting aside for the moment all of the negative connotations the word bureaucracy has today and focusing instead on the system's strengths, consistency, and predictability.

Rules. As *formal guidelines for the behavior of employees while they are on the job,* **rules** can help provide the discipline an organization needs if it is to reach its goals. Adherence to rules ensures uniformity of procedures and operations and helps maintain organizational stability, regardless of individual managers' or employees' personal desires.

Impersonality. **Impersonality** means that *employees are evaluated according to rules and objective data, such as sales or units produced.* Although the word *impersonality* can also have negative connotations, Weber believed that this approach guaranteed fairness for all employees—an impersonal superior doesn't allow subjective personal or emotional considerations to color evaluations of subordinates.

Division of Labor. The **division of labor** *refers to the splitting of work into specialized positions.* It enables the organization to use personnel and job-training resources efficiently. Managers and employees are assigned and perform duties based on specialization and personal expertise. Unskilled employees can be assigned tasks that are relatively easy to learn and do. For example, employee turnover at fast-food restaurants such as McDonald's and Wendy's is more than 150 percent a year. Because of the narrow division of labor, most fast-food jobs can be learned quickly and require only unskilled labor. Thus high turnover in this type of business may not create serious service problems.

Hierarchical Structure. Caliper Technologies Corporation, a manufacturer of lab-on-a-chip technology, uses a pyramid-shaped hierarchical structure, as shown in Figure 2.2. A **hierarchical structure** *ranks jobs according to the amount of authority (the right to decide) in each job.* Typically, authority increases at each higher level to the top of the hierarchy. Those in lower level positions are under the control and direction of those in higher level positions. At Caliper, optical employees report to the manager of chip manufacturing, who in turn reports to the vice president of product development. According to Weber, a well-defined hierarchy helps control employee behavior by making clear exactly where each stands in relation to everyone else in the organization.

Authority Structure. A system based on rules, impersonal supervision, division of labor, and a hierarchical structure is tied together by an authority structure. **Authority structure** refers to *who has the right to make decisions of varying importance at different levels within the organization.* Weber identified three types of authority structures: traditional, charismatic, and rational–legal.

- **Traditional authority** *is based on custom, ancestry, gender, birth order, and the like.* The divine right of kings and the magical influence of tribal witch doctors are examples of traditional authority.

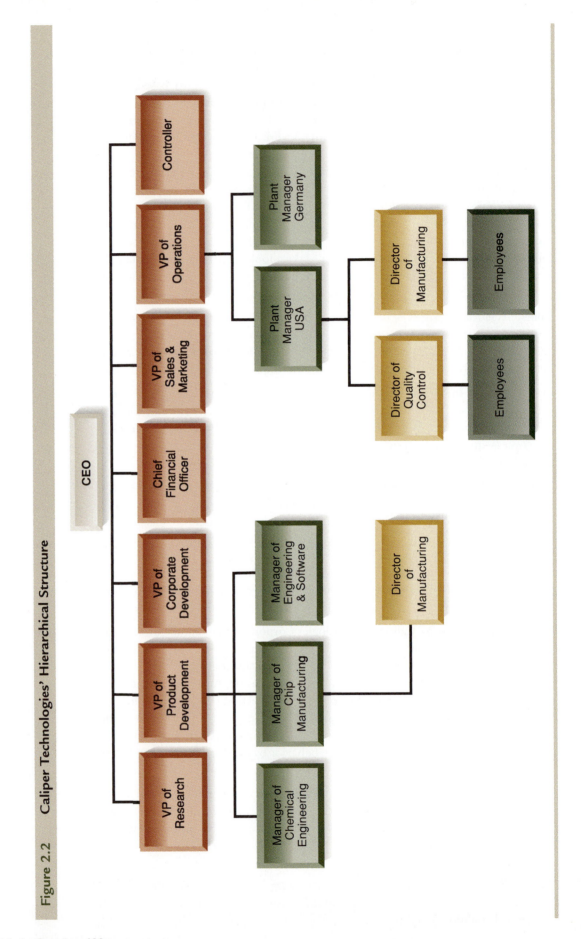

Figure 2.2   Caliper Technologies' Hierarchical Structure

- **Charismatic authority** *is evident when subordinates suspend their own judgment and comply voluntarily with a leader because of special personal qualities or abilities they perceive in that individual.* Charismatic leaders (e.g., Gandhi, Golda Meir, and Martin Luther King, Jr.) often head social, political, and religious movements. In contrast, business leaders seldom rely solely on charismatic authority, but some, such as Herb Kelleher (former CEO of Southwest Airlines), Anita Roddick (founder of The Body Shop), and Meg Whitman (president of eBay), have used their charisma to motivate and influence subordinates.

- **Rational–legal authority** *refers to the use of established laws and rules that are applied uniformly.* A superior is obeyed because of the position occupied within the organization's hierarchy. This authority depends on employees' acceptance of the organization's rules.

Lifelong Career Commitment. In a bureaucratic management system, employment is viewed as a **lifelong career commitment;** that is, *both the employee and the organization view themselves as being committed to each other over the working life of the employee.* Traditionally, Asian organizations, such as NEC, Samsung, and Toyota, have hired key workers with the expectation—by both parties—that a permanent employment contract was being made. In general, lifelong career commitment means that job security is guaranteed as long as the employee is technically qualified and performs satisfactorily. Entrance requirements, such as level of education and experience, ensure that hiring is based on qualifications rather than connections. The organization uses job security, tenure, step-by-step salary increases, and pensions to ensure that employees satisfactorily perform assigned duties. Promotion is granted when an employee demonstrates the competencies required to handle the demands of the next higher position. Organizational level is assumed to correspond closely with expertise. Managers in bureaucratic organizations, such as the civil service, often rely on the results of written and physical tests, amount of formal education, and previous work experience in making hiring and promotion decisions.

Rationality. **Rationality** *is the use of the most efficient means available to accomplish a goal.* Managers in a bureaucratic management system operate logically and "scientifically," with all decisions leading directly to achieving the organization's goals. Goal-directed activities then allow the organization to use its financial and human resources efficiently. In addition, rationality allows general organizational goals to be broken into more specific goals for each part of the organization. At UPS, for example, the overall corporate goal is to grow its e-Ventures business and develop other lines of business focused on supporting e-commerce businesses.

Ranking Organizations by Bureaucratic Orientation. We can use the seven characteristics of bureaucratic management to rank organizations from low to high with respect to bureaucratic orientation. As Figure 2.3 shows, government agencies (e.g., the Internal Revenue Service) and some private companies (e.g., Home Depot and

Figure 2.3   Bureaucratic Continuum

LOW Bureaucratic Structure	MIDRANGE Bureaucratic Structure	HIGH Bureaucratic Structure
DreamWorks	Sony	IRS
MP3	EDS	Home Depot
R&D Thinktank	Bank of America	Blockbuster Video

Blockbuster Video) rank high. Some creative and innovative companies (e.g., Dream-Works and MP3) rank low. Such rankings have to be interpreted carefully, however, because differences within organizations make precise measurement difficult. One organization may be highly bureaucratic in its division of labor but only slightly bureaucratic in its use of rules. In another organization these levels may be reversed. Are the organizations equally bureaucratic? No one can say for sure. Moreover, the degree of bureaucracy within an organization may vary considerably among departments and divisions. For example, Sony falls near the middle of the bureaucratic continuum, but its manufacturing plants, which produce standardized household goods (e.g., TVs, radios, clocks, and VCRs), tend to be more bureaucratic than its R&D departments, whose creativity would be stifled by too many rules.

Benefits of Bureaucracy. The expected benefits of bureaucratic management are efficiency and consistency. A bureaucracy functions best when many routine tasks need to be done. Then lower level employees can handle the bulk of the work by simply following rules and procedures. The fruits of their labor should be of standard (high) quality and produced at the rate necessary to meet organizational goals. At UPS, the use of rules and regulations for the size and weight of a package enable it to deliver more than 14 million packages daily throughout the world. The following Planning & Administration Competency feature provides an excellent example of how bureaucracy can lead to efficiency at call centers.[3]

PLANNING & ADMINISTRATION COMPETENCY

©Index Stock Imagery

Managing Call Centers

We call them to get some information and service and often get neither. Instead, the caller gets music, or much worse—push-button confusion, initiation into the call-transfer game, or simply a click. Call centers are one of the fastest growing industries: 3 percent of Americans now work at call centers, and some people predict that by 2010 the number of people could almost double. The United States has more than 4,000 call centers. The average call center costs $750,000 to build. Absenteeism and employee turnover are huge issues. In most call centers, 25 to 40 percent turnover is common and absenteeism ranges from 5 to 35 percent on a daily basis. The average cost to recruit and train a call center agent is about $6,500.

As a result, many firms are looking at call centers in the Eastern European and Far East markets. Call centers are now located in 52 countries. The reason is cheap labor.

Most call centers in the United States are staffed with middle-aged women who sit in windowless rooms with small partitions dividing each cubicle. Reasons for high job dissatisfaction include little opportunity for advancement; routine, nonchallenging jobs; and low pay. Physical complaints of aching backs, stiff shoulders, or a crick in the neck are commonplace. To ensure that these employees work efficiently and handle up to 1,400 calls a week, a call worker is tethered to the phone. They cannot physically move around a lot. A supervisor closely monitors each group of employees to ensure that they follow the correct procedures, such as answering a call before the fourth ring, taking no more than 2 minutes for every call, restricting rest breaks to 5 minutes during the hour, returning from lunch within 30 minutes, and electronically signing in and out. Electronic bulletin boards clearly display the productivity of each employee.

Costs of Bureaucracy. The same aspects of bureaucratic management that can increase one organization's efficiency can lead to great inefficiency in another. Managers at Caterpillar, Ericsson, Kodak, and other organizations report that the orderliness of a bureaucracy often leads to inefficiencies that cannot be tolerated by companies operating in today's changing times. The following are five, often unanticipated, drawbacks of bureaucratic management.

1. **Rigid rules and red tape.** Rigid adherence to rules and routines for their own sake is a frequent complaint of employees and customers of many organizations. Such a system leaves little room for individual freedom and creativity. This rigidity may foster low motivation, entrenched "career" employees, high turnover among the best employees, and shoddy work. A significant amount of time and money can be wasted.

2. **Protection of authority.** Managers in a bureaucratic organization may ignore issues of employee productivity while protecting and expanding their own authority. Caterpillar attacked the problem head-on. Management believed that the company couldn't afford to support a maze of corporate buck-passers, so it changed the system by focusing on customer satisfaction. Employees use their PCs to swap essential information and determine exactly what type of engine a customer wants. A computer-controlled monorail system and robots bring employees the engine, parts, and computer-generated information about what to do. This system requires 29 percent fewer people than the old system. Employees work on engines at their own pace and until they are satisfied that the job has been done right.

3. **Slow decision making**. Large, complex organizations depend heavily on timely decisions. In a highly bureaucratic organization, however, adherence to rules and procedures may take precedence over effective, timely decision making. When that happens, rules take on lives of their own. Formality and ritual delay decisions at every level until all the red tape has been cleared, petty insistence on power and status privileges has been satisfied, and any chance of blame for errors in judgment has been minimized.

4. **Incompatibility with changing technology**. Advancing technology may make bureaucratic management inappropriate. Audrey Van Drew, regional sales manager for Alcatel USA, believes that narrowly defined jobs based on rules and regulations generate little trust and sharing of information.[4] The technology changes rapidly, and employees must be able to go directly to the person who has the information they need to do their jobs.

5. **Incompatibility with workers' values**. More and more people are being hired by bureaucratic organizations to fill important decision-making positions. These workers' values include performing challenging work, serving clients and customers, and finding innovative solutions to problems. These values often are incompatible with the bureaucratic need for efficiency, order, and consistency. Bureaucratic authority is related to hierarchical position, but most professionals believe that authority stems from personal competence and technical knowledge. Cynthia Bland, regional director of accounting and finance for Marriott International, says she has to rely more on the professionalism and commitment of her people than on rules and regulations. Marriott is developing a performance appraisal system that allows team members, peers, and customers to evaluate employees' work. The company is having to do so because a manager might not know enough to evaluate a particular person's contributions.

Assessing Bureaucratic Management. Not all bureaucratic organizations are inefficient and unprofitable. In fact, bureaucratic management is still widely and successfully used. This approach is most effective when (1) large amounts of standard information have to be processed and an efficient processing method has been found (as in credit card and insurance companies, the IRS, and traffic courts); (2) the needs of the customer are known and aren't likely to change (as in the registration of drivers in most states); (3) the technology is routine and stable, so employees can be easily and quickly taught how to operate machines (as at Taco Bell and in toll booths); and (4) the organization has to coordinate the activities of numerous employees in order to deliver a standardized service or product to the customer (as is done by the IRS and the U.S. Postal Service).

Scientific Management

As manufacturing firms became larger and more complex in the late 1800s, not all managers could continue to be directly involved with production. Many began to spend more of their time on planning, scheduling, and staffing activities. Also, managers were hard-pressed to keep up with new technologies. As a result, a need was created for operations specialists who could solve the personnel and productivity problems that, if not addressed, could threaten operating efficiency.

Frederick W. Taylor. Thus the stage was set for Frederick Winslow Taylor (1856–1915) to do his pioneering work in scientific management.[5] **Scientific management** *is a philosophy and set of management practices that are based on fact and observation, not on hearsay or guesswork.* Scientific management is used by Microsoft, Kodak, Mattel, and other manufacturers in their plants, but it is also widely used in service-based organizations, such as FedEx, Delta Air Lines, and CIBC Oppenheimer.

Taylor, an American mechanical engineer, started out as a foreman at Midvale Steel Company in Philadelphia. He believed that increased productivity ultimately depended on finding ways to make workers more efficient by using objective, scientific techniques. When Taylor worked as a consultant to Bethlehem Steel, for example, he made a science of shoveling. Through observation and experimentation, he started a program that matched workers, shovel sizes, materials, and the like for each job. By the end of the third year his program had reduced the number of shovelers needed from 600 to 140 while the average number of tons shoveled per worker per day had risen from 16 to 50. Workers' earnings also increased from $1.15 to $1.88 a day.

Taylor used time-and-motion studies to analyze work flows, supervisory techniques, and worker fatigue. A **time-and-motion study** *involves identifying and measuring a worker's physical movements when performing a task and then analyzing the results.* Movements that slow production are dropped. One goal of a time-and-motion study is to make a job highly routine and efficient. Eliminating wasted physical effort and specifying an exact sequence of activities reduce the amount of time, money, and effort needed to make a product. Taylor was convinced that having workers perform routine tasks that didn't require them to make decisions could increase efficiency. Performance goals expressed quantitatively (e.g., number of units produced per shift) addressed a problem that had begun to trouble managers—how to judge whether an employee had put in a fair day's work.

Advocates of scientific management stress specialization. They believe that expertise is the only source of authority and that a single foreman couldn't be an expert at all of the tasks supervised. Each foreman's particular area of specialization therefore should become an area of authority. This solution is called **functional foremanship**, *a division of labor that assigned eight foremen to each work area.* Four of the foremen would handle planning, production scheduling, time-and-motion studies, and discipline. The other four would deal with machinery maintenance, machine speed, feeding material into the machine, and production on the shop floor.

What motivates employees to work to their capacity? Taylor believed that money was the answer. He supported the individual piecework system as the basis for pay. If workers met a certain production standard, they were to be paid at a standard wage rate.

Workers who produced more than the standard were to be paid at a higher rate for all the pieces they produced, not just for those exceeding the standard. Taylor assumed that workers would be economically rational; that is, they would follow management's orders to produce more in response to financial incentives that allowed them to earn more money. Taylor argued that managers should use financial incentives if they were convinced that increases in productivity would more than offset higher employee earnings.

The Gilbreths. Frank (1868–1924) and Lillian (1878–1972) Gilbreth formed an unusual husband-and-wife engineering team that made significant contributions to scientific management. Frank used a revolutionary new tool—motion pictures—to study workers' motions. For instance, he identified 18 individual motions that a bricklayer uses to lay bricks. By changing the bricklaying process, he reduced the 18 motions to 5, increasing a worker's overall productivity by more than 200 percent. Many of today's industrial engineers have combined Frank Gilbreth's methods with Taylor's to redesign jobs for greater efficiency.[6]

Lillian Gilbreth carried on Frank's work and raised their 12 children after his death. Concerned mainly with the human side of industrial engineering, she championed the idea that workers should have standard days, scheduled rest breaks, and normal lunch periods. Her work influenced the U.S. Congress to establish child-labor laws and develop rules for protecting workers from unsafe working conditions.

Henry Gantt. Taylor's associate, Henry Gantt (1861–1919), focused on "control" systems for production scheduling. His Gantt charts are still widely used to plan project timelines and have been adapted for computer scheduling applications. The **Gantt chart** *is a visual plan and progress report.* It identifies various stages of work that must be carried out to complete a project, sets a deadline for each stage, and documents accomplishments. Gantt also established quota systems and bonuses for workers who exceeded their quotas.[7]

Assessing Scientific Management. Taylor and other early proponents of scientific management would applaud the efforts of KFC, Honda, Canon, Intel, and other organizations that have successfully applied their concepts. Through time-and-motion studies, for example, KFC found that employees took almost two minutes to complete a customer's order. To improve performance, KFC instructed employees to acknowledge customers within 3 seconds of arriving at the drive-through window, fill a customer's order within 60 seconds, and arrive at an average service time of 90 seconds. To accomplish these objectives, KFC designed employees' workstations so that employees wouldn't need to take more than two steps to get what they needed, wouldn't lift anything, and from handy shelves could pull down napkins, straws, and other items needed to complete the order. Hundreds of other companies have used Taylor's principles to improve their employee selection and training processes and to seek the one best way to perform each task.

Unfortunately, most proponents of scientific management misread the human side of work. When Frederick Taylor and Frank Gilbreth formulated their principles and methods, they thought that workers were motivated primarily by a desire to earn money to satisfy their economic and physical needs. They failed to recognize that workers also have social needs and that working conditions and job satisfaction often are as important, if not more important, than money. For example, workers have struck to protest working conditions, speedup of an assembly line, or harassment by management, even when a fair financial incentive system was in place. Managers today can't assume that workers are interested only in higher wages. Dividing jobs into their simplest tasks and setting clear rules for accomplishing those tasks won't always lead to a quality product, high morale, and an effective organization. Today's employees often want to participate in decisions that affect their performance, and many want to be independent and hold jobs that give them self-fulfillment.[8]

Administrative Management

Administrative management *focuses on the manager and basic managerial functions.* It evolved early in the 1900s and is most closely identified with Henri Fayol (1841–1925), a French industrialist. Fayol credited his success as a manager to the methods he used rather than to his personal qualities. He felt strongly that, to be successful, managers had only to understand the basic managerial functions—planning, organizing, leading, and controlling—and apply certain management principles to them. He was the first person to group managers' functions in this way.[9]

Like the other traditionalists, Fayol emphasized formal structure and processes, believing that they are necessary for the adequate performance of all important tasks. In other words, if people are to work well together, they need a clear definition of what they're trying to accomplish and how their tasks help meet organizational goals.

Managers still use many of Fayol's principles of administrative management. For example, the **unity of command principle** *states that an employee should report to only one manager.* The reason for this principle was to avoid a person receiving conflicting work expectations from two different people. At Chapparal Steel the maintenance superintendent receives direction from the plant manager, the chief engineer, and the production manager—violating the unity of command principle. However, the maintenance superintendent has the authority to set priorities for plant maintenance. This illustrates the **authority principle**, *which states that managers have the right to give orders to get things done.*

Assessing the Traditional Viewpoint

Traditional management's three branches—bureaucratic, scientific, and administrative—still have their proponents, are often written about, and continue to be applied effectively. Table 2.1 highlights the points discussed.

Table 2.1   Characteristics of Traditional Management

Bureaucratic Management	Scientific Management	Administrative Management
Rules	Training in routines and rules	Defining of management functions
Impersonality	"One best way"	Division of labor
Division of labor	Financial motivation	Hierarchy
Hierarchy		Authority
Authority structure		Equity
Lifelong career commitment		
Rationality		
Focus		
Whole organization	Employee	Manager
Benefits		
Consistency	Productivity	Clear structure
Efficiency	Efficiency	Professionalization of managerial roles
Drawbacks		
Rigidity	Overlooks social needs	Internal focus
Slowness		Overemphasizes rational behavior of managers

Let's summarize what the three branches have in common and what some of their drawbacks are. All three emphasize the formal aspects of organization. Traditionalists are concerned with the formal relations among an organization's departments, tasks, and processes. Weber, Taylor, the Gilbreths, Gantt, and Fayol replaced seat-of-the-pants management practices with sound theoretical and scientific principles. Managers began to stress the division of labor, hierarchical authority, rules, and decisions that would maximize economic rewards.

The manager's role in a hierarchy is crucial. In organizations, the relationship between expertise and organizational level is strong. Because of their higher position and presumed greater expertise, superiors are to be obeyed by subordinates. Administrative and scientific management's emphasis on logical processes and strict division of labor are based on similar reasoning.

Although they may recognize that people have feelings and are influenced by their friends at work, the overriding focus of traditionalists is on efficient and effective job performance. Taylor considered the human side of work in terms of eliminating bad feelings between workers and management and providing employees with financial incentives to increase productivity. Traditionalists consider job security, career progression, and protection of workers from employers' whims to be important. However, they do not recognize informal or social relationships among employees at work. Taylor and Frank Gilbreth focused on well-defined rules intended to ensure efficient performance, the primary standard against which employees were to be judged.

In assessing the work of the early traditional theorists, you need to keep in mind that they were influenced by the economic and societal conditions facing them at the time. The United States was becoming an industrial nation, unions were forming to protect workers' rights, and laws were being passed to eliminate unsafe working conditions. Even so, most organizations operated in a relatively stable environment with few competitors.

BEHAVIORAL VIEWPOINT

During the Great Depression, the federal government began to play a more influential role in people's lives. By the time President Franklin D. Roosevelt took office in 1933, the national economy was hovering on the brink of collapse. To provide employment the government undertook temporary public works projects—constructing dams, roads, and public buildings and improving national parks. It also created agencies such as the Social Security Administration to assist the aged, the unemployed, and the disabled.

2. Explain the behavioral viewpoint's contribution to management.

In one of the era's most dramatic changes, unskilled workers greatly increased their ability to influence management decisions through organization and membership in powerful labor unions. During the 1930s Congress aided unions by enacting legislation that deterred management from restricting union activities, legalized collective bargaining, and required management to bargain with unions. As a result the labor movement grew rapidly, and the Congress of Industrial Organizations (CIO) was formed. In 1937, the autoworkers and steelworkers won their first big contracts. Eventually professionals and skilled workers, as well as unskilled laborers, formed unions to bargain for better pay, increased benefits, and improved working conditions. Following the depression and World War II, a new wave of optimism swept the U.S. economy.

Against this backdrop of change and reform, managers were forced to recognize that people have needs, hold to values, and want respect. Managers were now leading workers who did not appear to exhibit what the early traditional management theorists had thought was rational economic behavior. That is, workers weren't always performing up to their physiological capabilities, as Taylor had predicted rational people would do. Nor were effective managers consistently following Fayol's 14 principles. By exploring these inconsistencies, those who favored a behavioral (human relations) viewpoint of management gained recognition. The **behavioral viewpoint** *focuses on dealing effectively with the human aspects of organizations.* Its proponents look at how managers do what they do, how managers lead subordinates and communicate with them, and why managers need to change their assumptions about people if they want to lead high-performance teams and organizations.[10]

Follett's Contributions

Mary Parker Follett (1868–1933) made important contributions to the behavioral viewpoint of management. She *believed that management is a flowing, continuous process, not a static one, and that if a problem has been solved, the method used to solve it probably generated new problems.* She stressed (1) involvement of workers in solving problems and (2) the dynamics of management, rather than static principles. Both ideas contrasted sharply with the views of Weber, Taylor, and Fayol.[11]

Follett studied how managers did their jobs by observing them at work. Based on these observations, she concluded that coordination is vital to effective management. She developed four principles of coordination for managers to apply.

1. Coordination is best achieved when the people responsible for making a decision are in direct contact.
2. Coordination during the early stages of planning and project implementation is essential.
3. Coordination should address all factors in a situation.
4. Coordination must be worked at continuously.

Follett believed that the people closest to the action could make the best decisions. For example, she was convinced that first-line managers are in the best position to coordinate production tasks. And by increasing communication among themselves and with workers, these managers can make better decisions regarding such tasks than managers up the hierarchy can. She also believed that first-line managers should not only plan and coordinate workers' activities, but also involve them in the process. Simply because managers told employees to do something a certain way, Follett argued, they shouldn't assume that the employees would do it. She argued further that managers at all levels should maintain good working relationships with their subordinates. One way to do so is to involve subordinates in the decision-making process whenever they will be affected by a decision. Drawing on psychology and sociology, Follett urged managers to recognize that each person is a collection of beliefs, emotions, and feelings.

John Mackey, president of Whole Foods, a supermarket chain that sells only natural foods, believes that Follett's ideas have shaped his management practices. Each Whole Foods Market typically employs between 60 and 140 people and is organized into various teams to develop a sense of cooperation. Each team is responsible for doing its own work and selecting new team members. A candidate must be voted on by the team and receive a two-thirds majority to become a team member. Every four weeks, each team meets to discuss problems and make decisions.

Employees also practice self-responsibility. Mackey believes that, by placing responsibility and authority at the store and team level rather than at corporate headquarters, employees are encouraged to make decisions that affect their daily work. Mackey knows that employees will make mistakes because of their inexperience. However, the company is dedicated to learning and growing, and he believes that employees can learn from their mistakes. Recognizing that there are many different approaches to getting things done, Mackey encourages creativity and experimentation at each store and by each employee. He is convinced that only through experimentation can new information be gathered and communication increased among all employees.[12]

Barnard's Contributions

Chester Barnard (1886–1961) studied economics at Harvard but failed to graduate because he didn't finish a laboratory course in science. He was hired by AT&T, and in 1927 he became president of New Jersey Bell. Barnard made two significant contributions to management, which are detailed in his book, *The Functions of the Executive*.[13]

First, Barnard viewed organizations as social systems that require employee cooperation if they are to be effective. In other words, people should continually communicate with one another. According to Barnard, managers' main roles are to communicate with employees and motivate them to work hard to help achieve the organization's goals. In his view, successful management also depends on maintaining good relations with people outside the organization with whom managers deal regularly. He stressed the dependence of the organization on investors, suppliers, customers, and other outside interests. Barnard stressed the idea that managers have to examine the organization's external environment and adjust its internal structure to balance the two.

Second, Barnard proposed the **acceptance theory of authority**, *which holds that employees have free wills and thus choose whether to follow management's orders.* That is, employees will follow orders if they (1) understand what is required, (2) believe that the orders are consistent with organizational goals, and (3) see positive benefits to themselves in carrying out the orders.

The Hawthorne Contributions

The strongest support for the behavioral viewpoint emerged from studies carried out between 1924 and 1933 at Western Electric Company's Hawthorne plant in Chicago. The Hawthorne Illumination Tests, begun in November 1924 and conducted in three departments of the plant, initially were developed and directed by Hawthorne's engineers. They divided employees into two groups: a test group, whom they subjected to deliberate changes in lighting, and a control group, for whom lighting remained constant throughout the experiment. When lighting conditions for the test group were improved, the group's productivity increased, as expected. The engineers were mystified, though, by a similar jump in productivity upon reducing the test group's lighting to the point of twilight. To compound the mystery, the control group's output kept rising, even though its lighting condition didn't change. Western Electric called in Harvard professor Elton Mayo to investigate these peculiar and puzzling results.

Mayo and Harvard colleagues Fritz Roethlisberger and William Dickson devised a new experiment. They placed two groups of six women each in separate rooms. They changed various conditions for the test group and left conditions unchanged for the control group. The changes included shortening the test group's coffee breaks, allowing it to choose its own rest periods, and letting it have a say in other suggested changes. Once again, output of both the test group and the control group increased. The researchers decided that they could rule out financial incentives as a factor because they hadn't changed the payment schedule for either group.[14]

The researchers concluded that the increases in productivity weren't caused by a physical event but by a complex emotional chain reaction. Because employees in both groups had been singled out for special attention, they had developed a group pride that motivated them to improve their performance. The sympathetic supervision they received further reinforced that motivation. These experimental results led to Mayo's first important discovery: *When employees are given special attention, productivity is likely to change regardless of whether working conditions change.* This phenomenon became known as the **Hawthorne effect**.[15]

However, an important question remained unanswered: Why should a little special attention and the formation of group bonds produce such strong reactions? To find the answer, Mayo interviewed employees. These interviews yielded a highly significant discovery: Informal work groups, the social environment of employees, greatly influence productivity. Many Western Electric employees found their lives inside and outside the factory dull and meaningless. Their workplace friends, chosen in part because of mutual antagonism toward "the bosses," gave meaning to their working lives. Thus peer pressure, rather than management demands, had a significant influence on employee productivity.

The writings of Mayo, Roethlisberger, and Dickson that emerged from the Hawthorne studies helped outline the behavioral viewpoint of management. The researchers concluded that behavior on the job is determined by a complex set of factors. They found that the informal work group develops its own set of norms to satisfy the needs of individuals in the work setting and that the social system of such informal groups is maintained through symbols of prestige and power. As a result of their studies, the researchers recommended that managers consider the worker in a personal context (e.g., family situation, friendships, and membership in groups) in order to understand each employee's unique needs and sources of satisfaction. They also suggested that awareness of employee feelings and encouragement of employee participation in decision making can reduce resistance to change.[16]

The following Teamwork Competency highlights how TDIndustries use teams to recognize and reward people for directly contributing to the success of the organization. The importance of the relationship between the leaders and their subordinates is reinforced by the concept of servant leadership.[17]

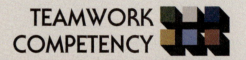

TEAMWORK COMPETENCY

TDIndustries

Many organizations say that people are their most important assets, but TDIndustries lives it. During the past 50 years, this organization has developed management practices that have enabled it to become one of America's most admired corporations, currently ranking fourth on *Fortune* magazine's top 100 companies to work for. TDIndustries has developed into a more than $200 million dollar mechanical/electrical/plumbing company that employs some 1,500 people, many of whom have been with the company for more than 10 years. CEO Jack Lowe believes that TDI's success can be related to its strong teamwork.

For TDI, creating a culture of teamwork that promotes high performance and longevity is based on the concept of *servant leadership*. The servant leader philosophy for TDI means that managers (servants) cultivate employees (leaders) by serving and meeting the needs of others. In his servant role, Lowe answers his own phone, has no reserved parking space, and works in an 8- × 11-foot cubicle just like everybody else. Keys to the servant philosophy include the following.

- People should work together to build a company. They are partners.
- Employees ranging from foremen to sheet metal hangers to safety directors hold TDI stock.
- Managers have to earn the recognition and respect of employees.
- Managers assume that their followers are working with them and must see things through their eyes.
- Managers are people builders, who don't hold people down but lift them up.

- Managers can be led. They are not interested in having their own way, but finding the best way.

To keep servant leadership central to TDI's teamwork concept, new employees are assigned to servant leadership discussion groups, which meet weekly for six weeks to discuss various aspects of servant leadership, such as sharing power, listening, and trusting others—and how they can apply these concepts to their particular jobs. TDI has also started a mentoring program designed to give all new hires a positive start at the company. A mentor adopts a new employee for the first six months, and the relationship continues as long as both employees work together on the same job site. If the new hire changes job sites, a different mentor is assigned.

Assessing the Behavioral Viewpoint

The behavioral viewpoint of management goes beyond the traditionalists' mechanical view of work by stressing the importance of group dynamics, complex human motivations, and the manager's leadership style. It emphasizes the employee's social and economic needs and the influence of the organization's social setting on the quality and quantity of work produced. The following are the basic assumptions of the behavioral viewpoint.

- Employees are motivated by social needs and get a sense of identity through their associations with one another.
- Employees are more responsive to the social forces exerted by their peers than to management's financial incentives and rules.
- Employees are most likely to respond to managers who can help them satisfy their needs.
- Managers need to involve subordinates in coordinating work to improve efficiency.

These assumptions don't always hold in practice, of course. Improving working conditions and managers' human relations skills won't always increase productivity. Economic aspects of work are still important to the employee, as Taylor believed. The major union contracts negotiated in recent years, for instance, focus on job security and wage incentives. And, although employees enjoy working with coworkers who are friendly, low salaries tend to lead to absenteeism and turnover. The negative effects of clumsy organizational structure, poor communication, and routine or boring tasks won't be overcome by the presence of pleasant coworkers. The human aspect of the job now is vastly more complex than those advocating the behavioral viewpoint in the 1930s could ever have imagined.[18]

The Competent Manager

"Teamwork is one of the most beautiful experiences in life. Teamwork is our core value and a primary way that the Container Store enriches the quality of employees' work life."

Kip Tindell
President
The Container Store

SYSTEMS VIEWPOINT

During World War II the British assembled a team of mathematicians, physicists, and others to solve various wartime problems. These professionals formed the first operations research group. Initially, they were responsible for analyzing the makeup, routes, and speeds of convoys and probable locations of German submarines. The team developed ingenious ways to analyze complex problems that couldn't be handled solely by intuition, straightforward mathematics, or experience. The British and Americans further developed this approach (called *systems analysis*) throughout the war and applied it to many problems of war production and military logistics. Later, systems analysis became an accepted tool in the Department of Defense and the space program, as well as throughout private industry.[19]

3. Describe how managers can use systems and quantitative techniques to improve employee performance.

System Concepts

A **system** *is an association of interrelated and interdependent parts.* The human body is a system with organs, muscles, bones, nerves, and a consciousness that links all of its parts. In the Preview Case, we described the UPS delivery process as a system with employees, teams, and departments that are linked to achieve its goals. An organization also is linked externally to suppliers, customers, shareholders, and regulatory agencies. A competent systems-oriented manager makes decisions only after identifying and analyzing how other managers, departments, customers, or others might be affected by the decisions.

The **systems viewpoint** *of management represents an approach to solving problems by diagnosing them within a framework of inputs, transformation processes, outputs, and feedback,* as shown in Figure 2.4. The system involved may be an individual, a work group, a department, or an entire organization.

Figure 2.4 Basic Systems View of Organization

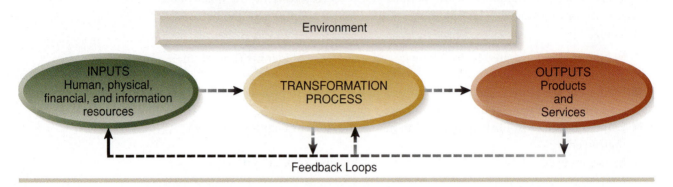

Inputs *are the human, physical, material, financial, and information resources that enter a transformation process.* At a university, for example, inputs include students, faculty, money, and buildings. **Transformation processes** *comprise the technologies used to convert inputs into outputs.* Transformation processes at a university include lectures, reading assignments, lab experiments, term papers, and tests. **Outputs** *are the original inputs (human, physical, material, financial, and information resources) as changed by a transformation process.* Outputs at a university include the graduating students. For a system to operate effectively, it must also provide for feedback. **Feedback** *is information about a system's status and performance.* One form of feedback at a university is the ability of its graduates to get jobs. In an organization, feedback may take the form of marketing surveys, financial reports, production records, performance appraisals, and the like. A manager's role is to guide transformation processes by planning, organizing, leading, and controlling.

System Types

There are two types of systems: closed and open. A **closed system** *limits its interactions with its environment.* At Solectron, discussed later, the production department operates as a closed system, producing standardized products in an uninterrupted stream. An **open system** *interacts with the external environment.* Nortel's marketing department constantly tries to identify new products and services to satisfy customers' telecommunications desires. It monitors what competitors are doing and then develops ways to deliver better quality and service at a lower price, constantly receiving feedback from customers as part of this process.

Communications processes—both internally with employees and externally with customers—are integral parts of a system. The following Communication Competency account reveals how the management of Solectron Corporation makes use of informal and formal communication processes to achieve a high level of performance. Solectron, a manufacturer of printed circuit boards and networking products for telecommunications companies, has 112 locations in the United States, 36 in Europe, and 24 in Asia. Its mission is to provide worldwide solutions to customers by utilizing the highest quality, lowest total cost, and integrated designs in manufacturing. Common processes enable it to deliver consistent quality, reliability, and on-time delivery and superior service to customers.[20]

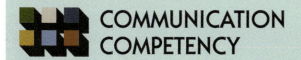

COMMUNICATION COMPETENCY

Solectron

Solectron tracks customer satisfaction weekly by means of surveys, with an 80 to 90 percent response rate. Scores for delivery, quality, and service are at or near the 90 percent satisfaction level across all locations. This satisfaction level is noteworthy because of the company's rating scale on which a C receives a score of 0 and a D receives a score of *minus* 100. Grades of B– or lower trigger Solectron's customer complaint res-

olution process. Within 24 hours, the account's program manager contacts the customer to acknowledge the complaint and arranges a visit with the customer to gain more information. Within 72 hours, an action plan is submitted to correct the customer's problem. Customer-satisfaction report cards are reviewed weekly by managers and employees at each location.

Solectron employees communicate with customers and suppliers at

the earliest stages of a product's design. The company bases its selection and regular reviews of its suppliers on several factors, including financial strength, technological leadership, total quality manufacturing systems, and compatibility with Solectron's values. By building a strong relationship with its suppliers on a foundation of full and open communication, Solectron's effectiveness is achieved.

Quantitative Techniques

While some advocates of systems analysis were suggesting that managers look at inputs, transformation processes, and outputs before making a decision, other systems advocates were developing quantitative techniques to aid in managerial decision making. Quantitative techniques have four basic characteristics.[21]

1. The primary focus is on decision making. Investigation identifies direct actions that managers can take, such as reducing inventory costs.
2. Alternatives are based on economic criteria. Alternative actions are presented in terms of measurable criteria, such as shipping costs, sales revenues, and profits.
3. Mathematical models are used. Situations are simulated and problems are analyzed by means of mathematical models.
4. Computers are essential. Computers are used to solve complex mathematical models, such as statistical process controls, that would be too costly and time consuming to process manually.

The range of quantitative decision-making tools available to management has expanded greatly during the past two decades. In the past, small businesses such as retail stores, medical offices, mom-and-pop restaurants, and farmers couldn't use systems analysis techniques—but today they can. Owners and managers now have inventory, statistical decision theory, linear programming, and many other aids for solving complex problems. Many of those tools are literally at their fingertips in the form of software that can be run on desktop computers. In the emergency room at Presbyterian Hospital in Dallas, a computer on the wall allows the staff to plug in different software modules, which relay the patient's functions to a display screen. Each type of sensor—pulse, blood pressure, and the like—is run by a piece of software in its module. Each computer has access to a high-speed local network, so that patient information can be monitored remotely. Thus each patient is monitored by a unique system of connected components that the staff can change as the medical needs of the patient change.

In the largest companies, groups of management scientists can tackle a broad range of business problems by devising their own sophisticated mathematical models for use on mainframe, networked, and personal computers. Such models help gambling casinos such as Caesar's Palace, Bally's, and Harrah's increase their profits and improve service.

Casinos provide millions of dollars of complimentary services (e.g., food, rooms, and transportation) for high rollers. To reduce the cost of these services and improve the odds that these people will gamble—and probably lose—in their establishments, casino managers utilize sophisticated information systems that analyze customers' favorite games, betting patterns, accommodation preferences, food and drink choices, and other habits.

Assessing the Systems Viewpoint

Systems analysis and quantitative techniques have been used primarily for managing transformation processes and for the technical planning and decision-making aspects of management. These methods can also be used to improve managers' ability to deal with human resources issues. For example, sophisticated staffing models can be used to map the flow of people into and out of an organization.

Organizations no doubt will continue to develop more sophisticated systems in order to increase productivity. Such systems will require changes in many aspects of day-to-day operations. These changes will not come without struggle and pain. Yet for organizations to survive managers must use increasingly sophisticated systems in making decisions.[22]

CONTINGENCY VIEWPOINT

4. State the two major components of the contingency viewpoint.

The essence of the **contingency viewpoint** (*sometimes called the situational approach*) *is that management practices should be consistent with the requirements of the external environment, the technology used to make a product or provide a service, and capabilities of the people who work for the organization.*[23] The relationships among these variables are summarized in Figure 2.5.

Figure 2.5   Contingency Viewpoint

Behavioral Viewpoint

How managers influence others:
• Informal group
• Cooperation among employees
• Employees' social needs

Systems Viewpoint

How the parts fit together:
• Inputs
• Transformations
• Outputs

Traditional Viewpoint

What managers do:
• Plan
• Organize
• Lead
• Control

Contingency Viewpoint

Managers' use of other viewpoints to solve problems involving:
• External environment
• Technology
• Individuals

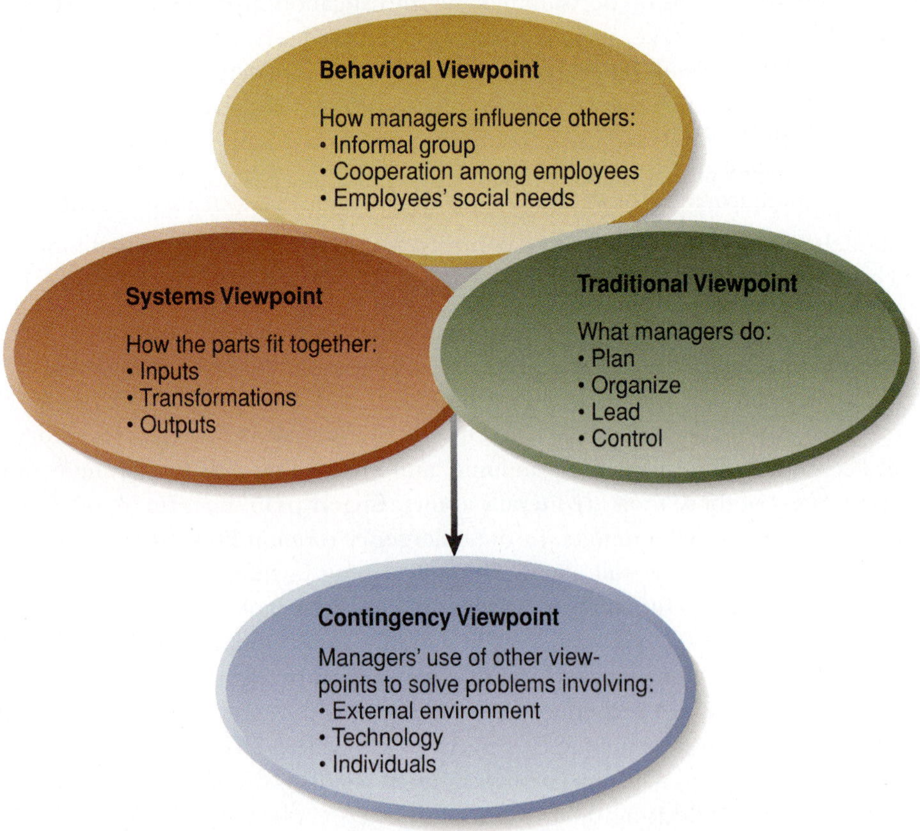

The contingency viewpoint of management emerged in the mid-1960s in response to the frustration of managers and others who had tried unsuccessfully to apply traditional and systems concepts to actual managerial problems. For example, why did providing workers with a bonus for being on time decrease lateness at one Marriott hotel but have little impact at another? Proponents of the contingency viewpoint contend that different situations require different practices. As one manager put it, the contingency viewpoint really means "it all depends."

Proponents of the contingency viewpoint advocate using the other three management viewpoints independently or in combination, as necessary, to deal with various situations. However, this viewpoint doesn't give managers free rein to indulge their personal biases and whims. Rather, managers are expected to determine which methods are likely to be more effective than others in a given situation.

Contingency Variables

The relative importance of each contingency variable—external environment, technology, and people—depends on the type of managerial problem being considered. For example, in designing an organization's structure a manager should consider the nature of the company's external environment and its ability to process customers' orders. Hence the IRS's structure is different from that of Solectron. The IRS has a fairly stable set of customers, most of whom must file their tax returns by April 15 each year. It hires many part-time people during the peak tax season to process returns and answer questions and then lays them off after the peak has passed. In contrast, Solectron has many locations scattered throughout the world and a constantly changing set of customers whose demands for high-quality manufacturing must be processed immediately.

Technology *is the method used to transform organizational inputs into outputs.* It is more than machinery; it also is the knowledge, tools, techniques, and actions applied to change raw materials into finished goods and services. The technologies that employees use range from the simple to the highly complex. A simple technology involves decision-making rules to help employees do routine jobs. For example, IRS clerks who enter tax information into computers perform routine tasks and work under such rules, requiring few (if any) independent decisions. A complex technology is one that requires employees to make numerous decisions, sometimes with limited information to guide them. A doctor treating an Alzheimer patient must answer many questions and make many decisions without having much guidance because the technology for treating the disease hasn't yet been perfected.

Assessing the Contingency Viewpoint

The contingency viewpoint of management is useful because of its diagnostic approach, which clearly departs from the one-best-way approach of the traditionalists. The contingency viewpoint encourages managers to analyze and understand situational differences and to choose the solution best suited to the organization, the process, and the people involved in each.

Critics argue that the contingency viewpoint really is nothing new. They say that it is merely a meshing of techniques from the other viewpoints of management. The contingency viewpoint does draw heavily from the other approaches. However, it is more flexible than the others, allowing managers to apply the principles and tools from those approaches selectively and where most appropriate. It holds that a manager can use principles from the traditional, behavioral, and systems viewpoints only after properly diagnosing the realities of the situation. Such a diagnosis looks at the nature of a situation and the means by which the manager can influence it.

QUALITY VIEWPOINT

5. Explain the impact of the need for quality on management practices.

Today's organizations are dynamic and, whether large or small, local or global, face a host of new management challenges. Organizations feel pressure from customers and competitors to deliver high-quality products and/or services on time, reward ethical behavior of employees, and develop plans to manage highly diverse workforces effectively. Customer demand for high-quality products and services may be the dominant theme for the foreseeable future. **Quality** *is defined as how well a product or service does what it is supposed to do—how closely and reliably it satisfies the specifications to which it is built or provided.* Managers in successful organizations are quality conscious and understand the link between high-quality goods and/or services and competitive advantage.

Total quality management (TQM) *is the continuous process of ensuring that every aspect of production builds quality into the product.*[24] Quality must be stressed repeatedly so that it becomes second nature to everyone in an organization and its suppliers. Moreover, training, strategic planning, product design, management information systems, marketing, and other key activities all play a role in meeting quality goals. For example, Solectron requires all employees to undergo hours of training at Solectron University to learn how to use statistical and other measurement tools to ensure quality in its products.

The godfather of the quality movement was W. Edwards Deming (1900–1993).[25] Initially, U.S. managers rejected his ideas, and not until his ideas had helped rebuild Japan's industrial might after World War II were they accepted in the United States. He taught eager Japanese managers how to use statistics to assess and improve quality. In 1951, Japan established the Deming Prize for corporate quality in his honor. Highly esteemed in Japan, this annual prize recognizes the company that has attained the highest level of quality that year. Deming believed that poor quality is 85 percent a management problem and 15 percent a worker problem.

The Quality Control Process

The quality control process generally focuses on measuring inputs (including customer expectations and requirements), transformation operations, and outputs. The results of these measurements enable managers and employees to make decisions about product or service quality at each stage of the transformation process.

Inputs. Quality control generally begins with inputs, especially the raw materials and parts used in a transformation process. For services, the inputs are based on the information the client provides. Recall that Solectron emphasizes quality control by its suppliers. For almost all parts, Solectron uses only one or two suppliers for each location, which is consistent with one of Deming's prescriptions. Tom Kennedy, vice president for quality at Solectron, realizes that its products are only as good as the weakest link in its supply chain. As a result, it developed a set of practices for working with suppliers so that both Solectron and the suppliers learn faster.

Transformation Operations. Quality control inspections are made during and between successive transformation stages. Work-in-progress inspection can result in the reworking or rejecting of an item before the next operation is performed on it.

The use of statistical process control is one of Deming's key prescriptions. **Statistical process control** *is the use of quantitative methods and procedures to determine whether transformation operations are being done correctly, to detect any deviations, and, if there are any, to find and eliminate their causes.*[26] Statistical process control methods have been available for decades but only in the past 20 years have they been used to any significant extent. They serve primarily as preventive controls.

Sigma *is a unit of statistical measurement, which in this context is used to illustrate the quality of a process.* The sigma measurement scale (ranging from two to six) describes defects in parts per million. To simplify the concept, let's consider the application of six sigma to writing a text. If defects were measured in misspellings, four sigma would be equivalent to one misspelling per 30 pages of text; five sigma, one misspelling in a set of encyclopedias; and six sigma, only one misspelling in an entire small library, such as a high school library.

Solectron, for example, has adopted the quality goal of six sigma, which means eliminating defects to the level of 1 per 3.4 million opportunities—or a process that is 99.99966 percent defect free. Five sigma is 233 defects per million, and four sigma is 6,210 defects per million. Most firms operate at the four-sigma level. A key theme in six-sigma programs is the reduction of waste. Solectron trains all employees to seek opportunities to reduce waste in seven areas. They include

- waste of overproduction (also irregular production such as end-of-month or end-of-quarter surges),
- waste of time on hand (waiting),
- waste in transportation,
- waste of processing itself,
- waste of stock on hand (inventory),
- waste of movement, and
- waste of making defective products.

Outputs. The most traditional and familiar form of quality control is the assessment made after completion of a component or an entire product, or provision of a service. With goods, quality control tests may be made just before the items are shipped to customers. The number of items returned by customers because of shoddy workmanship or other problems is one indicator of the effectiveness of the quality control process. Service providers, such as barbers and hairdressers, usually involve their customers in checking the quality of outputs by asking if everything is okay. However, the satisfactory provision of a service often is more difficult to assess than the satisfactory quality of goods.[27]

Determining the amount or degree of the nine dimensions of quality shown in Table 2.2 is fundamental to quality control. The more accurate the measurement, the easier comparing actual to desired results becomes. Quality dimensions generally are measured by variable or by attribute. **Measuring by variable** *assesses product characteristics for which there are quantifiable standards (length, diameter, height, weight, or temperature).* Consider the quality control process and technology used on the Mercedes-Benz M-class sport utility vehicle at the Mercedes factory in Vance, Alabama.[28] Carmakers have traditionally tracked their body-building accuracy by taking sample vehicles off the assembly line and physically checking a large number of their dimensions with special equipment. Mercedes still does so, running about every 100th body through a measuring machine that checks 1,062 dimensions with sensitive touch probes in a process that takes about 4 hours.

To spot flaws that can develop between those elaborate inspections on every 100th body, Mercedes uses a new vision system. At the end of the body-building line, a body-in-white vehicle—factory language for an unpainted body minus doors, hood, and liftgate—arrives at the vision station. In a process that takes just 45 seconds, 38 laser cameras mounted on a superstructure check 84 key measurements. Slight dimensional flaws can be identified and corrected before any out-of-tolerance bodies get built. "Before laser gauging, carmakers couldn't do 100 percent inspection. Now we do it," stated Mike Hill, leader of the measurement team.

Measuring by attribute *evaluates product or service characteristics as acceptable or unacceptable.* Measuring by attribute usually is easier than measuring by variable. When Tom Stemberg founded Staples, the office supply superstore, he decided to track customer purchases as a measure of customer loyalty. His solution was to create a membership card good for discounts and special promotions. The company encouraged all its customers

Table 2.2   The Meaning of Quality

Quality Dimension	Definition	Examples	
		Toyota Camry	**VISA Card**
Performance	Primary good or service characteristics	Miles per gallon, acceleration	Number of merchants who accept the card
Features	Added touches, secondary characteristics	Level of road noise	Credit provisions, interest rates
Conformance	Fulfillment of specifications, documentation, or industry standards	Workmanship, emissions level	Accuracy of monthly account statements
Reliability	Consistency of performance over time	Mean miles to failure of parts	Processing of lost card reports
Durability	Useful life	Miles of useful life (with repair)	Timeliness of automatic card renewals
Serviceability	Resolution of problems and complaints	Ease of repair	Resolution of errors
Responsiveness	Person-to-person contact, including timeliness, courtesy, and professionalism	Courtesy of auto dealer, repairs completed as scheduled	Courtesy of account agents in resolving problems
Aesthetics	Sensory effects, such as sound, feel, and look	Styling, interior finish	Enclosures with monthly statements
Reputation	Past performance and industry/customer regard	*Consumer Reports* ranking, owners' reviews	Advice of friends, *Kiplinger Magazine* ranking

to sign up and then entered their membership numbers at the cash register every time they made a purchase. If a customer forgot to bring the card, the cashier could access the account number simply by entering the customer's phone number. The membership application captured basic demographic information; cash-register data gave precise information about preferences, quantities, and frequency of purchase. Together the applications and purchase histories told Staples management which customers and customer segments accounted for most of each store's volume. Staples doesn't need mass mailings to entire geographic markets. Instead, it targets its coupons, mailings, and special promotions to specific customers who have purchased certain products.

The Importance of Quality

Producing high-quality products or services isn't an end in itself. Successfully offering high quality to customers typically results in three important benefits for the organization, as shown in Figure 2.6.[29]

Positive Company Image. A reputation for high-quality products creates a positive image for Maytag, Ritz-Carlton Hotels, Nordstrom's, Southwest Airlines, Lexus, and others. A positive image eases recruiting of new employees, increasing sales, and obtaining funds from various lending agencies. A positive company image can influence new customers who have little direct experience with the company to shop there. The Container Store, Chick-fil-A, Enterprise Rent-A-Car, among others, enjoy a positive company image that results in higher profits, lower employee turnover, and greater customer satisfaction than organizations with a poorer company image.

Lower Costs and Higher Market Share. At Solectron, higher quality increases productivity and lowers rework time, scrap costs, and warranty costs, leading to increased profits. Improved performance features and product reliability at Toyota enabled the

Figure 2.6   Importance of Quality

Camry to become the number one selling car in its class in the United States. Many have seen the TV advertisement for "The Lonely Maytag Repairman." In service settings organizations, such as State Farm Insurance, USAA, and Bergstrom Hotels, higher quality service can be used to attract and retain new customers. People are willing to pay for excellent service.

Decreased Liability. Product manufacturers and service providers increasingly face costly legal suits over damages caused by faulty, dangerous, and/or misrepresented products and services. Organizations that design and produce faulty products increasingly are being held liable in state courts for damages resulting from the use of such products. Successful TQM efforts typically result in improved products and product performance and lower product liability costs at Darden Restaurants, which operates the Olive Garden, Red Lobster, and other chains.

Decisions about quality should be an integral part of an organization's strategy—that is, how it competes in the marketplace.[30] A core strategy of quality consistently provides the best possible products in their price ranges in the marketplace. Quality therefore must be a basic component of the structure and culture of the organization. Quality isn't simply a program that can be imposed on employees by top management; it is a way of operating that permeates an organization and the thinking of everyone in the organization. The following Strategic Action Competency feature about the Bombardier Corporation illustrates the role quality plays in implementing a strategy.[31] Bombardier is a $14-billion-a-year Montreal manufacturer of business jets, railcars, outboard motors, and snowmobiles.

The Competent Manager	*"Generally speaking, whenever people get into trouble in business, it's because they are not anticipating consumer needs or are not taking proper care of their employees."* Joe Lee CEO and Chairman Darden Restaurants, Inc.

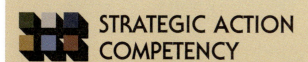

STRATEGIC ACTION COMPETENCY

Bombardier Corporation

Recently Bombardier faced a major challenge when it purchased the Outboard Marine Corporation (OMC), the maker of Evinrude and Johnson outboard engines. The quality of engines had declined and dealers stopped taking orders for them. OMC's share of the $2-billion-a-year

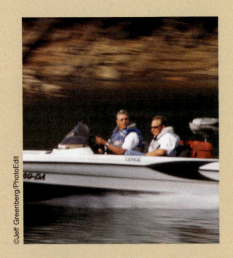
©Jeff Greenberg/PhotoEdit

outboard engine market had dropped from 55 percent in 1995 to 23 percent in 2001. The new engine that OMC developed had turned into a nightmare because manufacturing couldn't meet the demanding quality tolerances.

OMC had production plants scattered around nine plants in the United States, Mexico, and China. Component parts often spent three weeks in transit, boosting costs. For example, the engines' transmission housings were die-cast in Waukegan,

Illinois, machined and subassembled in Andrews, North Carolina, and then shipped to Calhoun, Georgia, for final assembly.

The first thing that Bombardier did to help solve these problems was hire Roch Lambert, an expert in quality control. He shut down two of the Southern plants and closed Waukegan's production plant. This consolidated operations and drastically shortened parts supply routes. A new plant was built in Sturtevant, Wisconsin, that would perform all the final assembly. Lambert and his plant manager received 6,000 applications for 300 job openings. They carefully selected workers whom they considered "team players" with problem-solving skills, rather than looking for employees who had prior work experience.

To ensure high quality, parts from all suppliers were checked. Bombardier brought in-house a crucial operation that was formerly done by a supplier at a cost of $1 million. Once parts pass inspection, they move to two separate assembly lines:

one for engine blocks and the other for the outboard's midsection and gear case. At every fourth or fifth assembly station, the assembled structure is taken aside and fully inspected. Engines travel inside carriers with electromagnetic cards that store data. A computer program reads the data and signals the assembly line to start building the correct powerhead to match up with a particular gear case. The two assembly lines eventually come together for final assembly. Employees spend as much as 20 percent of their time making sure that all operations were done properly. Once a day, a randomly selected engine, ready to be shipped, is taken out of its carton and inspected at 250 points for finish and workmanship. The engine is then attached to a boat and taken out for a test run on Lake Michigan.

What are the results? Impressed by high quality, dealers want to sell Evinrude and Johnson outboard engines again. More than 3,800 dealers of the original 4,600 have been reassigned to be distributors.

Integration of Management Viewpoints and Competencies

In Chapter 1, we identified six management competencies that are essential to your future success as a manager. Each of the five managerial viewpoints discussed here stresses at least one of those competencies more than others. Table 2.3 shows the relationships between the management viewpoints and the competencies.

The traditional viewpoint sought to identify management competencies that efficiently organized the work of employees. Each level of management was assigned specific goals and tasks to accomplish in an allotted time period. The structure of the organization governed relations between manager and employee. It was the manager's job

Table 2.3	Integration of Management Viewpoints and Competencies				
Managerial Competency	**Management Viewpoint**				
	Traditional	**Behavioral**	**Systems**	**Contingency**	**Quality**
Communication		X	X	X	X
Planning and administration	X			X	
Strategic action			X		X
Self-management					X
Global awareness			X		X
Teamwork		X		X	X
X = relatively high importance					

to plan, organize, and lay out the task for the employee; it was the employee's job to follow the manager's instructions. Employees were thought of as "rational" people who were motivated primarily by money.

The behavioral viewpoint focused on developing two competencies: communication and teamwork. It was the manager's job to acknowledge the social and emotional needs of employees and to develop harmonious relationships in the workplace. This viewpoint stressed that employees' behaviors are greatly affected by their interactions with peers. If managers communicated with employees and satisfied their workplace needs, the organization would be effective.

The systems viewpoint stressed that managers should focus on how various inputs, transformation processes, and outputs are related to the organization's goals. The organization was viewed as a "whole," rather than simply the sum of its various departments or divisions. This wholeness requires managers to develop their communication, strategic thinking and action, and global awareness competencies. To develop these competencies, managers use quantitative models to help them understand complex organizational relationships and make appropriate decisions.

The contingency viewpoint draws from each of the other viewpoints and involves a somewhat different set of competencies. Deciding whether to draw on one set of skills in a competency or on several skills across competencies is the job of the manager. How an organization is designed depends on its external environment, the skills of its employees, and the technology used to transform raw materials into finished products. The use of teams, for example, tests the manager's communication and teamwork competencies.

The quality viewpoint stresses meeting customers' expectations in terms of the value (performance and quality) of goods and services. Top management is responsible for putting systems into place to achieve quality. One way for top management to gain the support of employees in such an effort is to design TQM practices that reward employees for meeting quality goals. The TQM philosophy requires a high level of coordination throughout the organization. One way to achieve that coordination is through teamwork. In quality-conscious organizations, teamwork means sharing both responsibility and decision making. Managers delegate decision-making authority to employees, permitting them to manage themselves—but only after they have received the necessary training. Deming's philosophy of statistical quality control not only provides a method for analyzing deviations from standards, but it also provides a way to increase communication among employees.

Today, many managers are using these five foundation viewpoints to create new ways of thinking about managing their organizations. For centuries, owners of family business have passed on their wisdom, experience, and contacts to their children, master craftsman have taught their ideas to apprentices, and employees have exchanged know-how about the job with their fellow coworkers. In Chapter 9, we focus on how knowledge management is used by managers to create new ways of adding value for their organization. We indicate that different viewpoints of knowledge management result in different management practices. Knowledge managers share information with others to achieve innovation and best practices. The roots of some of these practices can be traced to the contributions of managers who advocated the systems and quality viewpoints. The challenge facing managers is to draw on traditional viewpoints to become decisive and action oriented.

Finally, since organizations are continuously changing, they must learn from the past in order to remain competitive. In Chapter 12, we discuss how managers can create learning organizations in which employees are encouraged and rewarded for sharing information and experiences that enable the organization to grow and prosper. Managers in learning organizations use certain practices to encourage employees to build effective teams. Many of these practices come from the behavioral viewpoint.

In this chapter we introduced several influential viewpoints and approaches that have shaped managerial thinking during the past 100 years. Ideas from bureaucratic, scientific, and administrative management greatly influenced early managerial practices. Later, new ideas of managing stressed the human or behavioral aspects of managing. During World War II, industry and the armed forces developed sophisticated management systems to coordinate war efforts. Then, as organizations grew and became global, none of the earlier management concepts seemed to apply totally to various situations. The contingency approach stressed that these concepts could be applied under some conditions but not under others. Today's managers are concerned primarily with the quality viewpoint of management as a way to meet consumer demand throughout the world for quality products and services.

1. Describe the three branches of the traditional viewpoint of management: bureaucratic, scientific, and administrative.

Max Weber developed a theory of bureaucratic management, which emphasizes the need for a strict hierarchy governed by clearly defined regulations and lines of authority. His theory contains seven principles: a formal system of rules, impersonal management, division of labor, a hierarchical structure, a detailed authority structure, lifelong career commitment, and rationality. Scientific management theorists tried to find ways to make workers more productive. Frederick Taylor thought that management's job was to make individual workers more efficient. That was to be accomplished by improving worker–machine relationships, based on time-and-motion studies. Frank and Lillian Gilbreth also studied how to make workers more efficient. Frank Gilbreth focused on the various physical motions workers used, and Lillian Gilbreth emphasized the welfare of workers. Henry Gantt thought that workers' performance could be charted and thus improved by setting deadlines. Administrative management theorists focused on principles that managers, rather than workers, could use to become more effective. Henry Fayol outlined four functions—planning, organizing, leading, and controlling—that he believed all successful managers use in their work.

2. Explain the behavioral viewpoint's contribution to management.

The behavioral viewpoint emphasizes employees' human and social needs. One of its first proponents, Mary Parker Follett, believed that management should coordinate the efforts of all employees to achieve organizational goals. Chester Barnard's contribution was similar to Follett's. He held, in part, that a manager doesn't have the authority to tell a worker what to do unless the worker accepts that authority. Studies conducted at the Hawthorne plant of the Western Electric Company led to the conclusion that social and human factors can be more important than physical and financial factors in influencing productivity.

3. Describe how managers can use systems and quantitative techniques to improve employee performance.

The systems viewpoint looks at organizations as a series of inputs, transformation processes, and outputs. A system may either be open or closed. Systems analysis advocates that managers use quantitative techniques to solve problems.

4. State the two major components of the contingency viewpoint.

The contingency viewpoint, or situational approach, encourages managers to use the concepts and methods of the traditional, behavioral, and systems viewpoints, depending on the circumstances they face at the time. The three key contingency variables that managers should consider before making a decision are the environment, technology, and people involved.

5. Explain the impact of the need for quality on management practices.

The quality viewpoint stresses the provision of high-quality products and services at all times. One of the founders of the quality movement was W. Edwards Deming. Long after he had helped Japanese managers make statistical analyses the basis for quality control improvements, his contributions were recognized by U.S. managers. His recommendations included planning for quality, striving for zero defects, using only a few suppliers who have demonstrated that they can deliver quality, and inspecting for quality during the process instead of after.

Acceptance theory of authority
Administrative management
Authority principle

Authority structure
Behavioral viewpoint
Bureaucratic management

Charismatic authority	Quality
Closed system	Rationality
Contingency viewpoint	Rational–legal authority
Division of labor	Rules
Feedback	Scientific management
Functional foremanship	Sigma
Gantt chart	Statistical process control
Hawthorne effect	System
Hierarchical structure	Systems viewpoint
Impersonality	Technology
Inputs	Time-and-motion study
Lifelong career commitment	Total quality management
Measuring by attribute	Traditional authority
Measuring by variable	Traditional viewpoint
Open system	Transformation processes
Outputs	Unity of command principle

QUESTIONS FOR DISCUSSION and COMPETENCY DEVELOPMENT

1. Why should you know about the evolution of management?

2. What principles of bureaucracy are illustrated in the UPS preview case?

3. Discuss the principles of scientific management used in call centers.

4. TDIndustries has been named by the editors of *Fortune* magazine as one of the best U.S. companies for which to work. What contributions from the behavioral viewpoint are illustrated?

5. What challenges face employees who are trying to implement aspects of the behavioral viewpoint in an organization?

6. Using systems concepts, describe the registration process used at your university to enroll students.

7. How has KFC used principles of scientific management to help employees increase their store's efficiency?

8. What types of problems does systems analysis tackle?

9. You have been asked to address a local business group on the subject of the contingency viewpoint of management. Prepare an outline of your talk.

10. What lessons did you take away from Bombardier quality movement?

11. Why is quality important?

CASE FOR COMPETENCY DEVELOPMENT

STARBUCKS

A few years ago, Howard Schultz, chairman and chief global strategist of Starbucks, indicated that his greatest challenge was to attract and manage a worldwide workforce. He believed that Starbucks could provide a motivational system that would cut costs while maintaining high quality. Evidently, he has done just that. Since going public in 1992, the company's stock has risen by more than 800 percent; its retail sales exceeded $3 billion in 2002; and its profits topped $215 million, a 19 percent increase over 2001. Starbucks products can be found in restau-rants, hotels, offices, airlines, and in more than 5,900 stores in over 20 countries throughout the world. By the end of 2005, the company is targeting revenue growth of approximately 20 percent per year, earnings per share growth of 20 to 25 percent per year, and 10,000 stores worldwide in 60 countries.

The Starbucks Support Center at Starbucks Coffee Company's headquarters in Seattle is packed with energy—not induced by a caffeine rush—but from associates being involved in a robust blend of teamwork, sense of mission, and challenge. As one of *Fortune* magazine's "100 Best Companies to Work for in America," not to mention one of the world's fastest growing purveyors of indulgence, Starbucks has been giving its employees a daily lift since 1971.

Woven into the company's mission statement is this goal: "Provide a great work environment and treat each other with respect and dignity." It takes more than company declarations to motivate and inspire people. So how does a young, developing company on an aggressive growth track motivate more than 54,000 people and inspire balance and a team spirit?

Starbucks purchases a line of Fair Trade–Certified beans, or "politically correct" coffee. It is grown on small farm cooperatives rather than large plantations. It sells for $1.26/lb, which goes directly to the farmers rather than to middlemen, who often pay growers less than $0.50/lb. The higher price paid directly to the farmers, who handpick their beans and carry them down the mountain in 100-lb sacks, means that the farmers can afford to send their children to school.

The Starbucks Foundation creates hope, discovery, and opportunity in communities where it does business with national nonprofits such as Jumpstart and America SCORES. Starbucks store partners (employees) have championed literacy efforts across America, and in 2002, distributed $1.7 million in literacy grants. Lauren Moore, Starbucks director of giving and community affairs, states, "The Starbucks Foundation is committed to supporting youth literacy for the long term."

Second is what Starbucks refers to as "a special blend of employee benefits" and a work/life program that focuses on the physical, mental, emotional, and creative aspects of each person. Starbucks developed an innovative work/life program to foster a committed organizational culture—and a long-term partnership. In fact, employees at Starbucks are called *partners*.

The company's work/life program includes on-site fitness services, referral and educational support for child care and elder care, an info line for convenient information, and the Partner Connection—a program that links employees with shared interests and hobbies. Starbucks has comparatively low health-care costs, low absenteeism, and one of the highest retention rates in the industry. Moreover, employees reap the benefits of the company's ongoing success.

Starbucks is committed to providing an atmosphere that breeds respect and values the contributions that people make each day, regardless of who or at what level they are in the company. All partners who work a minimum 20 hours a week receive full medical and dental coverage, vacation days, and stock options as part of the Starbucks Bean Stock program. Eligible partners can choose health coverage from two managed care plans or a catastrophic plan. They also can select between two dental plans and a vision plan. Because of the young, healthy workforce, Starbucks has low health-benefit costs. The company's health-care costs are approximately 20 percent lower than the national average.

The company also provides disability and life insurance, a discounted stock purchase plan, and a retirement savings plan with company matching contributions. These benefits provide a powerful incentive for partners, particularly part-timers, to stay with the company, thus reducing Starbucks' recruiting and training costs. "We have historically had low turnover, most of which can be attributed to the culture and a sense of community," says Joan Moffat, the Starbucks manager of partner relations and work/life.

A few years ago, the HR department began examining how it could become more attuned to employees. For instance, some employees who started with the company when they were in college are now buying homes and dealing with the realities of child care and elder care. Starbucks responded by providing flexible work schedules as part of its work/life program. "Our environment lends itself to meeting multiple life demands. By virtue of our strong sales and accelerated growth, flex schedules have not hurt productivity in the least," says Moffat. "Flexibility is particularly inherent in our stores because of our extended hours of operation and the diversity of our workforce— from students to parents—who need to work alternative hours."

Recent studies have shown that 60 percent of U.S. workers have child-care or elder-care responsibilities. Starbucks recognized—as many other companies have—that partners less encumbered by personal stress and obligations are more innovative and productive. Starbucks implemented several programs that specifically address the life stages and personal needs of its workforce. To help deal with the fast-paced and demanding environment at Starbucks, it also provides referral services for partners and eligible dependents enrolled in the medical plan. It connects them with information that helps make extraordinary life issues more manageable. In one particular case, a partner needed emergency child care for his ill son. The Starbucks Working Solutions program made prompt arrangements for a certified in-home caretaker, no work was missed, and Starbucks covered half of the cost.[32]

Questions

1. What viewpoint of management is practiced at Starbucks? Explain.

2. Visit a Starbucks coffee shop and, using the quality attributes in Table 2.2, rate Starbucks' product and service quality. How do they stack up against these criteria?

3. What systems concepts are illustrated by Starbucks' employees when they fill a customer's order?

4. Why has Starbucks grown to become the largest server of coffee in the world?

MANAGING AN ORGANIZATION

Although you might find it hard to do, try to answer each of the following 20 items with either a **mostly agree** or **mostly disagree** response. We'll talk about the scoring of the scale below.

	Mostly Agree	Mostly Disagree
1. I value stability in my job.	____	____
2. I like a predictable organization.	____	____
3. I enjoy working without the benefit of a carefully specific job description.	____	____
4. I'd enjoy working for a firm that promotes employees based on seniority.	____	____
5. Rules, policies, and procedures generally frustrate me.	____	____
6. I would enjoy working for a company that had 100,000 employees.	____	____
7. Being an entrepreneur would involve more risks than I'm willing to take.	____	____
8. Before accepting a position, I'd like to see a job description.	____	____
9. I'd prefer a job as a freelance landscape artist to one as a supervisor for the Department of Motor Vehicles.	____	____
10. Seniority should be as important as performance in determining pay promotions.	____	____
11. I'd be proud to work for the largest and most successful company in its field.	____	____
12. Given a choice, I'd rather make $90,000 a year as a VP in a small company than $100,000/year as a middle manager in a large company.	____	____
13. I'd feel uncomfortable if I had to wear an employee badge with an ID number on it.	____	____

	Mostly Agree	Mostly Disagree
14. Parking spaces in a company lot should be assigned according to job level.	____	____
15. I'd generally prefer working as a specialist instead of performing lots of tasks.	____	____
16. Before accepting a job, I'd want to make sure that the company had a good program of employee benefits.	____	____
17. A firm won't be successful unless it has a clear set of rules and regulations.	____	____
18. I'd rather work in a department with a manager than on a team where managerial responsibility is shared.	____	____
19. You should respect people's rank.	____	____
20. Rules are meant to be broken.	____	____

Scoring: Give yourself a point for each time you answered **mostly agree** to the following items: 1, 2, 4, 6, 7, 8, 10, 11, 14, 16, 17, 18, and 19. Give yourself a point for each time you answered **mostly disagree** to the following items: 3, 5, 9, 12, 13, 15, and 20.

Interpretation: Some norms have been developed to help you interpret your total number of points:

0–7	You would most likely be frustrated by working in a very formal organization, especially a large bureaucracy.
8–14	You would experience a mix of satisfaction and disappointment from working in a large formal firm.
15–20	Large, formal firms are more compatible with your style and preferences.[33]

Questions

1. What dimensions of the self-management competency are demonstrated in this exercise?

2. What dimensions of the planning and administration competency are demonstrated in this exercise?

©Photodisc/Getty Images

Managing the Environment

Chapter 3

©Eyewire/Getty Images

Environmental Forces

Learning Objectives

After studying this chapter, you should be able to:

1. Describe how economic and cultural factors influence organizations.

2. Identify the five competitive forces that affect organizations in an industry.

3. Describe the principal political and legal strategies used by managers to cope with changes in the environment.

4. Explain how technological forces influence changes in industries.

Chapter Outline

Ever since Ray Kroc purchased the rights to use the McDonald brothers' idea of serving fast-cooked, low-cost hamburgers, french fries, and shakes to customers in 1955, the restaurant industry has never been the same. It is now a $115 billion industry. Fast food is now served not only at restaurants and drive-thrus, but also at stadiums, airports, college campuses, Kmarts, Wal-Marts, gas stations, and hospital cafeterias and on cruise ships and trains. The McDonald's restaurant chain has grown to become a $15 billion dollar international chain of more than 30,000 restaurants operating in 121 countries. It has a 43 percent share of the fast-food market. More than 15 competitors have entered this industry since 1955, including Burger King, Wendy's, and Yum Brands, Inc. (owners of Kentucky Fried Chicken, Pizza Hut, and Taco Bell). All of these restaurants typically target customers willing to pay for a low-cost meal with a minimum of service and maximum convenience.

Despite the industry's growth rate of 3.7 percent a year, competition in this industry is fierce; newer rivals enter the industry to serve both existing tastes and create new ones. McDonald's had to close more than 175 restaurants in the Middle East and Latin America and lay off more than 600 employees because it couldn't profitably compete in these markets. Behind the rise in the number of fast-food restaurants are two important trends that may change the way restaurants in the industry compete. First, people are becoming more health conscious and selective about what they eat. New forms of "leaner" cuisine that emphasize balanced nutrition and good taste are affecting the ways restaurants are preparing and marketing their offerings. The baby-boomer generation (those born between 1946 and 1964) grew up on hamburgers. As this generation grows older, it is increasingly turning away from hamburgers to more ethnic foods, such as Chinese or Tex-Mex. The Generation-Xers (those born between 1965 and 1980) and Millennials (those born in 1981 or after) have been taught by their parents and others to seek healthier foods at restaurants.

Another major trend influencing the fast-food industry is that the average American family eats about half of its meals outside the home. Although this trend would appear to suggest continued growth in the fast-food industry, people are becoming more selective about what they want. People are not only more health conscious, but are seeking value from meals as well. In response, fast-food organizations now offer "value-based meals" or "value pricing" that seeks to add value to their meals. At the same time, new selections are being added to menus to feature "heart-healthy" or "lighter fare" foods. Many existing and newly entering restaurant chains find that these changes in demand and tastes present an opportunity for them to take market share away from McDonald's, Wendy's, and Burger King. More health-conscious customers are willing to try new leaner food, such as rotisserie-cooked chicken as opposed to fried chicken.[1]

THE ENVIRONMENT

1. Describe how economic and cultural factors influence organizations.

We were selective in choosing the environmental forces to address in this chapter. For example, the international arena is certainly a key part of most managers' environments—today more than ever. However, we mention international forces here only briefly because we devote Chapter 4 to this topic. Also, various groups are pressing for new forms and higher levels of ethical behavior by managers and for increased social responsibility by organizations. We allude to these forces here, but cover them in detail in Chapter 6. Generally, throughout this book, we discuss environmental forces and their management whenever they are relevant to the topic being considered.

We begin this chapter by introducing the basic features of the general environment within which organizations operate: economic and political systems, demographics, and cultural forces. We devote most of the chapter to three types of environmental forces that managers must monitor and diagnose because of their direct or indirect impact on organizations: competitive, political–legal, and technological forces.

The General Environment

The **general environment**, *sometimes called the macroenvironment, includes the external factors that usually affect all or most organizations.*[2] More specifically, as depicted in Figure 3.1, the general environment includes the type of economic system (capitalism, socialism, or

Figure 3.1   Forces Impacting Organizations

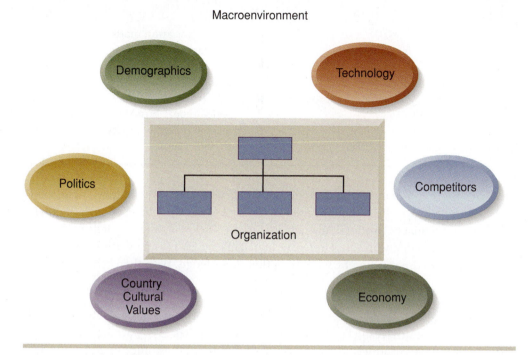

communism) and economic conditions (expansionary and recessionary cycles and the general standard of living); type of political system (democracy, dictatorship, or monarchy); condition of the ecosystem (extent of land, water, and air pollution); demographics (age, gender, race, ethnic origin, and education level of the population); and cultural background (values, beliefs, language, and religious influences). All of these aspects of the general environment have fundamental implications for managing organizations.

The Economy

Economics *is the discipline that focuses on understanding how people or nations produce, distribute, and consume various goods and services.*[3] Important economic issues are the wages paid to labor, inflation, the taxes paid by labor and organizations, the cost of materials used in the production process, and the prices at which goods and services are sold. Free-market competition, private contracts, profit incentives, technological advancement, and organized labor with collective bargaining rights are essential elements of the U.S. economic system and those of a number of other countries. The government (part of the political system) acts as a watchdog over business, providing direction in antitrust, monetary policy, human rights, defense, and environmental matters. Particularly challenging economic and political conditions include the fluctuation of inflation, unemployment, taxes, and interest rates and the environmental and safety regulations covering both the workplace and goods produced. Government ownership of enterprises is the exception, rather than the norm. The U.S. economy is not centrally planned, as in North Korea or Cuba.

Several trends are currently affecting the U.S. and Canadian economies. We briefly review four of these trends, which are shown in Table 3.1.[4]

Value Matters.   There is a major emphasis on value. The economies of the past—in the Agrarian Age or the Industrial Age—were characterized by the mass of their outputs, whether crops or steel. Value has shifted from the tangible to the intangible, from steel mills to know-how. Today, manufacturers use more software and less unskilled labor.

Table 3.1	Trends in the New Versus the Old Economy

New	Old

■ Value matters
  information is key
	■ Size of organization matters
	  manufacturing is key

■ New markets
  distance vanished
	■ Defined market segments
	  demographics

■ Customers buy activities, not products
  a click away
	■ Customers for a lifetime
	  loyalty, repeat business

■ Human capital
  rise of knowledge worker
	■ Physical and capital assets
	  tangible assets

They are more automated, networked, and integrated than ever before. Thus many manufacturers can reduce their heavy machinery ownership and concentrate on the software that manages production as an important source of value added. Software is created by knowledge workers. Therefore managers are increasingly thinking in terms of the value they are creating by increasing their knowledge. With the economy becoming less about goods and more about the transfer of information and delivery of service, companies in the new economy will focus on ideas and speed. For example, Wal-Mart provides Procter & Gamble (P&G) with daily information on what is selling in which stores. P&G, in return, restocks Wal-Mart's shelves as needed. Wal-Mart achieves greater sales because P&G products are not out of stock when a customer arrives and saves money because P&G carries the inventory. P&G increases its cash flow because it sends supplies only to those stores that need product, avoiding unnecessary distribution costs.[5]

Borderless Competition. The limitations of geographic borders apply less and less. Firms can increasingly reach customers directly without regard to their physical location or that of their customers. In an economy where most everyone has a computer, the shortest distance between a customer and the company can be a single mouse click. The Internet is revolutionary because it has dramatically reduced the cost of communication and coordination in business and personal transactions. Firms such as Travelocity (travel), Wells Fargo (banking), and Charles Schwab (investments) are reaching out directly to customers and in the process are challenging distributors, traditional retailers, and geographic borders. Customers can easily search, evaluate, negotiate, pay for, and take delivery of products at different times and from different providers.

New companies have been formed to provide information and advice to customers so that they can make better decisions. For example, http://www.theknot.com provides advice on wedding planning, including invitations, gift registries, honeymoons, and wedding-related travel. From http://www.garden.com customers can obtain gardening information, garden designs, gardening tips, and the like. More than 70 percent of new car buyers consult with Edmund's or CarPoint on the Internet before purchasing a new car. Edmund's uses Autobytel for dealer searches and negotiations, GEICO for insurance, and Warranty Gold for extended warranties. Customers accessing Edmunds Web site (http://www.edmunds.com) can gather and evaluate information, negotiate price and terms, and finance, purchase, and insure a car—all from this single source.[6]

Customer Convenience. Organizations in the new economy will succeed by creating convenience for their customers. For example, http://www.ebay.com, which calls itself the world's largest personal trading community, includes 50 million registered users. It has a market share of 64 percent, compared with UBid.com's 14 percent and Amazon Auctions with around 2 percent. With nearly 1 million items on sale at any time, eBay's Web site receives more than 22 million hits per month. More than 6.2 million people made purchases at online auction houses, making auction sales 10 percent of total e-commerce spending. What distinguishes eBay from your local flea market is not its sheer scale but the focus on convenience. The system is designed to allow buyers and sellers to search numerous categories and participate in auctions with as little friction as possible. Online tutorials lead customers through a simple four-step process: register, find stuff, bid, and sell. By bringing buyers and sellers together, it has created a huge market for resold goods, dramatically cutting the time needed for millions of buyers and sellers to find each other and transact business.[7]

Human Capital. In the old economy, the most important assets—capital, plant, and labor—were owned by the organization. To succeed in the new economy, organizations must manage knowledge, not just data or information. That is, knowledge is now an important asset too. **Knowledge management** *is the creation, protection, development, and sharing of information and intellectual assets.* In the new economy, human capital will have greater power because it is people who create and share knowledge. Knowledge workers in many organizations have positioned themselves to be independent entrepreneurs. Organizations will be forced to develop new ways to compensate employees because knowledge workers increasingly want to share in the wealth they create. Some 88 million N-Geners—the Net Generation (people between the ages of 2 and 22)—will enter the workforces in Canada and the United States between 2000 and 2020. The N-Geners thrive on collaboration and many find the notion of a "boss" somewhat bizarre.[8]

The Competent Manager

"Our assets leave on the elevator every night. Organizations do not own human capital; they can only rent them. In today's world, human capital will have greater power than other resources because it is the people who create knowledge."

Andy Grove
Founder and CEO
Intel Corporation

The Environment. Every firm exists in an environment. Although specific types of environmental forces and conditions vary from industry to industry, consider the rising consciousness of the need to protect the environment by all organizations. **Environmental stewardship** *is a policy that an organization adopts to protect or enhance the natural resources in the conduct of its activities.* The City of Calgary, Alberta, recently installed more than 11,000 new lower wattage streetlights that will save residents of this Canadian city $2 million per year while reducing carbon dioxide emissions of gas and coal-burning generators by as much as 16,000 tons per year. These new streetlights reduce light pollution (unnecessary light emitted into the sky) by using flat lens fixtures that reduce the amount of excessive light onto private residences. These new lights also reduce glare, which increases a driver's visibility and cuts down on accidents.[9]

Organizations must address the concerns of environmental groups such as Greenpeace, the Sierra Club, and the Union of Concerned Scientists. These groups question whether designer crops can do much to clean up pollution. They also keep a close watch on the manufacture and use of herbicides and other synthetic products. The Audubon Society has broadened its efforts from protection of wildlife to actively monitoring business practices that affect native plants and animals. It was the first organization to propose legal agreements requiring removal of significant amounts of phosphate from water used to refine sugar. The National Resources Defense Council has abandoned some of its earlier views—considered by some to be "fanatic and utopian"—and has displayed a greater understanding of the trade-offs involved in both economic and environmental survival. The organization has begun to move from confrontation to collaboration as a strategy. Nonetheless, some environmental organizations, such as Wise Use, continue to press legislators to adopt stricter laws and regulatory boards that enforce land use and waste disposal regulations to tighten their procedures.[10]

This renewed interest in serving the environment poses numerous challenges to business. With the passage of the U.S. Clean Air Act of 1990 and NAFTA, organizations faced more than a choice—they faced increasingly tough requirements. Meeting the needs of such legislation may add costs to doing business. For manufacturers of steel, aluminum, and copper—Nucor, Alcoa, and Phelps Dodge—meeting stringent new environmental standards has added millions of dollars to the cost of their products. It has also required them to design new manufacturing processes that will protect the environment.

Managers can take the following specific actions to respond to environmental concerns.[11]

- Give a senior-level person well-defined environmental responsibilities. This approach makes environmental concerns a strategic issue.
- Measure everything: waste, energy use, travel in personal vehicles, and the like. Set measurable goals and target dates for environmental improvements. Monitor progress.
- Consider reformulating products in order to use less toxic chemicals in the manufacturing process and cleanup. Try to use materials that won't harm the environment when the consumer eventually discards the product.
- Consider business opportunities for recycling or disposing of products, including having customers return them when the products have reached the end of their useful lives.
- Recognize that environmental regulations are here to stay and that they are likely to become more restrictive. Environmental awareness and behavior (*green behavior*) will have a lot to do with a firm's reputation in the future. Plan for that future by recognizing and acting on this reality today.

Environmental concerns have changed the way producers and consumers alike think about products, the raw materials used to make them, and the by-products of manufacturing processes. In fact, industries have developed a whole new generation of successful products in response to the Clean Air Act and reuse and recycling regulations. For example, Louisiana-Pacific makes various wood products, including particleboard, out of milling scraps.

Demographics

Demographics *are the characteristics of a work group, an organization, a specific market, or various populations*, such as individuals between the ages of 18 and 22.[12] Demographics—and in particular, changes in demographics—play an important role in marketing, advertising, and human resource management. Let's consider a few of the broad demographic changes that have occurred in the United States recently and that are expected to continue for the foreseeable future.

Increasing Diversity. The U.S. workforce is becoming more diverse. For example, people with disabilities—aided by passage of the Americans with Disabilities Act several years ago—have been finding more and more ways to become productive employees. Many gays and lesbians no longer try to hide their sexual orientation and want to be dealt with as employees who have rights equal to those of straight people. Older employees now have the right to refuse mandatory retirement and can continue to work as long as they are productive. Obese people are beginning to expect and gain some rights to be treated fairly and equally in the workplace.

By the end of this decade, more than 158 million people will be part of the U.S. labor force, an increase of 17 million from 2000. The share of women in the U.S. workforce will increase from 47 percent in 2000 to 48 percent in 2010. The percentage of Asians is expected to be at 5 percent, and the number of Hispanic Americans is expected to be at 13 percent, an increase from 10 percent in 2000. Hispanic men have the highest workforce participation rate, while Hispanic women have the lowest. This growth will result from continued immigration of young adults, high birth rates, and relatively few retirees. About 23 million baby boomers will retire by 2010, most of whom will be white men. However, many of these people will continue working in part-time jobs. Women and people of color will gradually represent a larger share of the labor force. The overall rate of labor force participation will barely creep upward by 2010, from 66.6 percent in 2000 to 67.1 percent. By 2010, the number of African-American workers will increase by 12 percent from 2000. All of these trends will make the labor force much more diverse than it is today.

Education and Skills. In the preceding section, we noted that the U.S. economy has shifted from industrial production to services and information analysis. This shift means that jobs of all kinds are more likely to require some type of specialized skill. One result is that people with little education or training will continue to have a hard time finding meaningful and well-paying work and will experience long spells of "labor market inactivity." Currently, knowledge workers, such as physical therapists, computer engineers and scientists, special-education teachers—all of whom must have education and training beyond high school—are among the workers in greatest demand.[13]

Managerial Challenges. Managers are likely to face new pressures from an increasingly diverse workforce as we will focus on in Chapter 13. One consequence of the massive downsizing of organizations has been an increase in the number of **contingent workers**, *employees who are independent contractors*, entering the workforce. For the most part, these are knowledge workers who have formed networks among themselves for trading jobs on the Web. A challenge of managers is to tap into this talent pool. They need to recognize this trend and learn how to manage people who may have once worked for the company and are now hired back on a "contingent" basis to complete a contract or initiate a new product for a customer.[14]

In response to the increasing diversity of the workforce, some organizations provide training to help employees at all levels be more tolerant of language, age, race, and ethnic differences but intolerant to sexual harassment; to identify and reject racial and gender preferences in hiring and promotion; and to be responsive to the needs of people with disabilities. Managers no longer can impose a traditional "Anglo male" organizational culture on workers. More and more workers from all backgrounds are interested in flexible scheduling that recognizes and accommodates the demands of modern families.

In addition, many new workers expect something more from their careers than simply earning a living—they want to feel that they are making a meaningful contribution to their employers and to society. These better educated employees want their individual and group needs recognized and met. They desire more control over their destiny, a say in decisions that affect them, and more flexibility in the terms and rewards of employment. They want a fair, open, flexible, and responsive work environment where they can enjoy the workplace, as well as be productive. Many expect to experience the excitement and stimulation of meeting challenging opportunities and problems and the security that comes from being appreciated and supported. People will be less willing to sacrifice personal and family life for career success.[15]

Cultural Forces

Underlying a society and surrounding an organization are various cultural forces, which often are not as visible as other general environmental forces. **Culture** *refers to the unique pattern of shared characteristics, such as values, that distinguish the members of one group of people from those of another.*[16] A **value** *is a basic belief about a condition that has considerable* *importance and meaning to individuals and is relatively stable over time.* A **value system** *comprises multiple beliefs that are compatible and supportive of one another.* For example, beliefs in private enterprise and individual rights are mutually supportive. Cultural values aren't genetically transferred. People begin to learn their culture's values from the day they are born, and this learning continues throughout their lives. As described in Chapter 18, cultural values differ across countries, across organizations, across ethnic groups, and even across organizations.

Managers need to appreciate the significance of values and value systems, both their own and those of others. Values can greatly affect how a manager

- ■ **views other people and groups, thus influencing interpersonal relationships**. In Japan male managers have traditionally believed that women should defer decision-making responsibilities to men. They belonged at home where they were responsible for raising and educating the children. Until recently, similar views prevailed in many U.S. organizations. But this situation has changed. Many more U.S. managers and government policies/laws view men and women as equals who should be recognized, consulted, and promoted because of their abilities and contributions, not their gender.
- ■ **perceives situations and problems**. Many U.S. managers believe that conflict and competition can be managed and used constructively by employees to solve problems. In France, employees take their different perspectives to their bosses who will then issue orders for settling a situation.
- ■ **goes about solving problems**. In Korea, managers at Samsung believe that team decision making can be effective. In Germany, managers at Hoechst Chemical believe that individuals should make decisions after thorough analysis and by following procedures.
- ■ **determines what is and is not ethical behavior**. One manager might believe that ethics means doing only what is absolutely required by law. Another might view ethics as going well beyond minimum legal requirements to do what is morally right.
- ■ **leads and controls employees**. In the United States, many managers believe in sharing information with employees and relying on mutual trust more than rigid controls. In Mexico, most managers emphasize rules, close supervision, and a rigid chain of command.[17]

By diagnosing a culture's values, managers and employees can understand and predict others' expectations and avoid some cultural pitfalls. Otherwise, they risk inadvertently antagonizing fellow employees, customers, or other groups by breaking a sacred taboo (e.g., showing the bottom of a person's shoe to a Saudi) or ignoring a time-honored custom (e.g., preventing an employee from attending an important religious ceremony in Indonesia).

A framework of work-related values has been used in numerous studies of cultural differences among employees in more than 50 countries. Geert Hofstede, director of the Institute for Research on Intercultural Cooperation, developed the framework for research on intercultural cooperation in the Netherlands while an organizational researcher at IBM. The findings reported here are based on his surveys of thousands of IBM employees in 50 countries. Hofstede's studies uncovered some intriguing differences among countries in terms of five value dimensions: power distance, uncertainty avoidance, individualism (versus collectivism), masculinity (versus femininity), and long-term versus short-term orientation. Before continuing to read this chapter, please take a few minutes and complete the questionnaire in the following Self-Management Competency feature. Think about the culture in which you now live and study.[18]

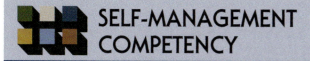

SELF-MANAGEMENT COMPETENCY

What Are Your Cultural Values?

Instructions

In the following questionnaire, please indicate the extent to which you agree or disagree with each statement. For example, if you *strongly agree* with a particular statement, you would circle the 5 next to that statement.

1 **Strongly disagree**
2 **Disagree**
3 **Neither agree nor disagree**
4 **Agree**
5 **Strongly agree**

<table>
<tr><td></td><td colspan="2" align="center">Strongly
Disagree</td><td colspan="3" align="center">Strongly
Agree</td></tr>
</table>

Questions

1. It is important to have job requirements and instructions spelled out in detail so that employees always know what they are expected to do. 1 2 3 4 5
2. Managers expect employees to follow instructions and procedures closely. 1 2 3 4 5
3. Rules and regulations are important because they inform employees what the organization expects of them. 1 2 3 4 5
4. Standard operating procedures are helpful to employees on the job. 1 2 3 4 5
5. Instructions for operations are important for employees on the job. 1 2 3 4 5
6. Group welfare is more important than individual rewards. 1 2 3 4 5
7. Group success is more important than individual success. 1 2 3 4 5
8. Being accepted by the members of the work group is very important. 1 2 3 4 5
9. Employees should only pursue their goals after considering the welfare of the group. 1 2 3 4 5
10. Managers should encourage group loyalty even if individual goals suffer. 1 2 3 4 5
11. Individuals may be expected to give up their goals in order to benefit group success. 1 2 3 4 5
12. Managers should make most decisions without consulting subordinates. 1 2 3 4 5
13. Managers must often use authority and power when dealing with subordinates. 1 2 3 4 5
14. Managers should seldom ask for the opinions of employees. 1 2 3 4 5
15. Managers should avoid off-the-job social contacts with employees. 1 2 3 4 5
16. Employees should not disagree with management decisions. 1 2 3 4 5
17. Managers should not delegate important tasks to employees. 1 2 3 4 5
18. Managers should help employees with their family problems. 1 2 3 4 5
19. Management should see to it that workers are adequately clothed and fed. 1 2 3 4 5
20. Managers should help employees solve their personal problems. 1 2 3 4 5
21. Management should see that health care is provided to all employees. 1 2 3 4 5
22. Management should see that children of employees have an adequate education. 1 2 3 4 5
23. Management should provide legal assistance for employees who get in trouble with the law. 1 2 3 4 5
24. Management should take care of employees as they would treat their children. 1 2 3 4 5
25. Meetings are usually run more effectively when they are chaired by a man. 1 2 3 4 5
26. It is more important for men to have professional careers than it is for women to have professional careers. 1 2 3 4 5
27. Men usually solve problems with logical analysis; women usually solve problems with intuition. 1 2 3 4 5
28. Solving organizational problems usually requires an active, forcible approach typical of men. 1 2 3 4 5
29. It is preferable to have a man in a high-level position rather than a woman. 1 2 3 4 5

Interpretation

The questionnaire measures each of the five basic culture dimensions. Your score can range from 5 to 35. The numbers in parentheses that follow are the question numbers. Add the scores for these questions to arrive at your total score for each cultural value. The higher your score, the more you demonstrate the cultural value.

Value 1: Uncertainty Avoidance (1, 2, 3, 4, 5). Your score _____. A high score indicates a culture in which people often try to make the future predictable by closely following rules and regulations. Organizations try to avoid uncertainty by creating rules and rituals that give the illusion of stability.

Value 2: Individualism/collectivism (6, 7, 8, 9, 10, 11). Your score _____. A high score indicates collectivism, or a culture in which people believe that group success is more important than individual achievement. Loyalty to the group comes before all else. Employees are loyal and emotionally dependent on their organization.

Value 3: Power Distance (12, 13, 14, 15, 16, 17). Your score _____. A high score indicates a culture in which people believe in the unequal distribution of power among segments of the culture. Employees fear disagreeing with their bosses and are seldom asked for their opinions by their bosses.

Value 4: Long-term/short-term (18, 19, 20, 21, 22, 23, 24). Your score _____. A high score indicates a culture in which people value persistence, thrift, and respect for tradition. Young employees are expected to follow orders given to them by their elders and delay gratification of their material, social, and emotional needs.

Value 5: Masculinity/femininity (25, 26, 27, 28, 29). Your score _____. A high score indicates masculinity, or a culture in which people value the acquisition of money and other material things. Successful managers are viewed as aggressive, tough, and competitive. Earnings, recognition, and advancement are important. Quality of life and cooperation are not as highly prized.

The following discussion focuses primarily on Hofstede's ranking of four regions of the world with respect to each dimension. These rankings are based on the dominant value orientation in each country. Figure 3.2[19] shows the rankings for Canada, Japan, France, and the United States.

Power Distance. *The degree to which less powerful members of society accept that influence is unequally divided is the measure of its* **power distance**. If most people in a society support an unequal distribution, the nation is ranked high. In societies ranked high (e.g., Mexico, France, Malaysia, and the Philippines), membership in a particular class or caste is crucial to an individual's opportunity for advancement. Societies ranked lower play down inequality. Individuals in the United States, Canada, Sweden, and Austria can achieve prestige, wealth, and social status, regardless of family background.

Managers operating in countries ranked low in power distance are expected to be generally supportive of equal rights and equal opportunity. For example, managers in Canada and the United States typically support participative management. In contrast, managers in Mexico, France, and India do not value the U.S. and Canadian style of participative management. Power is centralized and decisions are made from the top. Managers in the United States and Canada try not to set themselves too much apart from subordinates by appearing to be superior or unique. In countries with high power distance, however, a more autocratic management style not only is common but also is expected by employees. There is also a wide gap between executives and workers' compensation.

Uncertainty Avoidance. *The extent to which members of a culture feel threatened by risky or unknown situations is the measure of its* **uncertainty avoidance**. Laws and rules try to prevent uncertainties in the behavior of other people. Individuals in cultures ranked low on this dimension generally are secure and don't expend a great deal of energy trying to avoid or minimize ambiguous situations. In France and other cultures with high uncertainty avoidance, individuals often try to make the future more predictable by following established procedures and rules that foster tradition. In France, the younger person always approaches the older person for the *faire les bisous* or kiss. A violation of this formality is considered rude. In French organizations, such as Total Fina Elf and France Telecom, high uncertainty avoidance is often associated with built-in career stability (job security),

Figure 3.2   Cultural Value Rankings

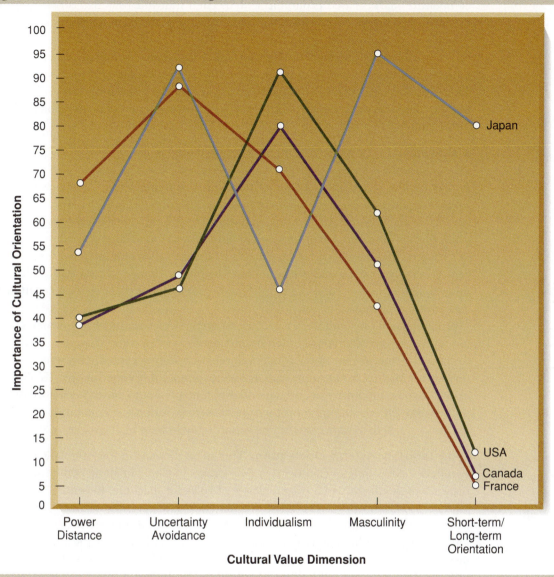

Figure 3.2 Cultural Value Rankings

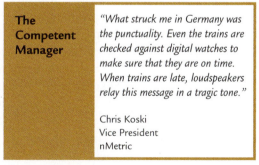

numerous rules governing behavior, intolerance of deviant ideas and behavior, belief in absolute truths, and overreliance on expertise.

In the United States and Canada, employees and managers ranked low on uncertainty avoidance, sharing a relatively high tolerance for uncertainty, compared with workers and managers in Japan and France. Thus Canadian and U.S. managers are more likely to be receptive to changing rules, open competition, and new ideas than are their counterparts in Japan and France.

Individualism. **Individualism** *is a combination of the degree to which society expects people to take care of themselves and their immediate families and the degree to which individuals believe they are masters of their own destinies.* The opposite of individualism is **collectivism**, *which refers to a tight social framework in which group (family, clan, organization, and nation) members focus on the common welfare and feel strong loyalty toward one another.*

In the United States, France, and Canada, employees ranked high on individualism, a result that agrees with the frequent characterization of these countries as "I" societies

The Competent Manager

"What struck me in Germany was the punctuality. Even the trains are checked against digital watches to make sure that they are on time. When trains are late, loudspeakers relay this message in a tragic tone."

Chris Koski
Vice President
nMetric

rather than "we" societies. A strong sense of individualism supports and maintains a competitive market-based economic system. High individualism also is consistent with the individual merit and incentive pay systems favored in the United States and Canada. Conversely, group incentives and strong seniority systems are likely to exist in countries with low individualism (high collectivism), such as Japan. Managers and employees in a high-individualism culture move from organization to organization more frequently. They don't believe that their organizations are solely responsible for their welfare, nor do they expect decisions made by groups to be better than decisions made by individuals.

Masculinity. In Hofstede's framework, **masculinity** *is the degree to which assertiveness and the acquisition of money and material things are valued, as well as the degree of indifference to others' quality of life.* The opposite of masculinity is **femininity**, a *more nurturing, people-oriented approach to life.* The masculinity dimension also reflects the division of labor among men and women in a society. Canada and the United States probably rank lower today on this dimension than they would have 20 years ago, largely because of the societal changes that have been taking place in role expectations for men and women. In recent years significant social pressures have begun to change stereotyped notions that men should be assertive and women should be nurturing or that gender roles should be clearly differentiated.

In high-masculinity cultures (e.g., Mexico, Japan, Austria, and Italy), women still do not hold many managerial jobs. Men dominate most settings, and an organization's right to influence the private lives of its employees is widely accepted. One researcher observed that Mexico, for example, rigidly defines gender-role expectations: The woman is expected to be supportive of and dependent on men—not to do for herself, but to yield to the wishes of others, caring for their needs before her own. A common belief in Muslim countries is that women should be subordinate to men in all aspects of their lives.

Long-Term/Short-Term Orientation. This value dimension was originally developed to reflect the teaching of Confucius, a civil servant in China in about 500 B.C. Known for his wisdom, he developed a pragmatic set of rules for daily life. Recently, Hofstede extended his earlier work and labeled this dimension **long-term/short-term**, *which reflects the extent to which a culture stresses that its members accept delayed gratification of material, social, and emotional needs.* In long-term oriented cultures (e.g., China, Hong Kong, Japan), families stress the importance of thrift, ordering relationships by status and observing this order, persistence, and education. We illustrate these rules by references to organizational life. First, the junior manager owes the senior manager respect and obedience; the senior manager owes the junior manager protection and consideration. Second, the family is the prototype of all social organizations. Members of organizations should learn to promote harmony by allowing others to maintain "face," that is, dignity, self-respect, and prestige, particularly in conducting business affairs. Third, people should treat others as they would like to be treated. First-line managers should encourage subordinates to acquire knowledge and skills to enable them to advance, just as these managers would like the middle managers above them to do. Finally, a person's tasks in life consist of acquiring skills and education, working hard, not spending more than necessary, being patient, and preserving the values of the society.

In high long-term cultures, management practices such as thrift, gift giving, good manners, and saving face are highly valued. Thrift leads to saving, which provides capital for reinvestment. Welcoming speeches by elder members of the organization and exchanges of small gifts prior to conducting business are important. Seniority is prized and is linked to the size of a person's office, pay, and other perquisites. Such practices emphasize the stability of authority relationships and respect. In the United States, Canada, and France, such management practices are not highly valued or practiced.

Managerial Implications. Understanding other cultures can make you a better manager even if you never leave your home country. In an increasingly global market, managers in every country must think globally. Even in the United States, most products face tremendous foreign competition. Global competition is a reality, and the number of managers and workers taking assignments in countries other than their own is rapidly increasing.[20] These workers bring aspects of their own cultures into their organizations, neighborhoods, school systems, and homes. Learning how to integrate these workers and their values and ways of doing things into the organization is essential. Although various cultural behaviors may appear similar on the surface, their meanings in different cultures may be quite different. Realizing the importance of these differences helps managers understand their international partners and ultimately to be better managers.

COMPETITIVE FORCES IN AN INDUSTRY

Organizations in any industry are directly affected by at least five competitive forces: competitors, new entrants, substitute goods and services, customers, and suppliers.[21] The combined strength of these forces affects long-term profitability, as shown in Figure 3.3. Managers must therefore monitor and diagnose each one, as well as their combined strength, before making decisions about future courses of action. As we noted in discussing the fast-food industry, companies have merged in order to influence character, magnitude, and impact of competitive forces in the industry. In this section, we continue to examine the fast-food industry to illustrate how companies compete.

2. Identify the five competitive forces that affect organizations in an industry.

Figure 3.3   Competitive Forces in the Task Environment

Competitors

Aside from customers, competitors are the single most important day-to-day force facing organizations. Bruce D. Henderson, founder and chairman of the Boston Consulting Group, comments: "For virtually all organizations the critical environment constraint is their actions in relation to competitors. Therefore any change in the environment that affects any competitor will have consequences that require some degree of adaptation. This requires continual change and adaptation by all competitors merely to maintain relative position." In the Preview Case, we noted that the fast-food restaurant industry has become fast paced and increasingly competitive. As a result of changes in customer tastes, this situation creates cutthroat product rivalry with leading companies, such as Yum Brands, Inc., and Diageo, that are attempting to gain market share through massive advertising campaigns. Fast-food restaurants spend more than $2.7 billion per year on advertising. This direct consumer advertising broadens people's awareness of new products.

New Entrants

New entrants refer to *the relative ease with which new firms can compete with established firms.* In an industry with low barriers to entry (e.g., the photocopy industry or the fast-food industry) competition will be fierce. The fast-food industry is a particularly interesting case because it has had both high and low barriers to entry during the past 10 years. Economies of scale, product differentiation, capital requirements, and government regulation are four common factors that need to be diagnosed in assessing barriers to entry. Let's see how they have affected the fast-food industry.

Economies of scale *are achieved when increased volume lowers the unit cost of a good or service produced by a firm.* The potential for economies of scale in the fast-food industry is substantial. The cost of advertising, buying supplies, training, and other administrative tasks at McDonald's is equally shared by its 30,000 restaurants, whereas Burger King's costs are spread over its 11,400 stores. Large purchasers frequently enjoy quantity discounts that smaller purchasers are not extended by suppliers.

Product differentiation *is uniqueness in quality, price, design, brand image, or customer service that gives one firm's product an edge over another firm's.* It's a tool that organizations can use to lock in customer loyalty to its products. Ronald McDonald, Happy Meals, and its "Golden Arches" serve to differentiate McDonald's from its competitors. Ninety-six percent of kids recognize Ronald McDonald. The only fictional character with a higher degree of recognition is Santa Claus. Kids are attracted to the toys found in happy meals and the eye-catching ads on the Cartoon Network and Nickelodeon television programs. McDonald's has recently teamed up with ConAgra to test a line of wrapped sandwiches made with Healthy Choice deli meat in an attempt to further differentiate itself from its competitors.

Capital requirements *are the dollars needed to finance equipment, purchase supplies, purchase or lease land, hire staff, and the like.* According to Jean Birch, vice president of operations for Taco Bell, the cost of opening a new restaurant is close to $1 million dollars. The cost of opening a multibranded restaurant (a combination of KFC and Pizza Hut) is roughly the same.[22]

Government regulation *is a barrier to entry if it bars or severely restricts potential new entrants to an industry.* The fast-food industry is not faced with a lot of government rules and regulations as is, say, the pharmaceutical industry.

Substitute Goods and Services

In a general sense, all competitors produce substitute goods or services, or goods or services that can easily replace another's goods or services. In the fast-food industry, a major substitute is the home-cooked meal. The introduction of desktop publishing systems by IBM, Apple, and Dell enabled graphic design companies to use personal computers (PCs) to design and typeset brochures, catalogs, flyers, and even books. Desktop publishing or typesetting software thus substitutes for the services of typesetting firms at a fraction of their cost. Many organizations (e.g., EDS, Citigroup, and Kinko's) commonly use fax, e-mail, and/or overnight delivery services as a substitute for long-distance telephone calls and the U.S. Postal Service. Substitutes are a powerful force in the pharmaceutical industry. The threat of substitution is largely based on the formula in the patent. The price difference between a "branded" and generic drug oftentimes is more than 100 percent.

Customers

Customers for goods or services naturally try to force down prices, obtain more or higher quality products (while holding price constant), and increase competition among sellers by playing one against the other. Customer bargaining power is likely to be relatively great under the following circumstances.

- **The customer purchases a large volume relative to the supplier's total sales.** People who eat at fast-food restaurants have little bargaining power over the prices charged at various restaurants. At another level, McDonald's is a customer of Simplot. McDonald's purchases almost all of the potatoes grown by Simplot. As their largest customer, McDonald's has tremendous power over Simplot to negotiate favorable prices and maintain quality standards.

- **The product or service represents a significant expenditure by the customer.** Customers generally are motivated to cut costs that constitute large portions of their total costs. Eating at fast-food restaurants normally does not constitute a big expense for the customer.

- **Large customers pose a threat of backward integration. Backward integration** *is the purchase of one or more of its suppliers by a larger organization as a cost-cutting or quality-enhancing strategy.* In the fast-food industry, there are no large customers to pose such a threat. If McDonald's decided to raise its own potatoes, this would be an example of backward integration.

- **Customers have readily available alternatives for the same services or products.** A consumer may not have a strong preference for one fast-food restaurant over another. Therefore, they have a huge choice of which restaurant to frequent. This means that they have alternatives and lots of power.

Suppliers

The bargaining power of suppliers often controls how much they can raise prices above their costs or reduce the quality of goods and services they provide before losing customers. As just mentioned, McDonald's has contracts with Simplot to buy all of its potatoes. Simplot in turn has contracts with more than 1,000 potato growers throughout the world to supply its needs. KFC has entered into long-term contracts with Pilgrim's Pride, Purdue, and other chicken raisers to supply its U.S. restaurants with chickens. These long-term contracts give McDonald's and KFC tremendous power over suppliers to keep costs down, maintain delivery schedules, and quality standards. In the pharmaceutical industry, copyrights and patents generally increase supplier (drug manufacturers) strength for defined periods of time. This protection prevents suppliers from copying branded drugs and distributing generic drugs. In general, high supplier strength in the pharmaceutical market tends to be relatively short lived.

The following Global Awareness Competency feature describes how KFC and Pizza Hut compete in China.[23] Both restaurant chains face similar problems, including unpaved roads in poor condition that increase delivery times and transportation costs and the lack of modern distribution warehouses and established networks of domestic suppliers. China has more than 600,000 miles of roads, but less than 40,000 miles of it are paved modern highways, so drivers can rarely cover more than 300 miles a day. Similarly, it takes about 17 days for a freight train to go from Shanghai to Guangzhou (1,125 miles), a city outside Hong Kong. Importing foodstuffs is too costly, so Yum Brands is working with a limited number of domestic suppliers and has been investing millions of dollars in them to improve their quality and size. It has relatively large suppliers of chickens, shortening, and flour, but must rely on local suppliers for all other staples.

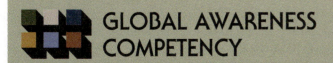

GLOBAL AWARENESS COMPETENCY

KFC in China

Samuel Su, president of KFC operations in China, faces numerous problems operating in China. When KFC initially went to China in 1987, it faced some startling conditions because it was the first company to introduce Western fast food to the Chinese. First, Chinese government

©Corbis Inc.

officials had no idea of what franchising meant. Intellectual property and franchise laws were weak, which permitted local officials to interpret the laws as they saw fit. Second, there were no known foreign brand names. Brands are unique symbols or product names that set them apart from the competition and provide the recognition factor that products need to succeed. KFC didn't want franchisees to buy the brand and then be able to sell whatever they wanted to with no legal recourse. Third, foreign multidivisional organizations learned quickly that they couldn't do business in China without government involvement. There are many hierarchical levels in local Chinese governments, and each bureaucrat wants "a piece of the action." As a result, KFC has 50 registered companies in China to help it move paperwork through the maze of bureaucratic procedures involved in opening a restaurant.

Another problem is developing a marketing program that will attract Chinese to KFC instead of McDonald's. Su knows that kids don't come alone, but instead bring their friends with them. To attract kids, he needed to tailor the menus (e.g., combo meals) and provide entertainment. Combo meals not only attract kids, but also simplify communication and choice. At KFCs, kids have a corner reserved for them. The corner is staffed with a professional hostess whose job is to talk with the kids. To ensure that they are having a good time, the hostess will sing and dance with them. The average KFC also hosts more than 430 birthday parties annually.

To compete in the fast-food industry, Su must differentiate his company's product not only from McDonald's, but also from millions of mom-and-pop restaurants. Therefore he needed to pay considerable attention to Chinese values. First, the opening of a restaurant is celebrated with a traditional "Lion Dance" to bring good luck and is attended by local politicians. Second, even though traditional Chinese fast-food restaurants have many choices on their menus and are cheap, controlling the standard of their cooking is difficult. KFC prides itself on the consistency of its offerings. Employees are trained to prepare food consistently by following rules and procedures spelled out in the operating manual. Third, the menu at KFC provides an important intangible: social freedom. In Chinese restaurants, what you order has social and status implications (e.g., "I can afford this"). The wrong order can cause the person to lose "face" with her friends. A standard and restricted menu with a limited price range frees the diner from this concern. Fourth, China has a strong desire to catch up with the rest of the world. Dining at an American restaurant enables Chinese people to feel connected to the rest of the world. Su notes that "For younger Beijing people who have higher incomes and wish to be 'connected' more closely to the outside world, eating at McDonald's or KFC or Pizza Hut is an integral part of their new lifestyle." Fifth, there is a shortage of management talent throughout China. Through its use of standardized recipes, cooking methods, and other practices, KFC is looked on by the Chinese people as a company that practices scientific management. This acknowledgment attracts consumers anxious to participate in the "modern" world.

POLITICAL–LEGAL FORCES

3. Describe the principal political and legal strategies used by managers to cope with changes in the environment.

Societies try to resolve conflicts over values and beliefs through their political and legal systems. For instance, in the United States and Canada the concepts of individual freedom, freedom of the press, property rights, and private enterprise are widely accepted. But legislative bodies, regulatory agencies, interest groups, and courts—often in conflict with one another—define the meaning and influence the actual interpretation of these concepts.

Many political and legal forces directly affect the way organizations operate. For the pharmaceutical industry in particular, changes in political forces have been especially significant during the past 25 years and will continue to be in the future. To achieve organizational goals, managers must accurately diagnose these forces and find useful ways to anticipate, respond to, or avoid the disturbances they cause.[24]

For many industries (e.g., financial services, pharmaceutical, chemical), government regulation is a central aspect of their environments. Consider, for example, how two federal credit laws affect lenders and borrowers in the United States.

- *The Equal Credit Opportunity Act* entitles the customer to be considered for credit without regard to race, color, age, gender, or marital status. Although the act doesn't guarantee that the customer will get credit, it does ensure that the credit grantor will apply tests of creditworthiness fairly and impartially.
- *The Truth in Lending Act* says that credit grantors must reveal the "true" cost of using credit—for instance, the annual interest rate the customer will be paying. In the case of a revolving charge account, the customer must also be told the monthly interest rate and the minimum monthly payment required.

As shown in Figure 3.4, managers can use five basic political strategies to cope with turbulence in their environments: negotiation, lobbying, alliance, representation, and socialization. These strategies aren't mutually exclusive, are usually used in some combination, and each often contains elements of the others. Negotiation probably is the most important political strategy because each of the other four strategies involves to some degree the use of negotiation.

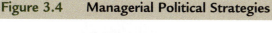

Figure 3.4   Managerial Political Strategies

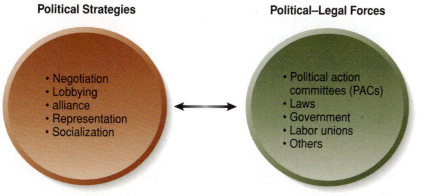

Negotiation *is the process by which two or more individuals or groups, having both common and conflicting goals, present and discuss proposals in an attempt to reach an agreement.*[25] Negotiation can take place only when the two parties believe that some form of agreement is possible and mutually beneficial. Recall that in 2002, management and the unions at United Airlines negotiated cuts in pay in an attempt to save the airline from bankruptcy. Negotiators representing the company and the union presented various proposals in an attempt to reach an agreement. Not until both parties realized that some agreement was necessary did they agree on and ratify a new contract. Unfortunately, it was too late to save United Airlines from bankruptcy.

Lobbying *is an attempt to influence government decisions by providing officials with information on the anticipated effects of legislation or regulatory rulings.*[26] Congress and regulatory agencies, such as the Securities and Exchange Commission, the Federal Communications Commission, and the Food and Drug Administration, are the targets of continual lobbying efforts by organizations affected by their decisions. Organizations whose stability, growth, and survival are directly affected by government decisions typically use their top managers to lobby for them. Motorola, Microsoft, and Coca-Cola, among others, lobbied Congress to allow favored nation trade status for China even after defiant student demonstrators were killed on Beijing's Tiananmen Square. These organizations agreed that human rights violations had occurred in China but that its market was too attractive to be ignored.

Only the largest organizations (e.g., NBC, AT&T, and Exxon) can afford to lobby for themselves. The most common form of lobbying is by associations representing the interests of groups of individuals or organizations. Approximately 4,000 national lobbying organizations maintain staffs in Washington, D.C. An additional 75,000 state and local associations and organizations occasionally lobby Washington's decision makers. Two of the largest associations representing business interests are the National Chamber of Commerce, with about 36,000 business and other organizational members, and the National Association of Manufacturers (NAM), with about 12,500 member corporations. The American Association of Retired Persons (AARP), with more than 30 million members, is the largest U.S. association representing individual interests. The AARP lobbies on behalf of U.S. citizens aged 50 and older and has a paid staff of 1,600, with headquarters in the heart of the nation's capital. In 2002 more than $1.45 billion dollars were spent by lobbyists, or more than $2.7 million in lobbying expenditures for each member of Congress. The biggest industries in the lobbying arena were pharmaceuticals and health products, followed by members of the insurance industry.

In 2002, many airline industry executives went to Washington in an effort to lobby Congress to help them rebuild their industry after the events of September 11, 2001. They were seeking more than $4 billion in additional relief. When Congress came to the airlines' rescue in 2001 with $5 billion in cash and another $10 billion in loan guarantees, many thought that the end was in sight. Instead, the industry lost $7 billion for the second year in a row. However, the cost of airport security and the decline in the number of passengers have cut deeply into the financial health of this industry.

An **alliance** *is a combined effort involving two or more organizations, groups, or individuals to achieve common goals with respect to a particular issue.*[27] Alliances, especially those created to influence government actions, typically form around issues of economic self-interest, such as reducing R&D costs in the pharmaceutical industry. Other issues include government policy (e.g., the control of raw materials or taxes), foreign relations (e.g., the control of foreign sales or investment in overseas plants), and labor relations (e.g., the control of industrywide salaries and benefits, as within the construction industry or the National Football League). Alliances often are used for the following purposes.

- **Oppose or support legislation, nomination of heads of regulatory agencies, and regulations issued by such agencies.** All companies involved in various aspects of HDTV development—AT&T, Zenith, RCA, Philips, and NBC—combined their various competing technologies into one Grand Alliance. The goal of this Grand Alliance is to gain agreement among all U.S. companies and pass legislation establishing a common digital standard for future HDTV broadcasts.
- **Improve competitiveness of two or more organizations through collaboration.** Nestlé and Coca-Cola formed a strategic alliance whereby both firms have benefited from using each other's distribution channels and marketing programs. Neither organization wants to manufacture the other's products, but they do need each other's marketing and logistical support to be competitive in their own markets.
- **Promote particular products or services, such as oranges, computers, and electricity.** For example, the Edison Electric Institute promotes both the use and conservation of electrical energy.
- **Construct facilities that would be beyond the resources of any one organization, such as new plants.** IBM has teamed up with Motorola and Toshiba to improve its semiconductor manufacturing ability to make superdense chips.

■ **Represent the interests of specific groups, such as women, the elderly, minorities, and particular industries.** The NAM lobbies Congress to pass legislation favorable to its members, including restricting imports of foreign goods such as shoes and automobiles, and trying to open new markets in foreign countries such as the sale of rice in Japan.

An alliance both broadens and limits managerial power. When an alliance makes possible the attainment of goals that a single individual or organization would be unable to attain, it broadens managerial power. When an alliance requires a commitment to making certain decisions jointly in the future, it limits managerial power. Members of OPEC periodically negotiate production levels and the price they will charge for oil. These agreements are intended to broaden OPEC's power by generating more revenue for its members. However, to be successful in this endeavor, OPEC members must abide by the agreed-on production limits.

A **joint venture** *typically involves two or more firms becoming partners to form a separate entity.* It is a common form of an alliance.[28] Each partner benefits from the other's expertise, which allows them to achieve their goals more quickly and efficiently. In the highly capital-intensive automobile industry, joint ventures are very common as firms seek to spread the high costs required to start a new plant. For example, General Motors uses joint ventures with Suzuki, Isuzu, and Toyota to produce many of its compact cars, including the Chevrolet Cavalier. Similarly, Motorola and IBM have created a joint venture in China to manufacture microprocessors and memory chips. One of the most visible joint ventures involves the production of the European Airbus. The Airbus joint venture has become the world's second largest aircraft manufacturer. Various parts are manufactured by participating companies in the United Kingdom, Germany, and Spain and flown over to Toulouse, France, where the planes are assembled by a thoroughly international team of employees.

Representation *involves membership in an outside organization that serves the interests of the member's organization or group.* Representation strategy often is subtle and indirect. School administrators often receive paid time off and the use of school resources to participate in voluntary community associations that might support the school system, such as the PTA, Chamber of Commerce, Elks, Kiwanis, Moose, Rotary, and United Way. A more direct form of representation, often based on some legal requirement, occurs when a specific group selects representatives to give it a voice in an organization's decisions. For example, union members elect officers to represent them in dealing with management.

Corporate boards of directors, the top-level policy-making groups in firms, are elected by and legally required to represent shareholders' interests. The National Association of Corporate Directors, however, suggests a much broader role for board members: They should ensure that long-term strategic goals and plans are established; that a proper management structure (organization, systems, and people) is in place to achieve these goals; and that the organization acts to maintain its integrity, reputation, and responsibility to its various constituencies. The board's responsibility to monitor and control the actions of the chief executive officer and others in top management is essential to its representing the interests of the shareholders.

Socialization *is the process by which people learn the values held by an organization and the broader society.* The assumption is that people who accept and act in accordance with these basic values are less likely to sympathize with positions that threaten the organization or the society. The so-called American business creed stresses the idea that a decentralized, privately owned, and competitive system in which price is the major regulator, should be continued and that citizens should oppose government actions that interfere with or threaten this system. Most U.S. and Canadian businesspeople subscribe to these beliefs and act on them.

Socialization includes formal and informal attempts by organizations to mold new employees to accept certain desired attitudes and ways of dealing with others and their jobs.[29] At its headquarters in Crotonville, New York, GE introduces thousands of its managers to the company's values and philosophy. These values include identifying and eliminating unproductive work in order to energize employees and encourage creativity and feelings of ownership at all levels. Conoco uses its virtual university to train managers. Employees can download courses from its Web site and/or attend courses at its Woodlands, Texas, location. Of course, top management's attempts may be offset or reinforced by the expectations of and pressures exerted by workers or other groups within the organization.

The use of socialization strategies by organizations is subject to broader cultural forces. In the United States and Canada the importance of individualism limits the extent to which organizations can use socialization strategies. Too much of what may be perceived as the "wrong kind" of socialization is likely to be met with resistance and charges of invasion of privacy or violation of individual rights.

The AARP uses many of these political strategies to gain support for its programs. Founded in 1958 by Dr. Ethel Percy, it now has more than 30 million members. Its goal is to be one of the most successful organizations in America for positive social change by educating older Americans (50 years old or older) on issues that face them, asking political candidates for clarification of their positions on issues that affect senior citizens, and increasing voter participation. AARP does not endorse political candidates or contribute money to their campaigns. However, it does organize forums at which candidates can discuss particular issues for older Americans. Working with and through various other organizations, AARP advises members about health, auto, and home insurance, investment opportunities, mail-order pharmacy services, travel, and legal services, among others, and provides discounts for its members for some of these services.

As the leading advocate for older Americans, AARP engages in legislative and consumer advocacy on many subjects.[30] The following Planning & Administration Competency feature describes how AARP uses various political strategies to communicate its goals in three areas: Social Security, Medicare, and long-term care. The political strategies are indicated in parentheses.

PLANNING & ADMINISTRATION COMPETENCY

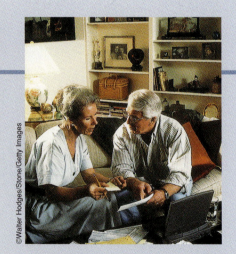

AARP

Few currently retired people or those who will retire by 2005 will outlive their Social Security benefits under the program as it is now constituted. By 2010, the first generation of baby boomers will begin to retire. By 2027, the burden on Social Security will be greater than the payments going into the trust fund. Approximately 28 percent of the people receiving benefits today are under 65, including more than 8.6 million children with a deceased or disabled parent. Although Social Security was never intended to be a person's sole retirement, 16 percent of its beneficiaries have no other income and more than 50 percent of older people rely heavily on Social Security income. To ensure that the system is properly funded, AARP has pressured Congress (*lobbying strategy*) to make adjustments in contribution rates, in annual cost of living adjustments, and investment of the trust fund. The organization has presented arguments against investing in the stock market, even though it routinely outperforms other investments, such as U.S. Treasury Bills. The argument presented is that most Americans with modest savings have little experience managing stock market investments and lack the skills needed to do so.

AARP was a driving force (*representation strategy*) for the 1997 Balanced Budget Act, which ensures that Medicare will be solvent through 2007. Under this act, Medicare makes regular monthly payments to certain health-care organizations that older people can use. It also supported the enactment of a medical savings account, which combines purchasing a catastrophic health insurance policy with an individual medical plan, something like an IRA.

AARP is also concerned about long-term care. More than 6 million elderly people need some help in caring for themselves. As people grow old, they grow more frail and often suffer from chronic and debilitating illnesses. Maintaining a person in a nursing home costs $35,000 to $50,000 per year, and each home visit by a nurse or physical therapist costs as much as $100. Medicare pays for such services only for a limited period of time after a person is released from a primary care facility (e.g., a hospital), and the remainder must come from a person's savings or from the person's family. Older people who go into a nursing home can be covered by Medicaid but only after they spend down their assets (e.g., sell their homes, stocks, and deplete almost all of their savings). AARP is trying to educate (*socialization strategy*) older people about different financing choices. But any financing program would require strong consumer protections and be easy for older people to understand and use. The organization is lobbying Congress to establish national standards to measure, assess, and ensure the quality of long-term care.

TECHNOLOGICAL FORCES

In Chapter 2 we defined *technology* as a transformation process that changes organizational inputs into outputs. Thus technology is the knowledge, tools, techniques, and actions used to transform ideas, information, and materials into finished goods and services. A technology may be as simple as making coffee at a restaurant or as complicated as driving the Pathfinder on Mars.

4. Explain how technological forces influence changes in industries.

Technological forces play an increasingly pivotal role in an organization's environment, building on the present and helping create the future. Many new technologies are radical enough to force organizations, especially in high-tech industries, to reconsider their purposes and methods of operation or face extinction. The United States and several other industrial societies have become information societies. This shift was made possible by the explosion of computer-based and telecommunications technologies. One example is the PC and its integration with mainframe computers and telecommunications systems to form supernets. Through them, organizations can collect, process, and transmit vast amounts of data quickly and economically. For instance, Kodak now supplies photographic dealers with a microcomputer and software system that enables them to order Kodak products directly rather than through wholesalers. The management of information technology is woven into various chapters of this book, but here we briefly examine technology's role in three areas: strategy, manufacturing, and distribution channels.

Technology's Role in Strategy

Computer-based information technologies are now essential in most organizations, which is one reason why we included technological forces in this chapter. In the 1970s, one of every two watches sold in the United States was a Timex product. By the mid-1990s, however, the company's market share was less than 5 percent. Seiko, Citizen, Pulsar, Accutron, and Swatch now dominate this market. Why? As the watch industry moved from mechanical to electronic, Timex didn't change its strategy and continued to build watches that relied on older technology. Innovations in quartz crystal chemistry and light-emitting diode semiconductors made Timex's technology obsolete. Electronic watches overwhelmed the marketplace and brought prices down, causing Timex to lose most of its market share. Similarly, in today's automobile industry, ceramic-based engines and sophisticated battery-powered systems hold the promise of greater efficiency and performance than internal combustion engines can provide.

Information technology creates options for managers that simply weren't feasible with older technologies.[31]

■ Computer-aided design linked to versatile, computer-controlled machines permits short production runs of custom designs with economies of scale approaching those of traditional large-scale manufacturing facilities.

■ Consumers can shop via home pages on the Internet and "electronic shopping malls" more easily than using the Yellow Pages and telephones and going to shopping centers or individual outlets.

■ With online, real-time financial management systems, managers can determine profit and loss positions daily, which was impossible with manual methods and earlier stages of computer technology.

■ Retail banking customers can perform numerous banking functions from remote locations, including shopping centers, apartment building lobbies, corporate offices, out-of-state banks, and even their homes with PCs.

Technology's Role in Manufacturing

Advances in design and manufacturing technology have made it possible to reduce substantially the amount of time required to introduce a new product into the market. The computers and statistical analyses in manufacturing have also boosted quality, with machines and processes integrated by means of common databases and routines that simplify procedures and reduce the potential for human error. Perhaps the most significant contribution of advanced manufacturing technologies is that of mass customization—that is, the ability to produce a wide variety of a product by using the same basic design and production equipment but making certain modifications to meet the demands of a broader market. For example, Levi Strauss has successfully used computer-assisted design systems to help design customized leather outfits and jeans for customers. Using an engineering workstation and advanced software, Levi Strauss can measure a customer's specific contours, body shape, weight, and preferences to create a customized pattern that becomes the basis for a perfectly fitting suit, pair of jeans, or dress in a short time. A customer's color and style preferences, as well as body measurements, are then directly fed into a computer that is electronically linked to a highly flexible stitching and finishing operation. Currently, most Levi Strauss outlets carry somewhere between 80 and 100 different varieties of jeans and outfits. With the use of new manufacturing and customization capabilities, company management believes that it will have between 400 and 500 variations on the shelves in the near future.[32]

The following Strategic Action Competency illustrates how Jeep uses technology to build its Liberty Jeep in its manufacturing complex outside of Toledo, Ohio. Jeeps started rolling out of this plant in 1941, but in 2001, Daimler-Chrysler undertook a $700 million renovation of the plant to take advantage of the latest information technology available to build Jeeps.[33]

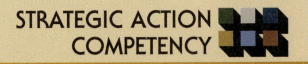

STRATEGIC ACTION COMPETENCY

Jeep

The assembly line is electronically connected to suppliers. Suppliers deliver parts and subassemblies just in time to the assembly line and exactly in production-line sequence. Each part bears the Vehicle Identification Number of the Jeep for which it was built. Half of the suppliers don't start building parts until they get e-mail that the painted body of the Jeep for which they're intended is heading into the first assembly-line workstation. Exactly how much time the supplier has to build a part varies by where that part is on the 239-workstation assembly line used to assemble a Jeep.

More than 1,300 parts are required to assemble a Jeep. During a normal workday, 420 trailer-loads of modules and parts arrive at the plant. Some parts travel 60 miles from a supplier to the assembly line. Most of these reach their designated place on the assembly line within minutes of arriving at the plant. The objective is to get the part at the proper place on the assembly line within two minutes of its arrival at

the plant. Using lanes marked "SPD" (Sequenced Parts Delivery), vehicles transport parts from the loading dock to assembly line. There's practically no inventory to serve against delayed deliveries. One Jeep is produced every 64.2 seconds. Automated equipment lifts and lowers the Jeep body from one assembly station to the next. When the assembly line is running, it produces 926 jeeps a day.

Suppliers get a daily updated forecast of production that extends to 10 days. The forecast is accurate and provides model mix data to each supplier. Suppliers have to meet the requirements of providing 10 exterior and two interior colors, three different engines, two- and four-wheel drive, manual and automatic

transmission, left- and right-hand steering, a half-dozen sound systems, and other options. Suppliers are subject to a heavy penalty if they stop the line. TRW has twice hired a helicopter to pick up some much-needed bolts at a supplier in Northern Michigan.

The order in which any particular Jeep is assembled is determined during a shift. Every 64 seconds a painted Jeep body is moved just outside the paint shop and directed to the first assembly workstation. Without any downtime, it takes about five hours from start to finish. A spring and shock-absorber package from TRW goes onto the painted body at one of the first stations. The radiator is installed near the end.

Technology's Role in Distribution

In the 1990s, perhaps the single greatest technological force was in changing the distribution of goods and services. The strong presence of the Internet and the World Wide Web, which made possible online ordering, distribution, and sales, changed the way many organizations competed for customers. When Jeff Bezos created Amazon.com, suddenly the Internet threatened established retail booksellers, such as Barnes & Noble and Borders. Internet brokerage houses, such as Ameritrade and E*Trade, allow customers to access their accounts directly to buy and sell stocks. These services bypass those offered by traditional firms. Internet shopping also has replaced the department store for many customers. Combining Internet access and traditional catalog sales has enabled Lands' End, Early Winters, Touch of Class, and L.L.Bean to reach customers whose specialized needs are not effectively satisfied by existing "brick-and-mortar" department stores and discount chains.

Pitney Bowes, a company best known for making postage machines, faced a challenge from the rise of the Internet. Since 1920, Pitney Bowes has provided organizations with machines that allow them to affix the right amount of postage to letters and packages. In late 1998, companies such as E-Stamp, Stamp Master, and many others started designing Web sites that enable customers to pay for postage over the Internet, download customer-specific sets of coded data into their computers, and print out their own mailing labels and envelopes. In effect, the Internet, with permission of the U.S. Postal Service, now allows customers to print their own stamps. In response, Pitney Bowes introduced its own version of user-friendly, Internet-based software to help customers order prepaid postage with greater ease.[34]

Building an international Information Superhighway now extends far beyond simple message systems and bulletin boards. Satellites, cellular towers, and fiber-optic telephone cables allow individuals and companies to exchange voice, data, and graphic messages in real time. Futurists speculate that within 5 to 10 years everyone will have personal numbers for all of the telecommunications devices they use; that wireless technology will replace twisted-pair, coaxial, and fiber-optic cable; and that telephone, fax, and computing will be integrated in handheld devices. In many countries, including the United

States, Sweden, Japan, and the United Kingdom, telephone customers already have personal cards that they can slip into such a device and receive calls anywhere in their calling areas. Malaysia, China, and other developing countries are bypassing wired systems in favor of cellular technologies. And personal communicators made by Toshiba, Sony, and others permit phone, fax, and computing with a pen-input screen. As a result, organizations have changed their business strategies to compete in the high-tech world.

While Congress debates U.S.–Chinese relations and China's human rights record, China is proving irresistibly attractive to the world's most advanced technology companies. Northern Telecom, Intel, and Philips now manufacture semiconductors in Shanghai. Sweden's Ericsson makes telephone switches in Nanjing, and IBM assembles PCs in Shenzhen.

The Information Superhighway via the Internet represents a significant change in technology for all companies. Like the computer-driven engineering technologies that revitalized manufacturing, the Information Superhighway has the ability to change the basic ways in which people communicate at work and home. Consider the International Cargo Management System. With this information system, Seal and other cargo carriers can send an electronic guard with cargo that will let the shipper visually inspect the product's location and condition. When the container is on land, the signal is sent via cellular carrier. When the cargo is at sea, the signal is sent via ship-to-shore radio or phone or global communication satellites. It is more than a cute gadget because theft is a major cost for shippers; more than $5 billion in losses are reported annually in the United States alone.[35]

The Information Superhighway will affect every organization in the years ahead. Because it represents new technology, this component of the environment undoubtedly will bring change to the political–legal arena, as customers and managers struggle with the problems of having confidential information travel around the world and with equipment and operator safety.

CHAPTER SUMMARY

The purpose of this chapter was to help you develop your planning and administrative, strategic thinking and action, global awareness, and communication competencies with respect to an organization's environment. We discussed and presented examples of various practices that organizations can use in coping with their environments. We indicated that an organization's environment can be broken into four segments: economy and culture, competition, politics, and technology. Various competitive forces have impacts on these segments, creating both opportunities and threats that will challenge you to use all of the competencies you acquire.

1. Describe how economic and cultural factors influence organizations.

The environment includes the external factors that usually affect organizations, either directly or indirectly. It encompasses the economic system and current economic conditions, political system, natural resources, and the demographics of the population within which organizations operate. Cultural forces, primarily working through value systems, shape the viewpoints and decision-making processes of managers and employees alike. Hofstede's work-related value framework has five dimensions: power distance, uncertainty avoidance, individualism, masculinity, and long-term/short-term orientation.

2. Identify the five competitive forces that affect organizations in an industry.

Managers must assess and respond to five competitive forces in the environment: competitors, new entrants, substitute goods and services, customers, and suppliers.

3. Describe the principal political and legal strategies used by managers to cope with changes in the environment.

Political–legal issues, which used to be in the background, now often directly influence the way organizations operate. Five political strategies that managers use in coping with political–legal forces in the environment are negotiation, lobbying, alliances, representation, and socialization.

4. Explain how technological forces influence changes in industries.

Technological forces in the environment are rapidly changing the specific knowledge, tools, and techniques used to transform materials, information, and other inputs into particular goods or services. We examined how techno-logical changes affect three areas of an organization: strategy, manufacturing, and distribution.

KEY TERMS and CONCEPTS

Alliance
Backward integration
Capital requirements
Collectivism
Contingent workers
Culture
Demographics
Economics
Economies of scale
Environmental stewardship
Femininity
General environment
Government regulation
Individualism
Joint venture

Knowledge management
Lobbying
Long-term orientation
Masculinity
Negotiation
New entrants
Power distance
Product differentiation
Representation
Short-term orientation
Socialization
Uncertainty avoidance
Value
Value system

QUESTIONS FOR DISCUSSION and COMPETENCY DEVELOPMENT

1. How might the four trends in the new economy affect your job prospects?

2. Choose one of the following industries: chemical, lumber, or utility. Why is environmental stewardship a concern for managers in that industry?

3. What political strategies affecting international organizations are being used by Greenpeace?

4. What implications do the changing demographic patterns in the United States have for managers in organizations such as Bank of America and Home Depot?

5. Pinault-Printemps-Redoute (http://www.pprgroup.com) is a fashion retail company with headquarters in France. What are some cultural values that you would

need to be aware of in order to be a productive employee at Pinault-Printemps-Redoute? What management competencies might you need to develop?

6. Using the five-force industry model, describe the key competitive issues in the fast-food industry.

7. How has Amazon.com used the Internet to change the technologies used in the retail book industry?

8. What political strategies have U.S. Sugar, Imperial Sugar, or Tate & Lyle, all sugar companies, used to control imports into the United States? Have these strategies been successful? To learn more about these companies, consult http://www.hoovers.com.

CASE FOR COMPETENCY DEVELOPMENT

THE MOVIE THEATER INDUSTRY

Since the late 1980s, movie-theater attendance has risen steadily partly because of advances in theater-exhibition technology that greatly enhanced the viewing experience and because of blockbuster films, such as *Titanic* and the Harry Potter films. In 2002 an estimated 1.5 billion people went to the movies, bringing in more than $9.1 billion. Theater admissions have grown steadily at 3 percent per

annum for the past 10 years. To meet this demand, studio movie output has increased. The major studios distributed 450 new films in 2002, up from 401 in 2001, and most studios plan to maintain this level of production. The cost of making movies ranges from $5 million to $55 million, but blockbuster movies, such as *Titanic*, cost more than three times that amount. In many instances, studios have failed to recoup their costs because of competition.

The industry is confronted by a number of competitors. Any leisure time activity can be considered a competitor, including college and major league sporting events. Challenges from video rentals, cable TV, and satellite programming have all made inroads in the entertainment industry in an odd way. According to Terrell Falk, vice president for marketing and communications for Cinemark Theaters, people who rent and buy CDs, DVDs, and videos are more likely to attend movies than those who do not make these rentals. About 32 percent of U.S. households own a DVD player, up from 25 percent in one year. It is estimated that by 2006, there will be more than 84 million DVDs in U.S. homes, and the forecast for the number in China will surpass that in the United States. With more people staying home, spending time with family, and keeping an eye on finances, the popularity of DVD players is expected to rise. As DVD players rise in popularity, the average price to purchase a DVD has dropped dramatically from around $500 to $150.

VCR usage has also increased dramatically during the past decade. Between 1995 and 2002, the number of households with VCRs has increased from 76 million to almost 150 million in 2002. Nearly 80 percent of all households with televisions also have a VCR.

Cable television subscriptions are also growing rapidly in the United States. Between 1995 and 2002, the number of households that received basic cable grew from 63 million to more than 73.5 million. In the United States, there are more than 9,000 cable systems that bring together more than 400 television stations. Cable systems have also created new options for consumers through the convergence of telephone and computer technologies.

Market research has shown that four major factors determine consumer movie going: (1) the film itself, (2) the location of the theater, (3) the starting time of the film, and (4) the overall quality of the theater. Screen size is important to moviegoers but technological features, such as digital sound, and quality of service have a less significant impact on attendance than the first three items. Reductions in ticket price do not dramatically increase attendance.

Because film selection is the most important determinant of attendance, theater companies license films with great care. Family-oriented movies have made a major return to the movie theaters because of the popularity of computer animation and a more conservative audience after September 11, 2001. Negotiations to license a film contain provisions for a fee paid by the movie house to the movie studio. Some of the factors that determine the fees that a movie theater pays a movie studio include the intensity of competition between movie theaters in the same region, and the perceived box-office potential of a film. Well-promoted productions with big stars often receive higher rental fees. For a new film, the percentage can range from 60 to 70 percent of box-office receipts in the first week and gradually decrease to 30 percent after four to seven weeks. Experienced buyers cannot always predict which films would most appeal to moviegoers. Attendance is also influenced by the timing of the release relative to other movies. Also, films such as *My Big Fat Greek Wedding* grew in attendance over time as a result of enthusiastic "word-of-mouth" recommendations. Initially, this low-budget film was shown in only eight markets. Multiplex theaters offer a wide selection of films and reduce the pressure to pick "winners" when licensing.

Movie houses obtained most of their revenue from theater admissions and concession sales. For the major movie houses, the average ticket price in 2002 was $5.85 and constitutes 69 percent of total revenues. Ticket prices depended on location, whether the film was first run or not, the age of the customer, and whether the customer held a discount pass. Admissions are difficult to predict. Therefore, multiplex theaters increase the flexibility of theater owners to balance screen capacity and moviegoer demand. Concessions revenue averages $1.50 per person and constitutes about 20 percent of the revenue . The gross margin is 90 percent on popcorn and beverages and 80 percent on candy. Concessions costs run about 32 cents per patron. The remaining revenue comes from electronic games located in theater lobbies and from on-screen advertising.

The United States and Canada have more than 5,800 theaters, but most theater operators have fewer than 10 screens. The top companies control more than 50 percent of all screens. Multiplexing and mergers and acquisitions have dominated the industry for the last decade. Some new multiplexes have 24 screens. As the number of screens per location increases, the average attendance at each screen decreases. Some of the major movie theater operators include Regal Cinemas (http://www.regalcinemas.com), which has more than 5,800 screens in 532 theaters; Carmike Cinemas (http://www.carmike.com), which has more than 2,300 screens in 323 locations; AMC Entertainment (http://www.amctheatres.com), which operates more than 3,300 screens in 235 multiplex theaters; Cinemark (http://www.cinemark.com), which operates more than 2,256 screens in 307 theaters, and Loews (http://www.loewscineplex.com), which operates 2,161 screens in 226 theaters.[36]

Questions

1. Describe the five competitive forces in this industry. Is this a good industry to enter?

2. How have demographics affected this industry?

©Corbis Inc.

Managing Globally

Learning Objectives

After studying this chapter, you should be able to:

1. State several characteristics of the global economy.

2. Describe how a country's culture can affect an organization's business practices.

3. Explain the impact of political–legal forces on international business.

4. Discuss how three major trade agreements affect global competition.

5. Describe six strategies used by organizations in international business.

Chapter Outline

Preview Case: Wal-Mart

THE GLOBAL ECONOMY

CULTURAL FORCES
>   Views of Social Change
>   Time Orientation
>   Language
>   Value Systems
>   Cultural Distance
>   Teamwork Competency: Motorola in Malaysia

POLITICAL–LEGAL FORCES
>   Assessing Political Risk
>   Political Mechanisms
>   Global Awareness Competency: The Paint Industry

GLOBAL TRADE AGREEMENTS
>   World Trade Organization
>   North American Free Trade Agreement
>   Planning & Administration Competency: Mabe
>   European Union

STRATEGIES FOR INTERNATIONAL BUSINESS
>   Exporting Strategy
>   Licensing Strategy
>   Franchising Strategy
>   Alliance Strategy
>   Multidomestic Strategy
>   Global Strategy
>   Strategic Action Competency: Imperial Chemical Industries PLC

Chapter Summary

Key Terms and Concepts

Questions for Discussion and Competency Development

Case for Competency Development: Esteé Lauder

Exercise for Competency Development: Cultural Preferences

The aisles are clean, the store is brightly lit, and "associates" in red polo shirts provide friendly service for customers who shop for low prices and a wide range of product offerings. Throughout the store are pictures of Sam Walton, founder of Wal-Mart. Next to the cash registers are tanks of crabs, fish, frogs, and shrimp that can be taken home live or be expertly gutted and cleaned on the spot. This is a Wal-Mart store in Shenzhen, a suburb of Hong Kong in China.

Because it has 40 stores in China, the company made the decision to introduce the Walton Institute. The Walton Institute offers programs to teach local managers Walton's three principles: respect for the individual, service to customers, and striving for excellence. At the local store in Shenzhen, managers hold Ping-Pong tournaments, stage fashion shows, and place clerks in front of large displays to sell certain products. The store has its own fight song ("My heart is filled with pride. . . . I long to tell you how deep my love for Wal-Mart is. . . .")

Wal-Mart is already operating more than 1,200 stores in nine countries. The sales from these stores account for $480 billion. As Wal-Mart tries to develop stores overseas, it is finding it difficult to export one of its biggest advantages. Its expertise in managing high-volume inventory and supply networks does not work well in Europe and Asia, where the highway systems aren't as good and stores are typically smaller than those found in the United States and Canada. The challenge for Wal-Mart is to become better at buying so that local managers can purchase products directly from the factory, instead of relying on outside vendors and imported products. According to Jody Ewing, replenishment manager, "We realize that the need to leverage international buying power is the key." The idea is to buy goods universally for all stores where feasible so the 20 locations in Brazil can get the same price and service as the 3,400 Wal-Marts in the United States.

By becoming a contractor, importer, and wholesaler, Wal-Mart expects to save money by buying directly from the factory, but also to cut down on inventory by speeding up the supply lines. For example, Wal-Mart gets most of its towels from India and reorders monthly. If one type of towel gets "hot" and sells out early, sales are lost. In going direct to the factory, Wal-Mart will make the factories in India a part of its Retail Link System that allows vendors like Sara Lee (makers of Hanes underwear) to tie into Wal-Mart's computers and track sales and replenish supplies constantly. At ASDA, the British chain Wal-Mart bought in 1999, the company was selling men's jeans for $24 after paying $14 per yard for 50,000 yards of material. Now it's buying 6 million yards at $4.77 per yard.

Fashion designers live in Bentonville, Arkansas, headquarters of Wal-Mart. When a new fashion is created, the design group sends orders to factories on how and what to make. No samples have to be sent back and forth across the ocean because the company uses computer color rendition and printing. Changes can be made quickly. The goal is speed and price. From the factories, garments can be sent around the world. Wal-Mart figures to take 20 percent of the cost out of the procurement process during the next five years by buying merchandise direct.[1]

THE GLOBAL ECONOMY

1. State several characteristics of the global economy.

Wal-Mart's situation illustrates the effects of several global forces that an increasing number of companies face—pressures on prices, the need for cost cutting, global expansion, and the impact of changes in the financial arena on profitability.

Table 4.1 highlights some of the more important trends in the global economy. In a global economy, products are shipped anywhere in the world in a matter of days, com-

Table 4.1	Global Economic Trends
■ Foreign exchange rates	
■ Importance of exports and imports	
■ Expanding nature of trade	
■ Worldwide communication	
■ Borderless organizations	
■ Worldwide labor pool	

munication is instant, and foreign exchange rates can dramatically effect the financial status of an organization. For example, more than 16 percent of Wal-Mart's revenue is generated by stores outside of the United States. Therefore what happens in the financial markets in Asia, Europe, Latin America, and Africa is of vital interest to Wal-Mart. The fall of the euro against the U.S. dollar in 2002 has been blamed for lower profits for Xerox, P&G, McDonald's, and Office Depot, among others.

Exports and imports of goods and services represent about 30 percent of the U.S. gross domestic product, up from less than 21 percent in 1992. Consider these 2002 statistics regarding global trade.

- The United States accounts for about 13 percent of the world's $6.4 trillion of imported goods and 18 percent of the world's $6.2 trillion exported goods. The European Union (EU) exported more than the United States did recently.
- The EU had more direct investment in the United States than did the United States in the EU.
- Of the more than $1.2 trillion worth of foreign direct investment in the United States, almost 75 percent comes from the EU.
- The United States exported some $180 billion in goods to Asia, imported $419 billion.[2]

Trade is now so important to the U.S. economy that one job in six depends on it. Yet a recent poll revealed that many people living in the United States thought that expanded trade led to a loss of U.S. jobs. When asked to identify the biggest threat to U.S. jobs, most people said that it was cheap foreign labor. This attitude reflects the fact that trade is often portrayed in the media as a war between nations in which countries that export more than they import win, whereas countries that import more than they export lose. Since 1995, U.S. exports of goods and services have soared 40 percent, accounting for much of the overall growth in the economy. However, imports have been growing more than exports, in part because the economy has expanded, which gave U.S. consumers more money to spend.

Increasingly, trade is taking place between different parts of the same corporation or through alliances (joint ventures). Asking whether a product—computer, car, or shirt—has been "Made in the USA" or "Made in Canada" has become almost meaningless. Grand Union, a large grocery chain that operates primarily in the eastern part of the United States, is 100 percent owned by Generale Occidentale of France, and A&P, which operates 700 grocery stores in the central and eastern United States, is 57 percent owned by the Tengelmann Group in Germany. Miles Laboratories, a major pharmaceutical company, is 100 percent owned by Bayer AG of Germany, and Alcon Laboratories is 100 percent owned by Nestlé, S.A., of Switzerland. Although many executives tend to think in terms of managing a U.S. company overseas, they may well find themselves employed by a non-U.S. organization as a local manager to run its U.S. affiliate. The production of components for cars, vacuum cleaners, PCs, and many products is increasingly scattered around the world.[3]

Another driving force is the information revolution that now permits instantaneous worldwide communication.[4] The globalization of business has placed a premium on information. Many organizations, especially in the United States, are spearheading the Internet boom, building fiber-optic networks, and offering myriad new products and services on the World Wide Web. Sun Microsystems offers 24-hour technical assistance throughout the world with a single phone number drawing on employee teams in California, London, and Sydney. The teams coordinate their efforts electronically through a sophisticated information system. Within the next 15 years, the number of computers and communications satellites is projected to double. The number of wireless communications networks will increase to several billion as people who live in China, India, and other developing nations expand their communication networks. The number of Internet users is expected to grow from 500 million in 2002 to more than 2 billion by 2005. These figures are astounding when you realize that one-half the world's population has never even used a phone!

The drive for increased openness—both economically and politically—is happening. The collapse of Communism in 1989 created a new group of rapid-growth countries in Central and Eastern Europe. The development of market institutions (e.g., banks and stock markets) that provide for effective corporate governance in many of these countries (e.g., Slovakia, Croatia, and Kazakhstan) have been developing slowly. The lack of strong legal frameworks has allowed increases in bribery and corruption. The lack of well-defined property rights that convey ownership and transferability has also led to problems. However, the rapid and widespread adoption of market-based policies in these emerging economies has been significant.[5]

Privatization permits organizations to adapt their strategies to meet the demands of the market and places the burden on top managers for managing their organizations effectively and efficiently. It also means an increasing number of joint ventures with foreign firms and usually the adoption of more modern management practices. When GE created a joint venture with a manufacturer of light bulbs in Hungary, GE managers with global experience were called in to help the Hungarian company improve its production to world-class standards.

As domestic policies are becoming more market oriented, governments are opening their countries to multinational trade and joining regional trade associations. New strategic partnerships of foreign and domestic organizations are emerging. Governments everywhere are pursuing market-based economic policies. Multinational corporations are accelerating the exchange of innovations across open borders. Global investors are pressuring companies to open their books. People are demanding stronger political and economic rights, as shown by Vicente Fox's election as president of Mexico. Mr. Fox's party, the National Action Party, won the election on the basis of improving educational opportunities for all Mexicans. The party hopes that, through education, more than 1.3 million unemployed Mexicans will be able to enter the labor force and make valuable contributions to society.

One of the most important factors that has fueled the growth of the global economy is the prevalence of labor and resources in different parts of the world.[6] Many textile, housewares, and toy manufacturers have opened overseas operations to take advantage of low labor costs. Toy companies, such as Mattel and Hasbro, have significant production operations in China where the average worker earns US $120 per month. Such low labor costs enable these companies to offer high-quality toys at low cost. The presence of these companies has also helped stimulate the development of local economies. Many U.S. firms are locating some of their most sophisticated operations in regions having abundant sources of highly skilled, technical personnel. Texas Instruments has established a state-of-the-art software development site in Bangalore, India, to work with highly skilled computer technicians. Of course, foreign businesses, such as Honda, Toyota, and Mercedes-Benz, have established manufacturing plants in the United States to take advantage of skilled labor and decrease transportation costs.

We discuss these and other forces that are driving and restraining the global economy throughout this chapter. Although any type of organization may act globally, most that do are for-profit businesses. Therefore the material covered in this chapter applies primarily to them.

The cultural forces that we discussed in Chapter 3 underlie the day-to-day competitive and political forces operating within and among nations. Five aspects of a culture that have direct implications for international management are views of social change, time orientation, language, value systems, and cultural distance. These five forces are shown in Figure 4.1.

2. Describe how a country's culture can affect an organization's business practices.

Figure 4.1	Five Aspects of Culture

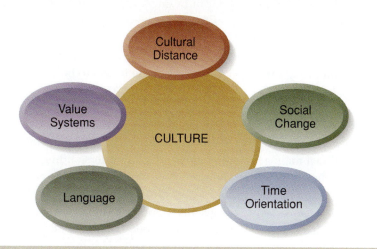

Views of Social Change

Different views of the need for social change and its pace can have a significant impact on an organization's plans for international operations.[7] The people of many non-Western cultures, such as those of India, Saudi Arabia, and China, view change as a slow, natural progression. For them change is part of the evolution of human beings and the universe and the attitude toward it tends to be passive (or even reactive). In contrast, the people of Western cultures tend to view change differently. For them change can be shaped and controlled to achieve their own goals and aspirations, and the attitude toward it tends to be active. Therefore Western managers assigned to non-Western countries often run into difficulty when trying to introduce innovations too rapidly. In cultures that hold a passive/reactive view of change, new ways of doing things often must go hand in hand with a painstaking concern for their effect on interpersonal relationships. Moreover, people in nations such as India, Italy, and Turkey that are characterized by high uncertainty avoidance also are likely to resist or react cautiously to social change. American managers plunged into these cultures have to recognize this viewpoint, plan for it, and manage change accordingly.

Time Orientation

Many people in the United States and Canada think of time as an extremely scarce commodity. They often say that "time is money" or that "there is too little time." Several popular books on time management show an almost frenetic concern with how managers should plan their days. The need to set and stick to tight deadlines for accomplishing tasks is a basic tenet of this style of management.

In some cultures, however, time is viewed more as an unlimited and unending resource.[8] For example, Hindus believe that time does not begin at birth or end at death. The Hindu belief in reincarnation gives life a nontemporal, everlasting dimension.

Because of such attitudes, employees, customers, and suppliers in some cultures are quite casual about keeping appointments and meeting deadlines—an indifference that can be highly frustrating to Canadian and U.S. managers who have to work with them.

Traditionally, the Mexican attitude toward time can best be summed up by the word *mañana*, meaning "not today"—but not necessarily tomorrow either! A manager in Mexico might say, "Yes, your shipment will be ready on Tuesday." You arrive on Tuesday to pick it up but find that it isn't ready. No one is upset or embarrassed; they say politely that the paperwork hasn't been processed yet or offer some other explanation. Time commitments are considered desirable but not binding promises. However, this attitude toward time is changing among Mexican businesspeople and professionals. As lifestyles become more complex and pressures for greater productivity increase, many more people in Mexico are paying attention to punctuality and meeting time commitments. However, the disregard for time can be found in many government offices where most procedures require long forms to be filled out, long letters to be filed, and endless waits in line.

Language

Language serves to bind as well as to separate cultures.[9] Fluency in another language can give an international manager a competitive edge in understanding and gaining the acceptance of people from another culture. However, the ability to speak a language correctly isn't enough: A manager must also be able to recognize and interpret the nuances of phrases, sayings, and nonverbal gestures. For example, many American managers communicate a relaxed atmosphere by "putting their feet up." The manager with his feet on the desk is saying, "I'm relaxing, and you can, too." However, people from other cultures may consider this rude or even insulting. Most German managers would consider putting one's feet on the desk uncivilized, and showing the soles of the feet is among the most outrageous insults to most Arabs.

In Mexico, managers are used to giving only positive feedback to their supervisors and to expressing views that only agree with their bosses. Mexican executives would consider it disrespectful of a subordinate to contradict them because they are essentially "people oriented." They judge superiors on their personal qualities. Mexican employees must feel that their boss is a *buena gente* (e.g., nice guy) before they give him their whole-hearted support.[10]

Value Systems

In Chapter 3, we discussed the importance of value systems and described five value dimensions: power distance, uncertainty avoidance, individualism (versus collectivism), masculinity (versus femininity), and long-term (versus short-term) orientation. Obviously, differences in cultural values affect how managers and professionals function in international business.

Anyone who has managed employees from different countries knows that being an effective manager requires an understanding of the country's value systems. Figure 4.2 rates the differences in importance of cultural values between a random sample of managers in Mexico and those in the United States.[11] What do these mean to you?

Americans prefer small power distances and Mexicans are comfortable with large power distances. Essentially, this implies that Americans believe inequalities should be minimized, that organizational hierarchies are established for convenience, and that bosses should be accessible. Middle and first-line managers usually answer their own phones and send their own e-mail. However, Mexicans view their relationship with their managers differently. The Mexican culture accepts large power distances between people. They believe that everyone has his or her place in an order of inequality. Managers and subordinates each view the other as different types of people. Subordinates believe

Figure 4.2   Cultural Values in Mexico and the United States

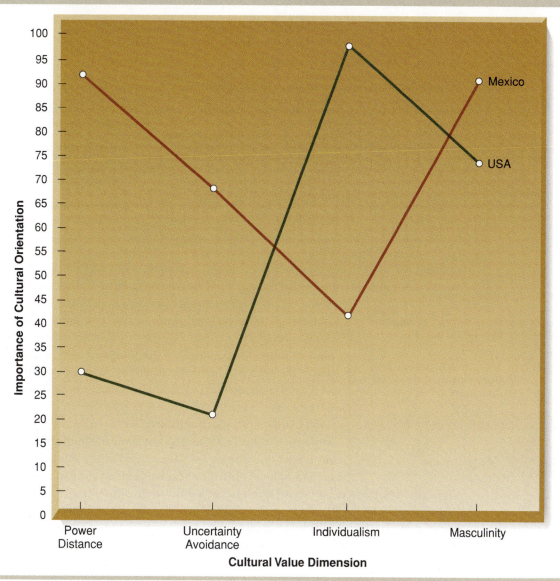

that their managers are there to provide direction and approve decisions and that they should be inaccessible. Superiors have certain privileges (e.g., reserved parking, large offices, the ability to take long lunches, and the like) by right. For example, titles are very important in Mexico. When Mexicans are answering phone calls, they normally identify themselves by title. Titles appear on business cards and elsewhere. For an American manager to decentralize decision making to his Mexican subordinates would be considered a violation of this value. Mexican employees would feel uncomfortable if a manager attempted to delegate decisions and share information. These are strictly management rights. The implication for American managers is to use a more directive leadership style because it is expected. Strong leadership from the top is expected to make change. Furthermore, those in power should look as powerful as possible. The managerial implications for differences in power distance between the United States and Mexico are summarized in Table 4.2.

Americans and Mexicans are also different with regard to uncertainty avoidance. Many Mexicans feel threatened by uncertain and ambiguous situations, and they struggle to develop security in their lives. In this regard, they feel a need for written rules and

Table 4.2 Managerial Implications of Power Distance Differences

Issue	United States	Mexico
Subordinates' dependence needs	Moderate dependence on supervisor	Heavy dependence on supervisor
Consultation	Expect to be consulted	Expect little consultation
Ideal superior	Democratic leadership	A benevolent autocrat or paternalistic father figure
Rules and regulations	Apply to all	Supervisors are above rules and regulations and take advantage of privileges
Status symbols	Are accepted as symbols of authority, but not necessary	Are very important evidence of the authority of superiors

procedures and rely on experts to provide them guidance. They also seek consensus and social harmony. To preserve harmony, saving face is important. Therefore, Mexicans as a rule do not wish to admit that they do not know something or that certain tasks assigned were, in fact, not done. Elaborate stories can be told to explain why the outcome was different than expected. The combination of high uncertainty avoidance and power distance produces the desire to have a powerful manager who can be blamed or praised. This satisfies their desire to avoid uncertainty.

The Competent Manager

"Teamwork in Mexico may appeal to workers as a way to reduce individual risk through collaboration. Mexicans feel a moral obligation to their team."

Jose Ramon Sida Medrano
Director General
Mexican Foundation
for Total Quality

The two cultures also appear different in relation to individualistic versus collectivist values. The typical American is more individualistic than the typical Mexican. Many people in Mexico place great emphasis on family and belonging to organizations. Friendships are determined by social relationships within their own social levels. There is an old saying in Mexico: "It is not what you know but who you know." The *grupo* form of organization, in which individual families control many companies and decision making is centralized, is a reflection of collectivism. Status and titles are keys to developing relationships. Few relationships extend across social levels (e.g., subordinates and managers do not usually mix.)

Cultural Distance

A country's cultural values determine how people interact with one another and with companies and institutions.[12] *Differences in religious beliefs, race, social norms, and language are all capable of creating* **cultural distance** *between two countries.* Some cultural differences between countries, such as language, are easily perceived and understood. Others are much more subtle. Social norms, the deeply rooted system of unspoken principles that guide individuals in their everyday behaviors, are often nearly invisible. The problems that S. K. Ko was having forming teams at Motorola in the following Teamwork Competency feature clearly illustrates this problem. She needed to realize that Malaysians are more interested in spending time with their families and friends than in earning overtime pay bonuses for attending team workshops.

Cultural differences also influence the choices that consumers make. Table 4.3 gives examples of situations in which cultural distance matters and lists some of the industries affected by this cultural distance. Color tastes, for example, are closely linked to cultural values. The word red in Russia also means "beautiful." The Japanese prefer automobiles and household appliances to be small, reflecting a social norm that is common in coun-

Table 4.3	Examples of Cultural Distance and Industries Affected by It

Aspects of Distance

- Different languages
- Different ethnicities
- Different religions
- Different social norms

Industries Affected by Cultural Distance Include:

- Consumer foods
- Tobacco products
- Products that have high linguistic content (TV)
- Auto (size, features)

tries where space is highly valued. For example, many families living in metropolitan Tokyo live in apartments of less than 700 square feet. The food industry is particularly sensitive to religious attributes. Hindus, for example, do not eat beef because it is expressly forbidden by their religion.

The following Teamwork Competency feature provides an additional perspective on the need to be aware of these cultural forces.[13] Motorola's experience in Malaysia illustrates how hard it was to develop a team approach that fit the Malaysian culture. The cultural mix in Malaysia is about 50 percent Malays (Muslims), 35 percent Chinese, 10 percent Indian and Pakistanis, and 5 percent other. A number of differences arising from this cultural mix are found in the Teamwork Competency feature.

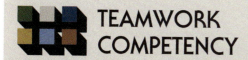

TEAMWORK COMPETENCY

Motorola in Malaysia

S. K. Ko, an American and the first female managing director in Malaysia for Motorola, immediately noticed that in Malaysia, employees strive to avoid making decisions. Malaysians believe that management has a right to make decisions and tell employees what to do. Therefore, the concept of shared decision making could not be part of teamwork. Second, women in Malaysia were supposed to follow their husband's direction at home. Ko encouraged women to speak out, but their husbands did not want them to. Therefore, few women spoke up in meetings. Self-managed or cross-functional teams were almost impossible to implement because of cultural barriers in the Malaysian culture caused by differ-

ences in gender, values, and religious beliefs.

To overcome these obstacles, Motorola designed a program entitled "Dignity and Respect." Because Malaysian production workers were uncomfortable working in teams with their managers, Motorola designed a program whereby engineers trained technicians and managers trained supervisors who in turn trained production workers. A "Critical Thinking Skills" program aimed at strengthening operators' learning capabilities was started. This program awarded advancements and certificates to participants. Separate classes were held for employees at different management levels.

Although monthly recognition awards were given to individuals, the awards arising from total customer

satisfaction were given to teams. Rewards and training also differed by technical complexity according to the specific process involved, with more highly skilled, better educated, and more capable workers being given more advanced training. Team training, structure, and awards varied by hierarchical level within the plant. Ko was people oriented and believed that it was important to "Treat your people with respect, as you would your own family; no yelling, no shouting, no finger pointing; give visible rewards to achievers; create enthusiasm; and share every success story." This approach worked in only one team where production workers and some supervisors were women, and most engineers and managers were men.

POLITICAL–LEGAL FORCES

3. Explain the impact of political–legal forces on international business.

Organizations that engage in international business must cope with a web of political and legal issues. Therefore management must diagnose these issues accurately in order to understand the risks and uncertainties involved in international business. Recall from Chapter 3 that managers may use one or more of five political strategies—negotiation, lobbying, alliance, representation, and socialization—to reduce political risk.

Political risk *is the probability that political decisions or events in a country will negatively affect the long-term profitability of an investment.* Of concern to all international and global corporations is the political risk associated with resource commitments in foreign countries.[14]

Assessing Political Risk

Political risk factors may be grouped into five principal categories: domestic instability, foreign conflict, political climate, economic climate, and corruption. As Figure 4.3 shows, managers may estimate the seriousness of the political risk associated with conducting business in a country by assessing various factors in each category.

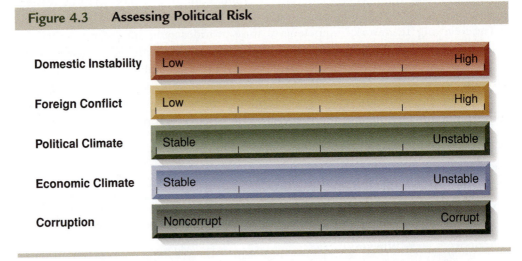

Figure 4.3   Assessing Political Risk

Domestic Instability	Low	High
Foreign Conflict	Low	High
Political Climate	Stable	Unstable
Economic Climate	Stable	Unstable
Corruption	Noncorrupt	Corrupt

Domestic instability *is the amount of subversion, revolution, assassinations, guerrilla warfare, and government crisis in a country.* Haiti and Fiji have histories of domestic instability that have generally discouraged foreign investment.

Foreign conflict *is the degree of hostility that one nation expresses to others.* Such hostility can range from the expulsion of diplomats to outright war. In 2003, President George W. Bush determined that the actions of the government of Iraq constituted an unusual and extraordinary threat to the national security and foreign policy of the United States. The government imposed a ban on trade with Iraq, which directly affected many firms, and requested that the United Nations send an inspection team into Iraq to look for weapons of mass destruction. The United States waged war in Iraq on March 20, 2003; therefore, the political risk for doing business in Iraq is very high.

Political climate *is the likelihood that a government will swing to the far left or far right politically.* Managers may evaluate variables such as the number and size of political parties, number of factions in the legislature, role of the military in the political process, amount of corruption in government, effectiveness of political leadership, influence of organized religion in politics, extent of racial and nationality tensions, and quality of the governmental bureaucracy. Currently, Nigeria is considered to have a risky political climate because of the instability of its government, opposing political forces, and widespread corruption. Recently 600 armed Nigerian women seized control of ChevronTexaco's Escravos oil terminal to protest the company's failure to hire local Nigerian men.

The **economic climate** *reflects the extent of government control of markets and financial investments, as well as government support services and capabilities.* These factors include government regulatory and economic control policies (wages, prices, imports, and exports); government ability to manage its own economic affairs (inflation, budget surpluses or deficits, and amount of debt); government provision of support services and facilities (roads, airports, electricity, water, and refuse and sewage disposal), often referred to as *infrastructure;* and government capabilities in general.

Corruption *refers to the degree to which institutions, including the government, are perceived to be untrustworthy, to be open to bribes, and to conduct fraudulent business practices.* Corruption in the United States, Canada, and other Western countries is viewed as wrong. Transparency International has compiled a Corruption Perception Index from research on 102 countries.[15] This list is based on perceptions rather than actual corruption, but it is a good indicator for corruption in a country. This index is widely used by organizations and the U.S. government in making judgments about business practices in countries. As shown in Table 4.4, both Finland and Denmark are ranked as less corrupt than the United States, and Indonesia and Bangladesh are viewed as being among the most corrupt nations according to Transparency International.

Table 4.4	Perceptions of Corruption
Country Rank	**Country**
1(Least corrupt)	Finland
2	Denmark and New Zealand
7	Canada
16	United States
20	Japan
25	France
33	Malaysia
50	Ghana
57	Mexico
70	Argentina
85	Vietnam
96	Indonesia
102 (Most corrupt)	Bangladesh

Political Mechanisms

Governments and businesses utilize a variety of political strategies, as we discussed in Chapter 3, to cope with political and legal forces. In this section, we go beyond those strategies to explain two significant types of international political mechanisms: (1) protectionism and (2) bribery and extortion. We support neither but want you to be aware of actual practices that you may encounter someday in international business.

Protectionism. **Protectionism** *refers to the many mechanisms designed to help home-based industries or firms avoid (or reduce) potential (or actual) competitive or political threats from abroad.* Tariffs, quotas, subsidies, and cartels are among the most widely used political mechanisms. Protectionism has both strong advocates and opponents. Generally, it works against consumers' interests because it results in higher prices. Advocates claim that it protects home-country industries and jobs against unfair competition from countries with subsistence wages and special subsidies. Therefore whether companies, business associations, and employee groups favor or oppose a particular protectionist measure depends on how it may affect their particular interests.

A **tariff** *is a government tax on goods or services entering the country.* The primary purpose of a tariff is to raise the price of imported goods or services. As a result, domestic goods and services gain a relative price advantage. In 2000, Congress passed the Continued Dumping and Subsidy Act, which allows manufacturers that successfully petition the U.S. Congress to impose tariffs on imports that they claim are being "dumped"—sold at less than fair market value. For example, Chinese candle makers must pay a 54 percent tariff on candles if they want to sell their products in the United States. Maui Pineapple Company also receives $500,000 in tariffs from Thai pineapple growers that are allowed to sell pineapples in the United States.[16]

A **quota** *is a restriction on the quantity of a country's imports (or sometimes, on its exports).* Import quotas generally are intended to guarantee home-country manufacturers access to a certain percentage of the domestic market. Most experts agree that, if protectionism is politically unavoidable, tariffs are preferable to quotas. The reason is that quotas fix the levels of imports entering a country and thus freeze markets. Labor unions and members of Congress have argued against further opening of U.S. markets at a time of trade deficits, arguing that quotas protect U.S. industries from low-cost manufacturing abroad. However, if quotas were lifted, domestic producers would then have to become more productive and efficient to maintain market share. Quotas are a hidden tax on consumers, whereas tariffs are a more obvious tax.

A **subsidy** *is a direct or indirect payment by a government to domestic firms to make selling or investing abroad cheaper for them—and thus more profitable.* Indirect payments are illustrated by some of the activities of the Overseas Private Investment Corporation. This self-sustaining U.S. government agency helps qualified U.S. investors establish commercial projects in developing countries by offering reinvestment assistance and financing. Its political-risk insurance program provides coverage for eligible projects against losses from a foreign government's seizure of assets; nonconvertibility of local currency into U.S. dollars; and damage caused by war, revolution, insurrection, or strife.

Global soft drinks producer Coca-Cola and South Africa's small-scale sugar cane farmers have teamed up against large commercial sugar producers in South Africa. Because this industry is dominated by large-scale sugar cane producers, Coca-Cola is lobbying for lower sugar prices, deregulation of the industry, scrapping of imports tariffs, and subsidies to small sugar cane producers. With such changes, Coke would pay a third less for the sugar it uses in its drinks.[17]

A **cartel** *is an alliance of producers engaged in the same type of business that is formed to limit or eliminate competition and control production and prices.* Governments impose tariffs and quotas and grant subsidies. In contrast, cartels operate under agreements negotiated between firms or governments, as in the case of OPEC (Organization of Petroleum Exporting Countries). A primary goal of any cartel is to protect its members' revenues and profits by controlling output and therefore prices. International cartels currently exist in oil, copper, aluminum, natural rubber, and other raw materials. The best known cartel is OPEC, which was formed in 1960. The recent history of the oil industry and OPEC clearly demonstrates that cartels often face uncertainty and have to cope with rebellion among their members. In recent years, OPEC hasn't been very effective in controlling oil production by member countries. Some members, especially Nigeria and Venezuela, often can't agree on prices or quantities to be produced. Law forbids U.S. firms from forming or participating directly in cartels because their purpose is at odds with preserving competitive markets and individual rights based on private property.

Bribery and Extortion. A **bribe** *is an improper payment made to induce the recipient to do something for the payer.* Bribes are illegal in Canada and the United States but not in some countries, such as Germany, Italy, and Brazil. By offering a bribe, the payer hopes to obtain a special favor in exchange for something of value (e.g., money, a trip, or a car). In recent years, the growing moral revulsion against bribery and other forms of corruption has swept politicians from office in Brazil, Italy, and Japan. In Italy, state prosecutors exposed an elaborate web of relationships among the Mafia, politicians, and business executives. Bids for highways, sewers, and other public projects now come in as much as 40 percent below past bids for comparable projects. However, this example is not to suggest that Italy—or any country for that matter—is now free from political and business corruption.

Extortion *is a payment made to ensure that the recipient doesn't harm the payer in some way.* The purpose of extortion is to obtain something of value by threatening harm to the payer. Recently, the United Nations launched an investigation into allegations that officials in Kenya were extorting thousands of dollars from refugees in exchange for settling them in America and Western Europe.[18]

Bribery and extortion are practiced throughout the world. These practices occur most frequently in Indonesia, Azerbaijan, Honduras, Tanzania, Yugoslavia, and several other countries. In fact, some countries culturally define certain forms of bribery and extortion as an acceptable, appropriate, and expected form of gift giving. Belgium, France, Sweden, Greece, and Germany allow or tolerate the tax deductibility of foreign bribes. The United Nations and the World Bank are attempting to get members to criminalize bribery and extortion—as has the U.S. government.

The U.S. Foreign Corrupt Practices Act of 1977 makes it a crime for U.S. corporations or individuals to bribe officials of foreign governments or companies for the purpose of obtaining or retaining business.[19] The act established specific record-keeping requirements for publicly held corporations, making difficult the concealment of political payments prohibited by the act. Violators—both corporations and individuals—face stiff penalties. A company may be fined as much as $1 million, and a manager who directly participates in or has knowledge of any violations of the act faces up to 5 years in prison and/or $100,000 in fines. Furthermore, the act prohibits corporations from paying any fines imposed on their directors, managers, employees, or agents.

The act doesn't prohibit grease payments to employees of foreign governments whose duties are primarily procedural or clerical. **Grease payments** *are small payments—almost gratuities—used to get lower level government employees to speed up required paperwork.* Such payments may be required to persuade employees to perform their normal duties. Some examples where grease payments are permitted under U.S. law include paying people to obtain a license, processing government forms, such as visas or work orders, mail pickup and delivery, installing phone service, and the like. Before HIH's $5.3 billion collapse, this Australian insurance company gave out $10,000 gold watches and $1,600 worth of cigars to government officials to ensure their clients got the very best services from people. Lavish trips to Australia's "Gold Coast" were also paid for by HIH for friends who helped the company out. Under U.S. law, these actions would constitute a form of bribe and would not be considered grease payments. However to Jerry Brown, manager of the Ethics Resource Center based in Washington, D.C., the difference between a bribe and grease payment is often difficult to define.[20]

The following Global Awareness Competency feature illustrates how paint manufacturers in Japan and France were able to keep foreign competitors from entering their market by using a variety of political mechanisms. When national competitors hold large market shares, they may engage in practices to block foreign manufacturers from entering the market.[21]

GLOBAL AWARENESS COMPETENCY

The Paint Industry

The paint industry in Japan is an $8 billion industry that is growing about 2 percent per year. There are nearly 200 paint manufacturers, with 3 manufacturers holding about 50 percent of the market: Kansai Paint (20 percent market share), Nippon Paint (20 percent market share),

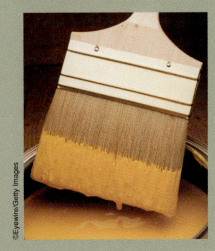

© Eyewire/Getty Images

Japanese market because customers there require just-in-time delivery and quick services. In addition, the Japanese paint industry has lobbied the Japanese Diet (similar to the Congress in the United States) to approve high tariffs and quotas. The high tariffs protect the industry from foreign competitors entering this market because of price. Japanese manufacturers also have successfully lobbied to establish quotas that serve to restrict U.S. and Chinese manufacturers from entering the market. To further protect this industry, the top paint manufacturers have entered into complicated distribution systems that are protected by local laws. The result is that Japanese customers import only the newest, state-of-the-art paint, which they

could not get from their regular Japanese suppliers. This type of paint represents 5 percent of the paint market.

In France, two paint manufacturers control the market for 20,000 tons of paint that are spread on roads each year. The only way to enter this market is to be certified by the government, and the certification process is very difficult (see Chapter 3 for a discussion of the cultural values of France). For example, in France, on-site certifications are required. That is, if the paint in the middle of the road is supposed to last 24 months, it needs to be certified for 24 months. Each month the paint on the roads needs to be monitored and certified by a qualified inspector.

and Dai Nippon Toryo (10 percent market share). Nippon Paint and Kansai Paint together supply more than 90 percent of the paint used in the Japanese automobile industry. It is very difficult for foreign firms, such as PPG or DuPont, to enter the

GLOBAL TRADE AGREEMENTS

4. Discuss how three major trade agreements affect global competition.

We discussed five competitive forces in Chapter 3: competitors, new entrants, substitute goods and services, customers, and suppliers. These forces apply whether a firm competes locally (say, in the Denver, Colorado, area), nationally (say, in Mexico), regionally (say, in Europe), or worldwide. In this section we briefly review three significant agreements that directly affect one or more of the five competitive forces. These agreements heighten the market-based competitive pressures on firms.

World Trade Organization

The **World Trade Organization** (WTO) was established in 1995 as an outgrowth of the General Agreement on Tariffs and Trade (GATT).[22] **WTO** *represents a series of negotiated understandings regarding trade and related issues among the participating countries.* Twenty-three countries signed the first GATT in 1947. Today, there are 144 member countries, accounting for more than 95 percent of the world trade. By 2005, world trade in merchandise and commercial services is forecasted to exceed $8 trillion (1 trillion is 1,000 billion), or $2 trillion more than in 2000.

The key functions of the WTO include

- administering WTO trade agreements,
- providing a forum for trade negotiations,
- handling trade disputes between nations,
- monitoring national trade policies,
- providing technical assistance and training for people in developing countries, and
- cooperating with other international organizations, such as the EU, the Association of South East Asian Nations (ASEAN), and the association formed as a result of the North American Free Trade Agreement.

WTO member countries receive many benefits:

- The agreement promotes peace by handling trade disputes constructively.

- Rules make life easier for all organizations to follow.
- Trade stimulates economic growth and reduces the cost of living.
- The system encourages good government.

Three principles are fundamental to WTO operations. The *most favored nation principle* means that when country A grants a tariff concession to country B, the same concession automatically applies to all other countries that are members of WTO. The *reciprocity principle* means that each member country will not be forced to reduce tariffs unilaterally. A tariff concession is made only in return for comparable concessions from the other countries. The *transparency principle* means that tariffs are to be readily visible to all countries. Presumably, tariffs are the only permitted form of restriction. WTO doesn't allow internal taxes and regulations to be applied to imported goods if they aren't equally applied to domestic goods. However, there are exceptions to these principles. For example, the escape clause provides that, if a product is being imported into a country in such increased quantities that it causes or threatens to cause serious injury to domestic producers of that product, the importing country may temporarily increase the tariff on that product.

The Competent Manager

"WTO members must address the problem of special and differential treatment for developing countries that lack the capacity to manufacture pharmaceutical drugs themselves. World health is at stake. I call on industry and governments to bridge their differences."

Supachai Panitchpakdi
Director-General
World Trade Organization

Under WTO provisions, trade negotiations also may take place directly between two or more countries. One significant trade dispute between the United States and Thailand and Malaysia has focused on intellectual property rights and pirated videos of movies. A deputy director-general of Thailand's Intellectual Property Office stated that the government had declared war on piracy. Heads of U.S. motion picture studios estimate that 75 percent of the Thai and Malaysian video industry is illegal. Government officials in both countries said a reward to encourage people to report pirates needs be introduced along with courts that are designed to hear and act on violations of intellectual property rights.

North American Free Trade Agreement

The **North American Free Trade Agreement** (NAFTA) went into effect in 1994 to increase free trade among the United States, Canada, and Mexico. **NAFTA** *essentially created a giant free-trade zone among the United States, Canada, and Mexico by removing barriers to trade, such as tariffs, quotas, and licenses.* This free-trade zone covers more than 8.2 million square miles, 400 million consumers, and $600 billion in annual economic activity. NAFTA represents an extension of the Canada–United States Free Trade Agreement, which went into effect in 1993. When Congress approved NAFTA, trade between the United States and Mexico was $81 billion. In 2002, trade reached $233 billion. U.S. exports to its NAFTA partners have increased more than 100 percent between 1993 and 2002, whereas U.S. trade with the rest of the world grew only half as fast. Today, the United States exports more to Mexico and Canada than to the countries that combine to form the European Union.[23]

NAFTA was intended to reduce and eliminate numerous tariffs and most nontariff barriers among the three countries. Although full elimination of certain tariffs will not take place until 2009, more than 70 percent of the goods imported from Mexico may now enter the United States without tariffs. At the same time, more than 50 percent of U.S. exports to Mexico are now tariff free. The agreement also realizes long-held goals of fostering trade in services and liberalizing foreign investment rules. NAFTA tightens the protection of intellectual property (copyrights, trademarks, and patents, in particular). More than 80 percent of Mexico's exports are now to the United States and Canada. The benefits to the United States and Canada are the ability of manufacturers to produce goods more cheaply, especially in *maquiladora* plants, and the ability to move raw materials easily among the three countries. ***Maquiladora* plants** *are foreign-owned industrial plants located in Mexico that border the U.S. states of Texas, New Mexico, Arizona, and California.* These plants employ more than 1 million people, account for roughly 40 percent of Mexico's manufacturing, and pay more than five times Mexico's minimum wage.[24]

Recently, organizations that produce electric and electronic goods have started to relocate their businesses from Mexico to China because of cheaper labor, which more than offsets the extra shipping charges. Managers at the *maquiladora* plants claim that the lack of clear regulations, increased tax costs, the deceleration of the U.S. economy and the strength of the peso have all contributed to this relocation.

Although NAFTA further opened Canadian and U.S. markets, the most significant liberalization applies to Mexico. NAFTA expanded Canadian and U.S. companies' ability to establish or purchase businesses in Mexico and increased their ability to sell if they wanted to leave. NAFTA loosened previous restrictions on expanding operations in Mexico and removed restrictions on transferring profits to other countries. U.S. exports to Mexico and Canada now support almost 3 million American jobs.

Despite much liberalization, NAFTA retains certain protectionist provisions, some of which may persist with no time limit. NAFTA temporarily protects sensitive industries (e.g., agriculture, minerals, banking, textiles, and apparel) by stretching out the phase-in time for lifting restrictions that apply to them. NAFTA also contains other types of protection that are permanent and appear to raise trade barriers above pre-NAFTA levels. In some industries—notably automobiles, textiles, and apparel—NAFTA imposes higher North American content rules. Under the previous Canada–United States Free Trade Agreement, for example, automobiles could be imported duty free if they contained at least 50 percent Canadian and U.S. inputs. For auto imports to receive NAFTA benefits, the North American rule is now 62.5 percent. For textiles or apparel to qualify for "free" trade under NAFTA, all components—beginning with the yarn or fiber—must be produced in North America.

The service industries that received the most attention during NAFTA negotiations were finance, insurance, transportation, and telecommunications. NAFTA doesn't change requirements for foreign banks' entry into the United States and Canada. But the opening of the Mexican financial system is among the agreement's most significant achievements. Requirements for entry into brokerage, bonding, insurance, leasing, and warehousing were liberalized even more than they were for banking.

NAFTA and WTO certainly don't eliminate all trade problems among the member countries. But they do provide frameworks through which such problems can be resolved. By increasing the competitive forces that act on firms, the ultimate goals of WTO and NAFTA are to achieve greater efficiency and consumer satisfaction. However, as legal documents that were politically negotiated, they contain provisions, loopholes, and exceptions that will be tested over the decades to come. The provisions of these agreements no doubt will be welcomed or resisted, depending on their effect on a particular country, industry, labor organization, or firm.

The following Planning & Administration Competency feature describes Mabe, a $1 billion a year manufacturer of appliances in Mexico that employs more than 15,000 people and has grown at annual rates of 15 to 20 percent since the passage of NAFTA.[25] Mabe exports refrigerators, ranges, heating elements, compressors, and washers to the United States, Canada, and Central and South American countries. Mabe manufactures these products for a variety of companies, including GE and IEM. It has been able to develop world-class manufacturing capabilities and innovative management practices under the CEO's leadership. This feature is based on remarks by Mabe's CEO, Luis Avalos, and highlights why Mabe located in Mexico instead of other Latin American countries.

PLANNING & ADMINISTRATION COMPETENCY

Mabe

With the passage of NAFTA, Mexico has become a very competitive nation because of the low cost of labor, good relationships with unions, and well-trained engineers. To remain competitive, Mabe had to locate plants in areas of a country where there was an educated workforce. For example, Mabe had to have employees who could make products that met GE's demands for six-sigma quality. In Mexico, it is easy to find workers with at least a high school education. A high school education provides them with a basis of general knowledge and level of mathematics that allows them to be trained. The engineering programs at Mexican universities are first rate.

To ensure a high-quality workforce, Mabe invests heavily in training. At least 6 percent of an employee's working hours are spent in training. This emphasis on training

allows employees to become more specialized in their areas of expertise or to develop managerial competencies. The average Mexican employee at Mabe works a 45-hour week. Therefore, in one year, that employee receives about three weeks of training. At the new $250 million Mabe factory designed to build side-by-side-door GE refrigerators for export to the United States, employees are assigned to self-managed teams. Employees are trained in setting production objectives and learn how to assume responsibility for six-sigma-level quality. They measure defects, the amount of scrap, and take care of equipment maintenance. Management clearly communicates Mabe's objectives, and team members become real doers.

Mexico does not have labor unions whose goals are based on antimanagement ideologies, such as those found in some other Latin American

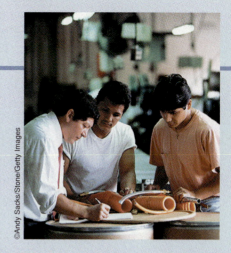

©Andy Sacks/Stone/Getty Images

countries. Currently, labor unions are focusing on promoting job stability for their members. The benefits for Mabe are that unions work with their members to help them arrive at work on time, be honest, and provide workplace stability. There is a sense of cooperation and consensus between management and unions. Mabe has also introduced scholarships for the unemployed in an area to help them develop the skills needed to enter or reenter the workforce.

European Union

The European Union, called the European Community until 1994, currently has 18 members: Austria, Belgium, Denmark, Finland, France, Germany, Greece, Iceland, Ireland, Italy, Liechtenstein, Luxembourg, the Netherlands, Norway, Portugal, Spain, Sweden, and the United Kingdom.[26] These countries are home to nearly 400 million consumers. In spite of the high unemployment rate in Europe, the EU has created 12 million new jobs since 1994 and is hoping for full employment by 2010. The EU introduced a common currency, the euro, in 2001. Its valuation against the U.S. dollar is monitored by an independent central bank in Frankfurt, Germany.

The **European Union (EU)** *is an organization with the goals of creating a single market among member countries through the removal of trade barriers (e.g., tariffs) and establishing the free movement of goods, people, services, and capital.* Implementation of activities to achieve these and other goals officially began at the end of 1992. In addition, the changes go beyond economic interests to include social changes as well. Educational degrees have already been affected. The EU Council of Ministers issued a directive that recognizes diplomas of higher education across national boundaries. This action makes it easier for professionals to work in different countries. Most member countries have developed master's degree programs in business administration that are compatible with those of other member countries and of the United States.

The EU clearly is more than an economic union: It is a state of mind and a political force. Eventually, it intends to reduce interference in economic activities by government in member countries. Meeting uniform quality standards and worker safety and environmental controls will be expected of all companies who trade in the EU. The **International Organization for Standardization (ISO)** *issues certification standards for excellence in quality.* This serves a purpose similar to that of the Deming Prize in Japan and the Baldrige Award in the United States, both of which recognize organizations for outstanding quality (see Chapter 2).

An essential stage of the EU program is to complete formation of a common internal market. That involves eliminating

1. physical barriers at each country's borders, which prevent the free flow of goods and people;
2. technical barriers, which prevent goods and services produced or traded in one member nation from being sold in others;
3. fiscal barriers, such as red tape and the different national tax systems, which hinder cross-border trade; and
4. financial barriers, which prevent the free movement of investment capital.[27]

The European Commission is the EU's executive body and sole initiator of legislation. The commission claims that 95 percent of the legislative measures set out in the 1992 program have been adopted. However, the toughest issues weren't addressed in the 1992 program, including agreement on a common immigration policy. Some member nations are concerned that they'll be flooded with immigrants as the result of an open-door policy. As unemployment has risen in Eastern Europe, the frontiers of the EU have been tightened. It is now virtually impossible to enter the member nations legally as an economic migrant. An applicant rejected by one member nation can no longer apply to any other member nation.

The EU has already increased market opportunities, fostered competition, and encouraged competition from the outside. The removal of transnational trade restrictions and the relaxation of border controls based on economic restraints have had a considerable impact on U.S. and Canadian companies. For example, NBC, with no previous global experience, acquired controlling interest in Europe's Super Channel. It is now beaming its programs to about 70 million homes and hotels throughout Europe.

Many non-Europeans continue to be concerned that the free market of Europe will be anything but free to outsiders. The European Commission has pressured U.S. and Japanese firms to conduct more R&D and production in Europe or face the risk of increased tariffs and other barriers. Restrictions still apply to non-EU banks and security firms unless foreign countries (e.g., the United States, Canada, and Japan) grant reciprocal rights. These restrictions range from limiting the right to acquire banks in EU countries to special taxes on foreign banks operating there.

Various alternative strategies are available to U.S. and Canadian enterprises. One strategy is to export goods and services to the EU. In general, though, North American firms have had only limited success in doing so. The most successful strategy has been to set up subsidiaries or branches in one or more of the EU countries. The advantages of subsidiaries have been demonstrated by well-established companies such as Opel (a subsidiary of GM in Germany), Ford, and IBM. Some companies have consolidated their previous positions in Europe. For example, UPS purchased 11 companies in EU nations to strengthen its market position.

STRATEGIES FOR INTERNATIONAL BUSINESS

5. Describe six strategies used by organizations in international business.

Organizations typically choose among six strategies for conducting international business.[28] They range from low to high in complexity and in resource commitment, as shown in Figure 4.4. *Complexity* refers to the structure of the organization (e.g., number of hierarchical levels, number of staff people, and number of departments) and the

Figure 4.4   Strategies for International Operations

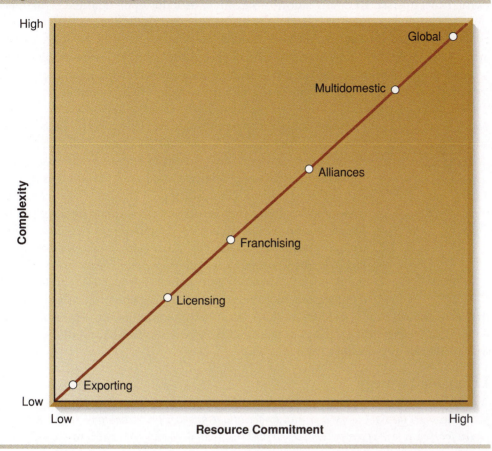

amount of coordination required to deliver a product or service to customers. *Resource commitment* refers to the amount of tangible financial assets (e.g., plants, warehouses, personnel) and information support systems that the organization dedicates to its global strategy.

Organizations can change their strategies over time as they learn from their experiences. Celanese Chemical Corporation used an export strategy to sell its chemicals in Thailand, China, Vietnam, and other Southeast Asian countries in the early 1990s. One person covered this territory and needed little support from the organization headquartered in Dallas, Texas. As its chemical business grew during the 1990s, Celanese changed its international strategy to become a global chemical company. As Celanese changed its strategy, its organizational structure became more complex and it committed larger amounts of resources to its far-flung operations. It built a $300 million dollar plant in Singapore and hired 100 local employees to staff that operation. The Singapore operation's output is coordinated with its other plants in Texas, Canada, and California to provide chemical products worldwide.[29]

Exporting Strategy

The **exporting strategy** *involves maintaining facilities within a home country and shipping goods and services abroad for sale in foreign markets.* When a domestic firm decides that it wants to move toward global operations, its first priority should be to build a global customer base. All that is necessary is a Web page and some promotion to direct potential customers to its location.

Exporting is a practical means for small or medium-sized organizations with little financial resources to invest but who are facing increased competition in their domestic markets. For many such firms, exporting is the primary strategy of international operations. Tim Luberski, CEO of California Sunshine, uses this approach. California Sunshine is a leading exporter of U.S. dairy products, including milk, eggs, yogurt, and sour cream. Extended product dating and rapid delivery allow them to be sold virtually around the world. California Sunshine customers can order products directly on the Internet at http://www.hiddenvilla.com. With three large warehouses located next to international airports, California Sunshine guarantees product delivery within 72 hours.

A variation on exporting (or importing) is **countertrade**, *an agreement that requires companies from the exporting nation to purchase products of equivalent value from the importing nation.* Countertrade continues to grow as a marketing tool for doing business in lesser developed countries.[30] The American Countertrade Association (aca@countertrade.org) indicates that countertrade eases trade and investments into countries that either have (1) difficulties trading in hard currency or (2) impose certain counterpurchase obligations on vendors that are selling their products into a country. Countertrade can also give a company a competitive advantage, improve customer relationships, and create goodwill with the importing country's government. For example, in Thailand, the government set a requirement that state projects worth more than 300 million bhat (US $7.03 million) would have to ask their foreign suppliers of equipment and services to accept at least half their payment in Thai products, such as frozen chicken, rice products, and furniture.

Licensing Strategy

A **licensing strategy** *involves a firm (the licensor) in one country giving other domestic or foreign firms (licensees) the right to use a patent, trademark, technology, production process, or product in return for the payment of a royalty or fee.*[31] This contractual arrangement also may involve the licensor in providing manufacturing, technical, or marketing expertise to the licensee. A simple licensing arrangement involves U.S. and Canadian book publishers giving foreign publishers the right to translate a book into another language and then publish, market, and distribute the translated book. The licensor doesn't have to worry about making large capital investments abroad or becoming involved in the details of daily production, marketing, or management. PepsiCo and Coca-Cola have licensing agreements with bottlers/distributors in most countries of the world.

Technological and market forces are combining to stimulate use of the licensing strategy. As a form of market entry, international licensing is more risky than exporting, but less risky than franchising. The licensor exports know-how instead of their product. Some of the reasons why organizations use a license are to generate extra income from existing technology, to spread the costs of R&D projects, to get into markets that have been closed or protected, to test new markets before making capital investment, and to minimize risks when entering foreign markets. Although there are potential benefits, there are also some risks. The licensee might become a competitor, fail to pay royalties, imitate the technology, or sell the license without the agreement of the licensor. Such risks are likely in the pharmaceutical and software industries.

Franchising Strategy

A **franchising strategy** *involves a parent organization (the franchiser) granting other companies or individuals (franchisees) the right to use its trademarked name and to produce and sell its goods or services.* It is a special type of licensing agreement whereby the franchiser not only provides the product, technology, process, and/or trademark, but also most of the marketing program. It is similar to licensing, but the franchiser usually has more control over the franchisee. In nearly any major city around the world, you are likely to find Burger

King, Kentucky Fried Chicken, or Marriott, among others. They are there because local entrepreneurs have bought franchises. Franchising permits companies to maintain marketing control while passing along many of the costs, risks, and responsibilities to the franchisees. The franchiser provides franchisees with a complete assortment of materials and services for a fee. Franchisees often function somewhat independently from the parent company but benefit from being part of a larger organization. However, the franchiser usually is actively involved in training, monitoring, and controlling certain actions of the franchisee to ensure that it conforms to the franchise agreement. For example, California-based New Horizons Computer Learning Center is the world's largest independent information technology training network. New Horizons provides Web-based training and computer-based training for the local franchisee. Because product quality is critical, New Horizons requires all franchisees to come to California for training several times a year.[32]

Alliance Strategy

An **alliance strategy** *involves an agreement between two or more organizations to pool physical, financial, and human resources to achieve common goals.* **Global strategic alliances** *are joint ventures that involve actions taken internationally by two or more companies contributing an agreed-on amount of resources.* This approach may be preferred when competition is tough or technology and capital requirements are relatively large for one partner. General Motors has global alliances with Suzuki, Isuzu, Daewoo, among others. Ford has alliances with Mazda. General Mills created a global strategic alliance with Nestlé in Europe, called Cereal Partners Worldwide, to compete against Kellogg's growing global market share. General Mills and Nestlé agreed to pool part of their product lines and distribution systems.

The following factors have stimulated the formation of alliances, especially joint ventures.[33]

- The need to share and lower the costs of high-risk, technologically intensive development projects, such as computer-based information systems. Toshiba, for example, is allied with several U.S. firms (United Technologies, Apple Computer, Sun Microsystems, and Motorola) and European firms (Olivetti, Siemens, Rhone-Poulenc, Ericcson, and SGS-Thompson). The partners are simultaneously owners investing capital, customers routing calls via satellites, and suppliers of technology to the venture.
- The desire to lower costs by sharing the large fixed-cost investments for manufacturing plants in some locations and in industries such as autos, steel, and appliances. To reduce manufacturing costs, Ford and Mazda have formed Auto-Alliance to manufacture the 2005 Ford Mustang. This $644 million dollar joint venture will enable Auto-Alliance to install flexible body systems on the assembly line that allows several models to be assembled at the same time.
- The desire to learn another firm's technology and special processes or to gain access to customers and distribution channels. The French publisher, Hachette, entered into an alliance with Pacific Publications of Australia to publish *Elle* and *Elle Cuisine* in Australia and New Zealand.
- The desire to participate in the evolution of competitive activity in growing global industries. Royal Crown Cola Company signed a joint venture agreement with Mexico's Consorcio Aga to help RC Cola boost its sales there. In addition to licensing its brands, RC Cola provides advertising, promotional, and technical support to Consorcio Aga.

Alliances provide entry into markets that are risky because of strict political requirements or great economic uncertainty. For example, China usually doesn't permit foreign corporations to establish wholly owned subsidiaries there—they must form some sort of alliance with Chinese participants. Finally, domestic partners are likely to have a deeper understanding of how to deal with great political and economic complexity in countries such as China and Russia.

Multidomestic Strategy

A **multidomestic strategy** *involves adjusting products, services, and practices to individual countries or regions* (e.g., Pacific Rim versus Western Europe versus North America).[34] Halliburton, General Mills, and PepsiCo all practice multidomestic strategies. Pressures for local customizing to respond to differences in customer demand, distribution channels, host government demands, and/or employee needs drive this strategy. It is based on the assumption that the benefits of local response will outweigh the extra costs of customizing. These companies view the world as a whole of unique parts and deal with each part individually. Thus a multidomestic company treats each market separately because of differences in tastes and competitive conditions.

Under a multidomestic strategy, each major overseas subsidiary usually is somewhat independent. Often each is a profit center and contributes earnings and growth according to its market opportunity. A **profit center** *is an organizational unit that is accountable for both the revenues generated by its activities and the costs of those activities.* Its managers are responsible for generating revenues and minimizing costs to achieve the unit's profit goals. Frito-Lay uses a multidomestic strategy in tailoring its snack foods to taste preferences around the world. For example, Janjaree Thanma directs marketing research for Frito-Lay in Thailand. Interestingly, after testing 500 flavors for its chips with Thai consumers, the results showed that their preference was for U.S. flavors, such as barbecue.

Global Strategy

A **global strategy** *stresses worldwide consistency, standardization, and relatively low cost.*[35] Subsidiaries in various countries are highly interdependent in terms of goals, practices, and operations. As much as possible, top managers focus on coordination and mutual support of the firm's worldwide activities. For example, a Black & Decker subsidiary in one country might manufacture certain parts for families of products; subsidiaries in other countries do the same with regard to other parts. The subsidiaries then exchange components to complete assembly of their particular products. Profit targets vary for each subsidiary, reflecting its importance to the company's total system.

The customers of global firms have needs that are basically similar in many countries. Thus primary marketing strategies are highly transferable across national boundaries. For example, the marketing of Intel's Pentium chips to computer manufacturers in various countries has many similarities. Customers' technical standards are relatively compatible, and, for the most part, governments don't regulate computer chip production and sales practices. American Express Company also realizes the benefits of a global strategy by emphasizing the ideas of quality, security, and safety. One of American Express's goals is to create the world's most respected brand name. Travelers around the world recognize the reliability and quality symbolized by the American Express logo. Travelers who encounter trouble can go to any American Express office for emergency replacement of travelers' checks or lost or stolen credit cards. In addition, all offices are equipped to send emergency telegrams and messages to families, consulates, and other contacts for people in need of such services.

An increasing number of multinational corporations are using global strategies, such as Caterpillar and Komatsu (heavy construction equipment); Kodak and Fuji (film); and Texas Instruments, Intel, and Hitachi (semiconductors). As demonstrated in the following Strategic Action Competency feature on Imperial Chemicals Industries PLC, the global form of organization is not without pitfalls. You might not recognize the name of

Imperial Chemical Industries, but you know its brands: Glidden, Ralph Lauren, DeVoe, and Color Your World. Located in London, it competes against Sherwin-Williams and Pittsburgh Plate Glass in coatings for cars, paint, liquid nails, and adhesives around the world. [36]

STRATEGIC ACTION COMPETENCY

Imperial Chemical Industries PLC

The sun never sets on the far-flung operations of Imperial Chemical Industries PLC (ICI). As one of the world's largest companies, ICI's sales exceed $9 billion. It has more than 200 manufacturing plants on six continents making paints, chemicals, explosives, film, and polymers, among other products.

In 1983, ICI began to abandon its traditional country-by-country organization and formed worldwide business units. Today, the company focuses its resources in locations where it has the strongest competitive advantage. Since 1983, ICI has bought and sold more than 50 businesses in an attempt to position itself in the industry. Today, it has four regional and industrial chemical centers. For example, of its $9 billion in sales, ICI gets more than 30 percent from sales in the United States. Therefore, ICI has established its headquarters in Wilmington,

Delaware. From this location, it makes many of its paint products. From its operations in Argentina, ICI provides chemicals to the wine industry and other related chemicals. From its India operation, it manufactures explosives, pharmaceuticals, and rubber chemicals. In Pakistan, it manufactures fibers and soda ash, a major component for making glass.

To avoid overlapping research, labs are given lead roles near their markets. For example, leather dye research went to Pakistan and advanced materials research was assigned to the United States. As a result, employees had to be outsourced or moved to another country. According to High Miller, an American, "It's hard on people who have built national empires and now don't have such allegiance. We are asking people to be less nationalistic and more concerned with what happens outside their country." The payoff, says Miller, is more efficient de-

cision making. "Before, each country would work up projects and you'd have warring factions competing in London for the same money. Now, with one person responsible for a global product line, it becomes immaterial where a project is located. Its profits will be the same. When you start operating in this manner, it takes a lot of steam out of country fiefdoms." In the wine industry, for example, better and quicker decision making from Argentina has helped ICI reduce the time it takes to introduce new chemicals used to fight insects that destroy grapes. These chemicals, subject to governmental approval, then can be used to fight insects in the United States, France, New Zealand, and other grape growing regions of the world. Similarly, ICI has been able to reduce the time for introducing new drugs into the pharmaceutical industry from six years to one or two by having focused all of its pharmaceutical operations in India.

Various needs must be addressed if a multinational's global strategy is to be successful.[37] The following are six such needs.

1. The firm needs to be a significant competitor in the world's most important regional markets—North America, Europe, and Asia.
2. Most new goods and services need to be developed for the whole world—such as American Express Company's financial services and Kodak's film and related products.
3. Profit targets need to be based on product lines—such as an ICI line of paint—rather than countries or regions of the world.
4. Decisions about products, capital investment, R&D, and production need to be based on global considerations—such as ICI's choice of strategic locations for plants for producing chemicals and related products in various regions of the world.

5. Narrow-minded attitudes—such as "this isn't how we operate here"—need to be overcome. Some ways to shape work-related attitudes and values include training employees to think globally, sending them to various countries for firsthand exposure, and giving them the latest information technology. Coca-Cola went so far as to ban the words *domestic* and *foreign* from its corporate vocabulary in order to bolster the image of a single global firm that had more than 80 percent of its sales from non-U. S. sources.

6. Foreign managers need to be promoted into senior ranks at corporate headquarters.

CHAPTER SUMMARY

In this chapter, we focused on various global considerations for those engaging in international business. Organizations and individuals—both as employees and consumers—are increasingly touched by global forces and issues.

1. State several characteristics of the global economy.

Organizations are becoming more global in their operations, and globalization of commerce will continue to accelerate. Societies also are becoming more global. During this next decade, these shifts will affect organizations in several important ways. First, communication is instant, placing a premium on information; second, organizations are becoming boundaryless, with operations spanning the globe; third, governments are becoming more democratic; and fourth, highly skilled labor is available in many different parts of the world.

2. Describe how a country's culture can affect an organization's business practices.

The primary cultural factors that can influence how an organization is managed include views of social change, time, language, value systems, and cultural distance. Special attention was given to understanding how cultural issues have led to differences in the management systems in Mexico and the United States.

3. Explain the impact of political–legal forces on international business.

International business operations create new complexities, risks, and uncertainties. Broad political–legal issues include domestic instability, foreign conflict, political climate, economic climate, and corruption. Political mechanisms utilized in international business include tariffs, quotas, subsidies, cartels, bribes, and extortion.

4. Discuss how three major trade agreements affect global competition.

The World Trade Organization helps open markets and reduce trade barriers (e.g., tariffs) among its 144 member nations. The North American Free Trade Agreement further reduces barriers, encourages investment, and stimulates trade among Canada, Mexico, and the United States. The European Union is an organization of 18 countries. Its primary goals are to create a single market and allow the free movement of goods, services, people, and capital among its members. The ultimate goal is to improve the standard of living and quality of life for the citizens of the member countries.

5. Describe six strategies used by organizations in international business.

The strategies used by many international businesses include exporting, licensing, franchising, alliances, multidomestic, and global. These strategies vary in terms of their relative complexity (reflected in organization design) and resource commitments required to effectively implement the strategy. Organizations use different strategies over time as they learn how to adjust their operations to the demands of their global marketplaces.

KEY TERMS and CONCEPTS

Alliance strategy
Bribe
Cartel
Corruption
Countertrade
Cultural distance
Domestic instability

Economic climate
European Union (EU)
Exporting strategy
Extortion
Foreign conflict
Franchising strategy
Global strategic alliances

Global strategy
Grease payments
International Organization for Standardization (ISO)
Licensing strategy
Maquiladora plants
Multidomestic strategy
North American Free Trade Agreement (NAFTA)
Political climate

Political risk
Profit center
Protectionism
Quota
Subsidy
Tariff
World Trade Organization (WTO)

QUESTIONS FOR DISCUSSION and COMPETENCY DEVELOPMENT

1. Identify at least three challenges facing Wal-Mart's global expansion.

2. What are some of the competencies you need to develop to become an effective global manager? How can your course work in school help you do so?

3. Describe the ways in which a rapidly changing competitive international environment has impacted global organizations.

4. What role do culture and society play in creating ethics for people in global organizations?

5. Suppose that Mabe wanted to open four new plants overseas. Name four countries that might represent a high degree of risk for such operations (go to

http://www.transparency.org/cpi/index.html#cpi). Would Mabe be better off exporting to those countries? Explain.

6. Has NAFTA been good or bad for U.S. manufacturing companies? What are two of the current problems for transportation companies under the NAFTA trade agreement?

7. Has the EU stimulated trade in Europe? How has it affected nations that are not members of the EU?

8. Describe three of the strategies for international business that organizations have used. State advantages and limitations of each strategy.

9. In Mexico, how important is punctuality? What nonverbal gestures are appropriate?

CASE FOR COMPETENCY DEVELOPMENT

ESTEÉ LAUDER

Esteé Lauder Companies, Inc., was founded in 1946 and has become one of the world's largest manufacturers and marketers of quality skin care, makeup, fragrance, and hair care products. The company's products are sold in 130 countries and its products include Esteé Lauder, Clinique, Aramis, Tommy Hilfiger, Origins, Aveda, and others. In 2002, its sales were $4.7 billion and the company recorded its 45th year of consecutive sales increases. It employs more than 20,000 people worldwide. It maintains research and development facilities in New York, Belgium, Tokyo, Ontario, and Minnesota. It manufactures all of its products from plants in the United States, Belgium, Switzerland, the United Kingdom, and Canada.

Esteé Lauder sells its products principally through limited distribution channels. These upscale department stores and specialty retailers account for the majority of sales, but stores on cruise ships, in-flight and duty-free shops in airports, and the company's own stores also sell the products. In 1998, the company also began to sell its

products over the Internet and created a new division, ELC Online, to coordinate all Internet sales. In 2000, it also formed a joint venture with Chanel and Clarins (http://www.Gloss.com), which sells all three brands.

Esteé Lauder serves three major markets: The Americas represent 61 percent of its sales; Europe, the Middle East, and Africa represent 26 percent of its sales; and the Asia/Pacific area represents 13 percent of its sales. Recently it has expanded into Russia and into the emerging markets of China and Eastern Europe.

Russia has proven to be an extremely attractive market for its products. An estimated 80 percent of its 65 million women use cosmetics regularly. In a move to strengthen sales, it has opened two shops in Moscow's prestigious GUM department store and a boutique in Saint Petersburg. It is attempting to adapt its colors to the tastes of Russian women while delivering high-quality products and services.

Gaining sales in Eastern Europe is a top priority of Esteé Lauder. Since being introduced in Romania in 1997, Clinique has dominated the upscale market, selling an average of two items per sale. Romania is a country with more than 23 million people. Its per capita income is $100 per month. Edward Straw, president of Esteé Lauder's Global Operations division, believes that this is a good market for Esteé Lauder because there are very few prestige cosmetics and there is "no such thing as service." The company uses a "free" gift with purchases of more than $40 to attract buyers. He recalls an employee seeing long lines of customers at 8:00 A.M. when Clinique offered a gift-with-purchase promotion at its Prague store.

To capitalize on the consumerism movement in China, it has opened 30 stores to serve the Shanghai market. Esteé Lauder has determined that Shanghai residents will spend money on upscale cosmetics, "brand" new clothes, and entertainment. To cater to this market, Esteé Lauder has also entered into joint ventures with major Chinese department stores. Although these shops generate a lot of interest, many customers cannot tell the difference between a $1 lipstick and a $10 lipstick.

In Japan, it has tested the open-sell concept in a major Tokyo department store, Odakyu, located in the Ginza district. Here, its cosmetics, fragrances, and accessories are available to customers who do not have time to talk to sales personnel. This self-service concept allows customers to purchase products at their leisure, with salespeople present only as support to answer questions and perform makeovers. The open-sell concept has been well received in Japan. Esteé Lauder's major competitor, Kao, is providing the same service.

Esteé Lauder continues to broaden its market by expanding its product offerings and adding new services, such as in-store spas. Straw says that the key to foreign markets hinges on employee training and customer service. Because customers may be unfamiliar with the product, Esteé Lauder salespeople will need to spend time educating customers on its value.[38]

Questions

1. What type of strategy has Esteé Lauder chosen to enter foreign markets?
2. What are some of the risks with this strategy?
3. How will cultural factors impact the selling process in Mexico?
4. What political–legal forces might impact Esteé Lauder's international growth?

CULTURAL PREFERENCES

Please complete this questionnaire to measure your cultural preferences. Ten pairs of statements are presented. Pick the statement in each pair that best represents your personal attitudes and preferences. There are no correct or incorrect choices.

1. a. Organizations should be organized like a family, with a focus on teamwork and cooperation.
   b. Organizations should be organized to serve the individual.

2. a. I usually base my decisions more on personal relationships than rules.
   b. I usually follow rules in making decisions.

3. a. It is important for managers to make decisions for subordinates.
   b. Subordinates should be allowed to make as many decisions as they feel qualified to make.

4. a. Title and position are more important than money.
   b. Money is a main status indicator and is a reward for achievement.

5. a. Who you are (your age, gender, education) is important in society.
   b. What you accomplish in your career is important in society.

6. a. Deadlines and commitments are flexible.
   b. Deadlines and commitments are firm.

7. a. Promotions should be based heavily on loyalty to my superior.
   b. Promotions should be based heavily on my performance.

8. a. Meaningful relationships need to be established before any productive discussions in a meeting can take place.
   b. Meetings should be short and to the point.

9. a. It's all right to show emotions at work and let emotions impact decision making.
   b. Emotions have little room in making business decisions.

10. a. Making money is good because it makes enjoying life possible.

b. Making money is good even if I do not have time to spend and enjoy it.

Interpretation: Count the number of (a) responses; they are considered to be stereotypical attitudes of traditional Mexican society and managers. Count the number of (b) responses; they are considered to be stereotypical attitudes of traditional U. S., society and managers.

Question

1. What dimensions of the global awareness competency are illustrated in this exercise?

©Courtesy of Burton Snowboards

Entrepreneurship

Learning Objectives

After studying this chapter, you should be able to:

1. Explain the role of entrepreneurs and how external factors impact their ventures.

2. Describe the personal attributes that contribute to entrepreneurs' success.

3. Outline the planning essentials for potential entrepreneurs.

4. State the role of intrapreneurs and how organizations can foster intrapreneurship.

Chapter Outline

Carolyn Minerich's dream of becoming an FBI agent took a different turn along the way when the former Marine Corps officer settled in Alabama and started a high-tech business with major corporate clients like Walt Disney World and Lord & Taylor. Arriving in Jacksonville, Alabama, in 1994 with her family, Minerich decided to start her own business from scratch. She had no customers, no experience in the field, no reputation, and no money. But Minerich states that the Marine Corps had taught her "not to think twice about doing things that had never been done or seen before."

Carmin Industries is a business that began with a mission to become an industry leader through the use of an innovative cutting technology—water! When Minerich and her family started Carmin Industries, a precision waterjet cutting and fabrication service, in 1996, she was the only employee. She could be found working on the shop floor by herself, running the machines, unloading trucks, and preparing products for shipment. Today, Carmin Industries has 15 full-time employees and has done work for Walt Disney World, Universal Studios, Lord & Taylor, the Smithsonian, and many other organizations.

During the first year Carmin Industries was in business, it cut very simple stainless steel plates that went into the entrance of the Hawaii Convention Center in Honolulu. Today, Carmin Industries cuts such things as a dinosaur bone that is 8 feet tall and 16 feet long for The Animal Kingdom at Disney World, and honeycomb-shaped aluminum that was made into steps for the space shuttle. As Minerich says, "We try to amaze at least one person each day with the wonderful things that water can do!"

Minerich credits her success to the Jacksonville Small Business Development Center, Compass Bank, which gave her a loan, and her husband Jon, who first heard about the waterjet cutting process on a Discovery Channel television program. He gave her professional advice as she was starting the company. Carolyn Minerich was recognized as the Alabama Small Business Person of the Year in 2002 by U.S. Small Business Administration.[1]

ENTREPRENEURS AND EXTERNAL FACTORS

1. Explain the role of entrepreneurs and how external factors impact their ventures.

Who Are Entrepreneurs?

Entrepreneurs *create something for the purpose of gain while accepting the risk and uncertainty associated with their ventures.* In launching a new business, entrepreneurs typically incorporate at least one of the following.[2]

- *Something new.* This could be a new product, service, or technology. Carolyn Minerich created precision waterjet cutting and fabrication services. Although her firm did not create this technology, it developed new services that employed the waterjet technology.
- *Something better.* This could be an improvement on an existing product or service encompassing more features, lower price, greater reliability, faster speed, or increased convenience. Jake Burton succeeded by improving on the design of a product that he first got to know as a 14-year-old. Shortly after college, he founded Burton Snowboards in Burlington, Vermont. He comments: "A lot of people think I invented snowboarding. But that's not true." The basic design for a snowboard had already been developed by Brunswick, the company that developed bowling alleys. But Brunswick never made the product a success. The philosophy of Burton Snowboards is to improve on what's available, based on an understanding of what customers really want. Burton states: "If the original product is a hassle for people, they'll fork over money for something that's better."[3]
- *An underserved or new market.* This is a market for which there is greater demand than competitors can currently satisfy, an unserved location, or a small part of an overall market—a niche market—that hasn't yet been taken over by other competitors. Sometimes, markets become underserved when large companies abandon or neglect smaller portions of their current customer base. Todd Greene invented a razor designed specifically for men who shave their heads. In 1999, he

tried to sell the concept to two large makers of men's grooming products, but was rejected outright. Greene decided to launch the innovative product on his own and formed HeadBlade Co., headquartered in Santa Monica, California. He has three patents on HeadBlade and others pending. HeadBlade also qualifies as being "something new." Many sales come through the firm's Web site (http://www.headblade.com).[4]

- *New delivery system or distribution channel.* New technologies, particularly the Internet, allow companies to reach customers more efficiently. This has created many new opportunities for businesses to provide products or services less expensively, to a wider geographic area, or with far greater choice. Kevin Grauman founded The Outsource Group (TOG), headquartered in Walnut Creek, California. Through heavy reliance on the Internet, TOG developed a new system for delivering human resource services, especially to small- and medium-sized firms. TOG has enabled its clients to substantially reduce the number of their employees devoted to increasingly complex human resource issues and to obtain virtually all of their needed specialized human resources services from one source. TOG is growing rapidly and serves 400 businesses. This e-business firm processes payrolls, manages benefits, helps clients comply with complex state and federal employment laws, negotiates on behalf of clients for health and other insurance benefits, and so on.[5] Grauman comments: "Our 'real work' is now associated with the wholesale rollout, acceptance and use of these technologies to move e-Businesses to the next level: enabling TOG's thousands of users (in client firms) to conduct millions of transactions on a true and seamless real-time Web-connected platform. And, to do so with a world-class customer service focus."[6]

These scenarios make clear that entrepreneurship is not limited to introducing something totally new. Successful entrepreneurs may begin by offering a higher quality product or service. They may make small modifications to what others are already doing. After they get started, they listen to customers or clients and come up with still other modifications. Then they quickly adapt what they're doing—and they repeat this process over and over. In brief, an entrepreneur is an innovator, decision maker, and organizational builder.[7] Typically, they get their inspiration through (1) previous work experience; (2) education or training; (3) hobbies, talents, or other personal interests; or (4) recognition of an unanswered need or market opportunity. Occasionally, the business idea comes from the experience of a relative or friend.

How Do External Factors Affect Entrepreneurs?

Chapters 3 and 4 provided a number of insights into how external forces impact all businesses, including those ventures launched by established organizations. In this section, we zero in on several key factors that are unique to entrepreneurship.

First, entrepreneurs require relatively open and free markets. Highly regulated and governmentally controlled markets, as are often seen in socialistic or communistic countries, severely limit opportunities for entrepreneurship. With the deregulation of markets in many countries during the past 15 years—including the United States, Canada, and other traditionally "free" market economies—the positive political climate for entrepreneurship has enabled millions of new entrepreneurs to flourish in the United States and globally. There has been an explosion in venture formation by women, immigrants, and members of minority groups.

One study found that 78 percent of respondents in the United States thought that entrepreneurship—through new startups or new ventures within existing organizations—would be the defining trend of the century.[8] As would be expected, the rates of entrepreneurship ebb and flow with changes in economic conditions. In the United States, entrepreneurship rates rose dramatically during the 1920s and then declined during the 1930s. They rose again after World War II but then declined from the 1950s into the late 1980s. The 1990s was another period of rising entrepreneurship, initiated by innovations in microelectronics, computers, telecommunications, and information technologies. With the softening of the economy, the rate of entrepreneurship was much lower in 2002 and 2003 than during the peak in 2000.

The support system for entrepreneurs also plays a role in the rate of new venture formation. The support system includes the current availability of investment capital, the availability of loans, tax rates and policies, and the availability of support services. The U.S. Small Business Administration, chambers of commerce, small business development centers, banks, venture capital firms, and other organizations provide a variety of services that are often helpful to entrepreneurs in the development, implementation, and growth of their ventures.

Business Incubators. According to the National Business Incubation Association, a **business incubator** *is an organization designed to accelerate the growth and success of entrepreneurial companies through an array of business support resources and services.*[9] There are approximately 550 business incubators in the United States. Local, regional, or state governments or other nonprofit organizations fund almost half of all incubators to stimulate economic development in their regions. Universities and colleges fund 13 percent of the incubators, private investors fund 12 percent, joint efforts of nonprofit and for-profit groups fund 18 percent, and other organizations fund 8 percent. Let's consider several of the features that are commonly found in business incubators.

- An existing building (few are newly built) is used that has been renovated to accommodate multiple tenants, as well as varying types of businesses.
- The tenants are offered below-market rent and flexible lease arrangements, including the opportunity to expand within the business incubator location.
- The incubator provides shared services such as telephone answering, access to a fax machine and copier, the use of a conference room or library, and on-site management consulting-business assistance by the incubator manager. Additionally, the incubator manager may serve as a liaison to contacts for financing or technology.
- Perhaps most important is the psychological or moral support that is fostered in an incubator. Often alone and unsure of themselves, entrepreneurs feel reduced anxiety and greater self-confidence when surrounded by other business owners experiencing similar struggles with their start-up ventures.

The incubator usually requires a written business plan, evidence of adequate financing, and a commitment by the business owner to relocate within the region upon leaving the business incubator facility.[10] Most new ventures stay in an incubator for two or three years, by which time the business has failed, chosen to expand within the incubator (if possible), or grown sufficiently enough to be able to move out of the incubator.

Is a Small-Business Owner an Entrepreneur?

Small-business owners may be entrepreneurs, but not all small-business owners are entrepreneurs. If small-business owners undertake one or more of the initiatives discussed previously, they are entrepreneurs. The U.S. Small Business Administration (SBA) defines a small business as a company employing fewer than 500 people. So, the term **small-business owner** *refers to anyone who owns a major equity stake in a company with fewer than 500 employees.* The SBA aids, counsels, assists, and protects the interests of small-business concerns, and advocates on their behalf within the U.S. government. It also helps small-business victims of disasters. It provides financial assistance, contractual assistance, and business development assistance. According to the SBA, there are more than 25 million small businesses in the United States. Since the 1990s, most of the employment growth in the United States has come from businesses with 500 or fewer employees.

Are Family Businesses Entrepreneurial Businesses?

When people think of a small business, they often think of a family business run by an entrepreneur. Actually a family business may be either large or small. It may or may not be an entrepreneurial enterprise. A **family business** *is one owned and managed mostly by people who are related by blood and/or marriage.* Often these businesses are passed down from one generation to the next. Kohler Company, which is known for its plumbing fixtures, is an example. Kohler was founded in 1873 by the inventor of the modern bathtub. Since then, this private company has diversified into furniture, small engines, and golf resorts. It is still controlled by the original family and employs many family members, including Herbert V. Kohler, Jr., who serves as the chairman of the board and president.[11]

As we explain later in this chapter, pressures to expand, adapt, and innovate can create a great deal of stress for entrepreneurs and the people who work with and for them. When those people also are family members, especially knotty problems can arise. Some families handle these pressures by turning over management of their firms to professionals. Some families find ways to keep their businesses changing while maintaining management and ownership control. Some families sell their businesses or close down. Only 35 percent of family businesses survive past the first generation of ownership. Only 20 percent survive to the third generation.[12]

ATTRIBUTES OF SUCCESSFUL ENTREPRENEURS

Few highly successful entrepreneurs start out with the goal of heading a rapidly growing company. When successful entrepreneurs are asked to explain why they started their own companies, the most frequent reason they give is to work for themselves and control their lives (41 percent). Other reasons include creating something new (12 percent), proving that they can do it (9 percent), not feeling rewarded in their old jobs (8 percent), being laid off (5 percent), and a variety of miscellaneous reasons (11 percent). The desire to be their own bosses increases when people discover that they can't accomplish their career goals in a large organization.[13]

The many studies of entrepreneurs that have been conducted over the years indicate that those who succeed have a cluster of attributes in common. These include some key personal attributes, strong technical attributes, and/or managerial competencies. As shown in Figure 5.1, the combination of all of these attributes increases the probability of entrepreneurial success.

2. Describe the personal attributes that contribute to entrepreneurs' success.

Personal Attributes

As suggested in Figure 5.1, the attributes that many entrepreneurs share are a strong need for achievement, a desire to be independent, self-confidence, and the willingness to make sacrifices for the sake of the business.[14]

Need for Achievement. The need for achievement—a person's desire either for excellence or to succeed in competitive situations—is a key personal attribute of successful entrepreneurs. High achievers take responsibility for attaining their goals, set moderately difficult goals, and want immediate feedback on how well they have performed. David McClelland and others have conducted extensive research into the human need for achievement. Their findings indicate that perhaps a low percentage of the U.S. population is characterized by a predominant need to achieve.[15] For many people, power needs and the need for affiliation are more important than the need for achievement. A strong drive to achieve is something that sets successful entrepreneurs apart from everyone else. Entrepreneurs set challenging but achievable goals for themselves and for their businesses and, when they achieve these goals, they set new ones.

Figure 5.1   Common Attributes of Successful Entrepreneurs

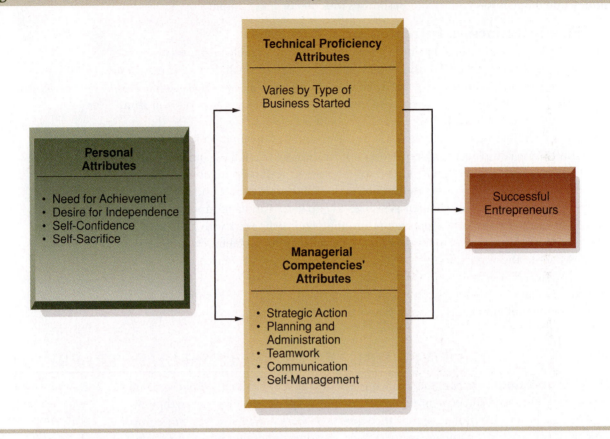

Desire for Independence. Entrepreneurs often seek independence from others. As a result, they generally aren't motivated to perform well in large, bureaucratic organizations. They have internal drive, are confident of their own abilities, and possess a great deal of self-respect.

Many of these feelings were familiar to Catherine Hughes. As CEO of Radio One, she became the first African-American woman in the United States to head a publicly traded company. Hughes got started in business about 25 years ago. That's when she took on the challenge of running Howard University's ailing radio station. Within a few years, she had bought her own station, WOL-AM, with the help of a $600,000 loan. The cost of servicing the loan was so steep that she had to live at the radio station. Hiring adequate staff was also a problem, so she filled in as a DJ and talk show host. Despite these hardships, Hughes was happy, saying, "I was thinking of programming ideas, recruiting people, putting together sales packages. It was finally my show." Today, the show that Hughes runs is a $250 million business with more than 60 stations around the country.[16]

Self-Confidence. A successful track record does much to improve an entrepreneur's self-confidence and self-esteem. It enables that person to be optimistic in representing the firm to employees and customers alike. Expecting, obtaining, and rewarding high performance from employees is personally reinforcing, and it also provides a role model for others. Most people want an optimistic and enthusiastic leader—someone they can look up to. Because of the risks involved in running an entrepreneurial organization, having an "upbeat" attitude is essential.

Self-Sacrifice. Finally, successful entrepreneurs have to be self-sacrificing. They recognize that nothing worth having is free. That means giving up the two-week vacation, the golf game every Saturday, or the occasional trip to the mountains. Success has a high price, and they are willing to pay it. For Catherine Hughes, living out of a sleeping bag at her radio station was a sacrifice. Having her car repossessed because she couldn't afford the payments on both her car and her station was a sacrifice. But perhaps her biggest sacrifice was selling a rare gold pocket watch because she needed the $50,000 it brought in. Made by slaves, the watch had belonged to her great-grandmother. Such sacrifices can be a tough reality for entrepreneurs.

Entrepreneurs: Made, Not Born. Although entrepreneurs are different from most people, they probably weren't born that way. They develop personal attributes over the years, but they acquire many of their key attributes early in life, with the family environment playing an important role. For example, women who were born first into a family tend to be more entrepreneurial than women born later into a family, perhaps because the first child receives special attention and thereby develops more self-confidence. Entrepreneurs also tend to have self-employed parents. The independent nature and flexibility shown by the self-employed mother or father is learned at an early age. Such parents are supportive and encourage independence, achievement, and responsibility.[17]

Changing personal attributes isn't easy, especially by the time people reach adulthood. Nevertheless, doing so may well be worth the effort. The best way is to engage in entrepreneurial behavior. Successful entrepreneurial experiences can lead to the development of new ways of thinking and can spur motivation.

The following Self-Management Competency feature provides a remarkable profile of personal attributes that were instrumental in the entrepreneurial success of Adrian Lugo, the founder and president of LUGO Construction, headquartered in Fife, Washington. Lugo established his firm in 1978 and it now completes approximately $50 million worth of projects annually. The company specializes in new construction and renovations of commercial and retail property; casinos and hotels; and industrial, institutional, and medical projects in both public and private sectors.[18]

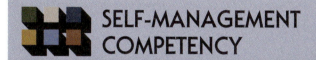

SELF-MANAGEMENT COMPETENCY

Adrian Lugo of LUGO Construction

Adrian C. Lugo, winner of an Entrepreneurial Success award from the SBA, could have been embittered by his encounters with racism and discrimination. Instead, he used them as catalysts to change for the better his own life and the lives of those around him. Lugo is of Hispanic and Native American heritage.

An army veteran of Vietnam, Lugo started college to become a teacher but encountered racial hostility that included one instructor specifically stating that he was not genetically suited for a teaching degree. Although he graduated cum laude, his experiences led him to forgo the graduation ceremonies.

Teaching was even more painful. Many of his peers would become silent or comment as if he weren't there when he entered the teachers' lounge. A few teachers did befriend Lugo—those of the campus improvement committee, of which he was a member. However, the constant negative comments and racially derogatory language convinced Lugo to leave teaching, which he actually loved. A teacher's pay could not compensate him for the constant attacks on his character. During summers, he had worked in construction and found the pay commensurate to

the work—and above his teacher's salary.

When he was rebuffed by the carpenters' and roofers' unions upon applying for work, Lugo determined he would be his own boss. LUGO Construction became a reality on

November 11, 1978. In forming the company, he promised himself three things: (1) to treat himself as well as his employees, (2) to treat his employees as well as himself, and (3) to treat his customers as he would like to be treated.

Two people mentored and supported Lugo in the early days of the company. Lugo contracted with Al Sether and Tom Morris, who appreciated the quality of his work. Lugo's careful attention to detail, however, was making it difficult to finish within specific time frames. Sether took it upon himself to constructively assess Lugo's lack of timeliness, encouraging him to complete the work on deadline. It was a valuable lesson, and today LUGO is known for both its high quality and on-time delivery. Morris personally posted $6 million in assets as a bond for Lugo's first major construction project, a flight simulator for the Navy.

Technical Proficiency Attribute

Many entrepreneurs demonstrate strong technical skills, typically bringing some related experience to their business ventures. For example, Joseph Sanda's passion for technology, his ability to envision its future, and his understanding of the importance of providing top-notch customer service are the keys that have unlocked the doors to business success for his company, Astute Solutions. This firm is headquartered in Columbus, Ohio, and has grown from a 2-employee operation in 1995 to more than 40 employees today.

As a full-service e-customer relationship management (eCRM) solution provider, Astute helps firms manage one-to-one customer relationships across multiple communication channels; including phone, Web, e-mail, and fax. Astute helps leverage Internet and telephone solutions for a completely integrated eCRM solution. Sanda's technical proficiency was essential to launching Astute solutions.[19]

MANAGERIAL COMPETENCIES

Managing a rapidly growing entrepreneurial company can be immensely challenging. To succeed requires drawing on the various managerial competencies described throughout this book. Of course, fundamental to these and all competencies is the self-management competency, as illustrated in features throughout this chapter.

Strategic Action Competency

Entrepreneurial success is often attributed to opportunistic behavior and being in the right place at the right time. Opportunity and luck may play some role in success, but sound strategic decisions also are important. A study of CEOs who have been winners of awards in the Ernst & Young LLP Entrepreneur of the Year Program reveal several strategic practices they used to sustain rapid growth for their companies. Five of the most common strategic practices identified include

- delivering products and services that are perceived as the highest quality to expanding market segments,
- using new products and services to expand revenue by about 20 percent annually,
- generating new customers that expand revenue by about 30 percent annually,
- focusing marketing expenditures on a high-quality sales force that can rapidly expand the company's geographic presence, and
- maintaining financial control of the firm.

> **The Competent Manager**
>
> *"At the end of every day ... I always ask myself two questions: Did we do what we said we were going to do? Was it what the customer wanted? Someone told me ... You're not selling anything.... You are finding a person who has a problem ... and you're helping them solve their problem! This was a dramatic turning point in how I look at business!"*
>
> Carolyn A. Minerich
> Founder and CEO
> Carmin Industries, Alabama

These common strategic practices are not necessarily formulated as goals early in the lives of their firms. For many, these practices emerged through their daily decisions. Making decisions that support growth is an ongoing activity that occurs day in and day out. Thus, a good approach is to treat a new venture like an experiment. It should be guided by a clear strategic plan focused on satisfying customers. Of course, decisions about how to achieve the goals should be based on trying various approaches and learning by observing what happens.

The following Strategic Action Competency reports on how Daniel Driesenga, who had a clear strategic vision in founding Driesenga & Associates, learned and adapted from experience. Founded in 1995, the firm now has four offices in western Michigan and a staff of more than 90 professionals, partly as a result of acquiring two other professional engineering firms.[20]

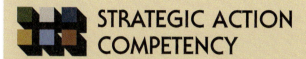

STRATEGIC ACTION COMPETENCY

Daniel Driesenga

While employed with an environmental engineering firm, Driesenga saw a need for more local services, especially construction materials testing, which was becoming a building code requirement. He suggested that the company expand its services in that area, but he was unable to convince the firm to do so. So Driesenga started his own company in 1995.

His engineering firm specializes in civil and geotechnical engineering, land surveying, construction materials testing, and environmental consulting. As the only firm in the Holland, Michigan, area to offer construction materials testing services, he has been able to provide quicker service at a lower cost than his out-of-state competitors. This has enabled him to gain a majority of the local market share.

At the end of the first year, the firm had sales of $450,000 and employed 7 people. Today, both figures have grown dramatically to approximately $6 million and 90 employees, with five Michigan offices in Holland, Grand Rapids, Kalamazoo, Spring Lake, and Whitehall.

But the road to success was not smooth. Within months of starting his business, Driesenga's largest customer, a state cleanup fund for underground storage tanks, ran out of money. This forced him to quickly shift focus and remarket the company. If this initial setback hadn't occurred, Driesenga might not have diversified into areas that have made him successful. He now realizes that he has gained an advantage by being in a constant state of innovation and change, offering a complete package of services, and focusing on excellent customer service.

Planning and Administration Competency

Though plans typically have to be changed along the way, planning is nevertheless important for entrepreneurial companies. Nearly 80 percent of successful entrepreneurs put their plans in writing. Their planning horizon is relatively short. Half the time it covers less than three years. Written monthly plans that cover periods of 12 to 24 months are common. As the time frame grows longer, the plans tend to become more general; for instance, they may merely state annual goals.

Administering the plan is important, too. For example, staffing activities can be key during the start-up phase. When funds are scarce and the company has no track record, attracting top-notch employees is difficult. Founders often do most of the crucial work themselves. But to grow, they soon must hire new talent. Once the talent has been brought on board, successful entrepreneurs tie a portion of management compensation to performance against the plan, on a monthly or quarterly basis. They also use the plan to work with employees to set job performance standards.

Recall the previous Strategic Action Competency on Daniel Driesenga. He described the best business tip and advice he received in these words:

Do your homework prior to starting the business. Make sure the market truly needs your service or product. Finally, make sure you can differentiate your service or product from the competition in a way that is beneficial to the customer. Stay focused on your goals, but be flexible enough to modify your business plan to match what the market is truly asking for. As evidence of why this is important: 75 percent of my firm's revenue today is from services we did not offer in my original business plan.[21]

Teamwork Competency

Successful entrepreneurs are extremely hard working and task oriented, but they aren't lone wolves—one person can do only so much alone. Unless they can build effective teams, their organizations' growth will eventually reach a limit. Successful entrepreneurs are self-starters who usually support subordinates and their programs enthusiastically. Entrepreneurs also maintain good relationships with their venture partners.

> **The Competent Manager**
>
> *"Surround yourself with the best managers and advisers. Communicate, challenge your team with new ideas and trust in their judgment. Thank and reward your team as often as possible."*
>
> Michael C. Hemphill
> Founder and CEO
> Michael Christopher
>   Designs of Delaware

The study of entrepreneurs previously described found that the majority of successful companies had a particularly effective top-management team. Only 3 percent of these CEOs acted alone in the top-management role. Such teams tended to be small, with 67 percent ranging in size from three to six managers, and diverse in terms of functional background. Team balance and innovation were achieved by mixing people who had previously worked closely together with people who hadn't. These management teams all used a collaborative decision-making style.

Communication Competency

For a budding entrepreneur with an idea and ambition, but little else to work with, being able to communicate effectively is essential to gaining the cooperation and support needed to turn a vision into reality.[22]

The communication that occurs in larger companies often entails speeches, written reports, formal proposals, and scheduled reviews. In new ventures, much communication is face to face, informal, and unscheduled. All of the interpersonal communication concepts and skills discussed in Chapter 16, Organizational Communication, apply as much to the entrepreneur as to a manager in a large organization.

Self-Management Competency

You may be wondering whether you have what it takes to be a successful entrepreneur. Obviously, no one can predict your success as a potential entrepreneur. The characteristics that many entrepreneurs have in common—including family background, motivation, and personality traits—may give you a rough idea of your potential. To learn more, complete the questionnaire presented in the following Self-Management Competency feature. Northwestern Mutual Life Insurance Company in Milwaukee prepared this questionnaire to help you and others like you to get an idea of whether you might have a head start or a handicap if you go into business for yourself.[23]

SELF-MANAGEMENT COMPETENCY

Your Entrepreneurial Quotient

Begin with the score of zero. Add or subtract from your score as you respond to each item.

1. Significantly high numbers of entrepreneurs are children of first-generation U.S. citizens. If your parents were immigrants, add 1. If not, subtract 1. _____
2. Successful entrepreneurs were not, as a rule, top achievers in school. If you were a top student, subtract 4. If not, add 4. _____
3. Entrepreneurs were not especially enthusiastic about participating in group activities in school. If you enjoyed group activities—clubs, team sports, and so on—subtract 1. If not, add 1. _____
4. Studies of entrepreneurs show that, as youngsters, they often preferred to be alone. Did you prefer to be alone as a youngster? If yes, add 1. If no, subtract 1. _____
5. If you started an enterprise during childhood—lemonade stands, family newspapers, greeting card sales—or ran for elected office at school, add 2 because enterprise usually appears at an early age. If you didn't initiate enterprises, subtract 2. _____
6. Stubbornness as a child seems to translate into determination to do things your own way—certainly a hallmark of proven entrepreneurs. So, if you were a stubborn child, add 1. If not, subtract 1. _____
7. Caution may involve an unwillingness to take risks, a handicap for those embarking into previously uncharted territory. Were you cautious as a youngster? If yes, subtract 4. If no, add 4. _____
8. If you were daring, add 4. _____
9. Entrepreneurs often speak of pursuing different paths—despite the opinions of others. If the opinions of others matter to you, subtract 1. If not, add 1. _____
10. Being bored with a daily routine is often a precipitating factor in an entrepreneur's decision to start an enterprise. If an important motivation for starting your own enterprise would be changing your daily routine, add 2. If not, subtract 2. _____
11. If you really enjoy work, are you willing to work long nights? If yes, add 2. If no, subtract 6. _____
12. If you would be willing to work "as long as it takes" with little or no sleep to finish a job, add 4. _____
13. Entrepreneurs generally enjoy their activity so much that they move from one project to another—nonstop. When you complete a project successfully, do you immediately start another? If yes, add 2. If no, subtract 2. _____
14. Successful entrepreneurs are willing to use their savings to start a project. If you would be willing to spend your savings to start a business, add 2. If not, subtract 2. _____
15. If you would be willing to borrow from others, too, add 2. If not, subtract 2. _____
16. If your business failed, would you immediately work to start another? If yes, add 4. If no, subtract 4. _____
17. If you would immediately start looking for a good paying job, subtract 1. _____
18. Do you believe entrepreneurship is "risky"? If yes, subtract 2. If no, add 2. _____
19. Many entrepreneurs put long-term and short-term goals in writing. If you do, add 1. If you don't, subtract 1. _____
20. Handling cash flow can be crucial to entrepreneurial success. If you believe that you have more knowledge and experience with cash flow than most people, add 2. If not, subtract 2. _____
21. Entrepreneurial personalities seem to be easily bored. If you are easily bored, add 2. If not, subtract 2. _____
22. Optimism can fuel the drive to press for success. If you're an optimist, add 2. If you're a pessimist, subtract 2. _____

Interpretation

A *score of 35 or more*: You have everything going for you. If you decide to become an entrepreneur, you ought to achieve spectacular success (barring acts of God or other variables beyond your control).

A *score of 15 to 34*: Your background, skills, and talents give you an excellent chance for success in starting your own business. You should go far.

A *score of 0 to 14*: You have a head start on the ability and/or experience

PLANNING ESSENTIALS FOR ENTREPRENEURS

3. Outline the planning essentials for potential entrepreneurs.

The Business Plan

Before starting a business, entrepreneurs who are successful typically plan more carefully than those who fail.[24] One tool that helps them do so is the business plan. A **business plan** *describes the basic idea that is the foundation for the start-up and outlines how that idea can be turned into reality*. Table 5.1 shows the major components of a business plan for new ventures with a few of the guidelines for developing each component. Chapters 7, 8, and 9 present a number of concepts, models, and tools that are useful in the planning process whether it is being done for a start-up or an established firm.

One of the challenges in developing a business start-up plan is to avoid exaggeration. Although somewhat tongue-in-cheek, we present four statements that are illustrative of this problem in statements by entrepreneurs within their business plans.

- "We took our best sales guess and divided by 2." *Reality:* We accidentally divided by 0.5.
- "We need only a 10 percent market share." *Reality:* So do the other 50 businesses getting funded.
- "Customers are clamoring for our product." *Reality:* We have not yet asked them to pay for it. Also, all of our current customers are relatives.
- "The project is 98 percent complete." *Reality:* To complete the remaining 2 percent will take as long as it took to create the initial 98 percent but will cost twice as much.[25]

In the remainder of this section, we address several issues that are central to planning for and implementing a new business.

The Competent Manager

"Develop a business plan, even if it is only one page. Outline all of your expected direct and indirect expenses needed for your business. A plan gives you a benchmark to look back on and improve, change and measure your progress."

Dave Ferkinhoff
Founder and CEO
Eastside Glass Company,
   Minnesota

Deciding to Buy, Start, or Franchise a Business

Prospective entrepreneurs who have the option to "start or buy" begin by weighing the advantages and disadvantages of each alternative. Sometimes, of course, the decision to start a business is made for them. If they don't have the financial resources necessary to purchase an existing company, they have no choice but to start their own. Even if they have the resources, suitable businesses may not be available. This situation is likely to be the case if an entrepreneur has a truly new idea.

Buy Strategy. If they have the resources, entrepreneurs often find that buying an existing company—perhaps one that the

Table 5.1 Essential Components of a Business Plan for New Ventures

I. Executive Summary

- What, how, why, where, and when must be summarized.

II. Business Description Component

- The name of the business.
- The potential and uniqueness of the new venture.

III. Marketing Component

- Convince investors that sales projections and competition can be met.
- Identify target market, market position, market share, pricing strategy.
- Evaluate all competition and state why and how you will be better than your competitors.
- Identify advertising plans with cost estimates.

IV. Location Component

- Describe the advantages of your location (zoning, tax laws, wage rates). List the production needs in terms of facilities (plant, storage, office space) and equipment (machinery, furnishings, supplies).
- Describe the access to transportation (for shipping and receiving) and labor.
- Indicate proximity to your suppliers.

V. Management Component

- Supply résumés of all key people in the management of your venture.
- Describe the legal structure of your venture (sole proprietorship, partnership, or corporation).
- Give information on how and how much everyone is to be compensated.

VI. Financial Component

- Describe the needed sources for your funds and the uses you intend for the money.
- Develop an estimated budget, cash flow statement, and profit and loss statement.
- Create stages of financing for purposes of allowing evaluation by investors at various points.

VII. Potential Critical-Risks Component

- Any potentially unfavorable industry-wide trends, such as price cutting by competitors.
- Design or manufacturing costs in excess of estimates.
- Sales projections not achieved.
- Product development schedule not met.
- Provide some alternative courses of action.

VIII. Milestone Schedule Component

- Develop a timetable or chart to demonstrate when each phase of the venture is to be completed.

IX. Appendix or Bibliography

Adapted from D. F. Kuratko, J. S. Hornsby, and F. J. Sabatine, The Breakthrough Experience: A Guide to Corporate Entrepreneurship (Muncie, IN): The Midwest Entrepreneurial Education Center, College of Business, Ball State University, 1999.

current owner is having difficulty managing—is a good idea. Leonard Riggio used this approach when he started Barnes & Noble in 1971. He secured a $1.2 million loan to purchase a failing 100-year-old bookstore on Fifth Avenue in New York City. Today, Barnes & Noble is the largest bookseller in the United States with 45,000 full- and part-time employees and more than 900 stores under the following names: Barnes & Noble, Bookstop, Bookstar, B. Dalton, Doubleday, and Scribner.[26]

Buying an existing firm is tricky and may involve considerable risk. The seller may not reveal some hidden problems—and may not even be aware of others. Also, many a new owner has thought that he or she was buying goodwill, only to have the previous owner open a competing firm and lure away the established clientele. A prospective buyer is wise to specify, in the purchase agreement, restrictions limiting the previous owner's ability or right to compete with the new owner. Such restrictions may limit the types of businesses that the previous owner can operate in a certain area and/or for a stipulated period of time.

Learning about businesses available for purchase and negotiating the purchase agreement often require the assistance of experts. Bankers, accountants, attorneys, and other professionals may be aware of an opportunity to buy a business before it is publicly announced. A business broker may help the prospective owner find a firm and act as intermediary for the sale. Usually, an attorney prepares or reviews the sale documents.

Start-Up Strategy. When deciding what types of business to own, people should begin by examining their competencies and the contacts they can bring to their possible ventures. Prospective entrepreneurs should carefully examine factors such as expected revenue, initial investment required, and intensity of competition. Such an analysis often turns up existing businesses that may be purchased. In addition to exploring the Internet, business magazines such as *Inc.*, *Entrepreneur*, and *Venturing* can be good sources of ideas for new ventures.

Franchise Strategy. A middle ground between starting a business and buying an existing business is to invest in and run a franchise. A **franchise** *is a business operated by someone (the franchisee) to whom a franchiser grants the right to market a good or service.* The franchisee pays a franchise fee and a percentage of the sales to the franchiser. In return, the franchisee often receives financial help, training, guaranteed supplies, protected market, and technical assistance in site selection, accounting, and operations management. McDonald's, Domino's Pizza, and Jiffy Lube, to name a few, all use franchises to market their products. Whoever enters a franchise agreement obtains a brand name that customers know. However, franchisees are their own bosses only to a degree. They can't run their businesses as they please. They have to conform to standards set by a franchiser, pay a fee to the franchiser, and often they must buy the franchiser's goods and services. But many people want to operate a franchise in the first place for these very reasons.

Other Strategic Options. Other strategic options the prospective entrepreneur may consider are suggested in the following questions.

- Is there a way that I can begin the enterprise in stages or with a limited investment?
- Can I run the business at first from my home?
- Can I continue working for someone else and put in time on my own business after hours?
- To what extent can I draw on relatives to help me, perhaps simply by answering the phone while I work at my regular job?

Assessing Affordable Loss

Successful entrepreneurs often use the **principle of affordable loss**—*the conscious determination of the amount of resources (money, time, and effort) entrepreneurs are willing to commit to an idea, which, in turn, influences the choice of strategies and methods needed to generate early revenues.* This principle helps potential entrepreneurs resolve the tension between excessive analysis versus quick action. Analysis increases a new business's chance of success but may decrease the probability of creating a business in the first place. Ironically, too much information and analysis only leads to more uncertainty and doubt about the opportunity.

In contrast, a bias toward quick action increases the probability of creating a business but decreases the probability of success. The rush to market often results in flawed strategies, poor goods and services, and insufficient resources. The principle of affordable loss helps entrepreneurs minimize risks while following their opportunity.[27] The dilemma facing potential entrepreneurs may be summed up by this saying: "Paralysis by analysis and extinction by instinct."

The planning process and market assessment techniques described in Chapters 7 and 9 may be overlooked in planning for business ownership. Entrepreneurs may be so excited about their business ideas that they assume others will feel the same way. Their market research may consist of asking the opinions of a few friends or relatives about the salability of a product.

Finding Funds

Entrepreneurs are likely to overestimate their income and underestimate their costs. The new-venture plan should identify anticipated costs of opening the business (e.g., deposits, fixtures, and incorporation fees). It should also include a month-by-month projection of the cost of goods or services sold and the firm's operating expenses for the first one to three years.

The entrepreneur must plan for obtaining funds to handle expenses associated with the start-up phase that revenues can't initially cover. Getting financial support is one of the most important activities that differentiates people who just think about having their own business from those who actually start one.[28] Furthermore, the larger the amount of resources obtained, the better the odds are of being able to continue in business for the long term.[29]

Common sources of funds and support include (1) the entrepreneur and other members of the team, family, and friends; (2) financial institutions such as banks; (3) venture capital firms; (4) business angels; and (5) perhaps business incubators. **Venture capitalists** *provide equity (ownership) financing.* In contrast, banks and other financial institutions provide debt (loan) financing. Venture capitalists get their funds and profits back only if their equity stake (ownership shares) rises in value and if dividends are paid. In brief, venture capitalists become part owners of the business by providing funds. Venture capitalists are organized as formal businesses.

Because venture capitalists aren't subject to the same state and federal regulations as banks, they can take greater risks when making investments. Generally, venture capitalists expect their investments to provide returns of 25 to 35 percent annually. To increase the likelihood of this, they get much more actively involved in the businesses they fund than bankers do. Indeed, according to one recent study, venture capitalists spend 40 percent of their time monitoring businesses they have funded and serving as consultants or directors.[30] To get information about venture capitalists, you can contact investment research firms, venture capital clubs, and vFinance.com (http://www.vfinance.com/home), among other sources.

A **business angel** *is a private individual who invests directly in firms and receives an equity stake in return.* Often such a person acts as a business adviser to the founder. Business angels may make less stringent demands than do venture capitalists on controlling the actions of the entrepreneur. Angels often truly enjoy seeing a business grow and watching a start-up venture mature into a viable business. Business angel Norm Brodsky has had this experience many times as an entrepreneur himself and now enjoys supporting others. "Yes, making money is important. I wouldn't go into deals unless I thought I could get my capital back and make a good return. But I really don't do this type of investing for the money anymore. I'm more interested in helping people get started in business."[31]

A sound business plan is essential to demonstrate to potential lenders and investors the viability of the proposed enterprise. Once funding has been obtained, entrepreneurs need to provide their financial backers with timely information and establish a trust relationship with them. This approach tends to reduce the extent to which investors intrude into the business, and it enhances the likelihood of their reinvesting in the future.[32]

Going Global

Most new-venture entrepreneurs begin with a domestic focus. A growing number, however, establish their firms as global start-ups or enter the international market through export firms. Exporting by small-business firms in the United States accounts for 31 percent of total merchandise and service export sales. The number of small-business firms engaging in export sales has more than tripled since 1987.[33] Because going global poses some special challenges to management, this strategic decision should be made only after very careful study and analysis. Figure 5.2 depicts the key factors affecting the decision about whether to establish a domestic or global start-up. Specific questions include the following[34]:

1. Are the best human resources dispersed among various countries? If yes, it may be easier to operate as an international company than to convince potential employees to move to your hometown.
2. Would foreign financing be easier or more suitable? If yes, consider whether the advantages of foreign financing are sufficient to offset the advantages of relying on domestic sources to meet other resource needs.

Figure 5.2   Factors That Favor a Global Start-Up

3. Do target customers require a venture to be international? If yes, a global approach may be necessary to acquire a reasonable share of the market.
4. Will worldwide communication lead to quick responses from competitors in other countries? If yes, the best domestic defense may be an international offense.
5. Will worldwide sales be required to support the venture? If initial expenses (e.g., R&D, manufacturing) will be high, worldwide sales may be necessary to generate sufficient revenue to support the venture.
6. Will changing the government policies, procedures, product designs, and advertising strategies of your established domestic company be more difficult than building a globally effective firm from the beginning?

Managing a Family Business

Family-owned businesses are an integral part of the U.S. economy.[35] Unfortunately, a family business too often results in family feuds, which can destroy both the family and the business. For the employees of such a firm, getting caught in the cross fire is an occupational hazard that no one really knows how to prevent.[36] Family feuding often leaves employees wondering whether to look for new employment. Karen Langley (not her real name) explains why she eventually left the small family-owned company that she once worked for. The father, his sons, and their cousins fought constantly over the business, engaging in behavior that could best be described as back-stabbing. "It was very uncomfortable," she says. Distrust within the family was high, and it eventually spread beyond the family. One family member began accusing employees of stealing and began lurking around trying to watch everyone. "It really became impossible for me to stay there," Langley explained.[37]

Not every family business has these problems, of course. Janice Bryant Howroyd started her family business, ACT*1 Personnel Services, in part to serve her family. It is headquartered in Torrance, California, with 67 offices nationwide. She employs eight brothers, sisters, nieces, and nephews who handle everything from marketing and accounting to technology. Her three children own 49 percent of the $20 million business (mom owns the other 51 percent).[38]

Figure 5.3 outlines the interlocking set of recommendations that increase the likelihood of a successful family business and one that will prosper from one generation to the next. These recommendations include the following.

1. *Settle conflicts as they come up.* If a family member does something on the job that makes another angry, correcting the problem requires that it be brought into the open quickly. This requires the use of the communication and teamwork

Figure 5.3   Recommendations to Ensure a Successful Family Business

Clear Job Responsibilities and Authority Relationships

Explicit Hiring Criteria for Family Members

Commitment to Resolving Conflicts Quickly

Plan for Management Transitions

Use of Outside Advisers/Directors

competencies. Particularly problematic is how to balance the need to make decisions that acknowledge both economic (rational) criteria and family obligation criteria. Various family members may feel differently about the importance of these two sets of criteria. This makes disagreements difficult to resolve through consensus if thought has not been given in advance as to how conflicts will be resolved quickly.

2. *Decide who is responsible for what and who has authority.* Jobs in family businesses probably shouldn't be too narrowly defined. Families should recognize each other's areas of expertise to determine who is best able to make decisions in various areas. Moreover, the types of decisions to be addressed by the family as a whole should be identified in advance.

3. *Agree on the hiring criteria to be used before considering any particular family member.* Being a daughter, son, spouse, uncle, etc., should not be enough. The competencies to ensure successful performance in the particular job must be present. It is better to experience the "hard feelings" that may come from not hiring a family member than the much greater harm to the business and "fights" involved in firing an unmotivated or incompetent family member.

4. *Use a board of advisers or board of directors to review and recommend key courses of action.* The outside advisers or board members can be especially helpful in providing guidance and a fresh perspective when assessing options.

5. *Develop a legal agreement.* It might address such issues as succession issues for management transitions when the current head of the business steps down or dies; the conditions for disposing of or reallocating the equity in the business; policies for the determination of salary levels, bonuses, and dividend payment; and how a decision will be made on whether and when to sell the business.

The effective use of a board of directors (or advisers) can assist a family business in forming and implementing all of the recommendations presented. Of course, boards of directors are useful for all private companies, not just family businesses. When operating well, the greatest advantages of such boards include (1) providing unbiased and unflinching advice; (2) forcing the top executives to focus on short-term and long-term goals, not just day-to-day operational issues; and (3) serving as a source of specialty advice, contacts, and business referrals.

The following Planning & Administration Competency provides a snapshot of how Dennis Gertmenian, the CEO, chairman, and founder of Ready Pac Produce Inc., has benefited from a board of directors. Gertmenian founded the produce-packaging company, headquartered in Irwindale, California, in 1969 and remains its sole owner. Today, the firm has about 2,500 employees. The five-person board of directors was established in 1982.[39]

PLANNING & ADMINISTRATION COMPETENCY

Ready Pac Produce's Board

Dennis Gertmenian, the founder and CEO of Ready Pac Produce, comments: "I was on the floor and in the plants. I wasn't taking the time to formally structure some of the areas of my company that needed atten-tion from a long-term point of view, such as: What are we doing with our banking relationship a year from now? What is our strategic plan? I had a plan, but it was in my mind, not written down." The board helped Gertmenian to systematically and thoughtfully address these and many other issues over the years.

In more than one case, the Ready Pac board has given him advice that caused him to reverse decisions that were on track to completion. Consider this example. Gertmenian told the board of the need to expand Ready Pac's operations with a new processing plant. He hired a project manager and entered into negotiations with the town of Soledad, California, to construct the plant there. He signed an economic development agreement with the town that gave him a discount on land in exchange for bringing a certain number of jobs to the area.

When he presented the deal to the board, one member asked a question that Gertmenian hadn't considered: "Weren't there any existing plants in the area that he could buy for less than it would cost to build one?" It turned out there were, and if Ready Pac moved into one in nearby Salinas, the cost would be half that of building a plant in Soledad. Also, the facility would be ready in a quarter of the time. It was a smart business decision, but not an easy one to explain to the Soledad local politicians. Ready Pac would have been the town's largest employer. "That was one of the toughest business calls I've ever made in my life," says Gertmenian. The board hasn't flinched from other tough calls and neither has Gertmenian.

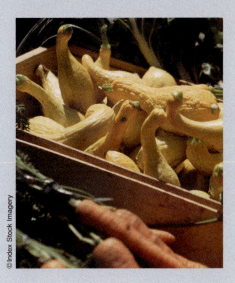
© Index Stock Imagery

CORPORATE INTRAPRENEURSHIP

Corporate intrapreneurship *refers to the fostering of entrepreneurial behavior within established companies to produce growth and profits.* Such behavior is essential for long-term survival. Once considered a contradiction in terms, corporate intrapreneurship has become widely accepted in successful companies, such as 3M, Intel, and Coca-Cola.[40]

Consider for a moment why an organization exists. It has a mission and goals to be accomplished, which require the efforts of more than one person. At the very least, a business has a long-term goal of satisfying customers so that it can become and remain profitable. Fundamental to organizing is dividing up the work. Managers may think that they have organized successfully when they have brought different people together, minimized conflict, increased stability, and reduced uncertainty. But they may overlook the effects of those organizing efforts on entrepreneurial tendencies. Is the new climate conducive to change? Will disruption be tolerated? Is redirection possible?

Large organizations are often formally structured for efficiency and operate through bureaucratic principles (see Chapter 2). Their managers may run operations in such a way that the same activities will continue indefinitely into the future. Obviously, this approach often is at odds with innovation and change. Employees come to take the working environment for granted, and individual efforts to foster change may be met with resistance. What then can be done to encourage entrepreneurship when a company needs to be revitalized? The answer lies in changing—perhaps even inciting a revolution in—an organization's practices. One way to do so is for the company to support intrapreneurs.

4. State the role of intrapreneurs and how organizations can foster intrapreneurship.

> **The Competent Manager**
>
> *"At P&G, we think of creativity not as a mysterious gift of the talented few but as the everyday task of making nonobvious connections—bringing together things that don't normally go together."*
>
> Craig Wynett
> General Manager of Future Growth
> Procter & Gamble

Intrapreneurs

An **intrapreneur** *is someone in an organization who champions turning new ideas into profitable realities.*[41] An example of intrapreneurship was the creation of CNNFN, which is CNN's financial news station. In that case, Lou Dobbs took the lead. He championed getting the station up and running. Dobbs also serves as the news anchor for the channel's daily financial news program, *Lou Dobbs Moneyline.*[42]

Not every employee can become a successful intrapreneur. Intrapreneurship requires unusually well-developed strategic action, teamwork, and communication competencies.

The person who is going to establish a new intrapreneurial venture must have a dream. Yet this dream, almost of necessity, is going to be at odds with what the rest of the organization is doing. So, to establish the new venture, the individual will have to sell that dream to others while simultaneously challenging the organization's beliefs and assumptions. Having successfully communicated a dream that others buy into, developing the venture requires that the intrapreneur build a team to work on the venture, crossing departmental lines, structures, and reporting systems. Intrapreneurial activities can cause some disruption, particularly in large organizations where each manager's "turf" has been staked out carefully over the years, so being diplomatic and avoiding win–lose conflicts is essential. Even organizational diplomats aren't immune to the frustrations that occur throughout the establishment of any new intrapreneurial venture. Thus, a strong support team is needed to carry the intrapreneur through endless trials and tribulations.

Fostering Intrapreneurship

Top management can foster an intrapreneurial culture by eliminating obstacles and providing incentives for intrapreneurship.[43] Organizations that redirect themselves through innovation have the following characteristics.

- *Commitment from senior management.* This commitment must include a willingness to tolerate failure. Top managers must regularly communicate their commitment to intrapreneurial activities—and back their words with actions.
- *Flexible organizational design.* Intrapreneurial organizations are designed for fast action. Management gives information—and the authority to make decisions—to those best positioned to react to changing market conditions. These people often are first-line managers.
- *Autonomy of the venture team.* Closely aligned with flexibility is maintaining a hands-off policy in day-to-day management of the team charged with implementing an innovation. Successful intrapreneurs usually are allowed considerable leeway in their actions.
- *Competent and talented people who exhibit entrepreneurial behaviors and attitudes.* A willingness to volunteer isn't sufficient reason to assign someone to a venture team—that person also must be competent in that or a related area. Competent volunteers usually have experience in, or have received training for, new-venture creation. Some companies conduct formal training programs; others establish mentor or coaching relationships. Even so, most intrapreneurs have experienced at least one failure before achieving successes that more than offset early losses.
- *Incentives and rewards for risk taking.* Intrapreneurs may not be willing to risk their careers and undergo the frustration of forcing change only for the satisfaction of giving life to their ventures. The developers of successful ventures should be generously compensated. Intrapreneurship should not be a dead-end activity; rather, it should be linked to an identifiable career path of advancement.
- *An appropriately designed control system.* Nothing is more stifling to an intrapreneurial activity than excessive bureaucratic controls. Nevertheless, despite the potential contradiction between strong controls and the intrapreneurial spirit, senior management can't give up its accountability for new-venture projects. Controlling internal innovations means collecting and analyzing data that enable management to predict, to a reasonable degree, where the new-venture team is headed. It also involves ensuring that the team understands the difference between intrapreneurial behavior and irresponsible risk taking.

Skunkworks are *islands of intrapreneurial activity within larger organizations.* The subculture within a skunkworks is similar to that in many incubator organizations. Formal rules and procedures are ignored in favor of experimentation and innovation. Violations of normal policies and rules are tolerated by top management, however, only as long as the team stays focused on helping the company bring new products and services to market ahead of competitors.[44] As is true for stand-alone new ventures, tying performance to rewards can keep a skunkworks team focused on its goal. Incentives should reward its cooperation with other parts of the organization and those in units that cooperate with and support the intrapreneurial project. Finally, in order for intrapreneurial activities to occur, top management must provide appropriate leadership. People generally are recruited to intrapreneurial activities by leaders who support norms and values that foster innovative activity.

Of course, a large organization isn't likely to support a particular skunkworks operation forever. If the effort succeeds, operations will be formalized, and the team might become the nucleus around which a new division is formed. If the effort fails to meet expectations, it might be closed down. A third possibility is to spin off the skunkworks and allow it to operate as a separate subsidiary. This approach allows the parent organization to obtain a return on its investment while keeping the entrepreneurial spirit alive.

CHAPTER SUMMARY

Entrepreneurial activity, whether through new business start-ups or corporate entrepreneurship, is one of the keys to long-term employment growth and rising standards of living.

1. Explain the role of entrepreneurs and how external factors impact their ventures.

Entrepreneurs are people who create new business activity in the economy. If they do so by starting a new company, entrepreneurs are also small-business owners. Other entrepreneurs create new business activity within large organizations. Often the reasons that entrepreneurs give for starting their own companies are to be their own bosses and have more control over their lives. When they start their companies, the goal of many entrepreneurs is for the business to grow slowly. When their companies grow rapidly for a sustained period of time, however, they are considered to be more successful. Rapid technological change, low interest rates, and high immigration rates all stimulate entrepreneurial activity. Local conditions that meet the needs of entrepreneurs—such as a good labor force and easy networking—also can stimulate entrepreneurial activity.

2. Describe the personal attributes that contribute to entrepreneurs' success.

Personal attributes of entrepreneurs include the need for achievement, desire for independence, self-confidence, and willingness to make personal sacrifices. These attributes often are developed early in life and seem to be shaped greatly by the family environment. Having a parent who was an entrepreneur and being involved in entrepreneurial activities increase the likelihood that a child will become an entrepreneur. Entrepreneurs usually are technically proficient in areas related to their businesses. Managerial competencies are as important for entrepreneurs as they are for other managers. Self-management, strategic action, planning and administration, teamwork, and communication competencies are especially important for entrepreneurs.

3. Outline the planning essentials for potential entrepreneurs.

Entrepreneurs can improve their chances for success by creating a business plan and following it. A few of the questions a prospective entrepreneur must consider include the following: (1) Have I developed a business plan that addresses all of the key issues? (2) Should I buy, start, or franchise a business? (3) What is my level of affordable loss? (4) How much will it cost, and where will I obtain the start-up funds? (5) Should I start a domestic or global organization? (6) What is involved in running a successful family business? Operating a family business leads to some unique opportunities and some special problems. Failure to manage them can spell doom for the company as well as the family.

4. State the role of intrapreneurs and how organizations can foster intrapreneurship.

Intrapreneurship involves turning ideas into marketable products and services within large organizations. Fostering intrapreneurship and successfully marketing new ventures require a commitment by top management, flexible organizational structures, autonomy of the venture team, competent and talented intrapreneurs, incentives and rewards for risk taking, and appropriate control systems. To encourage innovation and prevent formal rules and procedures from interfering with the development of new ideas, large organizations often set up skunkworks. Skunkworks activities are less formalized, and they usually have unique subcultures.

QUESTIONS FOR DISCUSSION and COMPETENCY DEVELOPMENT

1. "Opportunities rarely fall into an entrepreneur's lap; they must be discovered or created."[45] How did Carolyn Minerich of Carmin Industries discover or create her entrepreneurial opportunity?

2. What personal resources, other than money, did Carolyn Minerich have that were vital to the success of Carmin Industries?

3. How can a business incubator improve the chances of a new venture's success?

4. Is a small-business owner the same as an entrepreneur? Explain.

5. The self-management competency is said to be the most fundamental of all of the competencies needed to be a successful entrepreneur. Why is that thought to be the case?

6. Complete the "entrepreneurial quotient" questionnaire within the chapter if you have not done so. Do you think your entrepreneurial quotient is a reasonably accurate representation of whether you might have a head start or handicap if you go into business for yourself? Explain.

7. Why might an individual prefer to start a franchise business rather than launch an entirely new business?

8. Teamwork is important to any small business, including a family business. What are some of the special problems that family businesses seem to experience when it comes to working together as a team? Develop a short list of recommendations for families that want to maintain a positive team atmosphere.

CASE FOR COMPETENCY DEVELOPMENT

KINK BMX

Aaron Zack Phillips, the SBA Young Entrepreneur of the Year in 2002, is leaving his tracks on the American small-business scene. In this case, they are bicycle tracks. Phillips is the creator and owner of Kink BMX, a manufacturer and distributor of BMX bicycle parts and related accessories.

Phillips' work ethic surfaced early. His first job was as a paperboy at age 12, teaching him responsibility and money management. During the next four years, he worked several part-time positions at Burger King, Wendy's, and a local family restaurant. At 16, still in school, he was able to juggle a schedule that allowed him to work two part-time jobs totaling eight hours a day. By 18, he was the assistant manager for the lumber department at a home improvement store. He was responsible for payroll, scheduling, and inventory.

Phillips, who is now 26, started Kink in his hometown of Rochester, New York, when he was 16. A growing frustration with constantly breaking BMX bicycle parts helped him to spot a market need for more reliable components. Inquiring at a local machine shop to see if the parts could be made stronger, he determined to manufacture and sell his own at competitions and skate parks. In the summer of 1994, he sent for a media kit from a trade magazine and worked out an advertising budget, allowing him to sell the products from his apartment through mail orders.

At the age of 19, Phillips was offered a sales management position in North Carolina at Play Clothing, a clothing distribution company in the BMX industry. Negotiations led to Play becoming a distributor of Kink products, allowing Phillips to use the resources of an established wholesaler—a huge step.

Phillips left Play after a year to open a retail skateboard shop in Winston-Salem, North Carolina, and learn about business plans, the cost of goods, inventory control, profit margins, and markups. A year later, he moved back to Rochester, to oversee the manufacturing of the Kink product line. At the same time, he opened two other distribution companies to cover the Midwest and California.

As Kink grew, Phillips brought on a full-time employee to help him sell directly to retail shops and hired several part-timers to help with packaging. It wasn't long before he increased his staff to include a full-time advertising/Internet professional, a team manager, two salespersons, and two warehouse workers. In addition to these six employees, Kink employs five promotional bicycle riders who are paid on a contract fee basis.

The U.S. Small Business Administration has been instrumental in the growth of Kink. Mary B. Capone, vice president at JP Morgan Chase Bank in Rochester, said Phillips was originally turned down by Chase's Small Business Financial Services Group when he applied for his first business line of credit. His application failed in the normal channel of credit scoring. The local branch then asked Capone to look at the application and see if it would qualify with SBA's backing. She scheduled a personal call with Phillips and proceeded to secure an SBA guaranty for a $75,000 credit line under the then new pilot program, Community Express, which Chase operates under the Community Development Group's commercial lending unit.

The credit line was renewed in 2001, with a $40,000 loan and a 50 percent guaranty under SBA Express. Kink did not require additional technical assistance under the Community Express program. These funds were used to purchase the Blackout Distribution line from a German manufacturer, further diversifying the Kink line and offering another bike frame at a lower price.

Capone states: "What impressed me most about Phillips was his sense of business and his work ethic—here was a young man running a half-million-dollar company. We discussed his passion for the product, how he started the business (as a hobby, out of a backpack), and how dedicated he was not only to marketing his product—but to marketing upstate New York and Rochester in particular. On every mailing, logo, brochure, and marketing tool, 'Rochester Made Means Quality Made, is printed, along with archival prints of High Falls and Rochester."

Since 1999, Phillips has doubled his company's growth annually with sales reaching nearly $1 million as of 2002. Phillips now does business outside the United States and sells his products through distributors in Europe, Canada, Australia, and Japan.[46]

Questions

1. How did external forces play a role in the success of Kink BMX?

2. What personal attributes of Aaron Phillips appeared to contribute to the start-up success of Kink BMX?

3. What competencies does Phillips appear to possess?

4. What factors were probably important in the decision to sell Kink BMX products abroad?

©Woodfin Camp Associates

Ethics and Stakeholder Social Responsibility

LEARNING OBJECTIVES

After studying this chapter, you should be able to:

1. State the importance of ethics for individual employees and organizations.

2. Describe four forces that influence the ethical behavior of individuals and organizations.

3. Describe three approaches that people use when making ethical judgments.

4. Explain stakeholder social responsibility and how it influences managers' ethical decisions.

Chapter Outline

Preview Case: Nortel Networks' Code of Business Conduct

IMPORTANCE OF ETHICS

SHAPING ETHICAL CONDUCT

    Cultural Forces
    Legal and Regulatory Forces
    Organizational Forces
    Global Awareness Competency: Nortel Networks'
        Worldwide Rules on Bribes and Kickbacks
    Individual Forces
    Self-Management Competency: Douglas Durand's Journey

MAKING ETHICAL JUDGMENTS

    Utilitarian Approach
    Moral Rights Approach
    Communication Competency: State Farm Insurance Privacy Policy
    Justice Approach
    Combining Ethical Approaches

STAKEHOLDER SOCIAL RESPONSIBILITY

    Stakeholders
    Strategic Action Competency: Nortel Networks'
        Commitments to Stakeholders
    Stakeholder Pressures
    Protecting the Natural Environment
    Finding Win–Win Solutions
    Evaluating Social Performance

Chapter Summary

Key Terms and Concepts

Questions for Discussion and Competency Development

Case for Competency Development: Larry Hansen Speaks Out

Exercise for Competency Development: What Is Your Call?

The following is taken from a portion of Nortel Networks' *Code of Business Conduct*.

New ways of organizing people and work within Nortel Networks are giving each of us more decision-making responsibility. Given the complexity and constantly changing nature of our work and our world, no book of hard-and-fast rules—however long and detailed—could ever adequately cover all the dilemmas people face. In this context, every Nortel Networks employee is asked to take leadership in ethical decision making.

In most situations, our personal values and honesty will guide us to the right decision. But in our capacity as employees and representatives of Nortel Networks, we must also always consider how our actions affect the integrity and credibility of the corporation as a whole. Our business ethics must reflect the standard of conduct outlined in this document—a standard grounded in the corporation's values and governing Nortel

Networks' relationships with all stakeholders.

Our decisions as to what is ethical business practice in Nortel Networks context must be guided by the seven core values that form the fundamental basis of our conduct as a business. From these statements stem a series of commitments that we as Nortel Networks employees make to each other, to shareholders, customers, suppliers, and the communities in which we do business.

Integrity means "wholeness"—it means that all the parts are aligned and work together. It means, for example, that each individual within the corporation is doing his or her best to live by the standard of business conduct outlined in this Code.

"Acting with integrity" also means that while we may not always be sure of every answer, we will not say one thing and then do another. We will not make promises that we have no intention of keeping or cannot be reasonably sure we will be able to keep. We will strive to the best of our ability to support all the commit-

ments that the corporation has made to conducting business in an honest and ethical manner.

When individuals choose to disregard the Code, we all could suffer from damage to the corporate reputation and the ensuing loss of customers, community and employee goodwill, and profitability. Serious violations of the standards may result in termination of employment. Actions that are against the law may be subject to criminal prosecution.

- **You** have a personal responsibility to make sure that all your words and actions live up to these statements.
- **You** have a responsibility to ask questions when you have doubts about the ethical implications of any given situation or proposed course of action.
- **You** have a responsibility to report any concerns about business practices within the corporation that may violate this *Code of Business Conduct*.[1]

IMPORTANCE OF ETHICS

1. State the importance of ethics for individual employees and organizations.

In the Preview Case, Nortel Networks sets forth a strong statement of the ethical business conduct expected and required of all of its employees. This statement is only one part of the comprehensive standards and expectations outlined in Nortel Networks' *Code of Business Conduct*. Throughout the chapter, we will note various aspects of this code. Nortel Networks is recognized as having a strong commitment to ethics and corporate social responsibility. The importance of ethics to Nortel Networks is suggested in one part of the introductory statement to its *Code of Business Conduct*:

> At Nortel Networks, we recognize the importance of credibility, integrity and trustworthiness to our success as a business. We are committed to upholding high ethical standards in all our operations, everywhere in the world. We believe in the principles of honesty, fairness, and respect for individual and community freedoms.[2]

Nortel Networks Corporation is a global provider of networking and communication services with offices and facilities in more than 150 countries. It is headquartered in Brampton, Ontario (Canada), which is near Toronto.

The importance of ethical issues facing managers and employees has been magnified in recent years due to the unethical and illegal conduct of some of the top executives in various major U.S. organizations, including Enron, Arthur Andersen, WorldCom, Global

Crossing, Tyco, and Adelphia. William George, former chairman and CEO of Medtronic, Inc., comments:

> Every generation has its examples of corporate thieves who break the law to reward themselves. This time around the excesses are not limited to a few. While the majority of corporate CEOs are honest leaders dedicated to building their companies, far too many got caught up in the quest for personal gain and wound up sacrificing their values and their stakeholders. Call it greed, because that's what it is. It threatens the very fabric of our system.[3]

The notorious unethical and often illegal practices by the top executives of such organizations have resulted in bankruptcies, massive financial losses for shareholders, and loss of jobs by employees. The losses in individual firms have spilled over to a general loss of trust in business leaders. In one recent poll, 71 percent of the public felt that the typical CEO is less honest and ethical than the average person. Seventy-two percent of those polled rated the moral and ethical standards of CEOs of major corporations as either fair or poor.[4] A variety of studies indicate that effective ethics programs and practices help companies achieve (1) stronger financial performance over the long run; (2) greater sales, brand image, and reputation; (3) more employee loyalty and commitment; (4) less vulnerability to activist pressure and boycotts; and (5) fewer or no fines, court-imposed remedies, and criminal charges.[5]

In this chapter, we briefly describe four forces that shape ethical conduct; including cultural forces, legal and regulatory forces, organizational forces, and individual forces. Next, we invite you to consider your own approach to ethical problems. You will discover how much your personal judgments are influenced by utilitarian thinking, a concern for moral rights, and a belief in maintaining a sense of justice. Then, we review the stakeholder approach to the management of corporate social responsibility.

Throughout the chapter, we address ways for encouraging, expecting, and enforcing ethical conduct. For example, recall the clearly stated personal ethical responsibilities set forth in Nortel Networks' *Code of Business Conduct*. Also, recall the clear message that "Serious violations of the standards may result in termination of employment."

SHAPING ETHICAL CONDUCT

In the most basic sense, **ethics** *is a set of values and rules that define right and wrong conduct.* These values and rules indicate when behavior is acceptable and when it is unacceptable. What is considered ethical may depend on the perspective from which ethical issues are considered. Figure 6.1 identifies the four basic forces that influence the ethical conduct of individuals and organizations. Rarely can the ethical implications of decisions or behaviors be understood by considering only one of these forces.

2. Describe four forces that influence the ethical behavior of individuals and organizations.

Cultural Forces

As discussed in Chapter 3, *culture* refers to the unique pattern of shared characteristics, such as values, that distinguish the members of one group of people from those of another. Uncertainty avoidance, power distance, individualism, and masculinity were among the characteristics highlighted. A significant part of what is considered ethical comes from cultural values and the specific norms and traditions that flow from them. Within the American culture, fundamental personal values that are often cited as central to individuals include[6]

- honesty,
- integrity,
- trustworthiness,
- respect for other people,

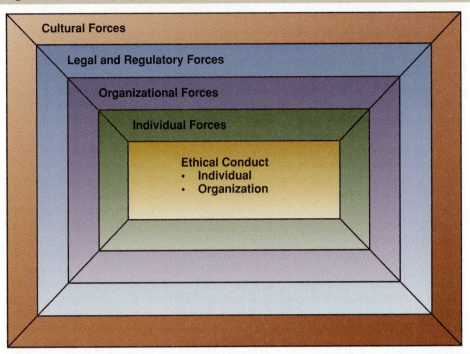

Figure 6.1   Shaping Ethical Conduct

Cultural Forces

Legal and Regulatory Forces

Organizational Forces

Individual Forces

Ethical Conduct
- Individual
- Organization

- self-respect,
- family,
- achievement,
- reliability,
- fairness, and
- loyalty.

A number of these values serve as anchors in ethical decision making and behavior. They reflect cultural ideals used to define ethical from unethical behaviors and decisions. For example, consider another of the comments by William George, the former chairman and CEO of Medtronics, Inc.:

> Our system of capitalism is built on investor trust—trust that corporate leaders and boards of directors will be good stewards of their investments and provide investors with a fair return. There can be no doubt that the leaders of these corporations, and possibly many more, have violated that trust. As a result, investors are losing confidence and withdrawing from the market. In the process, everyone is getting hurt, not just the perpetrators of the egregious acts.[7]

Clearly, George is emphasizing the personal and cultural values of honesty, integrity, and trustworthiness in his remarks. Other impacts of cultural forces will be noted throughout the remainder of this chapter.

Legal and Regulatory Forces

What a society interprets as ethical or unethical frequently ends up being expressed in laws, government regulations, and court decisions. **Laws** *are society's values and standards that are enforceable in the courts.* The legality of actions and decisions doesn't necessarily make them ethical, however. At one time, for example, U.S. organizations could legally discriminate against women and minorities in hiring and promotions. As a consensus developed that such discriminatory practices were unethical, laws such as the Civil Rights Act of 1964 were passed to stop the practices and ensure equal employment opportunities for all citizens. The legal concept of employment-at-will provides another example of the interplay between changing societal views and changes in the law. **Employment-at-will** *is a traditional common-law concept holding that employers are free to discharge employees for any reason at any time and that employees are free to quit their jobs for any reason at any time.* Historically, employers often dismissed employees without explanation (that is, "at will"). During the past 30 years, though, courts have modified the freewheeling notion that employees can be fired for any reason. Table 6.1[8] lists a few of the lawful and unlawful reasons for dismissing employees.

Table 6.1	Examples of Lawful and Unlawful Reasons for Dismissing Employees
Some Permissible Reasons	**Some Unacceptable Reasons**
■ Incompetence in performance that does not respond to training or to accommodation	■ Blowing the whistle about illegal conduct by the employer
■ Gross or repeated insubordination	■ Reporting Occupational Safety and Health Administration violations
■ Civil rights violations such as engaging in harassment	■ Filing discrimination charges with the Equal Employment Opportunity Commission or a state or municipal fair employment agency
■ Illegal behavior such as theft or physical violence	■ Filing unfair labor practice charges with the National Labor Relations Board or a state agency
■ Repeated lateness or unexcused absences	■ Engaging in union activities, provided there is no violence or unlawful behavior
■ Drug activity or drunkenness on the job	■ Complaining or testifying about violations of equal pay, wage, or hour law

When behavior is clearly unethical *and* illegal, employees also have clear knowledge of what's right and what's wrong. But in many areas of business practices, judgments about right and wrong fall within a gray area. How should employees behave when the laws are unclear or conflicting or when societal opinions have shifted and old laws are being questioned as unethical? Under these circumstances, employees must look to the standards, policies, and practices of their organization and to their personal values and beliefs.

During the past several years, a flurry of new laws and regulations have been passed within the United States at both the federal and state levels to reduce the discretion available to organizations and individuals as to what behaviors are both unethical and illegal. For example, the U.S. Congress enacted the Corporate and Criminal Fraud Accountability Act of 2002 in response to the numerous corporate scandals, such as those of Enron, WorldCom, Tyco, and Adelphia. It is part of the broader **Sarbanes-Oxley Act**, *which imposes rigorous auditing, financial disclosure, executive compensation, and corporate governance requirements on publicly traded companies.* The Sarbanes-Oxley Act does not merely reform and regulate corporate accounting practices—it has also created entirely new employment rights that expose both corporations and, in some cases, individual employees to civil and, under certain circumstances, even criminal liability.

Section 806 of the act creates a new federal cause of action designed to protect employees of publicly traded companies who act as corporate whistle-blowers. It protects employees who, among other things, "provide information, cause information to be provided, or otherwise assist in an investigation regarding any conduct which the employee reasonably believes constitutes" a violation of federal securities law, SEC regulations, or "any provision of Federal law relating to fraud against shareholders."[9] The act also contains a strict antiretaliation provision (Section 1107). It protects any individual from being retaliated against for providing any truthful information to a law enforcement officer in connection with the commission of a federal offense. Individuals who violate this provision by attempting to retaliate against any individual are subject to a fine and/or imprisonment of up to 10 years. Other provisions of this legislation make criminal various behaviors and decisions that previously would have been considered unethical, but not illegal.

Organizational Forces

Organizations influence employee actions both formally and informally. To provide formal guidance for employees, an organization can state clear policies that define ethical and unethical conduct. A **code of ethics** *states the principles that employees are expected to follow when acting on behalf of the organization.* Codes of ethics help employees understand the organization's norms and values, and they provide basic guidelines for deciding what behavior is acceptable. Additional formal guidance may be offered through training programs that describe difficult ethical situations that employees may face and offer advice about how to deal with them.

The basic informal source of guidance is top management's behavior, which demonstrates the ethical principles that are important to the organization. Unless top managers send very clear signals, employees can easily misinterpret what the organization values most. One survey of more than 4,000 employees found that 29 percent felt informal pressure to engage in conduct that violates their companies' business standards in order to meet profitability, sales, or productivity goals. About 25 percent reported that their managers looked the other way and ignored unethical conduct in order to achieve their goals.[10] New legislation and regulations, including criminal penalties, are likely to have some impact on reducing such informal pressures.

The Ethics Resource Center, headquartered in Washington, D.C., is a nonprofit, nonpartisan educational organization. Its mission is to be a leader in fostering ethical practices in individuals and organizations. To this end, it provides publications, videos, training, and consulting services to assist organizations in developing, implementing, and maintaining an ethical culture.[11] For example, several of its publications set forth the needed actions to ensure an ethical culture. A few of the recommended actions include the following[12]:

- *Create a formal ethics system.* The organization should create and implement a formal ethics system, including procedures and policies that explicitly define ethical expectations regarding employee behaviors to guide them in their day-to-day decision making. Examples of these systems include statements of values, codes of conduct, ethics policies and rules, ethics oversight committees, ethics surveys, employee "help lines," and other ethics management mechanisms.
- *Communicate ethical expectations.* Managers at all levels of the organization need to explicitly and implicitly communicate their expectations regarding employee behavior, reinforcing the explicit organizational expectations detailed through the formal ethics system and mechanisms. This includes the visible use of the ethics system in their own decision making and the requirement that subordinate employees do likewise.

The Competent Manager

"If your company is driven by core values that are strong—in our case that includes such values as integrity and fairness and respect and caring for people—those things can really bring out the best in your employee teams."

Joe Lee
CEO and Chairman
Darden Restaurants

Moral Rights Approach

The **moral rights approach** *holds that decisions should be consistent with fundamental rights and privileges (e.g., life, freedom, health, and privacy).* These rights are set forth in documents such as the first 10 amendments to the U.S. Constitution (the Bill of Rights) and the United Nation's Declaration of Human Rights.[26] A number of U.S. laws require managers and other employees to consider these rights as guides for decision making and behaviors.

Life and Safety. In the United States, many laws require businesses to comply with society's view of appropriate standards for quality of life and safety. Employees, customers, and the general public have the right *not* to have their lives and safety unknowingly and unnecessarily endangered. For example, this moral right in large part justifies the U.S. Occupational Safety and Health Act (OSHA) of 1970, which contains many requirements designed to increase the safety and healthfulness of work environments. Among other things, OSHA and its implementing regulations restrict the use of asbestos, lead-based paint, and various toxic chemicals in the workplace. Businesses operating in other countries often find that laws are less restrictive there, so they must choose whether to meet only the standards of the host country or exceed those legal requirements. General Motors chose to use a higher standard than required for its operations in Mexico. Although it wasn't legally required to do so, the company spent more than $10 million to install small stand-alone sewage treatment systems in towns throughout Mexico. According to Lee Crawford, a managing director working there, "It was just something we felt was the right thing to do. . . . Water is one of the biggest single problems in Mexico." As an indication of how important these projects were to that country, the Mexican government honored GM with its Aguila Azteca award for humanitarian service.[27]

Truthfulness. Employees, customers, shareholders, and the general public have the right *not* to be intentionally deceived on matters about which they should be informed. The classic legal concept of *caveat emptor*—"let the buyer beware"—used to be the defense for a variety of shady business practices. During the 1950s and 1960s, an increasingly aware public began to challenge the ethics of such a position. Shifting societal attitudes and values concerning *appropriate* behavior by businesses has led to a flood of U.S. consumer legislation. Today, quality improvement practices and customer-oriented practices make such an approach to customer relations risky. Nevertheless, the rapid speed of change inevitably means that there will always be opportunities legally to withhold information—and thereby deceive customers, shareholders, employees, and the general public.

Privacy. The moral right of citizens to control access to personal information about themselves and its use by government agencies, employers, and others was the basis for the U.S. Privacy Act of 1974. The act restricts the use of certain types of information by the federal government and limits those to whom this information can be released. The 1988 Video Privacy Protection Act is an example of a more specific law designed to ensure that privacy rights are respected. This act forbids retailers from disclosing video rental records without the customer's consent or a court order. For example, a customer who rents exercise videos from Blockbuster need not worry about getting on mailing lists for exercise equipment catalogs, fitness magazines, and the like.

With the availability of new information technologies (especially computers and surveillance equipment), enormous concern has been expressed about invasions of privacy.[28] A few of these privacy issues include drug testing, honesty testing, confidentiality of medical and psychological counseling records, monitoring of e-mail and work performed on computers, access to credit records, and the gathering and sale of personal information gleaned from the Internet.

Video monitoring is an example of the use of one technology that has become widespread, despite the negative reaction many people have to the idea of having everything they do recorded on tape. People react in a similar way when they hear about software programs designed to keep track of their accessing of Web sites via the Internet.

Due to legal requirements and in response to customer expectations, a number of companies have established specific privacy policies that are communicated to their customers on a regular basis. For example, the following Communication Competency feature presents a portion of the State Farm Insurance *Notice of Privacy Policy* that is distributed each year to its customers.[29]

COMMUNICATION COMPETENCY

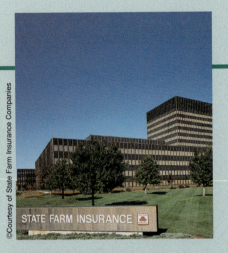

©Courtesy of State Farm Insurance Companies

State Farm Insurance Privacy Policy

We value you as a customer and take your personal privacy seriously. We will inform you of our policies for collecting, using, securing, and sharing nonpublic personal information ("customer information") the first time we do business and every year that you are a State Farm customer.

Our privacy principles:

■ We do not sell customer information.

■ We do not provide customer information to persons or organizations outside our State Farm family of companies who are doing business on our behalf, for their own marketing purposes.

■ We contractually require any person or organization providing products or services to customers on our behalf to protect the confidentiality of State Farm customer information.

■ We do not share customer medical information with anyone within the State Farm family of companies, unless you expressly authorize it, or unless your insurance policy contract with us permits us to do so.

■ We afford prospective and former customers the same protections as existing customers with respect to the use of personal information.

Types of information we may collect and how we gather it:

■ *From you.* On applications for our insurance, banking, and investment products, or on other forms, through telephone or in-person interviews, your State Farm agent, and our customer Response Center.

■ *From your transactions with us.* Such as your payment history, underwriting, and claim documents.

■ *From non-State Farm companies.* Such as your driving record and claim history.

■ *From consumer reporting agencies.* Such as your credit history.

Freedom of Conscience and Speech. Speech is one way for expressing matters of conscience. So freedom of speech is closely related to freedom of conscience. Employees have the right to refrain from carrying out orders that violate their moral or religious beliefs. They also have the right to criticize the ethics or legality of their employers' actions, as long as the criticisms are conscientious and truthful and do not violate the rights of others within or outside the organization.

The freedoms of speech and conscience have often been at the center of ethical debates associated with new media, such as the Internet. Should executives at Yahoo! accept advertisements from companies engaged in pornographic activity? Advertisements for pornographic products and services have long been banished from broadcasts of the major television networks. But the culture of the Internet supports aggressive adherence to principles of free speech. Permitting such advertising may be consistent with the principle of free speech for advertisers. However, parents whose children are exposed to pornography on the Web often express other concerns. Knowing of these concerns, a manufacturer of snacks that knows its logo might appear next to a pornography ad needs to think carefully about whether to advertise on that Internet site.[30]

As a guide to ethical decision making in organizations, the moral rights approach serves as an effective counterweight that protects society from overenthusiastic capitalists who strictly follow the utilitarian approach. However, as a guide to ethical behavior in organizations, the moral rights approach says more about what organizations should *avoid* doing—that is, violating the moral rights of employees, customers, and members of society—than it does about what *to* do. The justice approach provides more guidance in this regard.

Justice Approach

The **justice approach** *involves evaluating decisions and behavior with regard to how equitably they distribute benefits and costs among individuals and groups.*[31] To ensure just decisions and behavior, the proponents of this approach argue that three principles should be followed when designing management systems and making organizational decisions: the distributive justice principle, the procedural fairness principle, and the natural duty principle.

Distributive Justice Principle. The **distributive justice principle** *requires that individuals not be treated differently on the basis of arbitrarily defined characteristics.* It holds that (1) individuals who are similar in relevant respects should be treated similarly, and (2) individuals who differ in relevant respects should be treated differently in proportion to the differences between them. A legal regulation that supports the distributive justice principle is the U.S. Equal Pay Act of 1963. It made illegal the payment of different wages to women and men when their jobs require equal skill, effort, and responsibility and are performed under similar working conditions. Prior to the passage of this act, it was common for women to be paid at two-thirds the rate of men doing the same work. The practice of unequal pay for men and women doing equal work was a holdover from practices adopted during World War II, when many women entered the workforce to replace men who left the factories to go into the armed services. There is no suggestion that such discrepancies between men and women's pay for comparable positions have been eliminated. Betty Spence, president of the National Association of Female Executives, comments: "In my lifetime, there will still be a wage gap. It's up to women in senior positions to bring other women up or else it's not going to happen."[32]

Perceptions about what constitutes distributive justice also are behind recent concerns over the growing disparity between the compensation packages that CEOs receive and the pay levels of everyone else. Should the average daily compensation for CEOs be more than most workers make in an entire year? Is it fair for the average CEO's pay to be rising at a rate that is six or seven times the rate of increase for other workers? According to the distributive justice principle, these pay level rates of increase are ethical only if the contributions of a CEO are proportionately greater and if the value of the contributions has been increasing at a much faster rate than those of the average worker.[33]

Fairness Principle. The **fairness principle** *requires employees to support the rules of the organization as long as the organization is just (or fair) and employees have voluntarily accepted some benefits or opportunities in order to further their own interests.* Employees are then expected to follow the organization's rules, even though those rules might restrict their individual choices. For example, if an applicant for a store clerk position at 7–11 was informed that accepting a job offer would involve being video monitored, 7–11 could expect the employee to accept these conditions of employment. Under the fairness principle, both the organization and its employees have obligations and both should accept their responsibilities. Their mutual obligations can be considered fair as long as they were voluntarily agreed to, they were spelled out clearly, and they are consistent with a common interest in the survival of the organization.[34]

Perceptions of fairness often reflect people's reactions to the procedures used to make decisions. Acceptable processes lead to perceived *procedural justice*. A company's management practices are more likely to be perceived as fair when a formal process is in place for investigating employees' grievances and taking remedial actions, when needed.[35]

Natural Duty Principle. In exchange for certain rights, people must accept certain responsibilities and duties. The **natural duty principle** *requires that decisions and behavior be based on universal principles associated with being a responsible member of society.* Four universal duties are

- to help others who are in need or in jeopardy, provided that the help can be given without excessive personal risk or loss;
- not to harm or injure another;
- not to cause unnecessary suffering; and
- to support and comply with just institutions.

In exchange for accepting these duties or responsibilities, a person is entitled to certain rights. The natural duty principle complements the moral rights approach. For example, if a manager has the right to safety at work, as suggested by the moral rights approach, this right can best be ensured if employees also agree that they have a duty not to harm others. If everyone acted according to this principle, problems such as workplace violence would not occur. In addition, a manager's right to privacy should be complemented by a willingness to comply with privacy laws and regulations, as well as cultural norms regarding what constitutes invasions of privacy, in dealing with employees.

Combining Ethical Approaches

No approach to ethical decisions can be said to be the "best" approach. Each one has strengths and weaknesses.[36] Managers in many U.S. organizations regularly use the utilitarian approach when solving business problems. Consistent with this approach, which values the goals of efficiency, productivity, and profit maximization above all others, they consider issues of moral rights and justice only to the degree required by law. In many European countries, however, managers appear to be more likely to develop solutions that are relatively more consistent with the moral rights and justice approaches. These approaches give greater weight to long-term employee welfare than to quarterly profits. Although differences in cultural norms and values help explain some differences in how managers approach ethical decisions, there may be great variation among managers within any organization. Organizational cultures and differences in managers' personal perspectives help account for such differences.

Using all three approaches to ethical decision making increases the probability that decisions and behaviors will be judged as ethical by others holding a wide range of values and beliefs. Many organizational practices in the United States reflect solutions that were developed by managers who gave the most weight to the utilitarian approach but also believed that doing what was right was one way for the company to do well. Stakeholder social responsibility, as discussed in the next section, attempts to combine elements of all three ethical approaches.

STAKEHOLDER SOCIAL RESPONSIBILITY

Despite the preference for the utilitarian approach among many U.S. managers, most know that they also have many responsibilities for a wide range of activities. Even if they believe that the firm's financial considerations must always be given highest priority, they recognize that long-term success requires attending to the concerns and demands of different groups of people. A manager's job can be thought of as a series of attempts to address the concerns of these groups, or stakeholders.[37] Thus, **stakeholder social responsibility** *holds that managers and other employees have obligations to identifiable groups that are affected by or can affect the achievement of an organization's goals.*

4. Explain stakeholder social responsibility and how it influences managers' ethical decisions.

Three primary reasons often are suggested for embracing stakeholder social responsibility: (1) enlightened self-interest, (2) sound investment, and (3) interference avoidance.[38] Under the rationale of enlightened self-interest, management uses social responsibility to justify numerous decisions and actions. The general idea is that a better society creates a better environment for business. Under the rationale of sound investment, management believes that social responsibility has a positive effect on a company's net worth. As suggested in the opening section of this chapter, socially responsible firms, such as Johnson & Johnson, appear to have superior financial performance compared to those of less socially responsible firms over the long run.

The Competent Manager

"If you don't have honesty and integrity, you won't be able to develop effective relationships with any of your stakeholders."

Robert W. Lane
Chairman and CEO
Deere & Co.

Also, higher stock prices for socially responsible firms reduce the cost (interest rate) of capital and increase earnings. Under the rationale of interference avoidance, management aims to minimize control of company decisions by powerful stakeholders, such as government agencies and pressure groups. Industry self-regulation often is justified on the basis of interference avoidance.

Stakeholders

Individuals or groups that have interests, rights, or ownership in an organization and its activities are known as **stakeholders.** Those who have similar interests and rights are said to belong to the same stakeholder group. Customers, suppliers, employees, and shareholders are examples of primary stakeholder groups. Each has an interest in how an organization performs and interacts with them. These stakeholder groups can benefit from a company's successes and can be harmed by its mistakes. Similarly, an organization has an interest in maintaining the general well-being and effectiveness of stakeholder groups. If one or more stakeholder groups were to break their relationships with the organization, the organization would suffer.

For any particular organization, some stakeholder groups may be relatively more important than others. The most important groups—the primary stakeholders—are those whose concerns the organization must address to ensure its own survival. They directly impact the financial resources available to the firm. Secondary stakeholders are also important because they can take actions that can damage or assist the organization. Secondary stakeholders include governments (especially through regulatory agencies), unions, nongovernmental organizations (NGOs), activists, political action groups, and the media.

Figure 6.2 identifies the many primary and secondary stakeholders that may have an interest in a particular organization. Of course, the relative importance of each stakeholder group varies from one organization to the next and as issues come and go.

Figure 6.2   Common Stakeholders of Organizations

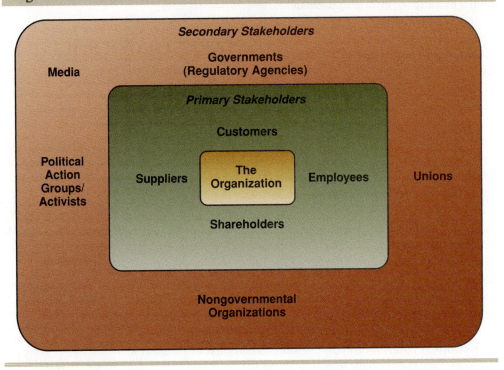

The following Strategic Action Competency feature reports on key sections of Nortel Networks' published statement of its commitments to primary stakeholders.[39] Throughout this chapter, we have used Nortel Networks to reveal some of the facets of a model comprehensive ethics program within a single organization.

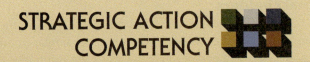

STRATEGIC ACTION COMPETENCY

Nortel Networks' Commitments to Stakeholders

This section outlines some of the key commitments that Nortel Networks makes to those with the most direct stake in the organization: its employees, shareholders, customers, and suppliers. It contains a lot of statements beginning with "Nortel Networks commits. . ." or "the corporation will. . . ."

Remember that the ethical conduct of "the corporation" is really the collective conduct of its employees, officers, and members of its board of directors. *Living the Commitments* provides specific guidelines on your role in making these statements more than just words.

To Employees. Nortel Networks values the contributions of all of its employees and treats each individual with respect. This includes safeguarding the confidentiality of employee records; respecting employee privacy—refraining from unnecessary intrusions; and supporting as far as possible employees' work-related aspirations. As a corporation, Nortel Networks is committed to informing employees quickly and fully on issues affecting them, and listening to their ideas and concerns.

The corporation strives to provide work that is satisfying and a work environment that is safe and pleasant. Wherever it operates in the world, the corporation offers salaries and benefits that are competitive and fair. The corporation provides employees with opportunities for continuing professional development.

In its hiring practices, Nortel Networks will be fair and equitable. Nortel Networks seeks to create a workforce that is a reasonable reflection of the diverse populations of the communities in which it operates. When the realities of the highly competitive global marketplace make it necessary for the corporation to downsize or phase out particular areas of business, Nortel Networks will respect the dignity of affected employees and ensure they are treated appropriately. Nortel Networks is committed to protecting and enhancing the health and safety of its employees.

To Shareholders. Profits are essential to the continued existence of the corporation and to the well-being of all who depend on it. The corporation seeks to provide value to shareholders, while maintaining financial prudence. Nortel Networks believes that shareholder value is delivered through satisfied and loyal customers, and that customer satisfaction is directly dependent on satisfied and effective employees. The corporation endeavors to act in what it perceives to be the shareholders' best interest, and informs them of major actions or decisions in a timely manner, in accordance with applicable laws.

To Customers. Customers deserve high-quality network solutions and services, including safe and environmentally responsible products. The business focus of all of the corporation's daily activities is to deliver market leadership through customer satisfaction, superior value, and product excellence. To maintain excellence through continuous improvement, the corporation invests substantial resources in research, design, and development of telecommunications products and services. The corporation maintains high ethical standards in all of its customer relationships, and upholds the Core Value: "We fulfill our commitments and act with integrity."

To Suppliers. Nortel Networks is fair in its choice of suppliers and honest in all business interactions with them. Purchasing decisions are made on the basis of such criteria as competitive price, quality, quantity, delivery, service, and reputation. The ethical and environmental standards and practices of suppliers also influence purchasing decisions. The objective is to procure those materials and services which will contribute most to the quality of products and the long-term benefit of the corporation.

Stakeholder Pressures

Each group of stakeholders has somewhat different expectations. That is, each cares more about some aspects of an organization's activities and less about others. The statements of Nortel Networks' commitments to stakeholders recognizes the different pressures by those it views with the primary stake in the organization—employees, shareholders, customers, and suppliers. In this and other chapters, we discuss the importance of primary and secondary stakeholders as managers identify and assess the many pressures and issues that must be considered in the decision-making process. Table 6.3 provides examples of these general types of pressures. All of these stakeholders are demanding to be treated ethically; with increasing pressures for truthfulness and fairness.

Protecting the Natural Environment

The protection of the natural environment is one of the key issue areas of growing concern and interest to a number of primary and secondary stakeholders. **Sustainable development** *involves conducting business in a way that protects the natural environment while making economic progress, thus meeting the needs of the present generation without compromising the ability of future generations to meet their own needs.*[40]

Norm Thompson, Inc., headquartered in Hillsboro, Oregon (near Portland), is a consumer specialty retailer of high-quality merchandise. It sells through mail-order catalogs, retail stores in Oregon, and its Web site. It has a specific environmental policy and is recognized as a leader in sustainable development. The firm states:

Norm Thompson is committed to having a positive impact on the environment. Our goal is to prove that sustainability is the right thing to do for the planet—and for commerce. We will, therefore, ensure that the choices we make in our day-to-day business take into account the environment around us, as well as our stakeholders and profitability.[41]

Norm Thompson, Inc., addresses sustainable development in a number of decision areas, five of which include efforts to accomplish the following[42]:

■ Promote products that are sustainable, safe, durable, and useful for society.

Table 6.3	Examples of Types of Pressures from Primary Stakeholders

Employees
- Pay and benefits
- Safety and health
- Rights at work/global labor standards
- Fair/ethical treatment in hiring, reviews, promotion, and related areas

Shareholders
- Demands for efficiency/profitability
- Viability (sustainability)
- Growth of investment
- Ethical disclosure of financial information

Customers
- Competitive prices
- Quality and safe products
- Respect for customers' privacy
- Concern for environment
- Truthful/ethical advertising and sales practices

Supplies
- Meet commitments
- Repeat business
- Fair trade practices/ethical treatment

- Develop packaging that is minimal, biodegradable, recyclable, reusable, and made from materials that have been recycled.
- Print catalogs with processes that avoid toxic materials and use resources wisely.
- Purchase paper with the highest level of available recycled content and virgin content sourced from sustainable forestry operations.
- Employ transportation methods that are based on renewable energy, and advance a product return system that closes the production loop.

Norm Thompson also indicates how it will attempt to influence its stakeholders to embrace sustainability and has set forth a set of measurable environmental goals to be achieved during the next five years.

In addition to voluntary actions, laws and regulations govern business actions related to pollution and the use of natural resources. International standards for environmental management have also been developed. The European Union's Eco-Management and Audit Scheme (EMAS) and the International Organization for Standardization's 14000 (ISO 14000) standards are examples of environmental policy statements designed to provide guidance to multinational businesses. By meeting the ISO 14000 standards, companies, such as the Lear Corporation and Volvo of North America, can certify that they have developed responsible environmental policies.[43] Numerous standards are in place that apply to numerous issues. For example, multiple standards address the issue of preventing and preparing for chemical spills. One of the standards calls for the use of secondary containment or oversized drums wherever possible. Another standard calls for always have someone check the MSDS (Material Safety Data Sheets) before storing any new chemicals. Many more such standards address this same issue.

Organizations that actively address environmental issues benefit in a variety of ways. Most obviously, they build reputations of being socially responsible. But they also develop new and valuable organizational capabilities. They learn to integrate the concerns of multiple stakeholders when making key decisions, and they also further develop abilities to innovate and learn.[44]

Finding Win–Win Solutions

Clearly, the primary pressures from various stakeholder groups differ, as do their views about the appropriate role of business in society. Some managers would agree with former Chrysler Chairman Robert Eaton, who said, "The idea of corporations taking on social responsibility is ridiculous. You'll simply burden industry to a point where it is no longer competitive."

Other managers would agree with the view of most people, who reject the idea that making money is the only role of business. In fact, they suggest that the path to long-term profitability requires taking into account the concerns of primary and secondary stakeholders in their decisions. The success of many companies support this view. Again, consider the performance of 13 well-known customer-oriented firms, such as FedEx and Intel. The performance of these firms to others in the same industries was compared. Over a period of five years, the revenues of these 13 companies grew 3.2 times faster than their competitors. Profits were 2.1 times as great as those of their competitors.[45]

Evaluating Social Performance

With heightened public interest in social responsibility, many organizations are discovering that they can't avoid having people evaluate how well they perform in this respect. Business publications such as *Fortune* magazine rank various aspects of organizational performance annually. Many stakeholders are pressuring business leaders to move away from the sole focus on the traditional, utilitarian approach of business and actively contribute to society. One approach to evaluating an organization's social and ethical performance is to consider whether it merely reacts to ethical pressures as they arise or anticipates and addresses ethical concerns proactively.[46]

Proactive Responsibility. A proactive stakeholder social responsibility approach involves five categories of initiatives.

- *Broad performance criteria.* Managers and employees consider and accept broader criteria for measuring the organization's performance and social role than those required by law and the marketplace. This is illustrated in our discussions of Nortel Networks and Norm Thompson, Inc.
- *Ethical norms.* Managers and employees take stands on issues of public concern. They advocate ethical norms for the organization, the industry, and business in general. These ethical norms are advocated even when they seem detrimental to the immediate profits of the organization or are contrary to prevailing industry practices.
- *Operating strategy.* Managers and employees maintain or improve current standards of the physical and social environment. For example, the Collins Companies is a private firm, headquartered in Portland, Oregon, that owns and operates forests, sawmills, and manufacturing facilities. It is one of the pioneers in implementing practices to ensure sustainable and renewable forest practices. Among many other practices, it has eliminated clear-cutting and carefully evaluates which trees can be cut from a tract each year.[47] Another operating strategy is for organizations to compensate victims of pollution and other hazards created, even in the absence of clearly established legal grounds. Also, managers and employees evaluate possible negative effects of the organization's plans on other stakeholders and then attempt to eliminate or substantially reduce such negative effects before implementing the plans.
- *Response to social pressures.* Managers and employees accept responsibility for solving current problems. They are willing to discuss activities with outside groups

and make information freely available to them. They are also receptive to formal and informal inputs from outside stakeholders in decision making.

- *Legislative and political activities.* Managers show a willingness to work with outside stakeholders for enactment, for example, of environmental protection laws. They promote honesty and openness in government and in their own organization's lobbying activities. For example, in one section of Nortel Networks' code of business conduct, the firm explicitly addresses how it relates to the political process in these words[48]:

> Nortel Networks does not abuse corporate power to influence public issues—nor does it become involved in unethical political activity. It does, however, express its views on local and national issues which affect its operations. The corporation respects and supports the right of all employees to participate in the political process. However, it does not reimburse employees for personal political contributions, nor does it permit employees to campaign on company time or property. Nortel Networks supports the political process as a corporation—by, for example, making limited contributions to political parties or candidates in jurisdictions where it is legal and customary to do so. All such contributions are reported to the corporation's auditors.

Social Audits. Managers measure what matters to them. Those who are concerned about their company's social performance should conduct a social audit. A **social audit** *identifies, monitors, and evaluates the effects that the organization is having on its stakeholders and society as a whole.* A social audit focuses on indicators, measurements, and goals relevant to key primary and secondary stakeholders, as identified earlier in Figure 6.2

General Motors (GM) is an example of a firm that conducts an annual social audit and reports its findings annually in a report entitled *Corporate Responsibility & Sustainability.*[49] The report documents GM's efforts to improve its operations and products and to integrate economic, environmental, and social objectives into its daily business. GM has been issuing this report since 1994, and was the first automaker to do so. GM's document addresses 90 specific topics. Table 6.4 provides a representative sampling of these topics which are, of course, of interest to various stakeholders.

Table 6.4	Thirty of Ninety Topics in GM's Corporate Responsibility and Sustainability Report
■ Accidental releases	■ E85 electric vehicle
■ Air emissions	■ Education—environmental
■ Alternative fuels	■ Education—biodiversity
■ Biodiversity	■ Emission to air
■ Child safety	■ Emission to water
■ Climate change	■ Energy efficiency
■ Diversity—management	■ Exhaust emissions
■ Diversity initiatives	■ Financial performance
■ Greenhouse gases—operations	■ Financial data
■ Greenhouse gases—products	■ Fuel cell
■ Hazardous waste	■ Philanthropic donations
■ Health and safety	■ Philanthropy initiatives
■ Human rights	■ Product design—safety
■ ISO 14001	■ Recycling—operations
■ Land management	■ Recycling—products

The following are just a few of the many indicators presented in GM's report[50]:

- The global energy team established a corporate goal of 10 percent energy reduction globally by 2005 from a 2000 baseline.
- The global environmental issues team set stretch goals in 2002 to reduce total waste (hazardous and nonhazardous) by 15 percent and increase recycling worldwide by 15 percent. The base year is 2000 and the target year is the beginning of 2006. Since 1997, facilities surpassed their five-year 50 percent reduction goal one year early and reduced the volume of their nonrecycled waste by 54 percent.
- Global facilities emitted 13.2 million metric tons of CO^2 (carbon dioxide) in 2001, a 9.6 percent reduction compared to 2000. Facility CO^2 emissions per vehicle produced decreased by 2.2 percent. CO^2 emissions are calculated from fuel and electricity use at each facility, which are the major sources of greenhouse gas emissions from GM operations.
- A stated goal is to put hydrogen-powered fuel cell vehicles on the road by 2010.
- From 1995 to 2002, the recordable injury rate per 100 employees for global operations dropped by 75 percent. Lost workday cases per 100 employees fell by 85 percent.

CHAPTER SUMMARY

In this chapter, we examined the importance of ethical and socially responsible business decisions. What is viewed as socially responsible is likely to vary among an organization's many stakeholders. Ultimately, individuals must accept responsibility for their own ethical conduct. Throughout the chapter, we presented concepts, policies, practices, and examples of how to behave in ethical and socially responsible ways.

1. State the importance of ethics for individual employees and organizations.

Due to recent events, major concerns have arisen about ethics in business. Many individuals say that they would prefer to work for organizations with good reputations for being ethical and socially responsible. At the same time, scandalous business practices were revealed in the business media, especially during 2002 and 2003. Managers and other employees must learn to recognize ethical issues and deal with them effectively by understanding the forces that affect ethical conduct and the key perspectives that can be used to make ethical judgments. Interestingly, there is good evidence that organizations with a reputation for being ethical tend to have superior financial performance over the long run.

2. Describe four forces that influence the ethical behavior of individuals and organizations.

The key categories of factors that influence a person's and organizations' ethical conduct are cultural forces, legal and regulatory forces, organizational forces, and individual forces. Cultural forces comprise shared values and norms that underlie standards for acceptable behavior. Legal and regulatory forces reflect societal standards that are enforceable in the courts. Organizational forces include both formal policies, such as a code of ethics, and cultural norms, such as how managers define acceptable employee performance. Finally, an individual's forces include the view of what is right and wrong and how that can influence a person's response to the other three forces.

3. Describe three approaches that people use when making ethical judgments.

Managers and employees commonly rely on one or some combination of three ethical approaches to guide decision making and behavior. The utilitarian approach focuses on decisions or behavior that are likely to affect an organization's profitability. For businesses, profits indicate financial and economic performance. The moral rights approach upholds a member of society's fundamental rights to life and safety, truthfulness, privacy, freedom of conscience, free speech, and private property. The justice approach advocates impartial, equitable distribution of benefits and costs among individuals and groups, according to three principles: distributive justice, fairness, and natural duty.

4. Explain stakeholder social responsibility and how it influences managers' ethical decisions.

The diverse values and ethical approaches prevalent in advanced economies introduce a great deal of complexity for managers of organizations that attempt to act in socially responsible ways. One approach that managers can use to ensure socially responsible actions is to consider how the organization's actions affect important stakeholders. Each group of stakeholders has different concerns. Sometimes these concerns conflict; at other times they mesh. Thus finding solutions that address the concerns of multiple stakeholders becomes an important strategic task.

Code of ethics
Distributive justice principle
Employment-at-will
Ethics
Fairness principle
Justice approach
Laws
Moral rights approach

Natural duty principle
Sarbanes-Oxley Act
Social audit
Stakeholder social responsibility
Stakeholders
Sustainable development
Utilitarian approach
Whistle-blowers

QUESTIONS FOR DISCUSSION and COMPETENCY DEVELOPMENT

1. In terms of the three approaches for making ethical judgments, what specific ethical concepts are illustrated in Nortel Networks' *Code of Business Conduct* as presented in the Preview Case? You should relate specific statements in the code to specific ethical concepts.

2. In our discussion of cultural forces, we identified 10 fundamental personal values that are often listed by individuals as central to them and the American culture. How would you rank these values in terms of their relative importance to you? What was the basis for your selection of the top three ranked values?

3. One way to simplify your approach to ethical decision making is to consider whether an action is legal or illegal. Is this a good approach to ethical conduct? Explain.

4. Think of an organization you have worked for. Did this organization follow the actions recommended by the Ethics Resource Center to ensure an ethical culture? Explain how it did or did not adhere to each of the recommended actions.

5. Under what specific conditions, if any, do you think you would act as a whistle-blower?

6. Managers are important in setting the ethical tone for employees. If you work for an unethical manager, chances are you may eventually feel some pressure to act in ways that you consider unethical. Suppose that you suspect that your boss is not completely honest when reporting the sales figures for your unit. What would you do?

7. As the boundaries of the workplace have become more fuzzy and flexible, so have the boundaries of private life. Many people take work home with them and stay in almost constant touch with their colleagues or customers via e-mail or voice mail. Similarly, they may conduct some of their private business from their office at work. What types of personal activities are routinely conducted while you're at work, if any? Is it fair for employers to expect employees to be constantly "connected" to their workplace, but not allow them to make personal telephone calls or shop on the Internet while at work? Explain.

8. Organizations communicate their ethical principles in a variety of ways: through the behavior of leaders, in writing, by offering training programs, through performance assessment methods, and so on. Visit the home page of any major organization of interest to you. Are the ethical principles of the organization communicated to people who visit this site? Are the perspectives of potential customers, employees, shareholders, and suppliers considered?

9. As a student, you are almost certain to work in a team with other students on some class assignments—for this course or other courses. What can you and the members of your team do to manage the ethical conduct of your team? Would it be useful to develop a code of conduct for your team? Explain your answer.

CASE FOR COMPETENCY DEVELOPMENT

LARRY HANSEN SPEAKS OUT[51]

Larry Hansen entered the employees' locker room prior to the starting time for his second shift at the northern Ohio plant of XYZ Manufacturing Co. He saw about a dozen of his coworkers just finishing the day shift. It seemed like an informal meeting was being held, and emotions were volatile. John Adams, the union steward, was trying to respond to complaints from several of the workers. Hansen took a seat nearby where he could listen to the discussion and get changed for his shift.

The gist of the discussion centered on an episode early in the day shift. Louis Brockington, a young journeyman machinist, had been fired by company management because he had been caught smoking a marijuana cigarette during a break from his work. "Brock" was being paid—considered "on the clock"—as well as being inside the factory. Because this was an obvious violation of the company's "drug-free" and "no smoking" policy for all employees, he had been immediately dismissed. He was even forced to leave the plant with his street clothes and personal items in a bag packed by management. He wasn't even given the opportunity to be sure all personal items from his locker were included.

Management informed union representatives of their action almost immediately and assured them that everything found in the locker belonging to Brockington was put into the bag he was given except for a small plastic bag, which had been stuffed into the toe of Brock's street shoes. The bag contained about half an ounce of the same substance Brockington had been found smoking. Management kept this item as "evidence" in case the union decided to formally protest Brock's rapid dismissal.

Many of the workers argued that management had violated Brockington's privacy by illegally searching an employee's locker without his permission and asked what was to prevent them from doing this to anyone working in the plant. Management would never think of searching the private areas of a manager's office. Also, Brock was a very popular worker who had a number of friends among nonmanagement employees. They also argued with the union steward that Brockington should have been given another chance.

Steward John Adams told the workers that, unfortunately, Brockington had been given a second chance by management. He had been caught doing the same thing three months earlier. Management quietly warned him at that time that a repetition of this misconduct would result in his dismissal. The company's "drug-free" policy also required that the union representative be informed of such action in writing. Adams had received such a notice about Brockington's first disciplinary action and also notice of his dismissal when Brockington violated his "second chance."

After hearing even his union representative say that Brockington had been "treated fairly by management when he got a second chance," Larry Hansen could no longer keep silent. He walked into the middle of the group of workers and said loudly to John Adams. "It's too bad that Brock wasn't a member of management—because then he would have gotten a third, fourth, and even fifth chance if he needed it!"

Quickly, several of the men asked Hansen what he meant by his remark. Hansen answered by asking, "Do you remember when we adopted this drug-free policy and put it in our work contract two years ago? Well, about a year later I found out from the executive day gate watch-man that one of the VPs used to frequently come back from lunch loaded to the gills. His excuse was he was buying 'liquid lunches' for good customers. But you all know that drinking during working hours is also covered under our glorious 'no drugs' policy." The locker room got very quiet as Hansen continued.

"The guard tells me that after doing this for over three months, he doesn't see this VP for about three or four weeks. And then, one day he shows up but parks in a different space from where he had been assigned. Also, he stops going to lunch by himself. He always has some other big brass with him, and now he comes back stone cold sober within an hour of when he left. The word the guard got was that after management told him to clean up his act, the guy kept right on doing it. And when he was gone for nearly a month, they sent him some place to dry out. When he came back, they gave him a different job."

"Guess the VP got bumped down a little, but he sure didn't lose his job. And he got a lot more than just two chances! If you guys ask me, the blue-collar men that make this place go don't get the same 'fair' treatment the bigwigs do under our 'no drugs' policy. If they screw up, they get special help, and they sure don't get fired!"

By the time Hansen had finished with his story about the company's VP, it was nearly time for the second shift to begin. "One thing," Hansen said to Adams, "the union sure ought to appeal this raw deal that Brock got. If we can't get the same treatment from management for our own members, what good is having this 'no drugs' agreement in our contract? They can go out and have a four-martini lunch and call it being sociable with a customer. What's wrong with us having the same rights? Let's put this on our agenda for next week's union meeting, and try to take care of Brock!" The group broke up with a loud round of "Yeah! Let's do that!"

Questions

1. What do you see as the major lesson that should be learned from this case? Is alcohol use during working hours with customers more or less detrimental to the company than substance smoking on the job? Should the privacy rights of employees preclude management from searching employee desks and lockers or reviewing employees' e-mail messages at will?

2. Do you think this case illustrates a dual standard for ethical conduct? Should the same rules exist for workers at all levels within a company's structure, or do members of management deserve special treatment? Why or why not?

3. When the union brings Brockington's dismissal appeal to management, how should management react if they sincerely desire an effective "drug-free" program in their company and an ethics policy by which all employees can live?

WHAT IS YOUR CALL?[52]

Scenario 1: The U.S. Patent Office recently issued a patent to Tiger Automotive for a device that has been proven to increase the average car's gas mileage by 45 percent. Given that Tiger is protected from direct competition by this patent, it has decided to price the new product at $45 to auto parts dealers. The device costs less than $1 to produce and distribute.

How would you rate this action on the following five-point scale?

1	2	3	4	5
Strongly Disapprove	Disapprove	Neutral	Approve	Strongly Approve

What ethical approach is the basis of your rating for scenario 1?

Scenario 2: A friend of yours is the president of a company in a highly competitive industry. Your friend learns that a competitor has made an important scientific discovery that will give the competitor an advantage and will substantially reduce (but not eliminate) the profits of your friend's company for about a year. Your friend learns that there is a possibility of hiring one of this competitor's employees who knows the details of the discovery and proceeds to do so.

How would you rate this action on the following five-point scale?

1	2	3	4	5
Strongly Disapprove	Disapprove	Neutral	Approve	Strongly Approve

What ethical approach is the basis of your rating for scenario 2?

Scenario 3: Jack Ward works in product development for an auto parts contractor. Last summer Ward's firm won a big contract to manufacture transaxles for use in a new line of front-wheel-drive cars to be introduced by a major auto manufacturer in the near future. Winning the contract was very important to the firm. Just before getting the contract, the firm had scheduled half its employees, including Ward, for an indefinite layoff—a plan that was jettisoned with the award of the contract.

Final testing of the assemblies ended last Friday, and the first shipments are scheduled to be made in three weeks. The manufacturer's specifications call for the transaxle to carry 30 percent more than its rated capacity without failing. While examining the test reports, Ward discovers that the transaxle tended to fail when loaded to more than 20 percent over rated capacity and subjected to strong torsion forces. Such a condition could occur with a heavily loaded car braking hard for a curve while going down a mountain road. The consequences would be disastrous. Ward shows the test results to his supervisor and the company president, who both indicate that they are aware of the problem but have decided to ignore the report. Chances of transaxle failure in ordinary driving are low, and there isn't enough time to redesign the assembly. If the company doesn't deliver the assemblies on time, it will lose the contract. Ward decides not to show the test results to the auto manufacturer.

How would you rate this action on the following five-point scale?

1	2	3	4	5
Strongly Disapprove	Disapprove	Neutral	Approve	Strongly Approve

What ethical approach is the basis of your rating for scenario 3?

Interpretations
Scenario 1: *Strongly disapprove or disapprove*—reflects the justice approach. *Strongly approve or approve*—reflects the utilitarian ethical approach. *Neutral*—reflects no preference.

Scenario 2: *Strongly disapprove or disapprove*—reflects the moral rights approach. *Strongly approve or approve*—reflects the utilitarian approach. *Neutral*—reflects no preference.

Scenario 3: *Strongly disapprove or disapprove*—could reflect the utilitarian, moral rights, or justice approach. *Strongly approve or approve*—might reflect utilitarianism (Ward has no responsibility beyond telling his supervisor or the president or the risk of death or injury is too low to hold up the sale).

©Corbis

Planning and Control

Chapter

7

©Stone/Getty Images

Planning and Strategy

Learning Objectives

After studying this chapter, you should be able to:

1. Explain the importance of the planning function.
2. Describe the core components of strategic and tactical planning.
3. Discuss the effects of degree of diversification on planning.
4. Describe the three basic levels of strategy and planning.
5. State the eight primary tasks of the planning process.
6. Explain the generic competitive strategies model.

Chapter Outline

Johnson & Johnson's (J&J) credo, established more than 60 years ago, continues to serve as a beacon and guide in its strategic planning. The Preview Case presents this credo and begins with a statement from top management of J&J.

Executive management of Johnson & Johnson, with the support and approval of the Board of Directors, has set the fundamental strategic direction of the Company to remain a broadly-based human health care company for the consumer, pharmaceutical and medical device and diagnostics markets. Strategic planning is guided by the ethical principles embodied in *Our Credo*, unifying our people worldwide behind a set of common values and providing a constant reminder of the Company's responsibilities to all of its constituents. The statement of *Our Credo* follows:

We believe our first responsibility is to the doctors, nurses and patients, to mothers and fathers and all others who use our products and services. In meeting their needs, everything we do must be of high quality. We must constantly strive to reduce our costs in order to maintain reasonable prices. Customers' orders must be serviced promptly and accurately. Our suppliers and distributors must have an opportunity to make a fair profit.

We are responsible to our employees, the men and women who work with us throughout the world. Everyone must be considered as an individual. We must respect their dignity and recognize their merit. They must have a sense of security in their jobs. Compensation must be fair and adequate, and working conditions clean, orderly and safe. We must be mindful of ways to help our employees fulfill their family responsibilities. Employees must feel free to make suggestions and complaints. There must be equal opportunity for employment, development and advancement for those qualified. We must provide competent management, and their actions must be just and ethical.

We are responsible to the communities in which we live and work and to the world community as well. We must be good citizens—support good works and charities and bear our fair share of taxes. We must encourage civic improvements and better health and education. We must maintain in good order the property we are privileged to use, protecting the environment and natural resources.

Our final responsibility is to our stockholders. Business must make a sound profit. We must experiment with new ideas. Research must be carried on, innovative programs developed and mistakes paid for. New equipment must be purchased, new facilities provided and new products launched. Reserves must be created to provide for adverse times. When we operate according to these principles, the stockholders should realize a fair return.[1]

THE PLANNING FUNCTION

1. Explain the importance of the planning function.

In the Preview Case, Johnson & Johnson sets forth the stakeholders and the responsibilities related to them that must be addressed and satisfied through its strategic planning. William Weldon, the chairman of the board and CEO of J&J comments:

> . . . we sustain our consistent performance through a culture that is based on a strong system of values. We expect the highest standards of ethical behavior throughout our global organization, achieved when each of us assumes responsibility for leadership and integrity. We are guided in that pursuit by Our Credo, the embodiment of our values, which has now been in place for 60 years. Our four-part strategic business model—broadly based in human health care, decentralized, managed for the long term, on a foundation of strong values—has served us well, yielding an enduring record of consistent growth and performance. It continues to light our way into the future.[2]

In this chapter, we discuss some of the fundamentals of planning and the strategies employed by J&J and other organizations. In Chapter 1, we defined *planning* as the determination of organizational goals and the means to reach them. We consider planning a basic general managerial function because it sets the framework and direction for the organizing, leading, and controlling functions. In addition, the ability of an individual, team, or organization to plan is an integral part in each of the six managerial competencies that we develop throughout this book.

Why plan? When used by competent leaders and managers, planning should assist them to (1) discover new opportunities, (2) anticipate and avoid future problems, (3) develop effective courses of action (strategies and tactics), and (4) comprehend the uncertainties and risks with various options. Planning should also improve the odds of achieving an organization's goals by creating desirable changes, improving productivity, and maintaining organizational stability. Realization of such goals enables the organization to achieve long-term growth, maintain profitability, and survive. If done properly, planning fosters organizationwide learning, including the discovery of key problems, opportunities, and new strategies.[3] A key goal of this chapter is to help you develop the ability to plan effectively.

Let's consider further the important role of planning at J&J. With more than 190 operating companies and 108,000 employees located throughout the world, Johnson & Johnson is organized on the principle of decentralized management. Each company is, with some exceptions, managed by citizens of the country where it is located. Senior management groups at U.S. and international operating companies are each responsible for their own strategic plans. Throughout the year, at meetings of the board and committees of the board, members of management and board members discuss the strategic direction and major developments of the various businesses in which the company is engaged. The process is an interactive, ongoing dialogue that provides insight into the activities and direction of the company's businesses.[4]

TWO TYPES OF PLANNING

In this section, we identify and describe the core components of two basic types of planning: strategic planning and tactical planning.[5]

2. Describe the core components of strategic and tactical planning.

Strategic Planning

Strategic planning *is the process of (1) diagnosing the organization's external and internal environments, (2) deciding on a vision and mission, (3) developing overall goals, (4) creating and selecting general strategies to be pursued, and (5) allocating resources to achieve the organization's goals.* Managers and others must take an organizationwide or divisionwide approach in the process of strategic planning. The focus is on developing strategies that deal effectively with environmental opportunities and threats in relation to the organization's strengths and weaknesses.

In most large organizations such as J&J and ExxonMobil, strategic planning includes **contingency planning**—*preparation for unexpected, major, and quick changes (positive or negative) in the environment that will have a significant impact on the organization and require immediate responses.* This process begins with managers developing scenarios of major environmental events that could occur. A contingency plan for a dramatic negative event could be developed for responding to a disaster (e.g., an earthquake, flood, or fire destroying a company's manufacturing plant) or for managing a crisis (e.g., terrorist attack).[6] A contingency plan may also be developed for a positive event, such as an increase in customer demand for products (goods and/or services) that overwhelms the firm's current capacity. Generally, managers should plan for three to five potentially critical and unanticipated events. The attempt to consider more events is likely to make the contingency planning process too time consuming and unmanageable. Contingency planning forces managers to be aware of possibilities and to outline strategies to respond to them. It supports orderly and speedy adaptation, in contrast to panic-like reactions, to external events beyond the organization's direct control.

If there was any doubt about the need to have a contingency plan to deal with the consequences of an unforeseen disaster, the tragic events of September 11, 2001, should put that doubt to rest. The following Planning & Administration Competency feature reports on how the September 11 experience led the Bank of New York to several new contingency planning insights.[7] The Bank of New York Company, headquartered in New York City, provides a complete range of banking and other financial services to corporations and individuals worldwide. The firm has more than 19,000 employees in multiple locations.

PLANNING & ADMINISTRATION COMPETENCY

©Photodisc/Getty Images

Bank of New York's Disaster Planning

On September 11, 2001, the Bank of New York had 8,500 employees working at four different sites, including a production data center, in and around lower Manhattan. Within a matter of hours, the bank was required to evacuate all four sites, relocate all of those employees, and reestablish data processing at several sites. Although the bank already had a well-conceived, thoroughly tested business contingency plan, the scale and extent of the damage from the attacks was far greater than anyone had anticipated. The bank was able to resume some of its mainframe and technology operations quickly, but the attack destroyed a considerable amount of telecommunications infrastructure, and its repair was beyond its immediate control. Ultimately, this adversely affected some clients.

The September 11 experience gave the Bank of New York a number of valuable business planning insights to develop responsive, flexible, risk-reducing contingency strategies. We note just a few that were adopted by them. When the Bank of New York lost access to its primary check-processing site in Manhattan following the terrorist attacks, it was able to resume check processing quickly because the bank had three other sites in the area with the same operational resources already in place. Since the attacks, the bank decided to use an "active-active" model for its most critical businesses. In this model, the bank performs the exact same business and processing functions in multiple sites rather than at one, central site.

The Bank of New York is placing greater emphasis on geographical diversity in its current contingency planning. From an operational standpoint, they decided it was unwise to have all critical business staff and processing functions in one location. The bank is now operating portions of several key businesses in different locations and is examining the feasibility of reducing the concentration in lower Manhattan. Its operations and data center processing were both in a single location that was severely impacted by the September 11 attacks. This created serious logistical hurdles for recovery efforts. The bank now maintains these two functional areas in different locations and has relocated staff performing key business functions to a number of geographically diverse areas in and around New York City. The staff is now cross-trained so that they can maintain key service capabilities if employees at another location cannot perform their duties.

Following September 11, the bank's contingency communications plan worked well. Division managers methodically went through their employee call sequences to verify that everyone was safe and to inform them about where to report for work in the following days. The bank set up a special toll-free number and Web site for distributing updated information to its employees and clients, and both of these proved helpful. Now, the Bank of New York has its telecommunications channels connected to each of its production sites through multiple access points, and the channels can be routed to multiple central offices for switching. The goal is to avoid using a single, central switching office that could create a single point of failure.

In Chapters 3 and 4 we discussed many forces—both domestic and global—in the environment that managers and others must understand in strategic planning and the daily management of their organizations. We now review the four main aspects of strategic planning that managers can directly influence: vision and mission, goals, strategies, and resource allocation.

Vision and Mission. A **vision** *expresses an organization's fundamental aspirations and purpose, usually by appealing to its members' hearts and minds.* A vision statement may add soul to a mission statement if it lacks one. Over time, traditional statements of mission (e.g., stating the business in which the organization is involved) may change, but the organization's vision may endure for generations.[8] The following statements represent the visions of three organizations[9]:

- **Lowe's:** Improving home improvement
- **eBay:** Serving as the world's online marketplace for the sale of goods and services by a diverse community of individuals and businesses
- **Dell Computer:** Bringing value to customers and adding value to our company, our neighborhoods, our communities and our world through diversity, environmental, and global citizenship initiatives.

Many organizations don't have a vision statement. They may have a mission statement only. A **mission** *is the organization's purpose or reason for existing.* A mission statement often answers basic questions such as these: (1) What business are we in? (2) Who are we? and (3) What are we about? A mission may describe the customer needs the firm aims to satisfy, the goods or services the firm supplies, or the markets the firm is currently serving or intends to serve in the future. Some mission statements are lengthy, but others are quite brief. The following statements illustrate how three organizations express their missions:

- **Lowe's:** To provide an unwavering commitment to homeowners pursuing their dream and the professionals who help them achieve it
- **eBay:** To provide a global trading platform where practically anyone can trade practically anything
- **Dell Computer:** To be the most successful computer company in the world at delivering the best customer experience in the markets we serve.

A mission statement is meaningful only if it acts as a unifying force for guiding strategic decisions and achieving an organization's long-term goals. The mission statement should encourage the organization's members to think and act strategically—not just once a year but every day.

Goals. **Organizational goals** *are the results that the managers and others have selected and are committed to achieving for the long-term survival and growth of the firm.* These goals may be expressed both qualitatively and quantitatively (what is to be achieved, how much is to be achieved, and by when it is to be achieved). Consider several of the corporate goals for J&J[10]:

- To provide scientifically sound, high-quality products and services to help heal, cure disease, and improve the quality of life.
- To achieve absolute reduction of CO^2 (carbon dioxide) emissions of 4 percent from 1990 to 2005 and 7 percent from 1990 to 2010.
- To be a world leader in health and safety by creating an injury-free workplace.
- To achieve one-third of sales from new products introduced during the previous five years and from existing products launched in new markets.

Strategies. **Strategies** *are the major courses of action (choices) selected and implemented to achieve one or more goals.*[11] In Chapters 3 and 4, we reviewed several competitive strategies that managers use to deal with threats and take advantage of opportunities in their businesses. They include the alliance strategy, exporting strategy, licensing strategy, multidomestic strategy, and global strategy.

A key challenge is to develop strategies that are at least partially unique relative to competitors or to pursue strategies similar to those of competitors but in different ways. Strategies will have the greatest impact when they position an organization to be different in one or more aspects from its competitors. Michael Porter, a professor at the Harvard Business School and widely regarded as one of the foremost thinkers on strategic management, comments:

> The essence of most good strategies is the need to make many choices that are all consistent—choices about production, service, design, and so on. Companies cannot randomly make a lot of choices that all turn out to be consistent. It's statistically impossible. That means companies need to grasp at least a part of the whole. As we study the histories of successful companies, we see that someone or some group developed insight into how a number of choices fit together. . . .[12]

The following Strategic Action Competency feature provides a glimpse of the competitive strategies employed by Dell Computer.[13] Dell Computer and most other successful organizations use multiple strategies that serve to complement and support each other.

STRATEGIC ACTION COMPETENCY

©Reuters New Media

Dell's Competitive Strategies

Dell Computer has developed four interrelated competitive strategies. In brief, they are speed to market; superior customer service; a fierce commitment to producing consistently high-quality, custom-made computer systems that provide the highest performance and the latest relevant technology to customers; and early exploitation of the Internet.

Michael Dell, chairman and CEO of Dell Computer, comments on some of these strategies in the remainder of this feature.

Dell's key competitive advantages are grounded in our unique, direct business model. We entered the business with no channel conflicts (e.g., selling through retail stores versus direct from us); we were and still are the entire channel, from procurement through service. As a result, Dell has one integrated process for managing the entire value chain, from component supplier to end customer—and we control all the aspects in between.

This integrated process provides lower cost by eliminating middlemen margins, as well as from the cost efficiencies of higher quality that result from greater control and "fewer touches" of both product and process. In fact, our ability to view the entire spectrum of a customer's experiences with Dell enables us to efficiently organize our company around well-defined customer segments. Each of our customer-oriented business segments controls its own product, manufacturing, sales, and support operations. Dell's ability to segment the market to provide closer understanding of distinct customer needs, and to tailor products and services accordingly, is the key to having the lowest cost and most effective service for each segment.

Any business is ultimately a series of transactions and interactions; the Internet is profoundly affecting the cost of transactions and the efficiency with which these interactions occur. Let me provide two examples. Each online purchase produces an average of 40 percent fewer order status calls for Dell (e.g., "Where's my order?"), and 15 percent fewer technical support calls which is a savings of $3 to $8 per call.

The Internet also is contributing to the cost savings that result from improved quality, as well as enhanced customer service. We have created Web-based links with our suppliers and customers to improve the speed of information flow throughout the value chain and literally bring supplies and customers inside our business. On the supply side, these Web-based links have greatly accelerated the speed of customer feedback on quality, as well as allowing suppliers to more rapidly adjust their product mix to customer demand, which improves their inventory and cost efficiency.

Resource Allocation. **Resource allocation** *involves assigning money, people, facilities and equipment, land, and other resources among various current and new business opportunities, functions, projects, and tasks.* As part of the strategic planning process, resource allocation generally boils down to earmarking money, through budgets, for various purposes. For example, Lowe's capital budget was $2.8 billion in a recent year. Approximately 96 percent of this capital budget was for store expansion and new distribution centers. One hundred and twenty-three new stores were opened in that year. This included the relocation of 11 older stores. Ninety-six percent were company-owned stores and 4 percent leased. Two regional distribution centers were opened.[14] Each of these projects had a detailed capital budget associated with it that set forth such budget categories as land, facility, technology, display, and related costs.

Tactical Planning

Tactical planning *involves making concrete decisions regarding what to do, who will do it, and how to do it—with a normal time horizon of a year or less.* Middle and first-line managers and teams often are heavily involved in tactical planning. It normally includes developing quantitative and qualitative goals that support the organization's strategic plan, identifying courses of action for implementing new initiatives or improving current operations, and formatting budgets for each department, division, and project within the guidelines set by higher level management.

Departmental managers and employee teams develop tactical plans to anticipate or cope with the actions of competitors; to coordinate with other departments, customers, and suppliers; and to implement strategic plans. The information presented in Table 7.1 demonstrates that tactical planning differs from strategic planning primarily in terms of shorter time frames, size of resource allocations, and level of detail. Of course, the two types of planning are closely linked in a well-designed planning process.

The Competent Manager

"As we manage our business, we are focused on meeting our financial targets the right way. Our actions are based on the company's long-term interests rather than on short-term, expedient solutions."

Kenneth I. Chenault
Chairman & CEO
American Express Company

DEGREE OF DIVERSIFICATION AND PLANNING

In this section, we review strategic considerations involved in making diversification decisions. They serve to define different types of firms and the complexity of planning associated with each type.

3. Discuss the effects of degree of diversification on planning.

Strategic Questions

Diversification *refers to the variety of goods and/or services produced by an organization and the number of different markets it serves.* The degree of diversification directly affects the complexity of an organization's strategic planning. Strategic changes in the degree of diversification should be guided by answers to questions that help top managers identify the

Table 7.1   Focus of Strategic and Tactical Planning

Dimension	Strategic Planning	Tactical Planning
Intended purpose	Ensure long-term effectiveness and growth	Means of implementing strategic plans
Nature of issues addressed	How to survive and compete	How to accomplish specific goals
Time horizon	Long term (usually two years or more)	Short term (usually one year or less)
How often done	Every one to three years	Every six months to one year
Condition under which decision making occurs	Uncertainty and risk	Low to moderate risk
Where plans are primarily developed	Middle to top management	Employees, up to middle management
Level of detail	Low to moderate	High

potential risks—and opportunities—that diversification presents. The following are four such strategic questions:

1. *What can we do better than other firms if we enter a new market?* Managers may base diversification or new start-ups on vague definitions of their businesses rather than on a systematic analysis of what sets them apart from current or potential competitors. Johnson & Johnson has made 52 acquisitions between 1992 and 2003 in the health-care area. Typically, these were firms already marketing successful drugs. For example, J&J recently acquired Scios, Inc., a biotechnology firm headquartered in Sunnyvale, California. One of the firm's key products treats congestive heart failure.[15]

2. *What strategic resources—human, financial, and others—do we need to succeed in the new market?* Excelling in one market doesn't guarantee success in a new one. The competencies required to be competitive in one type of business may not transfer to another type of business. One of the keys to J&J acquisitions is that they are broadly based human health-care companies. Acquisitions by some firms, especially when they involve significantly diversifying from what they do well, do not work.[16] When that problem is recognized, a firm may engage in **downscoping**—*a divestiture, spin-off, or some means of eliminating divisions and business lines that are unrelated to a firm's core businesses.* Dynergy Inc., headquartered in Houston, Texas, has downscoped its businesses to that of owning and operating divisions engaged in power generation, natural gas liquids, and regulated energy delivery. As a result of severe financial problems, Dynergy returned to its original business by selling off a number of unrelated businesses. Dynergy sold its data communication telecommunications services to the 360network Corporation. The sale included a high-capacity broadband network spanning 16,000 route miles with access points in 44 U.S. cities.[17]

3. *Will we simply be a player in the new market or will we emerge a winner?* Diversifying or new start-up companies may be outmaneuvered by current competitors. The reason is that managers may have failed to consider whether their organizations' strategic resources can be easily imitated, purchased on the open market, or replaced by other competitors. Also, entry by the firm may stimulate the current competitors to become much more effective and efficient. For example, several years ago, Toys 'R' Us, with more than 1,600 stores, responded aggressively when

several Internet-based toy retailers entered the market. The firm established its own Internet-based retailing arm and gave it great flexibility. For instance, if there were problems with an order, a customer could go to one of its "bricks-and-mortar" stores to return it. This approach eliminated the need for customers to return items through the mail. With its buying power, Toys 'R' Us was able to meet the price competition of the new competitors head-on. Most of its online competitors have now gone out of business. Although Toys 'R' Us initially had a variety of problems with its online sales and service, they have been resolved. However, Toys 'R' Us is now trying to cope with intense competition from Wal-Mart and Target.[18]

4. *What can we learn by diversifying, and are we sufficiently organized to learn it?* Astute managers know how to make diversification a learning experience. They anticipate how new businesses can help improve existing businesses, act as stepping stones to markets previously out of reach, or improve organizational efficiency. Dell's diversified from initially being a provider of just desktop PCs to a provider of laptops, servers, printers, storage devices, switches, and other products or services needed to assemble and run computer networks. This addition of these products and services are highly interrelated and have been added over a number of years.[19]

Types of Business Firms

An organization may be a single business in a market or diversified into related businesses or unrelated businesses. Figure 7.1 indicates that the degree of diversification and

Figure 7.1   Degree of Diversification and Planning

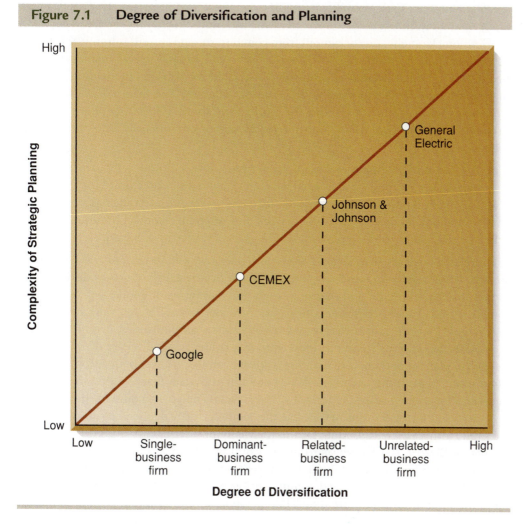

the complexity of strategic planning are directly related. A firm that produces varied goods or services for unrelated markets often must have a complex planning process. In contrast, a firm involved in a single product line or service needs a less elaborate planning process.

A **single-business firm** *provides a limited number of goods or services to one particular market.* Google is a privately held firm focused on search services. Google's mission is to deliver the best search experience on the Internet by making the world's information universally accessible and useful. The firm operates a Web site at http://www.google.com that is recognized by some as the world's best search engine. More than 200 million searches are answered daily through approximately 3 billion Web pages. The firm, headquartered in Mountain View California, has approximately 600 employees.[20]

A **dominant-business firm** *serves various segments of a market.* The term *market* refers collectively to the various users of a product line. CEMEX, headquartered in Monterey, Mexico, is the largest cement manufacturer and ready-mix producer in the Americas. With approximately 80 million metric tons of capacity, it has operations in 23 countries and trade relations with 60 others. CEMEX states that its overall business strategy is to

- focus on its core cement and ready-mix concrete franchise in the international markets it serves;
- primarily concentrate on the world's most dynamic markets, where the demand for housing, roads, and other needed infrastructure is greatest; and
- maintain high growth by applying free cash flow toward selective investments that further its geographic diversification.[21]

A **related-business firm** *provides a variety of similar goods and/or services.* Its divisions generally operate in the same or similar markets, use similar technologies, share common distribution channels, and/or benefit from common strategic assets. Johnson & Johnson is a related-business firm. It is a comprehensive and broadly based manufacturer of health-care products, as well as a provider of related services, for the consumer, pharmaceutical, and medical devices and diagnostics markets. The firm has 198 operating companies in 54 countries around the world with about 108,000 employees. It sells products in more than 175 countries. J&J is organized primarily into three major segments:

- The consumer segment makes nonprescription drugs, products for skin and hair care, baby care, oral care, first aid, women's health and nutrition.
- The medical devices and diagnostics segment makes products such as surgical equipment, medical monitoring devices, and disposable contact lenses.
- The pharmaceutical segment makes drugs for a vast array of ailments.[22]

An **unrelated-business firm** *provides diverse products (goods and/or services) to many different markets.* Often referred to as a *conglomerate,* such a firm usually consists of distinct companies that have little or no relation to each other in terms of goods, services, or customers served. Unrelated-business firms are not common, although they are typically very large. Hoover's, a firm that provides information on businesses, lists only 70 conglomerates worldwide.[23] For the most part, the volume and diversity of information needed to plan for and manage such firms are enormous. As a result, their top managers often revert to planning and controls through financial data that focus on the past and near-term for making strategic decisions. These factors help to account for the relatively few successful unrelated businesses and the tendency of firms needing to downscope over time if they diversify too much from their core businesses.

General Electric (GE) is among the successful unrelated business firms. Like many other firms, GE has faced tough times in recent years through at least 2003. GE is a diversified services, technology, and manufacturing company with approximately 300,000 employees worldwide and more than $132 billion in annual sales. GE has a broad range of 13 primary business units each with its own divisions. A few of the primary business units include GE Aircraft Engines, GE Commercial Finance, GE Consumer Products, GE Medical Systems, and NBC.[24] In the following Communication Competency feature, Jeffrey (Jeff) Immelt comments on principles and responsibilities of the board of directors to ensure and strengthen the corporate governance of GE. This feature includes only a portion of Mr. Immelt's statement.[25]

COMMUNICATION COMPETENCY

GE's Jeff Immelt on Corporate Governance

Sound principles of corporate governance are critical to obtaining and retaining the trust of investors—and to GE's overarching goal of performance with integrity. They are also vital in securing respect from other key stakeholders and interested parties—including employees, recruits, customers, suppliers, GE communities, government officials and the public at large.

We have revised our fundamental corporate governance documents: a statement of governance principles and the charters of our four board committees with a description of their key practices. The actions described in these documents—which the board have reviewed and approved—implement requirements of the Sarbanes-Oxley legislation and the proposed New York Exchange listing requirements, as well our own vision of good governance.

At the core of corporate governance, of course, is the role of the board of directors in overseeing how management serves the long-term interests of shareowners and other stakeholders. An active, informed, independent and involved board is essential for ensuring GE's integrity, transparency and long-term strength. As reflected in GE's statement of governance principles, the board has fundamental responsibilities:

- To select, evaluate and compensate the CEO and oversee CEO succession planning.
- To provide counsel and oversight on the selection, evaluation and compensation of senior management.
- To review, approve and monitor fundamental financial and business strategies and major corporate actions.
- To understand the major risks facing the company and approve steps to mitigate those risks.
- To ensure structures and processes are in place to protect and advance the company's integrity and reputation—the accuracy and completeness of its financial statements; its compliance with legal and ethical requirements; the quality of its relationships with employees, customers, suppliers and its other stakeholders.

I want directors to probe with hard questions which stretch management so that, within a context of mutual respect, board meetings deal in depth with the core issues GE confronts. By the same token, I expect directors to have even greater involvement and participation in GE, in understanding the company and advising the management team. Directors need to be our most constructive critics and our wisest counselors.

STRATEGIC LEVELS AND PLANNING

Plans and the strategies embedded in them are normally developed at three primary levels at dominant-business (e.g., CEMEX), related-business (e.g., Johnson & Johnson), and unrelated-business (e.g., General Electric) firms. Figure 7.2 shows some of the executives involved in planning at these levels for GE. For single-business firms, plans and strategies are developed at two primary levels—the business level and the functional level.

4. Describe the three basic levels of strategy and planning.

Corporate-Level Strategy

Core-Focus. Corporate-level planning and strategy guides the overall direction of firms having more than one line of business. The amount of diversification determines the complexity and scope of planning and strategy formulation required. **Corporate-level**

Figure 7.2   General Electric's Strategy and Planning Levels

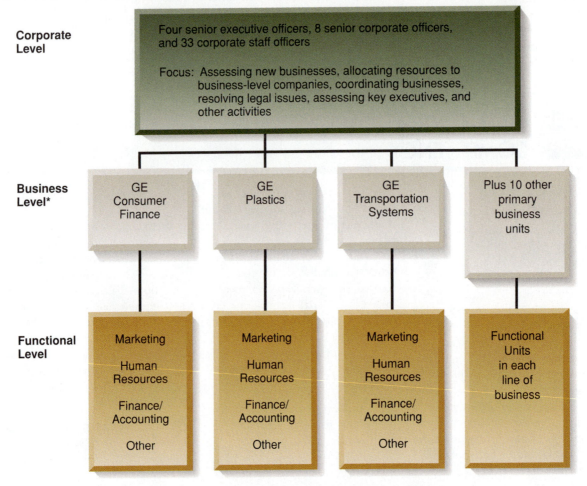

Corporate Level

Four senior executive officers, 8 senior corporate officers, and 33 corporate staff officers

Focus: Assessing new businesses, allocating resources to business-level companies, coordinating businesses, resolving legal issues, assessing key executives, and other activities

Business Level*

| GE Consumer Finance | GE Plastics | GE Transportation Systems | Plus 10 other primary business units |

Functional Level

Marketing	Marketing	Marketing	Functional Units in each line of business
Human Resources	Human Resources	Human Resources	
Finance/ Accounting	Finance/ Accounting	Finance/ Accounting	
Other	Other	Other	

*Each of the 13 primary business units has its own business functions.

strategy *focuses on the types of businesses the firm wants to be in, ways to acquire or divest businesses, allocation of resources among the businesses, and ways to develop learning and synergy among those businesses.* Top corporate managers then determine the role of each separate business within the organization.

One of GE's corporate-level strategies is to operate as a *learning company* that takes advantage of the diversity of markets and geographic areas served. As indicated in Figure 7.2, the corporate level at GE includes (1) 4 senior executive officers (chairman of the board and CEO and 3 vice chairmen of the board and executive offices); (2) 8 senior corporate officers (human resources, global research, general counsel/legal, information systems, corporate business development, finance, GE capital, and GE Asia); and (3) 33 corporate staff officers (a sampling of the roles include executive development, environmental programs, investor relations and corporate citizenship, and auditing).[26] The planning and strategy formulation process at GE's corporate level is complex and broad in scope.

One of the functions of corporate-level management is to guide and review the performance of strategic business units. A **strategic business unit (SBU)** *is a division or subsidiary of a firm that provides a distinct product or service and often has its own mission and goals.* An SBU may have a well-defined set of customers and/or cover a specific geographic area. An SBU is usually evaluated on the basis of its own income statement and balance sheet.[27] The top managers of each SBU are responsible for developing plans and strategies for their units. These proposals normally are submitted to corporate headquarters for review. Top corporate management, as at GE, is involved in determining which SBUs to start, acquire, or divest. Corporate-level management also decides whether to allocate the same, less, or more financial and human resources to the various SBUs.

Growth Strategies. Managers can use a variety of corporate-level growth strategies to reach their organizational goals. Five of the more common corporate-level strategies are forward integration, backward integration, horizontal integration, concentric diversification, and conglomerate diversification.

A **forward integration strategy** *refers to entering the business of its customers, moving it closer to the ultimate consumer.* This approach is sometimes called a *downstream strategy.* For example, Cisco Systems, headquartered in San Jose, California, is a major provider of routers and switches used to link networks and power the Internet. It primarily sells to other firms. To extend its reach into homes, Cisco purchased Linksys, headquartered in Irvine, California. Linksys makes networking equipment for homes and small offices, allowing consumers to connect two or more personal computers to a single high-speed Internet connection or printer. Linksys also makes devices to link computers wirelessly.[28]

A **backward integration strategy** *refers to entering the businesses of its suppliers, usually to control component quality, ensure on-time delivery, or stabilize prices.* This approach is sometimes called an *upstream strategy.* It is implemented by acquiring suppliers or by creating new businesses that provide the same goods or services as the organization's suppliers. Baxter International, headquartered in Deerfield, Illinois, is a global health-care company that provides critical drugs for people with life-threatening conditions. Recently, Baxter purchased an icodextrin manufacturing facility owned by ML Laboratories. Icodextrin is a key, raw material used to make Baxter's Extraneal peritoneal dialysis solution. This is a new solution that offers the potential for increased removal of fluid from the bloodstream during dialysis.[29]

A **horizontal integration strategy** *refers to acquiring one or more competitors to consolidate and extend its market share.* For example, Hewlett-Packard, headquartered in Palo Alto, California, acquired Compaq Computer Corporation, which had been headquartered in Houston, Texas. The rationale for the merger was based on such factors as (1) reducing duplication and competition between their overlapping product lines; (2) extending their complementary product lines and market share; (3) achieving cost efficiencies in production, administration, and marketing; and (4) providing more of the technology products and services needed by their customers.[30] As a result of the merger, Hewlett-Packard was reorganized into four core strategic business groups:

1. *Enterprise Systems Group (ESG)*—focuses on enterprise storage, servers, management software, and a variety of solutions.
2. *Imaging and Printing Group (IPG)*—focuses on printer hardware, all-in-one digital imaging devices such as cameras and scanners, and associated supplies and accessories; also is expanding into the commercial printing market.
3. *HP Services (HPS)*—focuses on know-how and a comprehensive portfolio of services to help customers realize measurable business value from their IT investment.
4. *Personal Systems Group (PSG)*—focuses on desktop and notebook PCs, workstations, thin clients, smart handhelds, and personal devices.[31]

A growing alternative to traditional forms of backward, forward, and horizontal integration is the *alliance strategy.* As suggested in Chapter 4, this strategy involves two or more organizations pooling physical, financial, human, technological, and/or other resources to achieve specific goals. For example, Johnson & Johnson has a strategic alliance with Merck & Co., headquartered in Whitehouse Station, New Jersey, through their joint venture, Merck Consumer Pharmaceuticals, headquartered in Fort Washington, Pennsylvania. This firm's prescription and over-the-counter products include Pepcid Complete and Pepcid AC. This alliance combines Merck's clinical research capabilities with J&J's sales and marketing expertise.[32]

A **concentric diversification strategy**, *sometimes called related diversification, refers to acquiring or starting a business related to the organization's existing business in terms of technology, markets, or products.* Frequently, a related-business enterprise acquires another company or starts a new venture. Some common thread must link the two firms, such as the same general set of customers and markets, similar technology, overlapping distribution channels, or similar goods or services. Cadbury Schweppes, headquartered in London, is one of the largest international beverage and confectionery companies in the world. It acquired Adams Confectionery, which had been a division of Pfizer. Pfizer decided to sell this division to focus on its core businesses in pharmaceutical, consumer, and animal health products. Key Adams' brands include Halls medicated confectionery, Trident sugarfree gum, Dentyne Ice chewing gum, and the Bubbas bubblegum range. Prior to the acquisition, a few of the Cadbury Schweppes brands included Canada Dry, Dr. Pepper, Snapple, and a variety of Cadbury candies. The rationale for the acquisition was expressed in these words by John Sunderland, the CEO of Cadbury Schweppes:

> Adams brings Cadbury Schweppes powerful brands, access to new geographies and significant scale in the fastest growing confectionery sectors. Together we are able to offer our customers and consumers a full range of products in every confectionery category which then gives us an excellent platform for growth and value creation.[33]

A **conglomerate diversification strategy** *refers to adding unrelated goods or services to its line of businesses.* A firm may acquire another company or start a venture in a totally new field. Diversified enterprises operating unrelated businesses most often purchase established companies. As mentioned previously, this corporate-level strategy is usually viewed with skepticism by financial and management experts. The acquiring firm seeks organizations that can enhance its growth, overall stability, or balance in the firm's total portfolio of companies, especially in terms of better use and generation of resources. General Electric and Berkshire Hathaway are among the few firms that have successfully used this strategy.

Berkshire Hathaway, Inc., headquartered in Omaha, Nebraska, is a conglomerate that owns approximately 38 subsidiaries engaged in a number of unrelated business activities. A few of these include Acme Brick Company, Benjamin Moore & Co., GEICO Direct Auto Insurance, International Dairy Queen, Inc., and See's Candies. William Buffet has been a key shareholder and chairman of the board of Berkshire Hathaway. The following Self-Management Competency presents a brief excerpt from his letter to the shareholders.[34] It provides a glimpse into him and why this firm has been one of the few successful conglomerates.

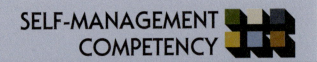

SELF-MANAGEMENT COMPETENCY

Warren Buffett
We continue to be blessed with an extraordinary group of managers, many of whom haven't the slightest financial need to work. They stick around, though: In 38 years, we've never had a single CEO of a subsidiary elect to leave Berkshire to work elsewhere. Berkshire's operat-

ing CEOs are masters of their crafts and run their businesses as if they were their own. My job is to stay out of their way and allocate whatever excess capital their businesses generate. It's easy work.

My managerial model is Eddie Bennett, who was a batboy. In 1919, at age 19, Eddie began his work with the Chicago White Sox, who that year went to the World Series. The next year, Eddie switched to the Brooklyn Dodgers, and they, too, won their league title. Our hero, however, smelled trouble. Changing boroughs, he joined the Yankees in 1921, and they promptly won their first pennant in history. Now Eddie settled in, shrewdly seeing what was coming. In the next seven years, the Yankees won five American League titles.

What does this have to do with management? It's simple—to be a winner, work with winners. In 1927, for example, Eddie received $700 for the 1/8th World Series share voted him by the legendary Yankee team of Ruth and Gehrig. This sum, which Eddie earned by working only four days (because New York swept the Series), was roughly equal to the full-year pay then earned by batboys who worked with ordinary teams. Eddie understood that how he lugged bats was unimportant; what counted instead was hooking up with the cream of those on the playing field. I've learned from Eddie. At Berkshire, I regularly hand bats to many of the heaviest hitters in American business.

Business-Level Strategy

Business-level strategy *refers to the resources allocated and actions taken to achieve desired goals in serving a specific market with a highly interrelated set of goods and/or services.* The focus is on using the firm's present and continuously developing core organizational capabilities in specific markets.[35] At Time Warner, business-level strategies are developed for America Online, Warner Brothers Studios, HBO, and its various other lines of business. Similarly, business-level strategies are developed for each of the numerous subsidiaries of J&J and GE. For a single-business firm, there is no distinction between business-level and corporate-level strategies. For example, the top managers at Lowe's focus primarily on business-level strategies because its activities and services are highly related.

Top managers of a firm or SBU focus on planning and formulating strategies for (1) maintaining or gaining a competitive edge in serving its customers, (2) determining how each functional area (e.g., production, human resources, marketing, and finance) can best contribute to its overall effectiveness, and (3) allocating resources for expansion and among its functions.[36]

A focus on customers is the foundation of successful business-level plans and strategies. This focus requires attention to three basic questions:

1. *Who will be served?* Customer needs and demand may vary according to demographic characteristics (e.g., age, gender, income, occupation, education, race, nationality, and social class); geographic location; lifestyle choices (e.g., single or married, with or without children); type of customer (e.g., manufacturers, wholesalers, retailers, or end customers); and so on. Lowe's focuses on selling to *do it yourself* customers, remodeling firms, and small-scale builders. It is estimated that Lowe's serves approximately 9 million customers a week.[37]

2. *What customer needs will be satisfied?* Lowe's serves primarily the needs of homeowners who want to beautify, maintain, repair, or enlarge their homes. Renters are served as well, but they do not purchase as wide of a range of Lowe's products and services. Remodeling firms and small-scale builders purchase items with the intent of serving homeowners and, to a lesser extent, small-scale businesses engaged in repair or renovation projects.

3. *How will customers' needs be satisfied?* Lowe's strives to satisfy customers by providing large, bright, clean, and well-organized stores with a comprehensive array of products and services to meet virtually all home improvement needs. A variety of special in-store services are offered, such as (1) professional installation services if the homeowner does not want to do it; (2) home delivery seven days a week; (3) free how-to-do it clinics, customer color matching, free computer-based designs for

kitchens, decks, and storage buildings; (4) custom cutting of lumber, mini blinds, pipe, rope, chain, and more; and (5) employee assembly of items (charges may apply).

Functional-Level Strategy

Functional-level strategy *refers to the actions and resource commitments established for operations, marketing, human resources, finance, legal services, accounting, and the organization's other functional areas.* Functional-level plans and strategies should support business-level strategies and plans. At the functional level, these tasks often involve a combination of strategic and tactical planning. Table 7.2 provides examples of the issues that management in various types of firms usually address in developing functional-level plans and strategies.

Table 7.2	Examples of Issues Addressed in Developing Functional Strategies
Sample Functions	**Sample Key Issues**
Human resources	■ What type of reward system is needed? ■ How should the performance of employees be reviewed? ■ What approach should be used to recruit qualified personnel? ■ How is affirmative and fair treatment ensured for women, minorities, and the disabled?
Finance	■ What is the desired mixture of borrowed funds and equity funds? ■ What portion of profits should be reinvested and what portion paid out as dividends? ■ What criteria should be used in allocating financial and human resources to projects? ■ What should be the criteria for issuing credit to customers?
Marketing	■ What goods or services should be emphasized? ■ How should products be distributed (e.g., direct selling, wholesalers, retailers, etc.)? ■ Should competition be primarily on price or on other factors? ■ What corporate image and product features should be emphasized to customers?
Operations (manufacturing)	■ What should be the level of commitment to total quality? ■ How should suppliers be selected? ■ Should the focus be on production runs for inventory or producing primarily in response to customer orders? ■ What production operations should be changed (e.g., automated or laid out differently) to improve productivity?

Operations strategies *specify how the firm will develop and utilize its production capabilities to support the firm's business-level strategies.* **Marketing strategies** *address how the firm will distribute and sell its goods and services.* **Finance strategies** *identify how best to obtain and allocate the firm's financial resources.*

In Chapter 13, we discuss a number of issues central to developing a functional plan and strategy in human resource management. Among others, these issues include the legal and regulatory environment, staffing, training and development, performance appraisals, and compensation.[38] For example, Lowe's human resource department develops and updates in-store job descriptions for 16 positions, including cashier, receiver, night stocker, and personnel/training specialist. The functional responsibilities for the personnel/training functional specialist in each store are stated as follows:

> Implements Lowe's Training Programs to ensure that all store employees are trained in company philosophy, policy, procedure and product knowledge. Coordinates employment, compensation and benefits, performance management, safety and other assigned programs to assure proper and consistent application and administration of human resources policies, programs, and practices. Reports to and completes other assignments as directed by the Assistant Store Manager.[39]

TASKS OF PLANNING

In this section, we expand on some of the concepts and issues discussed to this point and present them as tasks of business-level planning. We give more attention to functional-level planning and strategies in Chapters 9, 10, 11, and 13.

5. State the eight primary tasks of the planning process.

The planning process that we present applies primarily to single-business firms (or SBUs) and highly related-business firms. It comprises a sequence of eight primary tasks, which are summarized in Figure 7.3. However, these tasks do not necessarily have to be undertaken in strict sequence for the planning effort to be successful. In practice, managers and teams, such as at Lowe's, involved in business-level planning often jump back and forth between tasks, or even skip tasks, as they develop their plans.

Task 1: Develop Vision, Mission, and Goals

We noted previously that an organization's vision, mission(s), and goals are guided by considering questions such as these: What business are we in? What are we committed to? What results do we want to achieve? General goals provide a sense of direction for

Figure 7.3   The Planning Process

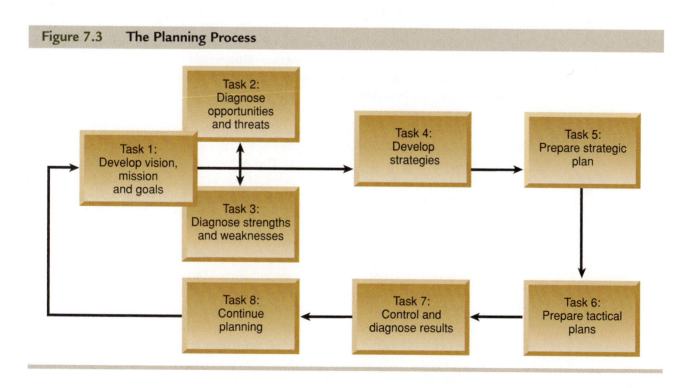

decision making and may not change from year to year. The vision, mission(s), and goals are not developed in isolation. They are affected by an assessment of environmental threats and opportunities (task 2) and strengths and weaknesses (task 3). Based on such an assessment, the top management of American Express decided on a set of long-term strategic goals, several of which include (1) 12 to 15 percent growth annual earnings per share, (2) 8 percent growth annual revenue, (3) 18 to 20 percent annual return on equity, (4) continue to expand the use of the Internet to serve customers, and (5) continue to diversify credit card spending by customers to lower the firm's reliance on the travel and entertainment sectors.[40]

Task 2: Diagnose Opportunities and Threats

In Chapters 3 and 4, we discussed environmental forces that can affect an organization. These forces represent both opportunities and threats for an organization. Strategic planning helps managers identify these opportunities and threats and take them into account in developing an organization's mission, goals, plans, and strategies. Political forces and stakeholders within and outside the organization play a key role in determining its mission and goals, as well as exerting pressures for changing them. Top managers negotiate with powerful stakeholders (boards of directors, banks, governments, major customers, and suppliers) in an attempt to influence those forces.

In Chapter 3, we reviewed the framework suggested by Michael Porter for diagnosing the competitive forces in an industry that a firm faces at any particular time. This framework (see Figure 3.3 and related discussion) includes five competitive forces: competitors, new entrants, customers, suppliers, and substitute goods and services. The combined strength of these forces affects the long-run profit potential of an industry. That, in turn, affects each individual firm's (or SBU's) overall profit potential, growth prospects, and even likelihood of survival. Strategic planning must include an assessment of these five forces. Numerous specific variables affect the strength of each force, but a review of all variables is beyond the scope of this book. Here, we simply review each force and highlight its potential impact on a firm's strategic planning.

Competitors. The rivalry among existing competitors in an industry varies with top management's view of threats or opportunities, the strategies a firm pursues, and competitor's reactions to those strategies. A few of these reactions include price increases or decreases, marketing campaigns, introduction of improved or new goods, and changes in customer service. Three of the variables affecting the strength of rivalry among competitors are the number of firms in the industry, the rate of industry growth, and level of fixed costs.

The many manufacturers (mostly assemblers) of personal computers, growth in demand for PCs, and ever improving computer-based capabilities have combined to create intense rivalry among firms in the industry. Through endless combinations of price cuts, improved features, and service enhancements, global and local suppliers of PCs have attempted to gain a competitive edge over their competitors. Some of the global PC firms operating today include Dell, Gateway, Hewlett-Packard, and IBM.

New Entrants. The entry of new competitors into an industry is often in response to high profits earned by established firms and/or rapid growth in an industry. The difficulties that new competitors experience are influenced by the barriers to entry and the reactions of established competitors. Barriers to entry are factors that make entering an industry relatively easy or relatively difficult. Two important barriers are economies of scale (lower costs as volumes increase) and capital requirements to enter the industry.

The Internet has created a revolution of new firms entering the market of traditional firms. For example, many brick-and-mortar travel agencies have closed, merged, downsized, or changed their strategies as a result of online travel services—such as

Expedia.com, Travelocity.com, and Travelzoo.com—and the major development of on-line passenger reservation systems by airlines.

Customers. The bargaining power of customers depends on their relative ability to play one firm off against another in order to force down prices, obtain higher quality, or buy more goods or services for the same price. As a result of deregulation, new computer-based technologies, digital convergence, and new competitors, the power of customers in purchasing telecommunications services has increased substantially during the past dozen years.

The bargaining power of customers is likely to be great in the following situations:

■ A small number of customers purchase relatively large volumes from the seller. Major automobile manufacturing firms buy tires from a few makers.
■ Customers purchase standard and undifferentiated goods or services. Customers perceive little difference between many telecommunications services, such as long-distance or wireless service.
■ Customers can easily switch from one seller to another. Long-distance telephone service providers, such as MCI, Sprint, and AT&T, make switching easy.

Suppliers. The bargaining power of suppliers increases when they can raise or protect market share, increase prices, or eliminate certain features of their goods or services with little fear of losing customers. The situations that tend to make suppliers more powerful are similar to those that make customers more powerful. The bargaining power of suppliers is likely to be great in the following situations:

■ A small number of suppliers sell to a large number of customers in an industry. Microsoft was found guilty by a federal court of abusing its supplier power.
■ Suppliers don't have to worry about substitute goods or services that their customers can readily buy. Microsoft was found guilty by a federal court of making its customers purchase its browser with its Windows products.
■ Supplier's goods or services are differentiated. Intel attempts to differentiate its microprocessors (computer chips) through mass advertising to PC purchasers.

Substitute Goods or Services. The threat of substitute goods or services depends on the ability and willingness of customers to change their buying habits. Substitutes limit the price that firms in a particular industry can charge for their products without risking a loss in sales. Cable television operators are being challenged by providers of digital satellite television transmission. Brinks and other armored car and guard operators were threatened by the increase in the number of electronic surveillance firms. As a result, Brinks and other traditional security firms have rapidly diversified into providing a wide range of technology-based security services, including those for the home.

Task 3: Diagnose Strengths and Weaknesses

The diagnosis of strengths and weaknesses enables managers to identify an organization's core competencies and to determine which need to be improved. This diagnosis includes the organization's market share, ability to adapt and innovate, human resource skills, technological capabilities, financial resources, managerial depth, and the values and background of its key employees. **Core competencies** *are the strengths that make an organization distinctive and competitive by providing goods or services that have unique value to its customers.* Core competencies fall into three broad groups: superior technological know-how, reliable processes, and close relationships with external stakeholders. A *reliable process* involves

The Competent Manager

"Diversity makes for a wonderful, rich development of ideas at Russell Athletic. We are selling apparel to our customers, and they are very diverse: male, female, old, young, Asian, Hispanic, African American."

Carol Mobe,
President and CEO
Russell Athletic, Atlanta, Georgia

delivering an expected result quickly, consistently, and efficiently with the least inconvenience to customers.[41]

Citigroup has sophisticated financial and market trading know-how (technological core competency). It uses local customer contacts in various countries and its global network of affiliates to develop international business (close relationships with external stakeholders core competency). As a result, Citigroup's 260,000 employees now provide numerous financial services through its global network to more than 200 million customers worldwide. Its mission is to provide its customers "any banking service, anywhere, anytime, in any currency in any way they choose" without losing transactions and without bureaucratic delay (reliable processes core competency). Citigroup has developed a solid reputation with customers for executing global transactions by assigning each customer a single contact person to build customer confidence in the handling of such transactions.[42] Ideally, a firm's core competencies make imitation difficult for competitors. For example, Citigroup's competitors do not have its ability or reputation for delivering easy foreign exchange trading to consumers. Many competitors are not as reliable as Citigroup because the competitors have a more limited network of affiliate banks around the world and must rely more on other banks, which also increases their costs.

Core organizational competencies represent strengths. Most managers find that assessing their organization's strengths is easier than assessing its weaknesses. Weaknesses often are blamed on specific managers, employees, or events. As a result, statements of organizational weaknesses may be perceived as personal threats to their positions, influence, and self-esteem. But weaknesses are not self-correcting and are likely to become worse if not fully addressed in the strategic planning process.

Outsourcing *means letting other organizations perform a needed service and/or manufacture needed parts or products.* An increasing number of firms are outsourcing part or all the tasks and functions that are not a core competency or represent a current or potential weakness. Partial outsourcing of information technology tasks to firms such as EDS, IBM, and Computer Science Corporation (CSC) has become increasingly common. For example, DuPont, the huge chemical firm, outsources 75 percent of its information technology tasks to CSC and Accenture.[43]

Table 7.3 provides a basic framework for beginning the assessment of some business-level and functional-level strengths and weaknesses. The framework is intended for a single-business firm or an SBU. In some firms, top-, middle-, and first-level managers develop statements of opportunities, threats, strengths, and weaknesses for their areas of responsibility. Issues assessed by mid-level plant managers usually are quite different from those considered by top managers. Plant managers are likely to focus on manufacturing opportunities, threats, strengths, and weaknesses, whereas top managers are likely to focus on current and potential competitors, legislation and government regulations, societal trends, and the like. The key issues, regardless of their source, need to be addressed in the organization's strategic plan.

Task 4: Develop Strategies

The development of strategies must be evaluated in terms of (1) external opportunities and threats, (2) internal strengths and weaknesses, and (3) the likelihood that the strategies will help the organization achieve its mission and goals. Firms such as J&J, GE, and Berkshire Hathaway have many SBUs. Thus, the development of corporate-level and business-level strategies for these organizations is very complex.

Three basic growth strategies are common to business-level planning. A **market penetration strategy** *involves seeking growth in current markets with current products or services.* A single-business firm or strategic business unit might increase market penetration by (1) encouraging greater use of its goods or services (e.g., getting current Marriott hotel customers to stay at its properties more often by taking advantage of a frequent guest in-

Table 7.3   Sample Factors in Diagnosing Strengths and Weaknesses

Instructions: Evaluate each issue on the basis of the following scale.

A = Superior to most competitors (top 10%).
B = Better than average. Good performance. No immediate problems.
C = Average. Equal to most competitors.
D = Problems here. Not as good as it should be. Deteriorating. Must be improved.
F = Major cause for concern. Crisis. Take immediate action to improve.

Category	Issue	A	B	C	D	F
				Scale		
Information technologies	Networking capabilities	___	___	___	___	___
	Service to customers	___	___	___	___	___
	Product features	___	___	___	___	___
Human resources	Employee competencies	___	___	___	___	___
	Reward systems	___	___	___	___	___
	Team orientation	___	___	___	___	___
Marketing	Channels of distribution	___	___	___	___	___
	Advertising effectiveness	___	___	___	___	___
	Customer satisfaction	___	___	___	___	___
Finance	Ability to obtain loans	___	___	___	___	___
	Debt-equity relationship	___	___	___	___	___
	Inventory turnover	___	___	___	___	___
Manufacturing	Per unit cost	___	___	___	___	___
	Inventory control	___	___	___	___	___
	Quality process	___	___	___	___	___

centive program), (2) attracting competitors' customers (e.g., getting Visa credit card customers to use an American Express credit card), and (3) buying a competitor (e.g., Comcast's acquisition of AT&T Broadband to create one of the largest U.S. cable TV operators).

A **market development strategy** *involves seeking new markets for current goods or services.* A single-business firm or strategic business unit might do this by (1) entering new geographic markets (e.g., Lowe's opening of stores in new cities and states), (2) entering target markets (e.g., Meredith Corporation's introduction of an online magazine—*Successful Farming*—for farmers because many of them have PCs connected to an Internet service), and (3) expanding uses for current products and facilities (e.g., Warner Cable's use of its cable lines to carry new multimedia products and services through the Internet, rather than just television signals).

A **product development strategy** *involves developing new or improved goods or services for current markets.* A single business firm or strategic business unit might do this by (1) improving features (e.g., Ford Explorer's new model with improved suspension to reduce risk of rollovers); (2) increasing quality in terms of reliability, speed, efficiency, or durability (e.g., introduction of the Itanium chip, which is Intel's first true 64-bit chip that is capable of dealing with up to 16 GB of main memory plus other new attributes); (3) enhancing aesthetic appeal (e.g., Kohler's introduction of a line of stylish shower faucets); and (4) introducing new models (e.g., Nissan's redesigned Maxima model with many new features).

Task 5: Prepare Strategic Plan

After developing alternative strategies and selecting among them, management is ready to prepare the written strategic plan.[44] The written plan should contain sections that address

- organizational vision, mission, and goals;
- goods and/or services offered, including what makes them unique;
- market analysis and strategies, including opportunities and threats and contingency plans if things don't go as expected;
- strategies for obtaining and utilizing the necessary technological, manufacturing, marketing, financial, and human resources to achieve the stated goals, including capitalizing on strengths and overcoming weaknesses, as well as contingency plans in these areas;
- strategies for developing and utilizing organizational and employee competencies; and
- financial statements, including profit-and-loss, cash flow, and break-even projections.

Task 6: Prepare Tactical Plans

Tactical plans are intended to help implement strategic plans. As suggested in Task 6 of Figure 7.3, middle and first-line managers and employee teams normally base tactical plans on the organization's strategic plan. (See Table 7.1 for a summary of the features of tactical planning.) Three factors are important in determining the successful implementation of a tactical plan: (1) achieving it at or under budget, (2) executing it by or under the scheduled time frame, and (3) meeting or exceeding the stated goals.[45]

First American Corporation (FAC) is a regional bank headquartered in Nashville, Tennessee. As a result of financial losses, changes in technology, and new sources of competition, management engaged in a major strategic planning process and developed a new strategy. The strategy selected was to become more "customer intimate"; that is, to know customers exceptionally well, better than any other financial institution. Management decided to focus on three market segments—consumer, small, and midsize businesses—where it felt that it could effectively compete. The customer intimacy strategy evolved into *Tailored Client Solutions (TCS)*, which is based on the idea that products tailored to meet customer needs will lead to stronger customer–bank relationships and long-term sustainable profits.

A number of tactical plans were developed to implement the strategic plan and the related TCS strategy. We note several of them. One tactical plan involved changing the processes at the branch level. The jobs of the customer service representatives have been expanded to handle routine tasks, such as changes of address that previously were done by the personal banker. The previous personal banker job was divided and handled by four broad categories of people. First, the personal banker job was changed. This person now handles walk-in traffic and tries to sell additional products. Second, there is a customer relationship manager, who performs an expanded personal banker role. People in this role have strong relationship skills and are entrusted with the bank's most valuable customers. Third, small-business relationship managers perform a similar role with the most valuable "mom-and-pop" type businesses. Fourth, the investment specialist is trained and licensed to sell an expanded set of investment products, which are key to moving the bank toward becoming a full financial services company.[46]

Task 7: Control and Diagnose Results

Controls are needed to ensure implementation of plans as intended and to evaluate the results achieved through those plans. If the plans haven't produced the desired results, managers and teams may need to change the mission and goals, revise the strategies, develop new tactical plans, or change the controls utilized. A thorough assessment of results will reveal specific changes that need to be incorporated in the next planning cycle. In Chapter 10, we discuss the controlling function in organizations. Controls help to reduce and correct deviations from plans and provide useful information to the ongoing planning process.

Task 8: Continue Planning

Planning is a continuing and ongoing process. The external (e.g., new competitors) and internal (e.g., expectations of new employees) environments are constantly changing. Sometimes these changes are gradual and foreseeable. At other times, they are abrupt and unpredictable, which was experienced by Bank of New York due to the acts of terrorism perpetrated on September 11, 2001.

GENERIC COMPETITIVE STRATEGIES MODEL

The **generic competitive strategies model** *provides a framework of four basic business-level strategies for a variety of organizations in diverse industries.*[47] This model is called generic because all types of organizations can use it, whether they are involved in manufacturing, distribution, or services. Figure 7.4 shows the basic parts of this model. The *strategic target* dimension (vertical axis) indicates how widely the good or service is intended to compete—throughout the industry or within a particular market segment of the industry. The *source of advantage* dimension (horizontal axis) indicates the basis on which the good or service is intended to compete—uniqueness as perceived by the customer or low cost (price) to the customer. The various combinations of these two variables, strategic target and source of advantage, suggest four different generic competitive strategies: differentiation strategy, focused differentiation strategy, cost leadership strategy, and focused cost leadership strategy. The three basic growth strategies for a single-business firm or SBU—market penetration, market development, and product development—can be used within each of these generic competitive strategies.

6. Explain the generic competitive strategies model.

Figure 7.4   Generic Competitive Strategies Model

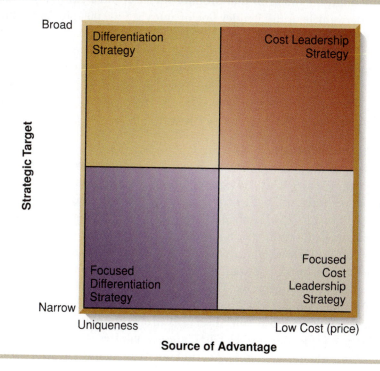

Differentiation Strategy

The **differentiation strategy** *involves competing by offering goods or services that customers perceive to be unique in ways that are important to them.* This strategy is dominant in much of the auto industry. Most automakers attempt to create unique value (benefits) by influencing customer perceptions and/or providing real differences for each automobile make and model. They use various strategies, including innovative product design (BMW), high quality (Toyota), unique brand image (Mercedes-Benz), technological leadership (Honda's four-wheel steering), customer service leadership (Lexus), an extensive dealer network (Ford and GM), and product warranty (Mazda's first introduction of the bumper-to-bumper warranty). The long-term effectiveness of the differentiation strategy depends on how easily competitors can copy the unique benefits provided by the firm. As soon as most or all competitors imitate the offering (such as bumper-to-bumper car warranties), it no longer is an effective means of differentiation.

A few of the requirements for implementing the differentiation strategy include (1) strong marketing, (2) effective integration among functions, (3) creative and innovative employees, (4) continuous development of new or improved products and services, and (5) reputation for quality and a commitment to continuous improvement in it. If successful, several benefits of this strategy include (1) fewer price wars, (2) customers who are less sensitive to price, (3) increased market share if quality is high, and (4) greater difficulty for competitors trying to copy the firm's goods or services.

Focused Differentiation Strategy

The **focused differentiation strategy** *involves competing in a specific niche by serving the unique needs of certain customers or a specific geographic market.* A *niche* is a specialized group of customers (e.g., undergraduate college students, heart surgeons, or military retirees) or a narrowly defined market segment that competitors may overlook, ignore, or have difficulty serving (e.g., an inner-city area being redeveloped or rehabilitated). Organizations attempt to create a unique image for their products by catering to the specific demands of the selected niche and ignoring other potential customers. Strategic actions associated with the focused differentiation strategy are adaptations of those associated with differentiation, but are applied to a specific market niche.

Within the auto industry, the firms that produce the 12-cylinder Rolls Royce Phantom at $360,000 plus per vehicle or the Bentley line of autos at $400,000 plus per vehicle employ the focused differentiation strategy. For example, the showrooms for the Bentley are eloquent in every respect. Salespeople are trained to weed out gawkers. They often look for Patek Philipe or other high-priced watches, hand-tailored suits, and the confident demeanor of a multimillionaire. Kenneth Tsang, the chief executive of Bentley Beijing, comments: "We provide meticulous, immaculate, 'wow' service."[48] Buyers are often provided a free trip to the Bentley factory in Great Britain.

Cost Leadership Strategy

The **cost leadership strategy** *means competing by providing goods or services at a price as low as or lower than competitors' prices.* This strategy requires a constant concern with efficiency (e.g., reduction in per unit costs). A few of the requirements for implementing the cost leadership strategy include (1) utilizing facilities or equipment that yield high economies of scale; (2) constantly striving to reduce per unit overhead, manufacturing, marketing, labor, and follow-up service costs; (3) minimizing labor-intensive personal services and sales forces; and (4) avoiding customers whose demands would result in high personal selling or service costs. High volume and/or rapid growth often are needed for profitability with the cost leadership strategy.

Online personal investing and financial services firms through the Internet, such as E*Trade, use the cost leadership strategy. E*Trade emphasizes its low commission and margin rates on its Web site by statements such as: "You simply get more for less at

E*Trade. Compare us to the competition. . . . Our combination of low costs and value-added resources is hard to beat."[49] Listed stocks may be traded for $19.99 per trade or as low as $9.99 for active traders. Active traders are defined as those who make 27 or more trades during a three-month calendar quarter.

Several potential benefits of a cost leadership strategy include (1) higher market share, (2) imposes discipline on competitors to not start price wars because they know there will be an immediate response, and (3) detracts competitors from entering the market because of the need to achieve very low costs in producing the good or service.

Focused Cost Leadership Strategy

The **focused cost leadership strategy** *refers to competing in a specific customer or geographic niche by providing goods and services at a price as low or lower than competitors' prices.* The requirements implementing this strategy are aligned with those of cost leadership, but the focus is on serving a subset of customers in an industry, such as furniture buyers, or set of customers in a particular geographic area, such as a local furniture store that focuses on low price. Gallery Furniture in Houston, Texas, is one such example of the latter.

Ikea, the Swedish furniture retailer, pursues a focused cost leadership strategy. Howard Davidowitz, the head of a retailing consulting firm, comments: "Not only does Ikea have monster stores and great prices, it has also created a unique niche."[50] Ikea's key strategy is to keep making furniture less expensive, without making it cheap. Ikea sells four basic and interrelated styles of furniture: Scandinavian (sleek wood), modern (minimalist), country (neotraditional), and young Swede (bare bones). In addition to appearance and utility, Ikea's designers and engineers focus on using materials as efficiently as possible and analyze the function of every furniture surface. This is done to determine which materials, finishes, and construction techniques will work best for the least amount of money. There are many other aspects to Ikea's focused cost leadership strategy. For example, its products are designed to ship disassembled, flat enough to be slipped into an SUV or safely tied to the roof of an auto.[51]

We do not want to leave you with the impression that any one strategy ensures success. A successful firm tends to develop and utilize a set of strategies that integrate functions, resources, and competencies to meet market demands, just as a symphony orchestra requires a score and conductor to integrate its many components to play in harmony.[52]

CHAPTER SUMMARY

This chapter focused on the development of your planning and administration and strategic action competencies. The features of strategy formulation and planning at the corporate and business level were emphasized.

1. Explain the importance of the planning function.

Planning is the most basic managerial function. It helps managers identify opportunities, anticipate problems, and develop appropriate strategies and tactics. If done properly, planning identifies risks and opportunities, facilitates entrepreneurship, and fosters learning.

2. Describe the core components of strategic and tactical planning.

Strategic planning focuses on the development of an organization's mission and vision, goals, general strategies, and major resource allocations. Tactical planning focuses on the shorter term detailed decisions regarding what to

do, who will do it, and how to do it. Tactical planning specifies the actions for implementing strategic plans.

3. Discuss the effects of degree of diversification on planning.

The primary degrees of diversification vary from single-business firm, to dominant-business firm, to related-business firm, and to unrelated-business firm. The complexity of strategic planning increases as an organization becomes more diverse in terms of the range of goods and services the firm provides and the markets it serves.

4. Describe the three basic levels of strategy and planning.

Corporate-level strategy focuses on the activities of various businesses (or product lines) within a parent organization. Corporate-level growth strategies include forward integration, backward integration, horizontal integration, concentric diversification, and conglomerate diversification. Business-level strategy focuses on the operations and performance of a single-business firm or strategic business unit (SBU). Functional-level strategy focuses on the actions for managing each specialized area. It specifies how each function will contribute to the organization's business-level strategies and goals.

5. State the eight primary tasks of the planning process.

The planning process includes eight interrelated tasks: (1) develop the organization's vision, mission, and goals; (2) diagnose opportunities and threats; (3) diagnose strengths and weaknesses; (4) develop strategies; (5) prepare a strategic plan; (6) prepare tactical plans; (7) control and diagnose the results of both strategic and tactical plans; and (8) continue the planning process.

6. Explain the generic competitive strategies model.

The generic competitive strategies model provides a framework of four basic business-level strategies (differentiation, focused differentiation, cost leadership, and focused cost leadership) that are applicable to various sizes and types of organizations in diverse industries.

KEY TERMS and CONCEPTS

Backward integration strategy
Business-level strategy
Concentric diversification strategy
Conglomerate diversification strategy
Contingency planning
Core competencies
Corporate-level strategy
Cost leadership strategy
Differentiation strategy
Diversification
Dominant-business firm
Downscoping
Finance strategies
Focused cost leadership strategy
Focused differentiation strategy
Forward integration strategy
Functional-level strategy
Generic competitive strategies model

Horizontal integration strategy
Market development strategy
Market penetration strategy
Marketing strategies
Mission
Operations strategies
Organizational goals
Outsourcing
Product development strategy
Related-business firm
Resource allocation
Single-business firm
Strategic business unit (SBU)
Strategic planning
Strategies
Tactical planning
Unrelated-business firm
Vision

QUESTIONS FOR DISCUSSION and COMPETENCY DEVELOPMENT

1. Review the Johnson and Johnson preview case at the beginning of this chapter. What managerial competencies are reflected in the J&J credo? You may find it helpful to review the section on *Managerial Competencies* in Chapter 1 before responding to this question.

2. If you were to develop a contingency plan for yourself, what three "environmental" factors would you include in it? Assume a three-year time period for yourself.

3. Review the Strategic Action Competency on Dell's competitive strategies. Based on the generic strategies model, what is the dominant generic strategy at Dell? Why? Does this competency feature suggest any other aspects of a generic strategy?

4. Think of a firm for which you have worked. What were its strengths and weaknesses?

5. With respect to the firm identified in Question 4, what were its opportunities and threats?

6. Does eBay have effective vision and mission statements? Explain.

7. Does Lowe's effectively address the three basic questions of (1) Who will be served? (2) What customer needs will be satisfied? and (3) How will customers' needs be satisfied? Explain.

8. Think of a firm for which you have worked. What was its generic competitive strategy? Did it seem to be effective? Explain.

9. Based on the self-management competency related to Warren Buffett, why do you think Berkshire Hathaway is a successful unrelated-business firm (conglomerate)?

GRUPO BIMBO[53]

Grupo Bimbo (hereafter GB) was established in Mexico City, Mexico, in 1945 as a small bread production and delivery company. Today, GB is the third largest baking company in the world and a leader among breadmakers in Mexico and Latin America. GB has expanded into the United States and 14 countries in Latin America and Europe. GB's 76 worldwide plants and 25,000-truck fleet allow products to reach 600,000 points of sale in the markets it serves. The majority of GB's 3,600 products are loaf bread, pastries, and cakes. GB has nearly 100 brands such as *Bimbo, Marinela, Tia Rosa,* and *Mrs. Baird's.* The company remains Mexico's largest commercial baking operation.

GB's mission states:

Produce and market food products, develop the value of our brands. A commitment to be: highly productive and people oriented; innovative and competitive and strongly oriented towards satisfying customers and consumers; and an international leader in the bakery industry with long-term vision.

GB has begun to expand into the United States through investments and numerous acquisitions. Believing that they have maximized growth in Mexico and Latin America, GB hopes to expand into the United States by gaining market share of the United States' bread market. The firm retains a 90 percent share of Mexico's packaged bread market. The company is recognized as the predominant bread producer in the region. GB is the leader in bread production in Mexico and many other Latin American nations. GB's *Plus Vita* brand holds a 21 percent share of Brazil's packaged bread market. Mexicans associate the GB name with high quality and dependable products.

GB's main competitors include ConAgra, Grupo Corvi, FritoLay, Haribo, Hershey, Nestlé, and Sara Lee Bakery Group. Many of these competitors are American-based firms. As competitors expand into the Mexican and Latin American markets, GB is faced with new challenges. Quality control has become an increasingly important aspect of food production. This is especially true in Mexico and Latin America where many consumers believe products to be of lesser quality than those produced in the United States. The company has committed itself to obtaining ISO 9000/1/2 certification in its plants. This certification helps to ensure quality control. GB has recently received certification in five of its plants for different production processes. Thirteen more plants are currently undergoing the certification process. GB is the first bakery business in Latin America to receive these certifications. By committing resources to achieving certification, the company is attempting to exhibit a commitment to a healthy product and a commitment to international quality. GB sees production quality and international recognition as vehicles for strengthening value and its competitive position.

International concerns for nutrition continue to grow. Competitors, such as ConAgra and Sara Lee Bakery Group, have begun to present their products as healthy and nutritious. GB is expanding its image as providing healthy and nutritious products. In advertisements, GB presents images of fresh ingredients used to make bread. GB enriches its bread with vitamins and minerals and uses enriched flour. The company has developed brands that target different segments of the market with a focus on nutrition. *Bimbo Xtreme* is a line of loaf bread with combinations of ingredients that "cater to the preferences of active young people who like to enjoy nature in all its splendor." *Bimbo Kids* is a brand created and marketed as a nutritious part of the daily diet of children.

GB attempts to compete by producing bread and other products at a lower cost and by trying to reach customers more efficiently than its competitors. The massive quantities GB produces allows the firm to produce each unit at a lower cost than competitors can. GB's extensive distribution network creates another competitive advantage for the firm. The firm's extensive distribution network allows GB's products to reach more points of sale than its competitors. These products also reach points of sale more quickly, making GB a fresher product.

GB expanded northward to capture the growing U.S. Hispanic population. The increasing Hispanic population in the United States has opened the door for GB. Many American firms have taken advantage of lowered trade barriers and expanded into Mexican markets. Latin American markets are generally more receptive to foreign business because they tend to be less developed (competitive) than markets in the United States. Being a Mexico-based firm, GB entered into the U.S. markets where there are large Hispanic populations, such as Texas and California. The "Latino food" market in the United States is growing at 6 percent per year. GB hopes to gain a significant share of this growth. Few Mexican firms have made a commitment to expand into the United States because they lack the resources needed to enter this fiercely competitive market.

Bimbo Bakeries USA has become a leader in Texas and the western United States. GB currently operates 16 plants and has operations in more than 22 states in the United States, offering brands such as *Oroweat, Mrs. Baird's, Entemann's, Thomas', Bobli,* and *Tia Rosa.* GB acquired some U.S. competitors (e.g., *Mrs. Baird's*) to increase sales. Expansion into U.S. markets has redefined GB's corporate strategy in the sense that the company now focuses beyond its traditional markets. Significant resource commitment, vis-à-vis investment and acquisitions in the United States, exemplifies this new growth strategy at the international level.

GB has also capitalized on the expansion of U.S. firms into Mexico. GB's distribution capability has appealed to a number of American firms because it allows products to reach a broad consumer base. For example, GB formed a strategic alliance with the Wrigley Company, the world's largest manufacturer of chewing gum. The alliance states that GB will be the exclusive distributor of Wrigley's chewing gum in Mexico. This strategic alliance was made possible by utilizing the company's established distribution channels.

Questions

1. What is the mission for Grupo Bimbo?
2. What are the key organizational goals for GB?
3. What growth strategies are being employed by GB?
4. What are the core competencies for GB?

CASE FOR COMPETENCY DEVELOPMENT

HARLEY-DAVIDSON[54]

Harley-Davidson, Inc. (Harley), headquartered in Milwaukee, Wisconsin, is primarily a motorcycle manufacturer and marketer of related accessories. Harley operates in two principal business segments: motorcycles and related products (the Motorcycles segment) and financial services (the Financial segment). The Motorcycles segment includes the group of companies doing business as Harley-Davidson Motor Company, subsidiaries of H-D Michigan, Inc., and Buell Motorcycle Company (BMC), which was acquired in 1998.

MOTORCYCLE SEGMENT

The primary business of the Motorcycles segment is to design, manufacture, and sell motorcycles for the heavyweight market. Harley offers motorcycle products and related parts and accessories under the Harley-Davidson motorcycle and Buell brand names. Harley's worldwide motorcycle sales generate 80 percent of the total net sales in the Motorcycles segment. Harley manufactures and sells 28 models of Harley's touring and custom heavyweight motorcycles. The touring segment of the heavyweight market was pioneered by Harley and includes motorcycles equipped for long-distance touring with fairings, windshields, saddlebags, and Tour Pak luggage carriers. The custom segment of the market includes motorcycles featuring the distinctive styling associated with classic Harley motorcycles.

Harley also offers replacement parts (Genuine Motor Parts), mechanical and cosmetic accessories (Genuine Motor Accessories), and General Merchandise, which includes MotorClothes apparel and collectibles. In addition, Harley provides a variety of services to its dealers and retail customers, including service training schools, customized dealer software packages, delivery of its motorcycles, owners club membership, a motorcycle rental program, and a rider training program that is available in the United States through a limited number of authorized dealers.

FINANCIAL SEGMENT

The Financial segment consists of Harley's wholly owned subsidiary, Harley-Davidson Financial Services (HDFS). It is engaged in the business of financing and servicing wholesale inventory receivables and consumer retail installment sales contracts, primarily motorcycles and non-commercial aircraft. Additionally, HDFS is an agency for certain unaffiliated insurance carriers providing property/casualty insurance and extended service contracts to motorcycle owners.

MISSION

Harley states its mission, as follows:

> We fulfill dreams through the experiences of motorcycling, by providing to motorcyclists and to the general public an expanding line of motorcycles and branded products and services in selected market segments.

The firm comments on its mission in these words: "It takes more than just building and selling motorcycles to fulfill the dreams of our customers. It takes unforgettable experiences. . . . If there's one secret to our enduring brand and the passion it ignites in our riders, it's that we deliver these experiences, rather than merely a collection of products and services. And we're dedicated to creating experiences and developing relationships with all of our stakeholders—customers, employees, investors, suppliers, governments and society."

CORE VALUES

The stated core values of Harley are:

- Tell the truth.
- Be fair.
- Keep your promises.
- Respect the individual.
- Encourage intellectual curiosity.

The firm comments on its values in these words:

These are our values. They are the heart of how we run our business. They guide our actions and serve as the framework for the decisions and contributions our employees make at every level of the Company. More than just a list of "feel good" buzzwords, our values define the character of Harley-Davidson just as much as the motorcycles that bear the Harley-Davidson name. They reflect how we relate to each other and to all of our stakeholders, including our customers, dealers and suppliers. The company fosters these values by actively communicating their importance and encouraging employee involvement and development. We believe that our business will be most successful if we tap the contributions of each of our people.

Questions

1. Based on this case and other information you may have about Harley, what do you think are its major strengths and weaknesses?

2. What are several of the potential opportunities and threats facing Harley?

3. Does Harley have a clear and well-stated mission?

4. In terms of the generic competitive strategies model, which of the four strategies does Harley appear to be following? Explain.

©Eyewire/Getty Images

Fundamentals of Decision Making

LEARNING OBJECTIVES

After studying this chapter, you should be able to:

1. State the conditions under which individuals make decisions.

2. Describe the characteristics of routine, adaptive, and innovative decisions.

3. Explain the three basic models of decision making.

Chapter Outline

Craig Barrett is the CEO of Intel Corporation. Intel supplies the computing and communications industries with chips, circuit boards, systems, and related products. This Preview Case presents excerpts of Barrett's remarks in response to interview questions related to how he and others at Intel make decisions.

- *What do you think is the purpose of decision making?* It's usually the transformation of information into some act. The purpose depends on how global you want to be. If we're talking really global, it's to "out-compete" the competition by moving faster, by making decisions faster, and by acting faster than the competition.

- *How do you determine the usefulness, accuracy, etc., of information?* I think you do that in a fairly structured way by being relatively careful to define exactly what decision you want to make up front. Then carefully analyze what information you think is necessary or appropriate to make that decision. You need to prioritize where you place your attention in terms of the significant data as opposed to the other mound of information that's potentially there.

- *Can you outline the steps most commonly used in your decision-making processes?* If you were to walk around Intel, you would see in a lot of our conference rooms a simple model, a six-step model. It really looks fine in the global sense. There are three big steps, which break down into six questions. The three steps are: (1) you basically have a free discussion of what's going on; (2) you generate some form of clear decision out of that discussion; and (3) you get everybody to buy into it. Either you agree and commit, or you disagree and commit to support that decision. Everybody then implements it until you decide maybe it was wrong. If it was wrong, you all agree to come back and revisit it. But below those three things, we ask everybody to ask themselves six questions: (1) What decision are you trying to make? (2) When does it have to be made? (3) Who will decide? (4) Who needs to be consulted before a decision is made? (5) After you make it, who needs to ratify it; in other words, who could potentially veto it? (6) And lastly, who needs to be informed of the decision?

- *Now is this at all levels of your organization?* This is essentially at all levels.

- *How do you determine the quality of your decision-making process?* During the process? We don't dwell on this on a daily basis. But while you're making decisions, you always try to answer: Does it make any sense? Did you follow the decision-making profile or methodology we have? We tend not to dwell extensively on "witch-hunts" after the fact. Once again, we have this "disagree-and-commit" mentality that drives the system. Nobody benefits by showing that a decision was wrong because once you've made a decision, everyone needs to support it and try to make it successful. So we tend not to have people who are preoccupied with "I didn't agree with that and I'm going to gloat when they crash and burn."

- *What do you do before you finalize a decision?* I think the usual process I go through is one of making sure that I understand the significant data and that I don't have any major blind spots. If I have blind spots, I try to fill them in. You can't always fill them in. Occasionally you just have to recognize that it's more important to get the decision made than it is to collect more data. And recognizing that you're taking a chance without all of the data, but it's more important to move forward than it is to sit there and gridlock.[1]

All of us make decisions every day. As indicated in Barrett's comments, thoughtful decision making typically involves the same underlying elements: defining the problem, gathering information, identifying and assessing alternatives, and deciding what to do. Barrett's remarks also suggest that a process is needed for addressing these underlying elements. At Intel, that involves "three big steps," which break down into six questions. Barrett's remarks also reflect another reality about decision making. No one decision may be agreed to by everyone, but a point is reached when a decision must be made and a commitment to that decision by everyone is essential.

Decision making *includes defining problems, gathering information, generating alternatives, and choosing a course of action.* We discuss how managers and employees can base various types of decisions on the nature of the problem to be solved, the possible solutions available, and the degree of risk involved.[2] Effective managers rely on several managerial competencies to make and implement decisions. In turn, decision making underlies most managerial competencies. For example, Barrett uses a decision-making process to develop strategies for achieving goals, which reflects the strategic action competency. Barrett uses his communication competency to indicate to others throughout Intel the expected decision-making process and, more importantly, to set expectations that everyone is to support a decision once made and make it successful. Barrett illustrates the self-management competency in this comment: "Occasionally you just have to recognize that it's more valuable to get the decision made than it is to collect more data." Barrett indicates the importance of the teamwork competency at Intel in these comments:

> Quite often our decision-making process is loud, egalitarian, open, and decisive. What we tend to do is empower, push it down to the lowest possible level. Anybody who engages their brain before they engage their tongue is allowed to speak their mind. You can have people that are three, four, five, or six different levels in the corporation, in the same room, jousting with one another about the pros and cons of this or that.[3]

DECISION-MAKING CONDITIONS

Numerous developments and events—often outside of the control of individuals—influence the results of individuals' decision making. In Chapters 3 and 4, we identified and discussed a number of domestic and global competitive, political, and cultural forces that must be considered when managers and employees make decisions. Many of these forces are beyond their direct control. In Chapter 6, we noted the impact that key stakeholders can have on decisions involving ethical and social responsibility issues. Thus decisions are affected by many forces. In addition to identifying and measuring the strength of these forces, managers must estimate their potential impact.

Cary Oswald is the director of risk operations and systems at Xcel Energy, Inc., headquartered in Minneapolis. He focuses on the impacts of market and political forces daily. His unit is responsible for buying and selling gas, electric power, and coal—100 to 200 times a day at prices set by volatile markets. He is aware of political/regulatory forces: "We can only charge so much, so if gas prices are too high we can't recover our full cost."[4] Oswald's unit also prepares daily reports on these developments for top management. Decisions top management might make based on these reports include adjusting inventory levels—raising them when prices are low or decreasing them when prices jump—or changing buy and sell commitments with suppliers and customers. Decision makers, such as Cary Oswald and Craig Barrett, have to base their decisions and recommendations on available information. Hence the amount and accuracy of information and the depth of the individual's managerial competencies (see Chapter 1) are crucial to sound decision making.

The conditions under which decisions are made can be classified as certainty, risk, and uncertainty.[5] These conditions are shown as a continuum in Figure 8.1. When individuals can identify developments and events and their potential impact with total predictability, they make decisions under the condition of certainty. As information dwindles and becomes ambiguous, the condition of risk enters into the decision-making

1. State the conditions under which individuals make decisions.

Figure 8.1   Conditions Under Which Decisions Are Made

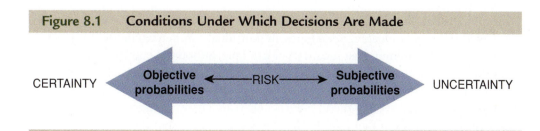

CERTAINTY ← Objective probabilities ← RISK → Subjective probabilities → UNCERTAINTY

process. Individuals begin to base their decisions on either objective (clear) or subjective (intuition and judgment) probabilities. A decision to reduce inventory levels of natural gas and coal at Xcel Energy is based on the subjective probability that prices will fall before the inventory must be restocked. The condition of uncertainty means that individuals have little or no information about developments and forces on which to base a decision. Because of that uncertainty, decision makers may be able to make only a reasonable guess as to possible outcomes from the decision.

Certainty

Certainty *is the condition under which individuals are fully informed about a problem, alternative solutions are known, and the results of each solution are known.* This condition means that both the problem and alternative solutions are totally known and well defined. Once an individual has identified alternative solutions and their expected results, making the decision is relatively easy. The decision maker simply chooses the solution with the best result.

Decision making under the condition of certainty is the exception for most managers. However, first-line managers make some day-to-day decisions under conditions of certainty or near certainty. Avis Rent A Car System, Inc., headquartered in Parsippany, New Jersey, has attempted to make the entire rental process as certain as possible. The process has been broken down into more than 100 incremental and prescribed steps. These steps are designed to take out the risk and uncertainty in decision making for both employees and customers at its 1,700 locations. Employees know exactly what to do and how to deal with problems that have already been anticipated. Customers know what to expect. Scott Deaver, executive vice president for marketing at Avis, comments: "We're constantly making little enhancements around the edges." For a number of years, Avis has been at the top of its category in the Brand Keys customer loyalty index. Brand Keys, a market research firm, surveys 16,000 consumers twice a year on their attitudes toward 158 brands in 28 categories.[6]

Risk

Risk *refers to the condition under which individuals can define a problem, specify the probability of certain events, identify alternative solutions, and state the probability of each solution leading to the desired result.*[7] Risk generally means that the problem and alternative solutions fall somewhere between the extremes of being certain and being unusual and ambiguous.

Probability *is the percentage of times that a specific result would occur if an individual were to make a specific decision a large number of times.* The most commonly used example of probability is that of tossing a coin: With enough tosses of the coin, heads will show up 50 percent of the time and tails the other 50 percent. Insurance companies make use of the probabilities in setting all kinds of premium rates.

The quality of information available to an individual about the relevant decision-making condition can vary widely—as can the individual's estimates of risk. The type, amount, and reliability of information influence the level of risk and whether the decision maker can use objective or subjective probability in estimating the result (see Figure 8.1).

Objective Probability. **Objective probability** *is the likelihood that a specific result will occur, based on hard facts and numbers.* Sometimes an individual can determine the likely result of a decision by examining past records. For example, although State Farm, Prudential, and other life insurance companies can't determine the year in which each policyholder will die, they can calculate objective probabilities that specific numbers of policyholders, in various age categories, will die in a particular year. These objective probabilities are based on the expectation that past death rates will be repeated in the future.

Subjective Probability. **Subjective probability** *is the likelihood that a specific result will occur, based on personal judgment.* Judgments vary among individuals, depending on their intuition, previous experience with similar situations, expertise, and personality traits (e.g., preference for risk taking or risk avoidance).

Ron Dembo is the founder, president, and CEO of Algorithmics, Inc., headquartered in Toronto, Ontario, with 15 offices worldwide. The firm focuses on developing risk management software—applications with names such as Risk Watch and Risk Mapper—for banks, insurers, and other firms that need assistance in measuring and managing financial and other risks. Dembo's comments:

> The world is much riskier today because everything is much more interconnected. . . . If you're not managing risk, you can't claim to be managing your business. . . . Managing risk means thinking about the future, not about the past. Some of the best minds in business misunderstand this point. We all get comfortable basing our strategies for the future on the past. That's why risks that we didn't anticipate can take us by surprise—and why it's so hard to reckon with events for which there is no precedent.[8]

The management of Intel recognizes many risks—and uncertainties—in its business. In the filing of its annual 10-K form with the Securities and Exchange Commission, Intel management annually identifies "risk factors," which actually include uncertainties as well, for review by all interested parties. This form is a public document and must be submitted for all firms traded on major U.S. stock exchanges. A few of the general risk factors—including uncertainties—that Intel management set forth in its submission of the 10-K form in 2002 were stated as follows:

> Our future results of operations and the other forward-looking statements contained in this "Outlook" section, and in our "Strategy" and "Critical Accounting Estimates" sections, involve a number of risks and uncertainties—in particular, the statements regarding our goals and strategies, expectations regarding new product introductions, plans to cultivate new business, market segment share and growth rate assumptions, future economic conditions and recovery in the communications business, revenue, pricing, gross margin and costs, capital spending, depreciation and amortization, research and development expenses, potential impairment of investments, the tax rate and pending legal proceedings. In addition to various factors that we have discussed above, a number of other factors could cause actual results to differ materially from our expectations.[9]

Intel's Form 10-K goes on to address a number of these categories of risk and uncertainty in more detail.

Uncertainty

Uncertainty *is the condition under which an individual does not have the necessary information to assign probabilities to the outcomes of alternative solutions.* In fact, the individual may not even be able to define the problem, much less identify alternative solutions and possible outcomes. As suggested in the high risks and uncertainties identified by Intel, the problems and alternative solutions are often both ambiguous and highly unusual. Dealing with uncertainty is an important facet of the jobs of many managers and various professionals, such as R&D engineers, market researchers, and strategic planners. Managers, teams, and other professionals often need to resolve uncertainty by using their intuition, creativity, and all available information to make a judgment regarding the course of action (decision) to take.

> **The Competent Manager**
>
> *"You and the people you work with cannot be sure what is going to happen tomorrow, never mind next year. The danger is that uncertainty can lead to paralysis."*
>
> George Conrades
> Chairman and CEO
> Akamai Technologies

Table 8.1 provides examples of possible crises that may be sources of uncertainty and high risk for organizations. Seventy-five percent of the *Fortune 500* companies are not prepared to handle unfamiliar crises, that is, those that involve uncertainty in terms of their likelihood of occurrence, potential impact, and means for dealing with them should they occur. Businesses often prepare to handle only the types of crises they've already suffered, and not even all of those. Ford might have averted or reduced the Firestone tire crisis in 2000 if it had paid attention to reports of its tires coming apart in Saudi Arabia and Venezuela. Instead, it wasn't until the crisis erupted in the United States and became headline news that Ford put together a 500-person task force to see if it faced similar problems elsewhere.[10] The potential crises facing an organization, such as those listed in Table 8.1 can't be totally eliminated. Through crisis anticipation and preparation, their likelihood of occurrence or severity of consequences can be reduced.

Table 8.1	Possible Crises That May Be Sources of Uncertainty and High Risk

Economic Crises Recessions Stock market crashes Hostile takeovers	**Information Crises** Theft of proprietary information Tampering with company records Cyberattacks
Physical Crises Industrial accidents Supply breakdowns Product failures	**Reputation Crises** Rumor mongering or slander Logo tampering
Personnel Crises Strikes Exodus of key employees Workplace violence	**Natural Disasters** Fires Floods Earthquakes
Criminal Crises Theft of money or goods Product tampering Kidnapping or hostage taking	

Sources: Adapted from I. I. Mitroff and M. C. Alpaslan. Preparing for evil. Harvard Business Review, April 2003, pp. 109–115; I. I. Mitroff. Crisis Leadership: Planning for the Unthinkable. New York: John Wiley & Sons, 2003.

The general types of business risk and uncertainty factors indicated previously for Intel are experienced by many firms. The following Strategic Action Competency reports on how Finbarr O'Neill, the CEO of Hyundai, resolved and managed the uncertainties of how to turn around the sales crisis facing Hyundai Motor America.[11]

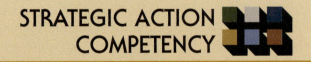

STRATEGIC ACTION COMPETENCY

Finbarr O'Neill's Crisis Leadership of Hyundai

Hyundai dealers were experiencing a business crisis in 1998. The Hyundai models had become the butt of jokes on late-night television. Overall U.S. sales were down to only 90,000 cars a year. Finbarr O'Neill, who had been the general counsel of Hyundai Motor America, was appointed chief operating officer in 1998 and chief executive officer shortly thereafter.

He began his leadership with a meeting of Hyundai dealers who all felt the firm was in a state of crisis.

Don Reily, one of the dealers, commented: "Fin got up and asked what direction we thought the company should be going in: We started throwing out suggestions, yelling out advice. Fin called time-out, left the room, came back with an easel with lots of paper on it, and started writing a bunch of things down." By the meeting's end, O'Neill had recorded 100 suggestions—and was facing less angry dealers. O'Neill stated: "I can't work on all of these at once, so let's pick the top 10, and that's where I'll start." Using disciplined thinking, attention to detail, and patience for steady progress, O'Neill began attacking the brand's problems one by one. Five years later, O'Neill is still CEO and leading Hyundai's transformation. Sales in the United States quadrupled to more than 360,000 cars by 2003 with the goal of selling 500,000 cars by 2006. In 2002, ground was broken for a billion-dollar plant in Alabama and Hyundai opened a $30 million design center in Irvine, California, in 2003.

O'Neill put Hyundai on a growth track by making a bold strategic decision. He understood that his first order of business as CEO was to address the company's biggest problem: worried customers. Put simply, he had to take the fear (uncertainty) out of buying a Hyundai. O'Neill thought that an eye-catching warranty would help relieve consumer anxiety about buying cars that Jay Leno liked to mention in the same breath as the Yugo. He also knew that such a warranty would involve some uncertainty for Hyundai. If the firm had to spend tens of millions of dollars fixing troubled vehicles, it would go out of business long before he could turn the brand around. The ultimate decision was to unveil what O'Neill and his executive team called "America's Best Warranty": 6 years of bumper-to-bumper coverage and 10 years of coverage on the car's engine and transmission.

Why was O'Neill prepared to make such a bold decision? He knew something that the comedy writers didn't: Hyundai had already started paying serious attention to quality. In the late 1990s, its cars were getting better and better, even as the brand's reputation sank lower and lower. What seemed like a brash

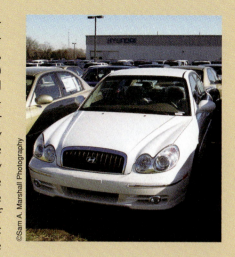

©Sam A. Marshall Photography

gamble was in fact a smart decision, but with uncertainty as to total costs and sales results.

O'Neill visits about 100 of the 600 U.S. Hyundai dealers each year. He comments: "I've got to know if there's anything Hyundai does that's standing in the way of them selling cars." O'Neill's more recent strategic initiative is to make Hyundai vehicles more fashionable. He remarks: "We want people to say at cocktail parties, 'It's okay to have a Hyundai in the driveway.'"

BASIC TYPES OF DECISIONS

No single decision-making method can be used in the various situations encountered by managers and employees. As a start, the decision maker needs to define accurately the problem at hand, move on to generating and evaluating alternative solutions, and finally make a decision. Doing so, however, is not this simple in reality.

2. Describe the characteristics of routine, adaptive, and innovative decisions.

The considerations of certainty, risk, and uncertainty provide an underpinning to the basic types of decisions—routine, adaptive, and innovative. They reflect the types of problems encountered and the types of solutions considered. Figure 8.2 presents the different combinations of problem types (vertical axis) and solution types (horizontal axis) that result in the three types of decisions. The diagonal line from lower left to upper right shows the related conditions of certainty, risk, and uncertainty.

Problem Types

The types of problems that managers and others deal with range from the relatively common and well defined to the unusual and ambiguous. The bank teller with an out-of-balance cash drawer at the end of the day faces a common and well-defined problem. In contrast, managers at Intel, Hyundai, and other organizations must deal with unusual and ambiguous problems, such as how to establish Hyundai as a brand or what type of new chip to develop. When the number of such problems escalates with short time

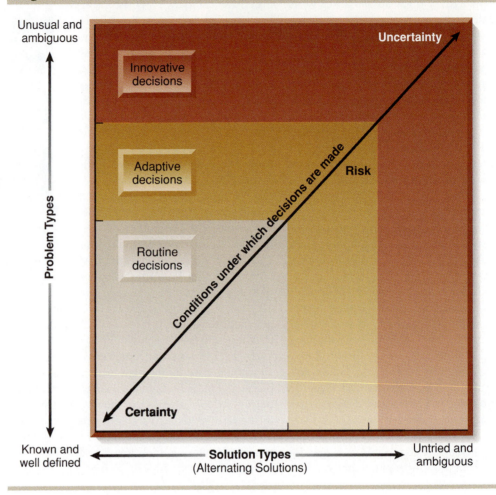

Figure 8.2   Framework for Decision Making

Unusual and ambiguous

Innovative decisions

Adaptive decisions

Routine decisions

Problem Types

Known and well defined

Uncertainty

Risk

Conditions under which decisions are made

Certainty

Solution Types
(Alternating Solutions)

Untried and ambiguous

---

frames for resolution, a pattern of *fire fighting* may occur with linked elements, such as the following, creating unsatisfactory results.

- *Solutions are incomplete.* Too many problems are patched, not solved. That is, superficial effects are dealt with, but the underlying causes are not fixed.
- *Problems recur and cascade.* Incomplete solutions cause old problems to reemerge or actually create new problems, sometimes elsewhere in the organization.
- *Urgency supersedes importance.* Ongoing problem-solving efforts and long-range activities, such as developing new processes, are repeatedly interrupted or deferred because fires must be extinguished.
- *Some problems become crises.* Problems smolder until they flare up, often just before a deadline.[12]

Solution Types

The types of solutions available also range from the known and well defined to the untried and ambiguous. What happens when a bank teller at a Bank of America branch has an out-of-balance cash drawer? In brief, the teller follows a specific, well-defined procedure—check all deposit slips against deposit receipts and cash tickets and recount all the cash. In contrast, managers often must develop solutions that are untried and ambiguous. More and more firms are finding it necessary to provide tailored solutions to fit customer preferences. The ABB Group, headquartered in Zurich, Switzerland, is a provider of power and automation technologies that enable utility and industry customers to improve performance while reducing negative environmental impacts. The firm operates in 100 countries and employs approximately 135,000 people. ABB provides customized solutions in power generation, such as at China's Three Gorges Dam, and in engineering and construction, such as at the Oslo airport. The firm often tailors the engineering and components of a project, integrating them into unique plants or systems, and shaping financing and performance guarantees to the project. ABB listens carefully to its clients to understand their needs. Also, it works closely with those clients to come up with customized solutions and approaches. At the same time, ABB's managers recognize the expense involved with such customization. They know that, whenever possible, it is important to learn from earlier projects so as to deal with new ones more economically and effectively.[13]

Routine Decisions

Routine decisions *are the standard choices made in response to relatively well-defined and common problems and alternative solutions.* As suggested in Figure 8.1, they are typically made under conditions of certainty through risk with objective probabilities. How to make various routine decisions is often covered by established rules or standard operating procedures or, increasingly by computer software, such as computerized airline reservation systems. Placing orders online, cleaning buildings, processing payroll vouchers, packing and shipping customers' orders, and making travel arrangements are but a few examples of tasks requiring routine decisions.

Managers and employees need to guard against the tendency to make routine decisions when a problem actually calls for an adaptive or innovative decision.[14] Doing so results in **active inertia**—*the rigid devotion to the status quo by attempting to do more of the same old thing better.* At times, even major companies, such as AT&T and American Airlines, become stuck in the routine ways of thinking and working that brought them initial success. When the competition changes, their once winning formulas bring stagnation, declining profits and shareholder value, or even failure.

Consider the following effective application of complex and sophisticated routine decisions and standards at Four Seasons Hotels and Resorts, headquartered in Toronto, Ontario. Four Seasons is a leading operator of midsize luxury hotels and resorts, managing 58 properties in 27 countries. To ensure that routine decisions are made in standardized ways, Four Seasons has established seven service culture standards expected of all staff all over the world at all times:

- *Smile:* Employees will actively greet guests, smile, and speak clearly in a friendly manner.
- *Eye:* Employees will make eye contact, even in passing, with an acknowledgment.
- *Recognition:* All staff will create a sense of recognition by using the guest's name, when known, in a natural and discreet manner.
- *Voice:* Staff will speak to guests in an attentive, natural, and courteous manner, avoiding pretension and in a clear voice.
- *Informed:* All guest contact staff will be well informed about their hotel, their product, will take ownership of simple requests, and will not refer guests elsewhere.
- *Clean:* Staff will always appear clean, crisp, well-groomed, and well-fitted.
- *Everyone:* Everyone, everywhere, all the time, will show their care for our guests.

These standards set the framework for making routine decisions. In addition to its service culture standards, Four Seasons has 270 core worldwide operating standards (routine decision rules). Table 8.2 provides some examples of these standards, all of which encourage routine decision making. Until 1998, there were 800 standards. These were overly complex and required too many exceptions. These decision rules are recognized by Four Seasons managers and employees as setting *minimum* expectations. Employees

Table 8.2 Examples of Decision Rules at Four Seasons Hotels and Resorts

Reservations

- Phone service will be highly efficient, including: answered before the fourth ring; no hold longer than 15 seconds; or, in case of longer holds, call-backs offered, then provided in less than three minutes.
- After establishing the reason for the guest visit, reservationist automatically describes the guest room colorfully, attempting to have the guests picture themselves in the room.

Hotel Arrival

- The doorman (or first-contact employee) will actively greet guests, smile, make eye contact, and speak clearly in a friendly manner.
- The staff will be aware of arriving vehicles and will move toward them, opening doors within 30 seconds.
- Guests will be welcomed at the curbside with the words "welcome" and "Four Seasons" (or hotel name), and given directions to the reception desk.
- No guest will wait longer than 60 seconds in line at the reception desk.

Hotel Departure

- No guest will wait longer than five minutes for baggage assistance, once the bellman is called (eight minutes in resorts).
- No guest will wait longer than 60 seconds in line at the cashier's desk.
- Staff will create a sense of recognition by using the guest's name, when known, in a natural and discreet manner.

Messages and Paging

- Phone service will be highly efficient, including: answered before the fourth ring; no longer than 15 seconds.
- Callers requesting guest room extensions between 1 A.M. and 6 A.M. will be advised of the local time and offered the option of leaving a message or putting the call through.
- Unanswered guest room phones will be picked up within five rings, or 20 seconds.
- Guests will be offered the option of voice mail; they will not automatically be routed to voice mail or they will have a clear option to return to the operator.

Source: Adapted from R. Hallowell, D. E. Bowen, and C. I. Knoop. Four seasons goes to Paris. *Academy of Management Executive*, 16(4), 2002, pp. 7–24.

are told repeatedly: "If you can do something for a client that goes beyond standards, do it."[15]

Adaptive Decisions

Adaptive decisions *refer to choices made in response to a combination of moderately unusual problems and alternative solutions.* Adaptive decisions typically involve modifying and improving on past routine decisions and practices. As suggested in Figure 8.1, they are typically made under conditions of risk that may range from objective probabilities to subjective probabilities.

Convergence. Adaptive decisions may reflect the concept of **convergence**—*a business shift in which two connections with the customer that were previously viewed as competing or separate (e.g., bricks-and-mortar bookstores and Internet bookstores) come to be seen as complementary.*

Those customer connections can include previously competing or separate sales channels, product categories, distribution channels, applications, features, and the like. Consider these two applications of convergence as examples of adaptive decisions.

Philips Consumer Electronics came up with the idea of removing the local display and all control buttons on its DVD players. In testing with employees and customers, the company found it could get by with just one button to control the most common functions. Buttons for the remaining operations could be moved to the graphical user interface, easily accessible by one button on the remote control. This helped counteract the tendency to add too many control buttons. It also contributed to an ultraslim DVD design. This communicated simplicity of operation to the user and differentiated Philips from the competition.[16]

Newell Rubbermaid is a manufacturer of a wide array of plastic-based molded products. It eliminated an annoying problem: the instruction sheet that was so often misplaced by customers. After exploring several options, the instructions are now printed on the product packaging for shelving products. This saved the paper costs of a separate booklet, simplified the packing process, and reduced the chance that instructions would be misplaced. There was also a marketing benefit. Rather than simply take up valuable space on the package surface and compete with the product sales message, the instructions actually help sell the product by showing how easy it is to assemble. This directly addressed customers' biggest complaint about shelving products.[17]

Continuous Improvement. Adaptive decisions also reflect the concept of **continuous improvement**—*which refers to a management philosophy that approaches the challenge of product and process enhancements as an ongoing effort to increase the levels of quality and excellence.*[18] Continuous improvement involves streams of adaptive organizational decisions made over time that result in a large number of incremental improvements year after year. The process resembles the wheel in a hamster cage—a ladder wrapped onto a cylinder, with no beginning and no end. Each "turn of the wheel" improves an existing product and/or process. Year after year the organization's products and processes keep getting better, more reliable, and less expensive. Continuous improvement is driven by the goals of providing better quality, improving efficiency, and being responsive to customers.[19]

Visa International Inc. has one of the largest worldwide financial processing systems, called VisaNet. The following Planning & Administration Competency feature focuses on the continuous efforts to adapt this system to meet new demands and threats.[20]

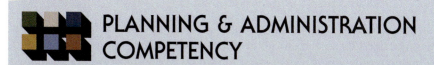

PLANNING & ADMINISTRATION COMPETENCY

VisaNet's Continuous Adaptations

Richard Knight is the senior vice president for operations at Inovant, Inc., the Visa subsidiary that runs VisaNet at its four major processing centers. Knight comments: "There is no such thing as 99.9 percent reliability; it has to be 100 percent. Anything less than 100 percent, and I'm looking for a job." The company has had eight minutes of downtime in the last five years. Visa continuously strives against outages and defects on two broad fronts. Its physical processing operations are protected by multiple layers of redundancy and backups. The company's IT staff conducts extensive and refined software testing.

Inovant makes 2,500 system changes to VisaNet per month and modifies 2 million lines of code annually. For example, Visa recently completed a three-year overhaul of its assembler-language-based clearing application, which processes 50 million to 100 million transactions each night to settle accounts among merchants and banks. In addition to unit and systems testing of the new code by the development staff, 50 people in two quality assurance groups put the software through numerous test applications. One quality assurance group tested 600,000 transactions, carefully selected from production data to represent each of 50 types of services. The other group ran full-scale tests using five days of production data—at 70 million transactions per day—and then compared the results with actual runs for those days.

Visa conducted user-acceptance testing among a sample of member banks, as well as life cycle testing in which 3,000 transactions (for example, a charge plus a later adjustment) were tracked over a seven-day period. Joel Mittler, a senior vice president for strategic projects, states: "About 40 percent of the entire project was devoted to these efforts. We added almost a year to the schedule when we realized the complexity of the testing."

Scrutiny of the new software didn't end when it went into production. A command center was set up for 30 days and staffed around the clock with senior technical people able to respond to problems. And the firm set up a help desk for customers who had problems with their own software, which had to be modified to interface with Visa's new system.

Each of the 2,500 system changes each month is assigned one of four risk ratings, with Level IV being the lowest risk and Level I the highest. Knight reviews those ranked I and II and routinely disapproves or reschedules any for which he feels the risk to system uptimes is too great. And he insists that changes be designed in such a way that they can be made or reversed in less than an hour, if necessary.

Innovative Decisions

Innovative decisions *are choices based on the discovery, identification, and diagnosis of unusual and ambiguous problems and/or the development of unique or creative alternative solutions.* As suggested in Figure 8.1, they are typically made under conditions that vary from risk with subjective probabilities to uncertainty. The solutions may involve a series of small, interrelated decisions made over a period of months or even years. In particular, leading-edge innovations may take years to develop and involve numerous specialists and teams. Because innovative decisions usually represent a sharp break with the past, they normally don't happen in a logical, orderly sequence. Such decisions are typically based on incomplete and rapidly changing information. Moreover, they may be made before problems are fully defined and understood. To be effective, decision makers therefore must be especially careful to define the right problem and recognize that earlier actions can significantly affect later decisions.[21]

Radical innovation typically comes from looking at the world through slightly different lenses. **Radical innovators** *are those individuals or organizations who do one or more of the following: Change customer expectations, change the bases for competition in an industry, or change the economic efficiency of an industry.* Let's consider several characteristics of radical innovators.

- Radical innovators challenge the prevailing dogmas and practices. Michael Dell questioned the need for dealers to sell its PCs. Charles Schwab questioned the need for high commissioned brokers to trade stocks. When most people think about the future, they often take 98 percent of current products and practices as a given.
- Radical innovators spot changing trends that have gone unnoticed by others. It has been suggested that managers should spend some time on the fringe—the fringe of technology, entertainment, fashion, and politics. Why? It's on the fringe where new possibilities are often found. Jeff Bezos founded Amazon.com after attending a book publishers' show in Los Angeles. He wondered why books were not being sold over the Internet instead of just bookstores.
- Radical innovators learn to live inside the "skin" of potential customers. Innovation often doesn't come from an expressed need. It comes from insights and understanding of people's frustrations or desires. Dell, Starbucks, and Amazon.com were not created by simply asking potential customers if they would like the services.[22]

Dr. Craig Bittner is the founder and medical director of AmeriScan, headquartered in Scottsdale, Arizona. He was a radiology fellow at Stanford Hospital in 1999 when the medical journal *Lancet* published a study that indicated a low radiation CT scan could detect early-stage lung cancer far better than a chest x-ray. San Francisco Bay Area smokers bombarded Stanford's radiology lab with phone calls, only to be turned away for lack of physicians' referrals. Dr. Bittner became a radical innovator by sensing the trend that a growing number of individuals desired to take a more direct role in their own health care. He quit his job and moved to Arizona where his parents live. Bittner scraped together $1.5 million in start-up capital to form AmeriScan. The firm now offers many imaging health screening services at 18 locations throughout the United States. These services do not require physician referrals. Currently, the services are not reimbursed by most health insurance plans. Services include CT full-body scan, CT coronary health scan, and MRI joint scan.[23] AmeriScan claims to empower its clients with the knowledge needed to have more control over their own health.[24] Within the prevailing practices and dogmas of the health-care industry, AmeriScan, under the leadership of Dr. Bittner, qualifies as a radical innovator.

MODELS OF DECISION MAKING

Our presentation to this point in the chapter provides the foundation for presenting three models of decision making: rational, bounded rationality, and political. These models have been developed to represent different decision-making processes. Each model provides valuable insights into those processes.

3. Explain the three basic models of decision making.

Rational Model

The **rational model** *prescribes a set of phases that individuals or teams should follow to increase the likelihood that their decisions will be logical and optimal.* A **rational decision** *results in the maximum achievement of a goal in a situation.* The rational model usually focuses on means—how best to achieve one or more goals. Moreover, this process may be used to assist in identifying, evaluating, and selecting the goals to be pursued.[25]

Figure 8.3 shows the rational model of decision making as a seven-step process. It starts with defining and diagnosing the problem and moves through successive steps to following up and controlling. When making routine decisions, individuals can follow these steps easily. In addition, people are most likely to utilize this process in situations involving low risk. That is, when they can assign objective probabilities to outcomes. Routine decisions under conditions that approximate certainty obviously don't require using all of the steps in the model. For example, if a particular problem tends to recur, decisions (solutions) may be written as standard operating procedures or rules. Moreover, individuals or teams rarely follow these seven steps in a strict sequence when making adaptive or innovative decisions.[26] Recall the Preview Case and Craig Barrett's discussion of how he and others at Intel think and make decisions. His discussion of their six-step model is one example of many frameworks for attempting to foster a rational decision-making process.

Step 1: Define and Diagnose the Problem. The rational model is based on the assumption that effective decisions (solutions) are not likely if people haven't identified the real problems and their possible causes. The task of problem definition and diagnosis involves three skills that are part of a manager's planning and administration competency: noticing, interpreting, and incorporating. *Noticing* involves identifying and monitoring numerous external and internal environmental factors and deciding which ones are contributing to the problem(s). *Interpreting* requires assessing the factors noticed and determining which are causes, not merely symptoms, of the real problem(s). Finally, *incorporating* calls for relating those interpretations to the current or desired goals (step 2) of an individual department or the organization as a whole. If noticing, interpreting, and

Figure 8.3   **Rational Decision-Making Model**

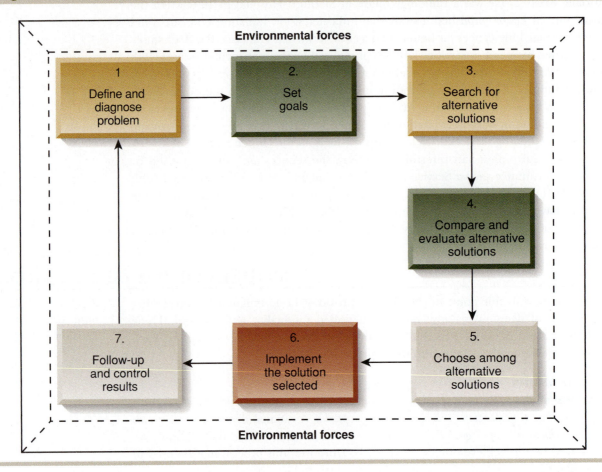

incorporating are done haphazardly or incorrectly, people are likely to incorrectly define and diagnose the problem.

A basic part of effective problem definition and diagnosis is asking probing questions. Consider the meaning of the word *question*. Our use of the word goes beyond the dictionary definition—an act or instance of asking—and is closer to the multiple meanings expressed by two creativity experts:

- A question is an invitation to creativity.
- A question is an unsettled and unsettling issue.
- A question is a beginning of adventure.
- A question is a disguised answer.
- A question pokes and prods that which has not yet been poked and prodded.
- A question is a point of departure.
- A question has no end and no beginning.[27]

Scott Hicar is the chief information officer for Maxtor Corporation, headquartered in Milpitas, California. The firm is a supplier of hard disk storage and related products. The company is committed to being a *real-time enterprise*, which is one that can provide decision makers with an enormous variety of data at any time of the day on any day of the week. Interestingly, the system that Maxtor created to solve the problem of data not being available on a timely basis created other problems. Hicar observed that Maxtor executives were creating real-time reports to be used at their executive meetings, but they were often slightly different from each other. Why? Because the reports were being produced at different times. Did this create a problem? Yes.

Executives were spending a lot of their meeting time comparing reports and puzzling over data rather than making decisions. After several meetings, the root cause of the problem was defined. The problem was easily solved by changing the software so that the real-time reports were based only on data at several set times throughout the day. Hicar comments: "Now people spend time acting on the information rather than questioning its validity. That was our early learning about the nature of real time. Every business and business process has different criteria about how timely *timely* is."[28]

Let's consider another example of the critical importance of careful problem definition and diagnosis. In the mid-1990s, Internet-based brokers seemed to invade the market of Edward Jones, a traditional office-based brokerage firm. The leadership of Edward Jones wondered if this development was a major problem that needed to be addressed by entering into Internet-based brokerage sales. After deep questioning, they decided not to enter the Internet brokerage business. Instead, Edward Jones focused on improving value-added products for its targeted customers; investing in its highly personal, face-to-face services in offices across the country. Edward Jones has increased its number of offices from 300 in 1980 to more than 4,000 today (more than any other U.S. brokerage firm). The company continues with its one-broker office strategy, which runs counter to that of virtually every other major U.S. securities organization. A managing partner, John Bachmann, stated: "You will not buy securities over the Internet at Edward Jones. That's going to be true as far as I can see into the future. . . . If you aren't interested in a relationship and you just want a transaction, then you could go to E*Trade if you want a good price. We just aren't in that business."[29]

Step 2: Set Goals. **Goals** *are results to be attained and thus indicate the direction toward which decisions and actions should be aimed.* **General goals** *provide broad direction for decision making in qualitative terms.* General goals for you may be to obtain a quality education and a good job upon graduation. One of the general goals of the Smithsonian Institute in Washington, D.C., is to serve as an educational resource for the people of the United States and the rest of the world. **Operational goals** *state what is to be achieved in quantitative terms, for whom, and within what time period.* A simple operational goal is "to reduce my weight by 15 pounds within three months." It specifies what in quantitative terms (15 pounds of weight), for whom (me), and a measurable time period (three months).

Management usually tries to rationally link goals between organizational levels and across units. This is no easy task and can be the source of many conflicts. A **hierarchy of goals** *represents the formal linking of goals between organizational levels.* A successful hierarchy-of-goals approach requires meeting the goal of the lowest level units in order to achieve goals at the next higher organizational level and so on until the goals of the organization as a whole are achieved.[30]

Figure 8.4 presents a simple hierarchy of goals for an organization with five organizational levels. It illustrates the use of operational goals. Figure 8.4 also shows that goals for the lowest level organizational units tend to become more detailed, narrower in scope, and easier to measure. The arrows pointing in both directions indicate that top management should not unilaterally set goals and impose them on employees. Setting goals often involves the back-and-forth flow of decisions between organizational levels, as well as across units at any given level.

We deliberately kept Figure 8.4 simple by *not* showing several aspects of setting goals. It doesn't show all of the performance goals normally found at each organizational level. Nor does it show the interaction between units at the same level, such as production and marketing.

Goals aren't set in a vacuum. Various stakeholders (e.g., customers, shareholders, suppliers, and government agencies) have an impact on an organization's goals. This impact

The Competent Manager

"The goals of leadership in sports, business, and the community are very similar. . . . My advice is to set high goals, to have strong values and demonstrate those values, work hard and be persistent."

Barbara Hedges
Athletic Director
University of Washington

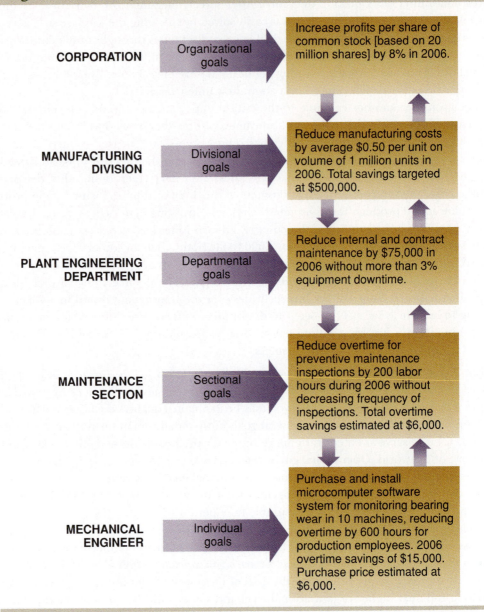

Figure 8.4   A Simple Hierarchy of Goals

CORPORATION — Organizational goals → Increase profits per share of common stock [based on 20 million shares] by 8% in 2006.

MANUFACTURING DIVISION — Divisional goals → Reduce manufacturing costs by average $0.50 per unit on volume of 1 million units in 2006. Total savings targeted at $500,000.

PLANT ENGINEERING DEPARTMENT — Departmental goals → Reduce internal and contract maintenance by $75,000 in 2006 without more than 3% equipment downtime.

MAINTENANCE SECTION — Sectional goals → Reduce overtime for preventive maintenance inspections by 200 labor hours during 2006 without decreasing frequency of inspections. Total overtime savings estimated at $6,000.

MECHANICAL ENGINEER — Individual goals → Purchase and install microcomputer software system for monitoring bearing wear in 10 machines, reducing overtime by 600 hours for production employees. 2006 overtime savings of $15,000. Purchase price estimated at $6,000.

is felt in the goal-setting revision process. As suggested previously in Figure 8.3, environmental forces, especially through stakeholders, play a crucial role in shaping the problems identified, goals selected, alternatives considered, and decisions made by managers and employees. The relative range of choices that organizations have in setting goals varies greatly, depending on the magnitude of stakeholder power.[31]

DuPont, headquartered in Wilmington, Delaware, is a major chemical manufacturer. The firm faced pressures from governmental agencies and environmental groups to reduce pollution from its various chemical-based products. DuPont has set a new general goal for its research center, named the Experimental Station, with 2,000 scientists and engineers. This goal is to create breakthroughs in bioscience. The new focus of the Experimental Station is on biological materials that are inexpensive, biodegradable, and easily accessible. DuPont's CEO, Chad Holliday, has set the ambitious operational goal of having 25 percent of sales come from renewable resources by 2010, up from 14 percent in 2003.[32]

Step 3: Search for Alternative Solutions. Individuals or teams must look for alternative ways to achieve a goal. This step might involve seeking additional information, thinking creatively, consulting experts, undertaking research, and taking similar actions. In the following chapter, we discuss the creative decision-making process for visualizing, generating, and identifying new and novel alternatives.

Gary Tooker is the former CEO and then chairman of the board of directors at Motorola. Motorola, headquartered in Schaumburg, Illinois, is a major manufacturer of integrated communications and electronic solutions used in products such as cell phones, pagers, digital video, and semiconductors. Tooker's reflections on the importance of searching for alternative solutions are instructive for all of us:

> . . . I think many people in a rush to make a decision do not have enough of the alternatives out in the open. So they have two of the alternatives and say, "Okay, I'm going this way," but they didn't think through it enough when there were possibly three or four alternatives. One of the hidden ones might have been the best, and so the issue is making sure that either all or enough of the alternatives are out in the open to allow you to make the best decision.[33]

Step 4: Compare and Evaluate Alternative Solutions. After individuals or teams have identified alternative solutions, they must compare and evaluate these alternatives. This step emphasizes determining expected results and the relative cost of each alternative.

The need to compare and evaluate alternative solutions is illustrated by British Airways' experience with its baggage-handling system. The negative consequence surfaced when some British Airways customers at London's Heathrow Airport asked a baggage handler how they could obtain yellow and black tags for their bags. The baggage handler asked them why they wanted these tags. They told him that bags with yellow and black tags always arrived at the luggage carousel first. Thus, they wanted their baggage tagged that way too. The baggage handler came to the realization that the people asking about the tags were first-class passengers. They deplaned first and were the first to arrive at the luggage carousel. However, these first-class customers had to wait on their bags while other passengers were getting their bags first.

The baggage handler didn't just ignore the problem. He asked questions about why this was happening. The answer from the operations people indicated that the stand-by and late passengers were the last to board the plane. Thus, their luggage was loaded last and then unloaded first. Ironically, stand-by and late passengers were receiving first-class luggage service. First-class passengers, who are highly profitable to the airline, had to watch and wait for their bags. The baggage handler offered a simple alternative solution. First-class luggage should be loaded last. Airline managers recognized the merit in his solution. However, the implementation of it required changing the British Airways luggage-handling procedures in airports all over the world. This would take time and money. Eventually, the procedures were changed. The average time for transporting first-class luggage from plane to carousel dropped from an average of 20 minutes to less than 10 minutes at all of the airports served by British Airways.[34]

Step 5: Choose among Alternative Solutions. Decision making is sometimes viewed as having made a final choice. Selecting a solution, as illustrated in the baggage-handling incident at British Airways, is only one step in the rational decision-making process.

Many managers complain that when recent college graduates receive a project assignment, they tend to present and propose only one solution. Instead of identifying and evaluating several feasible alternatives, the new graduate presents the manager with the option only of accepting or rejecting the alternative presented. The ability to select among alternative solutions might appear to be straightforward. However, it may prove to be difficult when the problem is complex and ambiguous and involves high degrees of risk or uncertainty.

Consider the complex and ambiguous problems that confront the Ladera Ranch team. These problems affect their choice of alternative solutions on a real-time basis. Ladera Ranch is a very large master planned community in Orange County, California. The Ladera Ranch team moves millions of cubic yards of dirt for the independent builders needing house pads, streets, water runoff areas, landscaping, and utilities. The major general goal is to decide which methods will move the least amount of soil the shortest distances possible. Geological studies exist to help. However, the moisture level and exact soil type are unpredictable. This creates a problem because moist earth requires more excavation and takes longer to settle before it can be built on. A project team might try to dry the dirt rather than delay selling lots. Also, some soil types may require different slopes for stability and that can affect the amount of flat area available for houses and streets. Sometimes, totally unexpected events—such as the discovery of prehistoric Indian ruins or a rare animal or plant species—can alter the operation completely.

The Ladera Ranch project management team is run on principles its project leader experienced in the U.S. Marine Corps. He states: "Every play we run is an option play. I want my people to be able to make decisions in the field without having to report back to me every time something comes up."[35] The team meets weekly to discuss whether the project or target path will change and, if so, how.

Step 6: Implement the Solution Selected. A well-chosen solution isn't always successful. A technically correct decision has to be accepted and supported by those responsible for implementing it if the decision is to be acted on effectively. If the selected solution can't be implemented for some reason, another one should be considered. We explore the importance of participation in making a decision by those charged with implementing it in Chapters 15 and 17.

Jeffrey McKeever is the chairman and CEO of Microage, Inc., a global provider of technology services that is headquartered in Tempe, Arizona. McKeever comments on the issue of implementation and participation:

> Remember that decisions have to be implemented. If you don't get people involved in the decision-making process, your chances of success are very, very small, especially if the decision is going to affect them. . . . I may float a question out to a group and let them all talk about it. I will tend to steer them towards my solution in as subtle a way as I can. In the process, they have a chance to understand the issues and begin to get clarity about why a certain choice is going to be made. And then, of course, if you keep your mind open you may in fact decide that this predetermined decision wasn't the right one after all.[36]

Step 7: Follow Up and Control the Results. Implementing the preferred solution won't automatically achieve the desired goal. Individuals or teams must control implementation activities and eventually follow up by evaluating the results of the decision. If implementation isn't producing satisfactory results, corrective action will be needed. Because environmental forces affecting decisions change continually, follow-up and control may indicate a need to redefine the problem or review the original goal. Feedback from this step could even suggest the need to start over and repeat the entire decision-making process. Jeffrey McKeever, the chairman and CEO of Microage who we previously cited, reflects the role of follow-up in these words:

> We do postmortems frequently. For instance, we have a national convention each year. After the convention we'll go back and review the processes to determine what went right, what went wrong. With the board of directors we certainly will review prior decisions and what went right and wrong. I have a saying: Success is never certain and failure is never final. I've seen too many people who, once they

make a decision, that's it. That's the only way to go. They have precluded a lot of chances to recover from bad decisions. Nimbleness is important.[37]

The following Teamwork Competency feature reports on various aspects of Dofasco's decision-making process, especially through the use of teams.[38] Dofasco, Inc., is headquartered in Hamilton, Ontario. It is Canada's most successful steel producer, serving customers throughout North America with high-quality flat rolled and tubular steels and laser-welded blanks from facilities in Canada, the United States, and Mexico. The firm has approximately 8,500 employees.

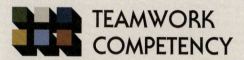

TEAMWORK COMPETENCY

Dofasco's Triple Bottom Line

Dofasco makes decisions based on a "triple bottom line": In addition to tracking financial numbers, Dofasco monitors its impact on society and on the environment. John Mayberry, the recently retired CEO of Dofasco, remarks: "These things all bleed into each other. How do you get happy shareholders? Start with satisfied customers. How do you get satisfied customers? Start with happy employees. How do you please employees? Try not to wreck the community they live in."

In reaction to two poor years in the early 1990s, the company changed how it operated. Mayberry cut out layers of management and put more decision making in the hands of first-line employees. Cross-functional teams with responsibility for quality control were added to balance its functional design. Mayberry comments: "People can make a phenomenal difference if you can tap into them, if you stop telling them to come to work, put their brains in a box, and do whatever the supervisor says. We've put the accountability

and reward right where it belongs: at the team level. And that's why we get great innovation."

Dofasco has placed a premium on setting and achieving environmental goals. In just 10 years, the company has cut the amount of energy it uses to produce a ton of steel by 22 percent.

Dofasco's environmental accounting not only helps the environment, it also boosts the company's competitive performance. In addition to reducing energy consumption, the new electric furnaces produced high-quality steel with less air pollution. In most mills, electric furnaces produce steel of a lower quality for different applications than steel made from traditional blast furnaces. At Dofasco, engineering teams worked with the new furnaces and with customers to improve quality and to find new uses for electric-furnace-produced steel. The company has been able to continue supplying its customers for high-end steel, as well as develop cheaper, more cleanly produced alternatives when appropriate. The move represented a leap from thinking about steel solely in

©Jeff Greenberg/PhotoEdit Inc.

terms of how it was produced to thinking also about customers' needs.

Norm Lockington, the vice president for technology comments: "We were able to make that jump in thinking because we rigorously return to our stakeholder model: How can we do better for the environment, for customers, for our community, for suppliers, for our shareholders? We're constantly examining problems from all perspectives as we try to solve them. And often, an improvement in one area that might initially look bad for another stakeholder actually pushes you to come up with solutions that are better all around."

The rational model might be thought of as an ideal, nudging individuals or teams closer to rationality in making decisions. At best, though, human decision making rarely approximates this ideal, especially under conditions of high risk or uncertainty. When dealing with some types of problems, people don't even attempt to follow the rational model's seven phases.[39] Instead, they apply the bounded rationality or political models.

Observations of actual decision-making processes in organizations suggest that individuals may modify or even ignore the rational model, especially when faced with making certain types of adaptive and innovative decisions.

Bounded Rationality Model

The **bounded rationality model** *contends that the capacity of the human mind for formulating and solving complex problems is small compared with what is needed for objectively rational behavior.*[40] Herbert Simon, a management scholar, introduced this model in the mid-1950s. It contributed significantly to the Swedish Academy of Sciences' decision to award him the 1978 Nobel Prize in economics for his "pioneering research into the decision-making process within economic organizations." This model emphasizes the limitations of rationality and thus provides a better picture of the day-to-day decision-making processes used by most people. It partially explains why different individuals make different decisions when they have exactly the same information. Figure 8.5 presents the key factors in the bounded rationality model.

Figure 8.5   Bounded Rationality Model

Decision Biases

Inadequate Problem Definition

Limited Search for Alternatives

Limited Information

Satisficing

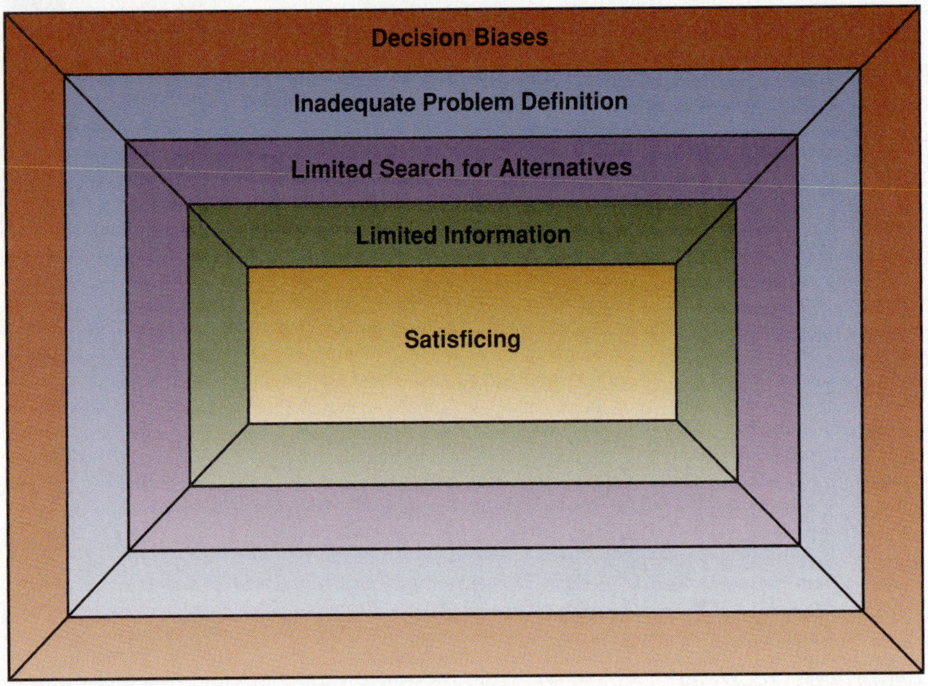

Decision Biases. People often fall prey to various biases when they engage in decision making. These biases cause individuals to use inadequate information in decision making. They can even influence what problems are recognized and how they are interpreted. The potential for such biases are most likely under conditions of high risk and uncertainty. A few of the biases that can influence one or more of the other elements in this model include the following[41]:

- The **availability bias** *refers to easy recall of specific instances of an event that may lead individuals to overestimate how frequently the event occurs and, thus, become a problem.* People who have recently seen a serious automobile accident often overestimate the frequency of such accidents.
- The **selective perception bias** *refers to people seeing what they expect to see.* People tend to seek information consistent with their own views and downplay conflicting in-

formation, thereby influencing what problems are perceived. Some people eagerly leap from a tower 100 feet above the ground with only a bungee cord between them and certain death. Yet these same people may not be willing to live near a closed plant that has been declared a completed Superfund cleanup site.

- The **concrete information bias** *refers to the recollection of a vivid, direct experience usually prevailing over more objective and complete information.* A single personal experience may outweigh statistical evidence. An initial bad experience on the job may lead an employee to conclude that most managers can't be trusted and are simply out to exploit their subordinates and, thus, are seen as problems for them.
- The **law of small numbers bias** *refers to the tendency to view a few incidents or cases as representative of a larger population (i.e., a few cases "prove the rule") even when they aren't.* Widely publicized, but infrequent, events of excessive use of force by a few police officers often trigger characterizations of most police officers as people who regularly engage in extreme use of force and aggression. Thus, police officers are likely to be seen as a problem to be reckoned with rather than as a source of protection.
- The **gambler's fallacy bias** *refers to people seeing an unexpected number of similar events that lead them to the conviction that an event not seen will occur.* For example, after observing nine successive reds turn up on a roulette wheel, a player might incorrectly think that chances for a black on the next spin are greater than chance. They aren't! Thus, the event not seen is interpreted as an opportunity rather than the continuing problem of having to deal with a random chance.

Competent and experienced decision makers attempt to minimize these biases. Their many experiences enable them quickly to gain an accurate sense of what's going on in the situation. They recognize typical and effective ways of reacting to problems. Their deep sets of experiences enable them to see patterns and anomalies that serve as warning signs. Competent individuals do not settle on the first thought—definition of the problem or solution—that comes to mind. They have typically encountered the adverse consequences of this approach in the past and have thus learned from experience.[42] On the other hand, experienced decision makers have to guard against preconceived notions. This is suggested by Jeffrey McKeever, the chairman and CEO of Microage whom we quoted previously. He comments on the importance of guarding against biases in decision making:

> . . . When someone comes to you, you often have a bias about what they are talking about. If you have been in business for 20 to 30 years, chances are you've been there and done that. Their idea is generally not so new or innovative as they think. You have a strong prejudice about outcomes. That is a dangerous thing. One of the things you have to do very cognitively to be a good leader is not let your biases or your filters totally cloud the message someone's trying to deliver.[43]

Limited Search for Alternatives. According to the bounded rationality model, individuals usually do not make an exhaustive search for possible goals or alternative solutions to a problem. They tend to consider options until they find one that seems adequate. For example, when trying to choose the "best" job, college seniors can't evaluate every available job in their field. If they tried to, they would probably reach retirement age before looking at every job possibility. In applying the bounded rationality model, students would stop searching for jobs as soon as they found an acceptable one.

Some research suggests that searching for more alternatives does not always yield better decisions. This result can be caused by several factors: the tendency to focus on problems that may only represent symptoms, the inability to process all of the information needed to evaluate a large number of alternatives, and the additional costs of searching for and evaluating a large number of alternatives that may not sufficiently improve the quality of the decision to justify those additional costs.[44]

Limited Information. Bounded rationality suggests that people frequently have inadequate information about the precise nature of the problems facing them and the consequences of each alternative.[45] These conditions create a condition of **ignorance**—*the lack of relevant information or the incorrect interpretation of the information that is available.*

S. C. Johnson Wax took advantage of the ignorance of its competitors when estimating sales potential in Central and Eastern Europe. Its competitors used official government data, which showed that Russia and Poland rank below Spain on per capita gross domestic product. However, the actual purchasing power in most East European countries is much higher than reported in government figures. The official data do not take into account unreported income and sales in that region. The unreported income is estimated to generate between 25 and 50 percent of all income. S. C. Johnson Wax capitalized on its competitors' ignorance of this fact. After just 5 years, its sales volume in Poland is already 50 percent of that in Spain where it has operated for more than 30 years.[46]

Satisficing. **Satisficing** *is the practice of selecting an acceptable goal or alternative solution rather than searching extensively for the best goal or solution.* An acceptable goal might be easier to identify and achieve, less controversial, or otherwise safer than the best available goal. As revealed previously in Figure 8.5, the factors that culminate in a satisficing decision are decision biases, inadequate or incorrect problem definition, limited search for alternatives, and limited information.

In an interview on the bounded rationality model, Herbert Simon explained satisficing this way:

> Satisficing is intended to be used in contrast to the classical economist's idea that in making decisions in business or anywhere in real life, you somehow pick, or somebody gives you, a set of alternatives from which you select the best one—maximize. The satisficing idea is that first of all, you don't have the alternatives, you've got to go out and scratch for them—and that you have mighty shaky ways of evaluating them when you do find them. So you look for alternatives until you get one from which, in terms of your experience and in terms of what you have reason to expect, you will get a reasonable result.[47]

But satisficing doesn't necessarily mean that managers have to be satisfied with whatever alternative pops up first in their minds or in their computers and let it go at that. The level of satisficing can be raised—by personal determination, by setting higher individual or organizational standards (goals), or by the use of an increasing range of sophisticated management science and computer-based decision-making and problem-solving techniques.[48]

Political Model

The **political model** *represents the decision-making process in terms of the self-interests and goals of powerful stakeholders.* Before considering this model, however, we need to define power. **Power** *is the ability to influence or control individual, team, departmental, or organizational decisions and goals.* To have power is to be able to influence or control the (1) definition of the problem, (2) choice of goals, (3) consideration of alternative solutions, (4) selection of the alternative to be implemented, and ultimately (5) actions and success of the organization. Political processes are most likely to be used when decisions involve powerful stakeholders, when decision makers disagree over the choice of goals, or when there is a failure to search for alternative solutions when conflicts arise.[49] Figure 8.6 presents a simplified political model of decision making. The factors in this model are highly interrelated.

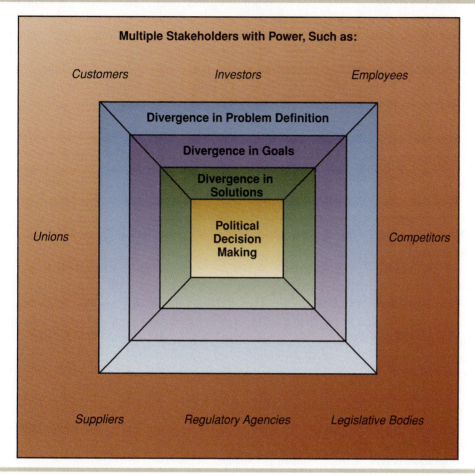

Figure 8.6 Political Model of Decision Making

Multiple Stakeholders with Power, Such as:

Customers   Investors   Employees

Divergence in Problem Definition

Divergence in Goals

Divergence in Solutions

Political Decision Making

Unions   Competitors

Suppliers   Regulatory Agencies   Legislative Bodies

Divergence in Problem Definition.   In the political model, external and internal stakeholders attempt to define problems to their own advantage. Conflicts occur when various stakeholders have different perceptions about the nature and sources of problems.

When things go wrong in a politically based organization, one or more individuals may be singled out as the cause of the problem. **Scapegoating** *is the casting of blame for problems or shortcomings on an innocent or only partially responsible individual, team, or department.* By implication, the other people who might be responsible for the problem are considered to be free from blame. Individuals or organizational units may use scapegoating to preserve a position of power or maintain a positive image.

Top management at Fluor Corporation used this tactic several years ago. When the company was charged with financial fraud during cleanup work at a closed nuclear-weapons fuel factory near Cincinnati, Ohio, Fluor blamed one of its engineers for causing its problems. The General Accounting Office—the investigative arm of Congress—cited Fluor for cost overruns, missing inspection records, leaking containers of hazardous waste, and substance abuse problems. Fluor originally denied the allegations, noting that they were overstated and highly prejudicial. It also alleged that the U.S. Department of Energy impeded the company's own internal investigation. Fluor eventually settled the lawsuit brought by the U.S. Justice Department to preserve the continuity of its operations.[50]

Divergence in Goals.   The political model recognizes the likelihood of conflicting goals among stakeholders. Thus an organization's choice of goals will be influenced by the relative power of these stakeholders. Often no clear "winner" will emerge, but if power is concentrated in one stakeholder, the organization's primary goals will likely reflect that stakeholder's goals.

A balance of power among several stakeholders may lead to negotiation and compromise in the decision-making process. Although a balance of power may lead to compromise, as in most union–management negotiations, it also may lead to stalemate. Recall that a common political strategy is to form a coalition (alliance) when no one person, group, or organization has sufficient power to select or implement its preferred goal. Many health-related organizations and associations—such as the American Cancer Society, American Heart Association, and American Medical Association—have formed an informal coalition with Congress to fight smoking and the tobacco interests.

Divergence in Solutions.   Some goals or the means used to achieve them may be perceived as win–lose situations; that is, my gain is your loss, and your gain is my loss. In such a situation, stakeholders often distort and selectively withhold information to further their own interests. Such actions can severely limit the ability to make adaptive and innovative decisions, which, by definition, require utilizing all relevant information, as well as exploring a full range of alternative solutions.

Stakeholders within the organization often view information as a major source of power and use it accordingly. The rational decision-making model calls for all employees to present all relevant information openly. However, managers and employees operating under the political model would view free disclosure as naïve, making achievement of their personal, team, or departmental goals more difficult.[51] To complicate the picture, information often is (1) piecemeal and based on informal communication (Did you know that . . . ?); (2) subjective rather than based on hard facts (Those computer printouts don't really matter around here.); and (3) defined by what powerful stakeholders consider to be important (What does the boss think? How will the board respond?).

Co-optation is one of the common political strategies used by stakeholders to achieve their goals. **Co-optation** *refers to bringing new stakeholder representatives into the strategic decision-making process as a way to avert threats to an organization's stability or existence.*[52] An example is placing a banker on a firm's board of directors when the firm needs to borrow money. Also, some organizations have created junior executive committees as a way to involve middle managers in selected strategic issues and gain their support in implementing a chosen course of action.

Despite the common view, the political model is not necessarily bad. As with the other two models—rational and bounded rationality—it can be useful and appropriate, especially for resolving conflicts among stakeholders with divergent goals and/or divergent preferences for actions to be taken. If the political model is implemented with an underpinning of basic ethical principles as discussed in Chapter 6, it is likely to lead to constructive decisions and outcomes.

The following Communication Competency reports on the application of the political model of decision making. This model was triggered as a result of questionable communications and decisions made by the top executives at AMR, the parent company of American Airlines.[53] As will be seen, the various parties, each with power, diverged over the key problems, goals to be achieved, and the preferred solutions. Through a political process, these differences were reduced to a level that enabled the various parties to arrive at a variety of acceptable decisions.

COMMUNICATION COMPETENCY

American Airlines' Failed Communications

The beginning of the end of Donald Carty's reign as the CEO of AMR, headquartered in Fort Worth, Texas, and the parent company of American Airlines, began on a Wednesday morning, April 23, 2003. It unfolded in the Meteor Room of the Hyatt Regency DFW, opposite American's busiest terminal at the Dallas/Fort Worth International Airport.

Carty arrived with two of his fellow executives. The labor representatives present were John Darrah, president of the Allied Pilots Association; Bob Ames, the pilots' union vice president; John Ward, president of the Association of Professional Flight Attendants; and Jim Little, head of the air-transport division of the Transport Workers' Union. Also present were four North Texas congressmen.

The unions were infuriated at Carty's failure to tell them about new lucrative executive pension and bonus plans. Forty-five top executives would be financially protected in the case of a bankruptcy filing. The new special bonuses and benefit protections for these top executives surfaced in the filing of a required and routine report to the Securities and Exchange Commission. This report was filed about two weeks after union members had narrowly voted to accept $1.62 billion worth of an-

nual wage and benefit concessions. Top managers at AMR had threatened that it would be necessary to file bankruptcy if these concessions were not approved. As a result of the perceived deception and self-serving actions by top executives, the union leaders were threatening to force a bankruptcy filing by either not signing concession agreements ratified a week earlier or by scheduling revotes that would probably nullify the concession agreements.

The four North Texas congressmen opened the talks, sitting first with the unions for an hour and then with management before putting the sides together at a long table. Rep. Joe Barton, R-Ennis, was reported to be the first person to tell Carty that he had to quit if there was any chance that the unions would trust AMR's management again.

When union leaders and management met face to face, Carty told them he was willing to quit. But he would only do it, he said, as a part of a deal where the unions would accept the $1.62 billion in annual concessions—with several new sweeteners—and stop any revoting. The room was quiet. None of the labor leaders took the offer. The congressmen left the Meteor Room about noon while both management and labor engaged in more talks. The

talks lasted until 8:45 P.M. that Wednesday, when all the negotiators—guarded by hotel security from reporters—left without any announcement. But the union leaders had left with a set of improvements to their concession agreements to present to their own boards of directors.

At 6:30 A.M. Thursday, AMR's 12 board members—including Carty—met privately. The board members had two tasks: Decide Carty's fate and wait for the unions to approve the sweetened concessions. A consensus emerged that Carty had to leave if the company had any hope of salvaging relations with the unions, much less staying out of bankruptcy. His misjudgment almost put the airline into bankruptcy. But a second mistake—repeatedly telling the board members that the unions were okay with the executive perks—ended up costing Carty his job.

Before the board meeting broke up about 4 P.M. on that Thursday, Carty volunteered to leave and the board members accepted his resignation. The boards of the various unions were also meeting on that day well into the evening. After more negotiations with the unions, especially with the flight attendants, an agreement was struck and announced on Friday morning.

CHAPTER SUMMARY

This chapter presented the basics of decision making. We discussed basic decision-making concepts and models that are used by managers and other professionals in organizations. Decision making involves identifying problems, gathering information, considering alternatives, and choosing a course of action from the alternatives generated. Decision-making abilities are needed to develop and

implement all six managerial competencies—communication, teamwork, planning and administration, strategic action, global awareness, and self-management. Managers and employees are required to make various types of decisions in a variety of situations daily. Chapter 9 presents several planning and decision aids that improve the ability and likelihood of making effective decisions.

1. State the conditions under which individuals make decisions.

Individuals make decisions under circumstances that represent the probability of events occurring over which they have no control but that may affect the outcomes of those decisions. Such conditions may be viewed as a continuum from certainty to risk to uncertainty. Decision making becomes more challenging with increasing levels of risk and uncertainty.

2. Describe the characteristics of routine, adaptive, and innovative decisions.

Routine decisions are relatively well defined and address common problems and solutions. Adaptive decisions address somewhat unusual problems and/or solutions of low to moderate risk. Innovative decisions address very unusual and ambiguous problems and/or solutions of high risk or uncertainty. In general, managers and professionals become more highly valued as they increase their ability to make effective adaptive and innovative decisions.

3. Explain the three basic models of decision making.

The rational model prescribes a sequence of seven phases for making decisions: (1) define and diagnose the problem, (2) set goals, (3) search for alternative solutions, (4) compare and evaluate alternative solutions, (5) choose among alternative solutions, (6) implement the solution selected, and (7) follow up and control the results. In contrast, the bounded rationality model describes a pattern that tends to be more descriptive of how managers and others often make decisions. It represents tendencies to satisfice, engage in a limited search for alternative solutions, have limited information, and use various biases to obtain and process information. This model recognizes the practical limitations on individuals when they make decisions. The political model emphasizes the impact of multiple stakeholders who have the power to make decisions. Political decision making is triggered when stakeholders hold divergent views about problem definitions, desired goals, and/or preferred solutions. Various political strategies, including co-optation and scapegoating, come into play under such circumstances.

KEY TERMS and CONCEPTS

Active inertia
Adaptive decisions
Availability bias
Bounded rationality model
Certainty
Concrete information bias
Continuous improvement
Convergence
Co-optation
Decision making
Gambler's fallacy bias
General goals
Goals
Hierarchy of goals
Ignorance
Innovative decisions

Law of small numbers bias
Objective probability
Operational goals
Political model
Power
Probability
Radical innovators
Rational decision
Rational model
Risk
Routine decisions
Satisficing
Scapegoating
Selective perception bias
Subjective probability
Uncertainty

QUESTIONS FOR DISCUSSION and COMPETENCY DEVELOPMENT

1. Read the Preview Case again regarding Craig Barrett's comment on Intel's expected approach to decision making. In what ways do Intel's six key questions relate to the rational model of decision making shown in Figure 8.3?

2. Do any of Barrett's comments suggest a recognition of the political model of decision making? Explain.

3. Identify two adaptive or innovative decisions that you have made during the past year or so. Describe how you made them.

4. What is the difference between the rationality of the decision and the rationality of the decision-making process? Cite a personal situation in which your decision seemed rational but the process you used didn't.

5. Give three examples of "personal" problems that you have encountered: one that involved the condition of certainty, one that involved risk, and one that involved uncertainty.

Why can managers, who are limited by the concept of bounded rationality, be expected to make reasonably *rational* decisions at times?

6. Did your decision to enroll in this course involve bounded rationality? Explain your answer.

7. What does your hierarchy of goals look like? Begin with this course as your most specific goal.

8. Think of an important decision that you have made during the past year or so. In what ways did your process of making the decision match or vary from each factor in the political model of decision making?

HENRY MANUFACTURING COMPANY

The setting is a board of directors' meeting of the Henry Manufacturing Company, a small company. A new corporate growth plan is the formal agenda item for the meeting. The location of the board meeting is the law office of Robert Harms, attorney and board member. The actors are Robert Harms (in his 60s), Gene Harms (in his 40s, the youngest brother, and chairman and president of the company), Clyde Brown and Carl Cutright (vice president of manufacturing and senior salesperson, respectively, both in their 50s), Debby McEwen (executive vice president, in her 40s), Bill Losey (vice president of finance, in his 30s), and Steve McEwen (executive vice president, in his early 40s).

Gene Harms had circulated the new plan prior to the meeting. The plan calls for a commitment to grow at the rate of 10 to 15 percent per year for the next five years and includes, among other things, three significant changes in sales operations. The first change is to move into global markets. The second is to hire a trained salesperson to sell a new product in the same territories as present sales personnel. The third is to stop commission (16 percent) for sales personnel and to pay them salaries (the going rate for selling industrial capital goods). The last change would reduce the income of three salespeople by at least 40 percent. Two of these three are Carl Cutright and Dick Harms, another brother.

Dick Harms had long been a member of the board of directors but had resigned earlier the same day because of the growth plan. He had discussed his feeling with both Carl Cutright and Steve McEwen before resigning. Dick had submitted his resignation in writing to Gene Harms. Gene and his younger colleagues, both on and off the board, created the growth plan. However, its preparation has generated obvious but undiscussed tensions among Gene and his brothers, and between the older and younger members of the board and their backers.

Gene Harms opens the meeting by acknowledging his brother's absence. He reads Dick's resignation aloud and reports a conversation with Dick, during which Dick stated that he would have taken the same action (developed the growth plan with its proposed changes) had he been in Gene's position as a major shareholder. (Gene and his wife together hold more than half of the corporation's stock.) Gene gives the impression that Dick's resignation is final, an unfortunate but understandable occurrence. However, Carl Cutright, Dick's sales colleague, moves that the board refuse Dick's resignation. Robert Harms seconds Cutright's motion, opening the motion to discussion.

Starting with Debby McEwen, each board member in turn offers an opinion. Debby argues against the motion, suggesting that the board's focus has been too narrow—that the same things could be accomplished through informal staff meetings at the plant. Carl Cutright favors inviting Dick back, saying further that growth should not be the primary purpose of the organization—that growth should be balanced with reality. This leads to an argument with Debby, who points to the absence of any formal growth plans to date. Gene Harms then tries to separate discussion of the growth plan from discussion of the motion regarding Dick's resignation, only to find himself further defending his growth plan. At this point, Robert Harms calls for a vote; Gene immediately asks Robert to speak on the issue.

Robert agrees with Carl that the board should not be a rubber stamp for staff decisions. Looking at Gene, he comments nostalgically that important decisions take time; that, in fact, it took years before they decided even to hire a chemist, which was before Gene entered the firm. Clyde Brown sides with Dick and Robert, arguing that Dick's conservative view is valuable. He also voices his concern over the dissension Gene's plan has caused and implies that the board's integrity has already been damaged by suggesting that Dick would not come back, even if invited. Bill Losey builds on Clyde's comment, but contrary to Clyde's view, views it as justification for voting against the motion. Bill bolsters his position by mentioning that he had talked to Dick the previous evening and learned that Dick was frustrated with the board; thus inviting him back would only put him on the spot. Thus three members favor the motion to invite Dick back and two do not.[54]

Questions for Discussion

1. Should Gene Harms vote against the motion, creating a deadlock, or diffuse the issue at least for the moment by voting with the majority? Why?

2. Are there any other alternatives to voting on Dick's resignation? Explain.

3. Which aspects of the bounded rationality decision-making model can you identify in this case?

4. Which features of the political decision-making model can you identify in this case?

DECISION-MAKING INCIDENTS

Four decision-making incidents appear below. Each one requests that you make decisions and apply various decision-making concepts.

Incident 1[55]

Susan is a front-line supervisor. One of her employees, Meg, has been in her department for eight months. Despite Susan's repeated efforts at training and coaching, Meg is performing below an acceptable level. Meg has been given average ratings in the past by the supervisors of three other departments. Susan has talked to these supervisors and has discovered that they rated her as they did in order to avoid Meg's emotional reactions. They explained that Meg files grievances and Equal Employment Opportunity (EEO) complaints on a regular basis. Susan's boss, Barbara, has told Susan to give Meg a superior rating and a glowing recommendation for a vacant position in another division.

Question

1. To the extent possible, apply the six key questions in the decision-making process described by Craig Barrett of Intel in the Preview Case. Of course, you need to decide what you will do.

Incident 2[56]

Your weekend staff is faced with a dilemma: The computers are down and a critical deadline is four hours away. The company's contract for computer repair has a minimum charge of $2,000 to get the system back on line for a weekend emergency. Just last week you were humiliated by the vice president's criticism for going over budget; he lectured you about the fact that margins are thin and money is tight. Your vice president is now out of town, and you feel reluctant to approve this new expenditure on your own.

An employee who is trying to be helpful suggests going around the service contractor by calling in his neighbor, who does the same work for another vendor, knows your computer system, will charge a lot less, and is available now.

Question

1. To the extent possible, apply the rational decision-making model to this incident. Of course, you need to decide what you will do.

Incident 3

The following are five common quotations: "Just do it." "Look before you leap." "Nothing ventured, nothing gained." "Slow and steady wins the race." "When in Rome, do as the Romans do."

Questions

1. Rank these quotations in order of your most favorite preferred (rank #1) to least favorite preferred (rank #5).

2. Do these quotes reflect your actual preference for risk and uncertainty? Explain.

Incident 4[57]

Your best salesperson has difficulty relating to peers. The position of sales manager is open, and this salesperson has told you that he/she plans to leave if not promoted. You consider these options:

a. Give the person the job.

b. Tell the person that he/she needs more management training.

c. Tell the person that you hate to lose a great salesperson to gain a questionable sales manager.

d. Ask the person what qualities he/she has to do a good job.

e. Tell the person to prove he/she can get along with others first.

f. Not give the person the job.

Question

1. Which option would you choose? Why? How might the bounded rationality model apply to this incident?

Chapter

9

©Corbis Inc.

Planning and Decision Aids

LEARNING OBJECTIVES

After studying this chapter, you should be able to:

1. Explain knowledge management and how it creates value for organizations.

2. Describe the basic features of the Delphi technique, simulation, and scenario forecasting aids.

3. Use Osborn's creativity model to stimulate adaptive and innovative decisions.

4. Apply three quality management decision and planning aids: benchmarking, the Deming cycle, and the balanced scorecard model.

Chapter Outline

Preview Case: SchlumbergerSema's InTouch Service

FOSTERING KNOWLEDGE MANAGEMENT
Knowledge Management Drivers
Knowledge Management Targets
Enabling Technology
Enabling Culture

FOSTERING FORECASTS
Delphi Technique
Communication Competency:
   Communicating Trends in Safety Management
Simulation
Planning & Administration Competency:
   The Industry Restructuring Simulation
Scenarios

FOSTERING CREATIVITY
The Creative Process
Osborn's Creativity Model
Teamwork Competency: IDEO Brainstorms

FOSTERING QUALITY
Benchmarking
The Deming Cycle
Balanced Scorecard Model
Strategic Action Competency: Southwest Airlines' Balanced Scorecard

Chapter Summary

Key Terms and Concepts

Questions for Discussion and Competency Development

Case for Competency Development:
  Mary Tolan's Energy Scenario and Proposal

Exercise for Competency Development: Personal Creativity Inventory

SchlumbergerSema is a supplier of information technology, system integration, and network services primarily to the energy industry. It is a subsidiary of Schlumberger Ltd., which is a global oilfield and information services company that employs 78,000 people of 140 nationalities who work in 100 countries.

The staff at a SchlumbergerSema oil-drilling site in Indonesia faced a serious problem: A field engineer had inadvertently programmed the wrong instructions into a computerized drilling tool, and the problem wasn't detected until after drilling had begun. Was there a way to save the situation without incurring the expense and lost time required to stop the drilling and start over?

At 5 P.M. in Indonesia, SchlumbergerSema engineers placed a call to the company's InTouch system. This is a program designed to put subject-matter experts in immediate contact with on-site employees who need an-swers. It was 4 A.M. in Houston. Within 15 minutes, the head of the department that oversees the drilling tool had worked out a solution and transmitted it back to Indonesia. An hour later, drilling was back on track.

The InTouch system is just one example of how companies are starting to use online decision aids to take knowledge management beyond its traditional role associated with chat rooms, data repositories, and FAQs (frequently asked questions). Although stored knowledge is still essential, these new aids also allow employees to tap into the most powerful problem-solving resource they have available: one another. So far, SchlumbergerSema's InTouch service has reduced the time it takes to resolve technical questions by 95% and saved the company more than $150 million annually—after factoring in the $50 million per year it costs to operate.

The InTouch service provides technical and operational support to field staff 24 hours a day, 7 days a week. The service is built on a number of elements: the Schlumberger global network infrastructure, a standard computer platform for all engineers, a single portal into the technical resource base, technical help desks in all technology centers, a knowledge repository, just-in-time online distance learning, and a centralized document authoring and publishing system. Kathryn Britt, a rig site controller at Schlumberger, comments: "Taking the knowledge, ingenuity, innovation, technology of Schlumberger and putting it at my fingertips, no matter where I am—desert, jungle, offshore, onshore. InTouch changes the way we think about accessing and using information, the way we do business, the value we bring our customer. Amazing!"[1]

Prior to 1999, the Schlumberger oilfield services organization operated largely as regional organizations operating in more than 100 locations across the world. Training and technology support was provided from the operational center in Houston. Procedures and technology were standardized across the world. However, communication between different operating regions could sometimes be slow. Also, engineers found that they needed to share experiences about working in the most challenging operating conditions (e.g., deserts, deep seas, jungles, frigid regions) to increase drilling efficiency. In such a demanding and dynamic environment, it was imperative that the Schlumberger oilfield services organization improve its knowledge management. Its InTouch service was created and provides an excellent example of knowledge management in practice.

Knowledge management (KM) *involves recognizing, generating, documenting, distributing, and transferring between persons useful information to improve organizational effectiveness.* It requires developing a system for collecting and maintaining data, information, experiences, and lessons, as well as facilitating communication.[2] In this chapter, we highlight and describe the features of KM. We also present seven planning and decision aids that can be used (1) at various organizational levels, (2) in virtually all functional areas (e.g., marketing, finance, human resources, and auditing), and (3) for aiding in the analyses essential to planning and decision making associated with many types of organizational issues and problems. However, we do not discuss general planning and decision aids (e.g., break-even analysis and payoff matrix) in this book. They are commonly presented and discussed in depth in other business courses (e.g., accounting, finance, and marketing).

We begin by discussing the fundamentals of knowledge management, which increases the likelihood of the effective use of the other aids. Next we review the basics and limitations of forecasting and the essentials of three commonly used forecasting techniques: the Delphi technique, simulation, and scenarios. Then we address the need for creativity in many situations by reviewing—from among dozens of aids—Osborn's creativity model. We conclude the chapter with three aids that are designed specifically to improve quality: benchmarking, the Deming cycle, and the corporate scorecard model.

FOSTERING KNOWLEDGE MANAGEMENT

Knowledge management is generally viewed as consisting of three main components:

1. Explain knowledge management and how it creates value for organizations.

- *Explicit knowledge:* published in internally generated reports and manuals, books, magazines and journals, government data and reports, online services, newsfeeds, and the like.
- *Tacit knowledge:* the information, competencies, and experience possessed by employees, including professional contacts and cultural and interpersonal dimensions—openness, the lessons to be gleaned from successes or failures, anecdotal fables, and information sharing. This knowledge may be subconsciously understood and applied, difficult to express, often developed from direct experiences and action, and typically shared through conversations involving storytelling and shared experiences.
- *Enabling technologies:* intranets, Internet, search engines, work-flow software.[3]

Knowledge Management Drivers

The Information Age has replaced the Industrial Age. The balance sheet, which typically measures physical assets (e.g., land, factories, equipment, and cash), is increasingly measuring a new asset—knowledge. Knowledge is becoming more valuable than physical or financial assets, or even natural resources. Information and knowledge (e.g., experience, advice, best practices, and communication) are the new competitive weapons.

The serious risks of not taking steps to manage knowledge assets and processes are driving organizations to reevaluate their knowledge strategies. In doing so, they are finding some rather severe shortcomings in their systems, including the following:

- *Productivity and opportunity loss:* a lack of knowledge where and when it is needed; a knowledge base that is not usable.
- *Information overload:* too much unsorted and nontargeted information.
- *Knowledge attrition:* according to some estimates, the average organization loses half its knowledge base every 5 to 10 years through obsolescence and employee and customer turnover.
- *Reinventing the wheel:* lack of standards and infrastructure for creating, capturing, sharing, and applying best practices or lessons learned.

Strategic importance must be placed on overcoming these and other such shortcomings to ensure that the right knowledge is available to the right person at the right time.[4]

Knowledge Management Targets

The application of KM has three natural targets: an organization's teams, customers, and workforce.[5]

Teams. Collaboration is often crucial to ensuring that goods and services are designed to meet customer needs. By obtaining input from sales, marketing, engineering, design, and other groups, KM provides a method for both the sharing of ideas and the identification of best practices across teams. By bringing together the ideas and information of each team, a project team can move ahead more quickly and efficiently. It becomes aware of work being done elsewhere in the organization, thereby reducing duplication and enhancing intergroup problem solving. Procter & Gamble (P&G)—manufacturer of numerous consumer products such as soap, toothpaste, and cosmetics—has researchers in 22 technical centers on four continents. One component of P&G's KM system is the *Innovation Net*, an intranet developed to provide them with specialized databases and knowledge. It also contains information on research being conducted throughout P&G, enabling researchers to identify others who are working on similar problems. Innovation Net also supports the creation of *communities* of researchers at P&G who are linked by their own broad professional interests, not just specific business needs or problems. Sixteen such communities operate through Innovation Net (e.g., life sciences and biotechnology, microbiology, and computer-aided design). Innovation Net supports and enhances face-to-face communication among these researchers; it isn't a substitute for them.[6]

Customers. Satisfied customers are the foundation of a company's continuing success. Tracking customers—their issues, buying patterns, and expectations—is essential for developing and improving those relationships. Knowledge management can help in this process. Organizations are challenged constantly to revise strategies affecting every area, from the supply room to the executive suite. Xerox is an example of this. Service technicians at Xerox faced an increasingly difficult job: They had to gain experience with a growing number of new copier models, resolve complaints immediately with the added complexity of network-integrated photocopiers, and find solutions to tricky errors that occur only occasionally. A technical network, dubbed "Eureka," created a breakthrough in service performance. Several years ago, the network converged around a knowledge base with more than 30,000 tips on products. Accessible from the customer's site, it provides essential tips and tricks when a technician encounters an unusual problem. The result: a 10 percent reduction in service time per case, a substantial decrease in very long or failed service operations, and significantly higher customer satisfaction. Within two years of implementation, Xerox achieved $150 million per year savings in spare parts and service time.[7]

Workforce. An organization's single most valuable asset is its workforce. Knowledge management can track employees' skills and abilities, facilitate performance reviews, deliver training, provide up-to-date company information, manage benefits, and improve employee knowledge and morale. Rapidly changing market conditions can catch a company short in terms of needed valuable employee skills. Knowledge management systems should be able to anticipate and identify skill gaps and provide mechanisms for training employees in new skills.

Clarica Life Insurance Co., a subsidiary of Sun Life Insurance Company of Canada, developed a knowledge management system to identify company experts on various topics and make them available to answer questions from other employees. Employees can query the system by keyword to find existing answers that might match their questions. If none can be found, the system provides a searchable list of subject-matter experts who can answer questions via e-mail or phone. "The question might be, 'How do I go about investigating this error that the client reported?' They're usually about a particular part of a process in a specific plan," states Hubert Saint-Onge, Clarica's senior vice president of strategic capabilities. The system also paid off after Clarica acquired Royal Trust Co.'s Canadian group retirement business in 2001. This resulted in 200 new employees. They had to learn to use Clarica's technology and methods while administering corporate pension plans, which tend to be very complex. Saint-Onge comments: "We estimated they would need three months of full-time training." However, the company was able to cut its training time by two-thirds.[8]

Enabling Technology

Technology is the KM enabler. It provides the foundation for solutions that automate and centralize the sharing of knowledge and fostering innovation. Recall the Preview Case feature on SchlumbergerSema's InTouch service. When the firm began to build its KM system in 1999, it already had a global intranet, called *SINET*, that provided secured connectivity between most of the company's sites as well as a corporate information hub to publish and disseminate information.

Choosing a set of technologies on which to build KM involves addressing at least two critical issues.[9] First, the technologies should deliver only the relevant information to users, but quickly and from every feasible source. A by-product of the speed at which technologies change is the creation and storage of knowledge in many different places. The technology used should support exploration of new ideas and solutions to problems and make existing knowledge easily available to both developers and users. Xerox's Eureka is an example of such technology. Second, because of the increasing mobility of knowledge workers, technologies used need to comprise a variety of devices—from telephone to laptop computers. The ability to obtain and deliver information is useless if it cannot be transmitted to where a decision needs to be made.

Expert Systems. In recent years, computer-based technologies have been developed to perform functions normally associated with human intelligence, such as comprehending spoken language, making judgments, and even learning.[10] Most business applications of such technologies involve what is called an expert system. An **expert system** *is a computer program based on the decision-making processes of human experts that stores, retrieves, and manipulates data, diagnoses problems, and makes limited decisions based on detailed information about a particular problem.* It helps users find solutions by posing a series of questions about a specific situation and then offering solutions based on the information it receives in response. The primary characteristics of an expert system include the following:

- It is programmed to use factual knowledge, if–then rules, and specific procedures to solve certain problems. If–then rules are logical steps of progression toward a solution.
- It is based on the decision-making process used by effective managers or specialists when they search among possible alternatives for a "good enough" solution.
- It provides programmed explanations, so the user can follow the assumptions, line of reasoning, and process leading to the recommended alternative.[11]

Expert systems have problem-solving capabilities within a specific area of knowledge. They vary in complexity, both in terms of knowledge and technology. An example of the simplest type of system is a personal budgeting system running on a PC. The thrust of basic expert systems is to improve personal decision making and thereby increase productivity. In contrast, strategic impact expert systems involve high levels of knowledge and technological complexity. Lincoln National's Life Underwriting System is an example. The process of underwriting an individual's life insurance application requires complex medical, financial, and insurance knowledge. Lincoln National also requires that an applicant's hobbies (e.g., mountain climbing) and vocation (e.g., one that might require frequent travel to politically unstable countries) be factored into policy evaluation and pricing. In many of these areas, the information that an underwriter receives needs to be clarified and interpreted. Lincoln National's four best senior underwriters spent much of their time for several years as consulting experts helping develop this expert system.[12]

Enabling Culture

Organizations consistently identify cultural issues as the greatest barriers to the successful implementation of KM.[13] There is an old saying that "knowledge is power." To overcome the hoarding of information as a source of power, an appropriate organizational culture needs to be in place or created. In later chapters, particularly Chapters 15 through 18, we discuss many facets of the type of culture and management practices that are necessary to ensure that knowledge management will flourish. As a start, a sense of trust in the organization is essential for members to actively share knowledge, especially tacit knowledge from one network member to another. There needs to be a belief that sharing one's expertise with another member will not be used against oneself.

To help create a sense of trust and positive cultural response in the InTouch service at SchlumbergerSema, the following implementation process was used:

- A *knowledge champion* was assigned as a focal point, and a steering committee was created to work with this person to set up and organize a useful design for storing and accessing the knowledge.
- Extensive input from the field employees was sought. They were kept informed of progress through designated local *knowledge champions* assigned in each operating location.
- A knowledge-sharing culture was developed among the oilfield services personnel. This is a culture where field experts systematically share their experience and incorporate the knowledge of their peers as a normal part of the everyday job. The factors that motivate individuals to share knowledge were identified. A system for rewarding the behaviors that support the culture was created.[14]

FOSTERING FORECASTS

2. Describe the basic features of the Delphi technique, simulation, and scenario forecasting aids.

Forecasting *involves projecting or estimating future events or conditions in an organization's environment.* Forecasting is concerned primarily with external events or conditions beyond the organization's control that are important to its survival and growth. A team of experts at Battelle, a renowned technology organization based in Columbus, Ohio, has developed a list of the 10 most strategic technological trends that will shape business and the world by the year 2020. As an overview to identifying these strategic technologies, Stephen Millett, manager of Battelle's technology forecasts, remarks:

> The 20th century was the time of big technologies, mass production, mass wars, and mass politics. But in the years ahead, new technologies will become much more personalized, and they will closely affect almost every aspect of our lives. We see advances in information and biological technologies bringing us into a more intimate relationship with nature and with each other. From cloned human organs, to personalized public transportation, to computers and sensors embedded in our bodies, we will become intertwined with technology.[15]

A presentation of the 10 strategic technologies is available at http://www.battelle.org/forecasts.

Most forecasting is based on some form of extrapolation, which is certainly an important factor in Battelle's forecasts of strategic technologies by the year 2020. Extrapolation is the projection of some trend or tendency from the past or present into the future. The simplest, and at times most misleading, form of extrapolation is a linear, or straight-line, projection of a past trend into the future.[16] For example, many investors were shocked and dismayed in 2000 when the forecasts of many stock market analysts in 1999 for continuing double-digit percentage stock market gains were not realized.

Cheryl Russell, a well-respected demographer and forecaster, warns of four forecasting pitfalls:

- *Listening to the media.* Tracking trends through headlines is asking for trouble. The media often distort trends, blow fads up into trends, or completely miss trends.
- *Assuming that things are going to return to the way they used to be.* The belief that trends are like a swinging pendulum—going one way, then the other—is a nice concept, but things really don't work that way.
- *Hearsay.* The neighbors are doing it, or everyone says that they know someone doing it, so therefore a trend must exist.
- *Tunnel vision.* The business media provide only a narrow view of what's going on in the world. Reading or obtaining material in other ways about other aspects of life provides an expanded view of the world.[17]

Even though forecasting is risky, it's still necessary. Managers and teams at all levels have to use whatever is available to them when trying to anticipate future events and conditions. Three forecasting aids—the Delphi technique, simulation, and scenarios—are often used in planning and decision making. Because all of them focus on understanding possible futures, they aren't mutually exclusive and may well be used with one another.

Delphi Technique

The **Delphi technique** *is a forecasting aid based on a consensus of a panel of experts.* The experts refine their opinions, phase by phase, until they reach a consensus. Because the technique relies on opinions, it obviously isn't foolproof. But the consensus arrived at tends to be much more accurate than a single expert's opinion. The Delphi process replaces face-to-face communication and debate with a carefully planned, orderly program of sequential impersonal exchanges. The first decision that has to be made involves the selection of a group of experts.[18]

Delphi Questionnaires. The heart of the Delphi technique is a series of questionnaires. The first questionnaire may include generally worded questions. In each later phase, the questions become more specific because they are built on responses to the previous questionnaire.[19] The following Communication Competency feature reports on the use of such questionnaires with safety professionals to forecast safety trends that could affect their employer's future profitability.[20]

COMMUNICATION COMPETENCY

Communicating Trends in Safety Management

For this Delphi study, a list of 120 American Society of Safety Engineers (ASSE) chapter presidents was obtained. These individuals served as the group of experts, known as the Delphi panel. They received a letter of introduction and explanation. The process continued for six months.

In the survey, respondents were asked an open-ended question regarding their predictions about safety for the remaining decade. Participants were asked to identify "up to 10 trends you feel the safety profession will experience over the next ten years." After four weeks—the end of round one—54 people had responded. Those who had not were

contacted again. Throughout the proceeding rounds, any participant who did not respond was contacted multiple times, since he or she had indicated some interest in participating based on responding to round one. The Delphi panel provided almost 200 predictions. Repeat predictions were consolidated. Predictions that were not safety related, not general to the entire field of safety, or incomplete were removed. This left a total of 168 predictions. In round two, panel members received the list of 168 predictions and were asked to identify their top 25 predictions. During round one, panelists had "brainstormed" ideas; this produced quantity. In round two, the focus was on quality, as the panel members identified which predictions were most likely to occur. A total of 35 ASSE chapter presidents completed round two. Results were tallied. The predictions falling into the top quartile—46 in all—were targeted for further study.

In round three, respondents were asked to rank the 46 predictions based on a scale of 1 to 4, of which 4 was "very likely"; 3, "somewhat likely"; 2, "not likely"; and 1, "very unlikely." Respondents ranked each prediction based on its likelihood to occur between now and the next 10 years. Thirty-three chapter presidents completed this round.

In round four, respondents were again presented with the 46 predictions, as well as information on how they had rated each during round three. In addition, respondents received the median and interquartile range. The median was used for consensus during the study because the median (as opposed to the mean) helps reduce the trend toward conformity. At the end of this round, 33 respondents remained in the study. An attrition rate of approximately 38 percent of those who initially agreed to participate is generally assumed. The rate for this study was 38.9 percent.

It is beyond our scope to go into each of the 46 predictions and the degree of agreement among panel members with each prediction. In brief, the panel sees a profession that will be more global as well as more reliant on computers. Professionals will increasingly be expected to explain how their efforts contribute to the bottom line, which will continue to be negatively affected by increasing medical costs and an aging workforce. The panel predicts little change in the way OSHA (Occupational Safety and Health Administration) operates. The panel anticipates certain new regulations (in areas such as ergonomics) from OSHA.

Phases. The Delphi technique typically involves at least three phases:

1. *A questionnaire is sent to a group of experts.* This process was illustrated in the previous communication competency feature. These experts remain unknown to one another. The questionnaire requests numerical estimates of specific technological or market possibilities. It asks for expected dates (years) and an assignment of probabilities to each of these possibilities. Respondents are asked to provide reasons for their expressed opinions. This process may be conducted via e-mail, fax, or regular mail.

2. *A summary of the first phase is prepared.* This report may show the median and quartile ranges of the responses. The report, along with a revised questionnaire, is sent to those who completed the first questionnaire. They are asked to revise their earlier estimates, if appropriate, or to justify their original opinions. The reasons for the possibilities presented in the first phase by the experts are critiqued by fellow respondents in writing. The technique emphasizes informed judgment. It attempts to improve on the panel or committee approach by subjecting the views of individual experts to others' reactions in ways that avoid face-to-face confrontation and provide anonymity of opinion and of arguments advanced in defense of those opinions.

3. *A summary of the second phase is prepared.* This report usually shows that a consensus is developing. The experts are then asked in a third questionnaire to indicate whether they support this emerging consensus and the explanations that accompany it. To avoid blind agreement, they are encouraged to find reasons for *not* joining the consensus.

Three phases generally are recommended. More phases may be used, as was the case in the Delphi study of safety management. However, experts often begin dropping out after the third phase because of other time commitments. The number of participating experts may range from only a few to more than 100, depending on the scope of the issue. A range of 15 to 30 is recommended for a focused issue. As the sample size (number of experts) increases, the amount of coordination required also increases, as do costs.

Simulation

A **simulation** *is a representation of a real system.* A simulation

1. imitates something real, but
2. is not real itself, and
3. can be altered by its users.

A simulation model usually describes the behavior of the real system (or some aspect of it) in quantitative and/or qualitative terms. Simulation often is used to forecast the effects of environmental changes and internal management decisions on an organization, department, or strategic business unit. The goal of simulation is to reproduce or test reality without actually experiencing it. Most simulations are intended to let management ask numerous "what if" questions. For example, What profits can we anticipate next year if inflation is 8 percent and we continue current pricing policies? Or What profits can we expect next year if inflation is 2 percent and we open two new plants? To answer such questions, analysts often develop complex equations and use computers to perform many of the step-by-step computations required. Such models can be used to simulate virtually any issue of interest (e.g., profits, sales, and earnings per share) for which a forecast is needed. Table 9.1 lists the common types of business simulation models.

Table 9.1	Examples of Business Simulation

Budget Models	**Operations Models**
■ All levels of organization	■ Inventory costs
	■ Materials costs
	■ Production costs
Treasury and Financial Models	**Human Resources Models**
■ Cash management	■ Compensation
■ Income statements	■ Optimum staffing levels
■ Cash flow projections	■ Measurements of productivity
■ Stock and commodity prices	
Marketing Models	**Strategic Planning Models**
■ Sales budgets	■ Scenario planning
■ Pricing	■ Political/economic forecasts
■ Market share projections	■ Business war-gaming
■ Advertising and marketing plans	

The senior management team of an electric utility had to face up to the industry restructuring of power generation. It was about to be transformed from a regulated monopoly into a fiercely competitive commodity industry. The following Planning & Administration Competency feature reports on the use of an industry restructuring simulation with the firm's senior managers to assist them in forecasting and planning.[21]

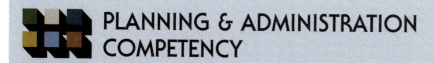

PLANNING & ADMINISTRATION COMPETENCY

The Industry Restructuring Simulation

New competition due to restructuring of the power generation indus-try meant the company would have to sell its output on the open market. Thus, it would have to reconsider its pricing policy. To gain a deeper understanding for planning in the new environment, senior management took part in a simulation.

©PhotoDisc/Getty Images

Each of the 13 participants represented one generating unit with fixed capacity. Combined, this capacity exceeded market demand. On each "day" of the simulation, the generating units submitted pricing bids to PoolCo, a body acting as an intermediary between buyers and sellers. Played by a computer, PoolCo ranked the bids by price and set the market price at the marginal bid that would meet market demand. All the units whose bids fell at or below the market price received that price for their energy. The other units stood idle, losing money because of their fixed costs.

The simulation consisted of 10 "days" of bidding, during which no conferring among participants was allowed. At the end of each day, players were shown their cash balances. It summed up their fixed costs and margins, if any. By the end of the simulation, several players had gone bankrupt.

Taking part in the simulation helped the senior managers understand and forecast what competition entailed and how the commodity nature of electric energy would affect market price. They learned to forecast that competitors were likely to price close to their marginal production cost to ensure that their facilities would not stand idle. They also discovered that marginal cost was the main factor in determining how competitive they could be.

Spreadsheet Simulations. Spreadsheets are often used to create hypothetical financial reports so that planners can experiment with how the future might look based on different sets of assumptions. They are simulations when used to create *pro forma* income statements and balance sheets, instead of real income statements and balance sheets.

ExperCorp is a business-planning consulting firm located in Naperville, Illinois. The company specializes in new venture strategy and marketing research for entrepreneurs entering the recreation and sporting goods markets. A key to small business planning is the development of good risk and reward estimates.[22]

First, the consultants estimate the size of the available target market. Then, they develop realistic assumptions for unit sales, selling price, production costs, and operating expenses in the first year of operation. An income statement spreadsheet is developed to create appropriate distributions for unit sales, production costs, operating expenses, and profits/losses.

The most critical and difficult aspect of venture planning is developing estimates of cash flow. Developing realistic statements for the first and subsequent years of operation along with determination of cash reserves is a task that all planners must face. This task is simplified with cash flow templates that plug into spreadsheets. The intent is to increase the precision of cash flow forecasts through these spreadsheet simulations.

Scenarios

Scenarios *are stories that help people recognize and adapt to changing features of their environments.* Scenarios provide a way to identify alternative paths that may exist for an organization in the future and the actions that likely are involved in going down each of those paths.[23]

Scenarios often involve answering "what if" questions. For example, considering the most pressing external forces our organization is likely to face, how can we spin them all together in a narrative story, or how can we weave in the risks and uncertainties of a future world to create new perspectives? A **competitor scenario** *presents a discussion that considers what a competitor (or set of competitors) might do over some specified time period, how the competitors would* *do it, and why they would choose to do so.* As with all scenarios, a competitor scenario presents a projection. It is not a prediction of what the competitor or set of competitors will do.[24] Table 9.2 presents some typical questions that are used in developing a "what-if" competitor scenario.

Table 9.2	Typical Questions in "What-If" Competitor Scenarios

- What if the competitor (or set of competitors) commits to a diversification of its product line (new products for existing and new customers) through a combination of current and new technologies?
- What if the competitor launches a series of new products?
- What if the competitor launches a sequence of extensions to its current product lines (with the specific aim of attracting new customers to the market)?
- What if the competitor suddenly divests a number of its product lines and/or pulls out of a number of geographic regions?
- What if the competitor moves rapidly to a focused differentiation strategy, as described in Chapter 7?
- What if the competitor fundamentally changes how it competes to win customers in the marketplace, such as moving from a differentiation strategy to a cost leadership strategy (see Chapter 7)?
- What if the competitor commits to gaining significant market share (and to do so as quickly as possible) without apparent regard to its long-term consequences (either for the firm itself or for the marketplace), such as through aggressive price cutting?

Source: Adapted from L. Fahey. Competitor scenarios. *Strategy & Leadership*, 31(1), 2003, pp. 32–44.

Some of the most creative, convention-breaking thinking occurs during the mapping of extreme scenarios—for instance, a fundamentally different but better world. However, the number of scenarios under consideration should be limited to prevent decision making from becoming unwieldy. The three most common categories of scenarios used in organizational planning are (1) the company's worst nightmare, (2) a fundamentally different but better world, and (3) more of the same (equivalent to the status quo) but better.

Planners at Ford, Wal-Mart, and other firms might use scenarios to address questions such as these: What future opportunities might exist for e-retailing? How could developments in e-retailing dramatically change traditional retailing distributions? What types of strategies might be useful in preventing, diverting, encouraging, or dealing with the possible future of e-retailing?[25]

Scenarios are quite useful in forcing those involved in planning to evaluate preliminary plans against future possibilities. John Bermingham is chairman of the board of directors of CitizensFirst Credit Union. It is headquartered in Oshkosh, Wisconsin, and has 30,000 members. Bermingham comments:

Scenario planning is a good way to develop the foundation for futurist thinking. Futurist thinking forces you to go back and look at your goals, then throw something at them that skews the current circumstances. . . . Scenario planning shakes things up. It helps people visualize what a scenario is like for another age group or market . . . it forces us to think outside of the box.[26]

The board of directors for CitizensFirst Credit Union (CU) had asked itself important questions during past scenario planning sessions, including "What if another large credit union opens a branch nearby?" That scenario helped the credit union avoid surprises when that possibility became a reality. When the competition came into the market, CitizensFirst CU already had decided that it would have to focus more on marketing, which it did. The seven-member board is used to looking at the future from an ever-changing perspective. Every 18 months the credit union does long-range planning from scratch. Bermingham states: "Then we throw different scenarios at our planning based on what's going on in the world. This gets the board thinking. It makes sense for a credit union board to examine different outcomes and interdependencies, even though none of them may come to fruition. In this way everyone helps shape today's decisions, which have implications for tomorrow."[27]

FOSTERING CREATIVITY

3. Use Osborn's creativity model to stimulate adaptive and innovative decisions.

All planning and decision making needs to be supported by creativity. **Creativity** *is the ability to visualize, generate, and implement new ideas.* Creative thinking increases the quality of solutions to many types of problems, helps stimulate innovation, revitalizes motivation and commitment by challenging individuals, and serves as a catalyst for effective team performance. For organizations, creativity is no longer optional—it is imperative. In particular, for innovative initiatives to succeed, managers and employees alike need creative thinking skills.

The Creative Process

The creative process, as suggested in Figure 9.1, usually involves five interconnected stages: preparation, concentration, incubation, illumination, and verification.[28]

The *preparation stage* involves thoroughly investigating an issue or problem to ensure that all of its aspects have been identified and understood. This stage involves searching for and collecting facts and ideas. Extensive formal education or many years of relevant experience are needed to develop the expertise required to identify substantive issues

Figure 9.1   Stages in the Creative Process

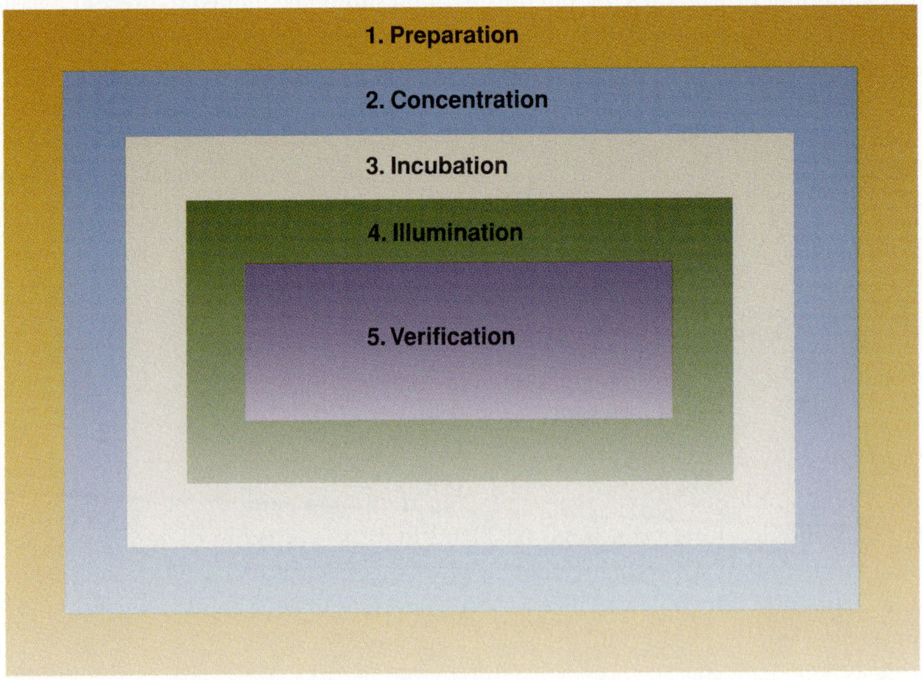

1. Preparation

2. Concentration

3. Incubation

4. Illumination

5. Verification

and problems. The preparation and concentration stages are consistent with Thomas Edison's statement that "Creativity is 90 percent perspiration and 10 percent inspiration." Edison was responsible for more than a thousand patents, the most famous of which is the electric light bulb in 1879.[29]

The *concentration stage* involves focusing energies and resources on identifying and solving an issue or problem. A commitment must be made at this stage to implement a solution.

The *incubation stage* is an internal and subconscious ordering of gathered information. This stage may involve a subconscious personal conflict between what is currently accepted as reality and what may be possible. Relaxing, sometimes distancing oneself from the issue, and allowing the subconscious to search for possible issues or problems and solutions is important. A successful incubation stage yields fresh ideas and new ways of thinking about the nature of an issue or a problem and alternative solutions.

The *illumination stage* is the moment of discovery, the instant of recognition, as when a light bulb seems to be turned on mentally. The mind instantly connects an issue or a problem to a solution through a remembered observation or occurrence.

The *verification stage* is the testing of the created solution or idea. At this stage, confirmation and acceptance of the new approach is sought. The knowledge and insights obtained from each stage of the creative process are often useful in addressing new issues and problems at the next *preparation stage*.

The Personal Creativity Inventory at the end of this chapter is a way for you to assess barriers to your own creative thought and innovative action. For now, we present A. F. Osborn's creativity model as an aid for fostering creative planning and decision making in organizations.

Osborn's Creativity Model

Osborn's creativity model *is a three-phase decision-making process that involves fact finding, idea finding, and solution finding*. It is designed to help overcome blockages to creativity and innovation, which may occur for a variety of reasons. It is intended to stimulate freewheeling thinking, novel ideas, curiosity, and cooperation that in turn lead to innovative decisions.[30] It can be used with all types of groups. Sufficient time and freedom must be allowed for the model to work well, and some degree of external pressure and self-generated tension are helpful. However, too much pressure or threats from the wrong sources (e.g., an order from top management to determine within 10 days why quality has deteriorated) can easily undermine the process.

Fact-Finding Phase. Fact finding involves defining the issue or problem and gathering and analyzing relevant data. Although the Osborn creativity model provides some fact-finding procedures, they aren't nearly as well developed as the idea-finding procedures.[31] One way to improve fact finding is to begin with a broad view of the issue or problem and then proceed to define subissues or subproblems. This phase requires making a distinction between a symptom of an issue or a problem and an actual issue or problem. For example, a manager might claim that negative employee attitudes constitute a problem. A deeper investigation might reveal that negative employee attitudes are only symptoms of a festering issue. The issue may be a lack of feedback on how well employees are performing their jobs.

Idea-Finding Phase. Idea finding starts by generating tentative ideas and possible leads. Then the most likely of these ideas are modified, combined, and added to, if necessary. Osborn maintained that individuals can generate more good ideas by following two principles. First, defer judgment. Individuals can think up almost twice as many good ideas in the same length of time if they defer judgment on any idea until after they create a list of possible leads to a solution. Second, quantity breeds quality: The more ideas that individuals think up, the more likely they are to arrive at the potentially best leads to a solution.

To encourage uninhibited thinking and generate lots of ideas, Osborn developed 75 general questions to use when brainstorming a problem. **Brainstorming** *is an unrestrained flow of ideas in a group with all critical judgments suspended.* The group leader must decide which of the 75 questions are most appropriate to the issue or problem being addressed. Moreover, the group leader isn't expected to use all of the questions in a single session. The following are examples of questions that could be used in a brainstorming session:

- How can this issue, idea, or thing be put to other uses?
- How can it be modified?
- How can it be substituted for something else, or can something else be substituted for part of it?
- How could it be reversed?
- How could it be combined with other things?[32]

A brainstorming session should follow four basic rules:

1. *Criticism is ruled out.* Participants must withhold critical judgment of ideas until later.
2. *Freewheeling is welcomed.* The wilder the idea, the better; taming down an idea is easier than thinking up new ones.
3. *Quantity is wanted.* The greater the number of ideas, the greater the likelihood that some will be useful.
4. *Combination and improvement are sought.* In addition to contributing ideas of their own, participants should suggest how ideas of others can be turned into better ideas or how two or more ideas can be merged into still another idea.[33]

These rules are intended to separate creative imagination from judgment. The two are incompatible and relate to different aspects of the decision-making process. The leader of one brainstorming group put it this way: "If you try to get hot and cold water out of the same faucet at the same time, you will get only lukewarm water. And if you try to criticize and create at the same time, you will not do either very well. So let us stick solely to *ideas*—let us cut out all criticism during this session.[34]

A brainstorming session should have from 5 to 12 or so participants in order to generate diverse ideas. This size range permits each member to maintain a sense of identification and involvement with the group. A session should normally run not less than 20 minutes or more than an hour. However, brainstorming could consist of several idea-generating sessions. For example, follow-up sessions could address individually each of the ideas previously generated. Table 9.3 presents the guidelines for leading a brainstorming session.[35]

Solution-Finding Phase. Solution finding involves generating and evaluating possible courses of action and deciding how to implement the chosen course of action. This phase relies on judgment, analysis, and criticism. A variety of planning and decision aids—such as those presented in this chapter and elsewhere in the book—can be used. To initiate the solution-finding phase, the leader could ask the team to identify from one to five of the most important ideas generated. The participants might be asked to jot down these ideas individually on a piece of paper and evaluate them on a five-point scale. A very important idea might get five points, a moderately important idea could get three points, and an unimportant idea could be assigned one point. The highest combined scores may indicate the actions or ideas to be investigated further.

Table 9.3   Guidelines for Leading a Brainstorming Session

Basic leadership role
- Make a brief statement of the four basic rules.
- State the time limit for the session.
- Read the problem and/or related question to be discussed and ask, "What are your ideas?"
- When an idea is given, summarize it by using the speaker's words insofar as possible. Have the idea recorded by a participant or on an audiotape machine. Follow your summary with the single word "Next."
- Say little else. Whenever the leader participates as a brainstormer, group productivity usually falls.

Handling problems
- When someone talks too long, wait until he or she takes a breath (everyone must stop to inhale sometime), break into the monologue, summarize what was said for the recorder, point to another participant, and say "Next."
- When someone becomes judgmental or starts to argue, stop him or her. Say, for example, "That will cost you one coffee or soda for each member of the group."
- When the discussion stops, relax and let the silence continue. Say nothing. The pause should be broken by the group and not the leader. This period of silence is called the *mental pause* because it is a change in thinking. All the obvious ideas are exhausted; the participants are now forced to rely on their creativity to produce new ideas.
- When someone states a problem rather than idea, repeat the problem, raise your hand with five fingers extended, and say, "Let's have five ideas on this problem." You may get only 1 or you may get 10, but you're back in the business of creative thinking.

Osborn's creativity model has been modified often and applied in a variety of ways.[36] The following Teamwork Competency feature highlights how IDEO Product Development, headquartered in Palo Alto, California, uses brainstorming.[37] The company is a renowned professional services firm that helps clients design and develop new products and, in the process, become more innovative. The creative process at IDEO is fostered through the extensive use of empowered design teams. These teams are staffed to take advantage of diverse perspectives, technical and creative skills, and ability to achieve goals jointly. Diverse views are encouraged and used to enhance the quality and creativity of decisions. At the same time, cooperation is fostered, and the teams are kept moving toward their goals.

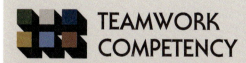

TEAMWORK COMPETENCY

IDEO Brainstorms

IDEO projects last from a few weeks to several years, with the average being 10 to 12 months. Depending on the client's needs, results can range from sketches of products to crude working models to complete new products. Clients vary from venture-funded start-ups to multinational corporations in North America, Europe, and Japan. IDEO has developed part or all of more than 3,000 products in dozens of industries, including Apple's first computer mouse, the Palm V, Polaroid's

I-Zone pocket camera, and Oral B's "Squish Grip" toothbrushes for children.

IDEO is unique in encouraging clients to participate in brainstorming sessions conducted by design teams. By going to a "brainstormer," clients gain insight and learn because they join IDEO designers in the creative process. Brainstorming sessions usually are initiated by a design team. The team members then invite other IDEO designers to help generate ideas for the project. These sessions are held in rooms with five brainstorming rules written on the walls: (1) defer judgment, (2) build on the ideas of others, (3) one conversation at a time, (4) stay focused on the topic, and (5) encourage wild ideas.

Designers who are also skilled facilitators lead the brainstorming sessions, enforce rules, write suggestions on the board, and encourage creativity and fun. Nearly all of the designers are experienced at brainstorming. Typically, project members (or clients) introduce the project and describe the design issue or problem they face (e.g., How do you make fishing more fun and easier for neophytes?). Participants then generate ideas (e.g., Use the "slingshot" method to launch lures), often sketching them on paper or whiteboards. Many new projects start with a flurry of brainstorming sessions. Clients often attend them to describe their existing products and the new products that they want designed. Clients may also give detailed demonstrations before a brainstormer to explain the product or service, such as clients from a chain of hair salons who did haircuts at the Palo Alto office to demonstrate their work process. Twenty or so IDEO employees may be invited to brainstorming sessions in the early weeks of a project.

Effectiveness. The Osborn creativity model is based on the assumption that most people have the potential for greater creativity and innovation in decision making than they use. Some research suggests that the same number of individuals working alone may generate more ideas and more creative ideas than do groups.[38] However, most of this research was conducted with students rather than employees and employee teams on the job. Unlike employees who have diverse knowledge and skills and who are brought together to brainstorm problems that have serious long-term consequences (as at IDEO), student groups are relatively homogeneous. Most students have a limited range of knowledge of the problems given to them and limited skills to apply to their solutions. Because students don't have to be concerned with real-world consequences, they may be less than fully committed to the process. Thus, whether group brainstorming in a work setting is more or less effective than individuals working alone to generate ideas remains an open question.

Some evidence suggests that, under certain conditions, electronic brainstorming may be a better way to generate ideas than traditional face-to-face brainstorming.[39] One condition is when individuals from different organizational levels are in the same brainstorming group. **Electronic brainstorming** *makes use of personal computers that are networked to input and automatically disseminate ideas in real time to all team members, each of whom may be stimulated to generate additional ideas.* For example, individuals may input ideas via the keyboard as they think of them. Every time an idea is entered, the team's ideas appear in random order on each person's screen. An individual can continue to see new sets of ideas in random order by pressing the appropriate key.[40] The random order format prevents the system from identifying who generates each idea.

FOSTERING QUALITY

4. Apply three quality management decision and planning aids: benchmarking, the Deming cycle, and the balanced scorecard model.

In Chapter 2, we defined *quality* as how well a good or service does what it is supposed to do—that is, how closely and reliably it satisfies the specifications to which it is built or provided. The most common meaning of *quality* is the extent to which a good or service meets and/or exceeds customers' expectations.[41] Consumers often apply the value dimension of quality when making purchasing decisions. *Consumer Reports* ranks goods and services on both quality and price to arrive at recommendations of "best buys." The various perspectives of quality are, of course, appropriate in different circumstances. We review three planning and decision aids that focus on improving quality: benchmarking, the Deming cycle, and the balanced scorecard model.

Benchmarking

Benchmarking *is a systematic and continuous process of measuring and comparing an organization's goods, services, and practices against industry leaders anywhere in the world to gain information that will help the organization improve performance.*[42] By identifying how such leading organizations achieved excellence in particular areas or processes, other organizations can determine how to develop their own strategic or tactical plans and processes to reach or exceed those levels. At the most fundamental level, benchmarking helps managers and employees learn from others.

Stages. As noted in Figure 9.2, benchmarking includes seven stages.[43] Stage 1 focuses on *defining the domain* to be benchmarked. This stage includes a careful assessment of the organization's own products and processes that are to be compared to benchmark products and processes. For example, common benchmarks used by airlines and rating services are percentages of on-time arrivals and amount of lost or misrouted baggage.

Figure 9.2   The Benchmarking Process

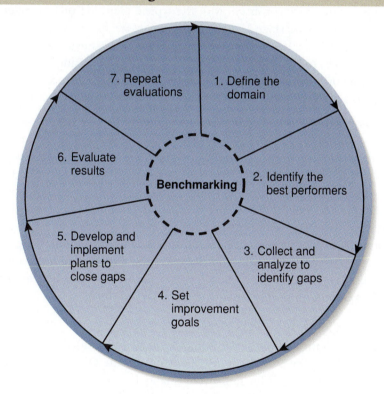

Manufacturing, finance, marketing, inventory management, transportation, accounting, legal services, human resources, and marketing processes may be benchmarked. Each function may be broken into more specific categories of processes for that purpose. For example, benchmarking in human resources may include the processes of recruiting, diversity enhancement, training, compensation, performance appraisal, recognition programs, and job design.

Benchmarking can be expensive and time consuming. Some experts recommend that benchmarking be directed at the specific issues and processes that are likely to yield the greatest competitive advantage (e.g., core strategic competencies, managerial competencies, and the like). Others, such as the American Productivity and Quality Center (APQC), suggest that benchmarking be applied to all functions and processes to instill total quality throughout the organization.[44]

Stage 2 focuses on *identifying the best performers*, or best-in-class, for each function, process, and product to be benchmarked. They may include organizations in the firm's own industry or in other industries. For example, Xerox compared its warehousing and distribution process to that of L.L.Bean, the catalog and online sales company, because of Bean's excellent reputation in this area.

Stage 3 focuses on c*ollecting and analyzing data to identify gaps*, if any, between the function, product, or process being evaluated and that of the best-in-class organizations. The data collected need to focus on specific methods utilized, not simply on the results obtained. It is one thing to know that Wal-Mart has a superb warehouse distribution system, yet it is another thing to learn how Wal-Mart has achieved this level of excellence. Many sources of information are available for learning about best-in-class organizations. They include customers, suppliers, distributors, trade journals, company publications, newspapers, books on quality, consultants, presentations at professional meetings, and even on-site interviews with people at the best-in-class organizations. This last source usually is easier to tap if the organizations aren't direct competitors.

The remaining steps are consistent with the typical planning phases: Stage 4 focuses on *setting improvement goals*; stage 5, *developing and implementing plans to close gaps*; stage 6, *evaluating results*; and stage 7, *repeating the evaluations as necessary*. Stage 7 suggests that benchmarking needs to be an ongoing process. Over time, the things benchmarked may remain the same or need to be revised. Revisions may include dropping and/or adding functions, products, or processes as issues, conditions, technology, and markets change.

Effectiveness. Benchmarking needs to be linked to other sources of information, such as changing customer expectations and preferences. Benchmarking always looks at the present in terms of how some process or quality dimension is being achieved by others. However, this approach may not be adequate for determining what should be done in the future or whether an organization should retain a function or process or contract it out. For example, an organization could contract out its computer operations to IBM or some other firm. When used simply to copy the best-in-class competitors, benchmarking may only lead to short-term competitive advantage. Finally, benchmarking needs to be used to complement and aid, not to substitute for, the creative and innovative efforts of the organization's own employees.[45] Benchmarking is often used to help an organization adapt, but less commonly to innovate.

The Deming Cycle

We provided some information on W. Edwards Deming, considered by some to be the "godfather" of the quality movement, in Chapter 2 (in the Quality Viewpoint section). One of the aids he advocated for improving quality is commonly known as the *Deming cycle*. Others refer to it as the *PDCA cycle* because it involves the four stages of plan (P), do (D), check (C), and act (A). As Figure 9.3 suggests, these stages unfold in sequence and continuously. Thus, the **Deming cycle** *comprises four stages—plan, do, check, and act— that should be repeated over time to ensure continuous learning and improvements in a function, product, or process.*

Three questions need to be answered during the plan stage of the Deming cycle: (1) What are we trying to accomplish? (2) What changes can we make that will result in improvement? (3) How will we know that a change is an improvement? The *plan stage* involves analyzing the current situation, gathering data, and developing ways to make improvements. The *do stage* involves testing alternatives experimentally in a laboratory,

Figure 9.3   The Deming Cycle

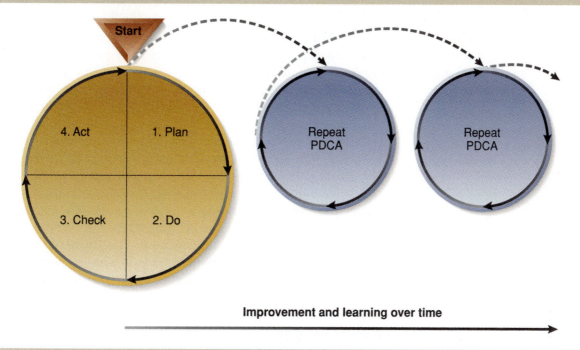

Improvement and learning over time

establishing a pilot production process, or trying it out with a small number of customers. The *check stage* requires determining whether the trial or process is working as intended, whether any revisions are needed, or whether it should be scrapped. The *act stage* focuses on implementing the process within the organization or with its customers and suppliers.[46] Benchmarking may be one of the aids used in the Deming cycle.

Application. Billie Boyd, the owner of Deluxe Diner in Midland, Texas, decided to do something about the long lines at lunchtime that occurred every day. During the *plan stage* she held several meetings with her employees. They identified four main aspects of this problem: (1) Customers were waiting in line for as long as 15 minutes, (2) tables usually were available, (3) many of the customers were regulars, and (4) those taking orders and preparing food were getting in each others' way.

The employees offered various ideas. Boyd developed a plan that involved the following changes: (1) Allow customers to fax their orders in ahead of time (rent a fax machine for one month), (2) install a preparation table for fax orders in the kitchen where there was ample room, and (3) devote one of the two cash registers to handling fax orders. To assess whether these changes had improved the situation, in the *do stage*, Boyd collected data on the number of customers in line, the number of empty tables, and the delay before customers were served. The length of the line and the number of empty tables were measured every 15 minutes during the lunch hour. When doing the 15-minute line check, she noted the last person in line and the elapsed time until that person was seated.

Next, the results of these measurements were observed for three weeks. Three improvements were detected during the *check stage*. Time in line dropped from 15 minutes to 5 minutes, on average. The line length was cut to a peak average of 12 people, and the number of empty tables declined slightly. Boyd held another meeting with her employees to discuss the results. In the *act stage*, they decided to purchase the fax machine, fill fax orders, and use both cash registers to handle walk-up and fax orders. Boyd thought that the Deming cycle was very helpful in resolving the problem and intends to use it again.[47]

Balanced Scorecard Model

The **balanced scorecard model** *provides a way for an organization to gain a wider perspective on its strategic decisions, which have an impact on quality, by considering the role of finances, customers, internal processes, and innovation/learning.*[48] The model takes into account financial and nonfinancial measures, internal improvements, past outcomes, and ongoing requirements as indicators of future performance. The balanced scorecard model attempts to measure and provide feedback to organizations in order to help in implementing overall goals and strategies. The model contends that long-term organizational excellence and quality can be achieved only by taking a broad approach, not by focusing solely on financials. The model can include the performance of entire organizations or business units. The balanced scorecard model is future oriented and not primarily a review mirror of performance, as is often portrayed in traditional financial reports such as income and balance sheet statements. The shift to a services and knowledge economy has increased the interest in the *intangibles* that are so important to organizational effectiveness.

Four Perspectives. As illustrated in Figure 9.4, the balanced scorecard model requires managers to look at their organizations' decision making from four strategic perspectives.[49] The intent is to link and balance the goals and related measures for each perspective to one another. The financial and customer perspectives are viewed as focusing on *outcomes*. The internal and innovation/learning perspectives are viewed as focusing on *activities*. Examples of the factors and questions addressed in each perspective include the following:

- *Financial perspective:* profitability, growth in profits, market value of firm. How do we serve and address stockholders' needs?
- *Customer perspective:* perceptions of service quality, trustworthiness, loyalty. How do customers see us?
- *Internal perspective:* productivity, employee motivation, organizational competencies, employee rate of defects/errors, employee competencies, safety record. How do we excel?
- *Innovation/learning perspective:* knowledge management, creativity, development of new goods and services, employee training and development. How can we sustain or accelerate our ability to change and improve?

Assessment. The potential suggested benefits of this model include these: It (1) helps align key performance goals and measures with strategy at all levels of an organization, (2) provides management with a comprehensive picture of business operations, (3) facilitates communication and understanding of business goals and strategies at all levels of an organization, and (4) provides strategic feedback and learning.[50]

The balanced scorecard model is consistent with the theme of the book—no one perspective or emphasis is adequate for creating a high-performance, quality organization. This model has the potential to serve managers well by requiring them to integrate important nonfinancial goals and measures into the planning process. The following Strategic Action Competency reports on the introduction of the balanced scorecard model for ground crews at Southwest Airlines Co., which is headquartered in Dallas, Texas.[51]

Figure 9.4   Balanced Scorecard Model

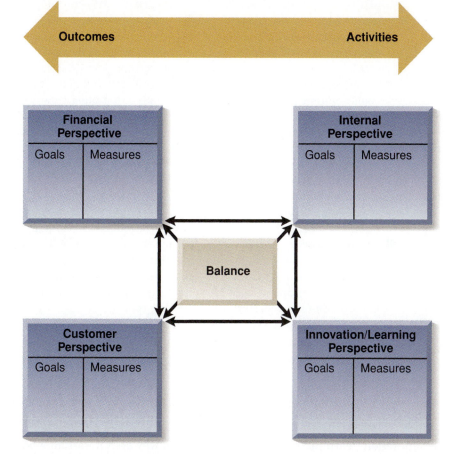

Outcomes ← → Activities

Financial Perspective		Internal Perspective	
Goals	Measures	Goals	Measures

Balance

Customer Perspective		Innovation/Learning Perspective	
Goals	Measures	Goals	Measures

Source: Based on R. S. Kaplan and D. P. Norton. *The Strategy-Focused Orientation: How Balanced Scorecard Companies Thrive in the New Business Environment.* Boston: Harvard Business School Publishing, 2000; R. S. Kaplan and D. P. Norton. *The Balanced Scorecard: Translating Strategies into Action.* Boston: Harvard Business School Press, 1996.

STRATEGIC ACTION COMPETENCY

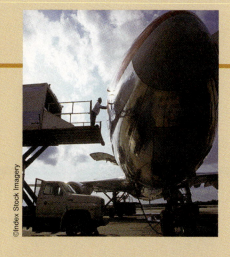
©Index Stock Imagery

Southwest Airlines' Balanced Scorecard

Southwest Airlines employs a number of scorecards, one of which relates ground-crew performance to company profitability. It arranges the four quadrants of the balanced scorecard—financial, customer, internal, and innovation/learning—that suggested the goals and measures in each perspective need to relate to one another.

Directly relating a financial measure, such as "lower costs," with an operations measure, "fast ground turnaround," is a relatively new idea according to Mike Van de Ven, vice president of financial planning and analysis. He states: "Historically, the budget system was the primary system to monitor costs. If you were an accountant, you got it. But if you were an operations person, and you weren't used to cost centers and general ledgers and budget-to-actual variances, it didn't make any sense to you."

The operations people had hundreds of measures dealing with things such as on-time performance or baggage delivery, but they weren't linked directly to the financial measures or the budget system. Van de Ven comments: "So what we have been doing over the past several years is putting these things together, and that neatly rolls into this balanced scorecard concept." Another advantage of the balanced scorecard approach is that it retains the hundreds of detailed measures for frontline supervisors but gives top management a "dashboard" displaying a few key measures. Van de Ven remarks: "We are trying to get more focused on key measurements that we want to stay on top of."

A sample of the goals and measures used in the Southwest Airlines balanced scorecard, primarily as it relates to ground crews, are as follows:

- *Financial perspective:* general goals—profitability, increased revenue, lower costs; measures—market value with operational goal of 30% compound annual growth rate; seat revenue with operational goal of 20% compound annual growth rate; plane lease cost with operational goal of 5% compound annual growth rate.
- *Customer perspective:* general goals—on-time flights and lowest prices; measures—Federal Aviation Authority on-time arrival rating with the operational goal of being ranked number 1; customer ranking based on market surveys with the operational goal of being ranked number 1.
- *Internal perspective:* general goal—fast ground turnaround; measures—time on ground with the operational goal of 30 minutes; on-time departure with the operational goal of 90 percent on time departures.

- *Innovation/learning perspective:* general goal—ground crew alignment with company goals; measures—percent ground crew who are stockholders with the operational goals of 70 percent in year 1, 90 percent in year 3, and 100 percent in year 5; percent ground-crew with training beyond new employee training with the operational goals of 70 percent in year 1, 90 percent in year 3, and 100 percent in year 5.

To date, Southwest Airlines has found the balanced scorecard approach to be effective in linking the four perspectives and related goals/measures to maintain and increase quality and profitability over the long run.

There are criticisms of the balanced scorecard model. We note several of them, as follows:

- The innovation/learning perspective is internal, so why does it warrant a box separate from the internal process perspective?
- Why aren't other stakeholders represented? Aren't financial measures also relevant to customers? In which case, why is finance on its own? Every organization has many internal processes. Which ones should be chosen for this perspective?
- Goals must be set for each of the four perspectives, but managers are not provided with any specific methodology or rationale on how to do it. They are left to their own devices.[52]

These criticisms, in our judgment, are useful in recognizing that there are limitations with the balanced scorecard model. Of course, this is the case with all of the planning and decision-making aids.

In this chapter, we focused on seven of the literally hundreds of planning and decision aids. They are aids that specifically foster knowledge management, forecasting, creativity, and quality management. These aids are useful in virtually all types of organizations, at all organizational levels, and in all functional areas.

1. Explain knowledge management and how it creates value for organizations.

Knowledge management (KM) is the art and practice of obtaining and transforming information and utilizing intellectual assets to create value for an organization's employees and customers or clients. A supportive and enabling organizational culture is a prerequisite for the introduction and use of KM. Its three major components are an information base, enabling technologies, and the skills and abilities of people. Information and knowledge are increasingly becoming more important assets and competitive weapons than an organization's physical assets. Knowledge management is most often applied to (1) collaboration among teams and departments, (2) improving service to customers or clients, and (3) tracking employees' capabilities, improving employee training, and performing other human resource functions.

2. Describe the basic features of the Delphi technique, simulation, and scenario forecasting aids.

Forecasting is the process of estimating future events and conditions in an organization's environment. The Delphi technique is a process of consensus building among experts to arrive at such estimates. Simulation involves the use of models of real systems to test alternatives, often on a computer. Scenarios are written descriptions of possible futures. All three methods are especially relevant as aids in the strategic planning process.

3. Use Osborn's creativity model to stimulate adaptive and innovative decisions.

Creativity is the ability to visualize, generate, and implement new ideas. The creative process usually involves five interconnected stages: preparation, concentration, incubation, illumination, and verification. Osborn's creativity model attempts to stimulate and reduce blocks of creativity and innovation. It helps decision makers address unstructured and ambiguous problems.

4. Apply three quality management decision and planning aids: benchmarking, the Deming cycle, and the balanced scorecard model.

Quality management is concerned with improving how well a good, service, or process does what it is supposed to do, as well as raising the standards and specifications for what it is supposed to do. In brief, benchmarking involves comparing an organization's functions, products, or processes with those of best-in-class organizations. This ongoing process is a sequence of seven stages: defining the domain, identifying the best performers, collecting and analyzing data to identify gaps, setting improvement goals, developing and implementing plans to close gaps, evaluating results, and repeating the evaluations. The Deming cycle includes four stages—plan, do, check, and act—that should be repeated over time to ensure continuous learning and improvement in functions, products, and processes. The balanced scorecard model is a quality aid and much more. It provides a way for an organization to gain a wider perspective on its strategic decisions, which have a direct impact on quality, by considering the role of finances, customers, internal processes, and innovation/learning.

KEY TERMS AND CONCEPTS

Balanced scorecard model
Benchmarking
Brainstorming
Competitor scenario
Creativity
Delphi technique
Deming cycle
Electronic brainstorming

Expert system
Extrapolation
Forecasting
Knowledge management
Osborn's creativity model
Scenarios
Simulation

QUESTIONS FOR DISCUSSION and COMPETENCY DEVELOPMENT

1. Review the Preview Case on knowledge management at SchlumbergerSema. Assume you are one of the 25,000 employees in this firm. What issues and concerns might you have with using its knowledge management system?

2. Describe two similarities and/or differences in the components of knowledge management involved in the functioning of a team-based student project of which you were a member.

3. In what ways has an organization for which you have worked used or failed to use KM? Explain.

4. How might the Delphi technique be used to develop a forecast of the possible impacts of the Internet on the learning process in higher education?

5. Describe a personal experience that you've had with virtual reality. Which of its features might apply in a business setting?

6. Develop a negative scenario on the impact of the Internet on the work environment for college graduates in 2015.

7. Describe a personal situation that occurred within the past six months for which Osborn's creativity model would have been useful. Why would it have been useful?

8. Describe how benchmarking could be used to help plan improvements in one service or process (e.g., registration, advising, or financial aid) at your college or university. Who might you benchmark? Explain why.

9. Think of an organization for which you have worked. Did management use the balanced scorecard model informally or formally? Explain. If not, do you think this model would have been helpful in improving the quality and performance of the organization?

MARY TOLAN'S ENERGY SCENARIO AND PROPOSAL[53]

Mary Tolan is the chief executive of Accenture's Resources Group. Accenture is a major management consulting and technology services company with more than 75,000 employees in 47 countries. It is headquartered in New York City. Portions of this case are based on her presentation to the 14th annual International Utilities and Energy Conference in 2003.

Tolan challenged the audience to understand the power of political will and its possible impact on restructuring our energy mix. To illustrate how change is possible, she outlined a scenario that could play out in an environment not very distant from the geopolitical situation of today. Tolan listed three factors that would drive this scenario: (1) a weak global economy, (2) oil price inflation with expectation of more inflation that could shave 1 to 2 percent off of the economic growth of major industrialized countries, and (3) geopolitical concerns leading to the view that the current petroleum dependence represents unacceptable risk. Tolan comments: "We have acute conditions developing that can accelerate change. But, we have a wild card, political will." She noted that, at present, the world lacks the political will to change our dependency on petroleum.

To help envision the potential implications of energy restructuring, she asked the audience to focus first on the transportation fleet where 50 to 70 percent of petroleum is consumed; in addition, typical forecasts call for increases in demand. Tolan described how hydrogen could achieve material displacement of petroleum: "It [hydrogen] can be created from many energy sources, and this diversity leads to greater security." She also noted that hydrogen offers a more efficient conversion of energy and results in a lower energy cost than that of conventional gasoline engines.

Assuming that all new vehicles were hydrogen fueled by 2013, transportation consumption of petroleum in the major industrialized countries could decrease by 15 million barrels per day from today. Tolan cautioned that such a scenario would require wholesale infrastructure redevelopment and large investments in commercializing fuel cells. To move to hydrogen, she said government subsidies on the order of $225 billion over a 10-year period would be required. While the dollar amount sounds high, she reminded the audience that many other subsidies and government programs spend this amount every year. "However, let me say, without political will, we should be unenthusiastic about this scenario," Tolan stated. Tolan did stress that such a positive outcome to this scenario requires fuel cell and automobile manufacturers to bring down the total cost of the vehicle. She stated: "The investment made today in preparing for the new hydrogen business environment is a bet on fuel cell technology."

With a $225 billion stimulus investment in the energy and transportation business, Tolan said hydrogen could deliver significant gains in productivity as well as an environmental benefit in emissions control. Reinforcing her view of the art of the possible being achievable, Tolan reminded the audience of historic challenges, in particular the U.S. "Man on the Moon" campaign. "Kennedy did not know what fuels could accomplish this. He didn't know what or who would have to come together to make this happen. He just took a leap of faith. Today, we know the fuel, the who and the what that have to come together. Now what is required is political will."

Under Tolan's scenario, the United States could completely wean itself off imported oil by 2015 by flooding the market with fuel-cell vehicles. Most of the hydrogen needed to power the cars would come from plentiful North American natural gas piped to existing filling stations, then processed into hydrogen. In little more than a decade, half the cars on American highways would run on clean-burning hydrogen costing 40 percent less per mile than gasoline. Tolan agrees that some unusual things would have to happen first: You'd need annual federal subsidies of $10 billion to $20 billion in the early years to make the cars affordable and to scale up production. Oil and gas companies and utilities would have to invest some $280 billion into hydrogen infrastructure in the United States alone. Tolan acknowledges that she's calling for a radical transformation that could expose energy industries to daunting technological and commercial risks and uncertainties.

Tolan contends that the costs of creating a hydrogen industry, while considerable, are far lower than the $1,000 billion (trillion) espoused by critics: $280 billion in the United States for hydrogen production and infrastructure. Her estimate includes $70 billion to expand the natural gas and ethanol supply, $40 billion to lay new pipelines, $40 billion to transport fuel to filling stations (via pipelines or trucks), and the $130 billion to retrofit filling sites. The scale of investment is in line with what major oil companies already spend on petroleum exploration and production. ExxonMobil, for instance, budgeted $100 billion for that purpose this decade.

At another energy conference in Houston, Tolan presented her scenario to 2,000 industry executives. "She got a lot of pooh-poohs," says Joseph Stanislaw, president of Cambridge Energy Research Associates, the conference sponsor. "But a lot of folks also said they know they've got to start thinking this way. Once you have first movers and quick followers, things can go very fast." He says that none of the big oil companies has committed significant capital to hydrogen, but all are studying its safety, feasibility, and cost.

Questions for Discussion

1. On what assumptions is Tolan's scenario based?

2. What aspects of Tolan's proposal are creative?

3. Would the use of the balanced scorecard model tend to discourage or encourage an energy firm in pursuing Tolan's proposal?

EXERCISE FOR COMPETENCY DEVELOPMENT

PERSONAL CREATIVITY INVENTORY[54]

This inventory provides you the opportunity to assess, reflect on, and reduce possible personal barriers to creativity. For each of the statements in the questionnaire, use the following scale to express which number best corresponds to your agreement or disagreement with the statement. Write that number in the blank to the left of each statement. Please do not skip any statements.

Strongly Agree 1	Agree Somewhat 2	Agree 3	Disagree 4	Strongly Disagree 5

_____ 1. I evaluate criticism to determine how it can be useful to me.

_____ 2. When solving problems, I attempt to apply new concepts or methods.

_____ 3. I can shift gears or change emphasis in what I am doing.

_____ 4. I get enthusiastic about problems outside of my specialized area of concentration.

_____ 5. I always give a problem my best effort, even if it seems trivial or fails to arouse enthusiasm.

_____ 6. I set aside periods of time without interruptions.

_____ 7. It is not difficult for me to have my ideas criticized.

_____ 8. In the past, I have taken calculated risks and I would do so again.

_____ 9. I dream, daydream, and fantasize easily.

_____ 10. I know how to simplify and organize my observations.

_____ 11. Occasionally, I try a so-called unworkable answer in hopes that it will prove to be workable.

_____ 12. I can and do consistently guard my personal periods of privacy.

_____ 13. I feel at ease with peers even when my ideas or plans meet with public criticisms or rejection.

_____ 14. I frequently read opinions contrary to my own to learn what the opposition is thinking.

_____ 15. I translate symbols into concrete ideas or action steps.

_____ 16. I see many ideas because I enjoy having alternative possibilities.

_____ 17. In the idea-formulation stage of a project, I withhold critical judgment.

_____ 18. I determine whether an imposed limitation is reasonable or unreasonable.

_____ 19. I would modify an idea, plan, or design, even if doing so would meet with opposition.

_____ 20. I feel comfortable expressing my ideas even if they are in the minority.

_____ 21. I enjoy participating in nonverbal, symbolic, or visual activities.

_____ 22. I feel the excitement and challenge of finding solutions to problems.

_____ 23. I keep a file of discarded ideas.

_____ 24. I make reasonable demands for good physical facilities and surroundings.

_____ 25. I would feel no serious loss of status or prestige if management publicly rejected my plan.

_____ 26. I frequently question the policies, goals, values, or ideas of an organization.

_____ 27. I deliberately exercise my visual and symbolic skills in order to strengthen them.

_____ 28. I can accept my thinking when it seems illogical.

_____ 29. I seldom reject ambiguous ideas that are not directly related to the problem.

_____ 30. I distinguish between trivial and important physical distractions.

_____ 31. I feel uncomfortable making waves for a worthwhile idea even if it threatens team harmony.

_____ 32. I am willing to present a truly original approach even if there is a chance it could fail.

_____ 33. I can recognize the times when symbolism or visualization would work best for me.

_____ 34. I try to make an uninteresting problem stimulating.

_____ 35. I consciously attempt to use new approaches toward routine tasks.

_____ 36. In the past, I have determined when to leave an undesirable environment and when to stay and change the environment (including self-growth).

Scoring

Transfer your responses to the statements above and record them in the blanks provided below. Then add the numbers in each column, and record the column totals.

A	B	C	D	E	F
1. _____	2. _____	3. _____	4. _____	5. _____	6. _____
7. _____	8. _____	9. _____	10. _____	11. _____	12. _____
13. _____	14. _____	15. _____	16. _____	17. _____	18. _____
19. _____	20. _____	21. _____	22. _____	23. _____	24. _____
25. _____	26. _____	27. _____	28. _____	29. _____	30. _____
31. _____	32. _____	33. _____	34. _____	35. _____	36. _____

Totals:

_____ _____ _____ _____ _____ _____

Interpretation

Take your scores from the scoring sheet and mark them with a dot in the score categories (cells) on the following graph. The vertical axis, which represents the possible column totals, ranges from 6 to 36. The horizontal axis represents the columns on your scoring sheet and ranges from A to F. The Key to Barriers legend at the end of this exercise identifies the category of barriers in each column. Connect the dots you have marked with a line. The high points represent your possible barriers to creativity as you see them. The higher the number in each column, the greater the barrier that factor represents in realizing your creative potential.

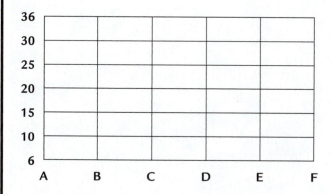

Key to Barriers

A = Barriers related to self-confidence and risk taking
B = Barriers related to need for conformity
C = Barriers related to use of the abstract
D = Barriers related to use of systematic analysis
E = Barriers related to task achievement
F = Barriers related to physical environment

Questions

1. Based on these results, are there any actions that you can and want to take to improve your creativity?

2. What managerial competencies are most linked to your potential creativity?

©John Neubauer/Photo Edit

Controlling in Organizations

Learning Objectives

After studying this chapter, you should be able to:

1. Explain the foundations of control.
2. Identify the six phases of the corrective control model
3. Describe the primary methods of organizational control.
4. Explain several key corporate governance issues and control mechanisms.

Chapter Outline

Waste Management, one of the largest trash haulers in the United States, was engaged in a major scandal several years ago. Regulators accused its top officers of engaging in massive fraud while pocketing almost $29 million in annual bonuses gained from insider trading. The company, which restated more than $1.7 billion in earnings over five years, went through five CEOs between 1996 and 1999, and its stock lost more than $25 billion in value. The turmoil allowed a smaller company, USA Waste Services, to take over the firm in a merger that later failed and resulted in more than $1.2 billion in charges.

In late 1999, Maurice Myers was selected as chairman, president, and CEO of Waste Management. He faced the enormous challenge of leading the firm out of a host of problems, including the lack of effective managerial control. After four years of effort as of 2003, Myers' effective leadership and controls have led to (1) reducing the company's debt by a third—to $8.3 billion, (2) increasing the stock price by 85 percent, (3) becoming the #1 solid waste firm with 25 million residential and 2 million commercial customers, and (4) rating agencies upgrading the firm's debt from junk to investment grade.

Myers was just one week into his position when he realized just how poor Waste Management's accounting, financial, and personnel controls

were. About 10,000 of the 55,000 paychecks sent out were incorrect, shortchanging those 10,000 workers. Myers immediately began visiting Waste Management employees around the country. Employees were upset not only with the paycheck problem, but also with the company's benefits plan. Within a few weeks, the firm had begun updating the payroll system and offering enhanced benefit options. Myers stated: "We quickly fixed the things we could fix, which showed the employees that we really did care about them. In a crisis like this, you don't want to risk losing valuable people who are critical to driving the recovery."

To get ahead of the rumor mill, Myers also launched a weekly company newspaper. It talked about real company issues, like customers the firm lost and why it lost them. To show that the new Waste Management valued doing the right thing, Myers created an anonymous hotline for employees to call to report improper behavior. This feedback control method has resulted in more than 4,600 calls since early 2001, leading to the termination of 60 employees and disciplinary actions for others. Myers also reestablished the position of ethics officer—who trains not only the workforce but the board of directors as well—as a preventive control method.

As months went by, it became clear to Myers that Waste Manage-

ment had another big control problem. The company had never fully integrated the thousands of small-scale garbage operations it had acquired during the 1980s and 1990s into its system. Waste Management also did not know how many landfills it owned and did not keep safety records. As a result, insurance costs and workers' compensation costs were high. Waste Management had been claiming for years that it was the best in the industry and that it completely satisfied its customers. This was found to be just wishful thinking. The company had no way to measure its performance and had never bothered to ask customers what they thought or wanted. Thus, the company began tracking numerous data—how long it took to answer a customer's call, how many customers reported billing problems, how many garbage pickups the company missed, how many accidents company workers had, and so on. Executives were stunned by what they discovered. For instance, 68 percent of the company's accidents were being caused by 12 percent of its drivers. Those drivers had typically worked at Waste Management for less than a year and usually were repeat offenders. The answers were simple: The company increased training and dismissed bad drivers. As a result, the driver accident rate fell 48 percent.[1]

FOUNDATIONS OF CONTROL

1. Explain the foundations of control.

The Preview Case reports on some of the changes in the methods of control, planning, and communication that helped turn around Waste Management. **Control** *involves the processes for ensuring that behaviors and performance conform to an organization's standards, including rules, procedures, and goals.*[2] To most people, the word *control* has a negative connotation—of restraining, forcing, delimiting, watching, or manipulating. With the threats of terrorism since the September 11, 2001, attack on the World Trade Center in New York City and the Pentagon in Washington, D.C., governments and business firms have substantially accelerated their use of security-based controls, especially through the increased use of security guards, surveillance cameras, computer monitoring, telephone monitoring, personal searches at airports, and scanning. Although most of these control methods have been reluctantly recognized as necessary, some controversy surrounds whether they have become too intrusive and threaten rights of privacy.

However, controls are both useful and necessary. Effective control was one of the keys to Waste Management's turnaround. We can illustrate the need for controls by describing how control interacts with planning:

- Planning is the formal process of developing goals, strategies, tactics, and standards and allocating resources. Controls help ensure that decisions, actions, and results are consistent with those plans.
- Planning prescribes desired behaviors and results. Controls help maintain or redirect *actual* behaviors and results.
- Managers and employees cannot effectively plan without accurate and timely information. Controls provide much of this essential information.
- Plans indicate the purposes to be served by controls. Controls help ensure that plans are implemented as intended. Thus, planning and control complement and support each other.

Preventive and Corrective Controls

The two general types of organizational controls are preventive and corrective.[3] **Preventive controls** *are mechanisms intended to reduce errors and thereby minimize the need for corrective action.* For example, most major banks and credit unions have developed methods to increase the security of their ATMs and the customers who use them. Jerome Sviglas, a credit card and electronic security consultant, says that financial institutions need to screen and rotate employees who maintain ATMs, place ATMs in well-lighted areas or inside 24-hour convenience stores, change the encryption key on ATMs every six months, and establish and advertise a rapid response to ATM abuse. Similarly, air traffic controllers help prevent crashes by ensuring that airline pilots follow well-defined standards, rules, and procedures during take-offs and landings.

Rules and regulations, standards, recruitment and selection procedures, and training and development programs function primarily as preventive controls. They direct and limit the behaviors of managers and employees alike. The assumption is that, if managers and employees comply with these requirements, the organization is likely to achieve its goals. Thus preventive controls are needed to ensure that rules, regulations, and standards are being followed and are working. Waste Management's ethics officer, who trains employees and the board of directors, serves as a preventive control by helping to avoid and reduce ethical and legal violations.

Corrective controls *are mechanisms intended to reduce or eliminate unwanted behaviors or results and thereby achieve conformity with the organization's regulations and standards.* An air traffic controller also exercises corrective control by instructing pilots who get off course to change altitude and direction to avoid other planes. At Waste Management, the tracking of numerous data—such as how long it took to answer customer calls, how many customers reported billing problems, and how many accidents employees had—provided input for corrective controls to reduce these problems. For example, the accident data led to termination or disciplinary action of some drivers. The company's anonymous hotline for employees to call to report improper behavior serves as both a preventive and corrective control mechanism. The existence of the hotline is intended to prevent or reduce improper behavior by making employees aware that such actions may be reported. It serves as a corrective control method when improper behavior is reported with the result of employees being disciplined or dismissed.

Sources of Control

The four primary sources of control in most organizations are stakeholders, the organization itself, groups, and individuals. These sources are shown in Table 10.1, along with examples of preventive and corrective controls for each.

Table 10.1 Examples of Different Sources and Types of Control

Source of Control	Types of Control	
	Preventive	Corrective
Stakeholders	Maintaining quotas for hiring personnel in protected classes	Changing recruitment policies to attract qualified personnel
Organization	Using budgets to guide expenditures	Disciplining an employee for violating a "No Smoking" safety regulation in a hazardous area
Group	Advising a new employee about the group's norm in relation to expected level of output	Harassing and socially isolating a worker who doesn't conform to group norms
Individual	Deciding to skip lunch in order to complete a project on time	Revising a report you have written because you are dissatisfied with it

Stakeholder control *is expressed as pressures from outside sources on organizations to change their behaviors.* Recall that stakeholders may be unions, government agencies, customers, shareholders, and others who have direct interests in the well-being of an organization. During the past two decades, organizations have been increasingly pressured to reduce pollution, save energy, and produce more environmentally safe goods. For example, the Environmental Protection Agency (EPA) takes actual measurements of air pollution concentrations at more than 5,000 sites across the country. The data from these readings identify outdoor air quality trends and are used to determine which areas meet the U.S. Clean Air Act standards.[4] Firms and government agencies in those areas found to be in violation of this and related legislation are then encouraged or required to take corrective action. More than a dozen major laws form the legal basis for the programs of the EPA. From the perspective of business leaders, this agency creates preventive controls for the firm by prescribing what should not be done to the natural environment—air, water, and land—and creates corrective controls by prescribing needed reductions in air, water, or land pollution by the firm.

Many consumers are demanding that companies provide environmentally safe products and often are willing to pay extra for "green-marketed" products. **Green marketing** *involves the marketing of goods and services considered environmentally friendly that make their organizations "environmentally responsible."* Organizations use green marketing not only to increase consumer approval, but also to cut costs. For example, McDonald's has reduced the amount of materials in its packaging by redesigning items or changing the material specifications to achieve significant packaging weight reductions. During the past 10 years, McDonald's has purchased more than $4 billion in recycled packaging materials. McDonald's has implemented a major energy-efficient fluorescent lighting program. This type of lighting also generates less heat than conventional incandescent lighting, thus reducing the energy required for air-conditioning equipment. Recently, McDonald's announced plans that call for its suppliers worldwide to phase out the use of antibiotics for animals that are also used in human medicine. These are among the few initiatives by McDonald's that are consistent with *green marketing* and stakeholder influence.[5]

Organizational control *comprises the formal policies, rules, procedures, and records for preventing or correcting deviations from plans and for achieving desired goals.* Many of the initiatives by Waste Management in the Preview Case involved some preventive and corrective organizational control. Much of this chapter focuses on organizational control. **Group control** *comprises the norms and values that group or team members share and maintain through rewards and punishments.* Examples include acceptance by the group or team and punishments, such as giving group members the silent treatment. A number of aspects of group or team control are discussed in Chapters 17 and 18.

Individual self-control *comprises the guiding mechanisms that operate consciously and subconsciously within each person.* Standards of professionalism are becoming an increasingly important aspect of individual self-control. Becoming a professional involves acquiring detailed knowledge, specialized skills, and specific attitudes and ways of behaving. The entire process may take years of study and socialization. In doing their work, certified public accountants, lawyers, engineers, business school graduates, and physicians, among others, are expected to exercise individual self-control based on the guiding standards of their professions.

Stakeholder, organizational, group, and individual controls form patterns that differ widely from one organization to another. Strong organizational cultures, the characteristics of which we describe in Chapter 18, usually produce mutually supportive and reinforcing organizational, group, and individual controls. The following Planning & Administration Competency reports on the organizational control practices at Siebel Systems, headquartered in San Mateo, California, with about 6,000 employees. This firm develops enterprise software for sales, marketing, and customer service systems. As you will see in this feature, organizational control drives and dominates the overall pattern of control at Siebel Systems.[6]

| The Competent Manager | *"My hardest decision comes whenever I have to fire someone. Those times (which, happily, haven't been often) have triggered some of my most self-reflective moments, because the decision is often as much a sign of the shortcomings of our human resource controls as of the person being let go."* |
| | Martha Jones Evans
President and CEO
The American Red Cross |

PLANNING & ADMINISTRATION COMPETENCY

Siebel Systems' Controls

Tom Siebel is the founder and CEO of Siebel Systems. He has a reputation for being a highly directive and top-down control-oriented executive. Under his direction, Siebel Systems developed a set of software programs, including 25 integrated applications known as *employee relationship management (ERM) software*. It has been fully implemented with Siebel's employees and is available for purchase by other organizations.

Siebel's ERM is a highly automated system that directs, informs, and tracks employees. Tom Siebel had it developed for internal use after surveys suggested that many of his employees were unsure about their roles. He came to think of the application as a kind of CEO dashboard. He thinks that "many companies will apply ERM to the problem of increasing return on investment in human capital."

©AP Photo/John Todd

Siebel's ERM is mostly about management command and control. The way it works at Siebel, for example, is that the software requires employees to set detailed goals and managers to conduct reviews on a fixed schedule each quarter. There is a strong top-down bias because the process begins with Tom Siebel setting his goals and then everyone else "aligning" theirs accordingly. Managers can check compliance from their desktops by calling up charts that show which departments, managers, or employees are on track. Employees are also required to take 5 of Siebel's 500 minicourses (mostly about Siebel products) every quarter and pass tests for each one. It's a system that reflects Siebel's own management style, which is buttoned-down—suits mostly a must, no lunch at the desk.

A major criticism of ERM software, such as that developed by Siebel Systems, is that too many tight and top-down organizational controls can stifle the individual's self-control in the workplace. This can lead to job dissatisfaction, higher employee turnover, and reduced creativity. Managers at Siebel and other organizations must weigh these potential costs against the anticipated performance improvements that greater formal controls might bring.

Linkage to Strategic Goals

Controls should be linked to the strategic goals of the organization. These goals often include improving customer service, protecting the organization's assets, and improving the quality of the goods and/or services it produces. Let's consider another example of this linkage at Waste Management, the company studied in our Preview Case. The company knew that missed pickups were often a result of cars blocking garbage bins. So Waste Management launched a program called Haul or Call. Now if drivers see something blocking containers, they call the local Waste Management office. The office then calls the customer and asks when they can reschedule a pickup, typically within 24 hours. Maurice Myers, the CEO, comments: "Our customers were shocked—literally shocked—when we started to call them, asking them when we could reschedule."[7] A good organizational control system has features such as those discussed in the following subsections.

Objective. An objective formal control is impartial and cannot be manipulated by employees for personal gain. In the United States, the Financial Accounting Standards Board (FASB) and several government agencies devote a great deal of effort to developing and monitoring principles and practices to attempt to ensure that financial statements objectively and as accurately as possible reflect reality. Unfortunately, in the early 2000s, the executives of some major corporations (e.g., Enron, Tyco, WorldCom) manipulated financial and accounting procedures and practices for their personal gain. However, the controls exerted by various external stakeholder groups did, eventually, lead to exposing the illegal and unethical practices by the top executives at such firms as Enron, Tyco, WorldCom, and Waste Management prior to Maurice Myers' leadership. Clearly, controls for assessing an organization's effectiveness must include multiple criteria.

Complete. A complete system of controls encompass all of the behaviors and goals desired by the organization. A purchasing manager evaluated solely on the basis of cost per order may allow quality to slip. A computer salesperson at IBM evaluated only on the basis of sales volume may ignore after-sales service. Thus, IBM balances quantitative (measurable) and qualitative (subjective) controls.

Timely. Timely controls provide information when it is needed most. Timeliness may be measured in seconds for evaluating the safe movement of trains and planes or in terms of months for evaluating employee performance. Computer-based information systems have played a major role in increasing the timely flow of information. The computerized cash registers at Target and many other major retailers give store managers and top-level executives daily data on each department's sales, as well as profitability measures for the entire store.

Acceptable. To be effective, controls must be recognized as necessary and appropriate. If controls are widely ignored, managers need to find out why. Perhaps the controls should be dropped or modified, should be backed up with rewards for compliance and punishments for noncompliance, or should be linked more closely to desired results. T. J. Rodgers is the founder and CEO of Cypress Semiconductor, which is headquartered in Palo Alto, California. The firm is a supplier of integrated circuits for network infrastructures and access equipment. Several years ago, Rodgers implemented computer-based controls for the firm's employees, dubbed *killer software*. It tracked detailed and daily goals and deadlines for each employee. When targets were missed, the software shut down the offending department's computers and canceled the manager's next paycheck. Rodgers ditched the scheme several years ago after realizing that it encouraged dishonesty and turned some employees into "checklist robots."[8] The employee relationship management software developed by Siebel Systems is not so draconian. However, Tom Siebel will need to monitor not only whether employees meet their goals, but also how they achieved them.

How Much Organizational Control?

One way to assess the amount of needed formal organizational controls is to compare the costs and benefits. Such a cost–benefit analysis addresses three basic questions:

1. For what desired behaviors and results should organizational controls be developed?
2. What are the costs and benefits of the organizational controls required to achieve the desired behaviors and results?
3. What are the costs and benefits of utilizing alternative controls to obtain the desired behaviors and results, such as greater reliance on group control or individual self-control?

Figure 10.1 shows a cost–benefit model for gauging the effectiveness of an organization's controls. The horizontal axis indicates the amount of organizational control, ranging from low to high. The vertical axis indicates the relationship between the costs and benefits of control, ranging from zero to high. For simplicity, the cost-of-control curve is shown as a direct function of the amount of organizational control. The two break-even points indicate where the amount of organizational control moves from a net loss to a net benefit and then returns to a net loss. Although the optimal amount of control is difficult to calculate, effective managers probably come closer to achieving it than do ineffective managers.

Managers have to consider trade-offs that affect the amount of organizational control to use. With too little control, costs exceed benefits and the controls are ineffective. As the amount of control increases, effectiveness also increases—up to a point. Beyond a certain point, effectiveness declines with further increases in the amount of control exercised. For example, an organization might benefit from reducing the average managerial span of control from 21 to 16 employees. However, to reduce it further to 8 employees would require doubling the number of managers. The costs of the increased control (managers' salaries) might far outweigh the expected benefits. Such a move might also make workers feel micromanaged. That, in turn, could lead to increased dissatisfaction, absenteeism, and turnover. Obviously, some of these costs and benefits can be difficult to quantify.

Figure 10.1   Cost–Benefit Model of Organizational Control

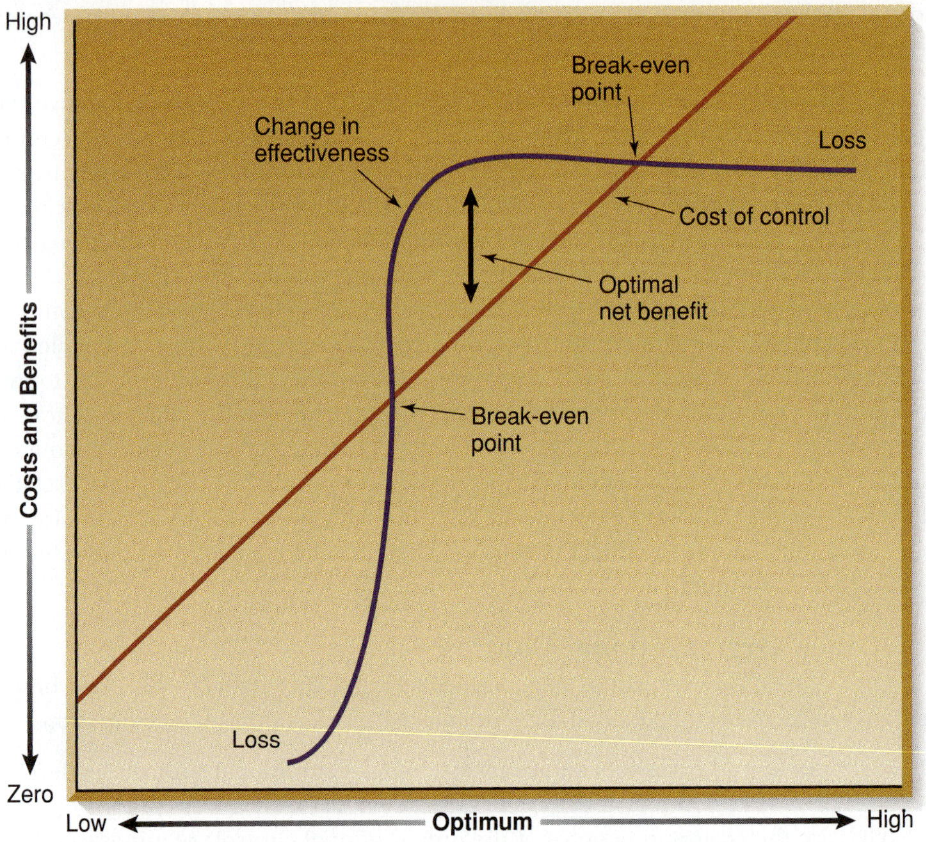

CORRECTIVE CONTROL MODEL

2. Identify the six phases of the corrective control model.

The **corrective control model** *is a process for detecting and eliminating or reducing deviations from an organization's established standards.*[9] This process relies heavily on information feedback and responses to it. As shown in Figure 10.2, the corrective control model has six interconnected phases: (1) define the system (an individual, a department, or a process), (2) identify the key characteristics to be measured, (3) set standards, (4) collect information, (5) make comparisons, and (6) diagnose problems and make corrections.

Define the System

Formal controls might be created and maintained for an employee, a work team, a department, a process, or an entire organization. The controls could focus on inputs, transformation processes, or outputs. Input controls often limit the amount by which raw materials used in the transformation process can vary from the organization's standards. For example, breweries use elaborate preventive controls (including inspections and laboratory testing) to guarantee that the water and grains they use to make beer meet predetermined standards. Such controls ensure that the correct quantity and quality of inputs enter the production process.

Many formal corrective controls are applied during production (the transformation process). For Budweiser, Coors, Miller, and other brewers, they include timing the cooking of the brew, monitoring the temperature in the vats, sampling and laboratory testing of the brew at each stage of the process, and visual inspection of the beer prior to final

Figure 10.2   Corrective Control Model

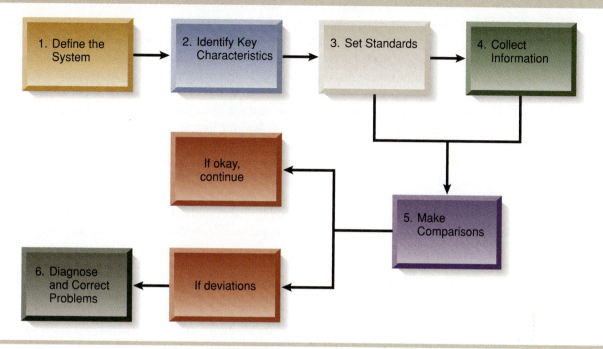

packing. Finally, output controls are used. For brewers, they range from specifying the levels of distributor inventories to monitoring consumer attitudes toward the beer and its marketing.

Identify Key Characteristics

The key types of information to be obtained about a person, team, department, or organization must be identified. Establishing formal corrective controls requires early determination of the characteristics that can be measured, the costs and benefits of obtaining information about each characteristic, and whether variations in each characteristic are likely to affect performance.

After identifying them, managers must choose the characteristics to be measured. The **principle of selectivity** *(also known as Pareto's law) holds that a small number of characteristics always account for a large number of effects.* In brewing beer, three characteristics that greatly influence the final product's quality are water quality, temperature, and length of brewing time. Failing to control these few vital characteristics can account for large variations in results.

Set Standards

Standards *are criteria for evaluating qualitative and quantitative characteristics and should be set for each characteristic measured.* One of the most difficult, but important, aspects of doing business in a foreign country is to adjust to differences in standards. Owing to the difficulties that they face in setting standards that apply in widely differing cultures and markets, many global organizations have adopted the strategy of *thinking globally, but acting locally.* Cisco, a computer networking organization, discovered that customer standards varied from country to country. In Japan, Cisco found that office buildings often lack the space required for installing the company's complex electrical equipment, so it had to design network routers that would fit under a person's desk. In France, buyers insisted that at least some product components be French made and demanded that Cisco use French-based organizations to test its products.[10] For food producers such as ADM, country-by-country regulations concerning labeling or possible restrictions on bioengineered ingredients must be taken into account.

Cultural and cross-cultural differences also are apparent in various human interactions, including language, nonverbal communication, religion, time, space, color, numbers, degree of materialism, customs, status symbols, and food preferences. For example, different time standards are reflected in differing approaches to work. U.S. and Canadian executives expect meetings to begin and end at certain times, but Latins typically arrive after the specified clock time and are not concerned about ending meetings at a clock-specified time. Why? Their standard for time is not based on deadlines, but rather on a series of events: First, they do a task; when that is finished, they move on to the next task; and so on. Similarly, Indonesians have "rubber time"; to them, time is elastic. If something comes up that is more important than business, such as a wedding, business gets postponed. In Nigeria, a starting time for a meeting is only an approximation, and "tardiness" is readily accepted. Thus, global organizations must observe standards set by the local cultures, rather than apply the standards the organizations are accustomed to and would prefer to set.[11]

Increasingly, controls are being based on performance standards (performance goals), of which many types are possible. Let's look at examples from five different functional areas:

1. *Inventory.* Monthly finished goods inventory should be maintained at the sales level forecast for the following three-month period.
2. *Accounts receivable.* Monthly accounts receivable should be no more than the dollar value of the previous month's sales, except for the month of December.
3. *Sales productivity.* The dollar value of sales per salesperson should be $1,000 greater than the comparable month for the previous year and $12,000 greater annually.
4. *Employee turnover.* The turnover of field sales personnel should be no more than 3 per 100 salespeople per month and no more than 30 per 100 salespeople annually.
5. *Production waste.* Waste should amount to no more than $100 per month per full-time production worker, or no more than $1,200 per year per full-time production worker.

Collect Information

Information on each of the standards can be collected manually or automatically. Examples of the latter are the electronic counting devices used at Disney World to count the number of people who use each ride or the turnstiles at many sports facilities that count the number of people who enter.

If the individual or group whose performance is to be controlled collects information, its validity must be checked. Employees and managers sometimes have an incentive to distort or conceal information if they will be criticized or punished for negative results. Moreover, when formal controls emphasize punishment, strong group controls (see Chapter 17) may emerge to distort the information reported to management. Such reporting may obscure responsibility for failure to meet standards or achieve goals.

Of course, rewards tied to results also create the possibility of individuals distorting information or groups pressuring others to avoid full disclosure of information. Consider what happened at the Lyondell-Citgo refinery, located in Houston, Texas, which produces light fuels. Employees heading into work at this refinery used to walk past a new four-door Ford pickup and Chevrolet Silverado parked at the front gate. The trucks, loaded with accessories, were a reminder that if the plant hit 1 million man-hours without a recordable injury, one lucky employee would win either the Ford or the Chevy or another \$30,000 vehicle of his or her choice in a drawing. Plant officials hoped that by giving away an expensive vehicle, like the Ford F150 pickup it awarded in 2002, the company could reinforce the importance of workplace safety. But to some employees, the display of the trucks was a subtle reminder not to report any injuries. Otherwise, they'd face the wrath of their peers, who'd like to park one of those trucks in their own driveway. David Taylor, a process operator, commented: "Unless you're bleeding or a bone is sticking out, most employees preferred to keep quiet and see their personal physicians." Several other operators indicated they were worried about the possible punishment from management if they reported an accident. One operator, who hid his pinched finger, remarked: "You get interrogated by ten to twelve people. Ninety to ninety-five percent of the time, they think it's your fault." A maintenance craftsman said he hasn't reported his cuts and bruises either. "They try to say it was your fault no matter what," he claims.

Under the discipline policy at the refinery, injured employees who do not follow established work rules, such as wearing gloves or using the correct tools, are first given a verbal warning. Repeat violators are warned in writing and then suspended and, finally, terminated. Lyondell-Citgo management is reconsidering its use of trucks as an incentive to reduce accidents.[12]

Make Comparisons

Comparisons are needed to determine whether what is happening is what *should be* happening. In other words, information about actual results must be compared with performance standards. Such comparisons allow managers and team members to concentrate on deviations or exceptions. At Tom's of Maine, an operator is supposed to package 81 tubes of toothpaste a minute. If all operators reach or surpass this goal, the production process is operating efficiently. If there is no apparent difference between what is and what should be happening, operations normally continue without any change.

Consider the comparisons in reportable injuries at the Lyondell-Citgo refinery before and after the truck incentive program along with its changed approach to safety, which places responsibility—and consequences—with individual employees. In 1998, the plant had 43 reportable injuries. In 2002, when the individual accountability approach had been fully implemented along with the vehicle incentive program, the refinery had 8 *reported* injuries.

Diagnose and Correct Problems

Diagnosis involves assessing the types, amounts, and causes of deviations from standards. Action can then be taken to eliminate those deviations and correct problems. However, the fact that a characteristic can be controlled does not necessarily mean that it should be controlled. Computer-based management information systems often help in overcoming inadequacies in corrective controls.

Suppose that you have just gotten your midterm examination back and have received a D. You immediately start typing an e-mail message to a friend, ranting about your terrible instructor and how you're thinking about getting other students to give him poor faculty evaluations at the end of the semester. You begin to have second thoughts, decide that complaining might be a dumb idea, and don't send the e-mail message. However, unbeknownst to you, every character you typed on your school's computer has been stored for the faculty to see. You get a call from the faculty member saying that he would like to see you after your next class.

Can something like that actually happen? It may not happen at a university, but if you work in a corporation, the answer is a definite yes! Many organizations are installing software that monitors their employees' computer activity, both online and off-line—every message sent, every Web site visited, every file formatted, and even every key stroke entered—to control abuses. Collecting such data is easy and cheap. For example, a company on the Internet at http://www.winwhatwhere.com sells surveillance software that does all of these things and more.

Corrective and preventive controls are essential to managing complaints well and restoring customers' satisfaction as well as repurchase intentions, trust, and long-term relationships. Interestingly, most customers are dissatisfied with the ways organizations handle their complaints.[13] The following Communication Competency feature reports on several of the key aspects of the complaint management process at Barclays Bank.[14] Barclays is one of the largest financial services organizations in the United Kingdom. It is headquartered in London and operates in 60 countries with more than 74,000 employees.

COMMUNICATION COMPETENCY

Barclays Complaint Management Process

Barclays has processes designed to provide a speedy response to complaints. They strive to acknowledge a complaint within 24 hours and, within five working days after an investigation, provide a full reply with an explanation of the causes and details of actions to be taken. The need for a speedy response is recognized by Barclays as vital if complaining customers are to be satisfied. In addition, they make a point of calling the customers on the phone whenever possible. This is done to provide a speedy acknowledgment of the complaint. More importantly, it gives Barclays an opportunity to present a human face to the customer, to ensure that the complaint process is seen as being genuine and caring rather than routine and impersonal.

Customers are encouraged to complain and comment, and systems are in place to make this as easy as possible. Barclays Bank relies on leaflets and posters informing customers that comments of any sort are welcome. These are readily available to their customers and well publicized in communications such as monthly statements and annual reports as well as in branches and offices.

Barclays does not provide any form of financial reward to employees for encouraging complaints. Doing so is seen to be unnecessary, even running counter to their desire to make encouraging complaints a part of normal practice. Furthermore, Barclays understands that not only are mistakes inevitable but that they are acceptable, except where repeated mistakes are being made. Barclays' *no-blame* culture encourages staff to take initiatives to satisfy complaining customers and to look for solutions without first thinking about whether they might be pun-

ished for going outside their job descriptions. There are limits as to what staff are allowed to suggest.

Barclays formally involves complaint-management professionals in their strategic planning sessions. This is done to ensure that their experiences of customer concerns are incorporated into planning at the bank. Top management views complaints as a contributor to operational improvement and Barclays' long-term success.

Complaints data at Barclays are compiled centrally. Regular reports (at least monthly) are circulated and discussed by managers, executives, and teams. Further, information on complaints are published in staff newsletters. Barclays' leadership is of the opinion that communicating complaint data is a good thing because it promotes awareness in employees of the problems and issues that are being faced and how they are performing in tackling them.

PRIMARY METHODS OF CONTROL

3. Describe the primary methods of organizational control.

Throughout this textbook, we have discussed various aspects of control and have indicated how a firm's strategy helps focus (control) employee behavior. For example, compared to the Ritz-Carlton, Marriott's Hampton Inns provide low-cost accommodations. Therefore, Marriott's control systems focus on maintaining a low-cost strategy. In terms of human resource management, performance appraisal systems help managers assess the behaviors of employees and compare them to performance standards. Deviations are noted and corrective controls are used to reduce or eliminate problems.

In this section, we explore six primary methods of organizational control. Two are basic to the type of organization: mechanistic and organic controls. One reflects external considerations: market controls. Two are functional: financial and accounting controls. And one is technological: automation controls. We also provide examples of specific control methods utilized by organizations.

As Figure 10.3 illustrates, all organizations utilize some combination of mechanistic and organic control methods in conjunction with their market, financial and accounting, and automation-based controls. The methods available have the potential for complementing one another or working against one another. Thus, management should select and assess control methods in relation to one another when deciding which to apply.

Figure 10.3   Primary Organizational Control Methods

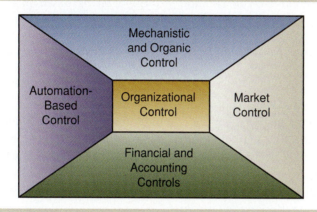

Mechanistic and Organic Controls

Mechanistic control *involves the extensive use of rules and procedures, top-down authority, tightly written job descriptions, and other formal methods for preventing and correcting deviations from desired behaviors and results.* Mechanistic controls are an important part of bureaucratic management (see Chapters 2, 11, and 18). In contrast, **organic control** *involves the use of flexible authority, relatively loose job descriptions, individual self-controls, and other informal methods for preventing and correcting deviations from desired behaviors and results.* See Chapter 11, especially Table 11.1, for more information on mechanistic versus organic organizations.

Organic control is consistent with a clan culture (see Chapter 18). In clan-type organizational cultures, such as Johnson & Johnson and Accenture, members share pride in membership and a strong sense of identification with management. In addition, peer pressure to adhere to certain norms is considerable. Teams of self-managed employees control themselves with little day-to-day direction from a supervisor. These self-managed teams use many organic controls, which create a supportive environment for members to learn new tasks. Table 10.2 contrasts the use of mechanistic and organic control methods.

Coca-Cola and other major organizations have large numbers of departments, which can differ widely in their use of mechanistic or organic controls. The use of mechanistic controls in certain departments and organic controls in others does not necessarily reduce a firm's overall effectiveness. At Coca-Cola, the syrup production units operate in a relatively stable environment, whereas the marketing units operate in a changing environment. Managers of these different types of units use different ways to divide

The
Competent
Manager

"As soon as people start to figure out they're being monitored and tracked, pretty much, you get what you ask for. If people feel they're the victims of bean counters who ignore quality and focus solely on numbers, they'll figure out how to drive numbers up without putting effort into quality."

Carla Lorek
Manager of Communication
  and Quality
Xerox's Information Management
  Division

Table 10.2	Mechanistic and Organic Control Methods

Mechanistic Control Methods	**Organic Control Methods**
Use of detailed rules and procedures whenever possible	Use of detailed rules and procedures only when necessary
Top-down authority, with emphasis on positional power	Flexible authority, with emphasis on expert power and networks of influence
Activity-based job descriptions that prescribe day-to-day behaviors	Results-based job descriptions that emphasize goals to be achieved
Emphasis on extrinsic rewards (wages, pensions, status symbols)	Emphasis on both extrinsic and intrinsic rewards (meaningful work)
Distrust of teams, based on an assumption that team goals conflict with organizational goals	Use of teams, based on an assumption that team goals and norms assist in achieving organizational goals

and manage the work. The syrup production managers use more mechanistic controls, and the marketing managers use more organic controls. One consequence of use of the organic controls was that marketing managers recognized that consumers in different countries did not perceive Coca-Cola the same way and had different product requirements. For example, in Spain, refrigerators are smaller than in other countries. As a result, two-liter bottles did not fit in the refrigerators, and sales were lost until marketing indicated a need to redesign the container.

Market Control

Market control *involves the collection and evaluation of data related to sales, prices, costs, and profits for guiding decisions and evaluating results.* The idea of market control emerged from economics. Dollar amounts provide standards of comparison. To be effective, market control mechanisms generally require that

- the costs of the resources used in producing outputs be measured monetarily,
- the value of the goods and services produced be defined clearly and priced monetarily, and
- the prices of the goods and services produced be set competitively.

Two of the control mechanisms that can satisfy these requirements are profit-sharing plans and customer monitoring.

Profit-Sharing Plans. As discussed in Chapter 13, **profit-sharing plans** *provide employees with supplemental income based on the earnings of an entire organization or a selected unit.*[15] The unit may be a strategic business unit, a division, a store in a chain, or other organizational entity. They are primarily a form of preventive control. Profit-sharing plans generally are used to

- increase employee identification with the organization's profit goals, allowing greater reliance on individual self-control and group controls;
- achieve a more flexible wage structure, reflecting the company's actual economic position and controlling labor costs;
- attract and retain workers more easily, improving control of selection and lowering turnover costs; and
- establish a more equitable reward system, helping to develop an organizational culture that recognizes achievement and performance.

At least three important factors influence whether the goals of a profit-sharing plan can be achieved. First, employees must think that the plan is based on a reasonable, accurate, and equitable formula. The formula, in turn, must be based on valid, consistently and honestly reported financial and operating information. Second, employees must think that their efforts and achievements contribute to profitability. Third, employees must think that the size of profit-based incentives will increase proportionally as profitability increases.

The major U.S. based automakers have profit-sharing plans for all of their employees, not just management personnel. For example, in a recent year, General Motors paid profit sharing of about $940, on average, to its 130,000 hourly employees in the United States. In contrast, Ford Motor provided a check of approximately $160 to each of its 95,000 hourly employees in the United States.[16] The difference is directly attributable to the difference in earnings by these two firms. In a survey of U.S. firms with profit-sharing plans, the most common feature is to have the firm contribute a portion of profits to the employee's retirement plan. On average, this amounts to 8 percent of the employee's pay for the year. The amount contributed to the employee's retirement plan varies by the amount of the firm's earnings up to a maximum allowed by law and the firm's own policies.[17]

Customer Monitoring. **Customer monitoring** *consists of ongoing efforts to obtain feedback from customers concerning the quality of goods and services.* Such monitoring is done to prevent problems or learn of their existence and solve them. As suggested in the Communication Competency feature on Barclays, customer monitoring is being used increasingly by organizations in their attempt to correct problems with service and quality.[18] Based on such assessments, management may take action to prevent the loss of further business because of customer dissatisfaction.

Service providers use customer monitoring often. Staples, the office supply chain, tracks consumer purchases by offering a membership card good for discounts and special promotions. This system allows Staples to know its customers' purchasing habits well. Because of its cash-register data, which tracks buying preferences, quantities, and frequency, Staples does not need to use mass mailings and generic coupons. Instead, it targets specific customer segments for selected coupons, mailings, and promotions. Fairfield Inn, a limited service motel chain and division of Marriott, focuses on a basic customer monitoring process that is considered to have great relevance throughout the organization. Guests are encouraged to rate three core aspects of service: cleanliness, friendliness, and efficiency. The three scores are aggregated to give an overall guest score. The accumulation of these guest scores may affect bonuses for everyone at a property—from guestroom attendant to Inn manager. The use of the guest scores to affect individual bonuses is left to the discretion of Inn managers.[19]

After purchases of their goods or services, many firms follow up with telephone interviews or mail questionnaires to obtain information from customers. Lexus reimburses dealers for performing 1,000- and 7,500-mile checkups at no cost to Lexus owners. After the car has been serviced, the customer is asked to fill out a survey regarding the adequacy of the service. An independent marketing research firm enters the data into a computer and then sends it on to Lexus headquarters in California by satellite transmission. As a result, Lexus can track all service work done anywhere in its system and compare the quality of service provided by its dealers.[20]

Financial and Accounting Controls

Financial control *includes the mechanisms for preventing or correcting the misallocation of resources.*[21] External auditors, usually certified public accounting firms (e.g., Ernst & Young, and KPMG) and/or internal auditing departments (e.g., accounting, controller, and treasure), monitor the effectiveness of financial control. The primary responsibility of external auditors is to the shareholders. The auditors' role is to assure shareholders that the firm's financial statements present its true financial position and are in conformity with generally accepted accounting principles.

Because so many financial control mechanisms exist, we focus on only three of the essential ones: comparative financial analysis, budgeting, and activity-based costing.

Comparative Financial Analysis. *Evaluation of a firm's financial condition for two or more time periods is called* **comparative financial analysis**. When data are available from similar firms, they are used in making comparisons.[22] Industry trade associations often collect information from their members and publish it in summary form. Publicly owned firms publish income statements, balance sheets, and other financial statements. These sources often are used by managers and outsiders to assess changes in the firm's financial indicators and to compare its financial health with that of other firms in the same industry. Companies that have multiple production facilities (e.g., Toyota and Bridgestone/Firestone), retail outlets (e.g., Pier 1 and Target), restaurants (e.g., Taco Bell and Olive Garden), and hotels (e.g., Marriott and Sheraton) compare the financial records of all units for control purposes.

The technique most commonly used is ratio analysis. **Ratio analysis** *involves selecting two significant figures, expressing their relationship as a fraction, and comparing its value for two periods of time or with the same ratio of similar organizations.* Of the many types of possible ratios, those most commonly used by organizations are profitability, liquidity, activity, and leverage. They are summarized in Table 10.3.[23]

Table 10.3	Examples of Commonly Used Financial Ratios		
Type	**Example**	**Calculation**	**Interpretation**
Profitability	Return on investment (ROI)	$\dfrac{\text{Net income}}{\text{Total investment}}$	Profitability of investment
Liquidity	Current ratio	$\dfrac{\text{Current assets}}{\text{Current liabilities}}$	Short-term solvency
Activity	Inventory turnover	$\dfrac{\text{Sales}}{\text{Inventory}}$	Efficiency of inventory management
Leverage	Debt ratio	$\dfrac{\text{Total debt}}{\text{Total assets}}$	How an organization finances itself

Return on investment (ROI) *generally is considered to be the most important profitability ratio because it indicates how efficiently and effectively the organization is using its resources.* A ratio value greater than 1.0 may indicate that the organization is using its resources effectively. The **current ratio** *usually indicates an organization's ability to pay bills on time.* A current ratio should be well above 1:1, and a ratio of 2:1 often indicates that a firm is financially sound. A low current ratio might mean that the organization has unnecessary inventory, a lot of cash sitting idle, or heavy accounts receivable that are difficult to collect. **Inventory turnover** *indicates the average number of times that inventory is sold and restocked during the year.* A high ratio relative to the industry means efficient operations—fewer resources are tied up in inventory as compared to competitors. A higher relative turnover enables the organization to use its resources elsewhere. **Debt ratio** *is computed to assess an organization's ability to meet its long-term financial commitments.* A value of 0.35 indicates that the organization has $0.35 in liabilities for every $1.00 of assets. The higher this ratio, the poorer credit risk the organization is perceived to be by financial institutions. Generally, organizations with debt ratios above 1.0 are considered to be relying too much on debt to finance their operations.

Financial ratios have little value unless managers know how to interpret them. For example, an ROI of 10 percent doesn't mean much unless it is compared to the ROIs of other organizations in the same industry. A firm with an ROI of 5 percent in an industry where the average ROI is 11 percent might be performing poorly. An inventory turnover rate of 5 per year at Pep Boys, Chief Auto Parts, and other auto-supply stores might be excellent but would be disastrous for Kroger, Grand Union, Safeway, and other large supermarkets for which an inventory turnover rate of 15 per year is common.

Budgeting. **Budgeting** *is the process of categorizing proposed expenditures and linking them to goals.* Budgets usually express the dollar costs of various tasks or resources. For example, at Toyota, production budgets may be based on hours of labor per car produced, machine downtime per thousand hours of running time, wage rates, and similar information. The main budget categories usually include labor, supplies and materials, and facilities (property, buildings, and equipment).

Budgeting has three primary purposes: (1) to help in planning work effectively, (2) to assist in allocating resources, and (3) to aid in controlling and monitoring resource utilization during the budget period. When managers assign dollar costs to the resources needed, they sometimes realize that proposed tasks are not worth the cost; they can then modify or abandon the proposals.

Budgeting for completely new tasks usually requires forecasting conditions and estimating costs. Budgeting for established tasks is easier because historical cost data are available. In either case, those who prepare budgets must exercise judgment about what is likely to happen and how it will affect the organization. Budgets often are developed for a year and then broken down by month. Managers, thus, are able to track progress in meeting a budget as the year unfolds—and to take corrective action as necessary.

The control aspect of budgeting may be either corrective or preventive. When budgeting is used as a corrective control, the emphasis is on identifying deviations from the budget. Deviations indicate the need to identify and correct their causes or to change the budget itself.

The power of a budget, especially when used as a preventive control, depends on whether it is viewed as an informal contract that has been agreed to or a club to bludgeon those who do not stay within their budgets. One study asked first-line managers about their companies' budgets. The question was: "Do you feel that budgets or standards are frequently a club held over the head of the manager to force better performance?" Twenty percent of the 204 respondents replied "yes" and 68 percent answered "no." Most managers and employees who must live by budgets accept their use by top management as a control mechanism. However, some managers and employees view budgets with fear and hostility. This reaction usually occurs when an organization enforces budget controls with threats and punishment.[24]

There is no single classification system for budgets. Specific individuals, sections, projects, teams, committees, departments, divisions, or SBUs may be given budgets within which they are expected to operate. The following are the most common types of budgets used in business.

- *Sales budget*—a forecast of expected revenues, generally stated by product line on a monthly basis and revised at least annually.
- *Materials budget*—expected purchases, generally stated by specific categories, which may vary from month to month because of seasonal variations and inventory levels.

- *Labor budget*—expected staffing and benefits levels, generally stated by number of individuals and dollars for each job category.
- *Capital budget*—targeted spending for major tangible assets (e.g., new or renovated headquarters building, new factory, or major equipment), often requiring a time horizon beyond a year.
- *Research and development budget*—targeted spending for the development or refinement of products, materials, and processes.
- *Cash budget*—expected flow of monetary receipts and expenditures (cash flow), generally developed at least once a year for each month of the year.

The types of budgets and budget categories used are strongly influenced by organizational design and organizational culture. An organization having a functional design usually has a budget for each function (e.g., marketing, production, finance, and human resources). However, an organization having a product design usually has a budget for each product line. For example, Dell Computers has a variety of product lines—servers, notebook, computers, workstations, switches, desktop PCs, printers, and so on. Product line budgeting enables Dell's control system to measure the contributions of each product line to sales, costs, and profits.

Activity-Based Costing. *Activity-based costing (ABC) is a system that focuses on activities as the fundamental cost centers.*[25] An *activity* is any event that drives costs, including energy consumed, miles driven, computer hours logged, quality inspections made, shipments made, and scrap/rework orders filled.

In contrast to most financial control mechanisms, ABC focuses on the work activities associated with operating a business. The number of these activities usually depends on the complexity of operations. The more complex the organization's operations, the more cost-driving activities it is likely to have. Equally important, managers have discovered that not all products have the same mix of these activities. If a product does not require the use of an activity, its cost would be zero for that activity.

At Carrier's air conditioning plant in Tyler, Texas, one low-volume product requires frequent machine setups, has many intricate parts that generate numerous purchase orders, and requires constant inspections to maintain quality. A second, high-volume product requires few machine setups, few purchase orders, and few quality inspections. If Carrier were to ignore the differences in these two products in terms of their cost-driving activities and simply assign a general overhead cost to the products on the basis of volume, the high-volume product would bear most of the overhead cost. This approach would seriously distort actual unit costs for each product. As a result, Carrier could make production mistakes, and overall profitability would hide the impact of these mistakes. The company could carry unprofitable products and customers because winners would more than offset losers. It could survive with misleading cost allocations and without knowing the real costs of its individual business processes—but profits would not be as high as they could be.

Figure 10.4 depicts a model of the flow of information in activity-based costing, which is viewed from two perspectives: cost and process. The *cost view* reflects the flow of costs from resources to activities and from activities to products and services. At a Lucent Technologies plant in Dallas, Texas, one of the activities is materials handling. The resources consumed in moving materials from one location to another at the plant are traced to each product, based on the number of times an item has been moved. This cost view is the key concept underlying activity-based costing: *Resources are consumed by activities, and activities are consumed by goods and services.*

Figure 10.4 Activity-Based Costing Model

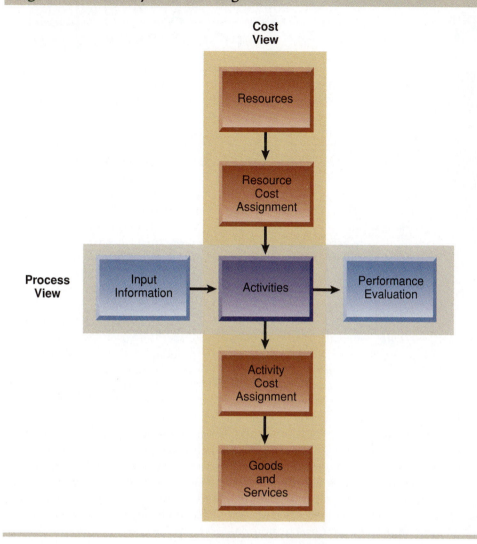

The *process view* reflects the lateral flow from costs of input information to activities and from activities to performance evaluation, or the observed transactions associated with an activity. In the case of materials handling at Lucent, information is gathered on the number of times that an item is moved to determine the extent of activity during a period. This information provides the activity data needed to complete the costing of products. It also provides the data needed to conduct performance evaluations.

Today some service organizations are also using ABC to communicate to their employees which activities are driving up costs. The Hospice of Central Kentucky (HCK) also used ABC to negotiate rates with insurance companies. The hospice operates under a managed-care model, with insurance companies providing per visit and per diem reimbursements. Shorter lengths of stay, higher costs for many terminal patients, and indigent care strain the resources of this managed-care facility. The following Strategic Action Competency feature highlights how HCK used the ABC approach to cut costs, manage its hospice more effectively, and negotiate more favorable rates with insurance carriers.[26]

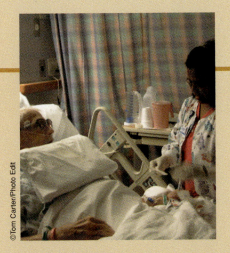
©Tom Carter/Photo Edit

ABC at Hospice of Central Kentucky

The Hospice of Central Kentucky (HCK) established a cross-functional team to determine the costs of things based on a patient day. The team realized that patients with lower acuity require less care and are subject to care over a longer period of time, whereas patients with higher acuity require more intense care over a shorter period of time. Because the per diem reimbursement does not vary in relation to acuity, the less acute cases subsidize the more acute cases.

To understand better the extent to which patients in various stages of acuteness demanded hospice resources, the cross-functional team identified activities at the hospice. The team traced costs for six months to get a good picture of them. To be useful, the resources required by a cost driver must be measurable or there must be some way to estimate them. The differences between the traditional way of accounting for costs and the activity-based costing system are shown in the following table. The data on the left are the *traditional* cost categories. These data tell managers whether they have overspent their budgets. The data on the right define the same costs in everyday language, providing cost information for managers and employees, not for accountants. Employees can relate much better to this language because it is easy to understand and logical.

The hospice was able to improve its efficiency by pinpointing activities that drove costs—accounting/finance, management, and information systems. Employees involved in these activities are much more intensely involved with the patients in imminent death situations than with other patients. For example, ABC analysis revealed that the cost per patient day dramatically increased as the patient approached death, rising from $35.53 for a patient not near death to $381.57 per day for a patient near death.

Communicating these results to all employees in the hospice let everyone know that total length of stay needed to be increased by admitting more patients at the less acute stage of illness because patients entering the acute phase strained the system financially. The hospice was also able to negotiate better contracts with private insurance carriers. Armed with more accurate information, HCK's management determined that the insurance carrier could select a payment type at admission, but couldn't change the payment type later. When faced with this choice, most insurance carriers selected the per diem type of payment that was financially advantageous to the hospice.

Traditional Costing		Activity-Based Costing	
Salaries	$ 70,000	Prereferral	$ 24,700
Benefits	16,000	Referral	10,900
Supplies	10,000	Admission	2,000
Depreciation	27,500	Postadmission	3,700
Pharmacy	5,000	Postdeath	1,500
Total	$128,500	Bereavement	12,700
		Postbereavement	15,100
		Patient Care	
		Medical services	23,300
		Reception	8,500
		Accounting/finance	13,600
		Information systems	6,200
		Billing	2,900
		Volunteer services	3,400
		Total	$128,500

Using activity-based costing yields at least four benefits.[27] First, all costs are pinpointed by activity instead of many of them being charged to overhead. Employees understand that their activities are translated into costs that define the performance level of their units and the organization as a whole. The system also gives them an incentive to think about how to reduce costs. Second, cost allocations are based on the portion of activities that can be directly traced to a finished product itself, as opposed to production volume. Third, costs associated with an activity for a particular product can now be traced. For example, at HCK, each activity was divided by the number of patient days associated with the cost. Prereferral interviews, testing, and similar activities cost HCK $322.58 per patient, whereas the receptionist who answered calls was charged $1.11 per patient. This result showed HCK managers that the best way to control costs is to control the activities that generate them in the first place. Managers can identify activities that are being performed that have little impact on profits but are costing a lot of money. Finally, the use of ABC shifts managers' thinking from traditional cost analysis to managerial decision making. Information technology is essential in gathering ABC information and combining not just cost information but also nonfinancial information and performance measures. As managers and employees become more aware of activity-based costing and the information available from it, they will become more proficient at differentiating between profitable and unprofitable activities.

The benefits of activity-based costing are offset somewhat by two limitations. First, managers must still make some arbitrary cost allocations based on volume. In many organizations, obtaining accurate product costs is difficult because so many costs relate to buildings, land, and equipment. Second, high measurement costs are associated with multiple activity centers and cost drivers. For example, at a hospital, automatically recording the results each time a nurse takes someone's blood pressure would be unreasonably expensive. Similarly, at Bank of America, recording the length of time that a teller and customer talk would be extremely difficult. Even if it were feasible, it might not be a good idea because most banks don't want tellers rushing customers and minimizing customer contact.

Automation-Based Control

Automation *involves the use of self-regulating devices and processes that operate independently of people.* Automation usually involves linking machines with other machines to perform tasks. **Machine control** *utilizes self-regulating instruments or devices to prevent and correct deviations from preset standards.* The use of machines in business has gone through several significant stages of development. Machines initially increased productivity by giving employees better physical control over certain tasks. Eventually, the interaction of employee and machine created a mutual control system. Then a new threshold was reached with automation.

Machine control of other machines takes over part of the managerial control function. That is, machines can now participate in the control process with managers. For example, computers in oil refineries collect data, monitor, and make automatic adjustments during refining processes. The impact of such automatic machine control on management has been reported in a number of studies. One researcher found that the introduction of an advanced automated system in one large factory reduced the number of middle management jobs by 34 percent.[28]

There has been a steady shift toward machine control in production operations. It began with machines being given control of some production tasks, such as when automatic sensors replaced visual inspection in steel production. With the advent of assembly lines and mass-production technology, machines supplemented rules and regulations as a way of directly controlling production workers. In continuous process or robotic operations, machines actually control other machines.

Air Products and Chemicals, Inc., is headquartered in Allentown, Pennsylvania. One of its product lines is gases, such as argon, hydrogen, nitrogen, and oxygen. These gases are provided to manufacturers, health-care facilities, and other industries. The company often distributes industrial gases by building on-site plants. At many of these on-site plants, Air Products and Chemicals uses what it calls a *lights-out system,* which is defined as an "unattended operation with remote access." The company no longer needs full-time operators at its many small plants that produce gases fed directly into larger, neighboring factories, such as steel mills. Instead, the company's machines send a signal to alert operators miles away when a motor overheats or a valve sticks. Safety systems automatically shut the plant down if a problem poses imminent danger.

An operator working from home and assigned to monitor several plants scattered in his region first will try to fix the problem from a computer at home by sending signals through a telephone line to restart processes, just as the operator would from inside the plant's control room. If that fails, the operator then drives to the site to fix the problem. "We can leverage one individual over a large geography this way," says David Fritz, general manager of North American product supply.[29]

Faced with the need to raise productivity to survive, especially against low-cost competitors in such nations as China, more companies are pushing toward so-called *lights-out* manufacturing. Once a science fiction dream, the phenomenon is emerging in plants and factories throughout the United States as machines become more reliable in making flawless parts on their own. New computer technologies also have broadened possibilities by linking plant equipment to the Internet where supervisors can check operations at any time and from any place—they can even do repairs from a distance.[30]

CORPORATE GOVERNANCE

4. Explain several key corporate governance issues and control mechanisms.

A **corporation** *is a government-approved form of organization that allows different parties to contribute capital, expertise, and labor for the benefit of all of them.* It is a legal entity separate from the owners, board members, executives, and other employees. There are many other legal features of a corporation, such as limited liability, but they are beyond the scope of our discussion.[31] Most of the examples throughout this text are from firms organized as corporations. **Corporate governance** *is the pattern of relations and controls between the stockholders, the board of directors, and the top management of a company.* These relations and controls are defined by the corporate charter, bylaws, formal policy, governmental laws and regulations, and the courts.[32] A few of the other terms that are central to corporate governance are defined as follows:

- **Annual meeting**—a company gathering, usually held at the end of each fiscal year, at which shareholders and management discuss the previous year and the outlook for the future, directors are elected and other shareholder concerns are addressed.
- **Annual report**—an audited document issued annually by all publicly listed corporations to their shareholders in accordance with Securities and Exchange Commission regulations. Contains information on financial results and overall performance of the previous fiscal year and comments on future outlook.
- **Board of directors**—the collective group of individuals elected by the shareholders of a corporation to oversee the management of the corporation.
- **Bylaws**—a document stating the rules of internal governance for a corporation as adopted by its board of directors.

- **Disclosure**—the public dissemination of material, market-influencing information.
- **Proxy statement**—a document sent by publicly listed corporations to their shareholders providing material information on corporate matters subject to vote at the general shareholders' meeting.[33]

Corporate governance includes a wide variety of issues and activities, such as (1) strategic and business planning, (2) risk management associated with major capital investments and the purchase of another firm or sale of a company/division, (3) performance assessment of the top executive and the firm as a whole, (4) compensation and benefits paid to executives and higher level managers, (5) CEO/management succession and appointment, (6) disclosure and reporting to stockholders and government agencies, (7) corporate values and corporate culture, (8) independent inputs from members of the board of directors, and (9) organization design.[34]

Clearly, many complex issues and activities fall under the umbrella of corporate governance. Our focus in this section is to provide a snapshot of the control aspects of corporate governance, as these relate to top executives and boards of directors.[35] The control aspects of corporate governance include *external* and *internal* mechanisms.[36] A few of the external control mechanisms include (1) laws and regulatory agencies, (2) the possibility of being acquired by other firms, (3) proxy statements in which stockholders vote on issues of interest to top executives, and (4) the possibility of being sued in the courts by stockholders or other stakeholders. A few of the internal control mechanisms include boards of directors, compensation contracts that attempt to align the interests of top executives with those of stockholders, and corporate bylaws that set ground rules for the responsibilities of top executives and board members. In the remainder of this section, we highlight several aspects of *external* and *internal* governance that apply particularly to publicly traded corporations in which there is a separation between the ownership and management of the firm. When a single individual or small set of individuals owns a firm, the issues of corporate governance are much less complex and problematic.

External Control: Sarbanes-Oxley Act

There are a variety of external control mechanisms in corporate governance. One of these mechanisms is enacted through the provisions of the Sarbanes-Oxley Act, which was passed by the U.S. Congress and signed by the president in 2002. This legislation, which is 66 pages in length, was prompted by the corporate scandals related to the extreme self-serving actions of some corporate executives and the lack of monitoring and control by some boards of directors. Many of the provisions of this act focus on defining the responsibilities of top executives and boards of directors to stockholders and the public at large. The act also defines the penalties for the failure to fulfill these responsibilities. In brief, executives and boards are required to be better agents or representatives of the interests of stockholders and the public.[37]

General Provisions. The act, which is named after its primary architects, Senator Paul Sarbanes (D–Maryland) and Representative Michael Oxley (R–Ohio), is organized into 11 sections. These sections deal with such issues as auditor independence, corporate responsibility, enhanced financial disclosures, conflicts of interest, and corporate accountability. The act also establishes a public company accounting oversight board.

The requirements of Sarbanes-Oxley may be divided into three categories: *certification, auditability,* and *disclosure.* Perhaps the best known provisions concern top management. It requires CEOs and CFOs (chief financial officers) of publicly traded companies to *certify* financial statements. Those who knowingly certify falsely are liable for criminal and civil penalties. This certification is the CEO's and CFO's personal guarantee that valid financial/accounting processes have been established to ensure the proper flow of financial disclosure.

The second mandate, *auditability*, requires companies to develop and publish internal processes so that outsiders can confirm the existence of appropriate controls. Finally, under the act's *disclosure* mandates, companies must report financial results and material changes in corporate financial condition or operations "on a rapid and current basis."

Accuracy and visibility are the two touchstones of Sarbanes-Oxley. Accuracy refers to the quality of the financial information a company reports to the public. *Visibility* means that the internal information processes that make accuracy possible must be transparent.[38]

The U.S. Securities and Exchange Commission has been charged with developing detailed rules and regulations to implement this legislation. This includes the establishment of a five-member Public Company Accounting Oversight Board. The purpose of this board is to oversee the audit of public companies to protect the interests of investors and further the public interest in the preparation of informative, accurate, and independent audit reports.[39]

Criminal Accountability. Criminal penalties for destroying, concealing, covering up, or falsifying records or documents may result in individual fines, imprisonment up to twenty years, or both. Fines on individual corporate officers may be up to $5 million.[40] These potential penalties are intended to serve as a strong preventive control mechanism to increase the likelihood of full compliance by corporate executives with the provisions of this act. If they fail as a preventive control, the penalties applied to those convicted of wrongdoing are intended to serve as a form of corrective control.

Whistleblower Protection. This act also protects employees of publicly traded companies who provide evidence of fraud on any rule or regulation of the Securities and Exchange Commission. The act has a number of provisions that serve to protect whistleblowers from retaliation or harm. For example, an employee who provides information regarding a possible violation of this legislation or a regulation of the Securities and Exchange Commission may not be dismissed, demoted, suspended, threatened, harassed, or in any other manner discriminated against in the terms and conditions of employment. An employee who is so discriminated against may seek relief through the Secretary of Labor or through the appropriate U.S. district court. Relief may include (1) the amount of back pay with interest; (2) reinstatement with the same status; (3) compensation for litigation costs, expert witness fees, and reasonable attorney fees; and (4) compensation for any other special damages.

Internal Control: Boards of Directors

Boards of directors are elected by stockholders. They are expected to act in the owners' interests by monitoring and controlling the top-level executives.

There are many proposals and new requirements for sharpening the accountability of boards of directors, especially in relation to their control role of top executives. Let's consider a few that may serve as an effective source of internal control.[41]

Independent Directors. The board should be composed of a substantial majority of independent directors. *Independence* means no present or former employment by the company or any significant financial or personal tie to the company or its management that could compromise the director's objectivity and loyalty to the shareholders. The board's three major committees—audit, compensation, and nominating and/or governance committees—should consist entirely of independent directors. All monetary arrangements with directors for services outside normal board activities should be approved by a committee of the board that is composed of independent directors and should be reported in the proxy statement.

The Competent Manager

"Board members must combine judgment, integrity and courage. They should be people who do speak up and won't back down if they don't get the answers to their questions."

Barbara Hackman Franklin
Head of Board Audit Committees
Aetna, Inc., and Dow Chemical Co.

Self-Assessment. The board should have ways to evaluate and improve its performance in representing the shareholders. At a minimum, there should be an annual review by the board of its overall performance, including the effectiveness of its committees. These committees should be evaluated against criteria defined in committee bylaws. The board should hold periodic executive sessions during which management, including the CEO, is not present.

Executive Compensation. Control of the executive compensation process is critically important. In one sense, it represents a window through which the effectiveness of the board may be viewed by shareholders and the public. The board should ensure that a fair compensation program is in place. Conversely, weak compensation practices—clearly excessive pay, unfairly enriching stock plans, or loose and subjective bonus awards for top executives—are likely to suggest a weak board. The board should ensure that the company describes clearly its overall compensation philosophy in the proxy statement to shareholders. It also should explain the rationale for the salary levels, incentive payments, and stock options granted to top executive officers.

Evaluation of CEO. Ensuring continuity of top-level leadership is also a primary responsibility of the board of directors. Accordingly, the evaluation of a corporation's chief executive officer is critical. A clear understanding between the board and the CEO regarding the expected performance and how that performance will be measured is essential. The board should establish a specific set of performance goals with the CEO annually. These should include concerns of shareholders, other investors, employees, customers, and the communities in which the company operates. Performance goals should include both annual and multiyear time periods. The board should establish an annual review process that incorporates CEO performance evaluation in executive session.

Resource Allocation. Every company needs to plan strategically to ensure future economic success. The strategic allocation of corporate resources to each of the company's businesses is critical to its future success and to the increased shareholder value needed for efficient capital formation. The board should discuss and evaluate the strategic plan of each of the company's major businesses at least annually.

Fiduciary Responsibility and Control. The board has a primary duty to exercise its fiduciary responsibility and control in the best interests of the corporation and its shareholders. This includes periodic review to ensure that corporate resources are used only for appropriate business purposes. To address some of the most important areas of fiduciary responsibility, the board should do the following:

- Ensure a corporate environment of strong internal controls, fiscal accountability, high ethical standards, and compliance with all applicable laws and regulations.
- Develop appropriate procedures to ensure the board is advised on a timely basis of alleged or suspected violations of corporate standards or of noncompliance and how management handled such violations.
- Appoint an audit committee of at least three independent directors, all of whom are financially literate. This is now required by rules of the New York Stock Exchange and the National Association of Securities Dealers. The audit committee should develop its statement of responsibilities and publish it in the company's proxy statement. The audit committee has both the authority and the responsibility to (1) select and evaluate the outside auditor and to ensure its independence, (2) review quarterly and annual audit statements, and (3) assess the adequacy of internal controls and internal risk management processes.

- Install a mechanism to review corporate operating and expense reimbursement policies and practices (e.g., travel and entertainment policy, executive perquisites) to ensure proper use of corporate resources.

Newell Rubbermaid, Inc., is a major consumer goods manufacturer of 24 branded products such as Rubbermaid, Sharplo (writing instruments), Irwin, and Calphalon. Recently, its board of directors adopted new corporate governance guidelines. We share a sample of these guidelines with emphasis on its audit committee bylaws, in the following Planning & Administration Competency feature.[42]

PLANNING & ADMINISTRATION COMPETENCY

Newell Rubbermaid's Audit Committee

The purpose of the Newell Rubbermaid Audit Committee (the "Committee") is to assist the Board of Directors (the "Board") of the Company in fulfilling its fiduciary obligation to oversee (1) the integrity of the Company's financial statements, (2) the Company's compliance with legal and regulatory requirements, (3) the qualifications and independence of the Company's independent auditors, and (4) the performance of the Company's internal audit function and independent auditors. The Committee also prepares the audit committee report required to be included in the Company's annual proxy statement under the applicable rules of the Securities and Exchange Commission (the "SEC").

Membership. The Committee consists of three or more directors designated by the Board, all of whom are to be "independent" under the Company's corporate governance guidelines and the applicable requirements of the Securities and Exchange Commission and The New York Stock Exchange, Inc. (the "NYSE"). Committee members may be removed or replaced by the Board at any time. Each of the members of the Committee is to be "financially literate" or must become "financially literate" within a reasonable period of time of his or her appointment to the Committee. At least one member of the

Committee is to have accounting or related financial management expertise.

Meetings. The Committee will meet with such frequency as it considers necessary to fulfill its responsibilities, but no less often than quarterly. The Committee will meet separately, on a periodic basis, with (1) management, (2) the Company's internal auditors and (3) its independent auditors. Meetings may take place in person or by teleconference, videoconference, or other means of electronic communication permitted under Delaware law. The Committee may invite the Company's independent auditors, outside counsel, or any officer or employee of the Company to attend any Committee meeting in order to provide information or advice in connection with the matters to be addressed at the meeting.

Authority and Responsibilities. This section of audit committee's bylaws is three single-spaced pages in length. We note just a few of the types of authority and responsibility for the committee. With respect to independent auditors, the audit committee will:

1. Have the sole authority to retain and terminate the independent auditors.
2. Be directly responsible for overseeing the work of the independent auditors (including the resolution of disagreements

between management and the independent auditors regarding financial reporting) for the purpose of preparing or issuing an audit report or related work. The independent auditor will report directly to the Committee.
3. Review and preapprove all engagements in connection with audit, review, and attest reports required under the securities laws.
4. Evaluate, at the time of the engagement and periodically thereafter, the independence of the independent auditors and report its conclusions to the Board.
5. Meet with the independent auditors before each audit to discuss the planning and staffing of the audit.
6. Evaluate the performance of the independent auditors and the lead partner and report its conclusions to the Board.

The audit committee bylaws go on to discuss responsibilities and authority regarding (1) oversight of the financial statements and financial disclosure, the annual external audit, and the internal audits; (2) oversight of the company's financial compliance with legal and regulatory requirements; and (3) other obligations such as reviewing and assessing its charter annually as well as its own performance.

CHAPTER SUMMARY

In this chapter, we examined how organizations use various controls to achieve their goals. We considered the basic foundations of control. Next, we looked at a corrective control model and detailed the steps involved in its use. We then discussed primary types of financial and nonfinancial controls, including activity-based costing. We concluded with a discussion of corporate governance with the primary emphasis on selected external and internal control mechanisms.

1. Explain the foundations of control.

The foundations of organizational control are (1) the type of control, (2) the source of control, (3) the pattern of control, (4) the purpose of control, (5) linkage of controls to strategic goals, and (6) the costs versus benefits of organizational controls. Preventive controls, such as rules, standards, and training programs, are designed to reduce the number and severity of deviations that require corrective action. In contrast, corrective controls are designed to bring unwanted results and behaviors in line with established standards or goals. The four sources of organizational control are stakeholders, the organization itself, groups, and individuals. Patterns of the different kinds of control vary from mutually reinforcing to independently operating to conflicting.

2. Identify the six phases of the corrective control model.

The corrective control model comprises six interconnected phases: (1) define the subsystem, (2) identify the charac-teristics to be measured, (3) set standards, (4) collect information, (5) make comparisons, and (6) diagnose and correct any problems.

3. Describe the primary methods of organizational control.

The primary methods of organizational control are (1) mechanistic, (2) organic, (3) market, (4) financial and accounting, and (5) automation-based controls. Effective managerial control usually requires using multiple methods of control in combination.

4. Explain several key corporate governance issues and control mechanisms.

Corporate governance focuses on the system of relations and controls between the stockholders, the board of directors, and the top management of a company. A wide variety of issues and activities are often included in corporate governance. A few of the internal and external control mechanisms, especially those related to the control of top executives, were noted. Key provisions of the Sarbanes-Oxley Act of 2002, which created new external controls, were discussed. The board of directors was discussed as a key source of internal control on top executives. Some of the key prescriptions for establishing effective boards were reviewed.

KEY TERMS and CONCEPTS

Activity-based costing
Annual meeting
Annual report
Automation
Board of directors
Budgeting
Bylaws
Comparative financial analysis
Control
Corporate governance
Corporation
Corrective control model
Corrective controls
Current ratio
Customer monitoring
Debt ratio
Disclosure
Financial control

Green marketing
Group control
Individual self-control
Inventory turnover
Machine control
Market control
Mechanistic control
Organic control
Organizational control
Preventive controls
Principle of selectivity
Profit-sharing plans
Proxy statement
Ratio analysis
Return on investment (ROI)
Stakeholder control
Standards

1. Identify the specific mechanisms that serve as preventive control, corrective control, or both in the Waste Management preview case.

2. Until recently, Waste Management used printed sheet maps to configure garbage routes. Now, the firm is using global positioning system technology in combination with route optimization software to develop more efficient schedules and routes for its 30,000 vehicles.[43] What type and source of control does this represent?

3. Evaluate Siebel Systems' employee relationship management system in terms of the criteria for effective controls, including *objective*, *complete*, *timely*, and *acceptable*.

4. Give three examples of organizational control in an organization in which you have worked or are now working. Within the same organization, give three examples of group and/or individual self-control that were present.

5. Based on the examples presented in Question 4, did any of these sources of control reinforce or conflict with one another? Explain.

6. Based on the cost–benefit model (see Figure 10.1), did the organization you identified in Question 4 have too much, too little, or ineffective control mechanisms? Explain.

7. Describe the key characteristics of the corrective control model as they apply to your bank.

8. Review the mechanistic and organic control methods in Table 10.3. Based on the organization you identified in Question 4, what was the relative emphasis on mechanistic versus organic control methods? Do you think that relative emphasis was effective? Explain.

9. Think of an experience in which you were highly dissatisfied and complained as a customer. Which of the mechanisms, if any, discussed for Barclays were used in dealing with your complaint? Was your complaint resolved to your satisfaction?

10. As of 2000, issues of corporate governance have been in the business and general news because of the revelations about extreme self-serving interests by some top executives at the expense of stockholders and other stakeholders. Reread the competency feature on Newell Rubbermaid's audit committee. Identify the preventive, corrective, sources, and methods of control that are implicit and explicit through the audit committee of the board of directors.

JEFF IMMELT OF GE ON CORPORATE GOVERNANCE[44]

Jeff Immelt is the chief executive officer of General Electric (GE). A new and revised set of governance principles, policies, practices, and mechanisms was announced for GE. At that time, Immelt issued a statement on corporate governance to GE's employees, shareowners, and customers. It is presented here. Immelt states:

Sound principles of corporate governance are critical to obtaining and retaining the trust of investors—and to GE's overarching goal of performance with integrity. They are also vital in securing respect from other key stakeholders and interested parties—including employees, recruits, customers, suppliers, GE communities, government officials and the public at large. We have revised our fundamental corporate governance documents: a statement of governance principles and the charters of our four board committees with a description of their key practices.

The actions described in these documents—which the board has reviewed and approved—implement requirements of the Sarbanes-Oxley legislation and the proposed New York Stock Exchange listing requirements, as well as our own vision of good governance. In preparing and making public these documents, we were guided by some basic ideas.

■ We should talk externally the way we run GE internally.
■ We should try to satisfy the spirit, not just the letter, of the new corporate governance requirements.
■ We should act promptly to implement changes in governance, and not wait for "formal" effective dates in the law, which may be many months in the future.

At the core of corporate governance, of course, is the role of the board of directors in overseeing how management serves the long-term interests of shareowners and other stakeholders. An active, informed, independent and involved board is essential for ensuring GE's integrity, transparency and long-term strength. As reflected in GE's statement of governance principles, the board has fundamental responsibilities:

- To select, evaluate and compensate the CEO and oversee CEO succession planning;
- To provide counsel and oversight on the selection, evaluation and compensation of management;
- To review, approve and monitor fundamental financial and business strategies and corporate actions;
- To understand the major risks facing the company and approve steps to mitigate those risks; and
- To ensure structures and processes are in place to protect and advance the company's integrity and reputation—the accuracy and completeness of its financial statements; its compliance with legal and ethical requirements; the quality of its relationships with employees, customers, suppliers and its other stakeholders.

To discharge such responsibilities in a company as diverse as GE requires board members with broad experience and independent judgment. All our board members, whether employee directors or non-employee directors, have that experience and judgment. Let me emphasize: they are persons of incomparable reputation and integrity who have nerve to speak their minds and advance shareowner interests. But, with respect to independence, we will take the following additional steps to meet current expectations of investors and regulators.

- A majority of the board will be "independent" under the NYSE rules, and it is our goal to have two-thirds of the board comprised of independent directors (which GE now has).
- Directors will be considered "independent" if the sales to, or buys from, GE are less than one percent of the revenues of companies they serve as executive officers, or if loans provided by GE to a company they serve as executive officers, and loans received by GE from such a company, constitute less than one percent of the total assets of such company. Moreover, if a GE director serves as an officer or director of a charitable organization, the GE director will be considered "independent" if GE donates less than 1 percent of that organization's annual charitable receipts.
- Whether directors meet these categorical independence tests will be reviewed and will be made public annually prior to their standing for re-election to the board.

- Under this approach, 11 of GE's 17 directors will be independent on January 1, 2003, future non-employee directors will be independent, and GE will seek to have a minimum of ten independent directors at all times. [This is now so.]
- Members of the audit committee must meet an additional "independent" test under the Sarbanes-Oxley legislation: their director's fees must be the only compensation which they receive from the company.
- GE will also apply that additional, stricter "independent" test to all members of the management development and compensation committee and to all members of the nominating and corporate governance committee, even though we are not required to do so by law.
- The non-employee directors will meet without management at least three times a year and more often if they wish to do so. The directors have determined that the chairman of the management development and compensation committee will serve as presiding director for these meetings.
- The non-employee directors will be expected to visit two GE businesses a year, without senior management being present, so they can interact freely and directly with business leaders of GE's core business units.

This approach to independence is just one of the changes embodied in the revised corporate governance documents. The changes in formal processes are only one means to a larger end—the effective functioning of the board to meet the dual challenge I have given it.

I want directors to probe with hard questions which stretch management so that, within a context of mutual respect, board meetings deal in depth with the core issues GE confronts. By the same token, I expect directors to have even greater involvement and participation in GE, in understanding the company and advising the management team. Directors need to be our most constructive critics and our wisest counselors. In short, they need to be engaged and committed partners in my task of continuing to make GE a great company, and a good company.

Cordially,
Jeff Immelt

Questions

1. Identify the comments in this statement that correspond to the guidelines for establishing boards of directors that serve as effective sources of internal control.

2. Give at least four examples of statements that reflect preventive control, corrective control, or both.

3. What statements by Immelt reflect external control mechanisms?

ETHICAL BEHAVIORS IN THE OFFICE[45]

The following questionnaire lists behaviors that you and others might engage in on the job. For each item, circle the number that best indicates the frequency with which you would engage in that behavior. Then put an X over the number that you think best describes how others you know behave. Finally, put a check mark beside that behavior if you believe that management should design a system to control that behavior.

Behavior	Most of the Time	Often	About Half the Time	Seldom	Never
1. Blaming an innocent person or a computer for errors that you made.	5	4	3	2	1
2. Passing on information that was told in confidence.	5	4	3	2	1
3. Falsifying quality reports.	5	4	3	2	1
4. Claiming credit for someone else's work.	5	4	3	2	1
5. Padding an expense account by more than 5 percent.	5	4	3	2	1
6. Using company supplies for personal use.	5	4	3	2	1
7. Accepting favors in exchange for preferred treatment.	5	4	3	2	1
8. Giving favors in exchange for preferred treatment.	5	4	3	2	1
9. Asking a person to violate company rules.	5	4	3	2	1
10. Calling in sick to take a day off when you weren't sick.	5	4	3	2	1
11. Hiding errors.	5	4	3	2	1
12. Taking longer than necessary to do the job.	5	4	3	2	1
13. Doing personal business on company time.	5	4	3	2	1
14. Taking a longer lunch hour without approval.	5	4	3	2	1
15. Seeing a violation and not reporting it.	5	4	3	2	1
16. Overlooking boss's error to prove loyalty.	5	4	3	2	1
17. Asking an aide to lie about your whereabouts.	5	4	3	2	1
18. Telling coworkers that you are going somewhere when actually you are going somewhere else.	5	4	3	2	1

Questions

1. What are the differences between the most and least frequently occurring behaviors?

2. What are the most important behaviors that should be controlled? Why? What do they reveal about your own preferences to control?

3. How would management go about establishing programs for controlling them?

Organizing

©Corbis Inc.

Organizational Design

Learning Objectives

After studying this chapter, you should be able to:

1. Describe the two fundamentals of organizing.

2. Explain the five aspects of an organization's vertical design.

3. Describe four types of horizontal design.

4. Describe two methods of integration.

Chapter Outline

Barnard Marcus and Arthur Blank founded Home Depot after they were fired from Handy Dan Home Improvement in 1978. They opened three stores in Atlanta in 1979 and now operate more than 2,500 stores in the United States, Canada, and Latin America. It is the largest home improvement chain and second largest retailer after Wal-Mart. Home Depot sales are more than $58 billion annually. How did it organize itself for growth?

Appealing to do-it-yourself home owners and contractors, Home Depot quickly established itself as a store staffed by professionals who could offer advice to the do-it-yourselfer, as well as the contractor. By 1981, it had expanded to Florida and, by 1986, sales exceeded $1 billion. Home Depot's sales continued to rise and, in 1994, it entered Canada by buying Aikenhead, a chain of home improvement stores. Operating more than 500 stores, in 1997, Home Depot bought National Blind and Wallpaper, a mail-order firm, and Maintenance Warehouse.

To continue to attract new customers, in 1999 Home Depot introduced Villager's Hardware stores, which are designed to compete with smaller hardware shops in urban areas. Unfortunately, it had to close these stores in 2001 because of their poor financial performance. With the purchase of Apex Supply, a plumbing distributor, and Georgia Lighting, Home Depot started to focus on home décor categories and added a new line of stores, EXPO design centers. At the same time, it opened a group of landscape design stores in Texas. In 2001, it acquired Total Home, a home improvement chain with stores in Mexico. In 2002, it acquired a four-store chain in Del Norte, Mexico, to increase its presence internationally.

Each time it acquired a competitor or created a new store, its organizational design came under pressure to evolve. For example, when Home Depot entered Mexico, it created a regional president position in charge of Mexico. This regional president, along with six other regional presidents, needed resources or information from one of seven vice presidents. Home Depot ended up with a huge bureaucracy that was not able to sustain its growth. Worse than that, Home Depot has not been able to find a new formula for large-scale growth like the one it used in the 1990s. It hopes to use existing Home Depot stores to aggressively push home services, such as air conditioning and flooring, and appeal more to the professional contractor. As a result of fierce competition from Lowe's, 84 Lumber, Sears, and Wal-Mart, the market for home improvement stores has become saturated. Although new stores boosted Home Depot's sales in the past, new store sales have increasingly come at the expense of existing older stores. Home Depot's financial performance has suffered as a result of these trends.

CEO Bob Nardelli and his executive team have engaged in an aggressive campaign to slash costs and redesign Home Depot's organizational structure. The growth of Home Depot was aided by its decentralized, free-wheeling management style. Nardelli centralized the chain's purchasing function and cut down the number of suppliers. To become more efficient, he consolidated the company's Mid-Atlantic and Southeast divisions to form one division that will have more than 600 stores and 110,000 employees.[1]

Most of you have probably visited a Home Depot store. The materials in the Preview Case give you some insights into Home Depot's struggles and plans for the future. While we did not go into every problem facing Nardelli, the case does highlight the important issues that we will cover in this chapter. In Chapter 7, we indicated that the strategy of an organization has a major influence on how an organization is structured.[2] Nardelli and his top management team are working hard to make certain that Home Depot's low-cost strategy and structure are aligned with each other.

In Chapter 1, we defined *organizing* as the process of creating a structure of jobs that enables employees to implement management's goals and plans. Organizing was presented as one of the four general managerial functions, the others being planning, controlling, and leading. The process by which management forms jobs and relationships is termed **organization design**, *which means quite simply the decisions and actions that result in a structure.*[3] All organizations have a set of jobs. In fact, the existence of structure is most visible in the familiar organization chart, but it is somewhat like the tip of an iceberg. Figure 11.1 shows the visible aspects of Home Depot's vertical and horizontal organization design.

Figure 11.1   Organization Chart for Home Depot

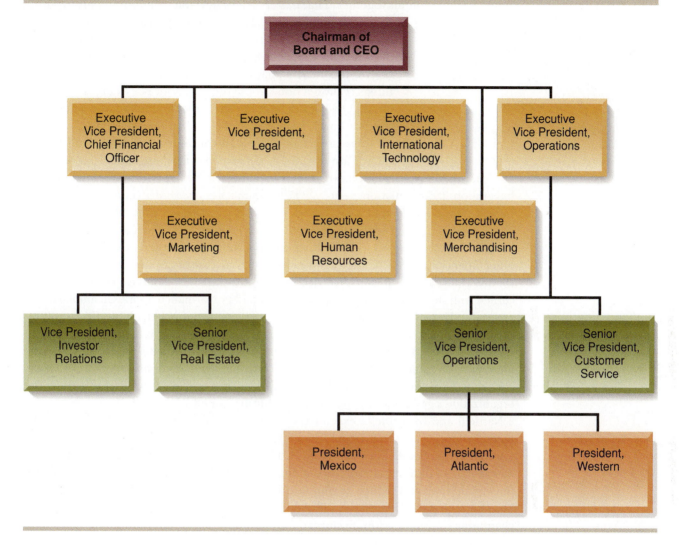

FUNDAMENTALS OF ORGANIZING

Managers often describe the structure of their organization by looking at its organization chart. The **organization chart** *is a diagram that illustrates the reporting lines between units and people within the organization.* We use the term *units* to refer to teams, groups, departments, or divisions. Basically, the organization chart is the skeleton of an organization. Figure 11.1 shows the general organization of Home Depot. This figure shows that the CEO has seven executive vice presidents reporting to him. Note that the chart conveys four kinds of information:

1. **Describe the two fundamentals of organizing.**

1. The boxes represent different units (marketing, legal, human resources).
2. The titles in each box show the work performed by that person.
3. Reporting relationships are shown by the lines connecting superiors and subordinates.
4. Levels of the organization are indicated by the number of vertical layers in the chart.

In this chart, we show three levels at Home Depot. For example, all presidents of the various regions (Mexico, Atlantic, Western) report to the senior vice president of operations, who in turn reports to the executive vice president of operations.

An organization chart provides several benefits. First, it gives some insight into how the entire organization fits together. That is, it indicates how the various functions relate to the whole organization. Thus everyone presumably knows who reports to whom and where to go with a particular problem. Second, the chart may indicate gaps or duplication of activities. A limitation of the chart is that it's just a picture and doesn't show how things really get done in the organization. For example, it cannot highlight what function has the most or least amount of political clout or how information flows between functions.

There are two fundamental concepts around which all organizations are organized: *differentiation* and *integration*.[4] An organization chart often reveals how an organization addresses the need for differentiation and integration. **Differentiation** *means that the organization is composed of units that work on specialized tasks using different work methods and requiring employees with unique competencies.* Carol Tome is the executive vice president and chief financial officer at Home Depot. In her job, she is concerned with the financial reporting systems used at Home Depot and other financial aspects of the organization, such as real estate and investor relations. Dennis Donovan is the executive vice president of human resources. Donovan is concerned with the selection, career progression, and performance appraisal, among other aspects, of Home Depot. Each person faces a unique set of problems, and each will organize his unit differently to handle these problems. **Integration** *means that the various units must be put back together so that work is coordinated.* Rules and procedures are one means used by managers to coordinate the ongoing activities of an organization. If departments have common goals, are organized similarly, and work together to achieve the organization's goals, the organization is highly integrated.

Nardelli and his team of executive vice presidents are struggling with these fundamental concepts at Home Depot in an effort to increase the performance of all stores. Combining the Southeastern and Mid-Atlantic regions to form a new region, Atlantic, is an example of differentiation. By combining these two divisions, he hopes to streamline the organization and reduce its complexity. By centralizing the merchandising function, he expects that this integration will reduce costs and improve the coordination of merchandising decisions across all stores.

Differentiation

Differentiation is created through a division of labor and job specialization. **Division of labor** *means that the work of the organization is divided into smaller tasks.* Look at the organization chart of Home Depot in Figure 11.1. There are seven executive vice presidents. Each one is in charge of performing a different set of tasks, such as finance, marketing, or legal. **Specialization** *is the process of identifying particular tasks and assigning them to departments, teams, or divisions.* Division of labor and specialization are closely related concepts. For example, at Home Depot, the senior vice president of operations is responsible for all operations of all 2,500 stores. He has organized stores according to their location—Mexico, Atlantic, Western, and so on. The president of each of these regions specializes in problems facing that location and is in charge of the day-to-day operations of stores in that location. The numerous tasks that must be carried out in an organization make division of labor and specialization necessary. Otherwise, the complexity of running the entire organization would be too great for any one person.

Integration

As organizations differentiate their designs, managers must be concerned with issues of integration. An organization is more than the sum of its parts; it is an integration of its parts. Because different units are part of the larger organization, some degree of coordination is needed among them for an organization to be effective. When Home Depot grew during the mid-1990s, for example, merchandising decisions were made by various regional presidents. With Lowe's, Sears, and other organizations entering the market, Nardelli recognized that Home Depot needed to become more efficient in its merchandising function. Therefore, he coordinated all merchandising decisions at Home Depot headquarters and put an executive vice president in charge of this function.

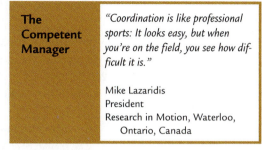

Now that we have introduced you to some fundamentals of organizing, we will discuss the vertical structure of an organization. There are few hard and fast rules for designing or redesigning an organization. An organization's vertical structure is often the result of many decisions and its past. It may reflect political biases, preferences of powerful external stakeholders, and historical circumstances. In one sense, an organization's vertical structure acts as a "harness" to guide employees' decision-making activities.

VERTICAL DESIGN

To understand the functioning of any organization, an understanding of the organization's vertical design is essential. We review five aspects in this section.

2. Explain the five aspects of an organization's vertical design.

Hierarchy

In Chapter 1, we discussed how organizations are structured. The **hierarchy** *is a pyramid showing relationships among levels.* The CEO occupies the top position and is the senior member of top management. The CEO and members of the top management team set the strategic direction of the organization. In Figure 11.1, this would include the CEO and the seven executive vice presidents at Home Depot. Reporting to these people are senior vice presidents in charge of specific areas, such as investor relations, real estate, and customer service. At the next level are presidents of the various regions in which Home Depot has stores. For example, the Atlantic president is responsible for more than 600 stores and 110,000 employees.

During the past few years, many U.S. companies, including GE, Wells Fargo Bank, and Farmers Insurance, have reduced the number of hierarchical levels in their organizations.[5] For example, GE used to have more than 20 hierarchical levels between the CEO and first-line employees. Today, it has 5. Why? Most executives think that having fewer layers creates a more efficient organization that can react faster to competition and is more cost effective. According to Andy Kolhberg, president of Kisko Senior Living Communities, with fewer levels, top managers can hear "bad" news more frequently and quickly and take immediate corrective action to solve the problem before it becomes a big one. Also, having fewer hierarchical levels permits more people to participate in the decision-making process.

Span of Control

The **span of control** *refers to the number of employees directly reporting to a person.* In the case of Home Depot, the CEO has a span of control of seven. The implications for different spans of control on the vertical design of an organization are clear. Holding size constant, narrow spans of control lead to more hierarchical levels. Wider spans create a flatter organization with fewer hierarchical levels. The span of control can either be too wide, too narrow, or appropriate. The optimal span of control is not so narrow that the manager "micromanages" subordinates or too broad so that the manager loses the ability to lead subordinates.

What is the optimal number of subordinates? There is no "correct" number of subordinates that a manager can supervise effectively. The following four key factors can influence the span of control in any situation[6]:

1. *The competence of both the manager and the employee.* If managers and/or employees are new to a task, they require more supervision than knowledgeable veteran managers and employees do.
2. *The similarity or dissimilarity of tasks being supervised.* At Starbucks, the span of control in the retail store area is broad because all managers can focus on one main product: coffee and its accessories. The more numerous and dissimilar the products, the narrower the span of control should be.
3. *The incidence of new problems in the manager's department.* A manager should know enough about the operations of the department to understand precisely the problems that subordinates are likely to face. The more the manager knows about these factors, the broader the span of control can be.
4. *The extent of clear operating standards and rules.* Clear rules and standard operating procedures (SOPs) leave less to chance and reduce the need for improvisation. At FedEx, extensive rules govern the tasks and behaviors of employees. The greater the reliance on rules and SOPs, the broader the span of control may be because the rules do part of the controlling.

Authority, Responsibility, and Accountability

Authority *is the right to make a decision.* Authority is the glue that holds the vertical and horizontal parts together.[7] Generally, but not always, people at higher levels have the authority to make decisions and tell lower level people what to do. For example, a first-line supervisor at Blue Bell Ice Cream has the authority to schedule worker overtime. The director of manufacturing also has the authority to tell first-line supervisors to schedule overtime.

Authority implies both responsibility and accountability. That is, by exercising authority, employees accept the responsibility for acting and are willing to be held accountable for success or failure. **Responsibility** *is an employee's duty to perform the assigned task.* Employees take on this obligation when they accept a job assignment. When giving an employee responsibility, the manager should give the subordinate enough authority to get the job done. Oftentimes, a manager is not able to give the person sufficient authority to get a job done. Under these conditions, the subordinate must use her informal influence instead of relying on formal authority.

When a manager delegates authority and responsibility to an employee, that person is accountable for achieving the desired results. **Accountability** *is the manager's expectation that the employee will accept credit or blame for his work.* No manager can check everything an employee does. Therefore managers normally establish guidelines and performance standards within which responsibilities are carried out. As such, accountability flows from the bottom to the top. The authors of this book are accountable to a department chair, the department chair to a dean, and a dean to a provost. Accountability is the point at which authority and responsibility meet and is essential for high performance. When either authority or responsibility are lacking, managers cannot judge a subordinate's accomplishments fairly. When managers are reluctant to hold their subordinates accountable, subordinates can easily pass the buck for nonperformance onto others.[8]

Delegation

Delegation *is the process of giving authority to a person (or group or team) to make decisions and act in certain situations.* In addition to holding an employee accountable for the performance of defined responsibilities, the manager should give the employee the authority to carry out the responsibilities effectively. Delegation starts when the design of the organization is being established and work is divided. Delegation continues as new jobs and tasks are added during day-to-day operations. Delegation should occur in conjunction with the assignment of responsibilities, such as when a company president assigns to an executive assistant the task of preparing a formal statement for presentation to a congressional committee or when the head of a computer department instructs a programmer to debug a new management reporting system. In each case, the manager is delegating authority to a subordinate.

Effective Delegation. The following practices are useful for achieving effective delegation[9]:

1. *Establish goals and standards.* Individuals or teams should participate in developing the goals that they will be expected to meet. Ideally, they should also agree to the standards that will be used to measure their performance.
2. *Ensure clarity.* Individuals or teams should clearly understand the work delegated to them, recognize the scope of their authority, and accept their accountability for results.
3. *Involvement.* The challenge of the work itself won't always encourage individuals or groups to accept and perform delegated tasks well. Managers can motivate them by involving them in decision making, by keeping them informed, and by helping them improve their skills and abilities.
4. *Expect completed work.* Individuals or teams should be expected to carry a task through to completion. The manager's job is to provide guidance, help, and information—not to finish the task.
5. *Provide training.* Delegation is only as effective as the ability of people to make the decisions necessary to perform the work and then actually to do the work. Managers should continually appraise delegated responsibilities and provide training aimed at building on strengths and overcoming deficiencies.
6. *Timely feedback.* Timely, accurate feedback should be provided to individuals or teams so that they may compare their performance to stated expectations and correct any deficiencies.

Barriers to Delegation. Delegation is only as effective as the ability of managers to delegate. The greatest psychological barrier to delegation is fear. A manager may be afraid that, if subordinates don't do the job properly, the manager's own reputation will suffer. Such a manager may rationalize: "I can do it better myself" or "My subordinates aren't capable enough" or "It takes too much time to explain what I want done." In addition, some managers also may be reluctant to delegate because they fear that subordinates will do the work their own way, do it too well, and outshine them!

Among the organizational barriers that may block delegation is a failure to define authority and responsibility clearly. If managers themselves don't know what is expected or what to do, they can't properly delegate authority and responsibility to others.

The six practices for achieving effective delegation that we presented earlier provide a strong foundation for reducing barriers to delegation. In addition, managers need to accept that there are several different ways to deal with problems and that their particular way of dealing with a problem is not necessarily the way their subordinates will choose to deal with it. Employees will make mistakes, but, whenever possible, they should be allowed to develop their own solutions to problems and learn from their mistakes.

The following Planning & Administration feature highlights how American Standard, based in the United States and specializing in the manufacture and sale of plumbing fixtures, air conditioners, and bath fixtures, used its planning and organizing skills when it invested in Bulgaria. American Standard chose Bulgaria in which to produce porcelain bathroom fixtures because it is strategically located and provides easy access to Western Europe and the Middle East and has labor costs about one-tenth of those in Western Europe.[10]

American Standard

When American Standard entered Bulgaria, it knew it would face significant political risks. To respond to these diverse political risks, it followed four management practices. First, it relied heavily on local suppliers. As a significant buyer, it has been able to convince suppliers from Germany, Austria, Spain, and Italy to open operations in Bulgaria to ensure rapid and dependable supply.

Second, American Standard has pursued direct contacts with the national government. These contacts have two major goals: management of day-to-day needs, such as licenses and certificate requirements, and lobbying activities that affect preferred tax and custom policies. American Standard also sponsored nonbusiness activities that show the government in a positive light.

A third management practice was to develop strong relationships with local stakeholders. American Standard is one of the few foreign investors not located in the capital, Sofia; instead, they are in a rural area. The company is recognized as a major force for development in this struggling area. Jobs at the plants are so plentiful that workers have to be bused in by the company from towns as far away as 35 miles. This benefits not only local governmental agencies interested in development, but also local cultural and recreational organizations that benefit from the growth in wages.

Finally, American Standard has created strong ties with its unions, employees, and other workers in the region. It directly employs more than 3,300 at its plants and indirectly employs about five times that many, including truck drivers and construction workers. The average salary ranges from $175 to $220 a month, which compares to Bulgaria's national average of $100. American Standard has invested in improving working conditions, pay scales, and social services for its workers.

Centralization and Decentralization

Centralization and decentralization of authority are basic, overall management philosophies that indicate where decisions are to be made. **Centralization** *is the concentration of authority at the top of an organization or department.* **Decentralization** *is the delegation of authority to lower level employees or departments.* Decentralization is an approach that requires managers to decide what and when to delegate, to select and train personnel carefully, and to formulate adequate controls.

No Absolutes. Neither centralization nor decentralization is absolute in an organization.[11] No one manager makes all the decisions, even in a highly centralized setting. Total centralization would end the need for middle and first-line managers. Thus there are only degrees of centralization and decentralization. In many organizations, some tasks are relatively centralized (e.g., payroll systems, purchasing, and human resource policies), whereas others are relatively decentralized (e.g., marketing and production).

Potential benefits to decentralization include the following:

1. It frees top managers to develop organizational plans and strategies. Lower level managers and employees handle routine, day-to-day decisions.
2. It develops lower level managers' self-management and planning and administration competencies.
3. Because subordinates often are closer to the action than higher level managers, they may have a better grasp of the facts. This knowledge may enable them to make sound decisions quickly. Valuable time can be lost when a subordinate or team must check everything with a manager.
4. It fosters a healthy, achievement-oriented atmosphere among employees.

Key Factors. A variety of factors can affect management's decisions to centralize or decentralize authority in various areas of decision making. We briefly consider five of these factors:

1. *Cost of decisions.* Cost is perhaps the most important factor in determining the extent of centralization. As a general rule, the more costly the outcome, the more likely top management is to centralize the authority to make the final decision.

2. *Uniformity of policy.* Managers who value consistency favor centralization of authority. These managers may want to assure customers that everyone is treated equally in terms of quality, price, credit, delivery, and service. At Home Depot, for example, a nationwide home improvement sales promotion on paint requires that all stores charge the same price. Uniform policies have definite advantages for cost accounting, production, and financial departments. They also enable managers to compare the relative efficiencies of various departments. In organizations with unions, such as Ford and General Motors, uniform policies also aid in the administration of labor agreements regarding wages, promotions, fringe benefits, and other personnel matters.

3. *Competency levels.* Many organizations work hard to ensure an adequate supply of competent managers and employees—an absolute necessity for decentralization. The Container Store, Harley-Davidson, and IBM, among others, believe that extensive training and practical experiences are essential to developing the competencies needed at lower levels. Also, they are willing to permit employees to make mistakes involving small costs so as to learn from them. Therefore, these organization decentralize many decisions to employees.

4. *Control mechanisms.* Even the most avid proponents of decentralization, such as DuPont, Cisco, and Marriott, insist on controls and procedures to prevent mistakes and to determine whether actual events are meeting expectations. For example, each hotel in the Marriott centralizes certain key data, including number of beds occupied, employee turnover, number of meals served, and the average amount that guests spend on food and beverages. Analysis of these data help managers control important aspects of the hotel's operation and compare it against the performance of others in the chain. If a hotel's operations don't fall within certain guidelines, top management may step in to diagnose the situation.

5. *Environmental influences.* External factors (e.g., unions, federal and state regulatory agencies, and tax policies) affect the degree of centralization in an organization. For example, laws and government regulations regarding hours, wages, working conditions, and safety make it difficult to decentralize authority in those areas.

In this section, we examined the five basic vertical parts of an organization. Issues of hierarchy, authority, span of control, delegation, and centralization/decentralization are important because they give you an idea of how managers and employees relate to each other at different levels. These five parts can be combined in many different ways to build a vertical design. Accordingly, managers need the right combination of hierarchical levels, spans of control, and delegation to implement the organization's strategy. Managers can use a number of practices, procedures, or rules to achieve consistent performance.

HORIZONTAL DESIGN

As organizations grow and become too complex to manage, they are divided into smaller units. In this section, we review the four most commonly used types of horizontal design: (1) functional, (2) product, (3) geographical, and (4) network.

3. Describe four types of horizontal design.

Functional Design

Functional design *means grouping managers and employees according to their areas of expertise and the resources they use to perform their jobs.* Functions vary widely according to the type of organization.[12] For example, Presbyterian Hospital doesn't have a production unit, but it has functional units for admitting, emergency rooms, surgery, and maintenance. Similarly, Boeing has production units, but doesn't have admitting and emergency rooms. Functional units are usually found in organizations that produce a high volume of a narrow range of products. Functional units are also particularly suited for small organizations.

As shown in Figure 11.2, Harley-Davidson has chosen a functional form of departmentalization.[13] Harley has more than 1,300 worldwide dealers, produces 28 different models of motorcycles, and has eight functional vice presidents as shown in Figure 11.2. Grouping activities by way of a functional structure is efficient and cost effective. That is, there is only one set of functional managers that oversee activities for the entire organization.

Figure 11.2   Harley-Davidson Organization Chart

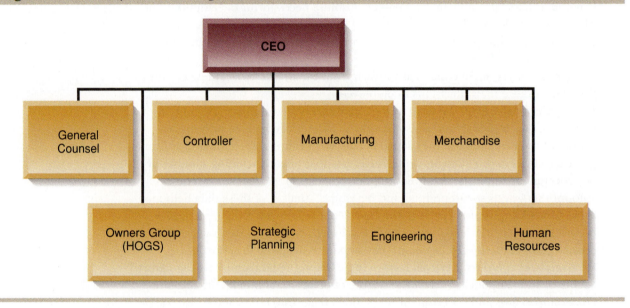

Potential Benefits. Designing by function is economical because it results in a simple structure. Management creates one department for each primary function to be performed (e.g., production, marketing, and human resources). This design keeps administrative expenses low because everyone in a department shares training, experience, and resources. Employees can see clearly defined career paths within their own departments. As a result, the organization can more easily hire and promote employees who have or develop good problem-solving skills in each area of specialization. In brief, the potential benefits of functional design include

■ supporting skill specialization,
■ reducing duplication of resources and increasing coordination within the functional area,
■ enhancing career development and training within the functional area,
■ allowing superiors and subordinates to share common expertise, and
■ promoting high-quality technical decision making.

Potential Pitfalls. The pitfalls of functional design become apparent when an organization provides highly diverse products (goods and/or services) or serves highly diverse customers. Making decisions quickly becomes difficult when employees have to coordinate with other units. For example, a sales rep at Hershey Foods may lose a good account because she has to wait for the sales manager to get the production manager to make a scheduling decision. In addition, when friction exists between units, managers have to spend time resolving the issues involved. Pinpointing the accountability and performance levels of employees who are performing separate functions may also be difficult. In other words, a top manager may not be able to determine easily which department—production, sales, or credit—is responsible for delays and declining profits.

Another pitfall is that top management may have a hard time coordinating the activities of employees in different units. At Pier 1 Imports, merchandising and marketing are located on different floors of the Pier 1 building in Fort Worth, Texas, and report to different managers, each of whom has different goals for their departments. Moreover, functional designs tend to de-emphasize the overall goals of the organization, with employees often focusing on departmental goals (e.g., meeting their own budgets and schedules). In brief, the potential pitfalls of functional design include

- inadequate communication between units,
- conflicts over product priorities,
- difficulties with interunit coordination,
- focus on departmental rather than organizational issues and goals, and
- developing managers who are experts only in narrow fields.

Product Design

As the organization expands into new products or businesses, the functional design loses many of its advantages. High product diversity leads to serving many different kinds of customers and a variety of geographic regions of the world. Many organizations regroup all of their functions into a single product line or division. **Product design** *means that all functions that contribute to a product are organized under one manager.* Product designs (sometimes labeled divisional structures) simply divide the organization into self-contained units that are responsible for developing, producing, and selling their own products and services to their own markets.[14] As illustrated in Figure 11.3, General Dynamics is organized into four product lines. Each product competes against competitors in its own market.

The
Competent
Manager

"A hierarchical organization structured around functions develops competing empires. Collaboration on creative approaches to customer problems are unthinkable and, at best, forced."

David Falvey
Executive Director
British Geological Survey, Nottingham, United Kingdom

Product design is the most commonly used design for companies in the Fortune 500. In large companies, such as Komatsu, Texas Instruments, or General Electric, these divisions remain fairly autonomous. Thus, managers and employees assigned to a particular product often become experts about that division's products and markets. Each product also has its own functional specialists and resources needed to support the product. Therefore, a product structure encourages decentralization of authority to the product manager by tailoring functional activities to the needs of the particular product. In the case of General Dynamics, the manager in charge of the Bath Iron Works has various functional managers, such as manufacturing, finance, and human resources, reporting to him.

Product designs are evaluated on the basis of their profit contributions to the entire organization. Because each division represents a product or group of products, senior management can measure the financial performance of each division. For example, at General Dynamics, the profitability of Bath Iron Works can be compared against the profitability of the Electric Boat division to see which division is more profitable. In many

Figure 11.3   General Dynamics Organization Chart

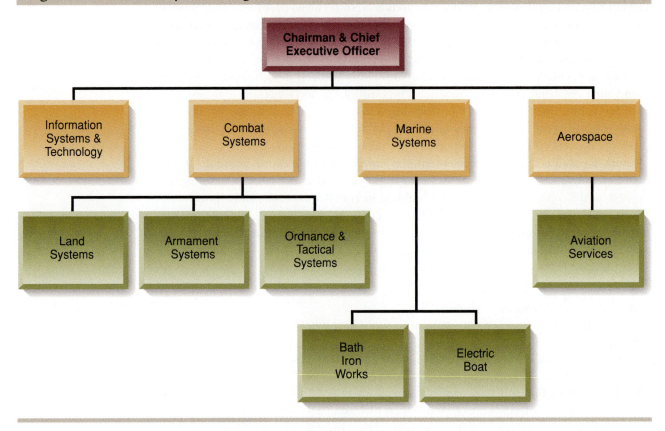

respects, separate divisions act almost as separate businesses and work independently to accomplish their goals and those of the organization.[15]

Potential Benefits. This form of organization enables managers and employees to become specialized and expert in a particular product (good or service) line. This benefit lessens only as the number and diversity of products provided by an organization increase. Management also can pinpoint costs, profits, problems, and successes accurately for each product line. In brief, the potential benefits of product design include

■ permitting fast changes in a product line,
■ allowing greater product line visibility,
■ fostering a concern for customer demands,
■ clearly defining responsibilities for each product line, and
■ developing managers who can think across functional lines.

Potential Pitfalls. Because some or many functions are duplicated for each product line, resource utilization may be relatively inefficient. In addition, products with seasonal highs and lows in sales volumes may result in higher personnel costs. Coordination across product lines usually is difficult. Employees tend to focus on the goals for their particular products, rather than on broader company goals. This situation may create unhealthy competition within an organization for scarce resources. In brief, the potential pitfalls for product design include

■ not allowing efficient utilization of skills and resources,
■ not fostering coordination of activities across product lines,
■ encouraging politics and conflicts in resource allocation across product lines, and
■ limiting career mobility for personnel outside their own product lines.

Geographical Design

Some organizations, such as Nestlé, Sheraton Hotels, and Celanese Chemical, operate in a number of geographic regions. Such organizations often find that functional and product designs are inefficient because they do not provide a way for managers to coordinate activities within a geographic region. **Geographical design** *organizes activities around location.* Geographical designs allow organizations to develop competitive advantage in a particular region according to that area's customers, competitors, and other factors. This form of horizontal design permits managers to specialize in particular markets. If each manager is in close contact with customers in his or her market, they can quickly adapt to changing market conditions. Geographical structures are extremely versatile.[16] Thus, the practices, procedures, and standards used can vary according to regional conditions, as well as the priorities senior management assigns to each region. Managers at local sites become familiar with local labor force practices, governmental requirements, and cultural norms that could impact their operations. For apparel firms, such as Nike and Adidas, locating near suppliers means that the organization is able to hire low-cost laborers to achieve a competitive advantage. Similarly, for manufacturing firms, such as Celanese and Motorola, locating plants near the source of raw materials saves transportation costs. As in the case with product designs, geographical designs also contain all of the necessary functional activities to reach the organization's goals.

Starbucks CEO Howard Schultz claims that Starbucks is everywhere. It operates nearly 6,000 coffee shops in a variety of locations (office buildings, airport terminals, hotels, supermarkets, bookstores) in 25 countries.[17] Started in Seattle in 1971 by three people who named the company for the coffee-loving mate in Moby Dick, Starbucks has grown to be the world's largest specialty coffee retailer and roaster in the world. Starbucks is also selling board games, CDs, and other products at its stores. It has found success with its Starbucks cards, which allow customers to prepay up to $500 on a card that gets swiped by the cashier. The following Strategic Action Competency describes Starbucks' organizational design.

STRATEGIC ACTION COMPETENCY

Starbucks

Starbucks is a $3 billion dollar organization that operates stores on three continents. Each store sells coffee beans, beverages, coffee-making equipment, pastries, and related products. Management likes to position stores in high-traffic locations. Starbucks is vertically integrated and controls its coffee sources, roasting, and retail sales to ensure adherence to its strict principles.

Figure 11.4 shows a portion of the company's basic organization chart. At its headquarters in Seattle, executive vice presidents report to the president. The president's job is primarily to focus on the company's

global strategy. The company's four executive vice presidents are organized by function. To ensure superior customer service in all 6,000 locations worldwide, Starbucks has established an executive vice president of the supply chain and coffee (i.e., the retail stores). Reporting to this person is the senior vice president of coffee. Four regional presidents (Japan; Europe, Middle East, Africa; North America; and International) report to that senior vice president. When Starbucks recently opened new stores in Germany, Spain, and Greece, for example, those managers reported to the European, Middle East, Africa president. Notice that

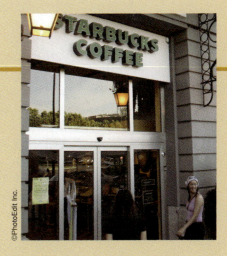

North America is further divided by various geographical regions with the United States. Within each of these regions, various district managers receive operating guidelines, ranging from roasting practices to sales training, but are accountable

for the specific operations and profitability of their specific regions. District managers are also responsible for all store operations, staffing, compensation, and all other functions related to store operations in their geographic area. For example, they are responsible for seeing that each new employee receives 25 hours of formal training. This training covers customer service, cash register operations, coffee brewing methods, and how to scoop coffee beans correctly.

Potential Benefits. Geographical designs allow an organization to focus on customer needs within a relatively small geographic area and to minimize the costs associated with transportation of goods or services. In brief, the potential benefits of geographical design include

- having facilities and the equipment used for production and/or distribution all in one place, saving time and costs;
- being able to develop expertise in solving problems unique to one location;
- gaining an understanding of customers' problems and desires; and
- getting production closer to raw materials and suppliers.

Potential Pitfalls. Organizing by location typically increases problems of control and coordination for top management. To ensure uniformity and coordination, organizations that use geographical designs, such as Starbucks and the IRS, make extensive use of rules that apply to all locations. One reason for doing so is to guarantee a standard level of quality regardless of location, which would be difficult if units in various locations went their own separate ways. In brief, the potential pitfalls of place design include

- duplication of functions, to varying degrees, at each regional or individual unit location;
- conflict between each location's goals and the organization's goals; and
- added levels of management and extensive use of rules and regulations to coordinate and ensure uniformity of quality among locations.[18]

Network Design

All organizations seek to combine the stability and efficiency of their existing designs with a capability for fast response to competitors. However, relying on functional, product, or geographical designs to attain such a balance is very difficult. To meet the dual needs of high efficiency and fast response, many organizations are becoming much more focused and specialized in what they will do in-house. As a result, some activities that used to be performed within the organization are now given to other firms.[19] Recently, a number of organizations have started to rely on a network design. A **network design** *subcontracts some or many of its operations to other firms and coordinates them to accomplish specific goals.*[20] Sometimes also called a *virtual organization,* managers need to coordinate and link up people (from many organizations) to perform activities in many locations. Contacts and working relationships in the network are facilitated by electronic means, as well as through face-to-face meetings. The use of computer-based technologies permits managers to coordinate suppliers, designers, manufacturers, distributors, and others on an instantaneous, real-time basis. Often, managers in a network design will work as closely with their suppliers and customers as they do with their own employees.

By connecting people regardless of their location, the network design enhances fast communications so that people can act together. Numerous organizations in the fashion, toy, publishing, software design, and motion picture industries have used this design. Organizing on a network basis allows the organization to compete on the basis of speed and ability to quickly transfer knowledge. For example, Cisco Systems outsources

Figure 11.4 Starbucks Organization Chart

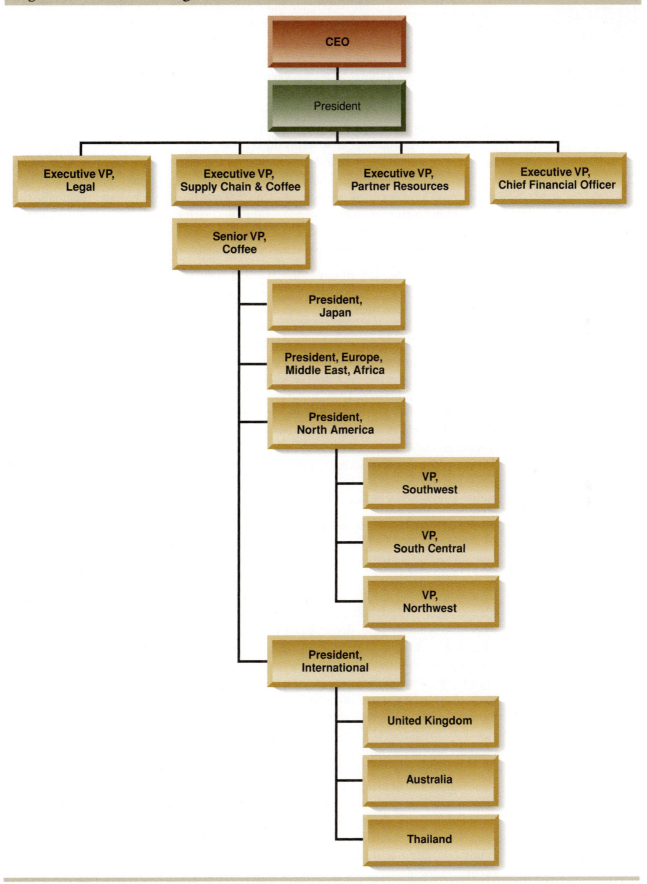

most of its manufacturing to other organizations that are better able to manage this function than Cisco. In turn, Cisco focuses exclusively on product development and customer relationships.[21]

The production of movies has for a long time illustrated many characteristics of a network design. Filmmakers, directors, producers, actors, agents, makeup artists, costume designers, special-effects artists, technicians, and lawyers come together from many different organizations and agencies to produce a film. Although they are all independent, the producer and director need to closely orchestrate and communicate with each of these to produce a film according to very exact specifications. After the production is complete and the film is released, these various people disband and then regroup (often with different people) to produce another film with a different set of actors, producers, directors, and so forth. Thus, the movie industry is actually composed of many different specialized organizations, each of which is critically dependent on the people, knowledge, and skills of other organizations to create a product that is often beyond the scope, capabilities, and means of any one firm.

Potential Benefits. The network design offers many advantages for an organization.[22] First, the organization brings together the special knowledge and skills of others to create value rather than hiring employees to perform this task. The network design enables managers to focus on one set of activities and rely on others to contribute. For example, Medical City of Dallas uses doctors from many specialty practices, such as radiology, oncology, and plastic surgery, to serve its patients. Second, the network design has the advantage of bringing together people with different insights into teams that work exclusively on a given project. Thus, network designs enhance the search for new ideas and creative solutions. Yet, it is important for employees working on such a project to have strong self-management, teamwork, communication, and planning and administration competencies. When a given project is completed, these teams will be disassembled. Third, organizations choosing a network design can work with a wide variety of different suppliers, customers, and other organizations. This gives managers a high degree of flexibility to respond to different circumstances.

Potential Pitfalls. With many people working from different locations and often linked by electronic means, some problems can surface. First, other organizations can sometimes fail to live up to the deadlines that were established. Because network designs work in real time, a delay in one part of the process has ripple effects throughout the system. How many times have you waited for a doctor in an office for an opinion? In instances where time is critical, delays can be very costly because the entire system must wait until a decision is made. Thus, dependence on other organizations can create an operational risk. Often, additional resources or coordination is needed, thus increasing the cost to the consumer. Second, since the network design does not provide managers with knowledge to complete the process on their own, they must constantly monitor the quality of work provided by those in other organizations. Since knowledge resides in people's minds, the network organization is only as competitive as the quality and resources assigned to the project by another organization. Assigning employees with weak communication and planning and administration competencies, for example, can lead to failure. Third, employees in the outsourced organization may not commit to the same values and sense of time urgency to which employees in the networked organization are committed. Therefore, it is crucial that all people working in a network organization understand the critical nature of the project. Last, since the network design requires managers working with many organizations, the lines of authority, responsibility, and accountability are not always clear. Therefore, projects are delayed and cost overruns do occur.

The following Communication Competency feature illustrates how DreamWorks SKG uses a network design to make movies.[23] Some of the benefits and pitfalls of the network design are illustrated in this example.

COMMUNICATION COMPETENCY

DreamWorks SKG

Created in 1994 by Steven Spielberg, Jeffrey Katzenberg, and David Geffen, this multibillion dollar company produced such mega box office hits as *Saving Private Ryan*, *Antz*, *Shrek*, and *A Beautiful Mind*. DreamWorks has also produced television shows, as well as music albums for a number of pop artists. With DreamWorks, the three men divide their responsibili-ties. Spielberg oversees the production of live-action movies, Katzenberg leads the animation division, and Geffen produces the soundtracks and other music activities. Headquartered out of offices at Universal Pictures, they have relied on a network organization design to produce movies as shown in Figure 11.5.

DreamWorks relies heavily on many other organizations to provide the critical resources, people, and skills needed to produce a film. As shown in Figure 11.5, makeup artists, costume designers, actors, and agents are not a part of DreamWorks. These people are hired at the time they are needed. Likewise, DreamWorks works with other specialized organizations to develop many of the newest technologies used to create computer-generated,

Figure 11.5   DreamWorks SKG Network Design

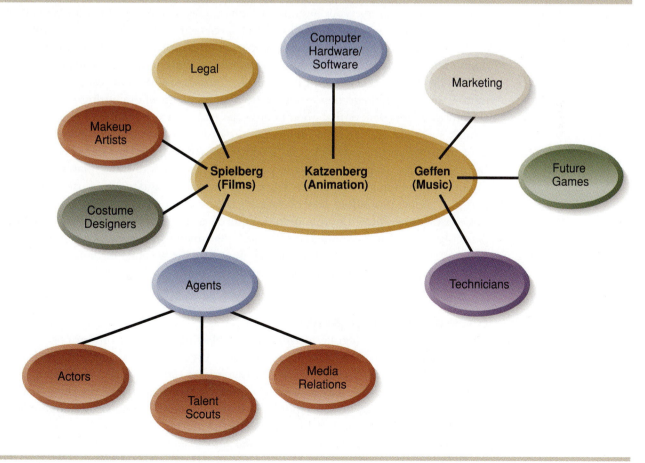

animated films. A central management task for Spielberg, Katzenberg, and Geffen is communicating with people from different backgrounds, expertise, and competencies to produce a blockbuster film.

As DreamWorks has grown during the past 10 years, so have the demands on the firm. For example, DreamWorks signed a deal in February 2002 with computer giant Hewlett-Packard (HP) to develop cutting-edge technologies for new forms of animation. HP will provide all of the computing resources for DreamWorks' next-generation digital studio at its Glendale, California, location. This facility will help DreamWorks create the latest computer-designed animation more quickly and more cost effectively than previ-

ous technology. HP will supply all of the workstations, servers, printers, and networking devices needed. In addition, HP will help DreamWorks develop technologies that foster even closer collaboration among producers, directors, animators, and other technicians working from many distant locations. In this relationship, Hewlett-Packard has effectively become a key provider of computer hardware and other technologies that will allow DreamWorks, which cannot develop the technology as effectively or in as timely a manner on its own, to produce even more realistic animation.

Many of DreamWorks' popular movies have become the basis for the newest video game ideas. Yet, DreamWorks does not currently

seek to invest in this industry alone, especially after having encountered some product failures in the late 1990s. DreamWorks realizes it does not have the skills or the resources to invest or compete in the video game industry. Yet, DreamWorks recognizes that the video game market is a new channel that could help spark interest in both current and future DreamWorks films. In January 2003, DreamWorks signed a deal with Activision to publish games based on three DreamWorks films: *Sharkslayer*, *Madagascar*, and *Over the Hedge*. In this relationship, Activision will help DreamWorks develop a video game franchise for interactive entertainment, but DreamWorks will not actually be developing the games.

ORGANIZATIONAL INTEGRATION

4. Describe two methods of integration.

Now that we have explored both the vertical and horizontal dimensions of an organization's design, we can turn our attention to how managers integrate the efforts of all employees. Specialization and division of labor refer to the fact that employees will think and act in ways that are good for their department, but may not be good for the entire organization. However, to achieve organizational goals, employees, projects, and tasks have to be coordinated. Without it, employees' efforts are likely to result in delay, frustration, and waste. Integration is one of the basic elements of organizing.

Many managers believe that good people can make any organization design work. Although such managers may be overstating the case, employees who work well together are extremely valuable assets. A good analogy is basketball, where teamwork is essential. During practice sessions, coaches try to transform the individual players into one smoothly functioning team. Players learn their functions—guards, forwards, center—as part of a cooperative effort, learn how each task relates to every other task, and relate these tasks to the whole. Coordination is required as the players execute their functions, particularly when they are called on to make adjustments in a game situation.

Managers can use a variety of methods to integrate the activities of their employees to achieve the goals of their organization. In this section, we review two methods: systems and technology.

Integration through Systems

When organizations integrate activities by establishing rules and routines, we say that they are using *systems*. We have identified two types of systems: mechanistic and organic.[24] A **mechanistic system** *is one in which management breaks activities into separate, highly specialized tasks, relies extensively on standardized rules, and centralizes decision making at the top.* This type of system may be most appropriate when an organization's environment is stable and predictable. Table 11.1 highlights these characteristics.

An **organic system** *encourages managers and subordinates to work together in teams and to communicate openly with each other.* In fact, employees are encouraged to communicate

Table 11.1 Organic Versus Mechanistic Organizations

Organic	Mechanistic
■ Tasks tend to be interdependent.	■ Tasks are highly specialized.
■ Tasks are continually adjusted and redefined through interaction and as situations change.	■ Tasks tend to remain rigidly defined unless changed by top management.
■ Generalized roles (responsibility for task accomplishment beyond specific role definition) are accepted.	■ Specific roles (rights, obligations, and technical methods) are prescribed for each employee.
■ Network structure of control, authority, and communication.	■ Hierarchical structure of control, authority, and communication.
■ Communication and decision making are both vertical and horizontal, depending on where needed information and expertise reside.	■ Communication and decision making are primarily vertical, top-down.
■ Communication emphasizes the form of mutual influence and advice among all levels.	■ Communication emphasizes directions and decisions issued by superiors.

with anyone who might help them solve a problem. Decision making tends to be decentralized. Authority, responsibility, and accountability flow to employees having the expertise required to solve problems as they arise. As a result, an organic organization is well suited to a changing environment. Table 11.1 summarizes the characteristics of an organic system.

The following Global Awareness Competency feature illustrates how Flextronics International has used many of the ideas of an organic organization to manufacture and assemble printed circuit boards for Motorola, Xerox, Ericcsson, and other networking and telecommunications equipment companies. Located in Singapore, the organization employs more than 78,000 people in more than 20 countries located in the Americas, Asia, and Europe. In the past seven years, its revenues have gone from $93 million to more than $13 billion by acquiring competitors.[25]

GLOBAL AWARENESS COMPETENCY

Flextronics International Ltd.

Ask Michael Marks, CEO of Flextronics, about his organization's procedures for making big capital investments and he is likely to refer you to the Corporate Policy Manual. It has 80 pages—all of them blank. Sometimes Marks lets subordinates do multimillion-dollar acquisitions without showing him the paperwork. He asks four questions: One, what is their line of business; two, what's their manufacturing capacity; three, how big and what is their customer base, and four, what are their cultural values? If his managers answer all of these questions, then the acquisition is verbally agreed on and as

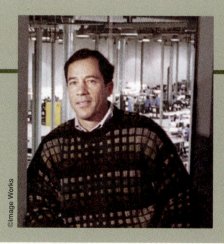
©Image Works

Integration through Technology

In previous chapters, we have frequently noted the importance of technology to a wide range of management issues, including organization design. Recall from Chapter 2 that *technology* is the method(s) used to transform organizational inputs into outputs. Technology greatly influences the size and shape of organizations and their products. Schools, banks, hospitals, governments, and retail stores all rely heavily on technology. Therefore we can analyze its impact on organization design in a variety of settings—and its importance cannot be overstated.

An organization's technology has a significant impact on how managers coordinate the organization's various activities because different types of technologies generate various types of internal interdependence. **Technological interdependence** *is the degree of coordination required between individuals and units to transform information and raw materials into goods and services.*[26] There are three types of technological interdependence: pooled, sequential, and reciprocal. Figure 11.6 shows how they operate to coordinate the efforts of employees in order to achieve desired results.

Pooled Interdependence. Illustrated in Figure 11.6(a), **pooled interdependence** *involves little sharing of information or resources among individuals within a unit or among units in the performance of tasks.* Although various departments contribute to overall organiza-

Figure 11.6   Three Types of Technological Interdependence

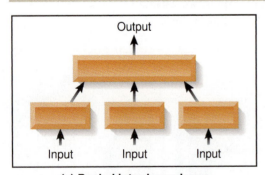

(a) Pooled interdependence

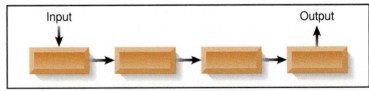

(b) Sequential interdependence

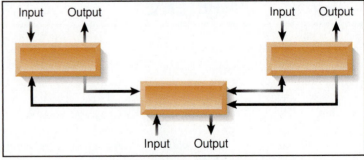

(c) Reciprocal interdependence

tional efforts, they work on their own specialized tasks. At a Bank of America branch, for example, the savings, consumer loan, and commercial loan departments work independently of one another. Bank of America achieves coordination by requiring each department to meet certain standards and follow certain rules. These rules are consistent for all its banks in various states and apply to all routine transactions, such as check cashing and receiving deposits, with few exceptions. Functional designs used pooled interdependence to coordinate various activities.

Sequential Interdependence. Illustrated in Figure 11.6(b), **sequential interdependence** *involves the orderly step-by-step flow of information, tasks, and resources from one individual or team to another within the same unit or from one unit to another.* That is, the output from department A becomes the input for department B, the output from department B becomes the input for department C, and so on. Mercedes-Benz uses standard methods and procedures at its Vance, Alabama, plant to manufacture its sport utility vehicles. These methods and procedures spell out the single exact and proper way to do every task. They were drawn up by engineers and posted at workstations for easy reference. Everything is spelled out, down to the proper way to tighten a lug nut. When an employee is finished with a hammer, guides (e.g., chalk body outlines) indicate exactly where it is to be laid. To ensure coordination of its workstations, managers must carefully schedule when parts arrive and leave each workstation.

Reciprocal Interdependence. Illustrated in Figure 11.6(c), **reciprocal interdependence** *involves the need for every individual and unit to work with every other individual and unit; information and resources flow back and forth freely until the goal is achieved.* For example, hospitals use resources from several departments (e.g., x-ray, nursing, surgery, and physical therapy) to restore a patient's health. Each specialist and department supplies some of the resources needed to help the patient. Doctors and professionals from each specialized area meet to discuss the patient's recovery. The method of coordination is mutual adjustment, achieved through team meetings.

Designing an organization to handle reciprocal interdependence and then managing it are extremely challenging tasks. The design of the organization must allow for frequent communication among individuals and units, and planning is essential. Because management can't easily anticipate all customer demands or solve all the problems that arise, managers must continually communicate to be sure that they understand the nature and scope of issues and problems—and to devise effective solutions. Usually managers choose a network design if various units are reciprocally interdependent.[27]

CHAPTER SUMMARY

In this chapter, we highlighted some of the basics of designing an organization. The two fundamentals of organizing, differentiation and integration, along with the vertical and horizontal ways of designing the organization were discussed. Two methods that organizations can use to integrate its activities were also highlighted. We also indicated that no organization is simply a static set of boxes and charts. Organizations are like motion pictures—they constantly change according to the demands placed on them by competitors, employees, governments, and many other stakeholders.

1. Describe the two fundamentals of organizing.

There are two fundamentals of organizing: differentiation and integration. Differentiation is created through a division of labor and job specialization. As organizations grow, they create departments to handle certain activities, such as payroll, manufacturing, and human resources. Because different units are part of the larger organization, some degree of integration (coordination) is needed among them for an organization to be effective. Integration is achieved through the use of systems and technology.

2. Explain the five aspects of an organization's vertical design.

The vertical design of an organization has five major parts. The hierarchy shows relationships among the various management levels in an organization. These relationships are shown in the organization chart. The span of control refers to the number of subordinates reporting to each manager. Authority, responsibility, and accountability are the glue that holds an organization together because these indicate who has the right to make a decision, who will be held responsible for the decision, and who is accountable for the results. Delegation is the process of giving authority to a person (or group) to make decisions. Delegation should go hand in hand with responsibility and accountability. Centralization/decentralization refers to the overall philosophy of management as to where decisions are to be made.

3. Describe four types of horizontal design.

The four primary types of design are (1) functional design—groups employees according to common tasks to be performed; (2) product design—groups employees by product or service in self-contained units, each responsible for its own goods or services; (3) geographical design—groups functions and employees by location; and (4) network design—subcontracts some or many of its operations to other organizations and coordinates them to accomplish specific goals.

4. Describe two methods of integration.

Ideally, an organization's design will help management to implement the development of key integration practices. We reviewed two basic ways in which an organization can integrate its activities: systems and technology. Mechanistic and organic systems refer to the use or absence of rules and regulations. Mechanistic or bureaucratic systems are used when customers' demands are well known and do not change. Organic systems use few rules and regulations, and they are found in organizations that must respond rapidly to changes in customer tastes, competitors' pressures, and the like. Three types of technological interdependence are pooled, sequential, and reciprocal. Pooled interdependence requires little sharing of information and other resources among individuals who work on specialized tasks. Sequential task interdependence serializes the flow of information and other resources between individual and departments to accomplish tasks. Reciprocal task interdependence encourages the constant flow of information and resources back and forth between individuals, teams, and departments to accomplish tasks.

KEY TERMS and CONCEPTS

Accountability

Authority

Centralization

Decentralization

Delegation

Differentiation

Division of labor

Functional design

Geographical design

Hierarchy

Integration

Mechanistic system

Network design

Organic system

Organization chart

Organization design

Pooled interdependence

Product design

Reciprocal interdependence

Responsibility

Sequential interdependence

Span of control

Specialization

Technological interdependence

QUESTIONS FOR DISCUSSION and COMPETENCY DEVELOPMENT

1. How is Home Depot organized? What are some of the advantages and pitfalls of this design?

2. What are the vertical and horizontal aspects of Starbucks' organization (see Figure 11.4)?

3. How is your university or college organized?

4. Discuss the advantages and disadvantages of a network design.

5. Why do some managers have a hard time delegating?

6. Would an organic or mechanistic system work best at DreamWorks SKG? Why?

7. Would you rather work in a functional or product design organization? Why?

8. What implications for managerial spans of control can be expected as organizations downsize? What additional managerial competencies might be placed on the managers who remain in a downsized organization?

9. Name sports that use each type of technological interdependence. What does this suggest for the design of effective organizations? For the managerial competencies needed in each type of technological interdependence?

KINKO'S

Kinko's has come a long way since its humble beginnings as a college town copy shop. It is the creation of Paul Orfalea, who started selling pencils and spiral notebooks on the campus of the University of California, Santa Barbara, in 1970. However, when he saw that it cost 10 cents per page to use the photocopy machine in the library, he realized that selling copies would be more profitable than pencils and notebooks. He borrowed $5,000 and opened his first Kinko's shop in a former taco stand near the campus. He sold school supplies and made copies on a copy machine that he moved outside when it was in use because the shop was so small. In 2003, Kinko's operated nearly 1,100 stores worldwide, including Asia, Australia, and Europe, as well as North America. Kinko's now offers a full range of services, including binding and finishing services, color printing, and Internet access. It primarily serves small office/school customers, but also provides digital document services to large companies and allows its customers to design their own products and place orders through its Kinkos.com Web site. Kinko's also acquired ImageX in 2003. ImageX marketed online business cards, stationery, and branded print materials for large commercial customers. Kinko's will offer these services in selected markets.

When Orfalea decided to expand his business into college towns nationwide, he didn't seek out local entrepreneurs to buy franchise rights. Rather, he invited his friends and relatives to become his partners. These partners enjoyed a large share of the store's profits, usually around 50%. Many of the partners shared profits with their employees. Kinko's had expanded to more than 80 shops in 28 states by 1979. Then in the early 1990s, Kinko's was no longer just serving colleges and small businesses. It established a partnership with Federal Express, and FedEx drop boxes were handily placed in all Kinko's outlets. An electronic document transfer system was introduced in 1995, enabling transfer of documents between various Kinko's locations. The company eventually grew to more than 150 videoconferencing centers in its branch shops.

In 1996, Orfalea started looking for a group of investors who were interested in reorganizing his company. He realized his organization had become somewhat unmanageable because it had outgrown its original design and structure. Orfalea, himself, was the hub around which the business ran. His partners relied on interpersonal relationships instead of formal authority and responsibility. Orfalea's charismatic leadership style had worked early on because very little coordination was needed among the partners.

Clayton Dubilier & Rice (CD&R) was a private investment firm that could see bright prospects for Kinko's, as long as some organization design changes were made. This new structure was created in 1997. CD&R purchased about 30% of the company for $219 million, with these funds to be used for new technology and expansion. CD&R later increased its stake to 73% of the company. As part of the deal, Kinko's established a highly integrated organization. Many of the decisions that had been made in the stores were now being made by top management. The company was reorganized by geographical region—East, West, Central, and International. Kinko's shops had been located in Japan and the Netherlands since 1992. Partners who owned the largest group of stores headed up their regional divisions.

After the reorganization, a search was begun for a new CEO. Gary Kusin joined the company in August 2001 in that position. Kusin decided to relocate the company headquarters from Ventura, California, to Dallas, Texas. The move was completed in 2002. Dallas was chosen because it was more centrally located in the United States and a less expensive city in which to do business than was Southern California. There was a strong senior executive labor force in Dallas, and Kusin planned to utilize this force to revamp the top management team.

All but three of Kinko's top executives had been replaced by the end of 2002. The common thread in the new top team was that each person was a strong team player, had previously been with a successful organization, and each held jobs with high accountability. The team had diverse managerial competencies and their primary job was to implement the programs that Kusin and his team had put together to improve the overall performance of Kinko's.

The team zeroed in on improving efficiency and reducing corporate overhead in each store in order to reduce costs. Management layers in the company's hierarchy were reduced from 12 to 6. Sue Parks was named executive vice president of operations for the retail side of the business. The vice president of marketing and two general managers for retail operations, operations support, and real estate reported directly to Parks. These general managers were put in charge of 18 operations directors, each of whom was responsible for the profit and loss in a distinct geographical market. Seventy-four district managers and the human resource and technology staff report directly to these operations directors. All 1,100 branches of Kinko's reported up through the individual districts.

Further expansion of Kinko's commercial business depended on its ability to utilize its store network. The stores had been reorganized into a hub-and-spoke configuration. Spokes were small stores that reported to larger facilities that had extensive capabilities and were open 24 hours a day. Each hub had one or two spokes. Kinko's also added two other categories to their stores—a flagship and a node. Flagship stores were large hubs in high-demand areas and each one had a broad range of technologies. Nodes were smaller stores that were staffed by one person. These nodes were designed for small and sporadic walk-in customers. They sometimes occupied only a corner in an office building. Nodes had low volume, but they were convenient to use and exposed more and more customers to Kinko's.

Large, commercial customers were not forgotten during the organizational redesign. Stand-alone locked facilities were built for large batch jobs. By 2003, four of these large facilities were in use, with four per district planned for the future. All stores were connected through the Internet so that jobs could be allocated, distributed, or shared, as the need arose. This was possible because Kinko's had calibrated all machines in these facilities so that all color copies were identical, regardless of where they were produced.

The senior vice president of sales is John MacDonald, who was hired in early 2003. He has 18 sales directors re-porting directly to him. Each sales director is responsible for profit and loss in his or her geographical district. There are now eight national account managers, responsible for large commercial accounts. They also report to MacDonald. Twenty-four digital sales consultants were added to call on clients and suggest money-saving processes to customers. These consultants report to the sales directors. Ten engagement managers have been located on-site at the largest Kinko's facilities, and there are 74 sales managers, all organized by district, who now report to the sales directors. The sales managers have nearly 500 sales reps, who, in turn, report to them.[28]

Questions

1. What type of horizontal design has Kinko's chosen? What are its benefits? Pitfalls?

2. Does Kinko's use an organic or mechanistic system to achieve integration? Defend your answer.

3. How has the technological interdependence among the stores changed over the years?

WHAT TYPE OF DESIGN IS YOUR ORGANIZATION?

In this competency exercise you are to focus on either your university or an organization for which you currently work in a full- or part-time capacity or for which you have worked in the past. Please circle the letter on the scale indicating the degree to which you agree or disagree with each statement. There is no "right" answer; simply respond according to how you see the organization being managed

Strongly Agree (SA)	Agree (A)	Neutral (N)	Disagree (D)	Strongly Disagree (SD)

1. People in this organization are urged to be innovative.

   SA   A   N   D   SD

2. There are a lot of rules to follow in this organization.

   SA   A   N   D   SD

3. People who pay attention to details are likely to get ahead in this organization.

   SA   A   N   D   SD

4. A person has a secure job in this organization.

   SA   A   N   D   SD

5. Precision in one's work is valued by the organization.

   SA   A   N   D   SD

6. This company operates with a stable set of competitors.

   SA   A   N   D   SD

7. People in this organization are urged to take risks and experiment with new ways of doing things.

   SA   A   N   D   SD

8. Jobs in this organization are very predictable.

   SA   A   N   D   SD

9. There are few rules in this organization.

   SA   A   N   D   SD

10. Employees are very careful in performing their work.

    SA   A   N   D   SD

11. Employees are treated impersonally by managers in this organization.

    SA   A   N   D   SD

12. Lines of authority are closely followed in this organization.

    SA   A   N   D   SD

13. Job opportunities in this organization are limited to employees who play by the rules.

    SA   A   N   D   SD

14. Being highly organized is expected and rewarded in this organization.

SA   A   N   D   SD

15. Being people oriented is a characteristic of this organization.

SA   A   N   D   SD

16. People are not constrained by many rules in this organization.

SA   A   N   D   SD

Scoring. On the scoring grid, circle the number that corresponds to your response to each of the 16 questions. Add the numbers in each column. Enter the total for each column on the line at the bottom of each column. Add the column totals and enter as a total score. This is your organization's score.

	Strongly Agree (SA)	Agree (A)	Neutral (N)	Disagree (D)	Strongly Disagree (SD)
1.	1	2	3	4	5
2.	5	4	3	2	1
3.	5	4	3	2	1
4.	5	4	3	2	1
5.	5	4	3	2	1
6.	5	4	3	2	1
7.	1	2	3	4	5
8.	5	4	3	2	1
9.	1	2	3	4	5
10.	5	4	3	2	1
11.	5	4	3	2	1
12.	5	4	3	2	1
13.	5	4	3	2	1
14.	5	4	3	2	1
15.	1	2	3	4	5
16.	1	2	3	4	5

Scores:_____   _____   _____   _____   _____

Total Score =   _____

Interpretation. A high score (90–64 points) indicates that your organization has many of the features characteristic of the mechanistic organization. A low score (32–16 points) indicates that your organization has more features usually associated with the organic organization. A score in the middle range (63–33 points) indicates that your organization incorporates features of both.[29]

©Stone/Getty Images

Organizational Change and Learning

LEARNING OBJECTIVES

After studying this chapter, you should be able to:

1. Describe four types of organizational change.

2. Explain the planning process for organizational change.

3. Identify four methods of organizational change.

4. Describe how innovation relates to organizational change.

5. Discuss how learning organizations foster change.

Chapter Outline

Almost everyone has seen one of the 13,000 orange trucks of the Yellow Freight System. They handle nearly 70,000 shipping orders every day. Bill Zollars spearheaded a major change effort at Yellow Freight System. Employees used to tell customers approximately when their shipment would be delivered and customers were left to plan their work schedules around that estimate. As long as a shipment arrived approximately when the customer was told to expect it, Yellow claimed it had done what it had agreed to. Before the cultural change, the efficient delivery of goods was Yellow's most important objective. Today when customers call, they tell a Yellow employee what services they need, and Yellow does everything possible to meet the customers' needs. Deliveries can be scheduled to arrive in hours, days, or weeks, and customers can specify the desired arrival times. According to Zollars, "We've gone from being a company that thought it was in the trucking business to one that realizes it's in the service business."

When Zollars was hired as the new CEO of Yellow Freight System in 1999, the company had just finished one of its worst years in its 70-year history. The company suffered losses of $30 million, two rounds of layoffs, and a major strike by the teamsters. Zollars was hired to help save the company, but he knew that he couldn't save the company on his own. He needed the help of all 25,000 Yellow employees. To gain their commitment to change, Zollars embarked on a road trip that lasted 18 months. He visited terminals all over the country and talked to thousands of dock workers, sales staff, and office employees. Zollars used town meetings to get the message out and explain why change was needed. The meetings took place wherever people were working. They took the form of one-on-one personal conversations between the CEO and employees at the site.

When Zollars set out to convince employees of the need for change, he used a communication style that was intentionally low tech and high touch. But sophisticated technologies are central to implementing Yellow's new customer-focused strategy. Customers can place their orders online, track shipments, and review their accounts. Dock workers and drivers can communicate instantly with each other and easily access schedule and delivery information using wireless, mobile data terminals. A sophisticated information system also allows sales representatives to instantly learn about a customer's company, the type of loading dock it has, and who needs to sign for deliveries, among other things.

Armed with all of the information they need, and supported by leaders who trust them to make decisions on their own, Yellow employees are now able to quickly spot and solve problems as they strive to satisfy customers. By reading the weekly company newsletter, employees get honest assessments of how Yellow is performing, and they also learn about trends in the industry. "We don't just talk about victories," says Zollars. "We talk about losing business, about claims problems. We want to give a clear picture." At Yellow Freight Systems, changing the company to meet customers' needs is now a way of life.[1]

TYPES OF ORGANIZATIONAL CHANGE

1. Describe four types of organizational change.

Organizational change *refers to any transformation in the design or functioning of an organization.* Effective managers understand when change is needed and are able to guide their organizations through the change process. Often, they learn by watching what other organizations are doing. For example, after seeing how total quality management (TQM) improved the effectiveness of manufacturing companies, executives at the Veterans Health Administration began to adopt TQM principles in their hospitals.[2] Other times, the environment jolts the organization into making major changes. If a substantially new and better method of production becomes available, adopting that new method is likely to require major organizational change. In the steel industry, the new minimill production method cut the time required to make a ton of steel by about 60 percent. Steel producers such as Nucor Steel spent millions of dollars to build new plants. But adopting the minimill production method also meant that the jobs of steelworkers and their managers changed significantly, as did the competencies needed to perform those jobs. More recently, development of the Internet has required managers in almost every industry to rethink and radically change the way their organizations function.

Degree of Change

Massive changes in the way an organization operates occur occasionally, but more often change occurs in small steps. The desire to improve performance continuously in order to stay ahead of competitors is a common reason for smaller organizational changes.[3] When Procter & Gamble (P&G) created a new cleaning mop, only minor modifications in production and sales activities were required. Though small in magnitude, those changes were essential to customer acceptance of the new product. Successful organizations are equally adept at making both radical and incremental changes.

Radical. **Radical change** *occurs when organizations make major innovations in the ways they do business.* Adopting a new organizational design, merging with another organization, or changing from a privately held to a publicly traded company are all examples of radical change. Radical change is relatively infrequent and generally takes a long time to complete. It can be stimulated by changes in the environment, by persistent performance declines, by significant personnel changes, or by a combination of all three factors. At Knight-Ridder, Inc., one of the largest newspaper chains in the United States, declining readership stimulated change. To rebuild its readership, the company launched a project called 25/43—so named because the goal was to increase readership among people between the ages of 25 and 43. Based on extensive input from readers, this project led to substantive changes in the format and content of the company's newspapers. Articles became shorter, topics were selected in part because of their potential interest to readers, and page layouts were redesigned. Equally significant was the change from a culture that gave priority to the preferences of editors and journalists to one that recognized that success required responding to the preferences of readers.[4]

Figure 12.1 illustrates a common framework for describing radical organizational change. Although it was introduced more than 50 years ago, most modern accounts of organizational change reflect the basic ideas shown. Developed by social scientist Kurt Lewin, the framework divides the change process into roughly three stages.[5] In stage 1—unfreezing—management plans and prepares the members of the organization for a major transformation. A primary objective in this stage is to convince members of the organization of the need for change and to reduce their tendency to resist the change. In stage 2—transitioning—most of the actual change occurs. Often this stage is described as the implementation process. Finally, in stage 3—refreezing—the change is solidified. Ideally, changes remain in place once they have been made. But people tend to be creatures of habit, and habits are difficult to change. During refreezing, therefore, monitoring the intended outcomes and providing support for new behaviors are essential to minimize relapses to the old way of doing things.[6]

Incremental. Radical change suggests that one "big bang" can transform an organization into something new. In contrast, **incremental change** *is an ongoing process of evolution*

Figure 12.1 Three Stages of Radical Change

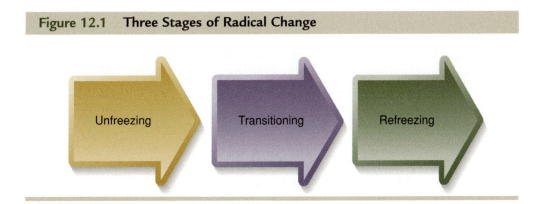

over time, during which many small adjustments occur routinely. After enough time has passed, the cumulative effect of these adjustments may be to transform the organization totally. Yet while they are occurring, the adjustments seem to be just a normal aspect of revising and improving the way in which work gets done. As we discussed in Chapter 2, total quality management is an approach that relies heavily on incremental organizational change. Employees routinely look for ways to improve products and services, and they make suggestions for changes day in and day out. The World Bank's Development Marketplace is another example of how to encourage incremental change. At the first marketplace, dozens of teams displayed ideas and answered questions from managers and executives who made on-the-spot decisions about which ideas to fund. By the end of the day, $3 million in funding was given to 11 new projects. At the second marketplace, which was held two years later, $5 million was awarded to fund 52 new projects. As each event grows bigger and bigger, the total effect of the many small changes being made has become substantial.[7] This approach to creating major change by taking many small steps in new directions seems to work well in bureaucratic organizations, where middle managers may feel threatened by radical change and try to block it.[8]

People who strive to create radical change but do so by prodding an organization to make many small incremental changes are called **tempered radicals**.[9] Their ideas are radical, but their approach is tempered. Tempered radicals understand that they can get more done by working as an insider in the system they want to change. Robert Redford, the well-known movie actor and director, is an example of a tempered radical. For two decades, he has worked to increase the diversity of films produced by supporting independent film makers at Sundance Institute, an artists community and film production studio located in Utah. Redford feels he has learned a great deal about creating change. His advice for how other tempered radicals can be successful in creating change is summarized in Table 12.1.[10]

Table 12.1	Working from Within to Create Change: Advice for Tempered Radicals

- Develop grass roots initiatives; chip away at standard operating procedures over time until you achieve real success.
- Earn credibility first, and then leverage it once you have it; if no one will listen to your ideas, it will be impossible to change the system.
- Develop your ability to compromise as well as persuade; accept small changes as making progress.
- Gather and accept support from others along the way; people who see you succeeding will want to join you; be willing to share the stage with supporters and don't turn them away.
- Be persistent; as you succeed in making small changes, set new goals and continue to strive for other improvements.

Timing of Change

In addition to the differences in the magnitude of change are differences in the timing of change. Organizations may make radical changes in response to a crisis or because leaders have a bold new vision of what the future *could* be like. Similarly, organizations may make incremental changes as a reaction to past events or in anticipation of trends that have just begun to develop. Figure 12.2 illustrates how the degree and timing of change combine to form different types of change.

Reactive. **Reactive change** *occurs when an organization is forced to change in response to some event in the external or internal environment.* New strategic moves made by competitors and new scientific or technological discoveries are common reasons for reactive change. De-

Figure 12.2   **Types of Organizational Change**

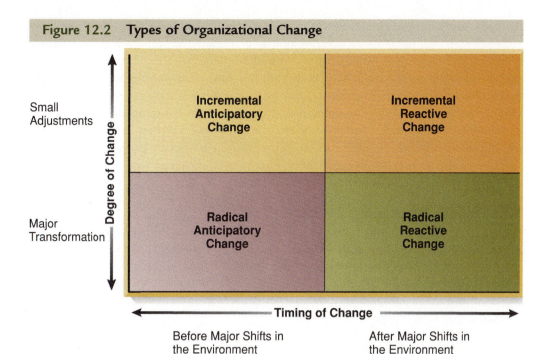

clining organizational performance is another common trigger for reactive change. When a business is in severe decline, often a new top management team is hired to develop and implement a turnaround plan.[11]

Reactive change can be incremental or radical. If an organization adapts to a change in the environment without undergoing a substantial reorientation in its strategy or values, the change is reactive and incremental. At General Electric, managers are encouraged to make incremental reactive change through a process called Work-Out. In a Work-Out session, groups of managers and employees from around the company work together in small teams to address problems. Often the teams focus on how to reduce unnecessary work. That is, they try to find ways to get work out of the system—for example, by reducing red tape and finding ways to be more efficient. Small teams work to develop solutions to problems, and then present their ideas in a Town Meeting. Attending the Town Meeting are other small teams and a senior manager with the authority needed to agree to implement the suggestions. During the Town Meeting, the manager discusses the ideas with everyone and makes an on-the-spot decision about whether to accept each solution that is recommended. If a change is to be made, volunteers are given assignments immediately and they are expected to be sure that the changes get implemented.[12]

Sometimes, reactive change takes the form of a new organizational design. When Dirk Jager became CEO of P&G, he tried to re-create that company to improve its sagging performance. His goal was to shake up the company's conservative and staid culture and turn it into a more entrepreneurial enterprise. Jager changed the company's processes for developing new products, conducting market tests, and making decisions about which products to promote. He closed several plants and cut thousands of jobs. Many of the managers who survived were moved into new jobs. New financial measures were adopted for assessing the company's progress. Unfortunately, Jager's reactive attempt to make radical change didn't succeed. A year after he began to make changes, the company's share price took a nosedive, falling 50 percent in 6 months, and Jager was replaced. Managers at P&G believed that Jager's biggest mistake was trying to change everything all at once. He didn't seem to realize how long organizations must plan and how carefully they must implement such radical transformations.[13]

Anticipatory Change. As the term suggests, **anticipatory change** *occurs when managers make organizational modifications based on forecasts of upcoming events or early in the cycle of a new trend.* The best run organizations always look for better ways to do things in order to stay ahead of the competition. They constantly fine-tune their policies and practices, introduce technological improvements, and set new standards for customer satisfaction. Often, anticipatory change is incremental and results from constant tinkering and improvements. Occasionally, anticipatory change is radical, however. Visionary leaders within the organization become convinced that major changes are needed even though there is no apparent crisis. Because there is no crisis, the change can be planned carefully and implemented gradually.

What Is Your Reaction to Change?

Some people thrive during change and even seek it out; others find change stressful and prefer to avoid it.[14] Before continuing, take a moment to answer the questions posed in the following Self-Management Competency feature. These questions are designed to provide insight into how you respond to change. After you have calculated your score, discuss it with other members of your class. Does everyone react to change the same way you do?

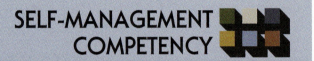

SELF-MANAGEMENT COMPETENCY

Is Change Your Friend or Foe?

Instructions

For each item, circle "T" if the statement is true or circle "F" if the statement is false. There are no right or wrong answers. Rather, the intent is to help you explore your attitudes about change.

Statement

T F 1. Among my friends, I'm usually the first person to try out a new idea or method.

T F 2. When I take vacations, I prefer to return to places I have been to already and know I will like.

T F 3. Compared to other people, I tend to change the way I look (hair, clothes) fairly often.

T F 4. I enjoy trying new foods, even if I'm not sure about the ingredients.

T F 5. I would prefer to work for many different companies rather than just a few during the course of my career.

T F 6. I am happiest when I'm working on problems that I'm quite sure I can solve.

T F 7. At work I get annoyed by people who seem to always have suggestions for how to change the way things are done.

T F 8. I seldom follow rules that I think are silly or ineffective.

T F 9. I believe that taking needless risks is irresponsible.

T F 10. I would prefer a job that I can master and become a real expert at doing, rather than one where I am always doing something new.

T F 11. Most of my friends are pretty similar to me in their general interests and backgrounds.

T F 12. In five years, I am likely to be working at something that is so different I can't even imagine doing it today.

T F 13. If I'm working on something new and run into a problem, I prefer to keep trying to solve the problem on my own rather than ask someone else for help.

Scoring

A. For the following items, circle those you answered "True." Then give yourself one point for each item you circled:

1
3
4
5
8
12

Total Points for Part A: _____

B. For the following items, circle those you answered "False." Then give yourself one point for each item you circled.

2
6
7
9
10
11
13

Total Points for Part B: _____

C. Add your points for parts A and B to get your total score:

_____ + _____ = _____(Total Points)

Interpretation
The higher your score, the more you enjoy change and the uncertainty associated with change. If you scored 10 or higher, you would enjoy working in an organization that offers cutting-edge products or services. Radical change drives you.

If you scored 4 through 9, you welcome incremental changes that do not disrupt your life. You would enjoy organizations that reward calculated risk taking and you prefer improving products rather than designing new ones.

If you scored 3 or less, you react to change as a burden and try to avoid changes that will cause you frustration. You would most enjoy working for organizations that provide clear performance measures and career guidelines.

PLANNING FOR ORGANIZATIONAL CHANGE

Organizational change can be unplanned and somewhat chaotic or planned and relatively smooth. By its very nature, chaotic change is difficult to manage. Nevertheless, large-scale organizational changes seldom occur without a bit of chaos. Organizations usually strive to minimize it by imposing some order on the change process. Change is most likely to be orderly when it has been planned. The planning process itself can help unfreeze the organization by convincing people of the need for change and involving them in decisions about how to change. The steps involved in planning for organizational change are shown in Figure 12.3. Although planned changes don't always proceed exactly as shown, planning generally precedes the implementation of major change initiatives.[15]

2. Explain the planning process for organizational change.

Figure 12.3   The Process of Organizational Change

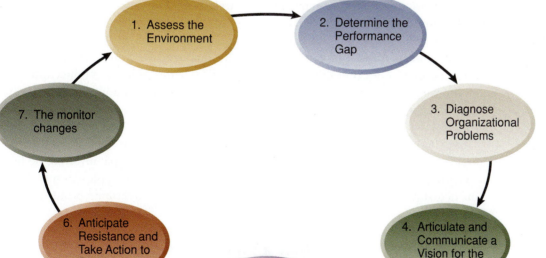

1. Assess the Environment
2. Determine the Performance Gap
3. Diagnose Organizational Problems
4. Articulate and Communicate a Vision for the Future
5. Develop and Implement an Action Plan
6. Anticipate Resistance and Take Action to Reduce It
7. The monitor changes

Assess the Environment

As we described in Chapter 3, both the degree and rate of change in the environment have implications for organizations. The four environmental factors most responsible for stimulating organizational change are customers, technology, competitors, and the workforce. Other factors that may pressure organizations to change include globalization, technological advances, and the actions of important stakeholders, such as shareholders, government regulators, unions, and political action groups.[16] Environmental scanning activities ensure that organizations become aware of changes as they occur. Marriott Hotels and Bank of America, among other firms, use customer satisfaction surveys and other forms of market research to assess customers' changing preferences. Similarly, employee surveys are a method of scanning the internal environment to assess the concerns of the workforce.

> **The Competent Manager**
>
> Ed Zander, president of Microsystems, Inc., used "whack-o-meter" sessions to assess the environment. Each week, key decision makers met to discuss competitors' moves and any implications that they may have for "whacking" the marketplace.

Determine the Performance Gap

A **performance gap** *is the difference between what the organization wants to do and what it actually does.* By determining the performance gap, managers provide clear answers to the question "What is wrong?" Bill Zollars' assessment of Yellow Freight System's environment led him to conclude that Yellow needed to address a major performance gap: Fundamentally, it was a service company that had failed to keep pace with changes in customers' desires. Long after competitors had shifted to a customer-focused approach to shipping and delivery, Yellow had continued to focus on the internal efficiency of the company. Meanwhile, competitors discovered that they could be more profitable by responding to customers who wanted faster and more predictable delivery times.

Diagnose Organizational Problems

The aim of **organizational diagnosis** *is to identify the nature and extent of problems before taking action in order to develop an understanding of the reasons behind gaps in performance.* It answers the question "*Why* do we have performance gaps?" The idea that diagnosis should precede action may seem obvious, but its importance is often underestimated. All too often results-oriented managers prematurely begin the change process and impatiently push for solutions before the nature of the problem itself is clear.

Organizations often hire outside consultants to assist with problem diagnosis. For example, interpersonal problems often require managers to gather sensitive information from employees. Outside consultants may be better able to conduct interviews and interpret data in an unbiased manner than insiders. In addition, consultants often have the expertise that the organization lacks to conduct and analyze attitude surveys properly.[17]

Tom Hawley, the human resource director at Food Ingredient Specialties, turned to employees to help diagnose organizational problems. To get people involved, he hired a blues band to perform during an off-site meeting. He then had employees spend some time actually writing and performing their own blues songs, describing problems in the company.[18]

Articulate and Communicate a Vision for the Future

Successful change efforts are guided by a clear vision for the future. Until leaders formulate a clear vision and persuade others to join them in being dedicated to that vision, they won't be able to generate the enthusiasm and resources needed for large-scale cultural change.[19]

To communicate the leader's vision, messages should be sent consistently and repeatedly through varying organizational channels by credible sources.[20] Communicating his vision at Yellow Freight Systems was one of the most important items on Bill Zollars' agenda during his first year as CEO. He went on a tour and visited sites all around the country. Zollars used face-to-face communication because he believed employees needed to hear directly from him about his vision. Because the company was quite large, he spent 18 months traveling to different locations and holding small on-site meetings to explain his new vision to employees.

Develop and Implement an Action Plan

Although investments made in planning often produce significant improvements in productivity, most companies begin substantial change efforts with a thoughtful, integrated plan of action. An **action plan** *articulates the goals for change and describes the specific measures to be used to monitor and evaluate progress toward those goals.* For major change efforts, the organization's action plan can be quite complex and not easily understood by most employees because it includes proposals for all levels and all units involved in the change effort. However, in an organization structured by functional department, each department should develop a more focused action plan based on the overall plan. In an organization structured by region, more detailed plans for each region should be developed, and so on. Regardless of the approach used, the action plan should be adopted only after considering the full range of alternative methods for fostering change, which we describe in more detail later in this chapter. Finally, the action plan provides a timetable for implementation and evaluation.

Consider Alternatives. When developing an action plan, management should consider all feasible alternatives, along with their advantages and disadvantages. In recent years, for example, many U.S. companies have had to cope with declining business due to a weak economy. To cut costs, many companies have resorted to laying off their employees. But some companies understand that the long-term effects of laying people off can be very negative, so they have used other methods of cutting costs. Some alternatives to layoffs include

- reducing the hours in a standard workweek, so everyone works and earns a little less,
- encouraging employees to take temporary leaves,
- not renewing contracts for temporary and part-time workers,
- job sharing, and
- reducing executive salaries and bonuses.

These alternatives to layoffs can reduce costs without imposing job losses on workers.

Early Involvement. For a plan to be effective, those who will be affected must buy into it. The best way to ensure that is through early involvement.[21] That employees should be involved in planning change seems obvious, but even experienced managers often forget this principle.

Task forces, focus groups, surveys, hot lines, and informal conversations are but a few of the ways that managers can involve employees and other stakeholders in assessing the alternatives for change. There is little disagreement among change experts about the importance of involvement. How you get people involved is less important than doing it. The use of teams as a way to involve employees in change efforts is described in the following Teamwork Competency feature.[22]

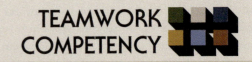

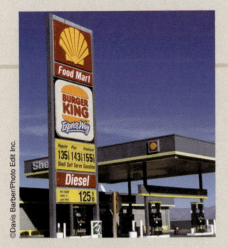

©Davis Barber/Photo Edit Inc.

Involving Employees at Royal Dutch/Shell

With 101,000 employees and $128 billion in annual revenues, Royal Dutch/Shell (known to many people simply as "Shell") is one of the largest companies in the world. Worldwide, it has more than 47,000 retail outlets, which serve more than 1 million customers daily. But Shell's size couldn't protect it from the intense competition being created by European hypermarkets, new competitors throughout the world, and business customers that needed a truly global supplier.

Recognizing the need for change, Shell began an initiative to transform the company. Beginning at the top and working down, managers at each level attended workshops that explained the changes needed. Over a period of two years, the company reorganized and downsized, but more fundamental change was still needed. Steve Miller, Shell's managing director, concluded that empowered employees would help the company find its way into the future. According to him, "Once the folks at the grass roots find that they own the problem, they find that they also own the answer—and they improve things very quickly."

One of the challenges facing Shell was figuring out how better to use its 47,000 retail outlets to boost sales of all of the company's products. To begin tackling that problem, Miller set up a five-day "retailing boot camp." Cross-functional teams (e.g., a trucker, a dealer, and a marketing employee) went to the "camp" and then went home to develop a new business plan for their retail outlets. Later they returned to camp and received feedback on their plans from their peers. After another cycle of revising their plans and getting more feedback, they went home to put their plans into action. After two more months, they returned to camp for a follow-up session that focused on what had worked, what had failed, and what they had learned. "The grassroots employees got to touch the new Shell, and participate in a give-and-take culture," Miller explained. "The energy of our employees spread to the managers above them. These frontline employees taught us to believe in ourselves again."

Miller is convinced that creating change is a bottom-up task. "As people move up, they get further away from the work that goes on in the field—and as a result they tend to devalue it. People get caught up in broad strategic issues, legal issues, stakeholder issues. But what really drives the business is the work that gets done down at the coalface [the frontline]."

Set Goals. For change to be effective, goals should be set before the change effort is started. If possible, the goals should be (1) stated in clear and measurable terms, (2) consistent with the organization's overall goals and policies, and (3) realistically attainable. For example, when a take-out pizza business in Virginia decided that it needed to improve driver safety, it began by collecting systematic information about behaviors (e.g., the extent to which drivers came to complete stops at intersections). Management shared the information with employees and asked them to set specific goals for improvement. During the months that followed, driving behavior was monitored and charts were used to inform employees of their progress toward meeting those goals. Employees participating in goal setting showed improvement in several areas of behavior, including some for which they hadn't even set specific goals.[23]

Anticipate Resistance and Take Action to Reduce It

Few planned organizational change efforts go as smoothly as managers would like. As we have already noted, most run into some amount of resistance. To deal successfully with resistance, managers must learn to anticipate it and then head it off, if at all possible.

Experienced managers are all too aware of the various forms that resistance can take: Immediate criticism, malicious compliance, sabotage, insincere agreement, silence, deflection, and in-your-face defiance, strikes, and output restrictions are just a few examples.[24] Some managers don't even initiate needed changes because they feel incapable of overcoming expected resistance. Successful managers understand why people resist change and what can be done to overcome such resistance.

Some resistance to change may actually be useful. Employees can operate as a check-and-balance mechanism to ensure that management properly plans and implements change. Justifiable resistance that causes management to think through its proposed changes more carefully may result in better decision making. Effective change efforts rest on the ability of managers to overcome resistance. The commonly used methods for doing so are education, participation, and incentives.

In general, individuals—and sometimes even entire organizations—tend to resist change for four reasons: fear, vested interests, misunderstandings, and cynicism.[25]

Fear. To be able to reduce resistance to change, managers first of all must not be afraid of resistance—and then help employees not to be afraid of change or its consequences. Some people resist change because they fear that they'll be unable to develop the competencies required to be effective in the new situation. A common obstacle to organizational change is the reluctance of managers and employees to change their attitudes and learn the new behaviors that the organization requires.

Even when employees understand and accept that they need to change, doing so often is difficult because they fear the consequences. When Mercedes-Benz Credit Corporation set out to restructure its operations in the United States, CEO Georg Bauer knew that fear could be a problem because restructuring often means downsizing. "It was absolutely essential to establish a no-fear element in this whole change process," he said. Rather than resist change, he wanted employees to help create a new, more efficient organization by expressing their ideas about where to cut and how to do work differently.[26]

The Competent Manager	Georg Bauer of Mercedes-Benz attacked the problems of fear and vested interests in two ways. He empowered employees to make decisions about how to change their work, and he used financial incentives to convince employees that even cutting their own jobs wouldn't harm them.

Vested Interests. Fear often goes hand in hand with vested interests. People who have vested interests in maintaining things as they are often resist change. This behavior seems to occur even when these people recognize the need for change. Convincing people that change is needed for the good of the organization does not necessarily reduce their resistance to it. They are likely to continue to resist the change if they believe that it conflicts with their own self-interests.[27]

Some managers initiate change believing that anyone with the same information would make the same decision. This assumption isn't always correct. Often top-level managers see change as a way to improve the organization. They may also believe that change will offer them new opportunities to develop their own competencies as they tackle new challenges. In contrast, employees may view proposed changes as upsetting the agreements between themselves and their employer. In particular, they may expect increased workloads and longer hours to be the only rewards for staying around to help implement a major organizational change.[28]

Empowering workers by giving them some control over the change process is an effective way to reduce the stress that employees experience during a change effort.[29] To align employees' self-interests with the goals of Mercedes Benz, Georg Bauer offered the security of a new—and probably better—job to anyone bold enough to eliminate his or her current position. In this successful change effort, four entire layers of management vanished at the suggestion of the managers themselves.[30]

Misunderstandings. People resist change when they don't understand its implications. Unless quickly addressed, misunderstandings and lack of trust build resistance. Top managers must be visible during the change process to spell out clearly the new direction for the organization and what it will mean for everyone involved. Getting employees to discuss their problems openly is crucial to overcoming resistance to change.

When wide-ranging changes are planned, managers should anticipate that misunderstandings will develop and take steps to minimize them. At Prudential Insurance, a specially designed board game (somewhat like *Monopoly*) was used to help employees understand the implications of the company's impending change from a mutual association to a public company. Small groups of employees at all levels and in all types of jobs throughout the company were brought together to play the game, which was both informative and fun. Top management was convinced that this approach to informing the workforce about the implications of the change they were about to experience would enable the change process to go smoothly—and it did.[31]

Cynicism. In some organizations, initiating change efforts is seen simply as something that new managers do to make their mark. Over time, employees see change efforts come and go much like the seasons of the year, as managers implement one fad after the other. Eventually, cynicism sets in and employees refuse to support yet another change "program." Without employee support the change efforts fail, which further contributes to cynicism.[32]

One way to reduce cynicism is to make *successful* change a normal part of daily life in the organization. Employees who are more accustomed to seeing changes occur around them become more open to new change initiatives.[33] Another way to reduce cynicism is by involving employees throughout the change process. Research shows that participation, especially when it is voluntary, usually leads to commitment.[34]

Monitor the Changes

As the process of change unfolds, managers need to monitor employees' reactions as well as results. Measures of employee stress, customer satisfaction, new-product development, market share, profitability, and other results should be tracked to assess both short-term and long-term consequences. The speed, degree, and duration of improvement should all be monitored. Ideally, the measures used for monitoring should be closely tied to the goals and timetables established in the action plan.

Because the continuous monitoring of change is costly and time consuming, assessments typically are made at predetermined intervals. If possible, the first assessment should be made before the change has been implemented. If that is not possible, it should be made as soon as the change process begins. To avoid jumping to premature conclusions, management should make several follow-up assessments. Sometimes a later assessment reveals that the positive effects of change have worn off. Alternatively, it could reveal delayed positive effects. Misjudging the amount of time needed to see the positive results of a change process is perhaps the most common mistake that managers make.

At Alberto-Culver, measures of sales and pretax profits were tracked in order to measure whether its attempts to change were effective. The company's experience is described in the following Planning & Administration Competency feature.[35]

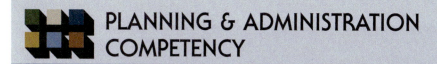

PLANNING & ADMINISTRATION COMPETENCY

Alberto-Culver's Makeover

Alberto-Culver Company may be best known for its VO5 hair care products, but the company also manufactures and markets many other personal care, specialty grocery, and household products worldwide. When Carol Lavin Bernick and her husband took over the leadership roles in the company founded by her parents, the company needed a makeover. Sales were flat, margins were slipping, and the competitive environment was getting tougher due to the emergence of power retailers (such as Wal-Mart). Bernick believed the best way to change the company's performance was to change its culture.

Like other companies, most of their employees understood little about how the company made money or how their jobs affected sales and profits. To change this, the company named 70 growth development leaders (GDLs) and charged them with creating cultural change at the small-group level. Each GDL mentors about a dozen people. As mentors, GDLs help employees understand how their work is related to achieving company goals, participate in performance reviews, and make sure employees understand and take advantage of the company's family friendly benefits. GDLs also meet with the CEO every six weeks or so. The GDLs bring their people's questions to the meeting and work with the top management team to develop solutions. Four years after the GDLs were estab-

lished, the company introduced an award to recognize those who were most successful. A year later, two other change initiatives were introduced: A formal statement of the company's cultural values was published and new employee performance measures were developed.

To assess whether the changes work, Bernick examines the effects on sales and pretax profits. Her analyses of these data have convinced her that the cultural changes being made during the past several years are responsible for the large increases in sales and pretax profits that have accumulated during the past eight years.

IMPLEMENTING CHANGE

Having decided that change is needed, managers have available to them many methods that they can use to make it happen. Here we discuss the four major methods depicted in Figure 12.4. Although we describe each method separately, some combination of these approaches is involved in most large organizational change efforts. Seldom can significant change be based on one of these approaches alone.[36]

3. Identify four methods of organizational change.

Technological Change

Technological change *involves incremental adjustments or radical innovations that affect workflows, production methods, materials, and information systems.* In 1908, Henry Ford changed the workplace by demonstrating how effective assembly-line technologies could be when he launched the mass production of cars. In that new age of mass consumption, the revolutionary assembly-line technology was ideal for making identical goods in volume.

Today, modern organizations are using information technology to achieve equally dramatic change. **Information technology** *(IT) comprises complex networks of computers, telecommunications systems, and remote-controlled devices.* As information technology continues to evolve, it is becoming increasingly easy for organizations to build links between suppliers, producers, distributors, and customers. At Wal-Mart, the electronic cash register monitors the goods sold, their prices, and the amounts remaining on hand (inventory). If the system recognizes that a store is low on Tide detergent, for example, an order is sent to the nearest distribution center to send more Tide to that store. When the distribution center's supply of Tide is low, the system automatically reorders it from P&G. IT also provides an efficient method for communicating with customers. In addition to

Figure 12.4   Methods for Creating Change

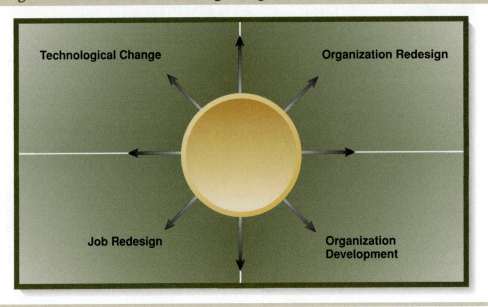

providing comments and feedback to companies, Web sites can be used to inform customers about changes in an organization's products and services. At the Yahoo! Web site, employees and customers hold a continuing electronic conversation about both the changes that customers request and the actions that Yahoo! takes in response.

Organization Redesign

Organization redesign *involves incremental adjustments or radical innovations focused on realigning departments, changing who makes decisions, and merging or reorganizing departments that sell the organization's products.* Recall our discussion of the fundamentals of organizational design in Chapter 11. The organization redesign approach may mean moving from one form of organization to another—for example, from functional to product departmentalization. Sometimes the need for redesign follows directly from implementing new technologies. As Mellon Bank's customers became more comfortable using ATMs, the bank found that it needed 30 percent fewer branches. The remaining branches were redesigned to focus more on selling new products and offering new services than on cashing checks.[37]

Two basic approaches to organization redesign are changing the organization's structure and changing the organization's processes. Regardless of the redesign chosen, the intent usually is to clarify what gives the organization its leadership position with its customers. In other words, design changes should capitalize on the capabilities that differentiate the organization from its competitors. Businesses, goods, or services that don't contribute to this goal are candidates for elimination or sale.

Structural Redesign. Restructuring *typically means reconfiguring the distribution of authority, responsibility, and control in an organization.* Authority, responsibility, and control change radically when entire businesses or divisions are combined or spun off. Thus, when Hewlett-Packard spun off its medical and instruments business, creating Agilent, it used structural redesign to create a radical organizational change.

Downsizing is another familiar approach to structural redesign. Downsizing is usually a reactive response to poor organizational performance, but this often-used method of change doesn't necessarily work. Although downsizing may improve financial performance in the short run, several studies have indicated that downsized firms end up in worse financial shape later.[38] However, no one knows whether such firms would have even survived without the changes undertaken. Regardless of how effective it may be in the long run, downsizing is a painful experience for both those who are let go and those who survive the cuts. The survivors often feel guilty because, somehow, they have been spared, but they also are anxious because they might be next. Survivors often have trouble maintaining a commitment to an organization when they might be "doing time" until the next round of layoffs is announced.[39]

Reengineering. When organizations want to improve their efficiency and the quality of their products and services, they often examine their internal production processes. If they decide to change those processes, they may create change through **reengineering**, *which focuses on creating new ways to get work done.* It often involves the redesign of processes related to logistics, manufacturing, and distribution. The goal is to design the most effective process for making and delivering a product.[40] Effective processes are those that cost the least while at the same time rapidly producing goods and providing services of excellent quality. Thus the starting point is to assess current processes from the customer's point of view.

Often, reengineering is interrelated with other key activities. Recall that many organizations are structured by function and that employees' reactions to change typically are based on its effect on their departments. Reengineering requires employees to think across functions. Reengineering can reduce the amount of "hand-offs" between departments by increasing the amount of resources brought together simultaneously to meet customers' needs. Benefits may include faster delivery time, more accurate billing, and fewer defective products that must be returned. By reengineering its insurance claims processes, National Grange Mutual was able to reduce its response time by 55 percent. This means that customers receive their money faster and with less hassle. After reengineering, customer satisfaction improved as did the company's overall growth rate.[41]

Job Redesign

Job redesign *involves modifying specific employee job responsibilities and tasks.* Whenever a job is modified—whether because of new technology or an organizational redesign—job designs also change. Two dramatically different ways of changing job designs are job simplification and job enrichment.

The oldest approach to job redesign is job simplification. **Job simplification** *involves the scientific analysis of tasks performed by employees in order to discover procedures that produce the maximum output for the minimum input.* Job simplication can involve changing the tasks to be performed, the work methods to be used, and the workflow. Like reengineering, job simplification is founded on engineering concepts. Recall that the scientific management techniques developed by Frederick Taylor defined jobs and designed tasks on the basis of time-and-motion studies (see Chapter 2). But there is a big difference between these two approaches to change. Reengineering focuses on an entire process, which may involve many employees working in many parts of the organization. In contrast, the focus of job simplification is the work done by employees in a particular job. For example, if McDonald's restaurants reengineered its facilities, it would redesign its stores in their entirety—including the order-taking technology, kitchen design, and eating areas. However, if the job of cashier needed to be changed, the company could simply undergo a job simplification.

The downside of job simplification is that it leads to low employee commitment and high turnover. Most current competitive challenges require a committed and involved workforce that is able to make decisions and experiment with new ways of doing things. Many people seek jobs that allow greater discretion and offer more of a challenge. Thus designing jobs with employee needs in mind requires a different approach.

Changing job specifications to broaden and add challenge to the tasks required and to increase productivity is called **job enrichment**. Job enrichment has four unique aspects. First, it changes the basic relationships between employees and their work. Job enrichment is based on the assumption that interesting and challenging work can be a source of employee satisfaction and involvement.

Second, job enrichment directly changes employee behaviors in ways that gradually lead to more positive attitudes about the organization and a better self-image. Because enriched jobs usually increase feelings of autonomy and personal freedom, employees are likely to develop attitudes that support the new job-related behaviors.

Third, job enrichment offers numerous opportunities for initiating other types of organizational change. Technical problems are likely to develop when jobs are changed, which offers management an opportunity to refine the technology used. Interpersonal problems almost inevitably arise between managers and subordinates and sometimes among coworkers who have to relate to one another in different ways. These situations offer opportunities for developing teamwork and communication competencies.

Finally, job enrichment can humanize an organization. Individuals can experience the psychological lift that comes from developing new competencies and doing a job well. Individuals are encouraged to grow and push themselves.

Organization Development

Many people-oriented methods for changing organizations are commonly grouped under the broad label of organization development. **Organization development** *(OD) is a planned, long-range, behavioral science strategy for understanding, changing, and developing an organization's workforce in order to improve its effectiveness.*[42] Although OD methods frequently include design, technological, and task changes, their primary focus is on changing people. Of the many OD methods available, three of the most commonly used are focus groups, survey feedback, and team building.

Focus Groups. When focus groups are used for organizational development, the objective is usually to learn about how employees feel about the current situation in their organization. Understanding the perspective of employees is important when designing change efforts. A **focus group discussion** *is a carefully planned discussion among several employees about a specific topic or issue of interest, which is led by a trained facilitator.* The facilitator's roles are to create an open, nonthreatening environment and to keep the discussion on track. Because the objective is to collect information systematically, several focus groups are conducted throughout the organization, and notes are taken at each focus group meeting. Figure 12.5 shows a typical setup for a focus group discussion.[43]

Survey Feedback. Focus groups can reveal a great deal about how employees think and feel, but they are not practical for gathering data from a large number of employees. When managers want to hear from several hundred or even thousands of employees, they may find that it is more practical to use survey feedback as a method for organization development. **Survey feedback** *is a process that allows managers and employees to report their thoughts and feelings about the organization and to learn about how others think and feel about their own behaviors.*[44] Such information becomes the basis for group discussion and the stimulus for change. Accurate feedback from others about behaviors and job performance is one of the primary bases of OD.

Feedback is obtained by means of a questionnaire developed and distributed to all employees, who complete it and turn it in anonymously. The content of the questionnaire depends on the areas of most concern to the organization. Typically, however, employee surveys tap into employees' feelings of commitment and satisfaction, their assessments of the climate for innovation, the degree to which they feel that the organization is customer oriented, and their attitudes toward supervision and management practices.

Figure 12.5   How to Set Up a Focus Group Discussion

The facilitator explains the topic to be discussed, the role of the scribe, and how the organization will use the results of the focus group discussion.

The participants come prepared to discuss a specific topic. If confidentiality is a concern, participants are chosen from different units of the organization, not the same work group.

The scribe takes notes about what is said, but not who says it.

When employee surveys are designed to address issues of strategic importance, they can be used to enhance the organization's competitive advantage.

When Intel recently conducted its employee survey, the company's 85,000 employees could respond to the survey over the Web, or they could fill out a paper version of the survey. Results from the survey were reported separately for each of the company's 36 business units around the world. After studying and discussing their results, and making comparisons to other units, managers were expected to develop action plans for improvements within their units.[45]

Team Building. As organizations become flatter and rely more on teams to get work done, the importance of team building has also grown. **Team building** *is a process that develops the ability of team members to collaborate effectively so they can perform the tasks assigned to them.* Team building activities often emphasize the importance of developing a group climate that is safe, where people trust each other and feel free to express their feelings and share their perceptions about daily experiences and hassles. Outdoor adventures and various types of games are popular approaches to team building. Hiding feelings or not being accepted by the group diminishes the individual's willingness to work constructively toward solutions to problems. Openness can be risky, but it also promotes creativity and can usually help people effectively plan solutions to problems and carry them out.[46]

Combining Methods of Change

Organizational change is a complex undertaking. Usually, large-scale change efforts involve the use of a combination of methods. Because information is integral to the functioning of most organizations, any restructuring effort is likely to have implications for the design and use of information systems. In fact a new term, *e-engineering*, has recently been suggested as a description of reengineering initiatives that use Web-based technology as the primary method for managing business-to-business processes (e.g., purchasing and account management). After it merged with Allied Signal, Honeywell International used e-engineering to improve the functioning of engineers working on product development. Using the Web, engineers located throughout the United States can work as a virtual team to design everything from airline cockpits to electron microscopes.[47]

Purchasing and installing enterprise resource planning (ERP) software is another management decision that often involves many forms of organizational change. ERP software is designed to be an enterprise-wide solution to all the information technology needs a company might have. It can pull together information about the company's financial performance, customer relations, human resources, manufacturing, distribution, and so on. Usually, it is extremely costly and can be difficult to implement well. Changing to an ERP system involves more than having employees learn a new software program. They often must also learn to do a variety of new administrative tasks. For example, salespeople may be asked to record information about the source of all new customers and the reasons for customers canceling their orders. The information doesn't help the salesperson directly, but marketing uses it to assess the productivity of advertising campaigns. When managers decide to purchase ERP software, they may think they are just making a change in the company's IT system. But that's a mistake. As described in the following Communication Competency feature, installing ERP software is a radical change that can affect the organizational design, the tasks people do, and the way employees feel about their employers.[48]

©Eyewire/Getty Images

COMMUNICATION COMPETENCY

Fairchild Semiconductor

Fairchild Semiconductor was created as a spin-off from National Semiconductor. After its birth, one of its first goals was to transition from National's data management system to one of its own. It chose an ERP application from Peoplesoft, and then set about adapting its processes to meet the software's requirements. The first step was to form teams of employees from all over the world to rework the company's business processes in finance, manufacturing, logistics, and human resources. The goal was to replace all of the customized business processes throughout the company with "plain vanilla" processes that fit the generic software system.

Once new processes were designed, extensive training was needed before and after the rollout of the new system. Besides teaching employees the new tasks they would be expected to perform, the training sessions explained why these new tasks were important. The goal was to ensure that employees understood how their own work was related to the overall business processes. The company felt that employees would be less likely to take short cuts to reduce their own workloads if they understood how their own contributions affected other people in the company and the bottom line. According to experts, this is a key step for companies that install new ERP software. For many companies, teaching employees about how their tasks are connected to basic business processes eventually leads to deeper cultural change in the organization.

To build employees' confidence in their ability to use the new system and reduce their fears, training sessions provided plenty of time for people to practice using the software and receive feedback. At Fairchild, installing new ERP software was a change that resulted in employees becoming more knowledgeable about the business and more excited about their own roles within the company.

ROLE OF INNOVATION IN ORGANIZATIONAL CHANGE

Innovation *is the process of creating and implementing a new idea.*[49] When Jeff Bezos founded Amazon.com, he invented a new way for people to purchase books—over the Internet. The new ideas that lead to innovation may come from inside the company, but often they come from somewhere else. For example, many companies copied Bezos's new invention and began selling products other than books over the Internet.

4. Describe how innovation relates to organizational change.

Although they are not the same, change and innovation are closely related. Change often involves new ideas of some sort. The new idea may be the creation of a new product or process, or it can be an idea about how to change completely the way business is done. But new ideas are not the only reason for creating organizational change. For example, a CEO may decide that the organizational culture needs to change in order to fit its global strategy, but the new culture that is created in the company does not depend on a truly new invention. Successful organizations understand that both innovation and change are required to satisfy their most important stakeholders.

Strategic Importance of Innovation

A dynamic, changing environment makes innovation and change as important—if not more important—for established organizations as they are for new organizations. Successful organizations can't rest on their prior successes. If they become complacent, competitors are sure to woo customers away. Organizational decline and even extinction may follow.

When a company fails to innovate and change as needed, customers, employees, and even the larger community can all suffer. Eastman Kodak, headquartered in Rochester, New York, was the biggest employer in the region and the country's best known name in photography. But when its main competitor, Tokyo-based Fuji, reduced the price of its color film by as much as 30 percent, Kodak's profits plummeted. To cut costs, Kodak announced that it would reduce its workforce by more than 10,000 people worldwide. Worried about job security, some of the 34,000 local employees cut back on their lunches at local restaurants, and when they did go to lunch they brought fewer smiles with them. George Fisher, who was CEO at the time, acknowledged the pain: "The anxiety that we create when we do things like we're doing is immense, and you can't help but generate some degree of ill will."[50] Eventually, Fisher himself became a victim of Kodak's lack of innovation and appropriate change efforts when he was asked to step down to make room for a new CEO.

Types of Innovation

Because new ideas can take many forms, many types of innovation are possible. Three basic types of innovation are technical, process, and administrative.

Technical. *The creation of new goods and services is one main type of innovation that is often referred to as* **technical innovation**. Many technical innovations occur through basic R&D efforts intended to satisfy demanding customers who are always seeking new, better, faster, and/or cheaper products. For example, numerous technical innovations have spurred the shift to wireless communications systems. Even in the absence of a new product, innovation can still occur, however.

Process. Process innovation *involves creating a new way of producing, selling, and/or distributing an existing good or service.* The introduction of do-it-yourself online stock trading represents a process innovation. At Toyota, *oobeya* (pronounced "ooh-bay-yuh") was a process innovation that enabled the company to dramatically lower the cost of producing automobiles. In Japanese, *oobeya* means "big open office." At Toyota, oobeya is a process for bringing together big teams of people involved in all aspects of the business to discuss how to cut costs out of the design, production, and sales processes. Before *oobeya* was introduced, each unit was given a budget. All they were expected to do was not go over their budget. With *oobeya*, which was used to design the new Matrix, cutting costs without reducing quality became the goal. By encouraging everyone to work together to cut costs, Toyota succeeded in producing high-quality cars that cost substantially less than similar models offered by competitors.[51]

Administrative. Administrative innovation *occurs when creation of a new organization design better supports the creation, production, and delivery of goods and services.* In the 1980s, many organizations began to experiment with flexible work schedules and telecommuting. Although these ideas had been around for some time, the widespread use of personal computers opened up new possibilities for implementing them on a large scale. Adopting a policy of flexible work schedules and/or telecommuting often means that an organization must find innovative ways to supervise and coordinate work effectively. Network and virtual organizations (see Chapter 11) are examples of more recent administrative innovations.

Convergence of Forms. Various types of innovation often go hand in hand. For example, the rapid development of business-to-business e-commerce represents process innovation. This new process required numerous technical innovations in computer hardware and software. As organizations began to use business-to-business e-commerce, administrative innovations soon followed. Implementation of process innovations required organizational change.

By necessity, doing something new means doing things differently. Thus innovation and organizational change go hand in hand. Table 12.2 illustrates how new technology for making paper led to numerous types of change at Champion International, a paper manufacturer.[52]

Occasionally, the convergence of many types of innovation can fundamentally alter the basis of competition within an industry. That's the kind of challenge that appeals to Ted Waitt, founder and chairman of Gateway, Inc., the computer company. In his vision of the future, Waitt imagines that computers will be about as exciting—and profitable—as telephones. The opportunities for value and wealth creation will lie "beyond the box"—not in the hardware of the computer but in related gadgets and the services to which the computer provides access.[53]

Architecture for Innovation

Because innovation is so important to success in a variety of industries, managers in all types of organizations are expected to help build infrastructures that encourage and support innovation and change. If an organization's basic infrastructure is in place before specific change initiatives are planned, the organization will be prepared to transform itself as needed. One of management's

Table 12.2 Organizational Changes That Followed Technical Innovations in Paper Manufacturing at Champion International

Key Changes Made at Champion International. . .

- New technology and restructuring of 10 of its 11 paper mills.
- Jobs redesigned for 7,500 of 24,000 employees.
- Hierarchical management structure changed to team-based structure, reducing management layers from five to two.
- Functional support groups (accounting, purchasing, marketing, etc.) restructured horizontally to support business processes.
- Shift to high-involvement management approach means employees now work with managers and customers to improve product and service quality.
- Employees participate in hiring process, evaluating peers on performance, and promotion decisions.
- Major investments made in training to improve business knowledge, technical skills, problem-solving and team operating skills.
- Introduced performance-based pay and gain sharing.
- New more cooperative approach to negotiations with unions results in more "partnership agreements" and fewer traditional labor contracts.

. . . And the Results

- Company moved up in *Fortune's* list of Most Admired Companies six years in a row.
- Reduced administrative costs.
- Mill production increased 32%.
- Productivity increased 47%.

---

primary concerns should be to ensure that the organization maintains a state of readiness so that it can move quickly and effectively when innovation is needed. Building an infrastructure and maintaining a state of readiness require an architecture for innovation. Table 12.3 summarizes several key features of that architecture. Briefly, managers should

- develop a learning environment and a learning orientation among employees,
- foster workforce resilience, and
- provide a support system for innovation.[54]

LEARNING ORGANIZATIONS

A **learning organization** *has both the drive and the capabilities to modify or transform itself and improve its performance continuously.* It learns from past experiences, it learns from customers, it learns from various parts of the company, and it learns from other companies.[55] In learning organizations, successful innovation and change aren't events with clear-cut beginnings and endings. Rather, they are never-ending processes that have become part of the daily routine. Innovation and change are not infrequent and special—they are simply a way of organizational life. As one manager observed, this way of life helps a learning organization avoid organizational stupidity.

When an organization's environment is unstable, learning may require a lot of exploration and experimentation. Failures may be frequent, but so are unexpected achievements. When an organization's environment is more stable, learning is more likely to occur through a systematic process of testing alternative approaches.[56] In either

5. Discuss how learning organizations foster change.

Table 12.3	Architecture for Innovation

Learning Orientation

■ Managers allow employees to identify and solve important problems.

■ Managers openly discuss organizational successes and failures with employees.

■ Formal and informal systems keep employees informed of customers' preferences and their evaluations of the services and products offered by the organization.

■ Small-scale experiments are used to resolve emerging problems before they reach the crisis stage.

Resilient Workforce

■ Hiring and promotion decisions are used to weed out people who resist change.

■ Employees are trained in the fundamentals of organizational change and innovation.

■ Because successful efforts are celebrated, employees have confidence in the organization's capacity for innovation and change.

Support for Innovation

■ Formal and informal systems facilitate the free flow of knowledge throughout the organization.

■ Reward and recognition systems encourage the development of competencies needed for innovation, including technical knowledge, teamwork, and communication.

■ Key measures are monitored to assess the effectiveness of the process of innovation and the outcomes of innovation.

situation, however, learning organizations change at a rate at least as fast as—or even faster than—the rate of change in their environments. Moreover, the learning process is managed systematically and professionally—it doesn't occur randomly.

Through continuous innovation and change, a learning organization creates a sustainable competitive advantage in its industry. Five distinctive features of learning organizations are illustrated in Figure 12.6:

■ shared leadership,
■ culture of innovation,
■ customer-focused strategy,
■ organic organization design, and
■ intensive use of information.

Shared Leadership

In learning organizations, responsibility for making decisions, directing operations, and achieving organizational goals is shared among all employees. These leadership tasks aren't the responsibility of top-level managers alone. *Everyone* is encouraged to find ways to improve the organization and its products.[57]

Empowerment provides a way to integrate tasks and allow employees to buy into the organization's goals. At Nantucket Nectars, a participatory leadership style encourages employees to learn by allowing them to make their own mistakes. The founders of this company adopted this approach because they believed that it would yield better quality beverages. When people discover better ways of doing their jobs, they see that their efforts *do* make a difference. That discovery in turn strengthens their involvement in making a better product and improving customer satisfaction.[58]

Figure 12.6   Characteristics of a Learning Organization

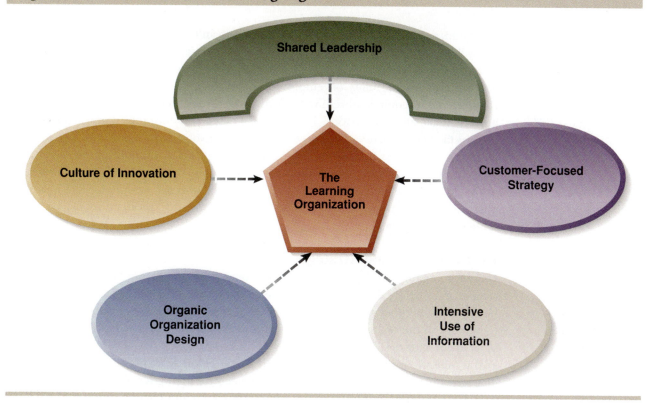

Culture of Innovation

Shared leadership goes hand in hand with a culture of innovation. For learning organizations, successful innovation is a never-ending process that becomes part of the daily routine. Instead of being an infrequent and special event that takes people's attention away from the central work of the organization, it is the central work of the organization. At Southwest Airlines, employees are always looking for better ways to meet customers' needs for low-cost, reliable air travel. When clerks suggested doing away with tickets, co-founder Herb Kelleher, who was the CEO at that time, encouraged them to experiment with this innovative idea on selected routes. Long before other airlines adopted the idea of electronic ticketing, Southwest Airlines' passengers made reservations over the phone and received only a PIN number—no ticket was issued. At the gate, the PIN number was exchanged for a boarding pass. Passengers who needed a receipt got one promptly through the mail.[59]

Community. Learning organizations nurture a sense of community and trust. Everyone works together, respecting each other and being able to communicate openly and honestly. Problems can't be avoided or handled by just passing them along to another department or up the hierarchy. Conflict and debate are accepted as responsible forms of communication. People willingly share the information and knowledge they have, so others can benefit from it.[60]

A sense of community also gives employees the feeling that they are important and are being treated fairly. Employees cooperate because they want to, not because they have to.[61] When people feel that they are part of a community, they are more willing to make the extra effort needed to find and fix problems. They also are more likely to share their solutions with their coworkers. As explained earlier in this chapter, Toyota uses *oobeya* as a means

The
Competent
Manager

"There are no taboos in oobeya. *Everyone in that room is an expert. They all play a part in building the car. With everyone being equally important, we don't confine ourselves to just one way of thinking our way out of a problem."*

Takeshi Yoshida
Chief Engineer
Toyota

for creating a sense of community among employees working in different parts of the company.

Continuous Learning. A learning organization can't succeed without employees who are willing to learn and change. Hence learning organizations encourage individual learning in numerous ways. One of the most successful ways is through empowerment, which places responsibility on employees for problem finding and problem solving.[62] Empowerment requires more involvement and learning than does simply having someone else make all the decisions. The flat, team-based structure found in learning organizations facilitates learning because employees are involved in a broad range of activities and work with others from whom they can learn. Formal training is another way to ensure continuous learning. For managers, in particular, continuous learning is essential to develop the competencies needed by generalists who are knowledgeable in several areas, as opposed to specialists who understand only finance, production, marketing, or some other function.

Customer-Focused Strategy

Learning organizations add value for customers by identifying needs—in some instances, even before customers have done so—and then developing ways to satisfy those needs. Customer-focused strategies reflect a clear understanding of how important customers are to the organization's long-term success and serve as the basis for aligning all of its major activities.

At a time when many organizations and shareholders look no farther than the next quarterly financial report, acceptance of the need for a long-term perspective is crucial for a learning organization. The processes of learning and change simply take time. At Knight-Ridder, for example, declining newspaper circulation was anticipated long before it became a reality. As early as the 1970s, the company began experimenting with other forms of news delivery, including TV broadcasts, but eventually abandoned them as failures. During the 1980s, the company experimented with online business services and again had little success at first. Eventually, the learning paid off. With several years of experience behind it, the company bought Dialog Information Services, which was the world's largest online full-text information service. With this acquisition, Knight-Ridder was transformed from a traditional newspaper company into a leader in the provision of online business information.[63]

Organic Organization Design

The design of learning organizations often reflects their emphasis on organic rather than mechanistic systems. In particular, they emphasize the use of teams, strategic alliances, and boundaryless networks.

Teams. In learning organizations, employees with dissimilar expertise form multidisciplinary teams. To encourage the free flow of ideas, these teams may be formed only as needed, on a project-by-project basis. "Bosses" are practically nonexistent. Team members have considerable autonomy to make key decisions and can take action without waiting for requests to crawl through a bureaucratic decision-making process. Compared to functional structures, team-based structures are more flexible and fluid. Knowledge flows more easily among members of the organization, which contributes to learning and creates opportunities for innovation.

Strategic Alliances. In addition to experimenting on their own, many learning organizations use strategic alliances with suppliers, customers, and even competitors as a method of learning. In Japan, Amgen, a biotech company, formed an alliance with Kirin Brewery. From Kirin, Amgen learned about fermentation processes, which are crucial for producing synthetic blood-clotting protein. From Amgen, Kirin learned about amino acid–protein combinations that can act as catalysts to speed up the brewing process.[64]

Boundaryless Networks. Network structures, which we described in Chapter 11, maximize the linkages among organizations. Such linkages in turn provide learning opportunities and generate innovation in goods and services.[65] Network structures seem to work in part because they create a sense of community among a larger pool of people who share their diverse knowledge and expertise, using it to find creative solutions to difficult problems.[66]

Intensive Use of Information

Information is the lifeblood of learning organizations. To be effective they must undertake extensive scanning, be measurement oriented, and foster shared problems and solutions.

Scanning the Environment. In learning organizations, managers strive to be creators of change. Staying attuned to emerging trends is their passion. To ensure that they don't miss an important trend or change, learning organizations aggressively scan both the external and internal environments for information. As a result, large amounts of information are obtained from the external environment about how customers are reacting to current goods and services, how customers compare them to those of competitors, and whether new competitors may be on the horizon. Such information is essential to judgments concerning the need to create new products to meet customer demand. Information obtained from the internal environment indicates how employees feel about the organization, whether their attention is focused on customers, whether they feel energized to solve difficult problems, and whether key employees are likely to defect to competitors.

Measurement Oriented. Organizations learn in order to improve. To judge improvement, an organization needs to know where it was before and where it is now. Systematic measurement makes assessing improvement possible. In learning organizations, employees have access to data about customer satisfaction, profit and loss, market share, employee commitment, and competitors' strategies, among other things. Data are gathered, monitored, disseminated, and used throughout the organization.

Pharmaceutical companies are good examples of learning organizations, because without continuous learning they would have no new products to offer the public. Furthermore, the process of developing new products and bringing them to market takes about eight years, on average. Throughout this time, pharmaceutical companies typically measure their learning progress in a variety of ways. For example, they keep track of the expertise of their scientists and engineers, the number of scientific papers published by their scientists, patent applications, and FDA drug approvals, among many other things. By monitoring measures such as these, pharmaceutical firms can better predict in advance how many new products they are likely to be able to introduce in future years.[67]

Communication. Numerical data (measurements) aren't the only type of information considered important in learning organizations. "Soft" information—sometimes referred to as *tacit knowledge* or *gossip*—is valued too. Employees who serve customers day in and day out may not need to read the results of monthly customer satisfaction surveys to know where problems lie. The anecdotal evidence they gather through dozens of service encounters may be enough to begin seeing a pattern of pieces that all seem to fit together, make sense, and suggest needed improvements. When Xerox wanted to improve its service for customers, it hired an anthropologist to study how service reps went about their jobs. The anthropologist concluded that informal storytelling and conversations around the water cooler were important activities for sharing problems and solutions.[68]

By sharing information about the problems they face and the solutions they discover, employees minimize the number of times they reinvent the wheel and speed up the process of organizational learning. This statement about the importance of communication is as true for executives as it is for front-line workers.[69]

Whether they are newly established or mature, organizations of all types maintain their vitality by innovating, changing, and learning from their experiences. As their external environments become increasingly competitive and turbulent, the most effective organizations will be those that build change, innovation, and learning into their normal operations.

1. Describe four types of organizational change.

Organizational changes vary in both degree and timing. In terms of degree, change can be radical or incremental. In terms of timing, change can be reactive or anticipatory. As shown earlier in Figure 12.2, combinations of these possibilities create four basic types of change: radical reactive change, radical anticipatory change, incremental reactive change, and incremental anticipatory change.

2. Explain the planning process for organizational change.

Although change often involves a bit of chaos, organizations can usually reduce its amount and impact by carefully planning for major change. Through planning, the organization begins to unfreeze and prepares for the change. The key planning activities are (1) assessing the environment; (2) determining whether a performance gap exists and, if so, its nature and magnitude; (3) diagnosing organizational problems; (4) articulating and communicating a vision for the future; (5) developing and implementing an action plan for the change; (6) anticipating and making plans to reduce resistance; and (7) developing a way to monitor change after the main initiatives have been implemented.

3. Identify four methods of organizational change.

Many approaches to implementing change are possible. Four general methods are technological change, organization redesign, job redesign, and organization development. Technological change often involves changing the way work is done by adopting new information technologies. The organization redesign method may involve changing the organizational structure and/or organizational processes. It normally affects large portions of an organization. Downsizing and reengineering are examples of this method. Job redesign involves changing employees' jobs by either simplifying or enriching them. Organization development can be used to change employee attitudes and behaviors. Focus groups and survey feedback permit managers and employees to provide information about a range of topics, including job satisfaction, organizational commitment, and perceptions of supervisory and managerial behaviors. Team building is used to improve the functioning of people who must work together to achieve assigned tasks. Change efforts often involve a combination of these methods.

4. Describe how innovation relates to organizational change.

Innovation is the process of creating and implementing a new idea. Three basic types of innovation are technical, process, and administrative. Organizational change refers to any transformation in the design or functioning of an organization. Generally, innovations require organizational change. Innovation and change are important to both new and established organizations, owing to the dynamic nature of the external environments of most organizations.

5. Discuss how learning organizations foster change.

Organizations are redesigning themselves to become learning organizations capable of quickly adapting their practices to satisfy the needs of their customers. The basic features of such organizations are leadership that is shared, a culture that supports innovation, a strategy focused on customers, an organic organization design, and an intensive use of information. In a learning organization, change is not a special event; it's a natural part of the organization's continuous attempts to satisfy customers.

Action plan
Administrative innovation
Anticipatory change
Focus group discussion

Incremental change
Information technology
Innovation
Job enrichment

Job redesign
Job simplification
Learning organization
Organization development
Organization redesign
Organizational change
Organizational diagnosis
Performance gap
Process innovation

Radical change
Reactive change
Reengineering
Restructuring
Survey feedback
Team building
Technical innovation
Technological change
Tempered radicals

QUESTIONS FOR DISCUSSION and COMPETENCY DEVELOPMENT

1. Which aspects of an organization's environment are more likely to lead to radical rather than incremental change? Explain.

2. Select one of the four methods of change described in this chapter. Is the method you selected better suited to anticipatory or reactive change? Explain

3. Evaluate the following statement: "We trained hard, but it seemed that every time we were beginning to form into teams, we would be reorganized. We tend to meet any new situation by reorganizing, and what a wonderful method it can be for creating the illusion of progress while producing confusion, inefficiency, and demoralization" (Petronius, 210 B.C.). Is the way you react to innovation and change a fixed aspect of your personality? Do you think you can develop the competencies needed to be effective in organizations experiencing change? Explain.

4. A manager once remarked, "No matter how much planning you do, the process of organizational change is always full of surprises." This is probably true, so why bother planning? Describe how planning can be useful even when anticipating everything that will happen during an organizational change is impossible.

5. Schools and colleges are supposed to be places of learning, but many fall short of being learning organizations. Choose a school or college with which you are familiar and explain how it could use one or more of the four basic change methods described in this chapter to become a more effective learning organization.

6. The process of organizational change requires extensive coordination among all parts of an organization. For global organizations, coordination can be particularly challenging. Describe how information technology can be used to address this issue.

7. Time is a precious resource to managers, especially when they are in the process of major organizational change. Knowing that communication is important at that time, many rely heavily on formal outlets such as speeches and mass e-mailings. Describe the main advantages and disadvantages of using formal (versus informal) communication channels during times of change. Should informal communication be emphasized over formal communication at certain stages of the change process? Explain.

CASE FOR COMPETENCY DEVELOPMENT

CHANGE AT HEWLETT-PACKARD

In Silicon Valley, Hewlett-Packard (HP) has long been revered as the area's first "garage start-up." Founded in the 1930s, it grew steadily to become a complex, global company. In fact, by the end of the 20th century, HP had become so complex that top management decided to split the company into more manageable parts. Reflecting just how much the company had changed, the split separated the core medical and instruments business on which the company was founded—which is now Agilent Technologies—from the computer side of the busi-

ness. At about the same time, then-CEO Lew Platt announced he would leave HP, to be replaced by Carleton (Carly) Fiorina. Formerly an executive at Lucent, Fiorina stepped into her new role as the first-ever outsider to serve as HP's CEO. Besides implementing the spin-off of Agilent Technologies, she was expected to lead HP through a radical transformation. Early in her tenure as CEO, one of the most radical aspects of the company's transformation was acquiring Compaq, another computer company.

A successful company by many standards, HP nevertheless had been experiencing significant problems. While the rest of the industry was focused on customers'

"Internet time," HP's product development process gave more weight to the preferences of the company's engineers than to the preferences of potential customers. And while other competitors were running on "Internet time" and experiencing rapid growth, both HP's decision-making processes and rate of growth lumbered along too slowly. According to Fiorina, the need for change at HP was urgent. "Time does not mean what it used to mean. In the Internet Age, things move very, very quickly. And we have to move quickly enough to catch up with that pace," she explained.

Fiorina's vision for change at HP was to preserve the best parts of the company and reinvent the rest. As part of HP's reinvention, it has entered into several new strategic alliances—a joint venture with Kodak, partnerships with Ford and Delta Air Lines, and a variety of strategic relationships with companies such as Yahoo!, Cisco, and Amazon.com. It also reorganized its existing businesses into fewer, more clearly focused units. At the center of it all were the HP labs.

For Fiorina, the best parts of the company are its technological know-how and its culture, which values respect, integrity, teamwork, and contribution. HP's culture is strongly rooted in the company's early garage days. Today, a poster of the "Rules of the Garage" reminds employees that Bill Hewlett and Dave Packard believed that bureaucracy and company politics were stupid and destructive. Inventing something significant was the goal. In an effort to avoid the problems of bureaucracy, HP's past leaders encouraged decentralization. To avoid politics, they used a high-involvement approach to decision making and sought to reach consensus about major issues. But for a large company operating in the Internet age, this approach is now considered too slow.

To speed things up at HP, Fiorina adopted a take-charge, fast-paced style. When making decisions, she gets input but then makes it clear that she will decide what to do and move ahead with it. This style was clearly evident as Fiorina charged ahead with her plan to acquire Compaq, HP's archrival, despite doubts among other executives and Wall Street analysts. She explains her approach this way: "If you want people to speed up, you speed up. You don't talk about it, you do it. If you don't walk the talk, nothing will matter to the contrary. In fact, worse, the result will be cynicism, and that would be devastating."[70]

Questions

1. Refer to Figure 12.2 and the related discussion. What type of change was HP undergoing?

2. What seemed to trigger the company's realization that change was needed?

3. Why are change and innovation important to HP?

4. Suppose you are an HP manager. What signs of resistance would you look for among your employees? How could you tell whether or not your employees were enthusiastic or reluctant to make the changes needed in your unit?

Managing Human Resources

LEARNING OBJECTIVES

After studying this chapter, you should be able to:

1. Explain the strategic importance of managing human resources effectively.

2. Describe several important laws and government regulations that affect how organizations manage their human resources.

3. Explain the objective of human resources planning and describe how organizations respond to the unpredictability of future business needs.

4. Describe the hiring process.

5. Describe several types of training and development programs.

6. Describe several principles for improving the accuracy of managers' appraisals of employee performance.

7. Describe the basic elements of a monetary compensation package.

Chapter Outline

To many people, Cisco is an $18 billion high-technology stealth company: the fastest growing company of its size in history, faster even than Microsoft, with a market capitalization of more than $150 billion. Cisco competes in markets where hardware is obsolete in 18 months or less and software in 6 months.

Cisco was founded in 1984 by Leonard Bosack and Sandy Lerner, a husband-and-wife team who invented a technology to link together separate computer systems at Stanford University. Today, it is ranked near the top of *Fortune's* list of the "100 Best Companies to Work For." Operating in more than 54 countries around the world, it provides products that enable computers to communicate with each other, offering customers end-to-end scalable network solutions. At company headquarters in the heart of Silicon Valley, where employee turnover averages al-

most 30 percent, the turnover at Cisco is around 8 percent.

As part of its approach to managing human resources, Cisco espouses five core values: a dedication to customer success, innovation and learning, openness, teamwork, and doing more with less. Each of these values is continually articulated by CEO John Chambers and reinforced in the mission statement, current initiatives, human resources policies and practices, and the culture of the company. To encourage openness, Chambers holds a monthly "birthday breakfast" meeting open to anyone with a recent birthday and answers every question put to him—no matter how tough the question. Teamwork is so important that disregarding it is one of three things that can get a person fired at Cisco. To reinforce the important link between business initiatives and the work that people do, every employee is expected to be able to recite the top initiatives.

Tremendous peer pressure ensures that employees know about these initiatives.

Cisco's human resources policies and practices are aligned with the business strategy and continually reinforced. The recruitment and selection system identifies exactly the kind of people they need. Cisco recruits at art fairs, microbrewery festivals, and other places frequented by potential employees. Rather than listing specific job openings, Cisco's ads feature their Web site address, which provides up-to-the-minute information about hiring needs. To select new employees, Cisco uses a minimum of five job interviews. The reward system is also carefully aligned with the strategy and values of the company. Stock options are distributed generously, with a full 40 percent of all Cisco stock options in the hands of individual employees without managerial rank.[1]

STRATEGIC IMPORTANCE

1. Explain the strategic importance of managing human resources effectively.

Human resources management *(HRM) refers to the philosophies, policies, and practices that an organization uses to affect the behaviors of people who work for the organization.* It includes activities related to hiring, training and development, performance review and evaluation, and compensation. The strategic use of all of these activities can improve organizational effectiveness. In fact, according to a recent study by Deloitte & Touche, the market value of companies with state-of-the-art human resources management is 43 percent higher than that of companies that do not use these practices.[2] This chapter describes several of the most valuable HR practices used by the best employers.

Activities related to managing human resources occur in all organizations, from the smallest to the largest. At a minimum, every company has jobs, which comprise a set of responsibilities. To get these jobs done, people are hired and compensated in return for the work they do. Few employers continue to pay a person who cannot or will not perform satisfactorily, so at least some measurement of performance generally occurs—even if it is just to keep track of how many hours were worked. To ensure that people know what they are supposed to do, some instruction and training are usually given, though these may be minimal.

Successful organizations see human resources as assets that need to be managed conscientiously and in tune with the organization's needs. Tomorrow's most competitive organizations are working now to ensure they have available tomorrow and a decade from now employees who are eager and able to address competitive challenges. Increasingly this means attracting superior talent and stimulating employees to perform at peak levels.

Gaining and Sustaining Competitive Advantage

As described in Chapter 7, a firm has a competitive advantage when all or part of the market prefers the firm's products and/or services. Companies seek ways to compete that can last a long time and cannot easily be imitated by competitors. Firms such as Cisco, Southwest Airlines, and The Container Store use their approaches to managing human resources to gain a sustainable competitive advantage. Several large research projects have generated substantial evidence linking human resources management practices to bottom-line profitability and productivity gains. For example, one study involved asking thousands of employees to describe their jobs and their organizations. The responses were used to form an index to reflect how much emphasis was placed on managing human resources. The research results showed a strong association between emphasizing human resources and profitability in subsequent years.[3]

To gain sustainable competitive advantage through human resources management, three conditions must be met:

■ employees must be a source of added value,
■ employees must be "rare" or unique in some way, and
■ competitors must not be able to easily copy or imitate the company's approach to human resources management.

Employees Who Add Value. Like most intangibles, the value of an organization's employees doesn't appear on a balance sheet. Yet, intangibles such as the knowledge that employees have and the way employees feel and behave can be used to predict financial performance. Investors seek companies with satisfied employees. These investors recognize that satisfied employees result in satisfied customers, especially in the services sector. Managers and employees who hate their jobs can't give the best possible service to customers. Conversely, when customers are happy, employees feel a sense of pride and satisfaction at being part of the company.[4]

Employees Who Are Rare. To be a source of sustainable competitive advantage, human resources must also be rare. If competitors can easily access the same pool of talent, then that talent provides no advantage against competitors. When Lincoln Electric Company in Cleveland, Ohio, announced it was planning to employ 200 new production workers, it received more than 20,000 responses. When BMW announced that it had selected Spartanburg, South Carolina, as the site for its first U.S. production facility, it received more than 25,000 unsolicited requests for employment. Numbers this large make it more feasible for Lincoln Electric and BMW to employ workers who are two to three times more productive than their counterparts in other manufacturing firms.

The Competent Manager

Tony Rucci, vice president of human resources for Sears, used data from 820 stores to determine that increased employee satisfaction predicted increased customer retention and customer recommendations to friends, which in turn improved financial performance. An increase of just two points on the annual employee survey translated into 0.5 percent increase in financial performance, which was worth millions to the company.

By being an employer of choice, organizations can gain access to the best available talent. In other words, "The Best Get the Best." Books and articles that purport to identify the "best" places to work are especially popular among students graduating from college, who view firms high in the rankings as desirable places to land their first postgraduation jobs. Dissatisfied workers who are looking for better employment situations read these lists too. Over time, a good reputation for attracting, developing, and keeping good talent acts like a magnet to draw the best talent to the firm.

An Approach That Can't Be Copied. Business practices that are easy for competitors to copy don't provide sources of sustained competitive advantage. Approaches to human resources management that have evolved over a long period of time to the specific needs of the organization are the most difficult to copy. Some companies continually scrutinize their approaches to managing human resources in order to improve continuously.

FedEx is one such company. Years of relentless attention to how people are managed have helped Federal Express maintain a position of leadership in a highly competitive industry. Larry McMahan, vice president of human resources at FedEx, explains it this way: "To create a culture where productivity can thrive involves integrating all elements of HR. It starts with having a realistic job match between the skills of the candidate and the requirements of the job. If you have a good match, the interest level and desire to be productive are already there." FedEx, which is considered one of the 100 best companies to work for in America, also provides extensive training. "The philosophy is that knowledge is power, and a better informed person is going to be better at what they do," according to McMahan.[5]

Bottom-Line Consequences

Estimating the dollar value of investments in human resources activities, such as systematic selection and training, is a topic of increasing interest to accountants and financial analysts. Until rules for making such estimates are developed, however, investors and shareholders must rely on their own judgments of how well a company manages its people. In organizations such as consulting firms and advertising agencies, there are few important tangible assets. Investing in these companies often means buying a customer list, some product brands, and to a large extent the hope that the best people working there will stay and invest their talents.[6] As one study of initial public offering (IPO) companies showed, companies that attend to human resources management issues are rewarded with more favorable initial investor reactions as well as longer term survival.[7]

Investors' judgments about the value of a company's human resources often are informed by reputation rankings, such as those published by *Fortune*, *Forbes*, and *Inc.*, and by other forms of the public recognition for excellence. For example, the Catalyst Award is given to organizations with outstanding initiatives that foster women's advancement into senior management. Another form of recognition for excellence in managing human resources is receipt of an Optima Award, sponsored by *Workforce* magazine. Wellpoint Health Networks received an Optima Award for its human resources planning system, which provides a systematic way for the company to identify possible candidates for promotion within the company. By identifying the talent that already is present in the company, this system ensures that excellent talent is promoted into leadership positions. It also saves the company money by eliminating fees paid to executive search firms. Simply by filling five executive jobs from within the company and not hiring a search firm, Wellpoint saved an estimated $1 million in a single year.[8]

Social Value

The financial consequences of how organizations manage human resources have received a great deal of attention in recent years, but these are not the only consequences that matter. During an era of seemingly constant restructuring and downsizing, many people have become more aware of the social consequences of different approaches to managing human resources. When a large employer in a community is forced to downsize because of declining sales and profits, the change can affect the entire community. Similarly, if employers discriminate unfairly against some groups when making hiring decisions, the consequences of those discriminatory practices can ripple through the community for many years.

Within the United States, society often judges organizations in terms of the fairness with which they treat their employees. People believe that fairness is a desirable social condition—we want to be treated fairly, and we want others to view us as being fair.[9] Companies that rank high as the best places to work generally emphasize fairness as part of their corporate culture because fairness creates the feeling of trust that is needed to "hold a good workplace together." When deciding which company to work for, a potential employee evaluates whether a company pays a fair wage. If they feel unfairly treated after being hired, employees are likely to "vote with their feet" and seek employment elsewhere.[10]

Some companies make a point of addressing basic concerns such as fairness even when doing so is costly and perhaps even reduces profitability. In addition, many legal regulations are intended to protect members of society from human resources management practices that are unfair and potentially harmful.

THE LEGAL AND REGULATORY ENVIRONMENT

Through elected government representatives, members of the labor force initiate and ultimately create federal and state laws. Through their tax payments, citizens pay for the operations of a vast array of government agencies and courts, which are responsible for interpreting and enforcing the laws. Thus, employment laws should be thought of not only as legal constraints; they are also sources of information about the issues that potential employees are likely thinking about as they decide whether to join or leave an organization. Some of the most important regulations affecting human resources management are described in Table 13.1.

2. Describe several important laws and government regulations that affect how organizations manage their human resources.

The numerous laws and regulations that affect how organizations manage human resources cannot all be discussed here but two major categories that deserve comment are equal employment opportunity and compensation and benefits.

Equal Employment Opportunity

The principle of **equal employment opportunity (EEO)** *states that job applicants and employees should be judged on characteristics that are related to the work that they are being hired to do and on their job performance after being hired,* and they should be protected from discrimination based on their personal background characteristics, such as gender, race, ethnicity, religion, and so forth. This general principle is the foundation of several federal and state laws that govern employment practices. In recent years, the number of EEO cases filed annually in federal courts has averaged about 23,000.[11]

One especially important EEO law has been **Title VII of the Civil Rights Act**. *As originally enacted in 1964, Title VII prohibited discrimination by employers, employment agencies, and unions on the basis of race, color, religion, sex, or national origin.* In 1991, a new version of the Civil Rights Act went into effect. The new law reinforces the intent of the Civil Rights Acts of 1964, but states more specifically how cases brought under the act should proceed. Other important employment discrimination laws cover age and disabilities.

Enforcement of U.S. EEO Laws. Power to enforce Title VII of the Civil Rights Act rests with the Equal Employment Opportunity Commission (EEOC). In carrying out its duties, the EEOC has the authority to make rules, conduct investigations, make judgments about guilt, and impose sanctions. In practice, this means that the EEOC has the responsibility and authority to prosecute companies that it believes are in violation of the law.

Following the terrorist attacks on September 11, 2001, employees thought to be of Middle Eastern ethnicity suddenly became targets of discrimination in the workplace, as well as elsewhere. This problem became so pervasive so quickly that dealing with it was already the top priority of the EEOC by December of that year. The EEOC quickly alerted employers to the responsibility they had to prevent any such discrimination in their organizations.

Failure to comply with EEO laws exposes a company to lawsuits. For example, the EEOC filed a suit against Allstate alleging that it engaged in age discrimination against its insurance agents when the company reorganized its sales force. As another example,

Table 13.1   Major Federal Employment Laws and Regulations

Act	Jurisdiction	Basic Provisions
National Labor Relations Act (Wagner Act; 1935)	Most nonmanagerial employees in private industry	Provides right to organize, provides for collective bargaining; requires employers to bargain; requires unions to represent all members equally.
Fair Labor Standards Act (FLSA; 1938)	Most nonmanagerial employees in private industry	Establishes a minimum wage; controls hours through premium pay for overtime; controls working hours for children.
Equal Pay Act (1963)	Most employers	Prohibits unequal pay for males and females with equal skill, effort, and responsibility working under similar working conditions.
Title VII of the Civil Rights Act (1964, 1991)	Employers with 15 or more employees; employment agencies; unions	Prevents discrimination on the basis of race, color, religion, sex, or national origin; establishes the EEOC; provides reinstatement, back pay, compensatory, and punitive damages; permits jury trials.
Age Discrimination in Employment Act (ADEA; 1967)	Employers with more than 20 employees	Prevents discrimination against persons age 40 and over; states compulsory retirement for some employees.
Occupational Safety and Health Act (OSHA; 1970)	Most employers involved in interstate commerce	Ensures as far as possible safe and healthy working conditions and the preservation of our human resources.
The Pregnancy Discrimination Act (1978)	Employers with 15 or more employees	Identifies pregnancy as a disability and entitles the woman to the same benefits as any other disability.
Worker Adjustment and Retraining Notification Act (WARN; 1988)	Employers with more than 100 employees	Requires 60 days notice of plant or office closing or substantial layoffs.
Americans with Disabilities Act (ADA; 1990)	Employers with 15 or more employees	Prohibits discrimination against individuals with disabilities.
The Family and Medical Leave Act (1993)	Employers with 50 or more employees	Allows workers to take up to 12 weeks unpaid leave for childbirth, adoption, or illness of employee or a close family member.

it recently joined in a lawsuit against Xerox alleging widespread discrimination against African-American sales employees. Such lawsuits can be extremely costly for a company. After the EEOC brought a discrimination lawsuit against Texaco, that company eventually agreed to pay some $140 million to current and former aggrieved employees—the largest settlement ever for a case of racial discrimination.

EEO in the Global Arena. Keeping up with legal requirements about employment practices requires making a commitment to the principles of equal opportunity. The challenge is even greater for international firms because laws take dozens of different forms in countries around the world. To provide a flavor for the international legal environment, consider the situation faced by Cirque du Soleil. When making hiring decisions around the world, Cirque du Soleil must understand the legal constraints that apply in each country, as well as cultural factors. Wherever it hires employees—which it does in every country where it performs—the company must ensure that it adheres to all local labor laws. Table 13.2 illustrates differences in discrimination laws—just one aspect of employment conditions.

Table 13.2	Who's Protected Where?					
Country	Age	Sex	National Origin	Race	Religion	Marital Status
United States	Yes	Yes	Yes	Yes	Yes	No
France	Some	Yes	Yes	Yes	Yes	Yes
Venezuela	No	No	No	No	No	No
Canada	Yes	Yes	Yes	Yes	Yes	Yes
Hong Kong	No	No	No	No	No	No
Japan	No	Yes	Yes	Yes	Yes	No
Indonesia	No	No	No	No	No	No
United Kingdom	No	Yes	No	No	No	No
Singapore	No	No	No	No	No	No
Greece	No	Yes	No	Yes	Yes	Yes

Compensation and Benefits

Compensation and benefits practices are shaped by a plethora of laws and regulations. These cover topics such as taxation, nondiscrimination, fair wages, the protection of children, hardship and overtime pay, and pension and welfare benefits. Recently, public discussion has centered on the question of whether to change the laws and regulations governing how companies expense stock options granted to employees. The debates are heated because any changes in these laws will have major consequences for how companies use stock in their compensation plans.[12]

Fair Labor Standards Act. Of the several laws that influence compensation and benefits practices, the primary one is the Fair Labor Standards Act (FLSA) of 1938. The **Fair Labor Standards Act** *is a federal law that specifies a national minimum wage rate and requires payment for overtime work by covered employees.* In 1938, the minimum wage was set at $0.25/hour. In 2003, it was $5.75. Individual states can, and often do, set higher standards than those set at the federal level. The FLSA also includes provisions to protect children. For example, it prohibits minors under the age of 18 from working in hazardous occupations.

Equal Pay Act. Another important regulation affecting compensation practices is the Equal Pay Act of 1963. The **Equal Pay Act** *requires men and women to be paid equally when* *they are doing equal work (in terms of skill, effort, responsibility, and working conditions) in the same organization.* Suppose for example, that a software company has mostly male programmers designing computer games and mostly female programmers designing Web sites for those games. If the levels of skill, effort, and responsibility are similar in these two jobs, the male and female programmers should be paid equally—despite the fact that they aren't doing identical work.

Many states have extended the logic of the Equal Pay Act to require that men and women be paid equally for doing *comparable work.* **Comparable worth** *legislation requires employers to assess the worth of all jobs and ensure that people doing jobs of comparable worth are paid similarly.* These state laws go beyond the narrow language of the federal law to state that work that appears to be quite dissimilar (e.g., nurses and engineers) can be of comparable worth. If one occupation tends to be dominated by women and the other by men, chances are high that the occupation dominated by women will be paid less. Such discrepancies may be due to historical factors, discrimination, or labor market conditions. For organizations covered by comparable worth laws, employers must demonstrate that pay discrepancies between men and women reflect differences in factors such as the skills and responsibilities associated with their work.

HUMAN RESOURCES PLANNING

3. Explain the objective of human resources planning and describe how organizations respond to the unpredictability of future business needs.

Human resources planning *involves forecasting the organization's human resources needs and developing the steps to be taken to meet them.* The primary objective is ensuring that the right number and type of individuals are available at the appropriate time and place to fulfill organizational needs. Human resources planning is tied directly to strategic planning (see Chapter 7). Typically, strategic goals are established first, followed by goals for managing human resources that will be consistent with the broader goals.[13]

At the heart of planning are two tasks: determining an organization's future human resource needs and developing a strategy to meet those needs. Typically, the organization's needs are determined using expert forecasts. More than 60 percent of all large firms utilize some type of expert forecasting to project HR needs. Such forecasts may not be very accurate, however, which makes it difficult to develop an effective strategy for meeting future needs. During times of growth, it is difficult to foresee changing conditions that may cause a downturn in the business. It also is difficult to predict when another business boom will occur. Realizing that the future is difficult to predict, some organizations stay flexible by employing contingent workers who understand that their jobs may be temporary. Other companies try to maintain a workforce of more permanent employees, but this strategy often means that layoffs become necessary when business declines.

Contingent Workers

Instead of hiring permanent workers to meet the demands of a growing business, many companies hire contingent workers. **Contingent workers** *are employees who are hired by companies for specific tasks or short periods of time with the understanding that their employment may be ended at any time.* Included among contingent workers are part-timers, free-lancers, subcontractors, and independent professionals of many types. Estimates place the number of contingent workers at about 8 percent of the U.S. workforce.

Members of the contingent workforce understand that they'll frequently be entering into and exiting from employment relationships. The temporary assignments generally last 3 to 12 months. Therefore, even when they are working on temporary assignments, they develop connections to a wide range of possible future employers. In effect, contingent workers must continually maintain their status as members of the applicant pool in order to ensure their continued employment.[14]

Layoffs

When business is slow, many companies reduce their workforce by laying off employees. During business downturns, companies may lay off 5, 10, or even 15 percent of their employees within a matter of weeks. Typically, the people who lose their jobs are those who were most recently hired and/or those whose performance is the lowest. Layoffs are typically a short-term solution to difficult economic conditions or an expected decline in the company's business. Often, sooner than they expected, companies that have conducted layoffs find that they need to rehire these same people. According to one large study, approximately 25 percent of the companies that had trimmed their workforces were rehiring people the next year—either for their former jobs or for new permanent jobs. The problem seems to be that managers use layoffs as a quick method of cost cutting. In the longer term, however, layoffs create problems because the overall trend is that the size of the labor force is growing very slowly. The historical trend is shown in Figure 13.1.[15] Therefore, as soon as business conditions improve, employers who have conducted layoffs quickly find that they must compete even harder to find new workers.

Figure 13.1   Historical Trend in Growth Rate of the U.S. Workforce

*Note: Values for 2010s are projections.

The true long-term consequences of layoffs are difficult to quantify. But experienced managers understand that layoffs should be a strategy of last resort. For example, to rehire a laid-off staff person, a company may have to offer higher pay. However, even though they may be paid better, such employees now feel less loyalty to the firm. So, if a better opportunity comes along, they may be more willing to change jobs than to stay put in anticipation of a promotion or pay raise. Figure 13.2 shows some of the other consequences of laying off workers. By laying off workers, companies may save some money in the short term, but in the longer term they may find that morale has gone down and labor costs up.[16]

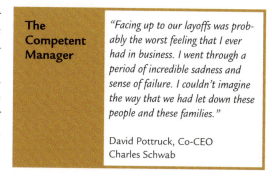

The Competent Manager

"Facing up to our layoffs was probably the worst feeling that I ever had in business. I went through a period of incredible sadness and sense of failure. I couldn't imagine the way that we had let down these people and these families."

David Pottruck, Co-CEO
Charles Schwab

Competency Inventories

In addition to matching the number of employees to the amount of work that needs to be done, human resources planning ensures that a company has the right types of

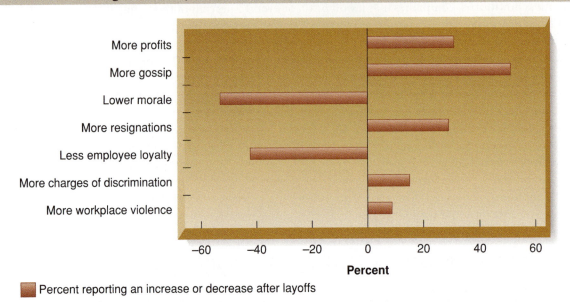

Percent

■ Percent reporting an increase or decrease after layoffs

employees—those with the competencies needed by the organization. One way to keep track of the skills present in a company's workforce is to use competency inventories. *A* **competency inventory** *is a detailed file maintained for each employee that lists level of education, training, experience, length of service, current job title and salary, and performance history.* Also included are assessments of the employee's competency levels in terms of the factors included in the competency model used throughout this book.[17] Our competency model is only one of many that could be used. In fact, a recent survey of 217 companies revealed a total of 148 different competency models in use. Of course, there was a great deal of overlap among the many models. The purpose of all of these competency models is the same: to keep track of the talent in the organization so that it can be nurtured and used effectively.[18]

Many organizations use computerized human resources information systems for storage and easy retrieval of such vital job-related information. For example, Texas Instruments (TI) maintains such files on its thousands of employees. These files help the firm's top managers spot human resources gaps. When gaps exist between the human resources needs of the organization and the current supply of talent in the organization, managers can use a variety of other human resources activities to fill the gaps. They can hire more (or fewer) people, or they can begin hiring people with different competencies. If the organization has the right number of people, but they need new skills, training activities may be used to address the gap. In the remainder of this chapter, we discuss these and other HR activities in more detail.

HIRING

4. Describe the hiring process.

The **hiring process** *includes activities related to the recruitment of applicants to fill open positions in an organization and the selection of the best applicants for a position.* Through hiring activities, employers ensure that the right person is in the right job.

As illustrated in Figure 13.3, recruitment and selection are stimulated by a vacancy in the organization. Vacancies may occur because employees move around in the organization. They may get promoted, or transferred to another location, or they may even be

Figure 13.3   Vacancies Stimulate the Hiring Process

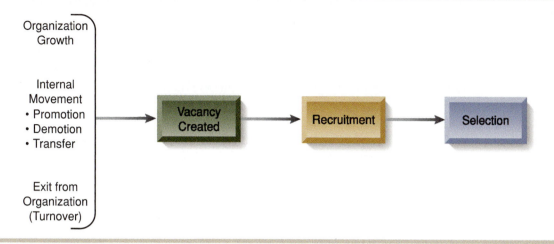

demoted. Often, when one employee moves within the organization, someone leaves the organization (turnover). Vacancies can also occur due to organizational growth. For example, each time Wal-Mart opens a new store, dozens of vacancies are created. By retaining productive employees as long as possible, employers can reduce the number of vacancies created by employee turnover and hence reduce the need to recruit and select new employees.

The link between the hiring process and employee retention is illustrated in the Communication Competency feature, which describes how Advanced Financial Solutions (AFS) ensures that both the company and its job applicants learn as much as possible about each other before committing to work together.[19] By communicating intensively during recruitment and selection, AFS avoids hiring people who will not work out as long-term employees.

COMMUNICATION COMPETENCY

Advanced Financial Solutions
Located in Oklahoma City, Advanced Financial Solutions must compete with the glamour of cities like New York, San Francisco, Boston, and even Paris, Brussels, and Tokyo when hiring software technicians. CEO Gary Nelson knows that keeping the people he hires is important to the firm's success, and he's proud of his record low turnover, which averages only about 1 percent. How does he make sure that the professionals he hires will like Oklahoma City and their new jobs well

enough to stay put? By investing heavily in recruiting and selecting new employees.

Early in the process, applicants participate in lengthy telephone interviews, and detailed reference checks are conducted. Then, when the company thinks it has found a good candidate, he or she is invited to spend one week visiting the company. Spouses also are encouraged to visit. Prospective employees visit all departments and meet everyone from the CEO to the support staff. Spouses are shown around the town

and company volunteers make an effort to answer their questions about life in Oklahoma City: How are the schools? What religious organizations are there? How good are the sports facilities? And so on. No job offers are made until applicants complete their one-week visit. The cost of this approach, which is about $7,500 per hire, is worth it, according to Nelson, who says "You can't put a price tag on [the] aggravation and grief" caused by hiring the wrong person.

Recruitment

Recruitment *is the process of searching, both inside and outside the organization, for people to fill vacant positions.* During recruitment, the organization develops a pool of job candidates from which to select qualified employees. After recruiting candidates, the organization selects those who are most likely to perform well on the job.[20]

In some organizations, recruitment activities are centralized in the human resources department, and professional HR staff members do most of the recruiting. In less centralized organizations, however, line managers often have most of the responsibility for recruitment. In organizations that rely heavily on teamwork, work team members may take most of the responsibility for hiring activities. At Advanced Financial Solutions, even the CEO is active in recruiting and hiring the technical professionals who are so vital to the success of that company.

The initial recruiting experience—when an employee is first considered for a position in the organization—is an employee's first exposure to the organization's recruiting activities, but it is not the last one. Employees may again become involved in recruiting activities as they help (or hinder) their employers' efforts to attract others to the company. When employees eventually consider applying for other jobs within the organization, they again become actively involved in recruitment activities. These experiences with the organization's recruiting activities may be especially important in determining whether talented employees are retained.

Employers inform potential applicants about employment opportunities using a variety of methods. They place ads, post notices on the company bulletin board, accept applications from people who simply walk in to their recruiting offices, and so on. Different methods may reach different sources of applicants. Posting announcements on company bulletin boards is a good way to recruit employees who are already working at the company but may be ready to move to another job. Placing ads in local newspapers or trade publications is a common method used to reach those in the external labor market. Instead of using just one recruiting method, most employers use multiple methods. This approach helps the organization generate a large, diverse pool of applicants

Electronic and Other Media. Virtually every company has a Web site to which applicants as well as customers can go to learn about the company. Many of these sites have specific information about job postings, required competencies, career progression programs, mentoring, diversity initiatives, and benefits. Increasingly, company Web sites accept—even encourage—electronic applications.[21] This saves a great deal of time and cost. It also enables the companies to be accessible to a wide range of applicants. New Horizons Computer Learning Centers likes Internet recruiting because it weeds out applicants who are not Internet savvy.[22]

Web-based recruiting is not a panacea, however. According to a recent study of business school graduates who were looking for jobs, poorly designed electronic recruiting sites can cause frustration. Figure 13.4 describes some of the most common problems encountered by electronic job searchers. How many of these problems would you put up with before deciding not to submit a job application?[23]

Job Postings. A **job posting** *prominently displays current job openings to all employees in an organization.* They are usually found on bulletin boards (cork as well as electronic). Job postings provide complete job descriptions, explain the competencies needed, and may also provide information about compensation and performance standards. Savvy employees observe postings over time to gain information about turnover rates in various departments, as well as information about the competencies that are most in demand.

Employee Referrals. **Employee referrals** *occur when current employees inform people they know about openings and encourage them to apply.* At The Container Store, 41 percent of new hires come from employee referrals. Companies such as New York Life Insurance facili-

Figure 13.4 Problems Encountered When Applying for Jobs on the Internet

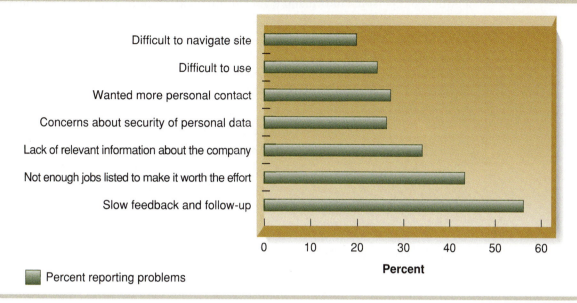

- Difficult to navigate site
- Difficult to use
- Wanted more personal contact
- Concerns about security of personal data
- Lack of relevant information about the company
- Not enough jobs listed to make it worth the effort
- Slow feedback and follow-up

0   10   20   30   40   50   60
Percent

▨ Percent reporting problems

tate employee referrals by supporting online alumni networks. Other companies make it easy for their employees to send electronic job announcements to their friends. This is a very low-cost approach. Some companies reward employees for referring qualified applicants. The financial incentives may be linked to a recruit's completion of an application, acceptance of employment, or working for a specified time period.

Employee referrals usually result in the highest one-year retention rates. One explanation for this success is that employees provide a balanced view of organizational life. The more information that is available, the better the referral decision is likely to be. Another explanation is that employees tend to recruit applicants who are similar to themselves in interests and motivations. Because employees are already adjusted to the organizational culture, this matching process increases the likelihood that applicants also will fit.[24]

Selection

Through recruitment, a company finds people who are potential employees. **Employee selection** *is a process that involves deciding which of these recruits should actually be employed and for which positions.*[25] The decision about who to select often takes into account a person's competencies and how well they fit into the organization. The most common sources of information for making selection decisions are

- résumés,
- reference checks,
- interviews, and
- tests.

Employers use the information they gain from these sources to select the best potential employees from a pool of applicants. Applicants, in turn, may draw inferences about the organization and the requirements of a job based on both the content of the selection procedures and the way the organization treats applicants throughout the selection process. Well-qualified applicants who react negatively to either the content or process used during selection may decline the organization's job offer.[26]

Résumés. A well-written résumé is clear, concise, and easy to read and understand. It gives (1) personal data; (2) career objectives; (3) education; (4) work experience, highlighting special skills and responsibilities; (5) descriptions of relevant competencies, activities, and personal information; and (6) the names, addresses, and telephone numbers of references. Many companies now accept electronic résumés, submitted over the Internet. These companies may specify a format for your résumé or even provide an electronic form for you to complete. In such cases, complying with all of the listed requirements for submitting your résumé is especially important because some of the companies also use software programs designed to scan for information and route your résumé to the appropriate person.

Reference Checks. Because résumés can be falsified easily, managers may request references and conduct reference checks. Many employers routinely check educational qualifications, including schools attended, majors, degrees awarded, and dates. Unfortunately, such checking often reveals that applicants have lied about their backgrounds.[27] An applicant's work experience is more difficult to check because employers often are reluctant to provide performance evaluations of former employees. Their concern stems from cases in which employees successfully sued their former employers for giving negative references. In fact, by law, organizations are required to provide only the job title and dates of employment of a former employee.

Interviews. In making a final selection, most organizations rely on a combination of interviews and tests. Although commonly used, interviews don't always predict on-the-job performance accurately. Research indicates that interviewers tend to decide about a person early in the interview and then spend the rest of the time seeking information to support that decision. But early impressions often are erroneous. Too often, managers form favorable impressions of candidates simply because they share superficial similarities with the manager—for example, where they grew up or where they went to school. Managers may also let their stereotypes affect their judgments about individual candidates. Problems like these were what made Home Depot decide to automate its hiring process. By using a computerized approach to screening all job applicants, it is now much more likely that a qualified female will end up in a job that uses all of her competencies instead of being put into a job that fits an interviewer's stereotype about what types of jobs women do best.[28]

Despite their potential drawbacks, well-structured interviews can be useful.[29] When you first enter the world of work, you probably will be interviewed many times before you're in a position to conduct interviews yourself. Typically, someone about to graduate from college goes through three types of employment interviews: on-campus, plant or office, and final selection. One of these interviews is likely to be a **situational** (also called *behavioral*) **interview**, *in which a manager or human resource professional role plays a situation you could face on the job*. Observers watch how you behave and give you a score. As one interviewer put it, "These are very vivid recreations. There's no time to put on an act."[30]

Tests. Many organizations use tests to screen and select candidates. The **cognitive ability test** *is a test that employers use to measure general intelligence; verbal, numerical, and reasoning ability; and the like*. Such tests have proved to be relatively successful in predicting which applicants are qualified for certain jobs.[31]

Written tests can also be used to measure personality. A **personality test** *assesses the unique blend of characteristics that define an individual*. In jobs that involve a great deal of contact with other people, such as sales agents and many types of service jobs, a personality characteristic referred to as *extraversion* is a good predictor of future job performance. Extraverts tend to be talkative, good natured, and gregarious—characteristics that facilitate smooth interactions with customers and clients. Another personality characteristic of interest to many employers is conscientiousness. Conscientious people seem to have a strong sense of purpose, obligation, and persistence—all of which lead to high performance in almost any type of work situation.

A **performance test** *requires a candidate to perform simulations of actual job tasks.* One example is a code-writing test for computer programmers. Another example is an in-basket exercise. In this case, job candidates receive a stack of letters, notes, memos, telephone messages, faxes, and other items and are told to imagine that they have been promoted to a new position. They are given a specific amount of time to deal appropriately with these items. In most cases they will have the opportunity to explain or discuss their decisions in a follow-up interview.[32] At the BMW auto plant in South Carolina, job candidates work for 90 minutes on a simulated assembly line. They don't actually produce cars that will be sold, but they perform many of the tasks that are needed in the job. To be selected, they must show more than their technical skills. They also must show the mental and physical stamina required to perform well in BMW's "aerobic workplace."[33]

Regardless of the specific procedures used to select employees, employers should be concerned with how applicants view them. It is important that hiring procedures *be* fair and also that they *feel* fair to applicants.

TRAINING AND DEVELOPMENT

When unemployment levels are high, it's relatively easy for employers to simply hire people who have the competencies needed to perform well in a job. But during labor shortages, it becomes much more difficult to solve problems by simply hiring new people. Instead, employers must take responsibility for helping the current employees develop the competencies needed by the company. **Training** *refers to activities that help employees overcome limitations and improve performance in their current jobs.* **Development** *refers to practices that help employees gain the competencies they will need in the future in order to advance in their careers.*

Even if a company hired only the very most qualified people available, the company would probably still need to invest in training and development activities. These activities range from one-day orientation sessions to personalized, long-term career development plans. Different approaches generally are used to achieve different purposes.

5. Describe several types of training and development programs.

Orientation Training

Almost all new employees need to "learn the ropes." Every company has its own way of doing things that is important for all employees to understand. A few hours of training during the first day or two on the job helps ease new employees into the company's way of doing things.[34] When a new employee is from a different country and culture, this initial training is especially important in helping new employees adjust. For many firms with a strong set of values and clear strategic objectives, orientation training provides the direction that new employees need in order to be successful in their jobs. As described in the Teamwork Competency feature, orientation training is extensive for new employees of the Ritz-Carlton hotel.[35]

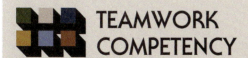

TEAMWORK COMPETENCY

Ritz-Carlton Hotel Company
Employees who work for the Ritz-Carlton hotel are proud of the fact that the company is a two-time winner of the Baldrige National Quality Award. The awards and the excellent customer service they represent don't happen by accident. It begins with the hiring process—the company

©Photodisc/Getty Images

tation comes next. This is the first step in creating a team of employees who all share the same vision and goals. During orientation, the company infuses new employees with the company's "soul," according to Horst Schultz, the former COO, president, and vice chairman. During orientation, Schultz would explain that every employee was essential to the company's success. If they didn't make checking in a pleasure, keep the rooms clean, and respond to the guests' every need, the company would suffer. In comparison, if Schultz didn't show up one day for work, it made very little difference!

After a general orientation program, Ritz-Carlton provides more

specific training for employees, reflecting their specific jobs. The training is designed and delivered by the five best employees in each job category. Working together, those who are best at doing each job develop a set of principles that everyone in that job needs to understand to perform it well. And the training never stops. For the first 10 minutes of each day, all employees participate together in the "line-up," which is used to remind all team members that they should strive to live the company's values throughout their workday. By constantly reminding employees what the company strives to achieve, it teaches them habits that will serve the guests and the company well.

knows what types of people perform well in each job, and it is careful to employ only the right people. Orien-

Basic Skills Training

Basic skills training may be needed by employees who are unable to read, write, do arithmetic, or solve problems well enough to perform even simple tasks. Such employees can't write letters to customers, read warning labels on chemical containers, or understand machine operating symbols. Organizations spend large sums of money on remedial training for employees because they believe that if employees can master certain basic skills, they can perform a variety of jobs and be able to deal with some of the new technologies.

E-Learning

Regardless of *what* is being learned, many companies are using electronic media to deliver training, instead of relying on traditional classroom approaches. *When training is delivered using Web-based technologies, it is commonly referred to as* **e-learning**. A major advantage of e-learning technology is it allows employees to develop their skills at their own pace and at a time that is personally convenient. At KMPG, a global consulting company, all employees—from senior partners to junior administrative assistants—take 50 hours of online training. Many people went through the curriculum just because they had to. But after they finished, some realized that it really helped them in their jobs. A marketing manager found that the course helped her think in new ways about how to help clients build an intranet. Other employees developed new research skills or gained new insights into issues of copyright laws. Perhaps most importantly, the company as a whole began to better understand the changes that their clients are facing as they too adjust to the Internet world. Such insights should improve the quality of service they provide to those clients.[36]

Team Training

When an organization downsizes, merges with another firm, redesigns its production process, or develops a new approach to serving its customers, it is likely that the jobs of many employees will change in fundamental ways. Training and development activities often are needed to help employees adjust to the organization. Because teamwork often increases as a result of these changes, training programs often seek to enhance teamwork competency.

When BP Norge decided to restructure around self-managing teams, its goals were to speed up decision making, reduce costs and cycle times, and increase innovation. Despite the strong business argument supporting a change to teamwork, the organization found that changing to teamwork was difficult. Nine months of frustration led management to conclude that a training initiative was needed. A team of American and Norwegian facilitators conducted two-day workshops, which were attended by a mix of people from all levels and functional specialties. Oil rig workers and senior managers sat side by side, as did Norwegians and Americans. Prior to the workshop, everyone watched a video that explained self-managed teams and showed how other organizations had used them successfully. They also interviewed a few colleagues to find out what they thought about self-managed teams. At the workshop, discussion focused on understanding the process through which teamwork develops. They also began practicing the behaviors needed in their new team environment—taking risks, communicating about their feelings, and teaching others as well as learning from others.[37]

Career Development

Most employees would not be satisfied with continuing to do the same job year after year. They want to grow in order to move into new jobs.[38] The intent of development programs is to improve an employee's competencies in preparation for future jobs. Before sending an employee to a development program, a needs analysis is made to identify that person's particular strengths and developmental needs. For beginning supervisors and managers, developmental needs often include inability to set goals with others and negotiate interpersonal conflicts.

Colgate-Palmolive is one company that takes development seriously. Its People Development unit conducted an extensive analysis of the external environment and had experts forecast Colgate's future personnel needs. Then they developed a profile of required leadership competencies, such as business savvy, use of personal influence, global perspective, strong character, people management, and entrepreneurial action. With a clear view of the types of leaders needed by the company, the People Development unit laid out a strategy for getting such people into place. The success of that strategy required (1) a commitment to identifying "high-potential" employees and giving them job assignments designed to develop their leadership competencies and (2) the active involvement of high-potential employees in their own career management. Table 13.3 describes the components of a tool kit developed to assist high-potential employees with their career management.

Many large companies, such as GE, McDonald's, Motorola, and Siemens, provide so many hours of development activities to so many employees that they have built company "universities," complete with classrooms, "dorm" rooms, and other amenities of a typical college campus. Organizations may encourage employees to attend these "universities" as part of a long-term strategy for developing a cadre of high-potential employees who, several years in the future, may eventually become upper level managers. The development experiences are intended to broaden these managers' perspectives and prepare them for general (as opposed to functional) management positions. A key objective often is to develop managers' strategic action competencies.[39]

One-on-One Mentoring and Coaching

Besides training employees in groups, some companies use more personal approaches, which include one-on-one mentoring and coaching.

Mentoring. **Mentoring** *occurs when an established employee guides the development of a less experienced worker, or protégé.* Mentoring can increase employees' competencies, achievement, and understanding of the organization. At Intel, the mentoring program is designed to help less experienced employees (called *partners*) develop specific knowledge

Table 13.3 Components of a Tool Kit for Individual Development at Colgate-Palmolive

I. Overview of the Individual Development Process

- Assess individual competencies and values.
- Define personal strengths, development needs, and options for career growth. Identify developmental actions.
- Craft individual development plan.
- Meet with manager to decide a course of action (based on preceding analysis).
- Accept the challenge of implementing the plan.

II. Worksheets for Individual Assessment

- Competency assessment worksheet: assesses strengths and weaknesses for a specified set of competencies.
- Personal values survey: assesses preferences for types of work environments, work relationships, work tasks, lifestyle needs, and personal needs.
- Development activities chart: describes on-the-job and off-the-job learning opportunities that can be used to develop key competencies.
- Global training grid: lists all formal training programs offered by the company and explains how each relates to key competencies.
- Individual development plan: developed by the employee, this describes specific development goals and a course of action to be taken to achieve those goals.

III. Defining and Understanding Global Competencies

This section of the tool kit is like a dictionary. It lists all the competencies considered to be important for various types of jobs throughout the company and describes the meaning of each competency. This section serves as a reference guide and encourages people across the company to use a common set of terms when discussing competencies and career development issues.

or skills with the help of an expert (the *mentor*). The company's intranet is used to match up partners and mentors, who then work together an average of six to nine months. Responsibility for setting up meetings, deciding what to talk about, and deciding when to end the relationship is in the hands of the partner and mentor.[40]

The Competent Manager

"We have a lot of people who are rocket scientists, great strategic thinkers, or great with clients. But very few business schools prepare people for the messiness of managing people, and a lot of coaching is about effectively managing people."

Alicia Whitaker
Managing Director
Credit Suisse First Boston

Coaching. For high-level executives and other employees who hold visible and somewhat unique jobs, traditional forms of on-the-job training are impractical. Yet, these employees often need to develop new competencies in order to be fully effective. In recent years, more and more executives have turned to personal coaching to address their training needs. With **coaching**, *an expert observes the employee in his or her job over a period of weeks or months and provides continuous feedback and guidance on how to improve.* Most coaches also encourage their "trainees" to discuss difficult situations as they arise and work through alternative scenarios for dealing with those situations. Although coaching is rapidly growing in popularity, it's a relatively new technique and few guidelines are available to evaluate whether a potential coaching relationship is likely to succeed.[41] Nevertheless, the evidence of its effectiveness is beginning to accumulate.

As described in the Self-Management Competency feature, an effective coaching program helps managers change themselves, but it requires their full commitment. Managers who are not truly interested in self-improvement are not likely to benefit much from coaching.[42]

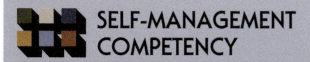

PERFORMANCE APPRAISAL

Performance appraisal *refers to a formal, structured system for evaluating an employee's job performance.*[43] Its focus is on documenting how productive the employee is and which areas of performance could be improved. One of the primary responsibilities of managers is appraising the performance of their employees.

6. Describe several principles for improving the accuracy of managers' appraisals of employee performance.

Uses of Performance Appraisal Results

Appraisal results influence who is promoted, demoted, transferred, and dismissed, and the size of raises that employees receive. Increasingly, employees also are being asked to appraise the performance of their managers.

Performance appraisal, which necessarily reflects the past, isn't an end to be achieved. Rather, it's a means for moving into a more productive future. For performance appraisals to achieve their potential, it's not sufficient to just *do* them; employees must *act* on them. Usually, supervisors have responsibility for communicating the results of appraisals to their subordinates and helping their subordinates improve in the future. Conversely, subordinates usually have responsibility for seeking honest feedback and using it to improve their performance.[44]

In **performance feedback sessions**, *managers and their subordinates meet to exchange performance information and discuss how to improve future performance.* In many organizations, the performance information that is discussed includes the employee's own assessments of his or her performance, the assessment of teammates, and even information from customers. Regular assessment of progress toward attaining goals helps employees remain motivated and solve problems as they arise. Regular feedback also encourages periodic reexamination of goals to determine whether they should be adjusted. This is true regardless of whether the manager is giving the feedback or getting it! In a study that tracked the performance of managers over five years, researchers found that some managers who received appraisals by subordinates improved more than others. The managers who improved the most were the ones who met with their direct reports to discuss the appraisal results and what they could do to improve.[45]

Much of the value of performance appraisals depends on accuracy. In order for managers and their subordinates to accept the decisions that are based on performance appraisals, such as who should be promoted or how much of a bonus an employee has earned, they must believe that the results of the performance appraisal process are accurate.

Performance Appraisal Accuracy

During the past 50 years, hundreds of studies have been conducted to learn how to improve the accuracy of managers' performance appraisals. Studies have examined the judgmental errors that managers make, problems that can be created by poorly designed appraisal forms, and even how employees use tactics such as ingratiation to influence their supervisors' evaluations of their performance.[46] A basic lesson that has been learned from all of this research is this: It is very difficult for managers to accurately assess the performance of their subordinates. Fortunately, there are several things organizations can do to help managers be more accurate when conducting performance appraisals, as illustrated in Figure 13.5.

Rating Scale Format. A **performance rating scale** *is used by managers to record their judgments of employee performance.* The rating process is similar to assigning a grade. At Sun Microsystems, for example, employees are rated as "Superior," "Sun Standard," or "Underperforming."[47] Performance ratings tend to be more accurate when the rating scales are precise. At TRW, four-point rating scales provide very specific descriptions of what each level of performance means. This system is described in the Planning & Administration Competency feature.[48]

PLANNING & ADMINISTRATION COMPETENCY

Managing Performance at TRW

TRW is a global business with nearly 100,000 employees worldwide working in four major businesses—automotive, aeronautical systems, space and electronics, and information systems. In 2001, responding to declining business conditions, management sought to revitalize the com-

pany by instituting numerous change initiatives. One change initiative was targeted at creating a companywide performance appraisal and career development system. Instead of several paper-based systems that were unique to each business unit, top management wanted a single, integrated approach that could be used to communicate the behaviors

needed for the company's profitability. These behaviors included creating trust, energizing people, embracing change, building teamwork, and being customer oriented. The global design team, which operated as a virtual team, recognized that an online system would be the best solution. However, because not all employees had access to the company's e-mail

Figure 13.5 Improving Performance Appraisal Accuracy

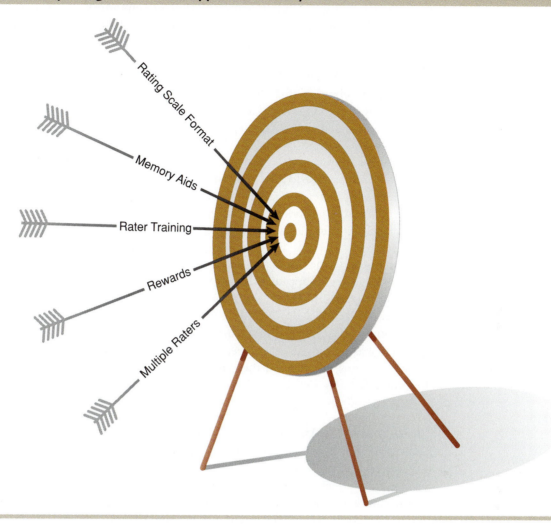

hub, a parallel paper-based system was also created. Within three months, a new four-page form had been created.

Besides evaluating performance against specific goals that had been set, managers rated their subordinates' performances against the key behaviors using a four-point scale. For each point on the scale, a paragraph explained what that rating meant. For example, the highest rating was:

Far Exceeds Expectations: *Organizational contributions and excellent work are widely recognized. Performance consistently exceeds all defined expectations,* *producing important and impactful results through superior planning, execution and creativity. Employee consistently demonstrated the rated TRM behaviors and/or initiatives at higher levels than expected.*

And the lowest possible rating was:

Needs Improvement: *Performance falls below expectations on one or more critical position competencies, objectives or tasks. While some responsibilities may be executed in a generally satisfactory manner, improvement is required for performance to become fully competent. Demonstration of the TRW behaviors and/or initiatives is inconsistent or at lower levels than expected.*

In another section, managers described the subordinate's performance goals and professional development activities for the upcoming year. The subordinate's perspective also was recorded. Subordinates described their strengths and areas they felt they could improve. They also assessed their own future potential and possible future positions. A year after the new system was implemented, the company reported that managers and subordinates alike found the new system to be both much more efficient and more effective in achieving a uniform and complete evaluation process.

Memory Aids. Everyone involved in making appraisals should regularly record behaviors or outcomes—good or bad—that relate to an employee's performance. Reviewing these records at the time of the performance appraisal helps ensure that the rater uses all available and relevant information.[49]

Rater Training. Rating accuracy can also be improved through training that focuses on improving the observation skills of raters.[50] Training also builds confidence. A good training experience helps raters see that they *can* rate accurately and *can* handle the consequences associated with giving negative feedback.

Rewards. One cause of rating inaccuracy is a lack of rater motivation. Without rewards, raters may find it easier to give high ratings than to give accurate ratings. A straightforward strategy for increasing rater motivation is to base salary increases, promotions, and assignments to key positions partly on performance as a rater. Managers who conduct performance appraisals in a timely and fair manner should be rewarded.

Multiple Raters. One popular way to assess performance is to conduct a 360-degree appraisal.[51] A **360-degree appraisal** *measures performance by obtaining assessments of the employee from a variety of sources—supervisors, subordinates, colleagues inside the company, people outside the organization with whom the employee does business, and even a self-appraisal by the employee.* The identities of specific individual assessors aren't disclosed to the employee. Multiple raters acting as a group may be especially effective in producing accurate ratings because discussion among members of the group helps overcome the various errors and biases of individuals.[52]

Performance Appraisals for Teams

Teams frequently take full responsibility for constructing and conducting their own performance appraisals. Team members are well acquainted with each other's strengths and weaknesses, so it makes sense that they become the primary performance evaluators. But team performance appraisal is fraught with challenges. When team members evaluate each other, they become concerned about creating conflict and hurting people's feelings. Because they will be working closely together in the future, fear of disrupting the team may be greater than the desire to provide accurate performance assessments. Using the team appraisal also is difficult. How should they use the information to provide feedback? Should someone outside the team conduct the feedback session? Should a team leader be designated for this task? Or should everyone on the team be involved in every feedback session?

The reality is that different teams handle appraisals and feedback in different ways. At Con-Way, everyone on the team participates in providing feedback to everyone else, and feedback is provided in a group discussion format. The goal is to incorporate feedback sessions into the normal work routine. Many other organizations provide feedback in a more private setting. Often the manager to whom the team reports is responsible for collecting performance information from the team and discussing it with each team member privately.

More important than who delivers the feedback is how they deliver it. Ideally, anyone who gives feedback has been trained in how to do so effectively. At Con-Way, teams are learning this invaluable skill by involving a professional facilitator in their feedback sessions. With sufficient practice and guidance, Con-Way teams may eventually develop enough skill and self-confidence to hold feedback sessions spontaneously and without assistance.

At Southwest Airlines and most other companies, the *total* compensation that employees receive for the work they do includes a mix of both monetary and nonmonetary compensation.

Nonmonetary compensation *includes many forms of social and psychological rewards—recognition and respect from others and opportunities for self-development.* For nine years Steve O'Donnell was David Letterman's head writer. He's the one who came up with the idea of the show's now-famous top ten lists. Did he ever get any special compensation tied to that particular contribution? "No. It never occurred to me," he says. "I'm probably the biggest simp about money of anybody over 12 years old. A pat on the back, making Dave happy, the thrill of hearing the audience laugh—that's what matters most."[53]

Nonmonetary compensation is certainly important to employees. As we describe in Chapter 14, money alone does not usually keep employees satisfied and motivated to do their best. In fact, nonmonetary compensation practices are central to employee satisfaction[54] and for creating an organization's unique culture (discussed in Chapter 18). The focus of our discussion here, however, is monetary compensation.

Monetary compensation *includes direct payments such as salary, wages, and bonuses, as well as benefits such as covering the costs of insurance plans.* Like many other aspects of an organization's approach to managing human resources, monetary compensation can facilitate (or interfere with) achieving various organizational objectives. Two objectives of particular relevance to compensation are (1) attracting and retaining the talent required for a sustainable competitive advantage and (2) maximizing productivity. In this chapter, we consider the role of compensation in attracting and retaining talent. In Chapter 14, the use of compensation for improving productivity is addressed.

7. Describe the basic elements of a monetary compensation package.

Importance of Pay Fairness

In conjunction with an organization's recruitment and selection efforts, monetary compensation can help ensure that the rewards offered are sufficient to attract the right people at the right time for the right jobs.[55] Effective compensation systems appeal to employees' sense of fairness. **Pay fairness** *refers to what people believe they deserve to be paid in relation to what others deserve to be paid.* Unless the compensation is perceived as externally competitive, the organization will have a difficult time attracting the best applicants. And unless it is internally fair, good employees (those the organization wants to retain) are likely to leave.[56] When evaluating whether a company's pay is fair, employees consider three basic components of the pay system: base pay, incentive pay, and benefits. These three components of the pay system are explained in detail next. Although the components are described separately, employees consider all three in combination with evaluating pay fairness.

Base Pay

In most organizations, being hired for a job means that you are guaranteed some basic level of pay, assuming you come to work and perform adequately. *The guaranteed pay offered for a job is called the* **base pay**. Employees who receive base pay that is on par with the market average—or even above the market—are more likely to feel fairly paid than those who are paid below the going rate. Ensuring that employees receive fair base pay has long been a major objective of organized labor unions. In general, the wages of unionized employees are higher than those of nonunionized employees doing similar work.[57]

Incentives

When monetary compensation is linked to the level of performance exhibited by employees it is referred to as **incentive pay**. Incentive pay is intended to encourage superior performance. Commissions, bonuses, and profit sharing are all forms of incentive pay. When pay is linked to strategically important behaviors and outcomes, it improves organizational productivity.[58] In addition to increasing performance, incentive pay can reduce turnover among good performers. High performers are more motivated to stay with an organization when they are rewarded more generously than poor performers. In addition, incentive pay can be cost effective. Savings result from productivity improvements and from the organization's ability to match compensation costs to performance levels. Because incentive pay is a very popular approach to increasing employee motivation, several types of incentive pay are explained in detail in Chapter 14.

Benefits

Employee benefits *are generally defined as in-kind payments or services provided to employees for their membership in the organization.* The employee benefits that companies provide usually include some health insurance, unemployment insurance, and some contribution to a retirement plan. Unlike direct compensation, which differs according to the job a person holds, full-time employees in an organization generally all receive the same benefits. In some organizations, part-time employees receive the same benefits as full-time employees, but that is unusual.

Some benefits are required by law. These include Social Security contributions, unemployment compensation, and workers' compensation. Other benefits are offered voluntarily by employers. Typically, larger organizations voluntarily offer health care, life insurance, disability insurance, and retirement pensions or savings plans. Benefits programs also include pay for time not at work—vacations, holidays, sick days and absences, and short breaks during regular workdays. Figure 13.6 illustrates the cost of benefits as a share of total labor costs for the "average" U.S. employee.[59]

For global companies, determining the number of vacation days to offer employees can be a real headache, due to large differences in national vacation practices.[60] As Figure 13.7 shows, American employees take relatively few official vacation days compared to employees in many other countries. Not surprisingly, many American employees do not feel that the balance between work and family life is healthy. Employees who

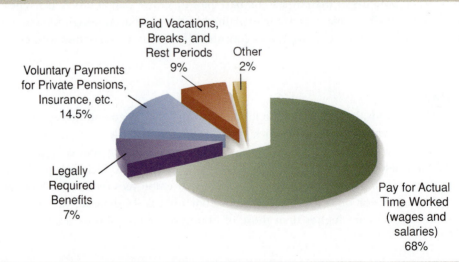

Figure 13.6   Average Annual Monetary Benefits and Earnings

Paid Vacations, Breaks, and Rest Periods 9%

Other 2%

Voluntary Payments for Private Pensions, Insurance, etc. 14.5%

Legally Required Benefits 7%

Pay for Actual Time Worked (wages and salaries) 68%

Figure 13.7   Vacationing Around the World

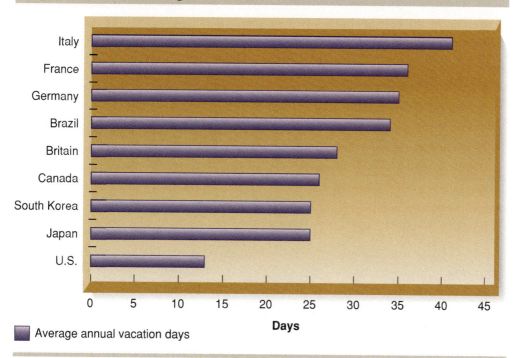

Average annual vacation days

feel crunched for time favor employers who offer benefits that enable them to enjoy a better lifestyle and more easily meet their social or personal obligations.[61] Flexible work schedules, telecommuting, compressed workweeks (e.g., 10 hours a day for four days), dependent care assistance, on-site child care, and dry cleaning services all fall into this category.[62]

CHAPTER SUMMARY

1. Explain the strategic importance of managing human resources effectively.

Human resources management (HRM) is concerned with the philosophies, policies, and practices that affect the people who work for an organization. The various HRM activities should help the organization achieve its strategic goals and achieve a sustained competitive advantage. Effective HRM has a positive impact on an organization's financial bottom line, employees, and the life of people in the local communities and the larger society.

2. Describe several important laws and government regulations that affect how organizations manage their human resources.

Many laws and regulations govern human resources management. Two major categories of laws and regulations are those that are intended to ensure equal employment opportunity and those that provide oversight of compen-

sation and benefits. A few of the major U.S. laws that managers need to understand are Title VII of the Civil Rights Act, the Fair Labor Standards Act, and the Equal Pay Act.

3. Explain the objective of human resources planning and describe how organizations respond to the unpredictability of future business needs.

Human resources planning should ensure that the right numbers and types of individuals are available at the appropriate time and place to fulfill organizational needs. At the heart of planning are two tasks: determining an organization's future human resource needs and developing a strategy to meet those needs. To stay flexible, some organizations hire contingent workers who work on a temporary basis and only as needed. An alternative is to maintain a workforce of more permanent employees, but this strategy often means that layoffs become necessary when business declines.

4. Describe the hiring process.

The hiring process includes two major activities: recruitment of job applicants and selection of the best applicants. When labor is in short supply, recruitment activities become more important. Selecting the right people from the pool of applicants helps improve productivity and reduce turnover. When selecting who to employ, the most common sources of information used are résumés, reference checks, interviews, and numerous types of tests. Of these, tests generally do the best job of predicting performance.

5. Describe several types of training and development programs.

Training programs help employees develop the competencies they need to perform their best in their current jobs. Orientation training, basic skills training, e-learning, and team training are all examples of programs that help organizations improve the performance of their workforce. Development programs help employees develop competencies that will enable them to continue to advance in their career over the longer term. They often provide employees with tools to assess their own strengths and weaknesses and develop personal plans for improvement.

6. Describe several principles for improving the accuracy of managers' appraisals of employee performance.

Performance appraisal is a formal, structured system for measuring job performance. During performance feedback sessions, managers and their subordinates meet to exchange performance information and discuss how to improve future performance. Performance appraisal and feedback are most effective when they are aligned with the organization's strategic goals, when managers make accurate judgments of performance, and when employees work with managers to use performance appraisal information as a basis for developing plans for performance improvement.

7. Describe the basic elements of a monetary compensation package.

Monetary compensation includes both direct compensation and indirect compensation. Direct compensation consists of the base wage or salary and incentive pay. Indirect compensation includes benefits that are mandated by law and those that employers provide voluntarily. Social Security, unemployment compensation, and workers' compensation are benefits that employers must provide. Insurance and vacation pay are commonly offered benefits that are not required by law.

KEY TERMS and CONCEPTS

360-degree appraisal
Base pay
Coaching
Cognitive ability test
Comparable worth
Competency inventory
Contingent workers
Development
E-learning
Employee benefits
Employee referrals
Employee selection
Equal employment opportunity (EEO)
Equal Pay Act
Fair Labor Standards Act
Hiring process
Human resources management

Human resources planning
Incentive pay
Job posting
Mentoring
Monetary compensation
Nonmonetary compensation
Pay fairness
Performance appraisal
Performance feedback sessions
Performance rating scale
Performance test
Personality test
Recruitment
Situational interview
Title VII of the Civil Rights Act
Training

QUESTIONS FOR DISCUSSION and COMPETENCY DEVELOPMENT

1. How does managing human resources effectively address shareholders' concerns?

2. How can organizations use human resources management to ensure that managers understand and abide by the primary laws and regulations that govern the hiring process?

3. Which types of training and development programs are likely to be most important for the following or-

ganizations: (a) a fast-food restaurant, (b) a software company located in New York City, and (c) a global consulting firm? Explain.

4. Some people believe that inaccurate performance appraisals are caused more by office politics and friendships than by any inability of managers to be accurate. Do you think managers sometimes intentionally give inaccurate performance ratings? If you think this happens, explain why it might happen.

5. Describe the ideal compensation package that you would like to receive. Which elements of the package are most important to you? Why?

6. Assume that you are a senior partner in Midland Ashby, a consulting firm. You are writing a proposal for an assignment in Indonesia. As part of the proposal you describe the members of the team that will work with your client, who you know has very "traditional" views about men and women. The person with the most expertise on the client's problem is a woman, so you list her as one of the team members. Your potential client states that a woman team member is unacceptable. Describe what you would do and why. Consider the ethical, legal, and business consequences of keeping her on the team versus removing her from consideration.

CASE FOR COMPETENCY DEVELOPMENT

INTERVIEWING JOB APPLICANTS

The following 10 questions might be asked during an employment interview. Some of them are illegal and should never be asked. Employers who ask illegal questions may be subject to legal prosecution for employment discrimination. Place a check mark in the appropriate column to indicate whether the question is legal or illegal. Before taking this quiz, visit the home page of the Equal Employment Opportunity Commission (EEOC) at http://www.eeoc.gov.

	Legal	Illegal
1. How old are you?	____	____
2. Have you ever been arrested?	____	____
3. Do any of your relatives work for this organization?	____	____

	Legal	Illegal
4. Do you have children, and if you do, what kind of child-care arrangements do you have?	____	____
5. Do you have any handicaps?	____	____
6. Are you married?	____	____
7. Where were you born?	____	____
8. What organizations do you belong to?	____	____
9. Do you get along well with other men [or women]?	____	____
10. What languages can you speak and/or write fluently?	____	____

Answers on the following page.

Answers

The following evaluations provide clarification rather than strict legal interpretation because employment laws and regulations are constantly changing.

1. **How old are you?**

   This question is legal but inadvisable. An applicant's date of birth or age can be asked, but telling the applicant that federal and state laws prohibit age discrimination is essential. Avoid focusing on age, unless an occupation requires extraordinary physical ability or training and a valid age-related rule is in effect.

2. **Have you ever been arrested?**

   This question is illegal unless an inquiry about arrests is justified by the specific nature of the organization—for instance, law enforcement or a position that requires handling of controlled substances. Questions about arrests generally are considered to be suspect because they may tend to disqualify some groups. Convictions should be the basis for rejection of an applicant only if their number, nature, or recent occurrence renders the applicant unsuitable. In that case the question(s) should be specific. For example: Have you ever been convicted for theft? Have you been convicted within the past year on drug-related charges?

3. **Do any of your relatives work for this organization?**

   This question is legal if the intent is to discover nepotism.

4. **Do you have children, and if you do, what kind of child-care arrangements do you have?**

   Both parts of this question are currently illegal; they should not be asked in any form because the answers would not be job related. In addition, they might imply gender discrimination.

5. **Do you have any handicaps?**

   This question is illegal as phrased here. An applicant doesn't have to divulge handicaps or health conditions that don't relate reasonably to fitness to perform the job.

6. **Are you married?**

   This question is legal, but may be discriminatory. Marriage has nothing directly to do with job performance.

7. **Where were you born?**

   This question is legal, but it might indicate discrimination on the basis of national origin.

8. **What organizations do you belong to?**

   As stated, this question is legal; it is permissible to ask about organizational membership in a general sense. It is illegal to ask about membership in a specific organization when the name of that organization would indicate the race, color, creed, gender, marital status, religion, or national origin or ancestry of its members.

9. **Do you get along well with other men [or women]?**

   This question is illegal; it seems to perpetuate sexism.

10. **What languages can you speak and/or write fluently?**

    Although this question is legal, it might be perceived as a roundabout way of determining an individual's national origin. Asking how a particular language was learned isn't permissible.

Leading

©Photodisc/Getty Images

Work Motivation

LEARNING OBJECTIVES

After studying this chapter you should be able to:

1. Describe four approaches that can be used to explain employee motivation and satisfaction.

2. Explain how managers can use goals and rewards to improve performance.

3. Describe how jobs can be designed to be motivating and satisfying.

4. State how the organization context affects motivation and satisfaction.

5. Describe how individual differences in needs can affect employees' work.

6. Describe how understanding motivation can help managers improve employee performance and satisfaction.

Chapter Outline

Located in Oxford, England, BMW's Mini factory produces one of the company's hottest new products. It's a big change from a few years ago, when Rover owned the factory. Then the buildings were crumbling and the plant was often half-empty. After acquiring the Rover factory, the first challenge for BMW was modernizing the facilities. They installed the newest production technology, expanded the parking lot, created more appealing landscapes, and in other ways created a more pleasant work environment. As employee Bernard Moss explained, "We had an open day for old employees and they just couldn't believe the transformation of the plant."

The improvements were badly needed, but they were costly, too. For the plant to become profitable, productivity had to improve. BMW relies on the factory workers themselves to find ways to cut costs and boost output. To motivate their employees and align their efforts with the needs of the business, BMW managers and union leaders designed a new pay system. It offers all employees an annual bonus of £260 (approximately $400) for their ideas. In order for the employees to receive the full bonus, they must come up with an average of three ideas per employee and the ideas must save an average of £800. Other changes were also made in the way employees were paid. Under the old system, when production stopped and employees didn't come to work, they were paid anyway. And when the plant was extra busy, they earned overtime pay. Now, when the plant is closed, employees are paid, but there is a new twist. The agreement is that they will make up the time by putting in extra hours when needed. When things are busy, the workers are expected to put in longer hours; but instead of overtime pay, they build up an account of extra days off.

The workers resented the new pay arrangements at first, but now they like it. According to Moss, "they [workers] are starting to see the advantages of long holidays." Today the plant is even more productive than BMW managers had hoped for. Employees offered more than 10,000 ideas for improvements, saving the company £6 million. Workers are generally happy, but morale is still a concern. "I would like to see the camaraderie back. If people are happy, they are more efficient. If they are unhappy, they are not going to bother [making] suggestions," says Moss.[1]

UNDERSTANDING MOTIVATION AND SATISFACTION

1. Describe four approaches that can be used to explain employee motivation and satisfaction.

Motivation *is a psychological state that exists whenever internal and/or external forces stimulate, direct, or maintain behaviors.* In organizations, the employee behaviors of interest include both productive and unproductive behaviors. By understanding employee motivation, managers can increase productive behaviors, such as arriving on time and putting in extra effort. An understanding of motivation also enables managers to decrease disruptive behaviors, such as tardiness, theft, and loafing.

Satisfaction *is a psychological state that indicates how a person feels about his or her situation, based on an evaluation of the situation.* Many managers assume that employee motivation goes hand in hand with employee satisfaction. As the saying goes, "A happy worker is a productive worker." Or, is it the other way around? As this chapter explains, the relationship between employee motivation and employee satisfaction is a bit complicated. Satisfied employees do perform their jobs somewhat better than dissatisfied employees.[2] But understanding satisfaction also is important for other reasons. For example, a dissatisfied employee may perform at an acceptable level while searching for another job at the same time.

Understanding employee motivation and satisfaction has long been of interest to managers and researchers alike. Because it is so important to managing effectively, it has been a topic of much debate. We have grouped the many different theories of employee motivation and satisfaction into four general approaches: the managerial approach, the job design approach, the organization approach, and the individual differences approach.

As illustrated in Figure 14.1, all four approaches help explain employee motivation and satisfaction. Figure 14.1 also suggests why managers care about employee motivation

Figure 14.1   Employee Motivation and Satisfaction

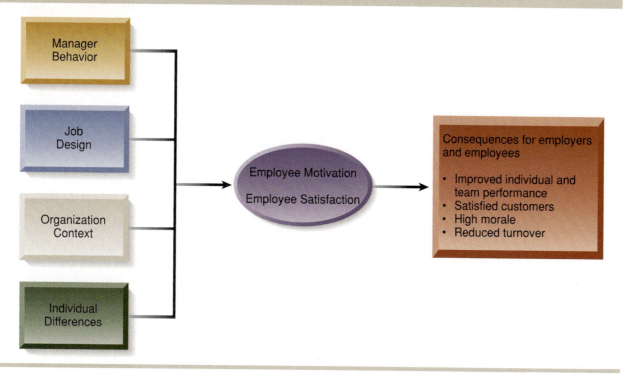

and satisfaction—namely, because motivation and satisfaction lead to other important consequences. Creating an organization filled with satisfied and motivated employees is not an end in and of itself. It is a means for achieving business success. Highly motivated employees outperform those who are less motivated. Research also shows that employee satisfaction results in higher customer satisfaction, lower employee turnover, improved safety, and greater profitability.[3]

Managerial Approach

The managerial approach focuses on how the behaviors of managers influence the satisfaction and motivation of their employees. Managers can directly motivate and satisfy employees through personal communication, by setting realistic goals, and by offering recognition, praise, and monetary rewards to employees who achieve those goals. According to this approach, the willingness of BMW employees to offer suggestions for cutting costs can be understood as resulting from the behaviors (e.g., setting goals, offering praise) of company managers.

Job Design Approach

A second approach to motivating employees emphasizes the design of jobs. Managers can sometimes design the jobs of the people they supervise, but not always. Often the design of jobs is determined by factors that cannot be easily changed without changing the technology or the structure of an entire work unit. As described in Chapter 12, enriched jobs are more motivating than jobs that are narrow in scope. Later in this chapter, we describe in greater detail how several aspects of job design determine whether employees experience their jobs as motivating and satisfying.

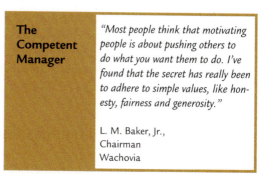

The Competent Manager

"Most people think that motivating people is about pushing others to do what you want them to do. I've found that the secret has really been to adhere to simple values, like honesty, fairness and generosity."

L. M. Baker, Jr.,
Chairman
Wachovia

Organization Approach

The broader organizational context also is important. As described in Chapter 13, human resource management policies and practices are generally an important aspect of the organizational context. The appropriate benefits (e.g., paid vacations, sick leave, insurance, and child or elder care), reward structure (e.g., bonuses, promotions), and development opportunities (e.g., education and mentoring) may attract new employees to the organization. Whether such policies serve to increase employee effort and desire to stay with the company depends partly on whether employees perceive them to be fair and equitable. At BMW, employees felt that the changes they had to make were fair given the investment that BMW had to make in order to transform the old Rover plant into a successful business. In this chapter, we describe in more detail how employees judge whether they are treated fairly, and how their judgments relate to feelings of satisfaction.

Individual Differences Approach

The fourth approach treats motivation and satisfaction as characteristics of individuals. Individual differences are the unique needs, values, personalities, and other characteristics that employees bring to their jobs. These differ from one individual to the next, which is why they are called *individual differences*. This view suggests that an employee who offers a lot of good suggestions for improving productivity at BMW would be likely to do the same if he worked at Ford or General Motors. Likewise, an employee who feels satisfied working at the BMW would probably feel fairly satisfied working at most other companies.

According to the individual differences approach, motivation and attitude are stable aspects of an employee's psychological makeup, and managers have limited ability to change them. How can managers motivate and satisfy employees if these are stable characteristics? The individual differences approach suggests that managers should use their understanding of individual differences to create organizations that are motivating and satisfying to people with a wide range of personal characteristics. Instead of treating everyone alike, managers should get to know their employees personally and treat them as unique individuals.

MANAGERIAL APPROACH

2. Explain how managers can use goals and rewards to improve performance.

Managers who are in direct contact with employees may be the most important influences on the motivation and satisfaction of employees. When the Gallup Organization interviewed 80,000 people about their work, they found that employees tolerate a lot of negative aspects of their work (low pay, ugly offices) if they work for a good manager. If they have a bad manager, however, they are likely to look for another job.[4] Good managers understand the unique characteristics of each employee and are responsive to these. But they also understand that there are a few basic principles they can follow to ensure that all employees are motivated to perform their jobs well. Good managers don't just make employees feel comfortable—they help them be productive. Three practical things managers can do to enhance the motivation of their employees are (1) to inspire employees through one-on-one communication, (2) to be sure that employees have specific and challenging goals that they accept and will strive to achieve, and (3) to provide employees with praise, recognition, or other rewards so they feel good about achieving those goals.

Communication Comes First

As we have seen throughout this book, effective communication is central to many aspects of managerial work. This is definitely the case when it comes to motivating employees. For William George, the former CEO of Medtronic Inc., communication is key to instilling employees with a sense of purpose and a meaningful mission. Medtronic is a medical technology company that produces devices such as pacemakers for heart patients and implants to control the tremors associated with Parkinson's disease. George believed that Medtronic's employees were motivated as much by a desire to contribute to improving the quality of people's lives as they were by the desire to simply earn a living. He reminded employees that doing their jobs well helped other people live better. Following a tradition set by the firm's founder, George traveled all around the world to meet individually with employees in all types of jobs—production, sales, service, and even high-level executives. In these one-on-one meetings, George reviewed the company's mission, which is "to restore people to fuller lives by alleviating pain, restoring health, and extending life." He took time to explain what this means and described some of the key events in the company's history. Then he presented a medallion to the employee, and encouraged the employee to keep the medallion somewhere in plain view throughout the workday. A picture on one side of the medallion is inscribed with the words "toward full life" and shows a person rising from an operating table and walking to a full life. The first sentence from the mission statement is shown on the back. Why would a CEO spend so much time communicating the company's mission to employees? As he put it, it's because "we have seen consistently high levels of performance from tens of thousands of people that can only come from a passion for a higher purpose or mission."[5]

Setting Goals

Besides instilling a sense of purpose, managers can further motivate employees through the use of goal setting. Put simply, **goal-setting theory** *states that managers can direct the performance of their employees by assigning specific, difficult goals that employees accept and are willing to commit to.* Done correctly, goal setting has been shown to be effective for increasing the performance of people working in a wide range of jobs. Today, many of the basic principles from this theory are accepted as standard management practice.[6] The Planning & Administration Competency feature describes how NCCI used goal-setting principles to improve the company's performance, which had begun to deteriorate after 75 years in business.[7]

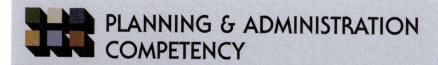

PLANNING & ADMINISTRATION COMPETENCY

NCCI's Goals Improve Performance

Located in Boca Raton, Florida, NCCI is a nonprofit consortium that employs 1,200 people. The organization provides workplace injury data to its customers, which include insurance companies, insurance brokers, and state officials in 40 states. When annual employee turnover reached 26 percent and customers began to express concerns about the service they were receiving, NCCI developed a new approach to motivating employees. Under the new system, employees meet with their managers twice a year to develop goals to be achieved during the next 12 months. In June, the meeting focuses on specific goals that the employee is to achieve. A billing analyst might have a goal of completing 100 percent of invoices on time. A marketing manager might have a goal of completing a project by a specific date and within a certain budget. How well an employee's goals are met determines her salary increase for the next year. In December, another goal-setting meeting is held, but this time the focus is on the employee's extra contributions to the organization. As Lisa Jarrot, a manager in the finance division puts it, "This is more an above-and-beyond sort of thing. Say that one of the corporate goals is to streamline performance to improve the bottom line. The billing analyst's part might be to seek efficiencies in the billing process to improve cycle time." How well an employee does in contributing to this "above-and-beyond" type of goal is used to determine the employee's annual bonus. Jarrot is convinced that the

Goal-setting practices like those at NCCI are quite common in U.S. companies because they have proven to be quite useful. At NCCI, the new approach to motivating employees helped reduce turnover—especially among the most experienced employees. It also helped improve efficiency and productivity and helped NCCI achieve a positive cash flow, thus making it possible for NCCI to give its customers price breaks worth $11 million.

Figure 14.2 illustrates how goal setting works. It shows that effective goals are specific, difficult, and accepted by employees. The exhibit also illustrates the four ways through which goals can result in better performance.

Figure 14.2 How Goal Setting Works

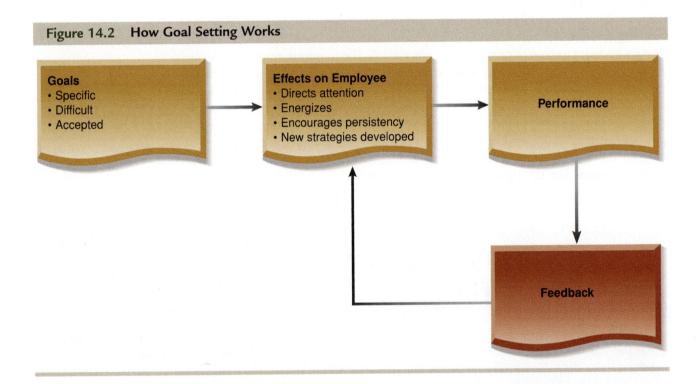

How to Set Effective Goals. Numerous studies have documented that performance is improved when managers set goals that are specific and difficult. In addition, employees must accept the goals as reasonable—that is, they shouldn't be so difficult that they are considered impossible to achieve.

In one of the most famous studies, goals were used to improve the efficiency of truck drivers hauling logs to Weyerhaeuser lumber mills. Before goals were introduced, loggers were carrying loads that were well below their trucks' legal weight capacities. Goals were introduced to encourage the loggers to transport fuller loads. At first, drivers were given a vague, easy goal that was stated as "do your best." This goal had almost no effect on the size of loads the drivers hauled. Three months later, drivers were given the *specific* goal of carrying loads that were 94 percent of their trucks' capacities. Within a month, the average load had increased from less than 60 percent to more than 80 percent of capacity. Six months later, truckers were carrying loads that averaged more than 90 percent of capacity. Specific goals also make it easier for employees to gauge how well they're doing. If a goal is specific, employees can quickly judge whether their efforts are paying off in terms of performance. Employees can then use this feedback to decide whether to continue using the same methods or try new approaches.[8]

Besides being specific, goals should be *difficult.* If goals are too easy, they don't give the employee any reason to exert extra effort. Difficult goals must also be *accepted* by employees, however, so they should not be too difficult. If employees reject their goals as impossible, they won't even bother trying to achieve them.[9] If they accept the difficult goals, employees will put in more effort and usually perform better. They may also feel a bit more fatigued by their jobs, but employees who enjoy achieving outstanding results will feel satisfied as a consequence of having performed well.[10]

When judging whether a goal is too difficult, managers and employees have no easy rules to follow. One way that managers try to be sure goals are accepted by employees is to involve the employees in the goal-setting process. At BMW, management works with union representatives when setting productivity goals as a way to ensure employee acceptance.

Management by objectives *(MBO) is a participative goal-setting technique used in many U.S. organizations.* Generally, the MBO process begins with a conversation between manager and employee. During this conversation, past performance is reviewed and objectives (goals) for the future are identified. The manager and employee agree to a set of goals that both parties accept as appropriate, with the understanding that future performance evaluations and rewards will reflect the employee's progress toward the agreed-on goals. NCCI is one example of an organization that uses management by objectives.

When employees are very competent and empowered, they may set their own goals. Because people generally feel committed to achieving goals they set themselves, this approach ensures goal acceptance. Universal Technical Institute (UTI), based in Phoenix, Arizona, believes in letting employees set their own goals. UTI provides technical training for people who work on climate control systems. Thus, a BMW dealer might send repair technicians to UTI courses to learn how to service its cars' air conditioning and heating system. When UTI decided to change its strategy, top executives didn't sit down and draw up a list of goals for its 1,100 employees. Instead, they set the objective of finding new ways to generate revenue and then involved all employees in creating a new strategic plan and developing accountability measures. When employees feel that they are capable of high performance, their self-set goals may actually be higher than those that a manager would assign. UTI's highly participative approach to goal setting helped increase profits by 44 percent while also improving employee morale.[11]

How Goals Work. First, goals help direct the attention of employees *toward* the most important work activities and *away from* irrelevant tasks. This is why effective managers invest so much time in communicating company goals. Second, goals energize employees to exert more effort. When employees accept a goal as something to strive for and then commit to achieving that goal, they essentially agree to exert the amount of effort required to do so. Assuming employees have the competencies needed to achieve the goals, then exerting greater effort usually leads to better performance. Third, goals encourage employees to be more persistent in their work efforts. For example, the desire to achieve a specific goal may encourage an employee to work extra hours instead of just putting in the minimum time required. Fourth, when employees are striving to achieve specific goals, they are more actively involved in thinking about alternative strategies to achieve that goal. If one approach doesn't work, they will try another approach in order to achieve their goal.[12]

Feedback. Goal setting works best when employees receive timely feedback about the progress they are making toward achieving their goals. As we explained in Chapter 13, performance feedback helps employees improve their performance. Even very simple forms of feedback (e.g., how well employees are doing compared to their goals) can be effective. When employees can see that they aren't performing well enough to reach their goals, they're likely to consider why and then change their methods or behaviors. One way is simply to try harder. If putting out more effort doesn't help, another way is to approach tasks differently.[13] Feedback is a signal that tells employees that they are doing well and should continue with their current approaches or that they aren't doing very well and should try new approaches.[14]

Team Goal Setting. Just as goals can improve the performance of individual employees, team goals can improve group performance.[15] Like individual goals, team goals work best if they are difficult, yet doable. To keep a team focused, it is best not to set too many team goals—usually no more than three to five. Also important in setting team goals is being sure that employees understand why it's important for them to achieve the goals.

The copper mining company of Phelps Dodge uses team goals throughout its six locations in North America. For truck maintenance workers, for example, a team goal is to shorten the time that trucks are off-line for maintenance. The goal is set participatively, using input from the maintenance crews and their supervisors. Miners at each location also have team goals designed to improve productivity. For achieving their team goals, employees receive extra compensation above their typical salary.[16]

Offering Incentives and Rewards

In some situations, managers can use goal setting to improve performance even if they don't offer any significant rewards to employees for achieving the goals. The idea of simply beating the goal may be all the motivation that some employees need. In most work situations, however, goals become more powerful when achieving them results in some type of tangible reward. Rewards for goal achievement increase motivation and performance because they strengthen the level of commitment that employees feel. Another explanation for the effectiveness of rewards is provided by reinforcement theory.

Reinforcement theory *states that behavior is a function of its consequences.* Positive consequences are referred to as *rewards,* and negative consequences are referred to as *punishments.* Psychologist B. F. Skinner developed and extended much of this approach to understanding what motivates behavior.[17] Skinner gained much public attention—and generated considerable controversy—when he revealed that he raised his children strictly by reinforcement principles.

Behaviors, Not Outcomes. Whereas goal setting focuses directly on improving performance outcomes, reinforcement focuses on changing behaviors. For this reason, *when the principles of reinforcement theory are used, it is sometimes referred to as* **behavior modification**. A manager who follows the principles of reinforcement will almost certainly be able to modify employee behaviors to some extent. Whether those changes in behavior result in better performance, however, depends on whether the manager actually knows which behaviors result in better performance.[18]

The basic principles of reinforcement are simple. They state that behavior followed by pleasant consequences is more likely to be repeated and that behavior followed by unpleasant consequences is less likely to be repeated. For instance, suppose that your job involves helping modify the company's Web site. You come to a staff meeting with a proposal for letting customers search the Web site using everyday language instead of the high-tech jargon used by the company's employees. If your manager praises your initiative and creativity, your behavior is rewarded. You probably will be motivated to come up with other innovations. However, if your manager gives you a disapproving look and says that the firm is perfectly happy with existing methods, you probably would feel put down or embarrassed in front of your colleagues. In effect, your behavior has been punished, indicating that you should modify that behavior in the future.

Figure 14.3 shows the process by which pleasant and unpleasant consequences influence behavior. A manager who wants to change an employee's behavior must change the specific consequences of that behavior.

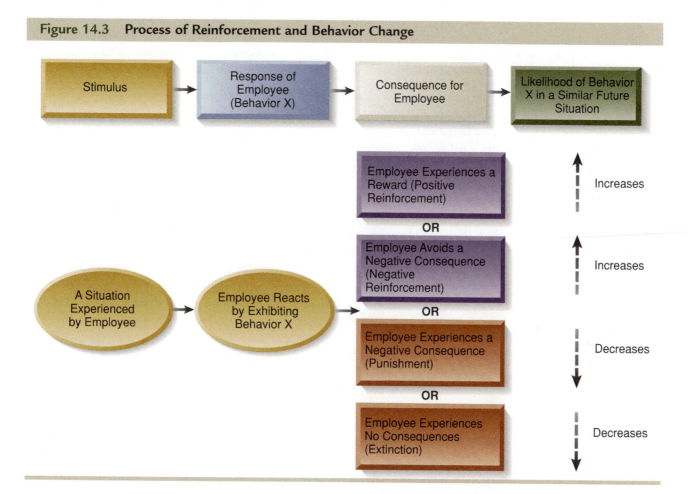

Figure 14.3   Process of Reinforcement and Behavior Change

Reinforcement principles don't require that managers actually tell employees what they should strive to accomplish. The theory assumes that employees will learn what is expected of them simply by experiencing the consequences of their behaviors. Employees also learn by observing what happens to others in the organization. Fortunately, not everyone has to be punished before most learn that some behaviors are best avoided. According to reinforcement theory, the behaviors of employees (e.g., helping each other out) occur because employees are being reinforced for them. If undesirable behaviors occur (e.g., harassment), it's because there are positive consequences for employees who engage in the undesirable behaviors. If desirable behaviors are absent (e.g., reporting harassment behavior), it is because those behaviors lead to no positive consequences for employees.

While it may be true that employees can learn what is expected simply by experiencing various outcomes and observing what happens to others, good managers recognize that it is important to communicate their expectations as clearly as possible. This is a simple matter of fairness. Employees should be told what they can do to receive reinforcement. If certain behaviors will be punished, employees should be told what those behaviors are and why they will be punished.

Behaviors that managers can most easily change by using reinforcement principles are those that can be easily measured.[19] Measurable behavior is action that can be observed and counted. Examples include smiling when a customer approaches, using a seat belt when driving a delivery truck, and wiping up spills when they occur on the shop floor. As Figure 14.3 suggests, a manager may increase the frequency of any of these behaviors by using positive reinforcement or negative reinforcement. To decrease any of these behaviors, a manager may use punishment or extinction. The concepts of reinforcement and punishment are easily understood because most individuals can readily recall at least one instance of a behavior being reinforced or punished. The concepts of negative reinforcement and extinction are sometimes more difficult to grasp, however.

Positive Reinforcement. **Positive reinforcement** *increases the likelihood that a behavior will be repeated by creating a pleasant consequence.* Any reward that encourages an individual to repeat a behavior can be classified as a positive reinforcer. Some common positive reinforcers used by organizations are praise, recognition of accomplishment, promotion, and salary increases. Most people regard these consequences as desirable.

Recognition programs are one common means to provide more positive consequences to employees who do a good job. Recognition programs provide a way for managers to acknowledge employees' efforts with small gifts and awards, without worrying about the many administrative and legal issues associated with awarding bonuses or salary increases. For example, when a garment factory decided it needed to improve employee attendance, it created a recognition program to provide several positive consequences to employees who came to work every day. For attending every day of the month, an employee's name was posted with a gold star for others to see. If perfect attendance continued for the entire quarter, the employee received a letter of recognition. At the end of the year, employees with perfect attendance were recognized at a plant-wide meeting where they were presented with a small gift (a silver necklace or penknife). Because the company wanted to see if this program was effective, they introduced it into only one of their plant locations. When they compared this plant to other locations, they found that absenteeism decreased 52 percent in six months. This compared to almost no change at the other locations.[20] Compared to the cost of absenteeism, which is estimated to cost about $1,000 per employee per year, on average, the cost of recognition programs is worth the investment.[21]

> **The Competent Manager**
>
> *"Recognition is like oxygen to employees; they can't survive without it."*
>
> John Farrell
> Senior Director of Client Strategy
> Carlson Marketing Group,
>   Minneapolis, Minnesota

Punishment. **Punishment** *involves creating a negative consequence to discourage a behavior whenever it occurs.* For example, disciplinary actions may be taken against an employee who comes to work late, fails to clean up the work area, or turns out too many defective parts. The disciplinary action might take the form of a verbal reprimand, a monetary fine, a demotion, or, if the employee persists, a suspension—all with the intention of discouraging the behavior.

Punishment is sometimes a useful way of eliminating unwanted behaviors, but it must be done carefully. To reduce the likelihood of the employee feeling resentment and possibly retaliating against the company, managers should avoid punishment that humiliates or embarrasses employees.

Extinction. **Extinction** *is the absence of any consequence—either positive reinforcement or punishment—following the occurrence of a behavior.* Usually, extinction occurs when the positive reinforcement that once normally resulted from the behavior is removed. Because the behavior no longer produces reinforcement, the employee stops engaging in it.

When extinction results in the decline of a disruptive behavior, the organization usually benefits. But extinction of beneficial behaviors occurs just as often, as illustrated in the following example. Jan Smith, a 7-11 store manager who seeks to reduce tardiness, puts in place a plan to reward employees for coming to work and not taking days off. Smith begins to offer a small monetary bonus for perfect attendance. Absenteeism goes down, as planned. Then Smith feels pressured to reduce costs and decides to eliminate the bonus program. Soon absenteeism is higher than ever. What happened? Unfortunately, Smith has gotten everyone to overcome any barriers they encountered in getting to work on time in order to receive their bonuses. Removing the bonus they received for doing so caused extinction of the behavior.

Negative Reinforcement. Notice that punishment, positive reinforcement, and extinction can be used only after a behavior has actually occurred. Employees experience **negative reinforcement** *when they engage in a behavior in anticipation of avoiding unpleasant consequences in the future.* Most students come to class on time to avoid a reprimand from the instructor. Similarly, most employees follow coffee break and lunch hour guidelines to avoid the disapproval of managers or coworkers. In both cases, these individuals are acting to avoid unpleasant results; when they are successful they are negatively reinforced. Whereas punishment causes a behavior to occur less frequently, negative reinforcement causes the behavior to be repeated.

Applying Reinforcement Principles. Positive reinforcement is the preferred approach for increasing desirable behavior in organizations, and extinction is the preferred approach for decreasing undesirable behaviors. Occasionally, punishment and negative reinforcement also may be needed, but managers often misuse these principles. The following is a typical example. Dan Caulfield, founder and CEO of a job placement firm, spent countless hours trying to move from print to electronic communication. When he was confident that his employees had all of the electronic tools they needed to work without paper, he became frustrated because employees weren't fully utilizing the new systems. He tried using punishment to change their behavior. He walked through offices removing yellow paper stickers from computer monitors, crumpled up papers that he found on people's desks, and scrounged through desk drawers looking for whatever paper he could find. He threw it all into a barrel, dragged the barrel to the fire escape, and set it ablaze as employees watched. Fines were introduced as a further deterrent: $1 per line for using the fax machine and 25 cents per page for printing a résumé. But as Caulfield eventually learned, this approach caused resentment among the employees.[22] With a better understanding of reinforcement, Caulfield would have known that offering rewards to the employees who used the least paper or found new ways to reduce the use of paper could have yielded the results he wanted.

Self-Management. Just as managers can use the principles of goal setting and reinforcement to change the behavior and performance of employees, so too can employees. With a bit of training, employees can learn to set their own goals, provide their own reinforcements, and even monitor their results over time. Taking an active self-management approach to job performance and career progress is one way to improve long-term outcomes, such as quicker promotions and higher salary levels.[23]

The effectiveness of self-management training was recently demonstrated for sales employees in an insurance company. During the period of a month, salespeople attended four training sessions that taught them about the principles of self-management. The salespeople were then monitored for a year. Compared to another group of salespeople who did not receive the training, those who completed self-management training reported that they felt better able to deal with difficult obstacles that might interfere with their jobs. They also greatly improved their sales performance. On average, they made 50 percent more sales calls, sold twice as many insurance policies, and generated three times as much revenue.

People who have confidence in their own ability to achieve their self-set goals can improve their performance in a variety of domains. Besides improving their work performance, they can improve their performance at school, they can perform better in athletic competitions, and they can even improve their own health outcomes.[24]

Using Performance Expectations to Motivate Employees

Experienced managers understand that keeping employees motivated and satisfied requires them to use a combination of goal setting and offering of incentives and rewards. This combined approach to motivation and satisfaction is evident in expectancy theory. **Expectancy theory** *states that people tend to choose behaviors that they believe will help them achieve their personal goals (e.g., a promotion or job security) and avoid behaviors that they believe will lead to undesirable personal consequences (e.g., a demotion or criticism).* Examples of choices that are related to work performance include whether to go to work or call in sick, whether to leave work at the official quitting time or stay late, and whether to exert a great deal of effort or to work at a more relaxed pace. Notice that these same behaviors might be explained by reinforcement principles. The two theories are somewhat similar, but there is one subtle difference to keep in mind. Reinforcement theory emphasizes changing behaviors after they occur, whereas expectancy theory emphasizes the initial decision to engage in a behavior.

As you can see, expectancy theory also includes some elements of goal-setting theory. But again, there are some subtle differences. One difference is that goal-setting theory emphasizes the importance of work-related goals, whereas expectancy theory emphasizes the personal goals of employees. Another difference is that goal-setting theory assumes that goals alone are motivating—they can influence performance even if there are no rewards or punishments tied to goal achievement. Corning has learned that team goals work well when they are tied to team rewards. At Corning and many other companies, this approach to motivating employees is called *goalsharing*. With **goalsharing**, *employees receive financial rewards when their business unit meets its goals.* The Strategic Action Competency feature describes how goalsharing works.[25]

STRATEGIC ACTION COMPETENCY

Goalsharing at Corning

When the telecommunications industry fell on hard times, Corning Inc. was one of the many companies that suffered. Due to huge declines in orders for fiber optic cable, Corning's stock price dropped nearly 99 percent and forced it to cut 16,000 jobs. Motivating employees in this type of business climate is tough, but Corning found a way. For the past decade, Corning has used a goalsharing system that employees helped design. Instead of tying employees' bonuses to the company's profitability, Corning sets specific performance goals for employees in each business unit and then rewards employees when those goals are met. In setting the goals, managers are expected to establish a clear "line of sight" to the corporate goal for each employee. The expectation is that every employee can improve each year, and that everyone has an equal chance of success.

The system emphasizes that the entire business unit must be successful in achieving its goals in order for each individual to be rewarded. Thus, goalsharing encourages em-

©Photodisc/Getty Images

ployees to cooperate with each other. Goalsharing also helps buffer employees from uncontrollable swings in the firm's overall financial performance. When bonuses are tied to a company's overall financial performance (as is done with profit sharing, for example), hard-working employees often feel discouraged when they receive no rewards because they feel the company's profitability is out of their control. Goalsharing recognizes that long-term success requires motivated employees who will help the company improve year after year, even when the company enters a downturn. If employees can meet the short-term (annual) goals set for their business unit, they deserve to be rewarded. With motivated employees, most companies can eventually succeed in executing a turnaround strategy.

Figure 14.4 illustrates how expectancy theory can be used to understand an employee's decision to exert more effort at work. When making such a decision, an employee would normally consider three questions.

1. *The expectancy question:* If I make an effort, will I be able to perform the behavior?
2. *The instrumentality question:* If I perform the behavior, what will be the consequences?
3. *The valence question:* How much do I value the consequences associated with the behavior?

Figure 14.4   Expectancy Theory

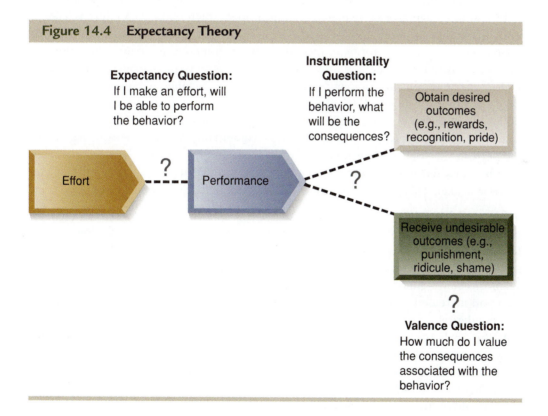

Expectancy Question:
If I make an effort, will I be able to perform the behavior?

Instrumentality Question:
If I perform the behavior, what will be the consequences?

Effort → ? → Performance → ?

Obtain desired outcomes (e.g., rewards, recognition, pride)

Receive undesirable outcomes (e.g., punishment, ridicule, shame)

Valence Question:
How much do I value the consequences associated with the behavior?

Expectancy. *Effort* is the amount of physical and/or mental energy exerted to perform a task or to learn something new. In other words, how hard is the employee trying? At Nordstrom department stores, a salesperson's attempt to find a medium-sized blue-striped shirt is an example of effort. Effort refers solely to the energy expended—not to how successful it is. **Expectancy** *refers to a person's estimate of how likely it is that a certain level of effort will lead to the intended behavior or performance result.* At Nordstrom, performance could involve making more sales, creating a satisfied customer, and/or helping another salesperson do his or her job more effectively.

Employees who believe that exerting more effort results in better performance generally show higher levels of performance than employees who don't believe that their efforts will pay off.[26] When employees feel their efforts are not likely to result in better performance, they don't even bother to put in the effort. For example, some older workers may not bother putting in the effort needed to learn how to use new technologies because they don't believe they are capable of performing the tasks required by new technologies.[27]

Instrumentality. To be willing to expend the effort needed to achieve the desired performance, employees must also believe that the performance will have some type of payoff. **Instrumentality** *refers to a person's perception of how useful the intended behavior or performance will be for obtaining desired outcomes (or avoiding undesired outcomes).* If Jackie develops an innovative product design at Texas Instruments, will she receive public recognition for this accomplishment? If Juan arrives at work on time at UPS, rather than being a few minutes late, will anyone else really care? If Max's employee performance rating is outstanding at Texaco, will he be paid more? According to a recent survey of U.S. workers, only about 35 percent of employees see a clear link between their job performance and important outcomes such as their pay.[28] Among that 35 percent are likely to be many managers, because managers appear to see their extra work effort as leading to higher compensation.[29]

Goalsharing and other forms of incentive pay are intended to create perceptions of high instrumentality. They don't always succeed, however. For managers whose pay is tied to movement in the company's share price, unpredictable market conditions or a single bad decision by the CEO can have devastating consequences for the company's bonus pool, despite overall excellent performance by most managers. Such events may result in a manager having a feeling of low instrumentality. When incentives are tied to the performance of a work team, a similar problem may occur—that is, individual team members may feel that the link between their own individual performance and their rewards is weaker. This problem seems to be more severe in larger work teams.[30]

Valence. **Valence** *is the value (weight) that an employee attaches to a consequence.* Valences are personal; the same outcome may have a high valence for one person and a low valence for another. For example, for Charlie Walter at the Fort Worth Museum of Science and History, a promotion from museum curator to the higher paying position of museum director would be appealing if he values (places a high valence on) financial gain and increased responsibility; it would be less appealing if he values creativity and independence.

As the Air Force recently discovered, the opportunity to accumulate hours of flying time is very valuable to young pilots. When the Air Force was preparing for war in Iraq, it was faced with the challenge of conducting a large number of unmanned reconnaissance flights, which are guided by remote control. The Air Force believed that trained pilots would perform these jobs best, but it was not easy to convince pilots to spend their time sitting at a desk. To motivate pilots to volunteer for the required training, the Air Force needed to find a way to link something of value to participating in the training program. The solution was to allow some of the time spent training for unmanned flights as "flying time." This meant that pilots could accumulate the flying hours they valued so highly in a new way—by flying via remote control.[31]

Because money is appreciated by most employees, it is often used by companies to reward employees for desired behaviors and for good performance. For money to be effective, however, the amount offered must be sufficiently large that employees will change their behavior in order to earn the money. Suppose you wanted to motivate employees to offer suggestions for how to cut costs so the company could save money. How much money would you offer? Keep in mind that the cost of getting employees to make suggestions shouldn't be too high—you are trying to cut costs! A hospital in Youngstown, Ohio, decided to offer an immediate payment of $50 and a personal response from the CEO for every qualified money-saving suggestion offered by its employees. In addition, each month, employees who offer the best suggestions are recognized at monthly management meetings and their suggestions are printed in the company newsletter. Finally, for ideas that the company believes it can implement, the employee receives 10 percent of the projected savings. Apparently, the hospital's employees value these outcomes. In one year alone, 390 suggestions were received from the hospital's employees and payouts were made for 80 percent of them.[32]

Applying Expectancy Theory. Expectancy theory gives great weight to how people think about the future. By understanding how employees think about the future, managers can find solutions to troublesome behavior problems, like theft. Theft is a major problem for many U.S. employers. The annual cost of theft for a forest products company in the Northwest was $1 million—or $833 per employee! The theft problem concerned the company managers because it cost nearly $1 million per year and had a significant impact on the bottom line. The theft problem concerned the union because their members had started to complain that they too were often the victims of theft. But getting answers from employees about what was going on proved difficult. No one was talking. To find a solution to their theft problem, the company enlisted the help of a consultant—an expert on employee motivation. The consultant suggested a procedure designed to discover how employees thought about theft. To find out, he interviewed employees, asking them questions such as these:

- What positive outcomes do you personally expect for honest behavior (at work)? Where is the win for you to be honest?
- What are the negative outcomes that you can expect for being honest? How will you get hurt for being honest? What are the downsides?
- What are the positive outcomes for you personally to steal (from the company)? What are the "wins" for you to steal? How will you come out ahead?
- What are the negative outcomes you can expect for engaging in theft? How might you get hurt? How might you lose?

The consultant used the employees' answers to create a scoreboard like the one shown in Figure 14.5. Given the employees' responses shown in Figure 14.5, what should the mill managers do to reduce theft? What would you do? Put in cameras for surveillance? Hire a private detective to masquerade as an employee? These were some of the ideas suggested by company managers. But the consultant believed these solutions might make the problem worse. His reasoning was that surveillance cameras and private detectives would simply make it more difficult to steal. And increasing the challenge might actually motivate the thieves even more. After all, as the challenge becomes greater, so does the thrill of succeeding.

After considering various options, the managers finally focused on the responses shown in cells 2 (negative consequences of honesty) and 3 (positive consequences of theft). Their solution was to set up a "library" system that allowed employees to borrow any type of tool or equipment that had previously been stolen. Employees did not steal things in order to sell them; they stole things to use them and for the fun of it. The library system removed the thrill and also made it easier for employees to get access to things that they might find useful to borrow for a home project. The company also created an amnesty day on which employees could return stolen material with no questions asked. On amnesty day, everyone would assume that the person returning an item was

Figure 14.5 Scoreboard for Understanding What Motivated Employees to Steal

	Responses to the Question **"What Are the Positive Outcomes You Expect?"**	Responses to the Question **"What Are the Negative Outcomes You Expect?"**
For Honesty	• "Nothing." • "You can look yourself in the mirror when you get out of bed in the morning." • "It is the right thing to do." • "I can live with myself." **Cell 1**	• "If you want to get along here, you better play the game." • "There's no harm. The company spills more milk at breakfast than you and I can steal in a year." • "See no evil, hear no evil." **Cell 2**
For Stealing	• "We are so good, we could steal a head-rig [which weighs more than a ton] from a sawmill." • "Doc, tell us what you want and we will get it out within 45 days." • "It takes real teamwork." • "It's a real thrill." **Cell 3**	• "If we got caught, we would get temporarily suspended." • "If someone got suspended, the guys would take a collection [to cover that person's pay loss]." **Cell 4**

doing it for "a friend," and no one would be expected to disclose the friend's name. The solution was a huge success. Employees returned truckloads of stolen items—so much was being returned that the company extended amnesty for three days. Almost everything that had been stolen was returned. Theft dropped to near zero and was still that low after three years. No other negative behaviors—such as graffiti or vandalism—crept up after the problem of theft had been resolved.[33]

As the scoreboard shown in Figure 14.5 revealed, employees who stole made rational choices about how to behave using the information available to them. Included in that information was some knowledge about how likely their efforts would be to affect their performance (as thieves) and how their performance (theft) would be related to certain outcomes, such as feeling "thrilled." Similarly, employees who knew about the theft but said nothing were thinking about their future and how people would react to someone who squealed.[34]

Danger: Money Ahead. Expectancy theory recognizes that tying monetary rewards to performance can be a powerful way to change how employees behave. Like any powerful instrument, it can be dangerous when used incorrectly. As described in Chapter 6, poorly designed incentive systems sometimes lead to behavior that is unethical and/or illegal.

The Occupational Safety and Health Administration (OSHA) worries that poorly designed incentives cause employees to hide injuries. Safety programs often include goals for reducing accidents and injuries, with rewards linked to goal achievement. When employees are injured, they may find themselves weighing the costs of reporting the injury and getting it treated quickly against the cost to themselves and their coworkers of not achieving their safety goals. Jenny-O Foods Turkey Store agrees that OSHA's concerns are valid. Jenny-O avoids that problem by setting goals and linking rewards to safety knowledge and behavior, not to reductions in injuries and accidents. Safety audits are used to check on dozens of workplace conditions that might cause accidents. Employees are randomly interviewed to check their knowledge of safety guidelines. Small rewards are given to employees who score well on these quizzes.

JOB DESIGN APPROACH

We have described how individual managers can affect motivation and satisfaction without saying much about how a specific job is performed by an employee. Characteristics of jobs also influence satisfaction and motivation. Job characteristics theory is the most popular and extensively tested approach to designing jobs that employees enjoy and feel motivated to perform well. Figure 14.6 illustrates the components of this theory.[35]

Job characteristics theory *states that employees are more satisfied and motivated when their jobs are meaningful, when jobs create a feeling of responsibility, and when jobs are designed to ensure that some feedback is available.* In essence, jobs should be designed to provide work that employees enjoy doing. People who enjoy doing their jobs may not need the extra motivation of high pay and impressive job titles. In fact, according to a recent survey of 1,200 U.S. employees, the nature of the work they did was the most important factor (ahead of direct and indirect financial rewards and career concerns) in determining how people felt about staying with their current employer and how motivated they were to work hard.[36]

3. Describe how jobs can be designed to be motivating and satisfying.

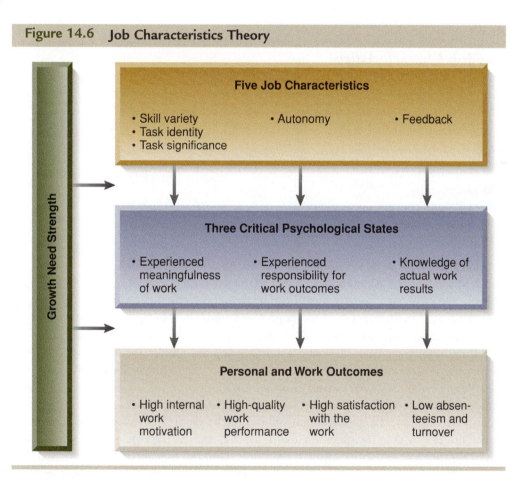

Figure 14.6   Job Characteristics Theory

Critical Psychological States

The job characteristics theory describes three attitudes or feelings that are essential for motivation. *The attitudes and feelings that must be present in order for employees to be highly motivated are referred to as* **critical psychological states**.

Experienced meaningfulness *is a critical psychological state that refers to whether employees perceive their work as valuable and worthwhile.* For example, people working in health care understand that their efforts can help save lives and improve the quality of people's lives. At Medtronic, managers understand how important it is for employees to experience their work as meaningful, and they use medallions to remind employees that what they do really matters.

Experienced responsibility *is a critical psychological state that refers to whether employees feel personally responsible for the quantity and quality of their work.* A surgeon who specializes in orthopedics is likely to experience a feeling of responsibility for the amount and quality of her or his work. Have you ever found a slip of paper among the packaging material of something you bought that said something like, "This product was inspected by Stacy Stamford"? Attaching a person's name to her work is one way that some companies use to increase employees' feelings of responsibility.

Knowledge of results *is a critical psychological state that refers to the extent to which employees receive feedback about how well they are doing.* Feedback can come from the task itself (e.g., successfully reviving a heart attack victim) or from other sources (e.g., the comments of colleagues or patient satisfaction surveys). At Lincoln Electric, knowledge of results can come directly from customers. When Lincoln Electric ships out an electric motor, for example, it includes the name of the employee who built it. If a customer has any complaints about the quality of the product, the employee who made it is informed of the problem and required to make the repairs.

Key Job Characteristics

Look again at Figure 14.6. How should jobs be designed to create the three critical psychological states? Job characteristics theory states that the critical psychological states are affected by five key job characteristics. **Key job characteristics** *are objective aspects of the job design that can be changed to improve the critical psychological states.* The five key job characteristics are

- skill variety,
- task identity,
- task significance,
- autonomy, and
- feedback.

Skill variety *is the degree to which the job involves many different work activities or requires several skills and talents.* **Task identity** *is present when a job involves completing an identifiable piece of work, that is, doing a job with a clear beginning and outcome.* **Task significance** *is present when a job has a substantial impact on the goals or work of others in the company.* **Autonomy** *is present when the job provides substantial freedom, independence, and discretion in scheduling work and determining the procedures to be used in carrying out tasks.* Finally, **feedback** *is present when the outcome gives the employee direct and clear information about his or her performance.*

At Whole Foods Markets, having jobs that are motivating fits the overall mission and values of the organization. The jobs are organized around self-managed teams. They're a natural extension of a management philosophy based on employee empowerment.[37] Teams are responsible for specific areas of a store, such as the fish section. One consequence is that each member of the team understands all aspects of running her or his area of the store, which creates *task identity*. Because the entire team shares the work in their section of the store, each person performs a variety of tasks which increases *skill variety*.

Teams are given goals that they're responsible for meeting, and then they're given a great deal of *autonomy* to find the best way to meet those goals. For example, if a holiday is coming up, a team decides how to arrange holiday schedules while also meeting the needs of customers. Another aspect of autonomy is that team members decide whether a new hire will stay on a team, based on their evaluations during an initial probationary period. Because of the autonomy given to Whole Foods Markets teams, feelings of *responsibility* seem to follow naturally.

Teams also get *feedback* about their results. If a team comes in under budget, the team gets to keep the difference and split it among the team members. If it comes in over budget, it builds up debt within the company, which can be erased by coming up with a plan to address the problem and showing some improvement. People get personal feedback, also. Team leaders know that they can be voted out at any time. To ensure that that doesn't happen very often, team members let leaders know clearly how the team feels about them, and leaders make the effort to get feedback without actually having to take a vote. Feedback in the form of financial results is plentiful, too. In fact, employees get so much financial information that they are "insiders" according to the Securities and Exchange Commission's definition.

Research conducted on employees in the Unites States shows that employees who work in jobs that include all five key job characteristics feel involved in their work and exert more effort, compared to those working in poorly designed jobs.[38] Studies in other countries reveal some cultural differences, however. For example, in Bulgaria, feedback seems to be less important than it is in the United States. For Dutch workers, task variety and task identity appear to be less important.[39] Clearly, managers working in countries outside the United States must be aware of such differences in order to be effective in motivating employees.

Growth Need Strength

Job characteristics theory considers individual differences to be important in determining how employees react to job content. In particular, employees' growth needs influence how they react to their jobs. **Growth need strength** *is a desire for personal challenge, accomplishment, and learning.* Employees with a strong growth need respond more favorably to enriched jobs, whereas employees with a weak growth need may experience enriched jobs as frustrating and dissatisfying. In other words, enriched jobs aren't for everyone. Nevertheless, many people thrive in an environment characterized by jobs designed to give them a sense of responsibility and meaningfulness.

People with strong growth needs are just the type of people that Jamba Juice looks for when hiring general managers to run its stores. In selection interviews, the interviewers look for people who "think the glass is half full"—that is, they see opportunities and are eager to make the most of them. When it finds the right people, Jamba Juice puts them in a situation that guarantees they'll feel a sense of responsibility. Besides the challenging task of being in charge of Jamba Juice stores—retail outlets that sell made-to-order smoothies and a variety of healthy foods—general managers who succeed at expanding their businesses also experience significant personal financial gain.[40]

ORGANIZATION APPROACH

The organization context includes many different elements, such as the organization design, pay plans, the organizational culture, and so on. Here we focus on a few elements of the organization context that are most important to understanding motivation and satisfaction. For small and medium-sized organizations, the organization context is usually similar for most employees working within a specific organization, regardless of what job a person has. In very large firms, such as GE and PepsiCo, the organization context may vary among different divisions or business units. To understand employee motivation and satisfaction, the immediate work context that an employee experiences on a daily basis is most relevant.

4. State how the organization context affects motivation and satisfaction.

Herzberg's Two-Factor Theory

According to Frederick Herzberg, the relationship between job satisfaction and motivation is a complicated one.[41] To gain an understanding of that relationship, Herzberg interviewed 200 accountants and engineers. He asked participants to describe job experiences that produced good and bad feelings about their jobs. He discovered that the presence of a particular job characteristic, such as responsibility, might increase job satisfaction. However, the lack of responsibility didn't necessarily produce dissatisfaction. Conversely, if lack of job security produced dissatisfaction, high job security didn't necessarily lead to satisfaction.

The study's results led to Herzberg's **two-factory theory**, *which states that two separate and distinct aspects of the work context are responsible for motivating and satisfying employees.* He used the terms *motivator factors* and *hygiene factors* to refer to these two aspects of context. Figure 14.7 illustrates these basic components of Herzberg's two-factor theory.

Figure 14.7 Two-Factor Theory

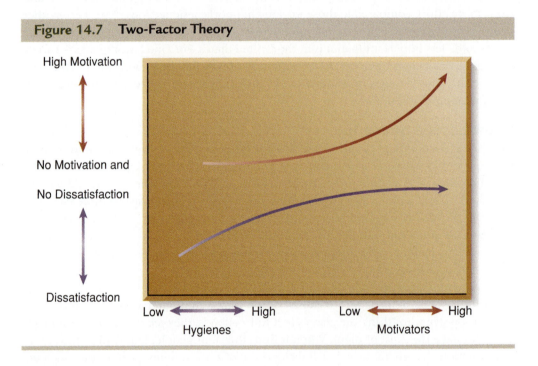

Hygiene Factors. The two-factor theory states that hygiene factors determine how satisfied employees feel. **Hygiene factors** *are the nontask characteristics of the work environment—the organizational context—that create dissatisfaction.* They include compensation, level of responsibility, working conditions, company policies, supervision, coworkers, salary, formal status, and job security. Hygiene factors need to be present, at least to some extent, to avoid dissatisfaction. The presence of hygiene factors alone will not motivate employees, however. That is, hygiene factors won't generate feelings of excitement about the job and organization. Nevertheless, hygiene factors help create a work setting that makes it possible to motivate employees. The absence of dissatisfaction is an essential, but not sufficient, condition for creating a motivated workforce. As described in Chapter 13, many of the fringe benefits offered by employers are attempts to remove potential sources of employee dissatisfaction.

Motivator Factors. Assuming hygiene factors are present and employees feel satisfied, then the presence of motivator factors results in employees who feel excited about their work. **Motivator factors** *are aspects of the organizational context that create positive feelings among employees.* Achievement, the challenge of the work itself, responsibility, recognition, advancement, and growth are all motivator factors. The presence of motivators alone doesn't guarantee that employees will be productive. Motivators lead to superior performance *only* if no dissatisfiers are present.

At Intuit, employees are generally satisfied, so motivator factors are used to increase motivation. Because employees are both satisfied and motivated, Intuit is one of *Fortune's* "Best Companies to Work For." Like many companies, Intuit uses recognition to motivate employees. As described in the Communication Competency feature, managers at Intuit understand that there are many ways besides a simple "thank you" to communicate how much they appreciate the efforts of their employees.[42]

COMMUNICATION COMPETENCY

Intuit

Headquartered in Silicon Valley, Intuit is the maker of well-known software programs such as Quicken and Turbo-Tax. But one program you may not have heard about is the company's Thanks Program.

With more than 6,000 employees, the company has 13 locations throughout the United States and Canada. At each site, giving out small awards is part of every manager's job. The company's philosophy is that awards should be given only to people who perform well above what is expected. Getting an award is special—it is a way to recognize excellence and communicate appreciation. Managers decide the criteria that will be used for giving awards, and they decide what awards to give. Examples of awards given include gift certificates to restaurants, movie tickets, written thank-you notes, and a Night-on-the-Town. Why do employees gets these awards? Some employees get awards for going beyond the call of duty to help out their colleagues. Some get awards for making suggestions that reduce bureaucracy. Some get awards for technical programming achievements or even for outstanding service to the community. Intuit gives managers the authority to make these decisions.

To make sure managers use good judgment when giving awards, Intuit developed a Web site designed to help them. It explains the importance of linking the awards they give to achieving business objectives. It also helps managers ensure that the awards given out are valued by employees. To monitor how employees feel about the Thanks Program, Intuit includes a question in the employee satisfaction survey that reads, "I am rewarded and recognized when I do a great job." As long as employees continue to agree with that statement, Intuit can be sure the Thanks Program is working.

The two-factor theory is based on the assumption that motivator and hygiene factors are similar for all employees. Individual differences among employees aren't recognized as being important. Therefore, in Herzberg's view, employers should be able to motivate all employees in the same way—by ensuring the presence of both hygiene and motivator factors. Studies that compare the importance of motivator and hygiene factors among different types of employees (e.g., those who work in the private sector versus the public sector or those who work in lower skill versus higher skill jobs) support this view.[43]

Recognizing the Power of Recognition. Perhaps you noticed that Herzberg's two-factor theory considers compensation a hygiene factor, whereas recognition is considered a motivator. In other words, the theory states that a person's compensation might cause them to feel more or less satisfied, but recognition is more effective for motivating employees. Some people argue that recognition programs are just a way for employers to avoid spending a lot of money on pay raises. Of course, spending *any* money on recognition programs would be a waste of money if they were not effective. But as Figure 14.8

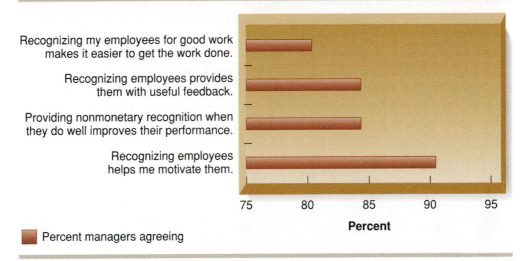

Figure 14.8   The Link between Recognition and Performance

Recognizing my employees for good work makes it easier to get the work done.

Recognizing employees provides them with useful feedback.

Providing nonmonetary recognition when they do well improves their performance.

Recognizing employees helps me motivate them.

75   80   85   90   95

Percent

■ Percent managers agreeing

shows, the evidence indicates that noncash recognition programs can be effective motivators. The data shown are based on the responses of employees in 34 organizations, including the U.S. Postal Service and Universal Studios. The same study found that managers also believed recognition programs could be effective. Of the managers, 73 percent said they got the results they expected from such programs almost immediately, and 99 percent believed they would get results eventually.[44]

Treating People Fairly

As Herzberg's two-factor theory suggests, employees are sensitive to many aspects of the organizational context. But the theory does not go into much detail about how employees think about all of these elements. According to equity theory, people evaluate their work experiences much like an accountant might. They consider everything they put into their work, everything they get out of their work, and then make a judgment about whether the balance of inputs and outcomes is fair. Even when the job itself is enjoyable and motivating, people will probably be upset if they feel that they're not being treated fairly.

In Chapter 13, we noted that compensation practices are one aspect of the organizational context that employees consider when evaluating whether they are fairly treated. When evaluating pay, they consider their salary or wage rate, bonuses and incentive pay, and the package of benefits offered by the organization. If their pay is judged as unfair, employees are likely to feel unmotivated and dissatisfied. But how exactly do employees decide what is fair?

According to **equity theory**, *employees judge whether they've been treated fairly by comparing the ratio of their outcomes and inputs to the ratios of others doing similar work.* Inputs are what an employee gives to the job (e.g., time, effort, education, and commitment to the organization). Outcomes are what people get out of doing the job (e.g., the feelings of meaningfulness and responsibility associated with jobs, promotions, and increased pay).[45]

Equity Ratios. Examples of equity ratios are shown in Table 14.1. In these examples, the outcomes and inputs are simply money and time, respectively. These are easy to quantify and the examples are easy to understand. In reality, the ratios and comparison can be quite complex. Employees consider many factors that are quite difficult to quantify and compare.

Table 14.1 Examples of Equity Perceptions

	Andy	Ally	Comparison	Andy's Equity Perception	Ally's Equity Perception
Situation A	Outcome: $500 Input: 50 hours work	Outcome: $800 Input: 80 hours work	$500/50 = $800/80 = $10/hour	Equitable	Equitable
Situation B	Outcome: $500 Input: 50 hours work	Outcome: $500 Input: 60 hours	$500/50 > $500/60	Feels over-rewarded (inequitable)	Feels under-rewarded (inequitable)

In situation A, Andy evaluates the pay he received and compares it to what Ally received. Ally received more pay, but she also worked more hours. Because the pay-per-hour worked is equal for Andy and Ally, Andy feels it is equitable and fair. In situation B, Andy also compares his pay to Ally's. In this example, Andy received the same pay as Ally. Both Andy and Ally know this. They also know that Andy worked fewer hours than Ally. Consequently, when Andy compares himself to Ally, he should feel overrewarded. When Ally makes the comparison, she is likely to feel underrewarded. In other words, Ally and Andy both view the situation as inequitable.

Feelings of being overrewarded are probably rare, but when they occur they have beneficial consequences for employers. Overrewarded employees tend to perform better in their jobs and are better members of the organization than employees who haven't been rewarded as well.[46] More typical are situations that result in employees feeling underrewarded. In those situations, employees feel dissatisfied and unmotivated.

Comparison Targets. As Table 14.1 makes clear, equity is a relative concept. Equity theory states that employees must make comparisons in order to decide whether their current balance of outputs-to-inputs is fair. Two common targets of comparisons are other employees and past situations you have experienced.

Perceived inequities often occur when employees compare outcomes such as their promotions, pay raises, and perquisites ("perks") to those received by others. Sometimes, these comparisons are quite simple, as in the example of Andy and Ally. The comparisons to others can become much more complicated, however. For example, imagine you are a U.S. manager working for Cisco as an expatriate in China. The business you work in is a joint venture between Cisco and a local Chinese company. When evaluating whether your pay is fair, you probably make the following comparisons: (1) your pay compared to the pay of other expatriate managers you know who are working for your company but in other countries, (2) local Chinese managers working in the same joint ventures as you, and (3) managers working in other state-owned Chinese businesses in your industry. If you give great weight to (1), you might feel underrewarded, because expatriates working in other countries would probably be paid more than you. But if you give more weight to (2) and (3), you would feel overrewarded, because U.S. expatriates working in China typically are paid more than local Chinese managers.

When employees make comparisons to others, they understand that not everyone deserves to receive exactly the same outcomes. Nevertheless, when their comparisons reveal that others are getting more, employees may question whether the inputs of other employees justify the better outcomes that those employees receive. When lower level employees compare their own pay and perks to those of the executives, they usually acknowledge that executives deserve more than they do. But how much more? In addition to salaries worth hundreds of thousands of dollars and bonuses worth millions, high ranking executives in many companies receive extravagant perks—daily limousine service, lavish lunches, offices adorned with expensive artwork, and so on. Can executives put in 500 times as much effort as someone lower in the hierarchy? Can they work 500 times as many hours? Can they have 500 times as much skill? If so, perhaps they deserve rewards worth 500 times more. But if not, people lower in the organization may feel underrewarded when they make the comparison. Herb Baum, CEO of Dial Corporation in Scottsdale, Arizona, recognized this when he said, "If you draw the line on your own greed, and your employees see it, they will be incredibly loyal and perform much better for you."[47]

Feelings of (in)equity can be stimulated by making comparisons between oneself and others, but such comparisons are not the only basis for judging whether your employer is treating you fairly. Another type of comparison employees make is how their current employer treats them compared to other employers in the past. Consider the situation faced by the thousands of people who have been laid off during the recent economic decline. Because jobs were few and far between, many laid-off employees felt they had to accept new jobs that paid less. When these recently laid-off employees compare their new situation to their old situation, two facts are salient: One fact is that they still have the same (or perhaps greater) level of competency, education, and experience that they had previously. In other words, their inputs to their work have not changed. The second fact is that their outcomes (pay) are less than they were in the previous job. Together, these two facts naturally lead such employees to experience feelings of inequity and dissatisfaction.[48]

Reactions to Perceived Inequity. Inequity can arise due to being either underrewarded or overrewarded. Either situation causes people to feel dissatisfied. When people are dissatisfied, they usually do something about it. How do employees react to inequity? Generally, six alternatives are available to employees who want to reduce their feelings of inequity. They can:

- increase their inputs (e.g., time and effort) to justify higher rewards when they feel that they are overrewarded compared to others;
- decrease their inputs to compensate for lower rewards when they feel underrewarded;
- change the compensation they receive through legal or other actions (e.g., forming a union, filing a grievance, or leaving work early);
- modify their comparisons by choosing another person to compare themselves against;
- distort reality by rationalizing that the inequities are justified; or
- leave the situation (quit the job) if the inequities can't be resolved.

Clearly, most of these reactions are harmful to the organization. For example, it can be quite costly to employers when high performers who feel that their pay is too low leave the organization. Not only does the company lose their productive talent, but they must exert time and spend money to find a replacement. If dissatisfied employees stay, they may react by withholding effort in order to restrict output or lower quality. Customers are not the only ones to suffer from such behavior; the morale of coworkers is also likely to suffer. Because feelings of inequity often cause frustration, they also lead people to behave in hostile and aggressive ways.

To be effective in their roles, managers must strive to treat all members of the organization fairly. Doing so can pay huge dividends. Employees who are paid and treated fairly are more likely to believe in and be committed to what they do. In turn, they will become more trusting, honorable, and loyal employees and will work harder to exceed the expectations that managers have of them. In team situations, equitable treatment improves cooperation among team members.[49]

INDIVIDUAL DIFFERENCES APPROACH

People differ from each other in many ways, having different abilities, personalities, values, and needs. During the past century, psychologists conducted thousands of studies designed to improve understanding of such differences.[50] Here, we describe one popular view of how individual differences affect employee motivation and satisfaction. This approach considers employees' needs to be the basis for differences in motivation and satisfaction.

5. Describe how individual differences in needs can affect employees' work.

Types of Needs

A **need** *is a strong feeling of deficiency in some aspect of a person's life that creates an uncomfortable tension.* That tension becomes a motivating force, causing the individual to take actions to satisfy the need, reduce the tension, and diminish the intensity of the motivating force.

Hierarchy of Needs.   Psychologist Abraham Maslow believed that people have five types of needs, as shown in Figure 14.9: physiological (at the base), security, affiliation, esteem, and self-actualization (at the top). He arranged these in a **hierarchy of needs**, *which describes the order in which people seek to satisfy their desires.* Satisfying the needs at the bottom level of the hierarchy comes first. As a person satisfies each level of needs, motivation shifts to satisfying the next higher level of needs.[51]

   Physiological needs *are those for food, clothing, and shelter, which people try to satisfy before all others.* For example, the primary motivation of a hungry person is to obtain food rather than, say, gain recognition for achievements. Thus people work for wages that will allow them to meet their physiological needs first.

Figure 14.9   Moving Up and Down the Needs Hierarchy

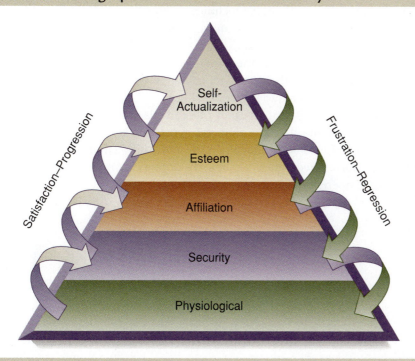

Security needs *include the desire for safety and stability, and the absence of pain, threat, and illness.* People deprived of the means to satisfy security needs are motivated to fulfill them. Some workers express their security needs as a desire for a stable job with adequate medical, unemployment, and retirement benefits. Such people are likely to be frustrated with current flexible staffing practices (e.g., emphasis on temporary workers to avoid providing benefits). Other workers express security needs as a desire for work that builds their competencies and ensures their long-term employability, and this concern is often more important than getting a bigger salary.

Affiliation needs *are the desire for friendship, love, and belonging.* Employees with high affiliation needs enjoy working closely with others. Employees with low affiliation needs may be content to work on tasks by themselves. When an organization doesn't meet affiliation needs, an employee's dissatisfaction may be expressed in terms of frequent absenteeism, low productivity, stress-related behaviors, and even emotional breakdown. A manager who recognizes that a subordinate is striving to satisfy affiliation needs might encourage others to work more closely with the employee and suggest that the employee participate in the organization's social activities.

Esteem needs *are the desire for self-respect, a sense of personal achievement, and recognition from others.* To satisfy these needs, people seek opportunities for achievement, promotion, prestige, and status—all of which symbolize their competence and worth. When the need for esteem is dominant, managers can promote job satisfaction and high-quality performance by providing opportunities for exciting, challenging work and recognition for accomplishments.

Self-actualization needs *are the desire for personal growth, self-fulfillment, and the realization of the individual's full potential.* Richard Branson, chairman of the Virgin Group, seems to be strongly motivated by the need for self-actualization. When explaining why he founded Virgin Atlantic Airlines and Virgin Records, he admits that part of the reason was to have fun but that it was also important to him to change things and make a difference. In the process of building new businesses, Branson himself developed and grew.[52] Managers who recognize this motivation in employees can help them discover the growth opportunities available in their jobs or create special growth opportunities for them. For example, at Merck, scientists can attend law school and become patent attorneys; at Hewlett-Packard, a parallel technical ladder was established so scientists can earn higher salaries without taking on management tasks. At both companies, managers also can offer employees special assignments, such as working on a task force that reports to top management. Such assignments often represent growth opportunities through which employees can develop their managerial competencies while continuing to utilize to the fullest their technical knowledge and skills.

Chef Anthony Bourdain is well aware of these needs and their consequences for his employees. Bourdain knows that his employees appreciate knowing that he is concerned about their needs and is looking after them. By addressing employees' needs, he motivates them to perform effectively as a team. His approach to managing is described in the Teamwork Competency feature.[53]

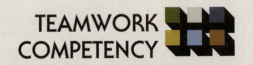

TEAMWORK COMPETENCY

Chef Anthony Bourdain
If you watch the Food Network channel, you know Chef Anthony Bour-

dain as the star of *A Cook's Tour*. But if you've visited New York, you may know him as the owner of Les Halles,

his popular brasserie. Les Halles' kitchen operates according to the classical French model, which has been described as "the brigade." The hierarchy is clear, with the chef firmly in control. Jobs are specialized, the rules are rigid, and compliance with the rules is absolutely mandatory. When the rules are followed, the result is that every dish the kitchen serves is excellent. In this environment, what motivates the kitchen staff? Bourdain believes that he makes the stressful life of working in his profession satisfying by attending to the needs of his staff. "It's important that the crew knows I care about them and will take care of them. They know that they can come to me and say, 'I got drunk last night . . . got into a fight . . . and the police are after me,' and I will help them out." By showing sincere concern about the difficulties employees face in their personal lives, Bourdain offers more than a secure paycheck to employees. In fact, he believes that the camaraderie enjoyed among

staff is one of the most satisfying aspects of working in a professional kitchen. "The kitchen's a place where you spend so much of your time that everyone knows everything about you. You're totally exposed, but also protected. In my kitchen, the intricacies and anomalies of one's love life are generally common knowledge—and openly discussed. Resentments are not allowed to simmer. . . . People are forced to get along, to cooperate, to come to understand one another." Teamwork drives the system, and in the process of building a team that is strong enough to get through any crisis, the staff members become friends. What about esteem needs? These are satisfied each time a cook "makes a really beautiful plate of food and puts it up in the window—the pass—to be taken into the dining room." The satisfaction doesn't come from the customer; it comes just before the food leaves the

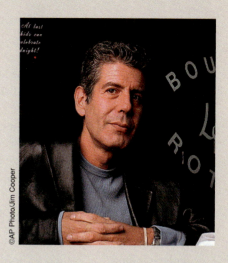

©AP Photo/Jim Cooper

kitchen, when the kitchen staff sees how perfect it is. When everything goes well, people feel a sense of achievement. One of the best feelings is sitting at the bar after a long night, enjoying a free drink, and reviewing the evening's events. "It's golden," says Bourdain.

Moving through the Needs Hierarchy

People often equate individual differences with fixed traits that don't change much over time. In contrast to this view, Maslow believed that people move through the needs hierarchy by considering which needs have been satisfied and which needs remain to be satisfied. For any specific person, a need that was dominant three months ago may no longer be dominant, and a need that is dominant today may not be dominant next year. In Maslow's original formulation of the needs hierarchy, he viewed movement as occurring much as it does when people are moving up on an escalator—the only way to go is up. However, later research showed that movement through the hierarchy could actually go in both directions.

Moving Up. To explain which need is dominant for someone at a particular time, Maslow proposed the satisfaction–progression hypothesis. The **satisfaction–progression hypothesis** *states that a need is a motivator until it becomes satisfied.* When a need is satisfied, it ceases to be a motivator and another need emerges to take its place. In general, lower level needs must be satisfied before higher level needs become strong enough to motivate behavior. Research supports Maslow's view that, until their *basic* needs are satisfied, people won't be concerned with higher level needs.

Moving Down. Maslow focused on the dynamics of satisfaction–progression. Later research showed that people can also move down the hierarchy.[54] The **frustration–regression hypothesis** *holds that, when an individual is frustrated in meeting higher level needs, the next lower level needs reemerge and again direct behavior.* For example, a finish carpenter who does highly creative trim work in houses may work for a contractor who builds from a limited number of floor plans with few trim options. Because the job doesn't provide a creative outlet, the frustrated carpenter may stop pursuing satisfaction of growth needs at work and instead regress to pursuing activities that satisfy his relatedness needs. An example would be socializing with other construction workers.

The frustration–regression hypothesis suggests that managers should try to determine the cause of an employee's frustration and, if possible, work to remove blockages to needs satisfaction. If blockages can't be removed, managers should try to redirect the employee's behavior toward satisfying a lower level need. For example, a company's production technology may limit the growth opportunities for people in their jobs. If employees are frustrated because they can't be creative or develop new skills, they could be encouraged to focus on relating to their coworkers, which can also generate feelings of satisfaction.

GUIDELINES FOR MANAGERS

6. Describe how understanding motivation can help managers improve employee performance and satisfaction.

Managers who understand what motivates employees and what detracts from employee motivation have a good basis for diagnosing and rectifying the causes of performance problems and dissatisfaction. Here we summarize some practical lessons suggested by the theories and research described in this chapter.

- **Clearly communicate the organization's mission to employees and explain how their contribution to the organization will help the organization realize its mission.** Effective managers understand that motivating employees involves two steps. The first step is setting a clear direction. Only when everyone is working toward the same results will their combined efforts move the organization forward. Assuming employees understand the big picture and how they fit into it, increasing the effort they exert should improve the effectiveness of the organization.

- **State the behaviors and performance achievements that are desired and explain how they will be rewarded.** By working with employees to set specific and measurable goals, managers can clarify their expectations for employees. These goals may include job-specific performance goals as well as behaviors that extend beyond job tasks but are necessary for the organization to function effectively. When setting goals, managers should be careful not to fall into the trap of focusing only on goals that are easily quantified, such as sales or absenteeism. They should also set goals for "soft" objectives, such as teamwork and being customer focused.[55]

- **Design jobs with high motivating potential.** Jobs designed to meet the principles of job characteristics theory tend to be more satisfying than other jobs. To determine whether jobs need to be redesigned, managers should assess the degree to which employees experience their work as meaningful, feel personally responsible for their work outcomes, and receive adequate feedback.

- **Provide frequent and constructive feedback.** When employees are performing well, telling them so spurs them on. When employees are performing poorly, telling them so suggests that they consider a different approach to the task or intensify their efforts. Giving appropriate feedback can be difficult, however. As a general rule, feedback should focus on task performance and be given immediately; avoid criticizing personal characteristics that are difficult for employees to change.[56]

- **Provide rewards for desired behaviors and outcomes.** Employees tend to repeat behaviors that are rewarded, and they strive to achieve goals to which rewards are attached. When a gap exists between actual and desired behaviors and goal achievement, rewards and punishments are likely to be misaligned. Effective managers ensure that the formal and informal rewards and punishments experienced by employees are aligned with the organization's desired behaviors and goal achievement.

■ **Provide rewards that employees value.** To be motivators, rewards must reflect the things that employees value. The rewards that employees want can be determined simply by asking them. Some employees value monetary rewards above everything else, whereas others value scheduling flexibility, the opportunity to work on special projects, training and development opportunities, and so on. Whenever possible, effective managers find ways to use various rewards to motivate a variety of employees.

■ **Provide equitable rewards.** Employees make two types of comparisons when evaluating whether they have been rewarded fairly. One involves assessing their own accomplishments in terms of the rewards they receive. The second involves assessing their own accomplishments and rewards in terms of those of other employees. Effective managers recognize that employees' assessments of equity and fairness are basically subjective perceptions. Perceptions may partially reflect objective facts, but inaccurate assumptions and beliefs often play a role, too. Effective communication about rewards is essential. A well-designed reward system will have little motivational value if employees misunderstand the system and rely on inferences and rumor when assessing whether the system is fair.

■ **Recognize that each person is unique.** Following the principles stated above should, on average, result in employees who are more motivated and more satisfied. But effective managers also must recognize the individual differences that make each person unique. Differences in employees' needs mean that rewards valued by one employee may not be valued by another employee. Similarly, although most employees seem to like enriched jobs, some employees find such jobs to be more stressful. Because individual differences play a part in shaping motivation and satisfaction, a manager needs to understand each employee.

CHAPTER SUMMARY

Ensuring that employees are motivated to work effectively is a primary managerial responsibility. Managers who are able to do so will be rewarded for their efforts with a workforce that expresses little dissatisfaction and exerts high levels of effort. To be effective, managers must understand the many factors that, in combination, can enhance or squelch motivation.

1. Describe four approaches that can be used to explain employee motivation and satisfaction.
The four approaches used to understand the motivation and satisfaction of employees are the managerial approach, the job approach, the organization approach, and the individual differences approach. None of these influences alone can fully explain employee motivation and satisfaction. Effective managers understand that the four approaches are most useful when used in combination.

2. Explain how managers can use goals and rewards to improve performance.
To use goals and rewards effectively, managers must begin by communicating a general direction to employees. To improve performance in a specific job, managers should set goals for employees. Performance improves when employees have specific, difficult goals that they accept and

to which they are committed. Providing feedback to employees about their progress toward those goals is important to their effectiveness. Reinforcement theory states that behavior is a function of its consequences. Positive and negative reinforcement should be used to encourage desired work behaviors, whereas punishment and extinction should be applied to discourage undesired work behaviors. Expectancy theory provides a framework for combining the principles of goal setting and reinforcement, while also taking into account the specific rewards that each employee values most. Expectancy theory states that motivation is highest when employees feel that their efforts lead to improved performance (expectancy) and when performance is rewarded with outcomes that they value (instrumentality).

3. Describe how jobs can be designed to be motivating and satisfying.
Job characteristics theory states that three critical psychological states—experienced meaningfulness, experienced responsibility, and knowledge of results—lead to high motivation and job satisfaction. These critical psychological states are created by well-designed jobs. Specifically, five job characteristics of job design are important—skill variety, task identity, task significance, autonomy, and feed-

back. Individuals with strong growth needs are likely to respond positively to jobs having these characteristics.

4. State how the organization context affects motivation and satisfaction.

Herzberg's two-factor model states that factors in the work situation strongly influence satisfaction and performance. Motivator factors such as challenging work, responsibility, recognition, achievement, and growth create high levels of motivation. The presence of motivators should enhance performance. Hygiene factors, such as good working conditions and benefits, are important determinants of satisfaction and dissatisfaction. Hygiene factors can hurt employee performance if not present but don't necessarily increase performance when present. Equity theory is based on the assumption that employees want to be treated fairly. Employees judge fairness by comparing their own inputs and outcomes to those of others in the workplace. When inequities exist, employees feel dissatisfied and their performance drops.

5. Describe how individual differences in needs can affect employees' work.

Maslow's hierarchy of needs includes physiological, security, affiliation, esteem, and self-actualization needs. Need satisfaction causes people to move up the hierarchy and need frustration causes them to move down. The importance of a category of needs at any specific time in a person's life determines how strongly it influences a person's behavior.

6. Describe how understanding motivation can help managers improve employee performance and satisfaction.

An understanding of employee motivation and satisfaction provides guidance concerning how managers should behave in their daily interactions, how to design jobs and organizations, and how to intervene when employees seem unmotivated or unsatisfied. To improve the performance and satisfaction of employees, managers should communicate the organization's mission, clearly state what employees are expected to do, design jobs with high motivating potential, provide feedback as well as rewards, and attend to employees' equity perceptions. In addition, they must recognize that each employee is unique. Due to individual differences among employees, their reactions to these approaches will not be identical.

KEY TERMS and CONCEPTS

Affiliation needs
Autonomy
Behavior modification
Critical psychological states
Equity theory
Esteem needs
Expectancy
Expectancy theory
Experienced meaningfulness
Experienced responsibility
Extinction
Feedback
Frustration–regression hypothesis
Goal-setting theory
Goalsharing
Growth need strength
Hierarchy of needs
Hygiene factors
Instrumentality
Job characteristics theory

Key job characteristics
Knowledge of results
Management by objectives
Motivation
Motivator factors
Need
Negative reinforcement
Physiological needs
Positive reinforcement
Punishment
Reinforcement theory
Satisfaction
Satisfaction–progression hypothesis
Security needs
Self-actualization needs
Skill variety
Task identity
Task significance
Two-factor theory
Valence

QUESTIONS FOR DISCUSSION and COMPETENCY DEVELOPMENT

1. Review the changes BMW made at its Mini factory. Which approaches to motivation did BMW seem to consider when making the changes described? Explain.

2. Pepper Oni manages a pizza shop. During the past few months, the pizza delivery drivers have received several traffic tickets and had three small accidents. No one has been seriously injured yet, but Oni is concerned. Using the principles of goal setting and reinforcement theory, develop a six-month plan to help Oni increase the frequency of safe driving behaviors and reduce the number of drivers' traffic tickets and accidents.

3. Think about a specific job that you've had. Use expectancy theory to explain your motivation to perform the job well. What aspects of the situation were motivating for you? What aspects of the situation interfered with your performance? How could a manager have used expectancy theory to improve your motivation and/or your performance?

4. When organizations downsize and lay off employees, the survivors of the downsizing often have increased workloads. According to equity theory, what are some of the possible reactions of the survivors that managers should expect? What can managers do to discourage negative reactions that employees may have if they feel that they're being treated unfairly?

5. Use job characteristics theory to analyze the motivational aspects of this course. What could your instructor do to enhance your feelings of meaningfulness, responsibility, or knowledge of results?

6. Review the five categories of needs shown in Figure 14.9. Which of these needs do you feel have been satisfied for you at this point in your life? Which needs are you still striving to satisfy? List three things you could tell your manager about how your need satisfaction (or frustration) is likely to affect you at work. What could a manager do (or not do) to show that she is taking your needs into account?

CASE FOR COMPETENCY DEVELOPMENT

MOTIVATING GEEKS AND GEEZERS

Professor Warren Bennis had a hunch that people who grew up during different eras would be motivated by different things. To find out if he was right, he conducted in-depth interviews with 25 "geezers" and 18 "geeks." The geezers were all 70 or older, and the geeks were all 35 or younger. Regardless of their ages, all of the people interviewed were accomplished leaders in their fields. But these two groups had very different experiences earlier in their lives.

The geezers had experienced the Great Depression and World War II. These events shaped the way they viewed the world and what was important to them. As children and young adults, they worried about their own security and how to satisfy their basic needs. For many of them, success meant making money and earning a steady paycheck. The meaning of a career was getting ahead in terms of increasing salary and rank. When they were young, geezers expected to work hard and "pay their dues" so that eventually they would get ahead. Some were entrepreneurs, of course, who built their own companies. For them, a primary motivation seemed to be gaining control over their own work lives. Balancing career and family was a matter people didn't talk about—at least not openly. Most of the geezers grew up in homes where fathers worked in an organization and the mothers managed the family and home.

The geeks were from Generations X and Millennials. In the families of their childhoods, it was much more common for both parents to earn income outside the home. Also much more common were divorce, second marriages, and blended families. As the geeks entered adulthood, the economic possibilities available to many seemed almost endless. Furthermore, they saw no reason why family life should have to suffer in order to realize those economic possibilities. Both men and women could have it all—a great job and a fulfilling family life. When asked what motivated them in their careers, the geeks sought to make a difference in the world. They were concerned with their own identities, they wanted to develop themselves as individuals, and they wanted to maintain a healthy balance between work and other aspects of life.

Although the geezers interviewed by Bennis were over 70 years old, most were still employed and actively involved in their jobs. They may be a bit older than your typical manager, but they are not so different from many CEOs of large U.S. companies. In these same companies, the middle and lower level managers are more similar to the geeks. And, of course, the geeks are managing some people from yet a later generation.[57]

Questions

1. In what ways do geeks and geezers seem to be similar when it comes to work motivation and satisfaction? How are they different?

2. Given the difference you identified, what are the implications for:

   a. The effectiveness of goal setting as a means to increase employee performance?

   b. The job characteristics that geeks and geezers are likely to be more concerned about?

c. The types of benefits packages that employers should offer in order to satisfy geeks versus geezers?

3. Imagine that you are working on a team project with a few geeks and a few geezers. Which of the guidelines for managers described in this chapter would be most useful for ensuring that the team makes satisfactory progress toward its goals? Give specific examples of how a manager could apply these principles to motivate the team.

HERE'S LOOKING AT YOU

You can develop a plan to change your own behavior and performance by taking the following steps. You may choose to focus on behavior related to your life at work, at school, or at home. Most important is that you focus on something fairly specific.

Step 1. Choose a behavior that you really would like to change (e.g., walking more and driving less). Briefly, I want to change this behavior:

_____

_____

_____

_____

_____

_____

_____

_____

_____

_____

Step 2. State a specific short-term goal for changing the behavior (e.g., within six months, I'll increase the number of times I walk to work from one to five times per week):

_____

_____

_____

_____

_____

_____

_____

_____

_____

_____

Step 3. Develop a procedure for monitoring the behavior (e.g., I'll make a chart and tape it to my bathroom mirror):

_____

_____

_____

_____

_____

_____

_____

_____

_____

Step 4. Create a plan to reward yourself for making progress toward your goal (e.g., each day I walk, I'll put $5 in a special reward fund, to be spent at the end of each month. Each day I drive, I'll remove $6):

_____

_____

_____

_____

_____

_____

_____

_____

_____

Step 5. Write a contract with yourself, specifically stating your goals, your plan for how to change, and any contingencies that you might want to consider (e.g., one of my contingencies is that on days when I have to travel beyond the office, I'll drive without removing any funds.):

_____

_____

_____

_____

_____

_____

_____

_____

_____

Step 6. Develop a plan for how you will deal with difficult obstacles (list five) that may interfere with progress toward your goal (e.g., I don't like to walk in the rain, so I'll purchase rain gear that makes it less of a problem for me to do so):

a. _____

_____

b. _____

_____

c. _____

_____

d. _____

_____

e. _____

_____

©Corbis Inc.

Dynamics of Leadership

LEARNING OBJECTIVES

After studying this chapter, you should be able to:

1. Explain what leadership means.

2. Describe the personal characteristics that enable leaders to be effective.

3. Describe the types of behaviors required for leadership.

4. Identify the contingencies that may shape how leaders behave.

5. State the key characteristics and behaviors of transformational leadership.

6. Describe how organizations develop leaders.

Chapter Outline

In Silicon Valley, Hewlett-Packard (HP) has long been revered as the area's first "garage start-up." Founded in the 1930s, it grew steadily to become a complex, global company. In fact, by the end of the 20th century, HP had become so complex that top management decided to split the company into more manageable parts. At about the same time, then-CEO Lew Platt announced he would leave HP, to be replaced by Carleton (Carly) Fiorina. Formerly an executive at Lucent, which had been spun off from AT&T, Fiorina stepped into her new role as the first-ever outsider to serve as HP's CEO.

A successful company by many standards, HP nevertheless had been experiencing significant problems. While the rest of the industry was focused on customers and moving at the speed of the Internet, HP's product development process was slow and deliberate. It reflected the preferences of the company's engineers more than the preferences of customers. According to Fiorina, the need for change at HP was urgent. "Time does not mean what it used to mean. In the Internet Age, things move very, very quickly. And we have to move quickly enough to catch up with that pace," she explained.

HP's culture is strongly rooted in the company's early garage days. HP's founders and past leaders encouraged decentralized decision making. They sought to reach consensus about major issues. In contrast to past CEOs, Fiorina adopted a take-charge, fast-paced style. She gets people's input, but then makes it clear that she will decide what to do and move ahead with it. She says, "If you want people to speed up, *you* speed up. You don't talk about it, you do it. If you don't walk the talk, nothing will matter to the contrary. In fact, worse, the result will be cynicism, and that would be devastating."

Fiorina's style was evident to everyone who watched the conflict between her and Walter Hewlett, the founder's son and a major shareholder. Fiorina wanted to acquire Compaq, the computer company. Hewlett was flat-out against it. The board was about evenly split before Fiorina set out to persuade them. She encouraged the board to think carefully about HP's strategy, the company's strengths and weaknesses, and the recent actions of competitors. Fiorina led board members to adopt her world view and helped them to see that acquiring Compaq was essential to HP's future success. She never convinced Walter Hewlett, however. For weeks, the news media provided in-depth coverage as Hewlett and Fiorina sought investors' votes. Once the conflict was over, Fiorina faced the challenge of selling HP's employees on the merits of the acquisition and convincing Compaq's top talent to stay after they were acquired. She spent weeks visiting facilities around the world. At Compaq, she walked more than a mile through a walkway that connected the 17 headquarters buildings. According to Antonio Humphreys, a Compaq employee at the time, "She was like this missive figure. She took pictures and put on hats. The fact that she was willing to do that for the common folks—that earned her a lot of points." So far, her leadership style seems to be working.[1]

THE MEANING OF LEADERSHIP

1. Explain what leadership means.

When people think of "leaders," they often think of famous people in positions of power. Carly Fiorina is pretty famous and has a lot of power. But fame and power are not what make Fiorina an effective leader. Leadership occurs at all levels in organizations. Long before she became CEO of HP, Fiorina was an effective leader at Lucent and AT&T. In her earlier jobs, she was constantly sent to trouble spots to fix things up. Back then, she wasn't famous and didn't have much formal power. Nevertheless, she was already an effective leader. **Leadership** *is an influence relationship among leaders and followers who strive for real change and outcomes that reflect their shared purposes.*[2] Because these three aspects of leadership—influence, shared purposes, and change—are so central to leading effectively, we explain them in more detail.

Influence

Influencing others is perhaps the most essential aspect of leadership. Fiorina knew she wanted HP to acquire Compaq. Even as the CEO, she had to convince others to support her plan. For weeks before the acquisition was final, the news media carried stories describing her meetings with HP's directors, customers, and employees. At first, Fiorina's view wasn't widely accepted. Business commentators speculated that she would have to step down as CEO if she could not influence others to accept her strategic plan. After dozens of meetings, her influence attempts succeeded in convincing key constituencies that acquiring Compaq was essential to the long-term success of HP.[3]

Managers can use many means to influence subordinates. They often use the authority of their *formal position* to influence subordinates. They may also use *rewards* to influence subordinates, as we described in Chapter 14.

Some managers use *coercion*. They obtain compliance by creating fear in their subordinates. Scott Rudin is a notoriously unpleasant producer of hit movies. He is infamous for verbally abusing staffers and throwing phones. One of his former employees commented, "I think the people that work there—most of them hate him. Nobody likes him, everybody's miserable." Rudin is able to verbally abuse his employees because there are 100 applicants for every job and he doesn't mind seeing his staff turn over every two years.[4]

Expertise is another source of influence that managers can use. If subordinates believe their managers have more knowledge or technical skill than they do, they will accept the manager's view more easily. When Fiorina joined HP, she had little relevant technical expertise and she didn't know the industry. Her background was in marketing and telecommunications. Thus, she could not use her expertise to influence her followers.

Finally, leaders can influence through personal *charisma*. Fiorina used her charisma to gain the support of her board of directors and employees. According to one director, she "dazzled" them. We return to the importance of charisma later in this chapter.

The means that leaders use to influence followers determines their effectiveness. Figure 15.1 illustrates how employees are likely to respond to each type of influence tactic.[5] Coercion often results in employee resistance. Rewards and formal position usually result in compliance, but not strong commitment. Leaders who use their expertise and charisma to influence followers are most effective in creating a sense of commitment.

Shared Purposes

Effective leaders understand that they need to do more than simply convince people to follow them. They strive to create a vision that reflects the concerns and aspirations of followers. When a leader and followers have shared purposes, each can count on the other to act in ways that move everyone toward the common goal. In the battle to acquire Compaq, Fiorina was not simply trying to have her own way. She knew she would need the support of others after the deal in order to make the new HP successful. When followers share the vision of their leader, they can be counted on to work toward the same goals and objectives. Dr. Eric Schmidt, CEO of Google, thinks too many managers don't recognize how important it is to ensure that followers share the same purposes. They give orders and expect their orders to be followed. According to Schmidt, "The problem is that smart people in most other organizations are likely to say, 'I've been thinking about this, and here's my opinion.' Until both leaders and followers agree to head in the same direction, little will be accomplished."[6]

Change

Change is the third key element in our definition of leadership. As we described in Chapter 12, the need for change seems to be constant in modern organizations. But, for a variety of reasons, employees often resist change. Andrea Jung, CEO of Avon, believes the ability to remain flexible and be open to change is essential for leaders. "There is a significant difference between being a leader and being a manager," she says. "Leaders lead from the heart. You have to be analytical and flexible. If you feel like it's difficult to change, you will probably have a harder time succeeding."[7] In contrast, managers focus on the technical aspects of their work and expect people to simply do as they're told.

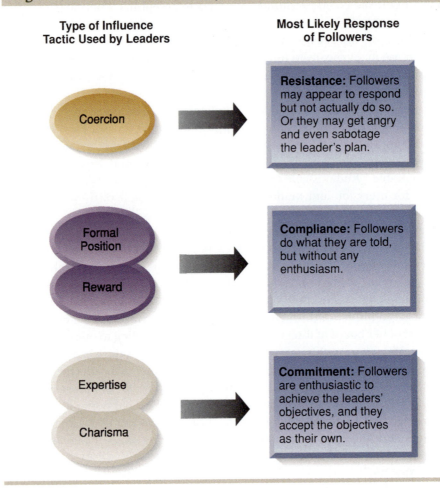

Figure 15.1   How Followers Respond to the Influence Tactics of Leaders

Type of Influence
Tactic Used by Leaders

Most Likely Response
of Followers

Coercion

Resistance: Followers may appear to respond but not actually do so. Or they may get angry and even sabotage the leader's plan.

Formal Position

Reward

Compliance: Followers do what they are told, but without any enthusiasm.

Expertise

Charisma

Commitment: Followers are enthusiastic to achieve the leaders' objectives, and they accept the objectives as their own.

For Fiorina, leading HP through an organizational change is her key responsibility. Acquiring Compaq was an easy change compared to the more fundamental cultural changes needed at her company. It took only a year for Fiorina to close the Compaq deal. That was a big achievement, but she knows that in the long run, people will judge her leadership effectiveness by whether HP succeeds in creating a new way of doing business and a new corporate culture for a new era.

In the remainder of this chapter, we present various leadership models that explain and prescribe how effective leaders influence others. There is no single or simple answer to which leadership approach works best. We have grouped the models into four main categories: personal characteristics, behavioral, contingency, and transformational. Each model provides some useful insights into what effective leadership involves. After explaining these models, we describe how organizations and individuals can develop their leadership capabilities.

PERSONAL CHARACTERISTICS OF EFFECTIVE LEADERS

2. Describe the personal characteristics that enable leaders to be effective.

The personal characteristics of leaders are the relatively stable attributes that make each person unique, including their physical, social, and psychological traits. A person can change some of her or his personal characteristics, but it is not easy to do so. Taken together, personal characteristics generally result in fairly predictable behavior over time and in various situations. Personal characteristics also create images in the minds of other people, and some of these images fit the stereotype of an effective leader.[8]

In recent years, the term *emotional intelligence* has received much attention for describing the personal characteristics of effective individuals, especially those in leadership roles.[9] **Emotional intelligence** *is a group of abilities that enable individuals to recognize and understand their own and others' feelings and emotions and to use these insights to guide their own thinking and actions.*[10] Like cognitive abilities, emotional intelligence may be affected by some aspects of our physiology. Not everyone is capable of being a mathematical genius, and not everyone can reach the highest levels of emotional intelligence. On the other hand, emotional intelligence is not fixed at birth. It develops over a period of many years as a person encounters various experiences and matures. Because emotional intelligence takes so long to develop, it is not easy for adults to change this aspect of their personal makeup.

As shown in Figure 15.2, emotional intelligence has four components—two that refer to awareness and two that address action. The model also recognizes two referents of awareness and action—one's self (e.g., the leader) and others (e.g., the followers).

Self-Awareness

The first component of emotional intelligence is self-awareness. **Self-awareness** *is the ability to recognize and understand your moods, emotions, and drives, as well as their impact on others.* To be effective as a leader, one must "know thyself"—that includes the good, the bad,

Figure 15.2   Four Components of Emotional Intelligence

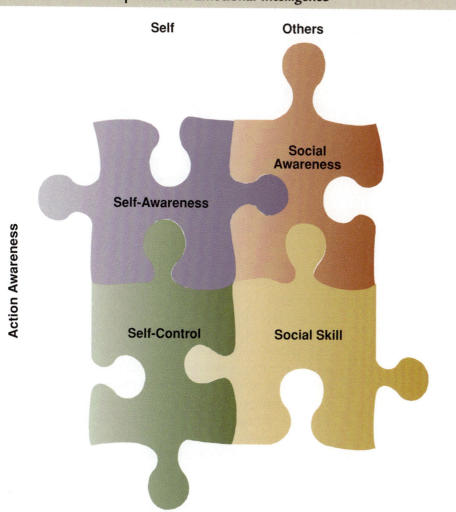

and the ugly! Self-aware people might know that social events create feelings of anxiety, and that deadlines make them short tempered. They also understand that those emotional reactions can have a negative impact on subordinates. Self-awareness also extends to understanding one's own motivation and goals. Self-aware people know what they want from their jobs and from life in general. They are honest with themselves and are able to see where two different goals may be in conflict with each other. They recognize that the desire to have it all can put stress on the people they care about most deeply.

Self-Control

Being aware of one's emotions and how they can affect others is essential to the development of emotional intelligence, but it is just the beginning. Emotional intelligence also requires an ability to control your emotions. Thus, the second component of emotional intelligence is **self-control**, *which is the ability to regulate and redirect one's own disruptive impulses and moods.* All of us experience negative moods and emotions. At times we feel frustrated and angry. At times our level of energy is low and we may feel that the challenges ahead are almost overwhelming. Effective leaders are not immune from such feelings. But when these feelings arise, they do not let the feelings take control. Instead, they take control of the feelings and use them for constructive purposes. When they feel angry, emotionally intelligent leaders analyze the causes of the anger and look for ways to remove those causes. When they feel overwhelmed by the amount of work that must get done, emotionally intelligent leaders take time out to reflect on their commitment to the objectives they have set to rejuvenate their enthusiasm.

Social Awareness

So far, we have focused on how emotionally intelligent leaders view and control their own emotions. Next we consider how they attend to the emotional states and needs of others. **Social awareness** *is the ability to understand the emotional makeup of other people, and the skill to treat people according to their emotional reactions.* Just as they are able to recognize their own emotional reactions, emotionally intelligent leaders have empathy for the feelings of their followers. They can read the signs of distress on people's faces. They anticipate the feelings of anxiety that followers will experience as they encounter major changes at work. And their actions take these emotional reactions into account.

Social Skill

The final component of emotional intelligence is social skill. Social skill is not simply the ability to get along well with others, nor is it mere popularity. **Social skill** *is the ability to build social networks, manage relationships, find common ground, and build rapport.* Socially skilled leaders are generally well liked and have a wide circle of acquaintances, but they are not satisfied just to be a friend. They use their relationships with people to get everyone moving in the same direction. They seem to have a knack for finding common ground. This doesn't just happen by luck. Socially skilled leaders use their emotional insights to understand people's concerns, motivations, feelings, and aspirations. This understanding, along with their ability for self-control, enables emotionally intelligent leaders to build collaborative relationships and effectively manage large teams of followers.

The Competent Manager	*"Leadership is about building camaraderie and trust."* Jamie Dimon CEO BankOne

Are you interested in assessing your own emotional intelligence? If so, complete the questionnaire shown in the Exercise for Competency Development, found on pages 443–444. Your scores will give you an estimate of how emotionally intelligent you think you are. Of course, other people may not agree with your self-assessment. When someone's emotional intelligence is assessed in a work setting, a neutral third party should conduct a 360-degree assessment to gain a more accurate view.

Behavioral models of leadership *focus on describing differences in the actions of effective and ineffective leaders.* They seek to identify and understand what leaders actually do.[11] Behavioral models of leadership assume that most people can learn to be effective leaders. Because effective behaviors can be learned, most individuals can become effective leaders with the proper encouragement and support.

3. Describe the types of behaviors required for leadership.

Theory X and Theory Y

The behavior of leaders is often influenced by their assumptions and beliefs about followers and what motivates their followers. Thus, differences in the behaviors of effective and ineffective leaders can be understood by looking at the different assumptions they make. One of the most widely cited and recognized models for describing differences in these assumptions was developed by Douglas McGregor in 1957. He coined the labels *Theory X* and *Theory Y* as a way to contrast two sets of assumptions and beliefs held by leaders. Theory X and Theory Y managers both understand that they are responsible for the resources in their units—money, materials, equipment, and people—in the interest of achieving organizational goals. What draws them apart are their assumptions about what motivates their subordinates and what are the best ways to carry out management responsibilities. Figure 15.3 summarizes the beliefs and assumptions of leaders who subscribe to Theory X and Theory Y.

Theory X. When McGregor developed his model of effective leadership, he knew many managers with the Theory X point of view. **Theory X** *is a composite of propositions and underlying beliefs that take a command and control view of management based on a negative view of human nature.* Theory X managers view management as a process that involves directing, controlling, and modifying their subordinates' behaviors to fit the needs of the organization. They view employees as basically lazy and self-centered. This perspective assumes

Figure 15.3 Assumptions Associated with Theory X and Theory Y

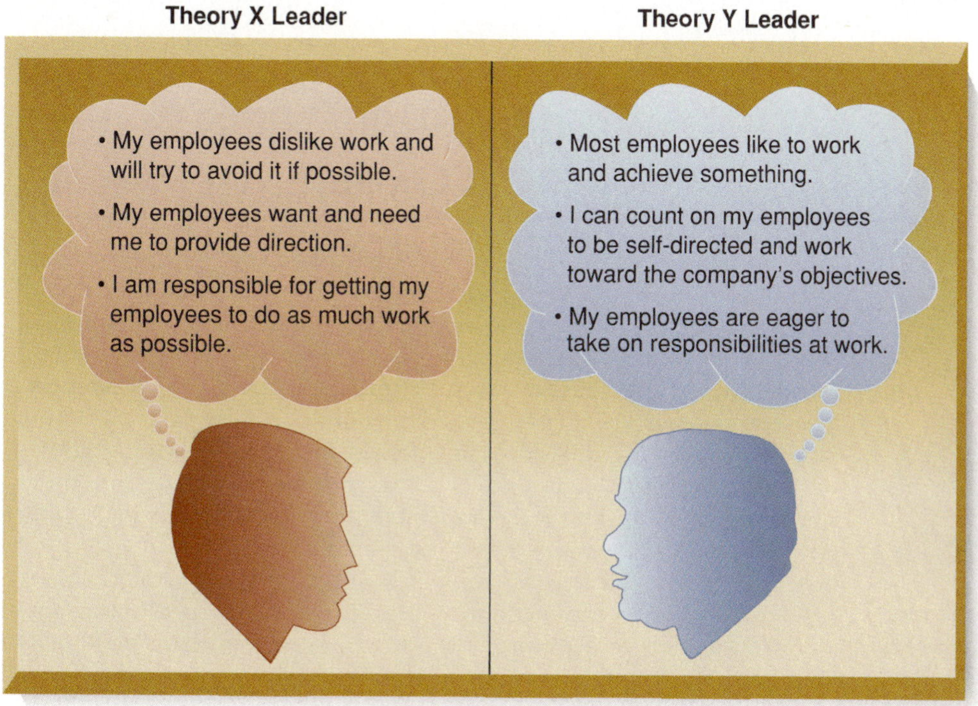

that, without the intervention of managers, most employees would be passive—even resistant—to organizational needs. Therefore, employees must be persuaded, rewarded, punished, and their activities tightly controlled. Doing so is management's primary task.[12]

McGregor believed that Theory X managers could be found everywhere in organizations, and that was a problem. According to him, management by direction and control was largely ineffective because it ignored the social, egoistic, and self-fulfillment needs of most employees.

Theory Y. McGregor concluded that a different view of managing employees was needed—one based on more adequate assumptions about human nature and human motivation. **Theory Y** *is a composite of propositions and beliefs that take a leadership and empowering view of management based on a positive view of human nature.* According to this view, employees are not by nature passive or resistant to organizational needs. They have become so as a result of their experiences in organizations. The motivation, the potential for development, the capacity for assuming responsibility, and the readiness to direct behavior toward organizational goals are all present in employees. Management does not put them there. It is management's responsibility to make it possible for people to recognize and develop these human characteristics for themselves. Whereas Theory X managers attempt to gain control over their subordinates, Theory Y managers rely on the self-control and self-direction of their subordinates.

McGregor's descriptions of the Theory X and Theory Y perspectives spawned many new leadership models, concepts, and approaches. Compared to 50 years ago, the assumptions of Theory Y and its concern for people are much more widely accepted among managers today. Nevertheless, many managers find it difficult to give up some of the assumptions that make up the Theory X perspective and its emphasis on management's top-down approach to accomplishing goals.

One organization that firmly believes in Theory Y leadership is New York's Orpheus Chamber Orchestra. As described in the Communication Competency feature, a concert master could never coax this orchestra to perform using a Theory X approach to leadership.[13]

COMMUNICATION COMPETENCY

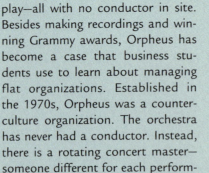

©Corbis Inc.

Orpheus Chamber Orchestra
When the Orpheus Chamber Orchestra begins a concert, some members of the audience are confused. Musicians tune their instruments,

warm up a bit, and then begin to play—all with no conductor in site. Besides making recordings and winning Grammy awards, Orpheus has become a case that business students use to learn about managing flat organizations. Established in the 1970s, Orpheus was a counterculture organization. The orchestra has never had a conductor. Instead, there is a rotating concert master— someone different for each performance. To develop a performance, the concert master works with a rotating core of section leaders and anyone else who wants to get in-

volved. A violinist might suggest a tempo change; a flute player might propose a different way to express a phrase. The philosophy of involvement doesn't stop at the concert hall. Musicians also serve as members of the executive board and the finance committee to be sure their views are heard whenever important decisions are made.

Members of the orchestra believe deeply in this high-involvement approach. These musicians would find it stifling to work under the traditional approach, as cellist Eric Bartlett explained: In a traditional orchestra, "the ideas are all his [the conductor's], therefore the responsibility is all his, and over time orchestra members give less and less." By not allowing one person to impose his or her view of how music should be performed, the orchestra believes that its members will give their best possible performance as a group every time. No one is passive. Everyone is involved and everyone accepts responsibility for the result. Debates are spirited, yet the members understand that their differences must be ultimately resolved amicably and in a timely manner for the organization to thrive.

Managerial Grid

In describing Theory X and Theory Y assumptions, McGregor described only two leadership perspectives. He assumed that managers behaved according to the assumptions of Theory X or Theory Y, but that a manager could not hold both points of view. A decade later, Robert Blake and Jane Mouton elaborated a more complex model. The **managerial grid** *identifies five leadership styles that combine different degrees of concern for production and concern for people.*[14] The five styles are plotted on the grid shown in Figure 15.4.

Impoverished. At the lower left-hand corner of the grid is the impoverished style, which is characterized by low concern for both people and production. The primary goal of managers who use this style is to stay out of trouble. They pass orders along to employees, go with the flow, and make sure that they can't be held accountable for mistakes. They exert the minimum effort required to get the work done and avoid being demoted or fired.

Figure 15.4   The Managerial Grid Model

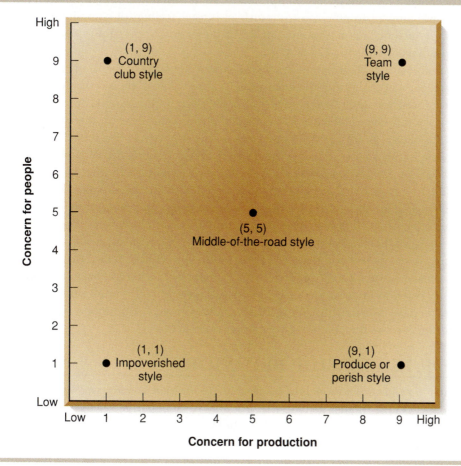

Country Club. At the upper left-hand corner of the grid is the *country club style*, which is characterized by a high concern for people and a low concern for production. Managers who use this style try to create a secure comfortable atmosphere and trust that their subordinates will respond with high performance. Attention to the need for satisfying relationships leads to a friendly, if not necessarily productive, atmosphere and work tempo.

Produce or Perish. A high concern for production and a low concern for people are reflected in the *produce or perish style* at the lower right-hand corner of the grid. Managers who use this style don't consider employees' personal needs to be relevant to achieving the organization's objectives. In addition to tying pay to performance, they use legitimate and coercive influence tactics to pressure subordinates to meet production goals. They believe that operational efficiency results from arranging the work so that employees merely have to follow orders. When a company's profitability is falling, showing more concern for production may seem like the best thing a manager can do to turn the company around. This style is consistent with Theory X.

<table>
<tr><td>**The Competent Manager**</td><td>*"It's important to be liked, but you can't get by just by being liked."*

Anne Mulcahy
CEO
Xerox</td></tr>
</table>

Middle of the Road. At the middle of the grid is the *middle-of-the road style*. Managers who use this style believe that the needs of people and organizations are in conflict and so it is difficult to satisfy both. The best one can do is to find an acceptable balance between workers' needs and the organization's productivity goals. Adequate performance is obtained by maintaining employee morale at a level sufficient to get an adequate amount of the work done.

Team. Finally, at the upper right-hand corner of the grid is the *team style*. It reflects high levels of concern for both people and production. Consistent with Theory Y, leaders who use this style attempt to establish teamwork and foster feelings of commitment among workers. By introducing a "common stake" in the organization's purposes, the leader builds relationships of trust and respect.

Katherine Hudson, chairman of the board and former CEO of the Brady Corporation in Milwaukee, Wisconsin, uses the team style. As she explains, "I was recently asked what one word would best describe the culture at Brady Corporation. For us, the word is 'YO!' It's our corporate cheer. It means saying 'yes' to change, information sharing and cooperation. All of us at Brady are committed to working together in this spirit."[15]

Behavioral models have added to the understanding and practice of leadership. The focus has grown from who leaders *are* (personal characteristics) to what leaders *do* (behaviors). However, leadership behaviors that are effective in one situation aren't necessarily effective in another. Certainly there are some cross-cultural differences in the behavior of effective leaders. For example, North American employees generally prefer leaders who give their followers great autonomy, but in China leaders who delegate too much are viewed as less competent.[16] Even within the United States, the same set of leader behaviors is not equally effective in all situations. Because behavioral models of leadership failed to uncover leadership styles that were effective in all situations, more complex models of leadership emerged. The next stage in the evolution of knowledge about leadership was the creation of contingency models.

CONTINGENCIES FOR LEADERSHIP BEHAVIOR

4. Identify the contingencies that may shape how leaders behave.

According to **contingency models of leadership**, *the situation determines the best style of leadership to use*.[17] These models assume that leaders can change the way they behave from one situation to the next. Effective leaders choose the behaviors that are most effective in a given situation. In other words, the behavior of effective leaders is contingent on the management situations they encounter. Leonard Shaeffer, CEO of BlueCross of California, understands the importance of contingencies for leadership behavior. Looking back over his 30-year career, he made the following observations:

> I've come to understand that leadership is about more than heavy-handed action from the top. Its defining characteristics change according to the needs and vagaries of the individual, the organization, the industry, and the world at large. In other words, leadership is . . . a journey. There aren't always sharp lines between one style of leadership and another—an autocratic leader sometimes has to be participative, and a reformer sometimes has to act like an autocrat. But by thinking clearly about the different roles I've needed to assume at different times, I've been able to tailor the way I make decisions, communicate with people, and manage my time so that I can address the most pressing needs of the organization at the moment.[18]

As Shaeffer realized, several aspects of a situation may determine the best leadership style to use. No single contingency model of leadership addresses all of these situational aspects in detail. Next we discuss two contingency models of leadership. The first model we discuss considers only one situational contingency, while the second model considers many more.

Situational Leadership® Model

The **Situational Leadership® Model** *states that the style of leadership used should be matched to the level of readiness of the followers.*[19] Like other contingency models of leadership, this one contains three basic components: a set of several possible leadership styles, a description of several alternative situations that leaders might encounter, and recommendations for which leadership styles are most effective in each situation.

Leadership Styles. According to the model, leaders can choose from among four leadership styles. These four leadership styles involve various combinations of task behavior and relationship behavior. Task behavior is similar to showing concern for production, and relationship behavior is similar to showing concern for people, as described in the managerial grid. More specifically, **task behavior** *includes using one-way communication, spelling out duties, and telling followers what to do and where, when, and how to do it.* Effective leaders might use a high degree of task behavior in some situations and only a moderate amount in other situations. **Relationship behavior** *includes using two-way communication, listening, encouraging, and involving followers in decision making, and giving emotional support.* Again, an effective leader may sometimes use a high degree of relationship behavior, and at other times use less. By combining different amounts of task behavior with different amounts of relationship behavior, effective leaders use four different leadership styles. The four leadership styles are called *telling, selling, participating,* and *delegating.* These styles are shown in Figure 15.5.[20]

Situational Contingency. According to this model, leaders should consider the situation before deciding which leadership style to use. The situational contingency in this model is the degree of follower readiness. **Readiness** *is a follower's ability to set high but attainable task-related goals and a willingness to accept responsibility for reaching them.* Readiness is not a fixed characteristic of followers—it depends on the task. The same group of followers may have a high degree of readiness for some tasks, but a low degree of readiness for others. The readiness level of followers depends on how much training they have received, how committed they are to the organization, their technical expertise, experience with the specific task, and so on.

Choosing a Leadership Style. As Figure 15.5 shows, the appropriate leadership style depends on the level of follower readiness. The curve running through the graph indicates the leadership style that best fits each readiness level of the individual or team.

Figure 15.5   The Situational Leadership® Model

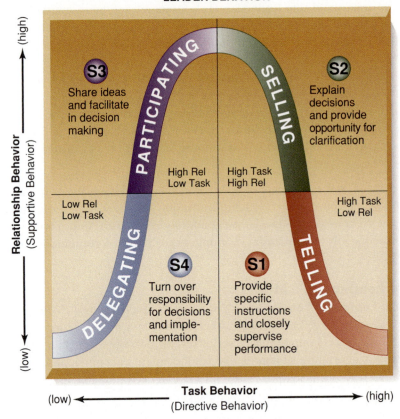

LEADER BEHAVIOR

S3 — Share ideas and facilitate in decision making

PARTICIPATING

SELLING

S2 — Explain decisions and provide opportunity for clarification

High Rel Low Task

High Task High Rel

Low Rel Low Task

High Task Low Rel

DELEGATING

TELLING

S4 — Turn over responsibility for decisions and implementation

S1 — Provide specific instructions and closely supervise performance

Relationship Behavior (Supportive Behavior) — (high) / (low)

Task Behavior (Directive Behavior) — (low) ← → (high)

FOLLOWER READINESS

High	Moderate		Low
R4	R3	R2	R1
Able and willing or confident	Able but unwilling or insecure	Unable but willing or confident	Unable and unwilling or insecure

Follower Directed

Leader Directed

Source: P. Hersey, K.H. Blanchard, and D.E. Johnson. *Management of Organizational Behavior: Leading Human Resources*, 8th ed. (Upper Saddle River, NJ: Prentice Hall, 2001), p. 182. Copyright © 2001, Center for Leadership Studies, Escondido, CA. Used with permission.

Note that high readiness levels appear on the left and low readiness levels appear on the right.

For a follower who is at the stage of low readiness for a task, a telling style is effective. In using a **telling style**, *the leader provides clear instructions, gives specific directions, and supervises the work closely*. The telling style helps ensure that new employees perform well, which provides a solid foundation for their future success and satisfaction.

As the follower's task-specific readiness increases, the leader needs to continue to provide some guidance behavior because the employee isn't yet ready to assume total responsibility for performing the task. In addition, the leader needs to begin using supportive behaviors in order to build the employee's confidence and maintain enthusiasm. That is, the leader should shift to a selling style. In using a **selling style**, *the leader provides direction, encourages two-way communication, and helps build confidence and motivation on the part of the follower.* Andrea Jung used the selling style when she became CEO of Avon. As described in the Strategic Action Competency feature, Avon really needed a makeover at the time, and Jung felt she knew what changes were in order for the company.[21]

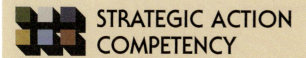

STRATEGIC ACTION COMPETENCY

Andrea Jung at Avon

It may be hard to believe, but when Andrea Jung became CEO of Avon in 1999, she was the first woman to head this 115-year-old company, whose workforce is almost all female. The company was in deep financial trouble at the time. The stock price had plummeted and people were questioning whether the company's business model of door-to-door sales had become obsolete. Within two years, the stock price, revenues, and profits were all growing again. She had proved that an Avon Lady could also be a world-class leader. In fact, it was her experience as an Avon Lady that helped her understand the company's problems and develop a plan to fix them. A month after becoming CEO, Jung laid out a turnaround plan and began selling it to Wall Street ana-

lysts, her board, and her employees. The plan included cutting costs by hundreds of millions of dollars, developing new blockbuster products, and launching a new line of business. At the time, analysts seemed to doubt the plan would work. But Jung had convinced her employees that the plan was one they could implement.

Susan Kropf, a veteran of 31 years, was put in charge of restructuring the company's operations. Kropf recalled that Jung "challenged us to really think about how we spend our money." When an initiative to sell Avon products through retail stores stumbled, Jung didn't blink. She kept selling her ideas: "I'm not changing any of our thinking. This turnaround is far from complete." One successful change involved an idea that had

©AP Photo/Tina Fineberg

been kicked around for years at the company, but no one else had ever sold it as well as Jung did. Referred to as "Leadership," the initiative is designed to grow the ranks of sales reps by providing rewards to reps who recruit new reps. After five years, no one questions Jung's leadership style. Ann Moore, a board member put it like this: "Her people would die for her."

When a follower feels confident about performing the task, the leader no longer needs to be so directive. The leader should maintain open communication but now does so by actively listening and assisting the follower as he or she makes efforts to use what has been learned. In using a **participating style**, *the leader encourages followers to share ideas and facilitates the work by being encouraging and helpful to subordinates.*

Finally, when an employee is at a high level of readiness for the task, effective leadership involves more delegation. In using a **delegating style**, *the leader turns over responsibility for making and implementing decisions to followers.* Delegating is effective in this situation because the follower is both competent and motivated to take full responsibility for their work. Even though the leader may still identify problems, the responsibility for carrying out plans is given to the follower. The follower who is fully ready for a project is permitted to manage the project and decide how, when, and where tasks are to be done.

Assessment. The Situational Leadership® Model helps leaders recognize that the same leadership style may be effective in some situations but not others. Furthermore, it highlights the importance of considering the followers' situation when choosing a leadership style. It has generated quite a bit of interest among practitioners and researchers.[22] The idea that leaders should be flexible with respect to the leadership style they use is appealing. An inexperienced employee may perform as well as an experienced employee if properly directed and closely supervised. An appropriate leadership style should also help followers gain more experience and become more competent. Thus, as a leader helps followers develop to higher levels of readiness, the leader's style also needs to evolve. Therefore this model requires the leader to be constantly monitoring the readiness level of followers in order to determine the combination of task and relationship behaviors that is most appropriate.

Like other contingency models, this one assumes that managers can accurately assess each situation and change their leadership styles to match different situations. Some people can read situations and adapt their leadership style more effectively than others. For those who can't, what are the costs of training them to be able to do so? Do these costs exceed the potential benefits? Before an organization adopts a management training program to teach managers to use this model of leadership, they need to answer questions such as these.

Vroom–Jago Leadership Model

We next consider another contingency model of leadership—one that is even more complex. Like other contingency models, this one states that leaders should evaluate the situation and then decide how to behave. The Vroom–Jago model also recognizes that various leadership styles have different costs and benefits associated with them. Some styles of leadership may save time and money in the short run, but in doing so they are less effective for developing followers. Others styles have the longer term benefit of being more effective for developing followers, but they require more resources (e.g., time) in the short term. The **Vroom–Jago leadership model** *states that leaders should choose among five leadership styles based on seven contingency variables, while also recognizing the time requirements and other costs associated with each style.*[23]

Leadership Styles. The focus of this model is on how leaders involve a team of followers when making decisions. This model identifies five basic leadership styles, which represent five different ways in which leaders can involve team members when making work-related decisions. Keep in mind that none of the five approaches to decision making is best under all circumstances. These five styles that leaders can choose among are as follows:

1. **Decide style:** *The leader makes the decision and either announces or sells it to the team.* The leader may use his or her expertise and/or collect information from the team or others whom the leader believes can help solve the problem. The role of employees is clearly one of providing specific information that the leader requests, rather than generating or evaluating solutions.
2. **Consult individually style:** *The leader presents the problem to team members individually, getting their ideas and suggestions without bringing them together as a group, and then makes the decision.* This decision may or may not reflect the team members' influence.
3. **Consult group style:** *The leader presents the problem to team members in a meeting, gets their suggestions, and then makes the decision.* This decision may or may not reflect the team members' suggestions.
4. **Facilitate style:** *The leader presents the problem to the team in a meeting and acts as a facilitator, defining the problem to be solved and the constraints within which the decision*

must be made. The objective is to get concurrence on a decision. Above all, the leader takes care to ensure that his or her ideas are not given any greater weight than those of others simply because of position on the team. The leader's role is much like that of chairperson, coordinating the discussion, keeping it focused on the problem, and being sure that all essential issues are discussed. The leader doesn't try to influence the team to adopt a particular solution and is willing to accept and implement any solution that the entire team supports.

5. **Delegate style:** *The leader permits the team to make the decision within prescribed limits.* The team undertakes the identification and diagnosis of the problem, developing alternative procedures for solving it and deciding on one or more alternative solutions. The leader doesn't enter into the team's deliberations unless explicitly asked, but behind the scenes plays an important role, providing needed resources and encouragement. This style represents the highest level of subordinate discretion and participation.

Situational Contingencies. The Vroom–Jago leadership model includes seven contingencies that leaders should assess before choosing which leadership style to use. To evaluate the situation, leaders should consider the following aspects of the situation:

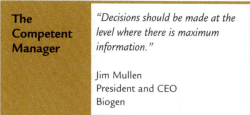

1. *Decision significance.* How important is the technical quality of this decision?
2. *Importance of commitment.* How important is it for followers to be committed to the decision? Can the decision be implemented even if followers don't agree that it is the best decision?
3. *Leader expertise.* Does the leader have the relevant information and competencies required to understand the problem fully and select the best solution?
4. *Likelihood of commitment.* If the leader makes the decision, will followers trust the leader's judgment? Would they be committed to implementing a decision made by the leader?
5. *Team support.* Do the followers share the goals to be achieved by solving this problem? Are the followers' interests aligned with those of the organization as a whole?
6. *Team expertise.* Does the leader believe that followers have the abilities and information to make a high-quality decision?
7. *Team competence.* Are the followers capable of handling their own decision-making process?

Choosing a Leadership Style. The matrix shown in Figure 15.6 integrates the model's seven contingencies with its five leadership styles.[24] In effect, the matrix represents a decision tree. The column headings denote the situational contingency that may or may not be present. The process of deciding which leadership style to use begins with the leader evaluating the significance of the problem—high (H) or low (L). Proceeding across the matrix, the leader records an H or L for only those contingencies that call for a judgment, until the recommended leadership style is reached.

To illustrate how you would use the tree, imagine you are in the following situation[25]:

You are the newly appointed director of a repertory theater company, with full responsibility for the financial and artistic health of the organization. You were a drama major in college and have 20 years of acting and directing experience. Your understanding of financial issues is fairly good because you recently spent a year heading up a task force charged with developing a long-term strategy that will ensure the theater company's long-term financial viability. Shortly after the task force disbanded, the former director left the company and you replaced her. The four other members of your management team, who all report to you, are in charge of

Instructions: The matrix operates like a funnel. You start at the left with a specific decision problem in mind. The column headings denote situational factors which may or may not be present in that problem. You progress by selecting High or Low (H or L) for each relevant situational factor. Proceed down from the funnel, judging only those situational factors for which a judgment is called for, until you reach the recommended process.

PROBLEM STATEMENT	Decision Significance?	Importance of Commitment?	Leader Expertise?	Likelihood of Commitment?	Group Supports?	Group Expertise?	Team Competence?	
	H	H	H	H	—	—	—	Decide
	H	H	H	L	H	H	H	Delegate
	H	H	H	L	H	H	L	Consult (Group)
	H	H	H	L	H	L	—	Consult (Group)
	H	H	H	L	L	—	—	Consult (Group)
	H	H	L	H	H	H	H	Facilitate
	H	H	L	H	H	H	L	Consult (Individually)
	H	H	L	H	H	L	—	Consult (Individually)
	H	H	L	H	L	—	—	Consult (Individually)
	H	H	L	L	H	H	H	Facilitate
	H	H	L	L	H	H	L	Consult (Group)
	H	H	L	L	H	L	—	Consult (Group)
	H	H	L	L	L	—	—	Consult (Group)
	H	L	H	—	—	—	—	Decide
	H	L	L	—	H	H	H	Facilitate
	H	L	L	—	H	H	L	Consult (Individually)
	H	L	L	—	H	L	—	Consult (Individually)
	H	L	L	—	L	—	—	Consult (Individually)
	L	H	—	H	—	—	—	Decide
	L	H	—	L	—	—	H	Delegate
	L	H	—	L	—	—	L	Facilitate
	L	L	—	—	—	—	—	Decide

Source: Reprinted from *Organizational Dynamics*, Spring 2000, Vol. 28, Victor H. Vroom, Leadership and the Decision-Making Process, pp. 62-94, (c) 2000, with permission from Elsevier.

production, marketing, development, and administration. In addition, the theater company employs about 30 artists with a variety of special skills. They are a talented and very committed team.

You have been implementing various suggestions of the task force and things seem to be going relatively well. You face one big problem, however. Production and labor costs have been rising faster than you expected. And audience size has been somewhat smaller than you expected. You believe the weak economy has kept some people from buying tickets. Because your mission is to serve the community, you've kept ticket prices low despite the rising costs. You need to decide what to do in order to resolve this situation.

Using the matrix shown in Figure 15.6, you might proceed as described below. Note that you must follow the rule, "*never cross a horizontal line*" as you go from left to right in the matrix.

1. First, you consider the significance of the decision. You rate it as highly important (H).
2. Next, you consider whether it is important that your management feel committed to whatever solution you choose. You feel that their commitment is essential (H).
3. You evaluate your expertise. Before the problem arose, you thought it was pretty high, but now you feel much less confident. You rate your expertise as somewhat low (L).
4. Now you consider whether it is likely that people would accept your decision if they were not involved in formulating the solution. You conclude the likelihood is low (L).
5. The next question to consider is whether your management team is strongly committed to the mission and goals of the theater. You know that they are very committed, so you rate this as high (H).
6. You consider next the issue of how much expertise is present among the members of your management team. You rate their expertise as quite high. Each has different skills but they all have many years of experience working in their professions (H).
7. Finally, you consider how well your management team works together. Your top managers actually do not work well together. There have been many conflicts during the past several months, and the team has been unable to resolve them. They all have very strong views and have not learned to collaborate and compromise when needed. You rate team competence as low (L).

Having evaluated the seven aspects of the situation, you can see that the recommended decision style is the *consult group style*. That is, you should present the problem to the team, have them offer suggestions, then make a decision. You may have two or three group meetings as you narrow down the options, but everyone understands that you will make the final decision. You will not delegate the problem and expect the management team to resolve the problem on their own.

To make it easier for leaders to use this matrix, Victor Vroom developed a computer program called Expert System. The program records the leader's judgments about each of the seven situational contingencies using a five-point rating scale. The program then uses these ratings to recommend the best leadership style.

Prioritizing Costs and Benefits. The matrix shown in Figure 15.6 should be used by leaders who are concerned about making decisions under time pressure. The matrix is designed to help leaders make a decision of acceptable quality with the maximum speed. Leaders often must make decisions when time is of the essence. For example, a decision about whether or not to purchase a particular software package may need to be made quickly because an attractive low price is being offered for a only a short time. Should the leader act alone and make a very quick decision? Or consult the team first and then decide? Or delegate the decision and let the team members decide on their own? When choosing a leadership style for this decision, the speed of the decision will be given high priority because there is a penalty for not deciding quickly enough.

Speed is not always the most important consideration when making decisions, however. Other priorities may be more important in some situations. For example, when there is less time pressure, a leader may give more priority to choosing a style that has the benefit of developing the followers. By using a more participative style, a leader can develop the technical and managerial competencies of employees, build teamwork, and foster loyalty and commitment to organizational goals. Here we have discussed in detail only the time-driven decision matrix. Other matrices are also available for leaders to use. Thus, a leader who wishes to give greater priority to developing followers could use a matrix for choosing the best style when development is of more concern than speed.

Assessment. If leaders can diagnose contingencies correctly, choosing the best leadership style for those situations becomes easier. These choices, in turn, will enable them to make high-quality, timely decisions. If the situation requires delegation, the leader must learn how to establish the desired goals and limitations and then let employees determine how best to achieve the goals within those limitations. If the situation calls for the leader alone to make the decision, the leader should be aware of potential positive and negative consequences of not asking others for their input.

This model does have limitations. First, most employees have a strong desire to participate in decisions affecting their jobs, regardless of the model's recommendation of a leadership style. If subordinates aren't involved in a decision, they are more likely to become frustrated and not be committed to the decision. Second, certain competencies of the leader play a key role in determining the relative effectiveness of the model. For example, in situations involving conflict, only leaders skilled in conflict resolution may be able to use the kind of participative decision-making strategy suggested by the model.[26] A leader who hasn't developed this competency may obtain better results with a more directive style, even though this style is different from the style that the model proposes.

At Conoco's LiquidPower flow improver plant in Bryan, Texas, managers are expected to coach, facilitate, and delegate—not decide. Because this requires some skill, team leaders receive 18 months of training before they are "thrown in" to a coaching or facilitating role. One visitor who saw this leadership style in action when an automation problem arose described it this way: "People came out of nowhere, nobody gave any orders, there was no supervision, everyone did the work that needed to be done, and when they were finished they all went back to their normal routine. What would have taken most facilities two or three hours to fix took only about twenty minutes."[27]

TRANSFORMATIONAL LEADERSHIP

5. State the key characteristics and behaviors of transformational leadership.

The leaders of some organizations have increasingly realized that leadership is more than a matter of personal characteristics, specific behaviors, or particular contingencies. It is all of those things, and much more. The people needed to guide organizations through needed changes are often called *transformational leaders.*

Transformational leaders *inspire others with their vision, often promote this vision over opposition, and demonstrate confidence in themselves and their views.*[28] Like Carly Fiorina, they take an active and personal approach to influencing others. Transformational leaders alter feelings, desires, and expectations of others.[29] They change perceptions of the possible and desirable. These leaders develop new approaches to long-standing problems and new options to open issues. Transformational leaders reflect excitement and enthusiasm and generate the same in others. They embrace risks to pursue new opportunities. They are empathetic and intuitive in their ability to relate with others and, in general, are high in emotional intelligence. As a result, they are highly trusted and their organizations perform better.[30]

Figure 15.7 outlines the interrelated characteristics and behaviors of transformational leaders. Each transformational leader is a unique mosaic of these characteristics. Although each transformational leader may be stronger in terms of some characteristics than others, all are likely to be present.[31]

Visionary

Perhaps the dominant characteristic that transformational leaders possess is their ability to create a *vision* that binds people to each other and creates a new future. Dr. Martin

Figure 15.7   Common Characteristics of Transformational Leaders

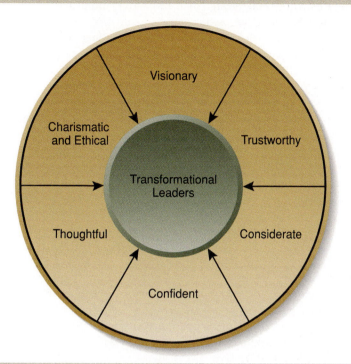

Luther King's famous "I Have a Dream" speech in 1963 galvanized a generation to support the civil rights movement in the United States. Business leaders can also galvanize people to act. Dr. Irwin Redlener's vision was to establish a "medical home" for every child who lacks continuous access to high-quality, comprehensive health care. A pediatrician, his vision was to "use health care as a lever to address the global needs of the most disadvantaged kids . . . [he wants to] unlock the future for millions of kids with no sense of hope . . . to ignite the imaginations of children and change their lives." Redlener's vision has become a reality at the Children's Hospital at Montefiore, in New York. The hospital combines Carl Sagan's cosmic world view with cutting-edge medical technology and the elaborate design artistry of a professional theatrical production. While being treated, children can learn about poetry, painting, chemistry, space, oceanography, and many other topics in an interactive bedside environment.[32]

As described in the Teamwork Competency feature, Samuel Palmisano's vision is to set the agenda for the computer industry in the 21st century by providing on-demand e-business. He didn't develop this vision alone, however. He won't implement it alone, either.[33]

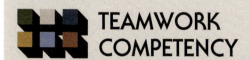

TEAMWORK COMPETENCY

Sam Palmisano at IBM

Before Sam Palmisano became CEO of IBM in 2002, Big Blue (as the company is known) had spent 10 years pulling itself back from the brink. A firm that revolutionized computing earlier in the 20th century seemed to have lost its way as that century came to a close. By the time Palmisano took the reins, IBM no longer needed a life support system. But it still needed a vision for how to become a truly great company again. Palmisano is eager to lead IBM back to greatness. In the future, he envisions IBM as the one-stop provider of on-demand e-business computing. He believes his industry is poised for another revolution. In the new era, he believes businesses will want efficient, extremely powerful, consolidated systems that run on open standards and meet the specific needs of an industry. The radical new idea is that a company will no longer own and house its own computing system. Instead, it will purchase computing power directly from a provider. As the provider of computing power, IBM will build supersized power grids that companies can tap into as needed. The idea is to manage and distribute computing power in a way that's similar to what we now do with electrical power. Coupled with the new technology will be powerful new software that captures and distributes an organization's base of knowledge.

Palmisano didn't develop this vision alone. He asked his top management team to join him in coming up with an idea that would be the type of major breakthrough that IBM made when it developed a mainframe computer 40 years earlier. The new vision is so radical that today only about 10 percent of the technology needed is actually available. The rest still has to be invented.

To make this vision a reality, Palmisano will continue to rely on other executives. One of his first moves as CEO was to abolish the bureaucratic corporate executive committee that held monthly meetings and oversaw every strategic initiative. In its place are three new teams in charge of operations, strategy, and technology. Made up of people from all levels of the company, he believes these teams will be the engines of creativity at IBM. "Creativity in any large organization does not come from one individual, the celebrity CEO. That stuff's B.S. Creativity starts where the action is—either in the laboratory, or in R&D sites, at a customer place, in manufacturing." According to Bruce Herrald, IBM's senior vice president of strategy, this new approach is a radical departure for the company. "Heads are spinning," he says. "He's reaching six levels down and asking questions." To demonstrate his commitment to a team-based approach to managing, Palmisano put his money where his mouth is. After naming his new top 20 managers, he asked the board to cut his own bonus and set the money aside as a pool to be shared based on team performance. One of the biggest challenges for the teams will be turning IBM itself into an on-demand e-business. To sell its new concept to others, first it must prove it can be done.

Like Palmisano, transformational leaders have more than just a vision. They also have a road map for attaining it. What is important is that followers "buy into" that vision and that the leader has a plan to energize them to reach it. Visionaries challenge old beliefs and ways of doing things. They strongly believe in their ideas, are able to communicate them clearly, and can use them to excite others.[34]

Charismatic *and* Ethical

Transformational leaders are charismatic, but not all charismatic leaders are transformational leaders. A **charismatic leader** *is a person who has the ability to influence others because of his or her inspirational qualities.* The Greek word *kharisma* means "divine gift." Leaders with charisma have the power to obtain the cooperation and devotion of followers. Followers of charismatic leaders attribute heroic and extraordinary abilities to them.[35]

Charismatic leaders may benefit or harm an organization or society. Adolf Hitler was a charismatic leader to his followers but not to most people. He was an unethical, unbalanced, and immoral charismatic leader who focused on his own needs and was not open to criticism or suggestions. Transformational leaders are charismatic *and ethical.* Ray Gilmartin, CEO of Merck, strives to be an ethical leader. He frequently quotes George Merck, the company's founder, whose philosophy was this: "Medicine is for the people. It is not for the profits. The profits will follow." While his competitors fight with tooth and nail to maintain high drug prices, Merck is donating vaccines to the Global Alliance for Vaccines and Immunization, helping to build a better health-care system in Botswana, and selling AIDS drugs at 85 percent discounts in the poorest countries. Critics of Gilmartin charge that "doing good" is a distraction for his company. But Gilmartin disagrees. He believes the best scientists want to work for a company that makes them feel proud.[36]

Like Palmisano and Gilmartin, transformational leaders listen carefully to followers, provide support and empowerment, and lead by example. They are flexible and open to criticism, but they will stand up for ideas even if they are unpopular.[37] Over time, transformational leaders inspire and develop their followers to become leaders.[38] These leaders do not make fun of the opinions of others, regardless of their status and position. In essence, transformational leaders are role models for followers to emulate. Transformational leaders are the individuals whom people describe when asked to think about someone who has had a major influence on their personal and professional development.

Trustworthy

Because transformational leaders strive to be ethical in their relations with others, they are viewed as trustworthy. Employees who do not trust a leader will hesitate in following that leader's expressed vision and will interpret inspirational messages with skepticism. Transformational leaders are often known for their honesty under pressure, including straight talking and keeping commitments. They "walk the talk." In addition to being perceived as trustworthy, transformational leaders show trust in their followers. These leaders empower and delegate tasks to followers. They actively encourage a two-way flow of information and dialogue.[39]

The Competent Manager

"If you say you're about a team, you have to be a team. You have to walk the talk, right? I can't have a big gap between me and my team."

Sam Palmisano
CEO
IBM

Thoughtful

Transformational leaders are agents of thoughtful change and innovation. They challenge followers to build on their vision by offering innovative solutions and new ideas. They encourage positive thinking and problem solving. These leaders embrace taking risks, but base their actions on thoughtful analysis and discussion. Creativity is encouraged. Followers are expected and encouraged to question long-standing assumptions and practices. These leaders often focus on the "what" and "why" of problems, rather than the "who" on which to place blame. For these leaders, nothing is too good, too fixed, or too political that it can't be challenged or changed.

Considerate

Transformational leaders care about the needs of others and have a great capacity for empathy. They actively listen to the concerns of employees, customers, suppliers, and the public. They are willing to accept responsibility when mistakes inevitably occur and do not look for scapegoats. They respect and value the contributions of all employees. Transformational leaders are often willing to sacrifice immediate personal gain for the benefit of others. They use their sources of power to move individuals and groups toward their visions but avoid the use of power for personal gain.[40]

Confident

Transformational leaders project optimism and self-confidence. Followers have to see that a leader is passionate about a vision and confident that it can be achieved—but not arrogant. Such leaders also exhibit confidence in their followers. They recognize that mistakes will be made and know that, if errors are not tolerated, followers will become too risk adverse.

Thus transformational leaders demonstrate a unique profile of personal characteristics, behaviors, and competencies. They aren't found only in top management positions in business organizations. They also are found in charitable organizations, civic and community groups, schools, student organizations, government agencies, small and large businesses, and every other type of organization. The individuals profiled in this chapter—Carly Fiorina of HP, Andrea Jung of Avon, Dr. Irwin Redlener of the Children's

Hospital at Montefiore, Sam Palmisano of IBM—can truly be called transformational leaders.

LEADERSHIP DEVELOPMENT

6. Describe how organizations develop leaders.

One recent poll of 700 employees working in dozens of different companies found that 83 percent believed there was a leadership vacuum in their organizations. Another study found that only 45 percent of employees have confidence in the job being done by their top executives. Trust in senior management has been falling steadily during the past few years.[41] Where have all the good leaders gone? How can organizations address the need for better leaders?

Some people believe that leaders are born, not made. Other people believe that a person's leadership capacity is learned during childhood and is pretty much set by the time they are working as managers. If these beliefs were true, all an organization could do is search for better leaders and hope they can find them somewhere. However, most CEOs seem to believe that leadership can be improved as a consequence of one's personal experiences, and research supports this view. That's why they invest both personal time and company resources in efforts to develop the leadership capacity of their employees. These investments fall into three general categories: assigning people to positions to promote learning on the job, sending employees to formal leadership assessment and training programs, and offering assistance through coaching and mentoring.[42]

On-the-Job Learning

As we noted in Chapter 1, on-the-job learning is important for all aspects of managerial work, and that includes learning leadership. Developing leadership on the job requires that employees take jobs or project assignments that include leadership responsibilities. Early in a person's career, working as an individual contributor on team projects provides many opportunities for learning how to be an effective leader. Being a formal leader of a project allows an employee to use different types of influence tactics and observe how people react to those influence attempts. Team leaders also can ask team members for candid feedback and suggestions for how to improve. Team members who aren't designated as the formal leader also can learn by observing the relationship between the leader and the team.

On-the-job learning is most effective for people who take personal responsibility for their own development. You will learn more through this approach if you understand your current approach to leadership, develop an action plan for improvement, and focus on carrying out the plan. Throughout this book, we have given you an opportunity to learn about yourself by completing various questionnaires, addressing various discussion questions, analyzing various cases, and reflecting on the textbook's various competency features. We hope that these activities are helping you develop your own leadership abilities.

Learning on the job is a first step to becoming an effective leader, but large companies seldom rely solely on this approach. They also invest millions of dollars in formal programs. Formal programs typically are built around the company's own view of what is required of its managers and leaders. As described in the Planning & Administration Competency feature, the 3M Company used the opinions of its own executives to develop its leadership model. Top-level executives understand that the CEO uses this model when he conducts his annual review of them. Managers at lower levels use the model as a guide when choosing developmental activities and assignments. Executives and managers also use the company's leadership model when setting performance expectations, judging performance, and discussing the development needs of their employees.

3M's Leadership Model

The decade of the 1990s saw increased global competition for 3M. The fierce competition, in turn, highlighted the need for highly effective leaders who could steer the company through a period of shrinking margins, pressures on pricing, and the ever-present demand for new innovations. This environment highlighted the importance of leadership development activities to promote the company's long-term viability. Due to the breadth of businesses and technologies within 3M, it takes years of experience before executives learn to function effectively. Thoughtful planning and job placements are needed to ensure that managers leverage their opportunities for leadership development.

The company's leadership model was developed by the company's human resource professionals who met with key executives to solicit their ideas and craft the model's wording. In addition to the CEO and his direct reports, 3M's leadership model reflects the views of representatives from Europe, Asia, Latin America, Canada, and the United States. The dimensions of leadership that 3M identified and now uses for developing future leaders are organized into three categories, as shown below.

■ *Fundamental leadership competencies:* New employees should possess these when hired and refine them through experience in successive managerial assignments:
  ■ Ethics and integrity
  ■ Intellectual capacity
  ■ Maturity and judgment

■ *Essential leadership competencies:* These competencies are developed through experience leading a function or department, and set the stage for more complex executive positions:
  ■ Customer orientation
  ■ Developing people
  ■ Inspiring others
  ■ Business health and results
■ *Visionary leadership competencies:* These competencies develop as executives take on responsibilities that require them to operate beyond the boundaries of a particular organizational unit, and are used extensively in higher level positions:
  ■ Global perspective
  ■ Vision and strategy
  ■ Nurturing innovation
  ■ Building alliances
  ■ Organizational agility

To meet the developmental needs of their employees, 3M and many other companies use many types of programs. Two common leadership development programs are (1) formal assessment and training and (2) coaching and mentoring.

Assessment and Training

Leadership assessment and training programs *generally include evaluating the individual's style of leadership and providing educational experiences designed to improve the individual's effectiveness as a leader.* Assessing a person's strengths and weaknesses helps set the stage for a formal training program. To assess their employees' leadership capabilities, organizations like Wells Fargo and Sara Lee use trained experts, self-assessments, and 360-degree feedback. For employees in roles that involve leadership, providing feedback is a good way to improve their effectiveness. Not surprisingly, most leaders see themselves in a more positive light than their followers do. The best leaders have a realistic view of themselves and use feedback about their behavior to make improvements. Formal assessment and training may be conducted at the organization's own educational facilities, at a college or university, or by organizations such as the Center for Creative Leadership, a nonprofit organization dedicated to leadership research and education.

FedEx conducts is own leadership assessment and training. Selecting and developing a person to enter a leadership role takes 14 months. Each year, some 3,000 FedEx employees interested in leadership positions enter the company's Leadership Evaluation and Awareness Process (LEAP). Only 20 percent make it to the final stage. Why? According to a senior official at the company, three reasons account for people dropping out. First, they come to realize that leaders put in very long hours. Second, they realize that leadership carries an unrelenting sense of obligation—they are always representatives of FedEx, even when they aren't at work. Third, they realize that leadership involves intensive interactions with people. The self-evaluation included in FedEx's LEAP program opens the eyes of many potential leaders. According to the managing director of the FedEx Leadership Institute, "Too many people get into leadership for all the wrong reasons. They want power. They think it's the only way to advance. LEAP is a gate that everyone has to pass through. And those who pass through it are attuned to what it means to lead and to work effectively with other people."[43]

Coaching and Mentoring

A relatively new approach to leadership development is the use of personal coaches. As explained in Chapter 13, coaching involves providing one-on-one, personalized feedback and advice for the purpose of enhancing the manager's performance and the organization's performance. Dell Computer uses coaches to help their best technically oriented managers develop their leadership skills. Abbott Laboratories uses coaches to help managers change from their old command-and-control (Theory X, task-oriented) style of leadership to the more egalitarian (Theory Y, relationship-oriented) style now preferred at the company.[44] When David Pottruck was moving up through the ranks at Charles Schwab & Co., he didn't think he needed a coach. "I thought I was a great leader," he says. "I didn't understand there was a problem." As he got close to the top, however, his problem got harder to ignore. Then, one day during a performance review session he learned that he was a very poor leader: "You are high maintenance—you are painful. Your peers don't like working with you—and they don't trust you." That's when Pottruck got a coach to help him improve his leadership style. "It's very hard to get better on your own," observed Pottruck. His coach was with him constantly—on the golf course, in his limousine, on wilderness trips, through a divorce, and through corporate scandals that hit Schwab after Pottruck became co-CEO. His coach provided constant feedback and advice while also helping him change his behavior.[45] Because personal coaches provide an intensive leadership development experience, they can be quite expensive.

In Chapter 13, we also discussed the value of mentoring for developing employees. For many managers, learning from a mentor is more feasible than hiring a coach. Mentors most often are managers or senior colleagues in the organization who provide advice and guidance about a variety of career-related concerns. For managers, talking with mentors about how to develop more effective leadership behaviors is important to career advancement. In particular, mentors can help managers understand how others respond to their behaviors and point out weaknesses or blind spots. Mentors also serve as role models that individuals can emulate, and they provide valuable advice concerning the styles of leadership favored in the organization. Finally, mentors often assist managers in developing leadership capabilities by helping them obtain assignments that will foster on-the-job learning. When Andrea Jung began working at Bloomingdale's during her first year after college, she sought out Joan Vass to act as her mentor. Vass had a fast-paced career, which she successfully balanced with a quiet family life. Jung saw Vass as an ideal role model who could teach her how to be tactfully aggressive, so she sought her out as a mentor. "Some people just wait for someone to take them under their wing," she commented. I've always advised that they shouldn't. They should take someone's wings to grab onto.[46]

CHAPTER SUMMARY

Leadership is central to the effectiveness of organizations. Employees at all levels of an organization can exercise leadership, which takes many forms. Because effective leadership is so important, numerous studies have been conducted in attempts to understand its nature. Each of numerous models explains some—but not all—aspects of effective leadership. Organizations interested in developing effective leaders often use these models as the basis for leadership development activities.

1. Explain what leadership means.

Leadership is an influence relationship among leaders and followers who strive for real change and outcomes that reflect their shared purposes. Leaders can influence others by using their formal position, rewards, coercion, expertise, and charisma. The most effective use of influence tactics results in followers who are committed to the leader's goals. The improper use of influence may result in mere compliance or even resistance.

2. Describe the personal characteristics that enable leaders to be effective.

A leader's personal characteristics include their physical, social, and personal attributes. Personal characteristics are not easy to change, and they generally result in fairly predictable behavior over a period of time. The presence and absence of certain individual characteristics enable some leaders to be more effective than others. Emotional intelligence is a set of four personal characteristics that appear to be useful for effective leadership. These characteristics are self-awareness, self-control, social awareness, and social skill.

3. Describe the types of behaviors required for leadership.

Behavioral models of leadership provide a way of identifying effective leaders by their actions. The Theory X and Theory Y model states that leaders' behaviors reflect their basic assumptions about people. Theory X and Theory Y represent two quite different ways that leaders view their subordinates and thus manage them. The managerial grid model identifies various combinations of concern for people and production. They provide the basis for deriving five different styles of leadership—country club, impover-

ished, produce or perish, middle of the road, and team. In this model the team style is viewed as the ideal leadership style to strive for.

4. Identify the contingencies that may shape how leaders behave.

The Situational Leadership® Model indicates that leaders must adapt their leadership style to the readiness level of their followers. This model prescribes different combinations of task and relationship leader behaviors for different levels of subordinates' readiness. It suggests four leadership styles—delegating, participating, selling, and telling. The Vroom–Jago leadership model prescribes a leader's choices among five leadership styles based on seven contingency variables, recognizing the time requirements and other costs associated with each style. The five core leadership styles are decide, consult individually, consult as a group, facilitate, and delegate. Contingency models assume that leaders can be highly flexible in their use of leadership styles.

5. State the key characteristics and behaviors of transformational leadership.

The transformational model of leadership views it as involving a combination of personal characteristics, behaviors, and contingencies. It is all of these things combined in unique ways. People who guide organizations through needed changes are often called transformational leaders. They inspire others with their vision, promote this vision over opposition, and demonstrate confidence in themselves and their views. In addition to having a vision for the future, they use their charisma to achieve ethical objectives, and they are thoughtful, considerate, trustworthy, and confident.

6. Describe how organizations develop leaders.

Organizations use three major approaches to develop leaders: placing employees in positions that promote learning on the job, providing employees with formal leadership assessments and training, and offering mentoring and coaching. Organizations invest in these leadership development activities because they understand that leaders are made, not born.

KEY TERMS and CONCEPTS

Behavioral models of leadership
Charismatic leader
Consult group style
Consult individually style
Contingency models of leadership

Decide style
Delegate style
Delegating style
Emotional intelligence
Facilitate style

Leadership
Leadership assessment and training programs
Managerial grid
Participating style
Readiness
Relationship behavior
Self-awareness
Self-control
Selling style

Situational Leadership® Model
Social awareness
Social skill
Task behavior
Telling style
Theory X
Theory Y
Transformational leaders
Vroom–Jago leadership model

QUESTIONS FOR DISCUSSION and COMPETENCY DEVELOPMENT

1. Evaluate the leadership of Carly Fiorina using the managerial grid. Based on what you have read, which style best describes her behavior?

2. Think of a leader that you know. Give examples of how this person influences others using formal authority, expertise, rewards, coercion, and charisma. Do you agree that people respond in different ways to these influence tactics? Explain.

3. Describe a manager you have worked for in terms of Theory X or Theory Y. Give some examples of this manager's behaviors and attitudes that seem to be consistent with Theory X or Theory Y.

4. In the Situational Leadership® Model, readiness of followers is a key contingency variable. Based on a recent job experience, did your manager appropriately recognize your "readiness" in work relations with you? Explain.

5. Think of a team decision-making situation in which you have been involved. Use the Vroom–Jago leadership model to analyze that situation (refer to Figure 15.6). Did the team leader use the correct leadership style based on this model? Did the leader seem to give more priority to making a speedy decision or to developing the team members? Explain.

6. Numerous organizations offer leadership development programs. Investigate the leadership training program offered by the Center for Creative Leadership by visiting their Web site. Which of the following does this organization offer: on-the-job learning, leadership assessment, formal leadership training, coaching, and/or mentoring?

7. Are leaders born or made? Defend your position.

8. Evaluate the emotional intelligence of Andrea Jung at Avon.

CASE FOR COMPETENCY DEVELOPMENT

KEN CHENAULT AT AMERICAN EXPRESS

American Express provides an array of financial and travel-related services, including the recent development of on-line banking, mortgage, and brokerage services. The firm has more than 88,000 employees and annual sales of some $23 billion. In 2001, Ken Chenault was appointed chairman and CEO of American Express. Immediately prior to becoming CEO, he served as the company's president and COO. In the 20 years before that, Chenault served American Express (AmEx) in a variety of positions, from director of strategic planning in the Merchandise Services division to president of the Consumer Card division. He displayed bold leadership during the early 1990s by persuading merchants—from airline companies to restaurants—not to leave the AmEx fold while internal feuds were being resolved at the company. As the executive handpicked to reduce costs, Chenault streamlined

four divisions, creating a productive business unit and saving a substantial amount in operating costs.

Harvey Golub, who preceded Chenault as chairman and CEO, recommended to the board of directors that Chenault be his replacement. He commented: "There are qualities in leadership that can only be observed over time—how an individual deals with others, how he deals with adversity and complex issues, how he organizes his time and efforts, and deals with external constituencies. And Ken has demonstrated amply over the years his abilities. He's more than capable."

Together, Golub and Chenault developed a three-prong growth strategy for the company's future. The plan called for expanding the company's card network through banks and financial institutions; expanding its financial and investment services; and increasing its market share in specialty segments, including small businesses and overseas markets.

Executing this strategy has meant transforming the company in a variety of ways. One major change is that technology is now at the center of the company's business. To execute the strategy, Chenault has had to help employees understand the new vision and what it means for each of their jobs. "Leaders must focus an organization on facing reality. Then they give them the confidence and support to inspire them to change that reality." Louise Parent, executive vice president of American Express, describes Chenault's leadership style as "relentless about performance and about measuring ourselves against the competition. He is the kind of person who inspires you to want to do your best. Part of the reason is his example."

David House, president of Establishment Service Worldwide for AmEx observed that he "has had tremendous courage in the face of adversity, and he's incredibly competitive. He really wants to win." According to House, he can persuade the proverbial Eskimo to purchase a cooler. He doesn't mean to suggest that Chenault is unscrupulous, however. In fact, House remembers how candid Chenault had been when House was interviewed by him several years ago. House says he had no intention of taking the job. He only accepted the interview because he wanted to meet Ken, whose name had come up several times in conversations at the company he was then working for (Reebok). To the surprise of House, Chenault outlined reasons why he shouldn't take the job. He pointed out that the card business was undergoing a major restructuring and that if his strategy didn't work, the company would go out of business. House states that "It was high risk, and that got me excited, along with the fact that [Chenault] had the integrity to tell me. Ken has the highest integrity of anyone I've ever met in business and personally, including my father."

Within a year of becoming CEO, Chenault's courage was really tested. The company's headquarters building in downtown New York was severely damaged by the terrorist attacks on September 11, 2001. Eleven AmEx employees were killed that day. Chenault was in Salt Lake City at the time and had to manage the crisis from there. Hundreds of decisions had be made on the spot and with little information. Besides the safety of his employees, his decisions following September 11 affected more than 560,000 customers who had been traveling at the time and were now stranded all over the country. These were tough times for Chenault, who acknowledges that he twice sought out the advice of a professional counselor to deal with his sadness, despair, and anger. His compassion was evident as he spoke with employees during a "town hall meeting" 10 days after the attacks. He told the audience, "I represent the best company and the best people in the world. In fact, you are my strength, and I love you." According to one observer, "The manner in which he took command, the comfort and direction he gave to what was obviously an audience in shock was of a caliber one rarely sees."[47]

Questions

1. In what ways does Ken Chenault reflect Theory Y assumptions?

2. Review the characteristics and behaviors of transformational leaders. Which of these are illustrated in this description of Ken Chenault?

3. What aspects of emotional intelligence does Ken Chenault reveal?

EXERCISE FOR COMPETENCY DEVELOPMENT

EMOTIONAL INTELLIGENCE

Instructions: Indicate how well the statements below describe you, using the following scale:

Strongly disagree 1	Somewhat disagree 2	Somewhat agree 3	Strongly agree 4

_____ 1. I know when to speak about my personal problems to others.

_____ 2. When I'm faced with obstacles, I remember times I faced similar obstacles and overcame them.

_____ 3. I expect that I will do well on most things.

_____ 4. Other people find it easy to confide in me.

_____ 5. I find it easy to understand the nonverbal messages of other people.

_____ 6. Some of the major events of my life have led me to reevaluate what is important and not important.

_____ 7. When my mood changes, I see new possibilities.

_____ 8. Emotions are one of the things that make life worth living.

_____ 9. I am aware of my emotions as I experience them.

_____ 10. I expect good things to happen.

_____ 11. I like to share my emotions with other people.

_____ **12.** When I experience a positive emotion, I know how to make it last.

_____ **13.** I arrange events others enjoy.

_____ **14.** I seek out activities that make me happy.

_____ **15.** I am aware of the nonverbal messages I send to others.

_____ **16.** I present myself in a way that makes a good impression on others.

_____ **17.** When I am in a positive mood, solving problems is easy for me.

_____ **18.** By looking at facial expressions, I can recognize the emotions that others are feeling.

_____ **19.** I know why my emotions change.

_____ **20.** When I am in a positive mood, I am able to come up with new ideas.

_____ **21.** I have control over my emotions.

_____ **22.** I easily recognize my emotions as I experience them.

_____ **23.** I motivate myself by imagining a good outcome to the tasks I do.

_____ **24.** I compliment others when they have done something well.

_____ **25.** I am aware of the nonverbal messages other people send.

_____ **26.** When another person tells me about an important event in their life, I almost feel as though I have experienced this event myself.

_____ **27.** When I feel a change in emotions, I tend to come up with new ideas.

_____ **28.** When I am faced with a challenge, I usually rise to the occasion.

_____ **29.** I know what other people are feeling just by looking at them.

_____ **30.** I help other people feel better when they are down.

_____ **31.** I use good moods to help myself keep trying in the face of obstacles.

_____ **32.** I can tell how people are feeling by listening to the tone of their voices.

Scoring:

1. Add your responses to questions 1, 6, 7, 8, 12, 14, 17, 19, 20, 22, 23, and 27. Put this total here_____. This is your *self-awareness* score.

2. Add your responses to questions 4, 15, 18, 25, 29, and 32. Put this total here_____. This is your *social awareness* score.

3. Add your responses to questions 2, 3, 9, 10, 16, 21, 28, and 31. Put this total here_____. This is your *self-control* score.

4. Add your responses to questions 5, 11, 13, 24, 26, and 30. Put this total here_____. This is your *social skills* score.

Interpretation: Emotional intelligence refers to how well an individual handles herself and others rather than how smart she is or how capable she is in terms of technical skills. Emotional intelligence includes the attributes of self-awareness, self-control, social awareness, and social skill. The higher your score is in each of these four areas, the more emotionally intelligent you are. People who score high (greater than 36) in *self-awareness* recognize their emotions and their effects on others, accurately assess their strengths and limitations, and have a strong sense of their self-worth and capabilities. People who score high (greater than 18) in *social awareness* are good at understanding others, taking an active interest in their concerns, empathizing with them, and recognizing the needs others have at work. People who score high (greater than 24) in *self-control* can keep their disruptive emotions and impulses under control, maintain standards of integrity and honesty, are conscientious, adapt their behaviors to changing situations, and have internal standards of excellence that guide their behaviors. People who have high (greater than 18) *social skills* sense others' developmental needs, inspire and lead groups, send clear and convincing messages, build effective interpersonal relationships, and work well with others to achieve shared goals.[48]

©Photodisc/Getty Images

Organizational
Communication

LEARNING OBJECTIVES

After studying this chapter, you should be able to:

1. Explain the main elements of the communication process.

2. Identify hurdles to communication and describe ways to eliminate them.

3. State the guidelines for fostering effective communication.

4. Discuss two ethical issues in communications.

Chapter Outline

CEO Kerry Killinger and the managers at Washington Mutual (WaMu) don't model their communication systems after Citigroup or Bank of America. Instead they look to Southwest Airlines and Wal-Mart for learning how to keep costs low, service high, and meet the needs of their customers.

Killinger's focus is on middle-class people who need a home mortgage and want free checking. WaMu found that there was a gold mine in "free checking." After 18 months of customer research, WaMu learned that thousands of its customers were likely to bounce as many as eight checks a year. In essence, customers were using their checking accounts as short-term credit. WaMu now charges $30 to cover checks with insufficient funds. With more than 7 million customers, WaMu learned that free checking can be a lucrative business.

To attract customers, mannequins in the windows are dressed in rustic casual clothes. Inside the bank, sales associates are dressed in Gap-like clothes: blue shirts, khaki pants, and navy sweaters. Sales associates are hired who share the WaMu attributes of being caring, dynamic, driven, and fair. Many WaMu branches also sell action "teller" dolls complete with mobile phones and banking uniforms. Resembling the corporate version of Action Man and Barbie, these dolls attempt to create a fan club among customers to say that WaMu's sales associates are not your average employees. If customers bring their children in with them, they can go to a location in the bank, called WaMu Kids, where they can amuse themselves with Nintendo games.

There are no teller windows or velvet ropes to keep customers in line. Instead there are teller towers, pedestals where sales associates stand in front of screens handling transactions. They handle no money. Customers who want cash are given a slip, which they take over to the cash-dispensing machine. This is central to the bank goal: having sales associates cross-sell products. Because sales associates are not tethered to a cash drawer, they can talk with customers and personally escort them to another area of the bank for service if needed.

WaMu has also established its own hotline that is open 24 hours a day, seven days a week. The goal is to address 90 percent of the customers' issues on the first call. It has extended its banking hours until 7 P.M. in some branches to service customers who cannot get to the bank during traditional banking hours. WaMu lets the local branch manager decide the product and staffing mix that meets its market. For example, in a transient market like Florida, the emphasis is on checking accounts, whereas in Seattle, a more stable market, the emphasis is on mortgage lending.

WaMu's communication strategy seems to have paid off. The bank's free checking has attracted more than 3.5 million new households since 1996. Four years after opening an account with a balance of $1,411, the average customer has relationships that are worth more than $23,360 in deposits, consumer loans, and mortgages.[1]

Killinger knows that even the best companies have trouble sustaining themselves because, once successful, they become sloppy and a little complacent. To make sure that this doesn't happen at WaMu, he constantly communicates with customers and employees. At times, he answers the customer's hotline and can be seen greeting customers as they walk into one of WaMu's banks to keep in touch. He constantly asks his staff: "What do you think real bankers would do?" When they answer, he asks them to think out of the box and say what they think Southwest Airlines President and Chief Operating Officer Colleen Barrett would do. He also knows that the "buck stops" with him. For example, when property taxes were paid late on 55,000 loans because of a banking error, he quickly instructed managers to reimburse customers without question. He then fired the vendor that sold WaMu its computer equipment and installed new equipment.

THE COMMUNICATION PROCESS

1. Explain the main elements of the communication process.

Whether the organization is a bank, school district, transportation system, or manufacturing plant, effective communication is essential. Communication is to an organization what the bloodstream is to a person. Just as a person can develop hardening of the arteries, which impairs physical efficiency, an organization can develop blockages of communication channels, which impair its effectiveness. Just as heart bypass surgery may be necessary to save a person's life, an organization may have to revamp its communications system to survive. And, just as heart patients can do more harm than good if they overreact to their health problems by exercising too strenuously, an organization may go overboard trying to repair a history of poor communication with employees.

Without *effective* communication, managers can accomplish little, which is why we included communication as one of the six key managerial competencies. Communication can be formal or informal, verbal or nonverbal, and may take many forms, including face-to-face interactions, phone calls, faxes, e-mail, notes posted on bulletin boards, letters, memos, reports, videos, and oral presentations. In this chapter, we examine how organizational communication takes place, identify key hurdles to communication, explore ways of improving communication in organizations, and highlight two ethical issues.

Communication *is the transfer and exchange of information and understanding from one person to another through meaningful symbols.*[2] It is a process of sending, receiving, and sharing ideas, attitudes, values, opinions, and facts. Communication requires both a sender, who begins the process, and a receiver, who completes the communication link. When the receiver provides feedback that the message was received as intended, the communication cycle is complete.

In organizations, managers use the communication process to carry out their four functions (planning, organizing, leading, and controlling). Because they must have access to relevant information in order to make sound decisions, effective managers build networks of contacts that facilitate information gathering, interpretation, and dissemination. These contacts help managers become the nerve centers of their organizations. Much like radar screens, managers scan the environment for changes that could affect the organization and share this information with others. Once made, decisions are quickly disseminated to those who will help carry them out.

In contrast, ineffective managers often leave employees in the dark about what is happening. Poor communication seems to be a particular problem during downsizing, when managers' and employees' stress levels soar. Poor communication allows rumors to replace facts, fosters animosities between departments and teams, and impedes successful organizational change. Under such circumstances, poor communication seems to be the single most important reason for poor strategy implementation.

Most managers spend a large part of their working day communicating with superiors, peers, customers, and others; writing and answering e-mails, letters, and reports; and talking with others on the phone. In doing so, they are engaged in the communication process, which involves six basic elements: sender (encoder), receiver (decoder), message, channels, feedback, and perception.

Figure 16.1 shows how these elements interact during the communication process.[3] Managers and employees who are concerned with improving their communication competency need to be aware of these elements and how they contribute to successful communication. We discuss the roles of the sender and the receiver first because they are the actors in the process.

> **The Competent Manager**
>
> *". . . the difficult and never-ending responsibility of a CEO is to communicate to every employee in every way possible just what it is that the company is in business to accomplish and what its core values are."*
>
> Russ Lewis
> President and CEO
> New York Times Company

Sender (Encoder)

The **sender** *is the source of information and the initiator of the communication process.* The sender tries to choose the type of message and the channel that will be most effective. The sender then encodes the message.

Encoding is the *process of translating thoughts or feelings into a medium—written, visual, or spoken—that conveys the meaning intended.* Imagine that you are planning to apply for a summer job. You will get the best response by first learning about the

Figure 16.1   The Communication Process

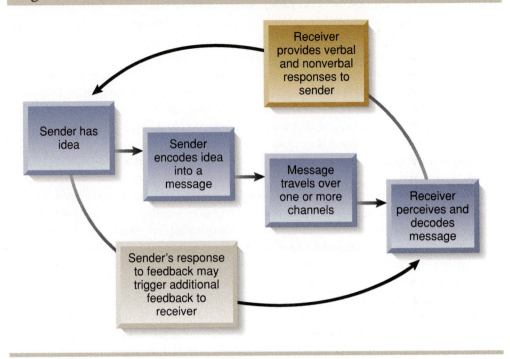

channels of communication used by the organization. Many employers now prefer to accept applications via the Internet, so you should begin by visiting the organization's Web site. From there, you often can determine which job openings exist and the procedures that the company uses to process applications for employment. If the organization accepts electronic applications, you're likely to get a faster response to your inquiry by using this method.[4] If the organization has no Web site, you can begin the process by calling to find out whether an opening exists, then writing a letter, and then phoning again to confirm that your letter has been received.

Regardless of whether you apply electronically or use a traditional letter, your application should convey certain ideas and impressions. For example, you should explain why you're interested in that particular company. You also need to provide background information about your qualifications for the job and explain how you think the job will further your career. When you transfer these ideas into speech or to an electronic memo or to paper, you are encoding your message. To increase encoding accuracy, apply the five principles of communication to the form of communication you're using:

1. *Relevancy.* Make the message meaningful and significant, carefully selecting the words, symbols, or gestures to be used.
2. *Simplicity.* Put the message in the simplest possible terms, reducing the number of words, symbols, or gestures used to communicate your intended thoughts and feelings.
3. *Organization.* Arrange the message as a series of points to facilitate understanding. Complete each point in a message before proceeding to the next.
4. *Repetition.* Restate key points of the message at least twice. Repetition is particularly important in spoken communication because words may not be clearly heard or fully understood the first time.
5. *Focus.* Focus on the essential aspects, or key points, of the message. Make the message clear and avoid unnecessary detail. In spoken communication, emphasize significant points by changing your tone of voice, pausing, gesturing, or using appro-

priate facial expressions. In written communication, underline or italicize key sentences, phrases, or words.

Receiver (Decoder)

The **receiver** *is the person who receives and decodes (or interprets) the sender's message.* **Decoding** *is translating messages into a form that has meaning to the receiver.* The person who receives your electronic application or letter about a summer job reacts to it first on the basis of whether the organization has any openings. If it doesn't, the receiver probably won't pay much attention to your inquiry. If there are openings, the receiver probably will compare what you wrote about yourself to the type of person that the organization wants to hire. Julia Sudduth, assistant vice president of Southwest Bank of Texas, is one of the bank's recruiters. Responsible for recruiting at more than 15 colleges and universities in the Southwest, she's learned to decode messages efficiently. She takes no more than a half a minute to judge a résumé. She prefers a standard résumé—if she receives one printed on pink paper with a color photo she'll "try to look beyond it." She searches for key information, including job experience, campus leadership, grades, and hometown. Why hometown? She says that it helps her judge the likelihood of a student's accepting a job in one of the cities where the bank has facilities.[5]

Both encoding and decoding are influenced by personal factors, such as education, personality, socioeconomic status, family, work history, culture, and gender.[6] Some research suggests that women are more concerned with the feelings and reactions of the person with whom they're speaking than men are. They focus on seeking and giving more support and try to gain consensus. When men use qualifiers such as *perhaps, maybe, sort of,* or *I guess,* they are often perceived as warm and polite; when women use such qualifiers, they are often perceived as weak and unassertive. Men are more concerned with status and trying to maintain the upper hand in a conversation. Men are more likely to interrupt others who are talking, and women are interrupted more often than men. Whereas women try to create intimacy in conversations, men focus on establishing their independence. For example, women are more likely to frame orders as questions ("Can you meet me at my office?" rather than "Come to my office."). Some of the important communication differences between men and women are shown in Table 16.1.

Table 16.1   Communication Differences between Men and Women

1. Men are less likely to ask for information or directions in a public situation that would reveal their lack of knowledge.
2. In decision making, women are more likely to downplay their certainty; men are more likely to downplay their doubts.
3. Women tend to apologize even when they have done nothing wrong. Men tend to avoid apologies as signs of weakness or concession.
4. Women tend to accept blame as a way of smoothing awkward situations. Men tend to ignore blame and place it elsewhere.
5. Women tend to temper criticism with positive buffers. Men tend to give criticism directly.
6. Women tend to insert unnecessary and unwarranted thank-yous in conversations. Men may avoid thanks altogether as a sign of weakness.
7. Men tend to usurp (take) ideas stated by women and claim them as their own. Women tend to allow this process to take place without protest.
8. Women use softer voice volume to encourage persuasion and approval. Men use louder voice volume to attract attention and maintain control.

One of the main requirements of the receiver is the ability to listen. **Listening** *involves paying attention to the message, not merely hearing it.* Of the 75 percent or more of their time that managers spend in communicating, about half is spent listening to others. Becoming a better listener is an important way for people to improve their communication skills. Studies have shown that most people can recall immediately only about 50 percent of what someone tells them. Two months later, they can recall only about 25 percent. That's why effective communication often involves the use of several media, such as written reports, memos, newsletters, and e-mail, in addition to the telephone, face-to-face conversations, and speeches.

Ten guidelines for effective listening are presented in Table 16.2. Try using them the next time you're having a conversation with someone. You'll be surprised at how much effective listening improves the communication process.

Table 16.2 Guidelines for Effective Listening
1. Remember that listening is not just about receiving information—how you listen also sends a message back to the message sender.
2. Stop talking! You can't listen if you're talking.
3. Show a talker that you want to listen. Paraphrase what's been said to show that you understand.
4. Remove distractions.
5. Avoid prejudging what the person thinks or feels. Listen first, then make judgments later.
6. Try to see the other person's point of view.
7. Listen for total meaning. This includes both the content of the words and the feeling or attitude underlying the words.
8. Attend to both verbal and nonverbal cues.
9. Go easy on argument and criticism, which put people on the defensive and may make them "clam up" or become angry.
10. Before each person leaves, confirm what has been said.

Message

The **message** refers to *the verbal (spoken and written) symbols and nonverbal cues representing the information that the sender wants to convey to the receiver.* Like a coin, a message has two sides, and the message sent and the message received aren't necessarily the same. Why? First, encoding and decoding of the message may vary because of differences in the sender's and the receiver's backgrounds and viewpoints. Second, the sender may be sending more than one message.

Recruiters such as Julia Sudduth, as well as managers and employees generally, use three types of messages: nonverbal, verbal, and written. The use of nonverbal messages is extremely important, although many individuals don't recognize this fact. Accordingly, we discuss nonverbal messages at greater length than the other two types.

Nonverbal Messages. All messages not spoken or written constitute nonverbal messages. **Nonverbal messages** *are facial expressions, eye contact, body movement, gestures, and physical contact (collectively often called* body language) *that convey meaning.* When people communicate in person, as much as 60 percent of the content of the message is transmitted through facial expressions and other methods of nonverbal communication.[7]

Recruiter Julia Sudduth sees each student for only 30 minutes, so every bit of information she can get is important. A smile and a strong handshake create an excellent first impression. Sudduth admits that first impressions based on nonverbal cues can be misleading but that they are hard to ignore. She uses her understanding of nonverbal communication to gather information about the candidate during the interview.[8] The ability to interpret facial expressions is an important part of communication. Eye contact is a direct and powerful way of communicating nonverbally. In the United States, social rules suggest that in many social situations brief eye contact is appropriate. However, if eye contact is too brief, people may interpret it as a sign of aloofness or untrustworthiness. Conversely, people often interpret prolonged eye contact as either a threat or a sign of romantic interest, depending on the context. A good poker player watches the eyes of the other players as new cards are dealt. Pupil dilation often betrays whether the card(s) just dealt improved the player's hand.

With regard to *body language*, the body and its movement—particularly movements of the face and eyes, which are very expressive—tell a lot about a person. As much as 50 percent of the content of a message may be communicated by facial expression and body posture and another 30 percent by inflection and the tone of speech. The words themselves may account for only 20 percent of the content of a message.[9]

The meaning of nonverbal communication varies by cultures. For example, the smile that Sudduth saw on the face of a candidate may indicate happiness or pleasure in the United States, but for Asians, it can also be a sign of embarrassment or discomfort. In the United States, maintaining eye contact is the sign of a good communicator; in the Middle East, it is an integral part of successful communication; but for the Chinese and Japanese, it can indicate distrust. Many Americans shake hands to greet people, whereas Middle Easterners of the same sex kiss on the cheek.

With regard to *space*, how close you are to another person, where you sit or stand, and how you arrange your office can have a significant impact on communication. **Proxemics** *is the study of ways in which people use physical space to convey messages.* Think about how you would feel if you walked into class midway through the term and someone was sitting in "your" seat. You'd probably feel angry because your space, or territory, had been invaded. To test how important your territory is to you, complete the questionnaire shown in Figure 16.2.[10]

The distances at which people feel comfortable when communicating vary greatly by culture. South Americans and Southern and Eastern Europeans prefer closeness. Asians, Northern Europeans, and North Americans prefer not to be as close. These behaviors reflect a culture's overall tendency to be *high contact* or *low contact*. People in high-contact cultures like to stand close and touch each other. High-contact cultures usually are located in warmer climates; there people tend to have greater interpersonal orientation and are perceived as interpersonally "friendly." Those from low-contact cultures prefer to stand farther apart and touch infrequently. These cultures are often found in cooler climates, in which people tend to be task oriented and interpersonally "cool." Figure 16.3 shows the approximate placement of various countries along the high- to low-contact culture continuum. For example, in Japan, strict rules of etiquette guide seating behavior. If businesspeople are traveling together on a train, the most senior executive sits next to the window, facing the direction in which the train is moving. In a taxi, the "top" seat is behind the driver and the most junior seat is next to the driver. In elevators, the senior person stands in the rear in the center facing the door and the most junior person stands near the buttons.[11]

Spatial arrangements in corporate offices in North America send many signals to members of an organization.[12] In some organizations, such as Ford Motor Company, Federated Department Stores, and Texas Instruments (TI), top managers have larger offices, windows with better views, plusher carpets, and higher quality furnishings than

Figure 16.2 How Territorial Are You?

Instructions: Circle one number to answer each question as follows:

1. Strongly agree
2. Agree
3. Not sure
4. Disagree
5. Strongly disagree

	1	2	3	4	5
1. If I arrive at my apartment (room) and find my roommate sitting in my chair, I am annoyed if he/she doesn't at least offer to get up immediately.	1	2	3	4	5
2. I do not like anyone to remove anything from my desk without first asking me.	1	2	3	4	5
3. If a stranger puts a hand on my shoulder when talking to me I feel uncomfortable.	1	2	3	4	5
4. If my suit jacket is lying on the back of a chair and another student comes in and chooses to sit in the chair, I feel that he or she should ask me to move my jacket or choose another seat.	1	2	3	4	5
5. If I enter a classroom and "reserve" a chair with a notebook, I am annoyed and offended upon my return to find my book moved and someone sitting in "my" seat.	1	2	3	4	5
6. If a person who is not a close friend of mine gets within a foot from my face to talk to me, I will either back off or uncomfortably hold my ground.	1	2	3	4	5
7. I do not like strangers walking into my room (apartment).	1	2	3	4	5
8. If I lived in an apartment, I would not want the landlord to enter for any reason without my permission.	1	2	3	4	5
9. I do not like my friends or family borrowing my clothes without asking me first.	1	2	3	4	5
10. If I notice someone staring at me in a restaurant, I become annoyed and uncomfortable.	1	2	3	4	5

To score and interpret your responses, add the numbers you circled for all 10 statements. Then compare your total with the following definitions:

10–25 points: *Highly territorial.* Your instincts for staking out and protecting what you consider yours are high. You strongly believe in your territorial rights.

26–39 points: *Ambiguous but territorial.* You may act territorial in some circumstances but not in others. You feel differently about different types of space.

40–50 points: *Not territorial.* You disagree with the entire concept of territoriality. You dislike possessiveness, protectiveness, and jealousy. The concept of private ownership is not central to your philosophy of life.

middle managers have. Meriting a personal assistant, a seat at the head of the table at meetings, a chauffeured limousine, use of a private dining room, and the ability to summon employees for discussion—all send messages via the use of space. Organizations that seek to have a more egalitarian culture, such as Whole Foods, The Container Store, and Wal-Mart, intentionally avoid these status symbols. Most managers don't have the op-

Figure 16.3   Examples of Cultures on the Cultural Contact Continuum

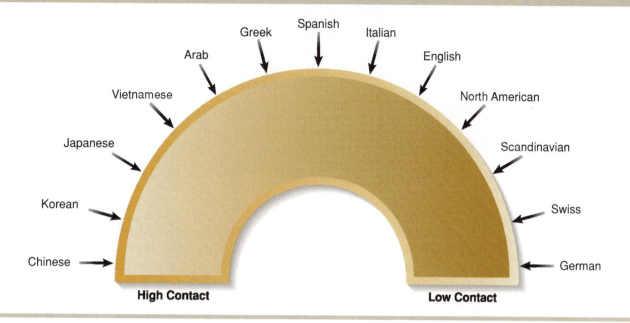

portunity to plan and design the buildings in which employees work. However, many do have the opportunity to plan floor layouts and the style and arrangement of office furniture, the tables and chairs used to furnish meeting rooms, and similar elements of work space.

Recently, some organizations, such as Citibank in Sydney, Australia and Concord Hospital in Concord, New Hampshire, have turned to feng shui to foster better communications. **Feng shui** *is a system for arranging everything around you in such a way that your environment works for you and with you.* Nearly 4,000 years ago, farmers in southern China recognized that how they arranged their fields, their crops, and their homes had significant effects on their lives. For example, they noticed that families whose huts faced north were hit by dust storms, whereas those with huts facing south were protected from wind and dust and enjoyed the warmth and light of the sun. The same principles have been adapted by managers to increase the flow of communications. Feng shui (pronounced "fung schway") is all about increasing chi ("chee") or energy and making sure it flows in the right direction. The implications for office design are highlighted in the following Planning & Administration Competency feature, which illustrates how the office of Northern Ontario Business in Sudbury, Ontario, used feng shui to ease communications.[13]

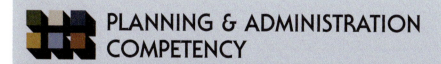

PLANNING & ADMINISTRATION COMPETENCY

Northern Ontario Business

To improve communications, Northern Ontario first arranged its office furniture to encourage people to informally communicate with each other. Sitting rooms were arranged so people could more easily communicate with each other. The less obstructed a person's view, the more likely communication is to take place. Second, because the office is right across the Canadian Pacific

©Index Stock Imagery

railway tracks, a concrete planter with evergreens was built. This buffered the noise from the passing trains and added some color to the walls. Third, offices were arranged so that people do not sit with their backs to the door, so they can see if someone is approaching. If a person cannot see who is approaching, he or she might become anxious and fearful. Employees' computer monitors were positioned to avoid glare, which strains the eye. Employees were asked to remove clutter from their desks because clutter means that they are surrounded by a bunch of decisions that have been postponed. Fourth, when a manager has been in an office for a long period of time and has to move to another office, the office is changed to adjust to this person's needs.

In terms of *personal appearance*, you've undoubtedly heard the expression "Clothes make the person." Style consultants for major corporations believe that the way a person dresses definitely communicates something to others. You should ask yourself: Is the way I'm dressed going to hurt or help my business relationships? Like it or not, people judge you partly on the basis of how you look. If you're dressed appropriately, customers and others may see you as a more competent person than someone who dresses inappropriately. This is especially true for people who are meeting for the first time. Of course, what is *appropriate* depends on the organization. A conservative suit fits in well on Wall Street, but looks out of place in a WaMu bank. In the arts and entertainment industry, fashionable clothes are more appropriate.

Posture also communicates meaning by signaling a person's degree of self-confidence or interest in what is being discussed. The more interested you are, the more likely you are to lean toward the person who is talking. Conversely, leaning away may communicate a lack of interest. Similarly, tension and anxiety typically show in a person's legs and feet. People often are able to hide tension from the waist up but may give themselves away by crossing their legs tightly and tapping their feet.[14]

Verbal Messages. Employees communicate verbally more often than in any other way. Spoken communication takes place face to face, over the telephone, and via other electronic media. Most people prefer face-to-face communication because nonverbal messages are an important part of it. But some people prefer written communications because it allows them to choose and weigh their words more carefully before sending the message. When emotions run high, or someone is writing in a second language, weighing words carefully can be advantageous.

Effective verbal communication requires the sender to (1) encode the message in words (and nonverbal cues) that will convey it accurately to the receiver, (2) convey the message in a well-organized manner, and (3) try to eliminate distractions. At WaMu, sales associates must be especially good at sending verbal messages. Many customer transactions involve the use of long written documents, filled with legal and financial jargon. Loan officers assume that most customers won't read these documents, even though they are required to sign them. Therefore sales associates take responsibility for conveying verbally the messages contained in the written documents. They translate the jargon into everyday language and then summarize what the documents say for the customer, checking to be sure that the customer understands the key points.

Written Messages. Although spoken communication is quicker than written communication and allows the sender and receiver to interact, organizations use many forms of written messages (e.g., reports, memoranda, letters, e-mail, and newsletters). Such messages are most appropriate when information has to be collected from or distributed to many people at scattered locations and when keeping a record of what was sent is necessary. The following are some guidelines for preparing effective written messages:

1. The message should be drafted with the receiver clearly in mind.
2. The contents of the message should be well thought out ahead of time.
3. The message should be as brief as possible, without extraneous words and ideas.
4. Important messages should be prepared in draft form first and then polished. If the message has to be long, a brief summary should be presented on the first page. This summary should clarify the main points and contain page references to details on each item.
5. The message should be carefully organized. The most important point should be stated first, then the next most important point, and so on. Thus, even if the receiver reads only the first few points, the essentials of the message will get across. Giving the message a title makes the subject clear. Using simple words and short, clear sentences make the message more readable and easily understood.

Channels

The **channel** *is the path a message follows from the sender to the receiver.* **Information richness** *is the information-carrying capacity of the channel.* Not all channels can carry the same richness of information.[15] Written communications are low in richness. Customer and employee surveys are a form of written communication that many organizations rely on heavily despite their lack of information richness. Surveys usually ask people to express their opinions about various topics by choosing from multiple-choice options. Customers might be asked to indicate whether they were delighted, just satisfied, or disappointed with the customer service they received. Employees might be asked to indicate whether they strongly agree, agree, disagree, or strongly disagree with a statement such as "My manager treats me with respect." This form of communication facilitates quantitative analyses, but it limits the type and amount of information received from customers and employees. Only the information written down is received. A channel low in richness is considered to be lean because it is effective mainly for sending specific data and facts.

As Figure 16.4 indicates, face-to-face communication is the richest communication channel. It conveys several clues simultaneously, including spoken and nonverbal information. Face-to-face communication also provides immediate feedback so that understanding can be checked and misinterpretations corrected. Managers can gather additional information about how customers and employees feel about the organization and its products by speaking with them personally. Focus groups are a structured form of

---

Figure 16.4   Information Richness of Channels

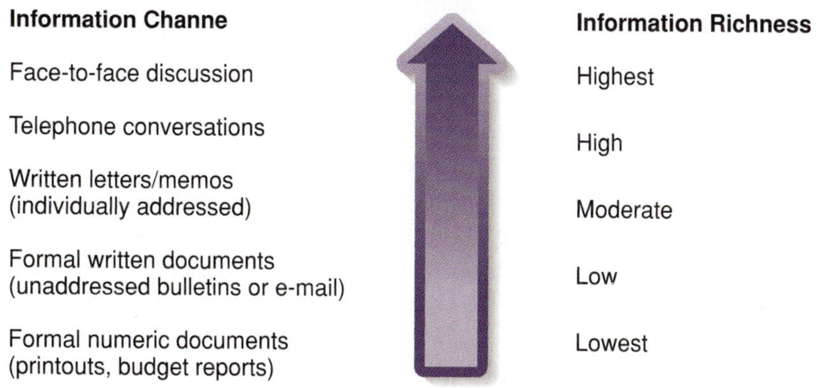

Information Channe		Information Richness
Face-to-face discussion		Highest
Telephone conversations		High
Written letters/memos (individually addressed)		Moderate
Formal written documents (unaddressed bulletins or e-mail)		Low
Formal numeric documents (printouts, budget reports)		Lowest

face-to-face communication that often are used to gauge customers' reactions to products. The telephone is somewhat less rich than face-to-face communication, but not as lean as written surveys. WaMu changed its approach to customer satisfaction surveys in order to obtain richer information. The bank discontinued its mail survey and began to conduct telephone surveys. Managers were trained to interview customers and were responsible for acting on their responses. Directly hearing the voices of customers added richness and perspective to the information provided.

In addition to selecting a channel that fits the level of information richness they need, individuals must choose among several *types* of channels for communicating with others. They include downward, upward, and horizontal formal channels as well as informal channels, such as the grapevine and networking or caucus groups.

Downward Channels. **Downward channels** *involve all the means of sending messages from management to employees.* For instance, the Freeport, Maine, mail-order headquarters of L.L.Bean, the $1.4 billion apparel and sporting goods cataloger, receives more than 350,000 communications (e.g., phone calls, faxes, and e-mail messages) a day during the holiday season for 20,000 outdoor items ranging from socks to flannel shirts to hunting bows to tents.[16] L.L.Bean recently opened a Japanese version of its e-commerce site (http://www.llbean.co.jp) that includes a Japanese pronunciation database for customer service representatives in Freeport and has an online payment system for the yen. To communicate effectively with L.L.Bean's 3,500 employees, managers use downward channels to convey

- how to handle special promotional items;
- job descriptions, detailing duties and responsibilities;
- policies and procedures, explaining what is expected of employees and the organization's rules and employee benefits;
- feedback about an individual's job performance; and
- news of activities and events that management believes employees should participate in (charitable organizations, blood drives, and the like).

Managers frequently use downward communication effectively as a channel, but it may be the most misused channel because it provides little opportunity for employees to respond. In fact, the fundamental problem with downward communication is that it is too often one way. It's a lean channel that doesn't encourage feedback from those on the receiving end. To correct this problem, managers should urge employees to use upward channels.

The Competent Manager	*"Sell good merchandise at a reasonable profit, treat your customers like human beings, and they will always come back for more."* Leon Leonwood Bean Founder L.L.Bean

Upward Channels. Some managers don't see the value of encouraging employees to participate in setting goals, planning, and formulating policies. The result is a failure to use upward channels of communication. **Upward channels** *are all the means used by employees to send messages to management.* Such channels may be the only formal means that employees have for communicating with higher level managers in the organization. Upward communication includes providing feedback on how well employees understand the messages they have received via downward channels. Moreover, it enables employees to voice their opinions and ideas. If effective, upward communication can provide an emotional release. At the same time, it gives employees a chance to participate, the feeling that they are being listened to, and a sense of personal worth. Most important, employees and customers often have excellent suggestions for improving efficiency and effectiveness. That is why WaMu's CEO Kerry Killinger frequently receives hotline calls, talks with customers, and chats with sales associates.

At Cirque du Soleil, upward channels are as strong as downward channels.[17] Specific methods for communicating upward include direct personal contacts and three publications circulated regularly within the company. One publication is *The Ball*, which features a column called BYOB—Be Your Own Bitch. Employees use it to complain, gripe, and rib without censorship. "This is part of the way we do things," explained Marc Gagnon, vice president of human resources. One message indicated that the writer felt that the Dutch employees were being treated better than the Canadians. This information was quite useful because it allowed the company to head off certain issues before they could become crises. *The Ball* also informs employees of events and activities taking place at company locations around the world.

Besides its publications, Cirque du Soleil uses employee focus groups to help design new initiatives and develop new policies. "We look for three things," explained Gagnon. "Make sure the proposed policy is clear and they understand it; see if they agree with it, or if they disagree with it and why; and see if we have any chance to get people to use it. People are allowed to say 'no' to a policy."

Upward channels provide many benefits, but managers need to be aware of the problems that can plague upward communication. First, most employees don't want their superiors to learn anything negative about them, so they may screen out bad news. Most employees try to impress their superiors by emphasizing their contributions to the organization. Some may even try to make themselves look better by putting others down. Second, an employee's personal anxieties, aspirations, and attitudes almost always color what is communicated. Would you tell a potential employer of the bad things you've heard about the organization? If you really wanted the job, you probably wouldn't be so bold. Finally, the employee may be competing for the manager's job and thus remains silent in the hope of being recommended for it when the manager is promoted and moves to another position.

Realizing that employees aren't always comfortable giving direct upward feedback has led many companies to provide another alternative—anonymously contacting a third party. At Pillsbury, employees can call a recording machine and sound off. Verbatim transcripts are prepared of each call and forwarded to the CEO and other top-level managers, with no identification about the gender or any other detectable caller characteristics. The objective was to let the company's senior managers hear the views of employees, without causing employees to be fearful of what might happen to them for voicing their concerns and criticisms. Employees began using the service to share all sorts of information. They noted that a clock in one bakery always ran 5 minutes fast, identified locations that didn't carry particular products on the shelves, suggested new pizza toppings, and complained so much about slow expense reimbursements that the company overhauled some of its accounting procedures. By calling to express their appreciation, employees also made a hero of a manager who closed down operations during a snowstorm.[18] Other companies that actively encourage upward communication include TDIndustries, Blue Nile, and The Container Store. In each case, the CEO encourages open griping and pays particular attention when the same comment is made repeatedly.

Horizontal Channels. **Horizontal channels** *are all the means used to send and receive messages across departmental lines, with suppliers, or with customers.* This type of channel is especially important in network organizations (see Chapter 11). Essential to the success of a network organization is maintaining effective communication among customers, suppliers, and employees in various divisions or functional areas. Nike outsources the manufacturing of its athletic shoes and apparel to manufacturers throughout the world. It needs effective horizontal communication channels to link suppliers with information about market demand in order to schedule production and shipping efficiently.

Horizontal channels are formal if they follow prescribed organizational paths. Messages communicated horizontally usually are related to coordinating activities, sharing information, and solving problems. Horizontal channels are extremely important in today's team-based organizations, where employees must often communicate among themselves to solve their clients' production or process problems.

Informal Channels. So far we have concentrated on formal channels of communication. Equally important, however, are informal channels of communication. **Informal channels** *are all the nonformal means for sender and receiver to communicate downward, upward, and horizontally.* The **grapevine** *is an organization's informal communication system, along which information can travel in any direction.* The term comes from a Civil War practice of hanging telegraph lines loosely from tree to tree, like a grapevine. In organizations, the path that messages follow along the grapevine is based on social interaction, not organization charts.

At Xerox's Palo Alto Research Center, informal channels are essential to its success. The company learned just how important informal channels were when it began looking for ways to boost productivity. Management hired a social anthropologist to observe closely the behavior of technicians who repaired copiers (tech reps) in an effort to improve efficiency. The consultant saw that tech reps often made a point of spending time with each other but not with customers. They would hang around the parts warehouse or the coffee pot and swap stories from the field. The consultant recognized the importance of these informal conversations to tech rep performance. Through their stories, the reps shared knowledge and generated new insights about how to repair machines better. Xerox concluded that tech rep performance could be improved by increasing this type of communication, so the company issued two-way radio headsets to the reps.[19]

Informal channels of communication have been recognized by many organizations as so important that they encourage and provide support for employees' efforts to strengthen them. **Employee network groups** *are informal groups that organize regularly scheduled social activities to promote informal communication among employees who share a common interest or concern.* In many organizations, network groups form to bring together employees who share common interests and concerns. For example, at Sara Lee, Motorola, IBM, and many other large organizations, numerous network groups (also called caucus groups) exist for members of particular ethnic groups. Caucus groups for women also are quite common. According to a survey of Fortune 500 companies, such groups have grown rapidly during the past decade. Participants benefit from the business information shared during meetings, as well as from the friendships they form and the contacts they make. At Sara Lee, women's leadership councils operate within specific divisions of the company to support career development and offer networking opportunities for women. To ensure their effectiveness, Steven McMillan, CEO, regularly reviews developmental activities of female and minority employees.[20]

External Networking. Managers and employees also spend considerable time meeting with peers and others outside the organization. They attend meetings of professional associations, trade shows, and other gatherings. As a result, they may develop various close, informal relationships with talented and interesting people outside the organization. People use these networks to help each other, trading favors and calling on each other's resources for career advancement or other types of information and support.

Consuella Guillory-Adams, contract supply manager at Lyondell Chemical, recognized how important networking is to a growing business. She organized a group that meets once a quarter in Houston to network and discusses business issues. The club's activities are supported by local professional groups. The goal is to provide quality control managers in the chemical industry with insights into new technological development. The group also has invited guests to speak at their meetings who provide them with some insights into problems and issues surrounding mergers and acquisitions in the industry.

Feedback

Feedback *is the receiver's response to the sender's message.* The communication cycle isn't complete until the sender receives feedback from the receiver. It's the best way to show that a message has been received and to indicate whether it has been understood. As Kerry Killinger and his top managers found out at WaMu, lots of information gets filtered and lost between top management and those who work daily with WaMu's customers. You shouldn't assume that everything you say or write will be understood exactly as you intend it to be. If you don't encourage feedback, you're likely to misjudge how much others understand you. Thus you'll be less effective than those who encourage feedback.

When managers are asked to rank the communication skills they find crucial to their success on the job, they consistently place feedback at the top of the list. Managers spend more than half their time listening to others. Because most people speak at a rate of 100 to 150 words per minute and the brain is capable of thinking at a rate of 400 to 500 words per minute, people often daydream. Therefore feedback is needed to ensure that messages sent are accurately received. The following Communication Competency feature allows you to assess your openness to receiving feedback.[21]

COMMUNICATION COMPETENCY

Are You Open to Feedback?

When answering these 11 questions, use the following rating scale:

1. Strongly disagree
2. Disagree
3. Slightly disagree
4. Slightly agree
5. Agree
6. Strongly agree

_____ 1. I seek information about my strengths and weaknesses from others as a basis for self-improvement.

_____ 2. When I receive negative feedback about myself from others, I do not get angry or defensive.

_____ 3. In order to improve, I am willing to be self-disclosing to others (i.e., share my feelings and beliefs).

_____ 4. I am very much aware of my personal style of gathering information and making decisions.

_____ 5. I am very much aware of my own interpersonal needs when it comes to forming relationships with other people.

_____ 6. I have a good sense of how I cope with situations that are ambiguous and uncertain.

_____ 7. I have a well-developed set of personal standards and principles that guide my behavior.

_____ 8. I feel very much in charge of what happens to me, good and bad.

_____ 9. I seldom, if ever, feel angry, depressed, or anxious without knowing why.

_____ 10. I am conscious of the areas in which conflict and friction most frequently arise in my interactions with others.

_____ 11. I have a close personal relationship with at least one other person with whom I can share personal information and personal feelings.

SCORING KEY

Skill Area	Total
Self-disclosure and openness to feedback from others (items 1, 2, 3, 9, 11)	_____
Awareness of own values, cognitive style, change orientation, and interpersonal orientation (items 4, 5, 6, 7, 8, 10)	_____
Grand Total	_____

COMPARISON DATA

Compare your scores to three standards: (1) the maximum possible (66); (2) the scores of other students in your class; and (3) the scores of a norm group consisting of more than 500 business students. In comparison to the norm group, if you scored

55 or above,	you are in the top quartile.
52–54,	you are in the second quartile.
48–51	you are in the third quartile.
47 or below,	you are in the bottom quartile.

Whenever a message is sent, the actions of the sender affect the reactions of the receiver. The reactions of the receiver, in turn, affect later actions of the sender. If the sender receives no response, the message was never received or the receiver chose not to respond. In either case, the sender is alerted to the need to find out why the receiver didn't respond. Upon receiving rewarding feedback, the sender continues to produce the same kind of message. When feedback is not rewarding, the sender eventually changes the type of message.

Receiver reactions also tell the sender how well goals are being achieved or tasks are being accomplished. However, in this case the receiver exerts control over the sender by the type of feedback provided. The sender must rely on the receiver for an indication of whether the message was received and understood. Such feedback assures the sender that things are going as planned or brings to light problems that have to be solved. Ricoh, Embassy Suites, Wachovia, and other companies have guidelines for providing effective feedback. According to these guidelines, feedback should have the following characteristics[22]:

1. *It should be helpful.* If the receiver of the message provides feedback that adds to the sender's information, the feedback is likely to be seen as constructive.
2. *It should be descriptive rather than evaluative.* If the receiver responds to the message in a descriptive manner, the feedback is likely to be effective. If the receiver is highly critical (or judgmental), the feedback is likely to be ineffective or even cause a breakdown in communication.
3. *It should be specific rather than general.* The receiver should respond specifically to points raised and questions asked in the message. If the receiver responds in generalities, the feedback may indicate evasion or lack of understanding.
4. *It should be well timed.* The reception—and thus the effectiveness—of feedback is affected by the context in which it occurs. Giving performance feedback to a person during a round of golf or at a luncheon is different from giving the same person this feedback in the office. Informal settings usually are reserved for social as opposed to performance-based feedback.
5. *It should not overwhelm.* Spoken communication depends heavily on memory. Accordingly, when large amounts of information are involved, spoken feedback is less effective than written feedback. People tend to "tune in and out" of conversations. They may fail to grasp what the speaker is saying if the message is too long and complex.

Perception

Perception *is the meaning given to a message by either sender or receiver.* Perceptions are influenced by what people see, by the ways they organize these elements in memory, and by the meanings they attach to them. The ability to perceive varies from person to person. Some people, having entered a room only once, can later describe it in detail, whereas others can barely remember anything about it. Thus the mental ability to notice and remember is important. How people interpret what they perceive is affected by their pasts. A clenched fist raised in the air by an employee on strike and walking the picket line could be interpreted as either an angry threat to the organization or as an expression of union solidarity and accomplishment. The attitudes that people bring to a situation color their perceptions of it.

Some problems in communication can be traced to two problems of perception: selective perception and stereotyping. **Selective perception** *is the process of screening out information that a person wants or needs to avoid.* Many people "tune out" TV commercials. Most everyone has been accused at one time or another of listening only to what they want to hear. Both are examples of selective perception. In organizations, employees sometimes do the same thing. Manufacturing employees pay close attention to manufacturing problems, and accounting employees pay close attention to debits and credits. Such employees tend to filter out information about other areas of the organization and focus on information that is directly related to their own jobs.

Stereotyping *is the process of making assumptions about individuals on the basis of their belonging to a certain gender, race, age, or other category.* Stereotyping distorts reality by suggesting that all people in a category have similar characteristics, which simply isn't true.

During the 1990s, organizations became increasingly sensitive to the potential negative consequences of stereotyping based on a person's gender, race, ethnicity, age, or sexual orientation. As they have sought to manage workforce diversity more effectively, many organizations—including State Farm Insurance and Citigroup—have developed training programs and other initiatives to reduce the negative personal and organizational consequences of stereotyping. We discuss workforce diversity further in Chapter 18.

In summary, then, the message sent, the channel of communication used, and the ability to respond all depend on a person's perceptions. Encoding and decoding skills are based on a person's ability to perceive a message and situation accurately. Developing the ability to send and receive messages accurately is central to developing your communication competency.

HURDLES TO EFFECTIVE COMMUNICATION

One of the first steps in communicating more effectively is to identify hurdles to the process. These hurdles hinder the sending and receiving of messages by distorting, or sometimes even completely blocking, intended meanings. We divided these impediments into organizational and individual hurdles—although there is obviously some overlap—and listed them in Table 16.3.

2. Identify hurdles to communication and describe ways to eliminate them.

Table 16.3 Barriers to Communication
Organizational
Authority and status levels
Specialization of task functions by members
Different goals
Status relationships among members
Individual
Semantics
Emotions

Organizational Hurdles

Channels of communication, both formal and informal, are largely determined by organization design. Hierarchical organizations have more levels of authority and greater differences in status among their members. Flat organizations have relatively few authority levels and tend to be more egalitarian in terms of status. The degree of specialization present in the organization also may affect clear communication, as can the presence of conflicting goals.

Authority and Status Levels. A person holding a higher formal position than another person has a higher level of authority. A person who is held in higher esteem than another person, regardless of their positions, has a higher status. Authority level and status often go hand in hand, but not always. **Status** *is a person's social rank in a group.* This is often determined by a person's characteristics, in addition to the person's formal position.[23] When status and authority level differ, communication problems are likely to occur.

The more levels in the organization—and the farther the receiver is from the sender—the more difficult effective communication becomes. Figure 16.5 illustrates the loss of understanding as messages are sent downward through a formal communication channel. To minimize this problem, top managers increasingly are using live video presentations to deliver the same message to employees at all of an organization's locations. In doing so, these managers use both verbal and nonverbal messages. Videos also increase the probability that the original messages will be received intact. Many organizations use videotapes to smooth the transition of managers to new locations. Such presentations can introduce the managers, reinforce the reason(s) for the relocation, and emphasize the need for employee cooperation during the changeover.

Figure 16.5   Levels of Understanding for a Message from the CEO

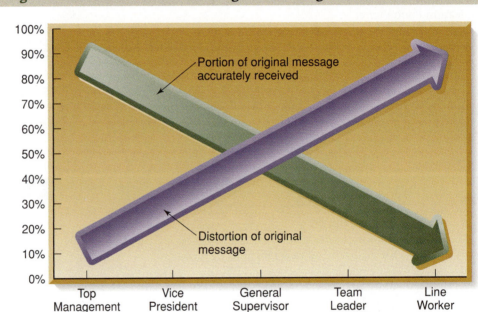

Even when communicating with others at the same level of authority, status can interfere with the process. In group discussions, members having higher status speak more and have more influence than members having lower status. This phenomenon is difficult to overcome, and it has been observed in exchanges of e-mail messages and face-to-face discussion groups. When computer-mediated group discussions were first introduced, many people expected them to decrease the effects of status on communication. Instead such information technologies often reinforce existing status relationships and magnify their effects on communication.

In organizations with flat hierarchies, such as Sun Hydraulics and Chaparral Steel, authority levels may not interfere with communication, but status is likely to come into play. Temporary employees, for example, often report feeling as if they are treated as second-class workers. Often they are excluded from meetings, not invited to social functions, and denied team-based rewards. They seldom hear news as it travels through the grapevine and miss the many advantages of being part of informal communication networks. Not surprisingly, then, nearly one of four managers reports that friction between permanent and temporary workers is a significant disadvantage of relying on temporary employees to create flexible staffing levels and reduce costs.

Specialization. As knowledge becomes more specialized, professionals in many fields develop their own jargon, or shorthand, to simplify communication among them. That often makes communication with people outside a particular field difficult. For example, a tax accountant and a marketing research manager might have trouble communicating successfully. Moreover, in an attempt to make themselves powerful, some people intentionally use the language of specialization to obscure what's going on. Employees often use specialized language when trying to "snow" others. When a plumber wrote to the U.S. Department of Housing and Urban Development (HUD) to find out whether using hydrochloric acid to unclog drains was safe, a HUD bureaucrat wrote back: "The efficacy of hydrochloric acid is indisputable, but corrosive acid is incompatible with metallic permanence." The plumber wrote back saying he agreed and was using it. A fax message from the bureaucrat arrived immediately at the plumber's shop. It read: "Don't use hydrochloric acid. It eats the hell out of pipes." Then the plumber understood.

Different Goals. If each department has its own goals, these goals can interfere with the organization's overall performance.[24] Colleen Barrett, chief operating officer of Southwest Airlines, doesn't set departmental goals because she believes that they would create conflicts between departments. Such conflicts can be direct consequences of competing interests, or they may simply arise from misunderstandings created by the different perspectives of the people involved. However, open communication between people with differing goals speeds problem solving and improves the quality of solutions. At ARAMARK, a large managed-services organization, each of its seven divisions—campus dining, business dining, sports and recreation, facilities management, maintenance, hospital, and correctional—has its own goals for revenue, account retention, and gaining new accounts. The goal of the campus-dining director is to serve student dining needs. Some colleges also outsource their maintenance and facilities needs, so it would be logical for the campus-dining director to look into a campus's needs in these other two areas. Unfortunately, most campus-dining directors narrowly focus on their own goals and neglect reaching out to help the organization reach its overall goals in the other areas. Why? Because their rewards are based on achieving their own unit's goals, not those of the entire organization.

Individual Hurdles

The Center for Creative Leadership at Greensboro, North Carolina, estimates that half of all managers and 30 percent of top managers have some difficulty communicating with others.[25] Through an intense training session at the center, managers can learn how to improve their communication competencies. The center's staff works with participants who believe that their messages are clear and effective when, in fact, they aren't. Their words, phrases, and references may be clear to some individuals, puzzling to others, and obscure to still others. These problems can be caused by semantics and emotions.

Semantics. *The study of the way words are used and the meanings they convey is called* **semantics**. Misinterpretation of word meanings can play a large role in communication failure. When two people attribute different meanings to the same words but don't realize it, a communication hurdle exists. Consider what happened when a sales rep phoned in a special order to her company's shipping department. She asked that it be shipped "as soon as possible," expecting these words to ensure that the order was given top priority. Five days later, the sales rep got a call from the irate customer wanting to know when the order would be delivered. Upon checking with the shipping department, the sales rep found that the order was being shipped that day. After some shouting, she realized that, in the shipping department, "as soon as possible" meant that the request did *not* need to be given top priority.

Problems caused by semantics are compounded when people who speak different languages attempt to communicate. As described in the following Global Awareness Competency feature, imprecise translations cause many blunders in international advertising campaigns.[26]

© Corbis Inc.

GLOBAL AWARENESS COMPETENCY

Lost in Translation

The largest numbers of blunders in advertising promotions are caused by faulty translation. Slang terms, idioms, and local dialects have all contributed to the many marketing mishaps that have occurred as or-

ganizations expanded into global markets. Here are some examples that illustrate how small language differences create big advertising blunders:

- Pepsi had a dominant share of the market in Southeast Asia until it changed the colors of its coolers and vending equipment from deep regal blue to light ice blue. In that part of the world, ice blue is associated with death and mourning.
- When Coors encouraged people to "Turn it loose," Spanish speaking people heard "Suffer from diarrhea."

- The soft drink Fresca was marketed in Mexico without a change in brand name. The company later discovered that *fresca* is slang for "lesbian" in Mexico.
- Purdue chicken's saying "It takes a tough man to make a tender chicken" in Spanish was interpreted as "It takes a sexually stimulated man to make a chicken affectionate."
- Tiffany sells glassware in sets of five in Japan because the word *four* translates to *shi*, which means "death" in Japanese.

To avoid such blunders, companies should routinely have messages translated back to the original language to ensure the accuracy of the original translation—a process called *backtranslation*. If the original message and the backtranslated version agree, the translated version probably will not have unexpected meanings. Even backtranslation is not foolproof, however, because the meanings of words often depend on the context in which they are used—especially in high-context cultures (e.g., Arabic, Japanese, and Chinese). In these cultures, communication involves sending and receiving many subtle cues. Nonverbal cues, slang subtleties, and inferences are all essential aspects of communication. The Japanese often talk around a point without ever stating it directly. From their perspective, it is the responsibility of the listener to discern the message from the context. German, Scandinavian, and Anglo cultures are low-context cultures that place more emphasis on the precise meanings of words and terms.

Emotions. An **emotion** *is a subjective reaction or feeling.* Remembering experiences, an individual recalls not only events but also the feelings that accompanied them. Thus when people communicate, they convey emotions as well as facts and opinions. The sender's feelings influence encoding of the message and may or may not be apparent to the receiver. The receiver's feelings affect decoding of the message and the nature of the response.

Misunderstandings owing to differences in what arouses people's emotions often accompany cross-cultural communication. In Japan, for example, feelings of embarrassment and shame are more easily aroused during social interactions than they are in Western cultures. Furthermore, these emotions aren't easily detected by people not socialized in the Japanese culture. Consequently, Westerners are likely to create situations that cause their Japanese counterparts to feel embarrassment and shame without realizing it—and thus seem insensitive. Although there are many other cultural differences in how people experience and express emotions, there are also many similarities. Rather than being hurdles to communication, these similarities aid communication. In particular, the antecedents of some emotions—anger, happiness, disgust, fear, sadness, and surprise—seem to be similar in most cultures, as are the facial expressions that accompany the emotions.[27] These similarities mean that nonverbal cues are less likely to be misinterpreted when emotions are involved.

Eliminating Hurdles

Regardless of how much information is needed to create feelings of overload in individuals, every organization is capable of producing that volume of information and more. Therefore managers should set up a system that identifies priority messages for immediate attention. One way of doing so is to ask others to bring you information only when significant deviations from goals and plans occur (known as *exception reporting*). When everything is going as planned, managers don't need a report. To empower subordinates, managers should let them know that they don't need to copy you on *all* of those e-mail messages.

Regulate the Flow of Information. If you receive too much information, you will suffer from information overload. How much information is too much varies from one person to the next and may even be different for today's Generation-X and Millennials. The Generation-Xers and Millennials have grown up in an environment where 10- to 30-second TV commercials are normal and students do homework with their MP3s turned on. MTV and video games that may lead to information overload by older people are normal for today's students.

Regardless of how much information is needed to create the sensation of information overload, every organization is capable of producing volumes of information. Therefore managers should set up a system that identifies priority messages for immediate attention. Some e-mail software packages allow senders to put "red flags" next to their messages, indicating urgency to recipients. In spite of this, between 35 and 50 percent of all e-mail received is regarded as unimportant. There is a lot of "spamming" going on. E-mail usage has been associated with a decrease in face-to-face communications and a feeling of employees being less connected with the organization.[28]

Encourage Feedback. You should follow up to determine whether important messages have been understood. Feedback lets you know whether the other person understands the message accurately. The sales manager who describes desired changes in the monthly sales planning report receives feedback from the report itself when it is turned in. If it contains the proper changes, the manager knows that the message was received and understood. Similarly, when you talk to a group of people, look for nonverbal feedback that will tell you whether you are getting through to them.

Simplify the Language. Because language can be a hurdle, you should choose words that others will understand. Your sentences should be concise, less than 15 words. Avoid jargon that others won't understand or that may be misleading. In general, understanding is improved by simplifying the language used—consistent, of course, with the nature of your intended audience.

Listen Actively. You need to become a good listener as well as a good message sender. Some organizations offer training programs to improve employee listening. Such programs emphasize that listening is an active process in which listeners and speakers share equal responsibility for successful communication. The following are some characteristics of active listeners[29]:

- *Appreciative:* Listens in a relaxed manner, seeking enjoyment, knowledge, or inspiration.
- *Empathic:* Listens without judging, is supportive of the speaker and learns from the experiences of others.
- *Comprehensive:* Listens to organize and make sense of information by understanding relationships among ideas.
- *Discerning:* Listens to get complete information, understand the main message, and determine important details.
- *Evaluative:* Listens in order to make a decision based on the information provided.

Restrain Negative Emotions. Like everyone else, you convey emotions when communicating, but negative emotions can distort the content of the message. When emotionally upset, you are more likely than at other times to phrase a message poorly. When you or others get angry and upset, call a halt until you and the other people involved can restrain your emotions—that is, until all of you can be more descriptive than evaluative.

Use Nonverbal Cues. You should use nonverbal cues to emphasize points and express feelings. Recall the methods of nonverbal communication that we've presented. You need to be sure that your actions reinforce your words so that they don't send mixed messages.

Use the Grapevine. As a manager, you couldn't get rid of the grapevine in an organization even if you tried, so you should use it to send information rapidly, test reactions before announcing a final decision, and obtain valuable feedback. Also, the grapevine frequently carries destructive rumors, reducing employee morale and organizational effectiveness. By being "plugged into" the grapevine, you can partially counteract this negative effect by being sure that relevant, accurate, meaningful, and timely information gets to others.

FOSTERING EFFECTIVE COMMUNICATION

3. State the guidelines for fostering effective communication.

To be an effective communicator, you must understand not only the communication process depicted earlier in Figure 16.1, but also the guidelines for fostering effective communication. These guidelines, presented throughout the chapter, are summarized in the following list. We have expressed them in terms of the American Management Association's seven guidelines that you can use to improve your communication skills.[30]

- *Clarify your ideas before communicating.* Analyze the topic or problem to clarify it in your mind before sending a message. Communication often is ineffective because the message is inadequately planned. Part of good message planning is considering the goals and attitudes of those who will receive the message.
- *Examine the true purpose of the communication.* Before you send a message, ask yourself what you really want to accomplish with it. Decide whether you want to obtain information, convey a decision, or persuade someone to take action.
- *Consider the setting in which the communication will take place.* You convey meanings and intent by more than words alone. Trying to communicate with a person in another location is more difficult than doing so face to face.
- *Consult with others, when appropriate, in planning communications.* Encourage the participation of those who will be affected by the message. They can often provide a viewpoint that you might not have considered.

- *Be mindful of the nonverbal messages you send.* Tone of voice, facial expression, eye contact, personal appearance, and physical surroundings all influence the communication process. The receiver considers both the words and the nonverbal cues that comprise your message.
- *Take the opportunity to convey something helpful to the receiver.* Considering the other person's interests and needs often presents opportunities to the sender. You can make your message clearer by imagining yourself in the other's position. Effective communicators really try to understand the message from the listener's point of view.
- *Follow up the communication.* Your best efforts at communication can be wasted unless you succeed in getting your message across. You should follow up and ask for feedback to find out whether you succeeded. You can't assume that the receiver understands your message; feedback in some form is necessary.

If you follow these recommendations, you will improve your ability to communicate effectively. Unfortunately, when communication does break down, people often waste time and energy trying to figure out who is at fault, provoking a defensive reaction that further inhibits effective communication.

ETHICAL ISSUES IN COMMUNICATIONS

Technology, especially in the area of communications, has raised two major ethical issues. The ability of employees to work at home or away from their office has enabled them to be more independent and productive. The price for increased employee independence has led some organizations to monitor employee's work. Also, it is tempting for employees to engage in personal activities, such as checking stock quotes, shopping, or looking for another job, while on the job. Advances in communications are likely to increase the pressures on both management and employees to develop a code of ethics.

4. Discuss two ethical issues in communications.

Computer Ethics

Computer ethics *is concerned with the nature and social impact of information technologies and the formulation of policies for their appropriate use.*[31] An increasing number of individuals and organizations are concerned with computer ethics. The ethical issues surrounding computers arise from their unique technological characteristics, including the following:

- Computers make mistakes that no human being would make.
- Computers communicate over great distances at high speed and low cost.
- Computers have huge capacities to store, copy, erase, retrieve, transmit, and manipulate information quickly and economically.
- Computers have the effect of radically distancing (depersonalizing) originators, users, and subjects of programs and data from each other.
- Computers may collect and store data for one purpose that can easily be used for another purpose and be kept for long periods of time.

The Computer Ethics Institute, a professional association headquartered in Washington, D.C., was formed because of growing concerns with the ethical use of computer technology. It has issued a "ten commandments" of computer ethics, which are listed in Table 16.4.[32] The commandments provide an ethical code of conduct for guidance in situations that may not be covered by law.

The following Self-Management Competency feature gives you an opportunity to assess and develop further your understanding of computer ethics.[33] Recall that the self-management competency includes (1) acceptance of responsibility for continuous self-development and learning; (2) willingness to learn and relearn continually, as changed situations call for new skills and perspectives; and (3) application of clear personal standards of integrity and ethical conduct.

Table 16.4   Ten Commandments of Computer Ethics

1. Thou shalt not use a computer to harm other people.
2. Thou shalt not interfere with other people's computer work.
3. Thou shalt not snoop around in other people's files.
4. Thou shalt not use a computer to steal.
5. Thou shalt not use a computer to bear false witness.
6. Thou shalt not copy or use proprietary software for which you have not paid.
7. Thou shalt not use other people's computer resources without authorization or proper compensation.
8. Thou shalt not appropriate other people's intellectual output.
9. Thou shalt think about the social consequences of the program you are writing or the system you design.
10. Thou shalt use a computer in ways that show consideration and respect for your fellow humans.

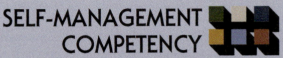

SELF-MANAGEMENT COMPETENCY

Computer Ethics Survey

Instructions

Twenty statements appear in this survey. You should evaluate each statement by using the following five-point scale:

1. **True**
2. **Somewhat True**
3. **Neither True nor False**
4. **Somewhat False**
5. **False**

If you think that a statement is *true*, record a 1 next to it. If you think that a statement is *neither true nor false*, place a 3 next to it, and so on. Don't skip any statement.

_____ 1. The courts have provided clear guidance on who should have access to e-mail at work.

_____ 2. Employees are usually informed by employers if their voice mail is going to be monitored.

_____ 3. Medical records are not available to employers.

_____ 4. Most organizations have clear written policies and procedures regarding the use of e-mail.

_____ 5. The confidentiality of faxes is generally well maintained.

_____ 6. Nothing inherent in computer technology raises unique ethical questions.

_____ 7. Public perceptions of computers and computer professionals generally have been good.

_____ 8. Computer professionals have a level of influence that is matched by equivalent levels of organizational controls and professional association guidance.

_____ 9. The best way to deter unethical behavior in the use of computers is through legal deterrents and remedies.

_____ 10. The best way to deter unethical behavior in the use of computers is through professional codes of conduct.

_____ 11. The majority of computer science graduates have had at least one course in computer ethics by the time they graduate.

_____ 12. There are many controls over what information is kept on private citizens, who keeps it, and who can access it.

_____ 13. The majority of businesses in the United States have well-documented policies regarding what employee information is kept in personnel databases and who has access to it.

_____ 14. Computerized medical records pose no greater danger to privacy and potential for misuse than do paper records.

_____ 15. Electronic bulletin boards are fairly well "policed" and do not contain potentially harmful information.

_____ 16. The majority of computer crimes are reported, and the violators are successfully prosecuted.

_____ 17. Computer abuse, such as gaining unauthorized access to a system or placing a virus or other potentially damaging

Privacy Issues

The amount and types of information available about most individuals in the United States and Canada to just about any business (or individual in that business) or government agency are astounding. Some of this information starts to be gathered when people borrow money, participate in a government program, or purchase goods with a credit card. Consumers and borrowers routinely give information voluntarily to retailers and creditors so that they can purchase goods on credit. At least once a month, banks, retailers, credit card companies, and mail-order houses send computer tapes or other electronic files detailing their customers' purchases and payment activities to credit bureaus.

The three large credit rating companies—TRW, Trans Union, and Equifax—maintain credit information on more than 170 million people in the United States. This information is accessible in a matter of seconds to merchants, clerks, and, in essence, just about anyone. In addition to credit ratings, a large amount of information on nearly everyone in the United States—ranging from medical histories and insurance information to buying habits—is stored in computer-readable form and widely disseminated among credit bureaus, resellers of data purchased from bureaus, and many businesses. The information that used to be inaccessible or very difficult to obtain is now instantly available for use by almost anyone. Protection of privacy through the legal system, organizational and managerial policies and practices, self-regulation through professional and trade associations, and consumer groups hasn't caught up with technological developments as we noted in Chapter 6 (Ethics and Stakeholder Social Responsibility).

One step in the direction of trying to reestablish online "rights of privacy" was taken by the Council of Better Business Bureaus, headquartered in Arlington, Virginia, in 2000. One component of their initiative is the "Privacy Seal Program," which participating and approved companies can use and display on their Web sites. For consumers, the program is designed to help Internet users identify companies that stand behind their privacy policies and have met the program requirements of notice, choice, access, and security in the use of personally identifiable information. Among other things, the program requires a site to disclose how it intends to use the information being collected, mandates that consumers be allowed to opt out of data collection, and requires site operators to obtain parental permission to collect data on children. The nation's largest online advertising agency, DoubleClick Inc., has been banned from tracking users without their knowledge. Though the company will continue tracking the movement of online visitors, it must now reveal its methods for retrieving and using this information and give individuals access to the profiles created about them.[34]

Some critics of the online invasion of privacy crisis assert that such voluntary industry efforts are inadequate. They contend that more governmental regulation and enforcement of privacy protections are needed for both consumers and employees. However, with the increased threat of terrorism since September 11, 2001, the efforts of the U.S. government have focused on gaining access to more private information than on privacy protection.

Effective communication is essential to many aspects of human endeavor, including organizational life. For managers, the communication competency is the foundation on which managerial effectiveness is built. Through communication, managers gather and interpret information that they then use to plan, set goals, and make strategic decisions. Strategic decisions, in turn, must be communicated throughout the organization, where they are used to guide planning and team activities. In cross-cultural situations, the global awareness competency supports effective communication.

1. Explain the main elements of the communication process.

The communication process comprises six elements: the sender (encoder), the receiver (decoder), the message, channels, feedback, and perception. Of the many possible forms of nonverbal communication, managers should be particularly aware of—and able to use effectively—space, physical appearance, and body language. Channels of communication are both formal and informal. Formal channels are downward, upward, and horizontal. Managers most frequently use downward channels to send messages to the various levels of the organization. Upward channels allow employee participation in decision making and provide feedback to management. Horizontal channels are used among peers in different departments and are especially important in network organizations. Informal channels—the grapevine and network groups—often are as important as formal channels of communication. Managers can never eliminate the grapevine and thus should learn to use it to send messages and receive feedback.

2. Identify hurdles to communication and describe ways to eliminate them.

Hurdles to communication hinder the sending and receiving of messages by distorting or even blocking intended meanings. Hurdles can be either organizational or individual. Organizational hurdles may result from the design of the organization itself, from differences in status, from the jargon that often grows up around highly specialized tasks, and from differing goals. Individual hurdles may result from conflicting assumptions on the part of the sender and receiver, from misinterpretation of meaning, and from misunderstanding of emotional reactions.

3. State the guidelines for fostering effective communication.

Guidelines for effective communication include clarifying ideas, examining the purpose of communicating, considering the setting, consulting with others, being mindful of nonverbal messages, taking the opportunity to convey something helpful to the receiver, following up, and being sure that actions taken support the communication.

4. Discuss two ethical issues in communications.

Many ethical issues arise from unique characteristics of computers and information technologies. The "ten commandments" of computer ethics reflect the need for radically different attitudes and actions of individuals. These commandments provide an ethical code of conduct for situations not covered by law. Privacy issues are also becoming more important because more and more individuals have access to information once considered private.

Channel
Communication
Computer ethics
Decoding
Downward channels
Emotion
Employee network groups
Encoding
Feedback
Feng shui
Grapevine
Horizontal channels
Informal channels

Information richness
Listening
Message
Nonverbal messages
Perception
Proxemics
Receiver
Selective perception
Semantics
Sender
Status
Stereotyping
Upward channels

1. What type of communication channels does Kerry Killinger of Washington Mutual use? When is each channel most effective?

2. Why are some people defensive about receiving feedback about their performance?

3. What are some of the downsides to sending messages via e-mail?

4. Why do communication difficulties arise in organizations?

5. The world is a busy and confusing place, and people are constantly bombarded by multiple messages. How do you simplify these messages in order to reduce the confusion?

6. What are some ways that managers can use to overcome hurdles to effective communication?

7. Besides taking foreign language lessons, what other activities could you participate in to avoid communication blunders overseas? What benefits would be associated with improving this competency?

8. What are some ethical issues that all of us face when we use e-mail?

9. How are upward communications affected by differences in gender?

CASE FOR COMPETENCY DEVELOPMENT

MAYO CLINIC

Going to the hospital is no fun. Nobody likes to do it. The experience is unnerving, often frightening, and a symbol of our own mortality. Also, it is difficult for the average person to judge the "quality" of the hospital, based on direct evidence. Therefore it is important to learn as much as possible about the competence, care, and integrity of a medical facility before entering it.

The Mayo Clinic doesn't leave this information to chance. Mayo tells a consistent and compelling story of its services to potential "customers." At Mayo Clinic, the patient always comes first. Hospital employees are hired and trained and facilities are designed with that in mind. Mayo offers patients and their family's concrete and convincing evidence of its strengths and values: competence, care, and integrity. Communicating these values to patients has resulted in exceptional positive word of mouth, and abiding customer loyalty has enabled Mayo Clinic to build the most powerful name in health care. It was done with very little advertising. It's called *evidence management*, an organized, explicit approach to presenting customers with easy-to-understand information and honest communication of the hospital's abilities. Evidence management is much like advertising, except that it turns Mayo Clinic into a living, breathing advertisement for it. And it's all done through communication.

A study was done on the communication process at Mayo Clinic. Researchers interviewed 1,000 Mayo employees and patients and observed hundreds of doctor–patient visits at Mayo. They even checked themselves in as patients. They got the message that Mayo was communicating: The patient comes first. However, verbal communication is not the only type of communication that works. Mayo Clinic has effectively designed a communication system that coordinates doctors' needs and patients' requests. The clinic communicates with patients and visitors through careful planning of space, light, color, sound, and the attitudes and personal appearance of staff members.

Many Mayo patients describe their care as being organized around their personal needs rather than the doctor's schedule, the hospital's processes, or any other factor. Mayo staff members clearly signal the patient-first focus. Patients are reassured by the kindness and concern shown by the staff. Their caring attitude is clearly communicated. The caring attitude applies not only to doctors and nurses, but is embodied by all staff members, including the receptionists when patients check in. This is due to the fact that Mayo consistently hires people who genuinely embrace the organization's values of quality, competence, integrity, and caring. This is reinforced to employees through training and ongoing seminars. William Mayo, one of the founders, stated in 1910, "The best interest of the patient is the only interest to be considered." This statement guides hiring practices and decisions to this day. People are not hired at Mayo because of intellect or technical skill alone. Those things are important, of course, but individual personality, personal values, and life experiences are equally important in the hiring process.

A story is told of a young woman whose wedding was scheduled to take place at a time when her mother became critically ill. The mother was not expected to live to attend her daughter's wedding in several weeks. Mayo came through. Nurses and staff members decorated the hospital's atrium for the wedding, provided a cake, nurses handled makeup and a hairstyle for the ill mother and wheeled her bed to the atrium. The hospital chaplain performed the ceremony, while hospital staff, family, and friends watched from the atrium balconies. The bride said they looked "like angels from above." That wedding signaled not only evidence of caring to the patient and her family, but also a strong reminder to the staff that the patients really do come first.

Because medical services are so intangible and technically so complex, patients are especially attentive to what they can see and understand in the physical environment. The questions for the Mayo Clinic's top administrators were "What does the Mayo Clinic communicate to customers?" "Do these clues convey the optimal message about our service?" From public spaces to exam rooms to laboratories, Mayo facilities have been designed explicitly to relieve stress, offer a place of refuge, create positive distractions, and convey caring and respect. For example, the outpatient facilities include quiet, darkened private areas for patients to rest between appointments. The pediatric unit in Mayo's St. Mary's Hospital Emergency Department, for example, transformed artwork by local school children into a colorful arrangement of wall and ceiling tiles. The resuscitation equipment in the examination rooms is hidden behind a large picture, which slides out of the way when the equipment is needed. Public spaces are made softer with natural light, color, artwork, music, and fountains.

The architect who designed Mayo Rochester's 20-story Gonda building said, "I would like the patients to feel a little better before they see their doctors." Mayo has used careful planning of space as a means of communicating that it cares about the people occupying that space. A well-designed physical environment also has a positive impact on employees, reducing physical and emotional stress—which is of value to patients as well. Visible employee stress communicates the wrong signals to patients. Mayo does not wish to convey the wrong signals. For example, on the main floor of the Gonda building, there is a multimedia Cancer Education Center. Its location was chosen to help take the stigma out of having cancer.

Mayo understands that the way employees present themselves also sends signals to patients. Doctors do not wear casual attire, nor do they wear the typical medical white coats. Instead, the more than 2,800 staff physicians wear business suits, unless, of course, they are wearing surgical scrubs. The suits convey professionalism and ex-

pertise and also communicate respect to patients and their families. The physician's area is near the patient's room and has a large sofa to hold the patient and family members. This arrangement removes the desk as a barrier to communication. The patient also may use the sofa to lie down while waiting for the doctor. This design helps communicate care, comfort, and compassion, showing commitment to patient well-being before the patient meets the doctor. The environment also inspires health-care professionals to deliver the high quality of care the patient is seeking.

Years ago, a young laboratory employee went to work one morning and her supervisor noticed and commented that the woman's white shoelaces were soiled. She was told to clean the shoelaces and to be more careful in the future. That young woman has since progressed to administrator of General Service and the office of Patient Affairs. Her name is Mary Ann Morris and she said, "Though I was initially offended, I realized over time that everything I do, down to my shoelaces, represents and communicates my commitment to our patients and visitors. Twenty-eight years later, I still use the dirty shoelace story to set the standard for the service level I aspire to for myself and my co-workers." Mayo believes that the personal appearance of its staff conveys the message of respect for the patient and instills a feeling of pride in the employees.

A dirty shoelace may seem minor, given the overall picture of caring for the patient, but a shoelace is something that a patient (customer) can see, while medical expertise and technical ability are not. It is a small part of the story that Mayo communicates to its customers—a story that puts each patient in a starring role—a story that communicates not only competence, but great caring, as well. What Mayo Clinic has done is identify a simple, consistent message and then manage the evidence—the buildings, the approach to care, and even the shoelaces—to support that message, day in and day out, year after year.[35]

Questions

1. What channels of communications are illustrated in this case?

2. What are the nonverbal clues that the clinic uses to communicate its mission to patients and their families?

3. What communication competencies are illustrated in this case?

COMMUNICATION INVENTORY

The following statements relate to how your manager and you communicate on the job.[36] There are no right or wrong answers. Respond honestly to the statements, using the following scale.

1. **Strongly Agree**
2. **Agree**
3. **Uncertain**
4. **Disagree**
5. **Strongly Disagree**

_____ 1. My manager criticizes my work without allowing me to explain.

_____ 2. My manager allows me as much creativity as possible in my job.

_____ 3. My manager always judges the actions of his or her subordinates.

_____ 4. My manager allows flexibility on the job.

_____ 5. My manager criticizes my work in the presence of others.

_____ 6. My manager is willing to try new ideas and to accept other points of view.

_____ 7. My manager believes that he or she must control how I do my work.

_____ 8. My manager understands the problems that I encounter in my job.

_____ 9. My manager is always trying to change other people's attitudes and behaviors to suit his or her own.

_____ 10. My manager respects my feelings and values.

_____ 11. My manager always needs to be in charge of the situation.

_____ 12. My manager listens to my problems with interest.

_____ 13. My manager tries to manipulate subordinates to get what he or she wants or to make himself or herself look good.

_____ 14. My manager does not try to make me feel inferior.

_____ 15. I have to be careful when talking to my manager so that I will not be misinterpreted.

_____ 16. My manager participates in meetings with employees without projecting his or her higher status or power.

_____ 17. I seldom say what really is on my mind because it might be twisted and distorted by my manager.

_____ 18. My manager treats me with respect.

_____ 19. My manager seldom becomes involved in employee conflicts.

_____ 20. My manager does not have hidden motives in dealing with me.

_____ 21. My manager is not interested in employee problems.

_____ 22. I feel that I can be honest and straightforward with my manager.

_____ 23. My manager rarely offers moral support during a personal crisis.

_____ 24. I feel that I can express my opinions and ideas honestly to my manager.

_____ 25. My manager tries to make me feel inadequate.

_____ 26. My manager defines problems so that they can be understood but does not insist that his or her subordinates agree.

_____ 27. My manager makes it clear that he or she is in charge.

_____ 28. I feel free to talk to my manager.

_____ 29. My manager believes that if a job is to be done right, he or she must oversee it or do it.

_____ 30. My manager defines problems and makes his or her subordinates aware of them.

_____ 31. My manager cannot admit that he or she makes mistakes.

_____ 32. My manager tried to describe situations fairly without labeling them as good or bad.

_____ 33. My manager is dogmatic; it is useless for me to voice an opposing point of view.

_____ 34. My manager presents his or her feelings and perceptions without implying that a similar response is expected from me.

_____ 35. My manager thinks that he or she is always right.

_____ 36. My manager attempts to explain situations clearly and without personal bias.

Communication Inventory Scoring and Interpretation Sheet

Place the numbers that you assigned to each statement in the appropriate blanks. Now add them to determine a subtotal for each communication category. Place the subtotals in the proper blanks and add your scores.

PART I: DEFENSIVE SCORES

Evaluation		Neutrality	
Question 1	_____	Question 19	_____
Question 3	_____	Question 21	_____
Question 5	_____	Question 23	_____
Subtotal	_____	Subtotal	_____

Control		Superiority	
Question 7	_____	Question 25	_____
Question 9	_____	Question 27	_____
Question 11	_____	Question 29	_____
Subtotal	_____	Subtotal	_____

Strategy		Certainty	
Question 13	_____	Question 31	_____
Question 15	_____	Question 33	_____
Question 17	_____	Question 35	_____
Subtotal	_____	Subtotal	_____

Subtotals for Defensive Scores

Evaluation	_____	Neutrality	_____
Control	_____	Superiority	_____
Strategy	_____	Certainty	_____

Total _____

Place an X on the graph to indicate what your perception is of your organization or department's communication. You may wish to discuss with others their own perceptions and interpretations.

18 25 30 35 40 45 50 55 60 65 70 75 80 85 90
Defensive Defensive to Neutral Neutral to Supportive Supportive

PART II: SUPPORTIVE SCORES

Provisionalism		Spontaneity	
Question 2	_____	Question 20	_____
Question 4	_____	Question 22	_____
Question 6	_____	Question 24	_____
Subtotal	_____	Subtotal	_____

Empathy		Problem Orientation	
Question 8	_____	Question 26	_____
Question 10	_____	Question 28	_____
Question 12	_____	Question 30	_____
Subtotal	_____	Subtotal	_____

Equality		Description	
Question 14	_____	Question 32	_____
Question 16	_____	Question 34	_____
Question 18	_____	Question 36	_____
Subtotal	_____	Subtotal	_____

Subtotals for Supportive Scores

Provisionalism	_____	Spontaneity	_____
Empathy	_____	Problem Orientation	_____
Equality	_____	Description	_____

Total _____

Place an X on the graph to indicate what your perception is of your organization or department's communication. You may wish to discuss with others their own perceptions and interpretations.

18 25 30 35 40 45 50 55 60 65 70 75 80 85 90
Supportive Supportive to Neutral Neutral to Defensive Defensive

Questions

1. What communication skills would you like to improve?
2. What did you learn about your communication competency from this exercise?
3. What steps will you take to become a more effective communicator?

©Digital Vision/Getty Images

Managing Work Teams

LEARNING OBJECTIVES

After studying this chapter, you should be able to:

1. Explain the importance of work teams.

2. Identify four types of work teams.

3. State the meaning and determinants of team effectiveness.

4. Describe the internal team processes that can affect team performance.

5. Explain how to diagnose and remove barriers to poor team performance.

Chapter Outline

Genomics, the study of DNA, is one of the biggest revolutions occurring in the pharmaceutical industries. By combining an understanding of genomics with knowledge about specific diseases, pharmaceutical companies are moving into an era of customized medicines. Instead of simply prescribing a drug based on the disease to be treated, prescriptions for customized medicines will match drugs up to the people who are most likely to benefit. Genomics is also creating a revolution in the way diseases are diagnosed. Until now, Roche's diagnostics and pharmaceutical businesses didn't have much in common. Scientists working on new approaches to diagnosis focused on their specialty and didn't concern themselves with developments related to new treatments. But genomics is changing that. According to Roche's CEO Franz Humer, "Diagnosis and treatment will come ever closer together."

Just as genomics has caused scientists to ask fundamentally new questions, it has also caused Roche to take a fundamentally new approach to the way it organizes scientific work. Until four years ago, scientists at Roche were divided into competing teams. Each team focused on its own project and the teams were expected to compete against each other for resources. Teams were fiercely committed to their projects, which made it nearly impossible for them to acknowledge that their project wasn't likely to produce a blockbuster drug—despite what their data might tell them. The competitive atmosphere also led to secrecy. Because scientists were in competition with each other, they seldom shared their expertise with other teams, fearing that it would damage their own chances of success.

Roche quickly realized that its competitive approach to teamwork was counterproductive. To prosper in the era of genomics, cross-discipli-

nary communication was essential. Multidisciplinary research teams were the answer. For example, the Genomics Oncology team includes seven researchers with specialties that include immunology, statistics, genetics, and oncology. Elsewhere in the company, new teams bring together plant geneticists, chemists, and diagnosticians. Restructuring into multidisciplinary teams hasn't been easy. "It isn't just a matter of turning on a light switch," says Klaus Lindpaintner, global head of genetics research. The new team structure means the company has had to create a new culture to support collaboration. Now it even looks for a different type of researcher. Instead of someone with 20 years of experience in their area of specialty, Roche wants people who can reinvent themselves as opportunities change. For Roche and many other pharmaceutical companies, genomics has changed everything.[1]

WORK TEAMS AND OTHER GROUPS

1. Explain the importance of work teams.

In everyday conversation, the terms *group* and *team* often are used interchangeably, but in this chapter we distinguish between the two. Here, *group* is the more general term, and *team* is a special type of group. Teams and groups are both important to organizational life, but for different reasons.

Organizational Groups

A **group** *is two or more individuals who come into personal and meaningful contact on a continuing basis.*[2] Many types of small and large groups can be found in most organizations.

Some of these are formal groups responsible for doing the work of the organization. Among the formal organizational groups that you learned about in Chapter 11 are departments, divisions, and business units.

Work Teams

Work teams are generally much smaller than formal organizational groups. A **work team** *consists of a small number of employees with complementary skills who collaborate on a project, are committed to a common purpose, and are jointly accountable for performing tasks that contribute to achieving an organization's goals.*

Not all groups of people who work together form a work team. To be a team, the members must have a shared goal that they can achieve only if they communicate and collaborate with each other. At Roche, a work team focuses on discovering knowledge that can be used to develop new pharmaceutical products for diagnosing or treating specific types of diseases. For example, the Genomics Oncology team is focused on using genetic information to diagnose and treat cancer.

To illustrate how organizational groups differ from work teams, consider how auto repair garages can be organized. In a traditional garage located at a Subaru dealership, the employees who provide maintenance and repair services belong to an organizational group with its own identity. Usually, the service manager controls the flow of their work assignments. As repair jobs come in, the service manager decides which technician will work on each job, and in what order they will do their work. Technicians often perform their jobs in relative isolation. Each technician has a task to do, and the various technicians who work on a particular repair are not held jointly responsible for the finished product. Compare this traditional organization to a team-based garage. In a team-based garage at a Lexus dealership, technicians work in small teams of about six people. A repair job is assigned to the whole team. Technicians do not specialize in specific repairs. The service manager's role is to act as a coach-player. He or she helps the team with special problems that arise and gives advice about how the team can be more effective. When the repair is finished, the team as a whole is held accountable for the parts they used, the time they billed, and for the customer's satisfaction. A study that compared traditional repair garages to team-based garages found that team-based garages were more profitable and their customers were more satisfied.[3]

Work teams go by many different names. A few of the terms used to describe work teams are shown in Figure 17.1.

One study revealed just how widely used teams have become in organizations. The researchers estimated that 50 percent or more of the employees work in teams at 80 percent of the Fortune 500 companies. Whereas work teams were found mostly in manufacturing operations a few years ago, they have now spread throughout the service sector.[4]

The importance of teams is reflected in the amount of time that managers and others spend in team meetings. Many top managers report spending 50 percent or more of

Figure 17.1 Terms for Work Teams

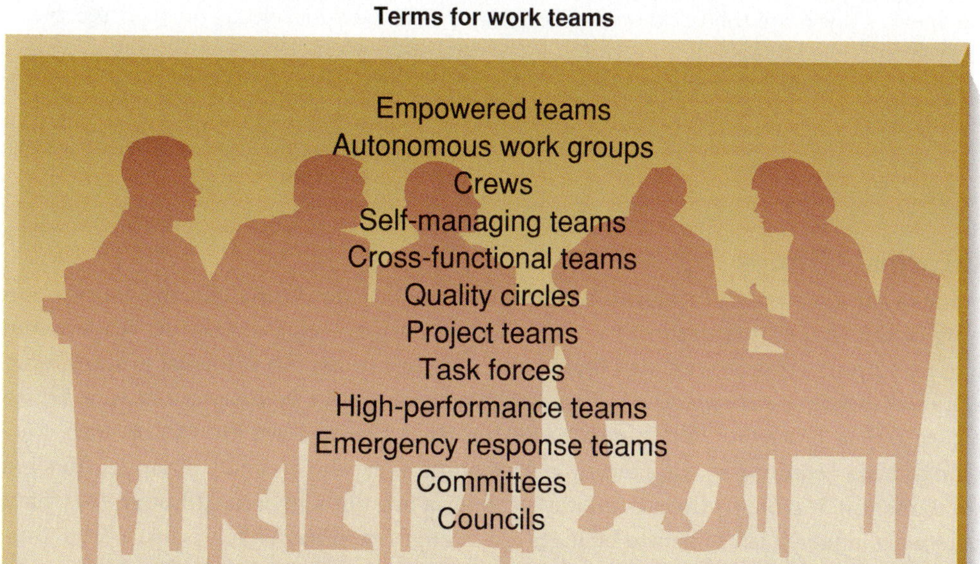

Terms for work teams

Empowered teams
Autonomous work groups
Crews
Self-managing teams
Cross-functional teams
Quality circles
Project teams
Task forces
High-performance teams
Emergency response teams
Committees
Councils

their time in team meetings; first-line managers and professionals may spend between 20 and 50 percent of their time in such meetings.[5] These team meetings range from quick huddles in someone's office to voice-mail exchanges to planning retreats that last several days. In some organizations, the importance of team meetings drives the physical design of the work space. As described in the Planning & Administration feature, the renovation of CommonHealth's buildings was partly guided by the types of teamwork needed among employees.[6]

PLANNING & ADMINISTRATION COMPETENCY

CommonHealth

CommonHealth is a communications agency located in New Jersey that focuses on developing advertising for health products. The company set out to renovate its three buildings, which included 90,000 square feet of work space. The goal in the renovation was to encourage better teamwork within departments and improve collaboration between departments. Susan DiDonato, the manager who oversaw the project,

commented: "We find the best ideas may happen in the hallways." To create more "hallways," the architects recommended an open office design. At first, senior managers resisted the idea of giving up their private offices. Budget considerations forced them to make a choice between keeping their private offices or including more areas for team meetings. They agreed that meeting spaces were more important.

The new design features many open areas, but it also includes semi-private alcoves furnished with table and chairs, and private meeting rooms where teams can go to thrash out ideas or hold problem-solving sessions. The teams assigned to manage different brands (e.g., Clarinex) are the backbone of CommonHealth. Each brand team is assigned its own work room, which gives the

team a place to concentrate. Brand teams are fairly stable, so it works to assign them their own meeting rooms. For many other CommonHealth employees, temporary task force assignments are more typical. The alcove spaces work well as places for task force members to gather on an as-needed basis. Because the types of teamwork needed in each of the company's 10 business units are somewhat different, the units all look different. "No one size fits all," observed DiDonato. To keep ideas flowing between teams of all sorts, CommonHealth's design includes areas that encourage employees to congregate informally—a kitchen, a bistro, a cappuccino bar. DiDonato seems to think the new arrangements are working well: "You can see the excitement of people when they're together."

Informal Groups

Some of the groups that form within an organization are not formed for the express purpose of doing the organization's work. Informal groups—such as bowling leagues and parent-support groups—can also be found in organizations. An **informal group** *consists of a small number of individuals who frequently participate together in activities and share feelings for the purpose of meeting their mutual needs.* Informal groups have little to do with completing tasks required by the employer. Five employees who by chance happen to sit at the same lunch table in their company's cafeteria are not a group. Although they have personal contact, it isn't likely to be highly meaningful and most likely is just a brief, one-time event. Suppose, however, that the five employees regularly seek each other out and almost always eat lunch together. As their interactions become more meaningful and they develop expectations for each other's behavior, the five employees become an informal group.

Informal groups may support, oppose, or have no interest in organizational goals, rules, or higher authority. When pilots at United Airlines decided not to work overtime because top management had not negotiated a new contract with them, they banded together in informal groups at United's major hubs in Denver, Chicago, and Los Angeles, and agreed to refuse to fly overtime. Angry customers who were left stranded at airports vowed never to fly United Airlines again.

An organization may encourage employees to participate in more positive informal groups, such as those based on shared hobbies or other interests. The friendships formed in such informal groups are greatly valued by many employees and may result in their feeling a greater sense of loyalty toward their employer. Members of work teams may develop close friendships that bind them together emotionally and increase their sense of loyalty, but this is not the primary objective of organizing employees into work teams.

Why Organizations Use Work Teams

Automakers estimate that developing a new model requires as many as 7 million engineering hours. The design and development of a new car at Toyota or Honda requires as many as 1,000 engineers working together for one to two years. At Microsoft, creating a new version of Windows requires writing more than 10 million lines of code, which may involve hundreds of people. Management's first challenge is figuring out how to divide the mountains of work involved in such complex projects. Its second challenge is integrating the efforts of the individuals and teams working on the projects to ensure that they achieve the organization's goals.

The specific goals to be achieved differ from team to team and from organization to organization. The goals depend partly on the needs of the particular customers being served. In one study, half the managers who responded believed that improving team processes to focus on customers was the strategic initiative having the greatest potential for ensuring their organizations' success.[7]

Although each work team has its own specific goals, the main reasons that managers give for organizing work around teams are generally similar. They include serving customers better through innovation, speed, cost reductions, and quality improvement.[8]

The Competent Manager

To attract creative scientists and increase the innovations coming from its labs, the top management team at Pfizer, a pharmaceutical company, decided to reorganize lab scientists into teams and give them more autonomy.

Innovation. Bringing together people who have a variety of experiences and expertise to address a common problem or task can increase creativity, which is the bedrock of new products.[9] At Microsoft, teams are essential to developing innovative products. Whether the product is another version of Windows or a new Internet service, managers at Microsoft address innovation and product development challenges by organizing employees into numerous work teams and then synchronizing their activities. Each team has a clear and limited product vision and a time limit for completing its work. Teams working on the same project are in constant communication with each other.

Speed. In addition to introducing more ideas, teams can reduce the time required for product development. They do so by replacing serial development with parallel development. In the past, the developmental process involved completion by one function (e.g., basic research) of a task and then forwarding of the product to the next function (e.g., prototyping), and so on until all functions had completed their tasks in sequence. With parallel development, many tasks are done at the same time and are closely coordinated among the functions. Parallel development cuts the amount of time spent in the developmental cycle, or what is often called *time to market*. In the pharmaceutical industry, new products are immediately patented so competitors cannot offer the same product for several years. As a consequence, being first to market with a new pharmaceutical product is absolutely essential to recovering the costs of developing the product and for generating profits from investments in R&D.

Cost. Like many other companies, reducing costs and responding more quickly to customers were key reasons for Jostens' decision to organize around teams. Jostens manufactures a variety of products, the best known being class rings and high school yearbooks. Before Jostens reorganized work around teams, employees were producing 16 rings per employee per day. After the entire manufacturing facility was switched to self-managing teams, the employees produced 25 rings per person per day. The entire process—from receipt of a work order to shipping of the finished product—was shortened from 30 calendar days to just 10 calendar days.

Quality. Excellent quality is a primary goal of some work teams. At GE/Durham, teams are expected to build perfect jet engines. Engines are produced by teams that carry out the entire production process. The engines they build will be used in airplanes that fly 10,000 miles without stopping. The drive for perfection really matters at this plant. As one employee put it, "I've got a 3-year-old daughter, and I figure that every plane we build engines for has someone with a 3-year-old daughter riding on it." A bad engine could destroy hundreds of lives and even alter the course of history.[10]

TYPES OF WORK TEAMS

2. Identify four types of work teams.

The strategic goals to be achieved by work teams—innovation, speed, cost reductions, and quality—may be much the same. The specific goals of work teams often differ greatly. Work teams differ in other important ways also, including their longevity and membership. The *longevity* of a work team may be quite short or it may be permanent. On the one hand, a short-lived team comprising lawyers, investment bankers, and other specialists might be formed to help a company go public and then disband after the initial public offering (IPO). On the other hand, NASA's mission control team has been in existence for several decades.

The *membership* of work teams can differ greatly from one situation to another. Sometimes all members of a team work in the same department. Other times, work teams include employees from several different departments or even people from different organizations, such as employees working with suppliers and customers. At Xerox Palo Alto Research Center (PARC), employees from Xerox and its customers work together in teams to design new Xerox products. In one team, for example, employees from Syntex, a customer engaged in drug research, are working with Xerox researchers, engineers, and marketers. Their goal is to find ways to use core technologies developed at PARC to manage the 300,000 reports that Syntex produces each year as it tests new drugs on volunteer patients.[11]

Different types of work teams suit different purposes. Problem-solving, functional, multidisciplinary, and self-managing work teams are four common types of work teams, and each has a different purpose.

Problem-Solving Work Teams

A **problem-solving work team** *consists of employees from different areas of an organization whose goal is to consider how something can be done better.* Such a team may meet for one or two hours a week on a continuing basis to discuss ways to improve quality, safety, productivity, or morale. Quality circles are the most familiar example of a relatively permanent and enduring problem-solving work team. Not all problem-solving teams have indefinite life spans, however. Temporary task forces are a familiar example of problem-solving teams that exist just long enough to deal with a specific problem. When Xerox needed to find a solution to a design problem for a product using photoreceptors that had to "rest" for 24 hours in the dark, it turned to a problem-solving team. The team discovered the causes of the problem, developed an improved design, and saved the company $266,000 the first year.[12]

Quality Circles. A **quality circle** *(also called a TQM team) is a group of employees who meet regularly to identify, analyze, and propose solutions to various types of production problems.* Meetings usually lasting an hour or so are held once every week or two during or after regular working hours. Quality circles at Navistar International, Johnson & Johnson, and ExxonMobil, among others, don't address just one problem and then disband. They are expected to look for and propose solutions to quality-related problems *continually.* Members often are given overtime pay if a quality circle meets after work. They normally receive eight or more hours of formal training in decision-making and team processes, which they apply in their meetings. Quality circles normally don't have the authority to implement their proposed solutions, which are presented to management for further consideration and action.

Task Forces. A **task force** *is a team that is formed to accomplish a specific, highly important goal for an organization.* Task forces often meet intensively during the course of a few weeks or months and then disband. Task force members usually are expected to continue working at their normal jobs during the duration of the task force. Also typical of task forces is diversity in the backgrounds and expertise of the members. Managers often create task forces to help achieve such goals as strategic reorientation, gathering data about the external environment, and designing approaches for implementing a new strategy.

Signicast Corporation used a problem-solving task force when management decided to build new facilities. Headquartered in Milwaukee, Wisconsin, Signicast manufactures precision castings of metal parts using blueprints supplied by customers such as Harley Davidson and John Deere. When top management decided to build a new facility, it set the goal of designing the best facility of its type in the world. To do so required taking advantage of everyone's expertise—from the top to the bottom of the organization. A team of five executives would develop an idea and then ask employees to evaluate it and suggest revisions. "Sometimes those meetings would go on for hours," recalled Robert Schuemann, a member of the executive team. "Sometimes there were even multiple meetings to discuss one item." Many policies and procedures were adopted only after the employees had an opportunity to vote on them.[13]

Functional Work Teams

A **functional work team** *includes members from a single department who have the common goal of considering issues and solving problems within their area of responsibility and expertise.* For example, at ConAgra, a diversified international food company, a functional team might consist of the purchasing manager and the purchasing agents in the department. Their goals might include minimizing costs and ensuring that beef supplies are available to stores when needed. To achieve their goals, these team members need to coordinate their activities constantly, sharing information on price changes and demand for various products. At Next Door Food Stores, the audit department formed functional teams to improve the company's relationships with customers. Radius, a Boston restaurant, also organizes the work around functional teams. There's a meat team, a fish team, a pastry team, and so on. Each team is responsible for everything related to its specialty. The fish team, for example, buys, cleans, and prepares the fish. In the true spirit of a team-based organization, the owner-chef believes that *Together Everyone Accomplishes More (TEAM)*.

Functional work teams formed for the purpose of completing their daily tasks are quite stable, enduring for as long as the organization maintains its same basic structure. In contrast, a functional work team brought together as a task force to look at a specific issue or problem disbands as soon as it completes its specific assignment.

Multidisciplinary Work Teams

A **multidisciplinary work team** *consists of employees from various functional areas and sometimes several organizational levels who collectively work on specific tasks*. In this respect, multidisciplinary teams are like task forces. However, they differ from task forces in one important way: They are the primary vehicles for accomplishing the core work of the organization. The work assigned to multidisciplinary teams at Lockheed Martin includes designing technology, meeting with customers and suppliers, and developing new products for the U.S. Navy. The use of such teams is spreading rapidly and crosses all types of organizational boundaries.[14] Multidisciplinary work teams provide several important competitive advantages if they are properly formed and managed. In particular, they often are used to speed design, production, and services processes or to enhance creativity and innovation.[15]

A product development team is a common type of multidisciplinary work team. It exists for the period of time required to bring a product to market, which could vary from a couple of months to several years. Roche, Pfizer, Merck, and other pharmaceutical companies use multidisciplinary teams to speed the process of bringing new drugs to the marketplace. In the telecommunications and electronics industries, multidisciplinary R&D teams bring together experts having a variety of knowledge and backgrounds to generate ideas for new products and services. To ensure that the products appeal to customers, the work teams may include representatives from marketing and the products' eventual end users.

Self-Managing Work Teams

A **self-managing work team** *consists of employees who work together daily to make an entire product or deliver an entire service*. The members all may be from a single functional area, but more often such teams are multidisciplinary, as illustrated in Figure 17.2. In the United States, manufacturers have been steadily moving to self-managing work teams during the past two decades.

The jet engine-building teams at GE/Durham are self-managing work teams. As mentioned earlier, each team "owns" the engines it builds—from the beginning of the assembly process to getting the engine loaded on a truck for delivery. As a team begins to build each engine, about the only instruction it receives is the date on which the engine is to be shipped from the plant. Instead of relying on a supervisor or support staff to order tools and parts, the team does it. Instead of having the human resource staff schedule vacations and overtime assignments, the team does it. Instead of having a quality control staff check the quality of the team's work, the team does it. In fact, decisions about almost anything related to building an engine are made by the team itself. The distinctive feature of a self-managing work team is the level of responsibility that the team itself has for various managerial tasks, including

- scheduling members' work and vacations,
- rotating job tasks and assignments among members,
- ordering materials,
- deciding on team leadership (which may rotate among members),

Figure 17.2 Members of a Self-Managing Work Team

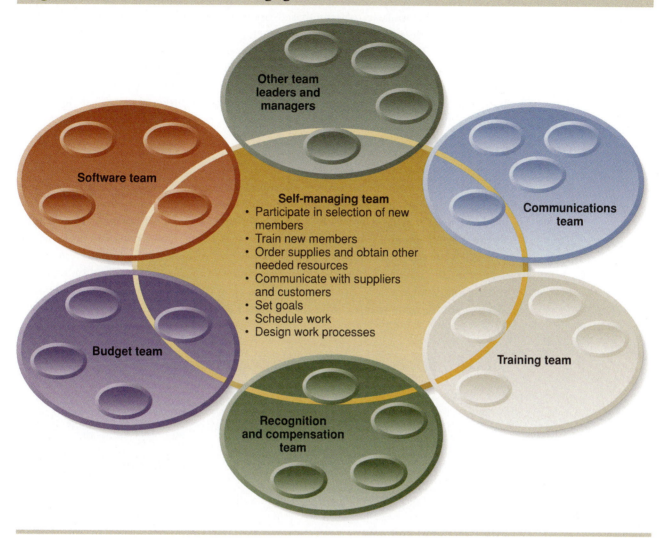

- providing feedback to team members,
- setting performance goals, and
- monitoring progress toward team goals.

To a large extent, the team as a whole—not just its leader—decides what the team needs to do and how to do it. As one employee at the GE/Durham plant explained, aviation mechanics at that plant enjoy a job that's unlike any other in the industry:

> I came from Northrop Grumman where I was working on a B-2 bomber. That plane, which used Stealth technology, was as high-tech as you can get. But someone else wrote the assembly process. Here, I write the process—at the mechanic level. There, I was on a "team," but I also had a supervisor. He had a boss. And there were other bosses above him. In two years of working there, I never saw the plant manager. Everyday, my boss would just hand me my job. I had no input at all—none. I'm much happier here.[16]

When it is truly empowered, a self-managing team does more than simply take over administrative duties. It also has a strong commitment to the organization's mission, the autonomy needed to control its own activities, belief in itself, and a chance to see directly the impact of its efforts.[17]

A FRAMEWORK FOR TEAM EFFECTIVENESS

3. State the meaning and determinants of team effectiveness.

The increasing popularity of team-based organizational designs reflects the view that teams can achieve goals that could not be achieved by the same number of individuals working alone. But as many organizations are discovering, the positive payoff from teams isn't automatic. Although teams offer great potential, that potential isn't always realized. Even when teams do fulfill their potential, team members and their organizations may experience unanticipated negative side effects, such as lingering political fights and turnover.

Effectiveness Criteria

The first step in fostering team effectiveness involves stating what effectiveness means. Figure 17.3[18] shows several effectiveness criteria for evaluating work teams. **Effectiveness criteria** *measure the outcomes achieved by individual members and the team as a whole.* A particular work team may be effective in some respects and ineffective in others. For example, a team may take longer than expected to make a decision. Thus, on speed and cost criteria, the team may seem ineffective. But the team's decision may be highly creative and make the team's primary customer feel very satisfied with the output. Thus, on creativity and customer satisfaction, the team would be viewed as effective. Similarly, individual members of the team may feel that their own work is slowed by having to get agreement

Figure 17.3   Effectiveness Criteria for Work Teams

Team Effectiveness

Task completion	Team development	Stakeholder satisfaction
Accuracy	Team cohesiveness	Customer satisfaction with team's procedures and outputs
Speed	Team flexibility	Team satisfaction with team's procedures and outputs
Creativity	Team preparedness for new tasks	Satisfaction of other teams with the team's procedures and outputs
Cost		

Individual Effectiveness

Task performance	Relationships with others	Personal development
Speed	Increased understanding of other perspectives	Develop competencies (teamwork, communication, strategic action, global awareness, planning and administration, and self-awareness)
Accuracy	Build others' trust in you	Develop network of colleagues within and outside the organization
Creativity	New friendships	Gain technical knowledge and skills
Efficiency		

from other team members before they proceed. But through discussion, individuals develop a better understanding of other perspectives and gain new technical knowledge and skills. Whether the work team is viewed as effective overall depends on the relative importance of the various effectiveness criteria applied.

Effectiveness Determinants

The second step in achieving team effectiveness involves knowing about the various factors that determine how well the team is doing with respect to the effectiveness criteria. Figure 17.4 illustrates several factors that work in combination to determine work team effectiveness. Effectiveness is determined by three main sets of influences: the external context in which the team operates, team design, and internal team processes. When teams are ineffective, managers must be able to diagnose and correct the causes of the teams' problems and poor team performance.[19]

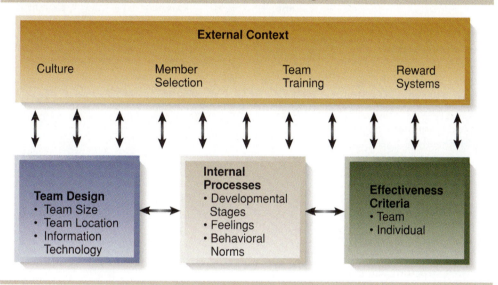

Figure 17.4   A Model of Work Team Functioning

Teamwork always presents challenges. Managers who understand its nature and challenges are in the best position to take advantage of teamwork and anticipate some of the problems that often crop up when teams are used. Internal problems—such as too much conflict—may be the most immediate cause of performance problems. When a team experiences internal problems, however, the root cause of those problems may lie elsewhere. The team members may be doing the best they can but under adverse circumstances. Their internal problems may be due to the design of the team or to aspects of the external context.

INTERNAL TEAM PROCESSES

Internal team processes *include the development of the work team over time, personal feelings, and behavioral norms.* In effective work teams, these processes support cooperation among team members and coordination of their work. When a team leader and individual team members learn how to manage the team's internal processes, they improve the likelihood of the team's being effective.[20]

A tool for assessing a work team's internal processes is presented in the following Teamwork Competency feature. Before continuing, take a few minutes to complete the Team Assessment Survey for a team to which you belong. If you were using this survey in

4. Describe the internal team processes that can affect team performance.

an organization, you would want to ask all members of the team you described to complete the survey.[21]

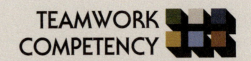

TEAMWORK COMPENTENCY

Team Assessment Survey

Instructions
This survey can be used to help a team assess its internal processes. It should be completed individually by each team member, who should indicate the extent to which he or she thinks the team exhibits the following characteristics and behaviors.

Questions	To a Very Small Extent		To Some Extent		To a Very Large Extent
1. Team members understand the range of backgrounds, skills, preferences, and perspectives in the team.	1	2	3	4	5
2. Team member differences and similarities have been effectively focused on achieving team goals.	1	2	3	4	5
3. The team cannot integrate diverse viewpoints.	5	4	3	2	1
4. Members view themselves as a team, not as a collection of individuals with their own particular jobs to do (e.g., they work interdependently, have joint accountability, and are committed to joint goals).	1	2	3	4	5
5. Team members have articulated a clear set of goals.	1	2	3	4	5
6. The team's goals are not motivating to members.	5	4	3	2	1
7. Team members agree on what goals and objectives are important.	1	2	3	4	5
8. The team has an effective work structure. It understands what work needs to be done, when work needs to be completed, and who is responsible for what.	1	2	3	4	5
9. It is not clear what each person in the team is supposed to do.	5	4	3	2	1
10. Team members have devised effective timetables and deadlines.	1	2	3	4	5
11. Team members have a clear set of norms that cover most aspects of how to function.	1	2	3	4	5
12. Team members take arguments personally and get angry easily.	5	4	3	2	1
13. Every team member does his or her fair share of the work.	1	2	3	4	5
14. A few members do most of the work.	5	4	3	2	1
15. A few people shirk responsibility or hold the team back.	5	4	3	2	1
16. Team members are imaginative in thinking about new or better ways to perform team tasks.	1	2	3	4	5
17. All team members participate in decision making.	1	2	3	4	5
18. Team members have the resources, information, and support they need from people outside team boundaries.	1	2	3	4	5

Questions	To a Very Small Extent		To Some Extent		To a Very Large Extent
19. Team meetings are well organized.	1	2	3	4	5
20. Team meetings are not productive.	5	4	3	2	1
21. Coordination among members is a problem. People seem not to know what to do and when to do it for smooth team functioning.	5	4	3	2	1
22. Team members express their feelings freely in the team.	1	2	3	4	5
23. Team members support each other.	1	2	3	4	5
24. Team members are not effective at decision making.	5	4	3	2	1

Scoring and Interpretation

To assess the overall quality of the team's internal processes, simply add all of the numbers you circled and divide by 24 (the total number of items in the survey). This is your effectiveness score. A score of 4 or higher indicates that you judge the team's internal processes as generally quite positive. A score less than 4 but greater than 2.5 indicates that you feel the team is functioning in a satisfactory manner overall but that several areas need improvement. A score of 2.5 or lower indicates that you believe the team's internal functioning is quite poor.

The team leader should compute the team's average score for each question. For example, suppose that a team had four members and that they gave these responses to question 1: The first person circled 3, the second person circled 4, the third person circled 5, and the fourth person circled 4. Then the team's average for question 1 is $(3 + 4 + 5 + 4)/4 = 4$.

After computing the average score for each question, the team leader should provide feedback to the team. Effective feedback involves acknowledging the things that the team seems to be doing well (e.g., questions with an average of 4 or higher), and identifying the things that need to be improved immedi-ately (e.g., questions with an average of 2.5 or lower).

After setting priorities for the areas needing improvement, the team leader and team members should agree on a schedule for making those improvements. At the end of that time, the leader should again ask team members to respond to the Team Assessment Survey. When the reassessment results have been calculated, team members should determine whether satisfactory progress has been made in addressing the issues previously identified. If they find that it hasn't, they should continue to make adjustments and reassessments, as needed.

People with little experience working in teams often expect a team to be fully functioning immediately, but that rarely happens. Observations of newly formed work teams reveal that coordination and integration tend to develop over a period of time. Team members usually need to spend some time together before the team can jell—knowing this fact of team life reduces needless frustration. The establishment of trust and clear behavioral norms usually precede effective task completion.[22]

Developmental Stages

A team's internal processes usually change over time. Like individuals, teams develop their skills the more they use them. Team functioning generally improves after the team has been together awhile. The developmental stages that teams commonly go through are shown in Figure 17.5. The vertical axis indicates that work teams develop along a *continuum of maturity*, which ranges from low, or immature (e.g., inefficient and ineffective), to high, or mature (e.g., efficient and effective). The horizontal axis represents a *continuum of time together*, which ranges from start (e.g., the first team encounter) to end (e.g., the point at which the team adjourns).[23] In general, the speed of team development seems to reflect the team's deadlines. Work teams tend to develop slowly at first. Then, as deadlines approach, team members feel more pressure to perform and often

Figure 17.5   The Development of Work Teams

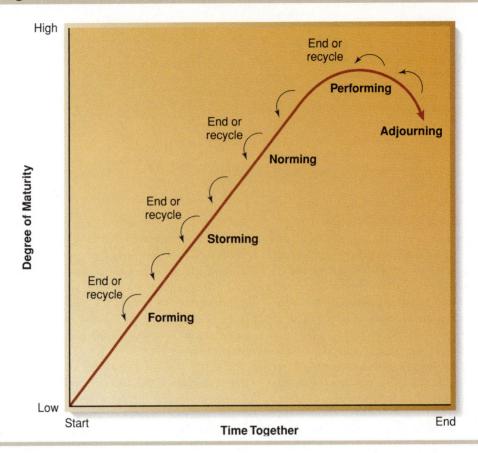

respond by resolving or setting aside personal differences in order to complete the task.[24]

No particular period of time is needed for a team to progress from one stage to the next. For example, a work team whose members have effective interpersonal skills and high initial commitment to the team's goals could move rapidly to the performing stage. In contrast, a committee that is skeptical about whether its work is really valued by the organization and which also experiences early conflict among its members may never make much progress and even disband without producing a recommendation or report.

A work team may adjourn in a variety of ways. It may simply stop meeting, or it may meet rarely and engage only in routine tasks. Its membership may change (e.g., adding, losing, or changing members), weakening its purpose or commitment. It may be terminated officially by the manager who created it.

Figure 17.5 also shows the possibility of a team ending at each stage or recycling to a previous stage. For example, a mature work team could lose the majority of its members in a short period of time due to promotion, retirement, and/or rotation of membership. With so many new members, the team may recycle to an earlier stage of development. The stages identified represent general tendencies, and teams may develop by going through repeated cycles rather than linearly, as shown. Also, each stage simply reveals the *primary* issues facing team members. Behaviors from other stages may occur at times within each stage.

Forming.   During the **forming stage**, *a work team focuses on orientation to its goals and procedures.* The amount of information available and the manner in which it is presented are crucial to work team development. Most members may be anxious about what the team is supposed to do. In newly formed teams, relationships often are guarded, cautious, and noncommittal. Understanding leadership roles and getting acquainted with other team members facilitate development.

Storming. The **storming stage** *begins when competitive or strained behaviors emerge.* Initially, the storming process may involve resistance and impatience with the lack of progress. A few dominant members may begin to force an agenda without regard for the needs of other team members. Team members may challenge the leader, or they may isolate themselves from team discussion. If conflict spreads, frustration, anger, and defensive behavior (especially the self-serving "look out for yourself" kind) may appear. Team mem-

bers might think: Our problem is that we don't want to resolve our conflicts; we thrive on them, and though it may be counterproductive, conflict seems to be a way of life for now.

If conflict is suppressed and not permitted to occur, resentment and bitterness may result, which in turn can lead to apathy or abandonment. Although conflict resolution often is the goal of work teams during the storming stage, conflict management is generally achieved instead. In fact, conflict management is a more appropriate goal because maintaining conflict at a manageable level is a desirable way to encourage a work team's growth and development.[25]

Norming. In the **norming stage**, *team members become increasingly positive about the team as a whole, the other members as individuals, and what the team is doing.* At the beginning of the norming stage, the dominant view might be: We are in this together, like it or not, so let's make the most of it. Thus the team members may begin to develop a sense of belonging and commitment. Members increasingly are committed to their team. Problems are resolved through cooperation, open communication, and the acceptance of mutual influence. The rules of behavior that are widely shared and enforced by team members develop. If the work team gets to the end of this stage, most members may like their involvement a great deal.

Sometimes, however, the work team focuses too much on "we-ness," harmony, and conformity. When that happens, team members may avoid task-related conflicts that need to be resolved to achieve optimal performance. That in turn may cause the quality and/or quantity of performance to slip.

Performing. By the **performing stage**, *members usually have come to trust and accept each other and are focused on accomplishing their goals.* As deadlines and due dates approach, teams often shift into a mode of productive performance.[26] To accomplish tasks, diversity of viewpoints (rather than we-ness) is supported and encouraged. Members are willing to risk presenting "wild" ideas without fear of being put down by the team. The processes of listening carefully and giving accurate feedback to others focus team members on the team's tasks and reinforce a sense of clear and shared goals. Leadership within the team is flexible and may shift among members in terms of who is most capable of solving a particular problem. The team accepts the reality of differences and disagreements and works on them cooperatively and enthusiastically. The team tries to reach consensus on important issues and to avoid internal politics. The following characteristics lead to high levels of team performance:

■ Members direct their energies toward the twin goals of getting things done (task behaviors) and building constructive interpersonal ties and processes (relationship behaviors).

■ Members use procedures for making decisions, including how to share leadership.

- Members trust each other and are open among themselves.
- Members receive help from and give help to one another.
- Members are free to be themselves while feeling a sense of belonging with others.
- Members accept and deal with conflicts.
- Members diagnose and improve their own functioning.[27]

The degree to which one or more of these characteristics is absent determines the extent to which teams are likely to be ineffective.

Adjourning. The **adjourning stage** *involves terminating task behaviors and disengaging from relationships.* This stage isn't always planned and may be rather abrupt. However, a planned team conclusion often involves recognition for participation and achievement as well as an opportunity for members to say personal good-byes. Adjournment of a work team charged with a particular task should be set for a specific time and have a recognizable ending point. However, many work teams (e.g., the executive committee of an organization's board of directors) are ongoing. As members turn over, some recycling through earlier stages rather than adjournment may occur. Staggered terms of appointment can minimize the amount of recycling required.

Feelings

Throughout the stages of a work team's development, team members experience a variety of psychological reactions, emotions, or feelings. As we use the term here, **feelings** *refers to the emotional climate of a group.* The four feelings most likely to influence work team effectiveness and productivity are trust, openness, freedom, and interdependence. The more these feelings are present, the more likely the work team will be effective and the members will be satisfied.[28] These feelings probably are present in a formal or informal group to which you belong if you *agree* with the following statements:

- *Trust:* Members have confidence in each other.
- *Openness:* Members are really interested in what others have to say.
- *Freedom:* Members do what they do out of a sense of responsibility to the group, not because of pressure from others.
- *Interdependence:* Members coordinate and work together to achieve common goals.

The greater the degree to which the four feelings are present, the greater the level of group cohesiveness.

Cohesiveness *is the strength of members' desires to remain on the team and their commitment to it.* It is a reflection of the members' feelings toward one another and the team as a whole.

Team members may feel strongly committed to the team, even if they don't feel strongly committed to the organization.[29] Cohesiveness can't be dictated by managers, team leaders, or others. A cohesive team or group can work effectively for or against organizational goals. For example, a cohesive team or group with negative feelings toward the organization may promote performance standards that limit productivity and pressure individual members to conform to them. In contrast, a cohesive team or group with positive feelings toward the organization may support and reinforce high quality and increased productivity.

As described in the Strategic Action Competency feature, Ken Neishi, vice president of operations at Michael Foods, understood that managing feelings within teams can be essential to business success. Michael Foods is a company that has grown through acquisitions. As it acquires companies, it seeks to preserve their entrepreneurial nature by allowing them to remain fairly autonomous after being acquired. This was the strategy followed when Michael Foods made its biggest acquisition ever—Papetti's Hygrade Egg Products, located in New Jersey.[30]

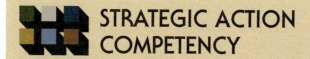
Michael Foods

When Michael Foods acquired Papetti's Hygrade Egg Products of New Jersey, it acquired a major competitor of its own Waldbaum division. Although Papetti's and Waldbaum were in the same industry, their organizational cultures were vastly different. Papetti's was a family-run business, and the owners did not share much information with employees. Waldbaum's operated as a division of a big corporation that valued open communication. For the first three years after the acquisition, Michael Foods allowed the Papetti group to preserve their culture. When Arthur Papetti, the president and patriarch retired in 2000, executives at Michael Foods decided that Papetti's employees should be integrated into the larger corporation and become real members of the company team. Up until then, there was little communication between Waldbaum's and Papetti's. Now it was time to bring together the oper-

ations of the two divisions. This task fell to Ken Neishi, vice president of operations.

Neishi's goal was to create a new business that incorporated the best aspects of each division. To reach his goal, he knew that members of the two divisions had to build a relationship and learn to trust each other. He started the process by visiting Papetti's plant and getting to know the top-level managers. These visits were followed with a team-building session, held at a neutral location. Neishi and a member of the Papetti family co-led the session. When the session began, feelings of suspicion and skepticism filled the room. According to Neishi, "It was like a union negotiation, with eight guys on one side of the table and eight guys on the other staring each other down." The goals for these 16 managers were to identify the best practices in each division and develop a plan to build a new business team. The process was painful at first, but

gradually the leaders helped the group accept the norms of allowing everyone to talk and showing respect for everyone's ideas. During this session, cross-functional teams that included members from both divisions were created. Another outcome of this session was that the participants set a goal of saving $15 million in operating costs—a goal they soon achieved.

Three years after that first session, managers of the consolidated egg products division continue to hold team-building meetings. Now it is impossible to tell who came from Papetti's and who came from Waldbaum's. Brad Cook, an executive vice president, comments: "It was difficult. There was a lot of negativity between the two divisions. Each thought it was better than the other. [But] by sharing respect for our differences, a new culture has arisen. Together we are pursing a vision of the future."

Behavioral Norms

How people feel is an important aspect of teamwork. How people actually behave may be even more important. **Behavioral norms** *are the rules of behavior that are widely shared and enforced by members of a work team.* Their main function is to regulate and standardize the behaviors viewed as important by team members.

Norms may specify how much work to do, how customers should be treated, the importance of high quality, what members should wear, what kinds of jokes are acceptable, how members should feel about the organization, how they should deal with their managers, and so on. Two important types of norms are those governing performance and those governing how team members deal with conflict.

Performance Norms. A performance norm exists when three criteria have been met.[31] First, there is a standard of appropriate behavior for team members. Second, members must generally agree on the standard. If most members have widely varying opinions about how much work is enough, for example, the team doesn't have a productivity norm. Third, the members must be aware that the team supports the particular standard through a system of rewards and punishments. Norms such as these reduce the chances of one team member being a free rider. A **free rider** *is a team member who isn't contributing fully to team performance but still shares in team rewards.*

Norms for Managing Conflicts. Norms concerning how to handle conflicts within the team are important for teams engaged in a lot of problem solving and decision making. Social pressures to maintain friendships and avoid disagreements can lead to work team members agreeing to a decision based more on personal feelings than on facts and analysis. When team norms stifle conflict, groupthink can develop. **Groupthink** *is an agreement-at-any-cost mentality that results in ineffective work team decision making and may lead to poor solutions.* The fundamental problem underlying groupthink is pressure on members to concede and accept what other members think. The likelihood of groupthink increases when

- peer pressure to conform is great,
- a highly directive leader presses for a particular interpretation of the problem and course of action,
- the need to process a complex and unstructured issue under crisis conditions exists, and
- the group is isolated.[32]

Instead of stifling conflict, a better approach to handling disagreements is to engage in productive controversy. **Productive controversy** *occurs when team members value different points of view and seek to draw them out to facilitate creative problem solving.* To ensure constructive controversy, work team members must establish ground rules to keep them focused on issues rather than people and defer decisions until various issues and ideas are explored. They should frame decisions as collaborations aimed at achieving the best possible results and follow procedures that equalize sharing of power and responsibility. By following these norms, team members can focus on their common goal and avoid becoming embroiled in battles of egos.

A study of executive teams revealed that norms concerning conflict differed greatly from one team to the next. About half the teams studied reported that the team members argued most of the time. In these teams, everyone felt free to voice opinions and share ideas. One executive described his team's pattern for handling conflict this way: "We scream a lot, then laugh, and then resolve the issues." In several other teams, however, there was little open conflict—in fact, some teams actually had too little conflict.[33]

Managers Help Establish Norms. Effective managers understand that they can shape the norms that develop within work teams. During the team-building session at Michael Foods, the managers helped the team establish norms that ensured everyone's ideas would be listened to and considered respectfully. At AeroMexico, CEO Barahona and his top management team wrote their norms on paper. They came up with a list of 10 things they agreed were important. Barahona gave the list to everyone and had each of them sign it. When one of the team members violated a norm, Barahona pulled out his list and said, "What you did violated Norm 3 right here." After a few instances like this, he never had to do it again.[34]

Owner and Chef Michael Schlow of Radius uses frequent staff meetings to develop and sustain the norms that account for some of his restaurant's popularity with diners. Recall that employees at Radius work in functional teams. With this design, effective teamwork among staff members is essential. Each week, employees attend a series of meetings that reinforce many of the norms required for the teams to perform effectively. These meetings usually involve people from several different functional teams. A weekly meeting of chefs, waiters, and food runners focuses on how to describe and present each course of the meal. Schlow uses daily meetings of all kitchen staff to remind his employees that they should always be thinking about ways to use as much of each ingredient as possible to cut down on waste. A nightly meeting of service staff is used to reinforce the importance of recognizing repeat customers. Schlow also thinks that continual learning is important to his restaurant's success. One way that he supports the norm of learning is by assigning one person each day the task of researching a bit of information about food and presenting what she or he learned to the others of the restaurant's staff. And Schlow gives them occasional tests to see how much they've learned! Do Schlow's efforts make a difference? According to a recent graduate of the Culinary Institute of America, the norms at Radius are immediately noticeable. "The first time I walked into Radius, the whole atmosphere was beautiful," he said. "You could tell people really believed in what they were doing. I knew this place was for me."[35]

DIAGNOSING THE CAUSES OF POOR TEAM PERFORMANCE

When teams fail to perform as well as they are supposed to, there may be many reasons. Internal team processes are the first thing that people usually think about as the cause of poor performance. Effective teams and their leaders consider whether negative internal team processes are responsible for poor performance, but they don't stop there.[36] Teams don't exist in a vacuum, and their internal processes don't unfold in isolation. The external forces acting on a team may also be the cause of team performance problems. A team's **external system** *comprises outside conditions and influences that exist before and after the team is formed.* Important features of the external system to consider include team design, culture, team member selection, team training, and the reward system.[37]

5. Explain how to diagnose and remove barriers to poor team performance.

Team Design

The design choices involved in creating a work team are numerous. When teams are designed well, they are more effective in managing their work, their members are more satisfied, and they perform better.[38] Here we focus on three design choices: team size, team location, and information technology.

Team Size. As the number of team members increases, changes occur in the team's internal decision-making processes. A good rule of thumb to remember is that understaffed teams tend to outperform overstaffed teams.[39] In other words, it is better to have a team with fewer people than you think might be needed, rather than adding an extra member to help get the work done. Members of teams with more than a dozen members generally have difficulty communicating with each other. Increasing team size also causes the following effects:

- Demands on leader time and attention are greater. The leader becomes more psychologically distant from the other team members. This problem is most serious in self-managing work teams, where more than one person can take on leader roles.
- The team's tolerance of direction from the leader is greater, and the team's decision making becomes more centralized.
- The team atmosphere is less friendly, the communications are less personal, more cliques form within the team, and, in general, team members are less satisfied.
- The team's rules and procedures become more formalized.
- The likelihood of some members being free riders increases.[40]

For innovative decision making, the ideal work team size is probably between five and nine members.[41] If a work team has more than nine members, separate cliques might form. If larger teams are required for some reason, the use of subteams may be a solution to the problem of size. The purpose of subteams is to encourage all team members to share ideas when analyzing problems, information, and alternative solutions. The full team can then meet to discuss subteam assessments and recommendations. In some instances, different subteams work on the same set of problems and then share and discuss their conclusions with the entire team. The leader of a large work team needs to be aware of the possibility that subteams, or cliques, may form on their own, each with its own leader and agenda. Although more resources are available to large teams, these resources can create a backlash that hurts overall team effectiveness if each unofficial sub-team or clique lobbies strongly for its own position.

Team Location. **Team proximity** *refers to the location of a team's members.* Two aspects of team location are (1) proximity to other work teams and members of the organization and (2) team members' proximity to each other.

The ideal proximity among teams depends on the work being done. When many teams are working together on a single project, close coordination among the teams is needed. At Microsoft, teams benefit from being near others in the organization. Members of different teams can meet at the snack shop or water cooler to fill each other in on developments within their respective teams. Problem solving readily occurs as the need arises. For some work teams, however, performance is improved when the team is removed from the daily activities of the organization. Recall the discussion of corporate intrapreneurship in Chapter 5. Innovation and creativity are essential to successful intrapreneurship, but the bureaucracy and political intrigue often found in large corporations can stifle them. Consequently, intrapreneurial teams at 3M and Apple frequently set up skunkworks operations in a remote location—such as an old warehouse or someone's garage. Isolated from outside distractions, the intrapreneurs are able to focus on the future without having to battle the status quo.

The location of team members may depend on where the talent needed for a task happens to be. A **virtual work team** *meets and does its tasks without everyone being physically present in the same place or even at the same time.* In virtual teams, team members usually work in widely scattered geographic locations. IBM began to use virtual teams in the 1970s. Today, about one out of three IBM employees participates as a member of at least one virtual team. Virtual work teams can be functional, problem solving, multidisciplinary, or self-managing. As described in Chapter 11, virtual teams often are essential to the functioning of network organizations.

> **The Competent Manager**
>
> *"As we attract, retain, and develop the best talent, we have to assess employees on a continuing basis for flexibility and adaptability to work in a virtual environment—that is the twenty-first century workplace."*
>
> Joy Gaetano
> Senior Vice President
> USFilter, Palm Desert, California

Information Technology. Where team members are located and the information technologies they use are intertwined. As members become more spread apart geographically, they rely more heavily on electronic communications instead of face-to-face communications. Technologies such as the Internet, voice mail, and videoconferencing allow the members of virtual work teams to work together even though they may be separated by physical and cultural boundaries. Sabre, the company that invented electronic commerce for the travel industry, switched from functional teams to cross-functional virtual teams in 1999. Their goals were to become more customer focused and to improve customer service. As described in the Global Awareness Competency feature, Sabre discovered that global virtual teams encounter some unique challenges and must find solutions that fit their special virtual environment.[42] Sabre processes more than 400 million travel bookings annually—that's 40 percent of the world's travel reservations.

As Sabre learned, many of the principles of effective teamwork that apply to face-to-face team activities also apply to virtual work teams. However, other principles for designing and managing virtual work teams address their special nature.[43] As organizations expand into global consumer and labor markets, managing virtual work teams that cross international borders will be an increasingly important managerial responsibility. The challenges associated with managing virtual teams with members from many different cultures and living in many different time zones are even greater than those faced by Sabre in North America. Some of the current best practices for managing domestic and global virtual work teams are shown in Table 17.1[44] on page 500.

©Micael Newman/PhotoEdit Inc.

Sabre's Virtual Teams

You may have never heard of Sabre, but if you ever booked a reservation through Travelocity.com, which Sabre owns, you've done business with them. More than 60,000 travel agents in 114 countries also use the company's services. Sabre's North American division relies heavily on multidisciplinary virtual teams, each with about eight members located all over the continent. Account executives sell the reservation system, field service technicians install it, training representatives teach customers how to use it, and so on. Members of the team occasionally work alongside each other at a location, but most of the time they work in isolation. A whole team meets face to face only about once per year. To coordinate their activities, teams use e-mail, telephones, videoconferencing, and Web-based conferencing.

Interviews with members of Sabre's global virtual teams revealed that they experienced several special challenges. These challenges and Sabre's solutions to them are described below.

Challenges

Building Trust: Team members are often strangers with few opportunities for personal bonding.

Creating Synergy: Because team members do not see each other often, it's difficult to clarify roles and spot problems before they become serious.

Feeling Isolated: In face-to-face teams, people share personal stories and family pictures, take breaks together, celebrate birthdays, and so on. When such social activities don't occur, people feel detached and isolated.

Balancing Technical Skills and Communication Competencies: At first, Sabre believed technical skills were almost all that mattered. They soon realized that communication competencies were much more important than they had thought.

Performance Management: Sabre discovered that traditional methods of measuring and rewarding performance didn't work when managers seldom saw the people they were managing.

Solutions

Establish Norms for Reliable Performance: Team members developed trust when they responded rapidly to each other's communications and agreed to norms for how to communicate.

Team Building and Team Training: Before a team's launch, members receive classroom training to help them develop a team mission and values statement, set objectives, clarify roles, and build relationships. They also complete 15 CD-ROM training modules.

Member Selection: Sabre uses interviews to screen out people who may not enjoy virtual teamwork, provides realist previews, and allows candidates to opt out of isolating positions if they become dissatisfied.

Member Selection: Sabre assesses communication and teamwork competencies before hiring virtual team members. Team members and managers use teleconferencing to conduct panel interviews and assess a candidate's fit with the team.

Use Multiple Performance Measures: Sabre invested in developing new measures of team effectiveness, including customer satisfaction ratings, electronic monitoring of team discussions, and 360-degree performance assessments.

Culture

The societal and organizational cultures within which work teams operate are important aspects of the external context.[45] Differences in the language people use to describe work teams and differences in norms for team behavior often reflect differences in national culture. In some cultures, such as China, Malaysia, and Thailand, societal values

Table 17.1 Guidelines for Managing Virtual Teams

Managers of virtual teams can improve the effectiveness of the team as a whole and individual team members by following these guidelines:

- *Use a variety of communication technologies.* Software designed especially for electronic meetings can be a good way to supplement video or telephone conference calls. Software that facilitates language translations can make written communication easier for global team members.
- *Pay attention to the quality of the communication transmissions.* Low-quality voice transmissions are frustrating and demotivating for team members, especially when they are listening to a person with a strong accent. Video images should be clear and large enough to reveal subtle expressions and body language.
- *Encourage the team members to discuss cultural differences.* These differences usually become apparent quickly when people meet face to face. They may be less noticeable during electronic meetings, but they are no less important.
- *Be sure that someone is responsible for facilitating the communication process.* A good facilitator doesn't allow anyone to be a passive observer. A good facilitator may also occasionally contact participants individually to be sure they feel that their opinions are being heard.
- *Encourage team members to interact one on one, without feeling obligated to copy every e-mail message to the entire team.* This approach can help prevent misunderstandings from needlessly escalating into crises.
- *Train team members to match their choice of technology to the task.* Fax, e-mail, and a company's intranet work well for disseminating information. Conference calls and videoconferencing are more appropriate for holding important discussions and making major decisions.

For virtual teams that will be working together for several months or years, a few additional principles should be followed, within time and budget constraints:

- To help the team members develop trust more quickly, hold an initial face-to-face meeting. Discuss the team's purpose and clarify the roles and responsibilities of each team member.
- Whenever possible, individual team members should visit others, even if the entire team can't be assembled.
- Schedule periodic face-to-face meetings to refresh connections and minimize "out-of-site, out-of-mind" attitudes.

---

support striving for harmony and cohesiveness and avoiding open conflict. In the more individualistic cultures of the United States and Canada, people feel more comfortable when they are able to express their opinions and have their views taken seriously by other team members. At the same time, U.S. and Canadian cultures value friendly relationships among coworkers, so too much conflict feels uncomfortable. In an international work team, the natural tendency of team members is to behave according to the norms of their countries. When different cultures are present, misunderstandings are the likely result if team members are not familiar with the cultures represented on the team.[46]

Regardless of national cultures, work teams can function well if they are supported by the organization's culture. Organizations that support participation by lower level employees increase the likelihood that work teams will embrace organizational goals and authority relations, rather than attempt to undermine them. When individualistic employees are empowered through self-managing work teams, they gain more control and influence over their work. Because having control is important in individualistic cultures, employees working in self-managing teams often report being very satisfied with their work.

Team Member Selection

The characteristics needed in an employee who works in relative isolation are different from those needed in an employee who must work in a team environment. In work teams, the personality trait of *agreeableness* and *conscientiousness* seem to be especially important.[47] People with agreeable personalities seek to find areas of common understanding with the members of the team. When areas of agreement are known, team members may also be able accept their differences more easily. People who are conscientious tend to stay focused on the task and seem to be good at organizing and coordinating activities.

Of our six managerial competencies, communication and teamwork are essential for working in *all* types of teams. If the team is self-managed and everyone shares all aspects of a task, more technical skills often are needed by each team member. The planning and administration competency also is extremely important for members of self-managing teams. When teams are used to coordinate the activities of organizational units spread throughout the world, the global awareness competency is especially important.[48]

Personality traits are difficult to change, and both technical skills and managerial competencies develop slowly over time. For these reasons, team-based organizations often use intensive and sophisticated selection procedures when hiring new employees. The GE/Durham jet engine plant is a good example. When the plant was started, management decided that all job candidates would have to be FAA-certified mechanics. FAA certification requires two years of training and is something that no other GE plant requires of all job candidates. First-rate mechanical skills are just one of the 11 criteria that job applicants must meet to get a job. Others include helping skills, teamwork, communication, coaching, and flexibility. As one current employee remembers, the interview process—lasting eight hours—was especially grueling: "That was one heck of an experience. I talked to five different people. I participated in three group activities with job candidates. I even had to do a presentation: I had fifteen minutes to prepare a five-minute presentation." Through these activities, GE assessed the teamwork and communication competencies that these mechanics would have to rely on day in and day out in doing their new jobs.

The value of paying attention to teamwork competencies appears to hold for many types of teams. When Roche redesigned its research activities around multidisciplinary teams, they realized they would also need a different type of scientist to work on those teams. Paying attention to teamwork competencies pays off despite the level of technical skill involved in the work. A study of cardiac surgery teams found that the process used to select members of the team predicted the team's subsequent performance. When team members participated more in the selection of new members, and when they took both teamwork competency and technical skills into account, cardiac surgery teams were more effective.[49]

Team Training

Even in organizations that do a good job of selecting employees who are capable of working well in teams, additional team training can be beneficial. Perhaps more than any other organization, NASA understands that training comes before effective teamwork. Before astronauts are sent into space to live in a community that relies heavily on teamwork for survival, NASA has them working together every day for a year or two in order to become a team. They share office space, spend countless hours together in flight simulators, and rehearse everything from stowing their flight suits to troubleshooting malfunctions. Formal training in procedures is part of the experience, but it isn't everything. NASA realizes that teamwork training also involves helping teammates get to know each other and develop confidence in each other.

Most organizations can't afford to give team members a year or two of training before teams begin working to achieve their goals. They look for quicker ways to achieve the same goals that NASA has for its training program. For example, at Mabe, an appliance manufacturer with plants located throughout Latin America, employees receive two to three weeks of training each year. To support teamwork, the training teaches employees about setting goals, learning how to measure results, and deciding what needs to be measured.[50] Regardless of how many hours of team training organizations require, their goals usually are the same—to train team members to perform a variety of managerial and leadership activities and to enhance team cohesiveness. Organizations that invest resources to train teams can increase both team and organizational effectiveness.[51]

Management and Leadership Training. Work teams of all types are being empowered to perform tasks that previously weren't employees' responsibility. Figure 17.6 shows a wide range of tasks that may be assigned to a work team. The vertical axis indicates the degree to which the team is self-managing. The greater the degree of self-management, the more the team has authority, responsibility, and general decision-making discretion for tasks. The horizontal axis indicates the amount and range of competencies required

Figure 17.6   Examples of Tasks Performed in Self-Managing Work Teams

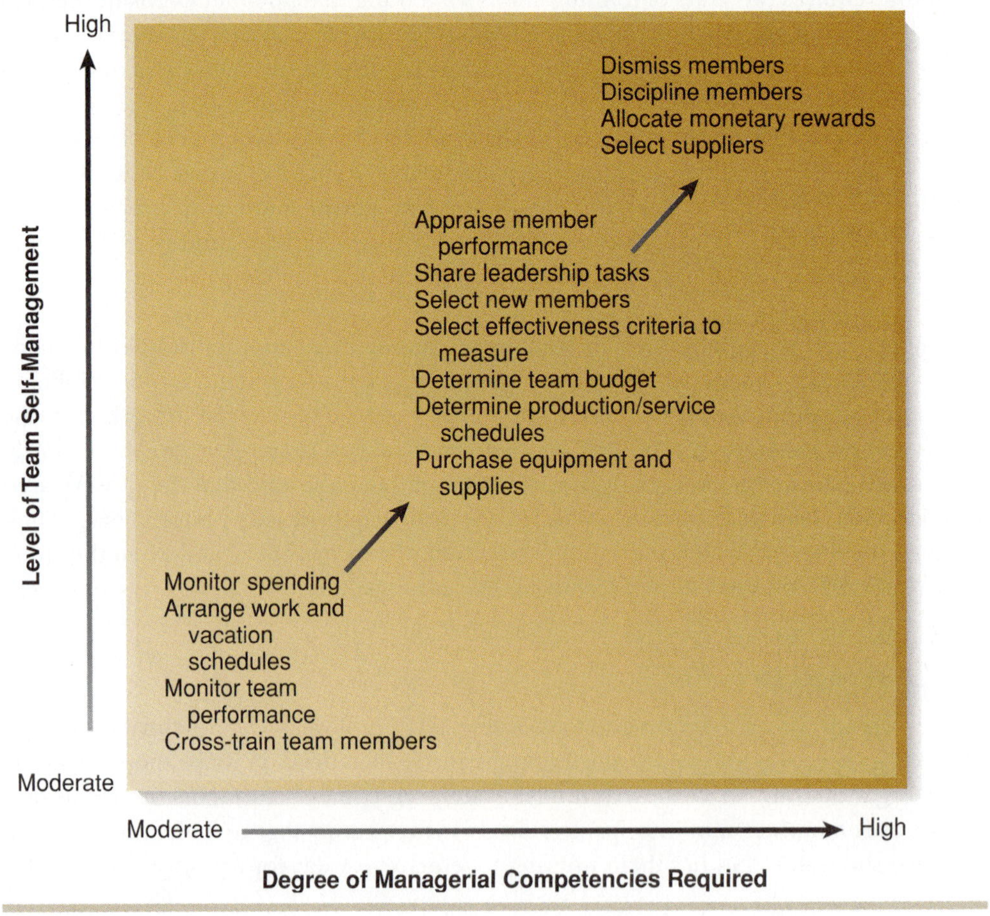

Level of Team Self-Management

High

Dismiss members
Discipline members
Allocate monetary rewards
Select suppliers

Appraise member
   performance
Share leadership tasks
Select new members
Select effectiveness criteria to
   measure
Determine team budget
Determine production/service
   schedules
Purchase equipment and
   supplies

Monitor spending
Arrange work and
   vacation
   schedules
Monitor team
   performance
Cross-train team members

Moderate

Moderate ⟶ High

Degree of Managerial Competencies Required

of team members for handling an increasing number and complexity of tasks. The more self-managing a team is, the more important it is for team members to receive training that will enhance their management competencies. The more confident team members feel about the team's ability to perform, the more likely it is that the team actually will perform well.[52]

We've already described leadership development in some detail in Chapter 15. That discussion applies particularly to situations where there is one designated leader. Often, however, the task of leadership is shared among all members of the team. In such circumstances, all can benefit from a discussion of the key leadership responsibilities that they'll be sharing, which include the following:

■ *Managing meetings.* People who resist teamwork often point to time wasted in meetings as a big source of dissatisfaction. True, teams do need to meet, one way or another, but team meetings should never be a waste of time. Training team members to run meetings properly can make meetings more efficient. Team members can then share the key leadership role (e.g., scheduling a meeting, developing an agenda, recording ideas and decisions, and communicating with others outside the team), rotating through these responsibilities during the life of the team.

■ *Supporting disagreement.* A skillful team leader supports disagreement that stimulates innovative solutions while minimizing the risk of bad feelings. Disagreement can be productive if members are open to differences within the team and if they separate idea generation from idea evaluation. Team members also need to understand that the absence of disagreement on a work team may be as destructive as too much disagreement to the team's proper functioning. The use of decision-making aids, such as the brainstorming, the nominal group technique, devil's advocacy, and dialectical inquiry, creates productive controversy and can result in better quality decisions that team members can fully accept.[53]

■ *Committing to a team decision.* Making a final decision when team members disagree can be relatively easy if final decisions ultimately rest with a team leader. Reaching a final decision that everyone will endorse is more difficult when there is no designated leader. For teams that make most decisions by reaching a consensus, it is helpful to train the team in how to come to a consensus and the importance of moving ahead once the consensus is reached. Such training helps team members understand that they won't be allowed to moan or drag their feet after the team's decision has been made.

■ *Using group-based technologies.* For virtual teams as well as some co-located teams, training may be needed to develop the teams' abilities to use technologies that support their work. Group decision support systems (GDSS) can be particularly useful. A GDSS is an interactive, computer-based system that combines communication, computer, and decision-making technologies to support group meetings. Using such a system can help a team effectively process information when making a group decision.[54]

Building Team Cohesiveness. To develop team cohesiveness, many organizations use experientially based adventure training. Such training often is held in a camplike environment and includes navigating river rapids, scaling cliffs, or completing a ropes course. Evart Glass Plant, a division of Chrysler Corporation, involved its entire 250-person staff in such training as a way to prepare its employees for working in self-managed work teams. Union members and managers trained side by side during employees' normal work hours. A hi-lo driver (similar to a forklift operator), a maintenance person, a shift supervisor, and a receptionist found themselves working together as a team throughout their training. After each activity, trainers led a discussion about the experience to identify the lesson to be learned from it. Table 17.2 describes a few of the activities and associated lessons from the company's specially designed one-day program.

Table 17.2 Examples of Team Training Activities and Objectives	
The Challenging Activity	**The Teamwork Lesson**
Juggle several objects simultaneously (e.g., tennis balls, hackey sacs, and koosh balls) as a team.	Although everyone has a different role, each person touches and affects the outcome.
Find the path hidden in a carpet maze and move each member through it in a limited amount of time.	Teams must find and use each individual's hidden strengths (e.g., a good memory and the abilitiy to move quickly). Doing so allows the team as a whole to succeed.
Balance 14 nails on the head of a nail that has been pounded into a supporting block of wood, creating a free-standing structure without supports.	Things that may seem impossible can be achieved when people work together.
Draw a vehicle that represents the training team and signify which part of the vehicle each member represents.	Each member has different strengths and bringing these strengths together leads to task success.

Was the training effective? Surveys and personal interviews were conducted to assess employees' reactions, and the results were positive. Employees commented that people now were going out of their way to help others and felt that people were doing a better job of seeking opinions from employees at all levels. Employees also got to know each other. Explained one engineer, "Personally, I hadn't been on third shift very long and found there were three people on that shift that I had the wrong opinion of. I saw they were real go-getters and they stayed positive throughout the experience; I was surprised." Overall, the training helped break down personal walls that people had built around themselves and helped them see the benefits of being a contributing member of a team.[55]

Experiential training is an effective way to develop cohesiveness, but used alone it isn't likely to result in optimal teamwork. Teams can also benefit from more formal training. In addition to covering organization-specific procedures for obtaining resources, cost accounting, progress reports, and the like, team members may benefit from learning about the stages of team development. If they understand how teams normally develop, they are less likely to become easily frustrated during the early forming and storming stages of their own team's development. Formal team training can also help members realize the importance of norms to their performance and stimulate the team to develop norms that aid rather than hinder it.

Reward Systems

As described in Chapters 13 and 14, reward systems inform employees about how to direct their energies and reinforce them for making valuable contributions to the organization. When employees work in a single team most of the time and it is essentially the employee's entire job, establishing team performance measures and using them to determine rates of pay is relatively easy. In most organizations, however, people aren't assigned full time to a single team. Their primary responsibilities may derive from a job that they perform essentially as an individual, with work team participation added to their regular duties. Or most of a person's regular duties may require working on teams. During the course of a year a person may serve on five or six different teams.

Most experts agree that different team designs call for different reward systems. Thus, rather than prescribing a specific approach to rewarding work teams, understanding the basic choices involved in tailoring a reward system to an organization's situation is more useful. Regardless of the details of a team-based reward system, employees need to understand it and managers need to endorse and support it.[56] Table 17.3 lists several questions that managers should consider when designing and evaluating team reward systems. With so many choices, perhaps the best way to develop an appropriate reward system is to assign the task to an empowered, multidisciplinary, well-trained work team.

Table 17.3   Choices in Designing Reward Systems for Work Teams

- How can nonmonetary rewards be used to recognize excellent team performance?
- What portion of a person's total monetary rewards should be linked to performance of the team (versus the performance of the individual or the business unit)?
- If rewards are to be linked to results, which effectiveness criteria should be used to evaluate team results? Individual results?
- How should rewards be distributed among the members of a team? Should they all receive equal rewards? If not, on what basis should people receive differential rewards?
- Who should be responsible for the allocation of rewards among team members: team members, a team leader, someone outside the team?
- For global teams, how should cultural differences among members of the team and the pay systems used in different countries be addressed?

CHAPTER SUMMARY

One of the most striking things about today's organizations is their reliance on work teams. The trend toward greater reliance on team-based structures is the reason why teamwork competency is one of the six key managerial competencies. The discussion of work team functioning presented in this chapter is intended to help you improve your teamwork competency.

1. Explain the importance of work teams.
The popularity of team-based organizational structures reflects the belief that teamwork offers the potential to achieve outcomes that couldn't be achieved by individuals working in isolation. Several strategic objectives lead organizations to design their structures around work teams, including customers' demands for innovation, faster response times, better quality, and lower prices.

2. Identify four types of work teams.
A work team is a special type of group. Most work teams consist of a small number of identifiable, interdependent employees who are held accountable for performing tasks

that contribute to achieving an organization's goals. Members of a work team have a shared goal and must interact with each other to achieve it. The four most common types of work teams are problem-solving, functional, multidisciplinary, and self-managing teams. Three key differences among work teams are the nature of their goals, their duration, and their membership. Different types of work teams suit different organizational purposes.

3. State the meaning and determinants of team effectiveness.
The primary components of a model of work team functioning are the external system, team design, internal team processes, and criteria for assessing the team's effectiveness. Effectiveness criteria measure the outcomes achieved by individual members and the team as a whole. A particular work team may be effective in some respects and not in others. Internal processes include the development of the work team over time, personal feelings, and behavioral norms. Through these processes, team members develop and integrate their behaviors. The choices involved in

creating a team, including goals, membership, size, location, and duration, are numerous. Virtual work teams are an increasingly common choice in global and high-tech organizations. A team's external system comprises outside conditions and influences that exist before and after the team is formed. Its components include the societal and organizational culture, member selection, team training, and reward system.

4. Describe the internal team processes that can affect team performance.

Teams develop over time, moving through several developmental stages. These stages include forming, storming, norming, performing, and adjourning. Teams may move through these stages in a variety of ways. In effective teams, members develop feelings of trust, openness, freedom, and interdependence. These feelings allow team members to cooperate and coordinate their actions. Behavioral norms also develop within a work team. They function to regulate and standardize behaviors within the team. Norms concerning how to handle conflict and controversy are especially important for effective team decision making.

5. Explain how to diagnose and remove barriers to poor team performance.

When teams are ineffective, the source of the problem may be internal team processes. However, poor internal processes may be caused by factors in the team's external system. Managers who accurately diagnose the causes of work team problems will be able to take appropriate corrective actions.

KEY TERMS and CONCEPTS

Adjourning stage
Behavioral norms
Cohesiveness
Effectiveness criteria
External system
Feelings
Forming stage
Free rider
Functional work team
Group
Groupthink
Informal group
Internal team processes

Multidisciplinary work team
Norming stage
Performing stage
Problem-solving work team
Productive controversy
Quality circle
Self-managing work team
Storming stage
Task force
Team proximity
Virtual work team
Work team

QUESTIONS FOR DISCUSSION and COMPETENCY DEVELOPMENT

1. Explain why Roche organized its R&D employees into multifunctional teams. What specific goals were these teams designed to achieve?

2. Choose two organizations with which you are familiar (e.g., your school, your employer, a local community group, or a department store in your town). For each organization, list the work teams that appear to be present, identify the types of teams (functional, multidisciplinary, problem solving, or self-managing), and explain why the organization needs those particular types of teams.

3. Think about two teams in which you were a member. Pick a team that you think was very effective and one that was less effective. What role did the following factors have in shaping the effectiveness of these two teams: internal team processes, team design, culture, team member selection, and the reward system?

4. Describe how work teams develop. What dangers are present at each stage of development?

5. As the owner of a small business that offers marketing services, you believe that your staff needs to understand how to work effectively in teams, including teams whose members are mostly the employees of your clients. You plan to send several of your employees to a teamwork training program. You have found three consultants who provide team training. List four questions you would want these consultants to address before deciding which one to hire.

MANAGING GE'S JET ENGINES

In Durham, North Carolina, 170 GE employees work in nine teams to produce the GE90 jet engines that Boeing will install in its new, long-range 777 aircraft. Each team "owns" the engines they build—from the beginning of the assembly process to getting it loaded onto a truck for delivery. As they begin each engine, about the only instructions these teams receive is the date on which the engine is to be shipped out from the plant. Getting the engine produced is the team goal, but that goal can be reached only if the teams effectively manage themselves. Besides producing an 8.5-ton jet engine out of 10,000 individual parts, team members order tools and parts; schedule their vacations, training and overtime; make adjustments to the production process to improve their efficiency; monitor their product quality; and take responsibility for diagnosing and resolving problems that arise among members of a team.

Decisions about these and all other issues that the teams face are made by consensus, which was a founding principle for the plant. Each employee understands that living with ideas that they don't necessarily agree with is part of the job. They don't blame others when things go wrong, because they make the decisions. The process of reaching agreement on decisions is so much a way of life here that people routinely talk about "consensusing" on this or that.

The one boss in this plant—plant manager Paula Sims—keeps everyone's attention focused on the common goal: making perfect jet engines quickly, cheaply, and safely. Her job is to make sure that the efforts of all teams are coordinated so that together their decisions optimize the plant's performance, and then to free up resources for growth and improvement.

In her four years as the plant manager responsible for GE's jet engine production teams, Sims has learned that communicating what you intend to isn't always easy. She describes her plant manager's job as "the most challenging four years of my life—and also the most rewarding. To do it well requires a different level of listening skills—significantly different. More and more of what I do involves listening to people, to teams, to councils, to ideas, trying to find common themes."

In this culture of continuous feedback, one reason Sims listened so carefully was to monitor her own effectiveness. She learned early that her actions could be easily misinterpreted. Recalling an incident from her early days, she explained, "An employee came to me and said, 'Paula, you realize that you don't need to follow up with us to make sure we're doing what we agreed to do. If we say we'll do something, we'll do it. You don't need to micro-manage us.'" At most plants, following up was just part of a manager's job. But here it was sending the wrong message. Because she always followed up, people concluded that she didn't trust them. The real problem was that she had not yet learned the plant's norms about decision making.

Sims also listens when the plant is trying to solve a problem. At other companies, the title of manager almost means "decision maker." At GE/Durham, however, the manager actually makes only about a dozen major decisions each year. All other decisions either rely heavily on input from, or are actually made by, the other plant employees. The plant manager is responsible for making sure plant employees know about problems, and for informing the GE managers that she reports to about the solutions. But to get the solutions, the plant manager is expected to listen, not decide. For major issues, such as reducing costs or improving safety, a task force is formed to decide how to address the problem. The plant manager educates the task force and everyone else about the problem and explains why it is important. Then the task force takes responsibility for finding solutions. When they have a plan for the future, the plant manager informs those above her about how the plant will proceed and makes sure the higher-ups are on-board with the plan.[57]

Questions for Discussion

1. What work team effectiveness criteria seem to be most important to GE's engine-building teams?

2. Review the six managerial competencies described in Chapter 1. How important is each of these for Paula Sims? Provide a rank order, where 1 = the most important managerial competency for Sims and 6 = the least important managerial competency for Sims. Explain your rationale.

3. Suppose that you were in charge of campus recruiting for GE/Durham. What qualities would you look for in job candidates and how would you determine whether a candidate possessed those qualities? Consider the qualities needed for team members as well as those needed by the plant manager.

4. What aspects of the external system at GE/Durham are likely to be important to the success of its work teams?

NORMS FOR VIRTUAL TEAMS

Virtual teams are becoming quite common. Nevertheless, many managers have very little experience with virtual teams. Assume you are in charge of a newly formed virtual brand team at CommonHealth. The team is in charge of developing an Internet site for a new pharmaceutical product called IVYOUT, which is used to treat skin rashes caused by poison ivy and other toxic plants. Your office is in Parsippany, New Jersey, but you often work at home. The team members include

- two employees of your client—one who works in Basel, Switzerland, and one who works in Palo Alto, California;
- two CommonHealth colleagues who work in the same building as you;
- a freelance graphics design specialist who works in Orlando, Florida; and
- a software engineer who specializes in e-commerce Internet programming and works in Bangalore, India.

All of the team members speak English fluently, but English is a second language for four members of the team.

This is the team's first project, and it also is the first time you have been responsible for managing a virtual team. The team is working under a tight schedule, and team members will not be able to hold a face-to-face start-up session. You know that it is important to help the team members establish strong norms to guide their behavior. Your plan is to propose a list of about 20 norms for the team to consider adopting. You expect the team members to participate in modifying your draft, but you need something to get them started.

Using the worksheet on the following page, prepare the draft list of norms for your team to consider.

Questions

1. What competencies do you need to effectively manage your virtual team?

2. Imagine that it is one month since the team started working together. One member of the team continues to exhibit some negative behaviors that everyone agreed should not be exhibited. How would you deal with this problem?

General Aspect of Team Life to Which the Norm Applies	Norms Describing Positive Behaviors that Team Members Can Exhibit	Norms Describing Negative Behaviors that Team Members Should Not Exhibit	Norms that Apply Specifically to the Team Manager (Positive or Negative Behaviors)
Using e-mail communications			
Managing personal relationships among team members			
Managing conflict within the team			
Managing cultural differences			
Managing unanticipated individual problems that affect the team's work			
Managing due dates and deadlines			
Other:			

©Index Stock Imagery

Organizational Culture and Cultural Diversity

LEARNING OBJECTIVES

After studying this chapter, you should be able to:

1. Describe the core elements of a culture.

2. Compare and contrast four types of organizational culture.

3. Discuss several types of subcultures that may exist in organizations.

4. Describe several activities for successfully managing diversity.

Chapter Outline

Founded in 1971 by six college bud-
dies, today GSD&M Advertising is a
highly successful and very visible
company in Austin, Texas. The company's ambitious mission is nothing
less than this: "To foster, harness,
and focus the scarcest resource in
business: great ideas." At GSD&M,
the organizational culture supports
creating and harnessing great ideas.
Great ideas make for happy customers—which include Southwest
Airlines, Anheuser-Busch Theme
Parks, and Master Card—and happy
customers keep the firm in business.
Ideas are so important to Roy
Spence, Jr., a cofounder and president of GSD&M that he campaigned
to have the city of Austin adopt
the slogan "The City of Ideas." So far,
Austin is keeping its slogan of "Live
Music Capital of the World."
GSD&M's founders have had to be
content with calling their headquar-
ters building Idea City.

The GSD&M building is designed
to look and feel like a small city. The
business development department is
located in the city's financial district.
Employees go to the community center to socialize or have a meal. To
speak with top-level managers, employees head for the city center,
where windowless executive offices
were located in order to make them
as accessible as possible. As employees walk around their "city," they are
constantly reminded of GSD&M's
core values: community, winning,
restlessness, freedom, responsibility,
curiosity, and integrity. These words
are carved in stone at the "city center," and they show up in various
other forms throughout the work
areas.

When they tell the story of
GSD&M's beginning, the founders
make it clear that risk taking and
great ideas are what the company is
all about. Six college kids chose to
bypass job opportunities at established ad agencies and instead
started their own firm in a small
Texas town. They were rebels then,
and now they want rebels as employees. The founders were also a team,
and GSD&M still considers teamwork to be the best way to do creative work. "Big ideas come from
small groups" is a phrase everyone
at GSD&M understands. Another
key saying at GSD&M is "Ideas
are serious fun." Employees are expected to work hard in order to help
their clients achieve their goals. To
align employees with their clients'
perspective, idea teams work in "war
rooms" filled with clients' artifacts—
a section from a Southwest passenger plane, a realistic mock-up of
Chili's Grill and Bar, and so on. The
message is clear to every employee.
Each employee is expected to be im-
mersed in the client's world. They are
to sit where their clients sit and think
the way their clients might think. A
saying used to capture this norm is
"Your butt is connected to your
head."[1]

THE ELEMENTS OF A CULTURE

1. Describe the core
   elements of a
   culture.

A **culture** *is the unique pattern of shared assumptions, values, and norms that shape the socialization, symbols, language, narratives, and practices of a group of people.*[2] As illustrated in Figure 18.1, assumptions, values, and norms form the base of a culture but they can't be observed directly. They can only be inferred from a culture's more visible elements—its
socialization activities, symbols, language, narratives, and practices.

At GSD&M, stories about the firm's founding and the physical building where people
do their work are crafted to communicate and sustain a culture that supports creativity.
Roy Spence may not talk a lot about culture, but he clearly understands its importance
at his firm. Herb Kelleher, founder and chairman of Southwest Airlines, also understands that his company's culture is a key to its success. When asked whether the real secret to his success wasn't simply keeping costs low, Kelleher slammed his fist on the table
and shouted back that culture has everything to do with Southwest's success because
competitors can't copy its culture.[3] At both GSD&M and Southwest Airlines, a powerful
organizational culture is a key aspect of the company's overall strategy.[4] Effective management of these companies begins with understanding the elements of their cultures.

Assumptions

Shared assumptions *are the underlying thoughts and feelings that members of a culture take for
granted and believe to be true.* At GSD&M, one shared assumption seems to be that creative

Figure 18.1   The Culture Iceberg

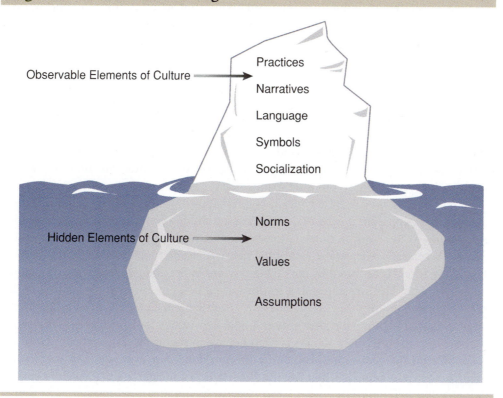

ideas are stimulated by the environment—they don't just develop inside a person's head. Members of the loose-knit "open source" community of Linux software programmers share the assumption that software code should be openly available so that anyone anywhere can modify it or create new code to enhance the software's capability. This assumption contrasts sharply with the assumption held by most software producers who believe that code should be proprietary and that secrecy is required in order to make a profit.

Values and Norms

A **value** *is a basic belief about something that has considerable importance and meaning to individuals and is stable over time.* Creativity and big ideas are highly valued at GSD&M. At Southwest Airlines, "having fun" is a value shared by the airline's employees and customers alike. After the terrorist attacks on September 11, 2001, the custom of flight attendants cracking jokes was suspended for more than a year. But gradually letters from customers began to trickle in saying they missed the jokes. Soon the humor that is so much a part of Southwest's culture returned.[5] Nonprofit professional theatres typically value artistic creativity and independence as well as community education and outreach.[6] As we described in Chapter 6, many contemporary organizations are striving to ensure that all employees value ethical and socially responsible conduct.

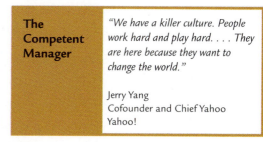

The Competent Manager

"We have a killer culture. People work hard and play hard. . . . They are here because they want to change the world."

Jerry Yang
Cofounder and Chief Yahoo
Yahoo!

Norms are rules that govern the behaviors of group members. In Chapter 17, we discussed norms as elements of the internal processes of work teams. When a norm is widely shared throughout the organization, it becomes an element of the organization's culture. The main function of norms in organizations is to regulate and standardize behavior. When members of an organization engage in behaviors that violate the norms, they can expect expressions of disapproval. When behavior conforms to the norms, members receive the approval of their peers and others in the organization.

Socialization

Socialization *is a process by which new members are brought into a culture.*[7] The most powerful way to do so is through consistent role modeling, teaching, coaching, and enforcement by others in the culture. At the societal level, socialization takes place within the family, in schools and religious organizations, and through the media. At the industry level, socialization often occurs through organized activities conducted by industry associations. In the Linux open source community, socialization occurs over the Internet, where norms such as "don't dump on others" and "make nice" are posted electronically.

In organizations, socialization typically begins subtly during the hiring process. It then becomes more apparent during orientation and training events soon after the new hire begins work. At Ritz-Carlton hotels, room-service waiters attend formal training sessions and assist a veteran waiter who coaches the new waiter and inculcates the hotel's service philosophy, which is captured by the saying "We are ladies and gentlemen serving ladies and gentlemen." The formal training sessions teach new employees the story of how the hotel began and ensures they are familiar with each sentence of the firm's Credo—three paragraphs that capture the firm's most important values and principles. On-the-job coaching sessions teach new waiters how to behave in their jobs. Emphasis is placed on *how* people do their jobs, not just getting the job done. For example, new waiters are taught how to use language that fits the Ritz-Carlton's image (e.g., "Please accept my apologies," rather than "I'm sorry," and "Certainly, my pleasure" instead of "Okay"). Coaching also teaches new hires to think about situations from the customer's perspective, imagine their emotional reactions, and anticipate (rather than respond to) each customer's concerns. Ultimately, the hotel's goal is to create a workforce whose attitudes and habits are perfectly aligned with the hotel's values.[8]

Symbols

A **symbol** *is anything visible that can be used to represent an abstract shared value or something having special meaning.* Symbols are the simplest and most basic observable form of cultural expression. They may take the form of logos, architecture, uniforms, awards, and many other tangible expressions. At GSD&M, the entire building serves as a symbol of the organizational culture. The office building is designed to be an "idea city." Artifacts from customers are used to remind employees that their objective is to assist customers in advancing their businesses.

For some companies, a song or anthem is an important symbol. Consider this one, which was popular at IBM during its early years, when the founder Thomas Watson still ran the show. The lyrics were sung to the tune "Singin' in the Rain":

Selling IBM, selling IBM.

What a glorious feeling, the world is our friend.

We're Watson's great crew; we're loyal and true.

We're proud of our job, and we never feel blue.[9]

As described in the Planning & Administration Competency feature,[10] a simple scoreboard became a powerful symbol for Setpoint's employees. They began each week with a "board meeting." The meetings served a business purpose of ensuring that everyone understood their priorities for the week and also strengthened the personal friendships among employees.

PLANNING & ADMINISTRATION COMPETENCY

Setpoint

If you like roller coasters, chances are you have enjoyed a product that was manufactured by Setpoint, which is in the business of producing amusement park entertainment. The Super Saturator at Paramount Carowinds park is one of their latest creations. Imagine taking a roller coaster ride and having people take aim at you with water shooters. You would get soaked as your roller car plunged through a forest of shooting water, but you would laugh and scream throughout the entire ride. Creating experiences like these is the mission of Setpoint.

When Steve Petersen first visited Setpoint, he was curious about how this manufacturing company really worked. They made fun rides and, from what he had heard, they had fun doing it. Petersen wasn't thinking about an acquisition or a merger when he visited Setpoint that first time. But Setpoint's powerful culture made such an impression on him that he soon starting thinking that merging his company with Setpoint would be a solution to his own problems. During a casual visit, Setpoint's CEO, Joe Knight, took Peterson on a tour of his manufacturing company's facilities. "I knew right then that Setpoint had what we needed, and somehow we had to get it," recalled Petersen. "It" was the business, the management system, and the cul-

ture. What impressed Petersen most about Setpoint's culture was the degree of alignment between the way employees thought about their work and Setpoint's strategic objectives.

From the beginning, Setpoint's culture embraced employee involvement. It used an open-book approach to management. Regardless of their specific jobs, employees were given financial training and expected to participate in enhancing the firm's financial performance. During its first few years, Setpoint's practice was to distribute financial spreadsheets to employees on a monthly basis. But now the numbers are displayed on "the board." By studying the board, anyone can figure out what stage a project is at and its financial success. For each project, employees can track operating expenses and gross profits per hour. And because everyone understands how the company makes money, they can interpret the figures to understand how their projects are doing compared to other projects. Every Monday morning, the board is the focus of a company "huddle," where projects are reviewed and tactics are discussed to ensure that goals are met. Petersen had the board explained to him by a young technician wearing a baseball cap who happened to be in the area during his tour. Petersen was amazed by the employee's explanation. "He

knew the board inside and out. There was no hesitation. He knew what was up there. I could see that the board was a cherished possession."

Petersen liked what he saw so much that he approached Joe Knight about acquiring Setpoint. Petersen explained, "I talked to several of them and I just couldn't get over the positive attitude they had and their understanding of the business. That openness—we started with it [but] you lose that feeling over time. We want to get it back. It's something to strive for." Of course, "the board" wasn't responsible for all of the positive attitude that Petersen observed. Some of it reflects a history of people working together and helping each other out though the tough times that most start-ups endure. In addition, employees have fun together outside of work. About half are dirt-bike fanatics who go riding together and show off their antics by posting photos of themselves in the shop.

At Setpoint, the scoreboard that was the focus of so much employee attention symbolized the open and trusting relationships that managers and other employees shared. At the same time, the board and the huddles that took place around it strengthened the company's culture. But Petersen was mistaken to think that he could transform his own company's culture simply by acquiring a firm that already had the culture he desired.

Language

Language *is a shared system of vocal sounds, written signs, and/or gestures used to convey special meanings among members of a culture.*[11] At GSD&M, key words were carved in stone to remind people of the company values. Roy Spence's appreciation for the importance of language is still evident today. When talking about what his company strives for, he says that he wants his employees to be "status go," not status quo. At the Mayo Clinic, a medical complex in Rochester, Minnesota, the use of language reinforces the value placed on teamwork. Mayo doctors work in patient-centered teams, which typically include other doctors and may also include social workers, spiritual advisers, and psychiatrists. At Mayo, all doctors use the term *consultants* to refer to each other. To describe the socialization practices that they've all been through, they say they have been "Mayo-ized."

Vernon Hill, CEO of Commerce Bank, understands the link between language and culture. He likes to use the word "Wow" as often as possible. "Wow" isn't a word many people associate with banking. For Hill, that's just the point. He doesn't think very highly of the organizational culture found in most banks—too bureaucratic for him. He preferred the culture found at retailers such as Home Depot and Starbucks. Commerce Bank branches are open seven days a week, typically from 7:30 A.M. to 8:00 P.M. On Fridays, the drive-thru window is open until 10 minutes past midnight. His goal is to wow his customers, not just meet their basic needs. At Commerce, "wow" is so important that there's a Wow Department. There's also a Dr. Wow at Commerce Bank. Employees and customers are encouraged to send their compliments and complaints to Dr. Wow, who sorts through them and then sends them along to the appropriate staff member. If the message happens to be a letter describing the great service a customer received, it might be delivered with a bouquet of red balloons. Two other important symbols of the company's culture are its mascots—Mr. C and Buzz—the bank's walking logos. Mr. C is a big red letter with white gloves and a jolly personality. Buzz is a human-sized bee who helps ensure that workers are creating buzz in the branches. According to Hill, his biggest concern is "Culture, culture, culture. You have to have a service cult."[12]

Narratives

Narratives *are the unique stories, sagas, legends, and myths in a culture.* They often describe the unique accomplishments and beliefs of leaders over time, usually in heroic and romantic terms.[13] The basic story may be based on historical fact, but as the story gets told and retold, the facts may be embellished with fictional details. The story of how Art Fry, a 3M employee, developed Post-It Notes is a well-known saga that's told over and over at 3M and many other innovative firms. According to the story, Fry became frustrated when the bits of paper he used to mark pages in a hymnal kept falling out. To solve the problem, he needed an adhesive that would stick long enough to keep his pages marked without leaving a residue on the hymnal. When such an adhesive was found in one of 3M's labs, he suggested the idea of marketing the product that eventually became Post-It Notes. But market surveys yielded negative results and potential distributors couldn't see the product's potential. Undaunted, Fry gave out samples to 3M secretaries and executives. Eventually, everyone—at 3M and elsewhere—was hooked on Fry's new product. Fry was rewarded with a promotion to the highest level possible in the technical career ladder. At 3M, this story is used to teach employees three important lessons: (1) They should look everywhere for new ideas; (2) when they have a great idea, they should be persistent; and (3) 3M rewards employees for great ideas.

In organizations that value innovation, stories that illustrate the value of persistence are quite common. A manager in a jet engine plant likes to tell the story of how employees reacted when he first suggested using two-way radios to improve communication and speed the production process. In this case, the innovation influenced the process used to put together the parts that make up a very complex product: "I got radios for everyone. All the major functions had radios. Two-way radios. And that was something that had never been done here before. And [people said] *'it will not work, it can't work, we've never done that.'* Well, I went ahead and did it. Now, they won't give up the radios. We were asked to do the job one month early by our customer. We did it."[14]

Practices

The most complex but observable cultural element is *shared practices*, which include taboos and ceremonies. **Taboos** *are culturally forbidden behaviors.* A taboo at Johnson & Johnson is to put profits ahead of ethical responsibilities to doctors, nurses, and patients. When people join the company, they receive a copy of the Johnson & Johnson credo (presented in Chapter 7), which states this taboo.

Ceremonies *are elaborate and formal activities designed to generate strong feelings.* Usually they are carried out as special events.[15] In most societies, ceremonies celebrate the birth, marriage, and death of the society's members. In many organizations, ceremonies are used to recognize special achievements and honor the retiring employee. At Ravenswood winery, company meetings are held at a *CawCaw*. People gather around a barbecue pit to enjoy a meal and sample various company products. When Ravenswood was bought by Constellation Brands, a CawCaw was held to discuss the decision. According to Kimberly Dreyer, a Ravenswood manager, a CawCaw "gives people a chance to ask questions, cry, or jump for joy." It's an important part of their culture. According to Dreyer, Constellation Brands "saw that our approach worked. They knew that it was what made us unique, so they left the culture intact."[16]

BASIC TYPES OF ORGANIZATIONAL CULTURES

Cultural elements and their relationships create a pattern that is distinct to an organization, just as a personality is unique to an individual. As with a classification of individuals that share some common characteristics, several general types of organizational culture can be described. Figure 18.2 shows one approach to describing different types of cultures. The vertical axis reflects *formal control*, ranging from stable to flexible. The

2. Compare and contrast four types of organizational culture.

Figure 18.2 Types of Organizational Cultures

horizontal axis reflects the *focus of attention*, ranging from internal functioning to external functioning. The four quadrants represent four pure types of organizational culture: bureaucratic, clan, entrepreneurial, and market.[17] In a culturally homogeneous organization, one of these basic types of culture will predominate.

Different organizational cultures may be appropriate under different conditions, with no one type of culture being ideal for every situation. However, some employees may prefer one over another. As you read about each type of culture, consider which best fits your preferences. An employee who works in an organization that fits the person's view of an ideal culture tends to be committed to the organization and optimistic about its future.[18]

Bureaucratic Culture

In a **bureaucratic culture**, *the behavior of employees is governed by formal rules and standard operating procedures, and coordination is achieved through hierarchical reporting relationships.* Recall that the long-term concerns of a bureaucracy are predictability, efficiency, and stability. The focus of attention is on the internal operations of the organization. To ensure stability, the tasks, responsibilities, and authority for all employees are clearly spelled out. Rules and processes that apply to most situations are developed, and employees are socialized to believe that their duty is to "go by the book" and follow legalistic procedures. Behavioral norms support formality over informality.[19]

Bureaucratic cultures often are found in organizations that produce standardized goods and/or services, such as Pizza Hut, the IRS, and Farmers Insurance Company. They are particularly common in local, state, and federal governments. Governments create rules in their efforts to ensure that all citizens are treated the same, regardless of their backgrounds, wealth, or status. These same values often are reflected in the organizational cultures of such organizations.

Clan Culture

An internal focus also characterizes a clan culture. However, compared to a bureaucratic culture, in a clan culture control over behavior is more subtle. Few formal rules and procedures exist. Instead, in a **clan culture** *the behaviors of employees are shaped by tradition, loyalty, personal commitment, extensive socialization, and self-management.* Members of the organization recognize an obligation beyond the simple exchange of labor for a salary. They understand that contributions to the organization (e.g., hours worked per week) may exceed any contractual agreements. The clan culture achieves unity with a long and thorough socialization process. Long-time employees serve as mentors and role models for newer members. These relationships perpetuate the organization's values and norms over successive generations of employees. Members of a clan culture are aware of their unique history and they have a shared image of the organization's style and manner of conduct. They have a strong sense of identification and recognize their need to work together. Shared goals, perceptions, and behavioral tendencies foster communication, coordination, and integration. Peer pressure to adhere to important norms is strong.

The Ritz-Carlton hotel has many elements of a clan culture. "Putting on the Ritz" is a phrase most Americans recognize and associate with luxury and elegance, so employees can bask in the hotel's excellent reputation. Employees who approach their jobs as a simple economic exchange would not last long. Ritz employees understand that providing outstanding services requires making a deeper emotional commitment. Extensive training and socialization practices teach new employees how to make that commitment and the value of doing so.

Entrepreneurial Culture

In an **entrepreneurial culture**, *the external focus and flexibility create an environment that encourages risk taking, dynamism, and creativity.* There is a commitment to experimentation, innovation, and being on the leading edge. An entrepreneurial culture suits a new company's start-up phase. An entrepreneurial culture also fits well with the demands faced by employees who are seeking to create and develop new products within the environment of a larger company. GSD&M has an entrepreneurial culture. This culture doesn't just quickly react to changes in the environment; it creates change. Effectiveness means providing new and unique products and rapid growth. Individual initiative, flexibility, and freedom foster growth and are encouraged and well rewarded.

Regardless of whether an organization is a start-up company or a more established firm, this focus on the external environment will be evident in an entrepreneurial culture. However, for managing products and services that have already been brought to market and may be entering later stages of the product life cycle, a market culture may be more appropriate.

Market Culture

In a **market culture**, *the values and norms reflect the importance of achieving measurable and demanding goals, especially those that are financial and market based (e.g., sales growth, profitability, and market share).* Hard-driving competitiveness and a profit orientation prevail throughout the organization. EDS, Frito-Lay, and Oracle, among others, share many elements of a market culture.

A market culture doesn't exert much informal social pressure on an organization's members. Superiors' interactions with subordinates largely consist of negotiating performance-reward agreements and/or evaluating requests for resource allocations. Social relations among coworkers aren't emphasized, and few economic incentives are tied directly to cooperating with peers. Managers in one department are expected to cooperate with managers in other departments only to the extent necessary to achieve their performance goals. As described in Chapter 15, a primary objective of HP's CEO, Carly Fiorina, has been to change that company's clan culture to one that is much more market oriented.

Organizational Implications

Organizational culture has the potential to enhance organizational performance, individual satisfaction, the sense of certainty about how problems are to be handled, and other aspects of work life.[20] Many managers pay attention to culture. Some managers are concerned about building or maintaining their existing culture. Other managers are concerned about changing their organizational culture in order to improve their future performance.

Building a Strong Culture. An organization is said to have a **strong culture** *when the more observable cultural elements project a single, consistent message.* In such organizations, managers and employees share a common behavioral style. They use the same basic approach to solve problems, meet goals, and deal with important customers, suppliers, and other stakeholders. They share common norms that guide how they relate to one another. Results are measured the same way throughout the organization, and a common set of rules governs the use of rewards and punishments.[21] GSD&M and Ritz-Carlton both have strong cultures. A strong organizational culture results in predictable, well-specified behavior patterns. When an organization's business environment is relatively stable, strong cultures that support strategic goals contribute to firm performance.[22]

A strong organizational culture doesn't just happen. It's cultivated by management, learned and reinforced by employees, and passed on to new employees. For organizations such as Setpoint, Southwest Airlines, Yahoo!, and Commerce Bank, having a strong culture is essential for business success. MBNA is another organization with a strong culture. As described in the Communication Competency feature, they have conveyed a culture that fits the financial services industry quite well.[23]

MBNA

In Wilmington, Delaware, MBNA—the world's largest independent credit card company—is new to the area. In this city, the DuPont family and their company have been influential for more than 200 years. MBNA was founded less that 25 years ago. Like their histories, the cultures of these two companies are completely different. Everyone in town sees the difference as they go about their daily lives. According to William Lee, a retired judge, "There is a clash of cultures." What is the MBNA culture, which is shared by the 11,000 people who work for Delaware's largest employer? Some people describe it by comparing it to DuPont's culture; a realtor explains: "DuPonters have always kept a low profile. They don't

buy fancy cars, even though they could afford to. The MBNAers do." Some people describe the culture as hard driving and friendly. Some people call it intense. Some people describe it as being "a cult." One employee recalls walking along the street with her children. She was carrying her purse, which had an MBNA badge pinned to it. Seeing her badge, a couple stopped her and said, "Oh my God—you work there? I heard that's a cult." Whatever words are used to describe the culture of MBNA, people agree that it is a strong culture. "Our people do share a similar attitude. [But] we certainly don't believe that it is a cult," says Bruce Hammonds, MBNA America's chairman.

In Wilmington, even the way MBNAers look and dress is distinctive.

The company never adopted the casual dress style, favored by workers at many DuPont facilities. MBNAers look a bit like traditional bankers, but they're not stodgy. One reporter described the men as being easy to spot because they look like Secret Service agents—they tend to be youngish (mid-20s to mid-40s), physically fit and trim. They usually wear suits—often gray, with blue shirts. Men and women alike almost always wear a gold MBNA pin on their left lapel. And, it seems, MBNAers really like having fun together at group activities. Each year, thousands of employees and their families participate in a walkathon that benefits the company's charitable foundation.

Changing an Organizational Culture. Not all organizations have a strong culture. As we discuss later in this chapter, many organizations have several subcultures. Such organizations may undergo cultural change in order to meld together the different subcultures. In other words, one reason for change is to create a stronger, more consistent organizational culture. Another reason that organizations may want to change their organizational culture is because the external environment has changed. In the United States during the 1980s, many companies began changing their cultures to be more responsive to customers' expectations for high-quality products and excellent customer service. During the 1990s, when unemployment levels reached historic lows and labor shortages made it difficult for organizations to take advantage of market opportunities, many top managers began to reassess how well their organizational cultures fit the expectations of their workforces. By 2002, a sharp economic decline and revelations about unethical and illegal accounting practices pressured many firms to reassess their organizational cultures. Going forward, rapid rates of globalization, the shift toward knowledge-based competition, and the continuation of merger and acquisition activities has focused attention on the importance of understanding, assessing, and melding differing organizational cultures.[24]

Before an organization can improve its overall culture, it must first understand the culture that is present now in the organization. When an organization focuses on understanding its culture, it is likely to discover that it doesn't have one organizational culture. Instead, it probably has several subcultures. Next we discuss the reasons why an organization might have several different subcultures. Later in this chapter, we describe some steps that organizations are taking to change their organizational cultures.

SUBCULTURES WITHIN ORGANIZATIONS

An **organizational subculture** *exists when assumptions, values, and norms are shared by some—but not all—organizational members.* Organizational subcultures occur for a variety of reasons. Here we discuss three reasons why many organizations have subcultures:

■ The organization was created from a merger or acquisition.

■ Departments and divisions within the organization have their own subcultures.

■ A diverse workforce creates subcultures.

3. Discuss several types of subcultures that may exist in organizations.

Subcultures Due to Mergers and Acquisitions

When one firm acquires another firm, or when two firms merge, it is likely they will discover that the two firms had different cultures. This is what happened when AOL Time Warner (now known simply as Time Warner) was created. AOL had a strong entrepreneurial culture that was characteristic of the dot.com companies that emerged during the 1990s. Time Warner had more of a market culture. When these companies merged, many Wall Street analysts doubted that the managers would be able to meld the different cultures. Their doubts were not unfounded. In fact, incompatible cultures is the most frequently cited reason for why mergers and acquisitions (M&As) fail, as shown in Figure 18.3.[25] When organizational cultures of the two firms are similar, the chances of success increase. Likewise, the success of joint ventures and other strategic alliances is greater when the firms involved have similar organizational cultures.[26]

Figure 18.3   Reasons for M&A Failures

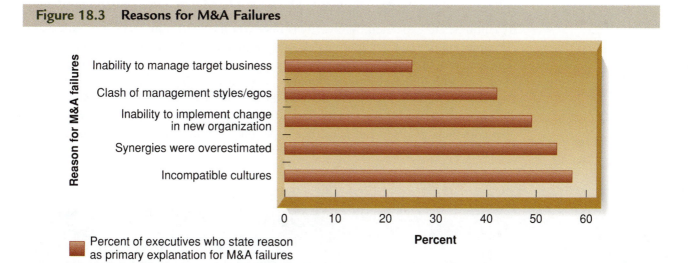

Percent of executives who state reason as primary explanation for M&A failures

---

Departmental and Divisional Subcultures

Suppose a company hasn't experienced any mergers or acquisitions and it isn't involved in other forms of strategic alliances. Do such organizations also have subcultures? Yes, they usually do. Different subcultures often are found in different departments of an organization. These subcultures may reflect departmental specialties, regional locations, or they may be created by the managers in charge of the departments.

Occupational Subcultures. Recall that in Chapter 11 we described several forms of organizational design, for example, design by function, by product, and by place. In organizations that are organized into functional departments, employees with the same occupational specialty are grouped together. Departments in the organization have names like manufacturing, R&D, accounting, marketing, human resources, and so on.

Occupational socialization practices can be strong sources of cultural indoctrination, especially for professionals. For them, the socialization period begins in college and continues as long as they identify with their chosen professions. Professional associations often formulate their own mission statements, codes of ethics, and standards for professional practice. Together, these values and norms can create a shared world view that is understood and generally accepted within the profession—but is largely unknown to outsiders. Organizational designs that group members of a profession together reinforce and sustain occupation-based subcultures.

Geographically Based Subcultures. Many organizations have facilities and operations spread across several geographic regions. As we described in Chapter 11, these organizations often rely on a geographical structure. If places in which units are located each have distinct cultures, then the organization is likely to have place-based, or regional, subcultures.

Regional subcultures are common in global organizations. At each location, the societal culture combines with the organization's culture to create a distinct subculture. The result is that different subcultures are found in each country where the company has operations. IBM has a strong organizational culture. But the IBM organizational culture is not identical all around the world. The subculture found at each IBM location is a combination of the IBM organizational culture and the culture of that country.[27]

Mercedes-Benz managers learned to manage the subcultures found in different geographic locations when it developed its M-Class SUV. In fact, when CEO Andreas Renschler decided to set up a new facility in Alabama, his goal was to create a new corporate culture. This new culture would incorporate the best elements of many different country cultures. He explained, "I strongly believe you have only one chance to establish a corporate culture and that it ultimately sets the tone for your entire organization. By design, we brought together people with a variety of experiences, with a lot of different ideas, and with different ways of thinking." Experts from Japan, the United States, and Germany all worked together to develop the new organization. When the Alabama facility was up and running, it had its own distinct subculture, which was different from the Mercedes-Benz plants in Germany. The experiences of Mercedes-Benz are described in the Global Awareness Competency feature.[28]

GLOBAL AWARENESS COMPETENCY

©Corbis Inc.

Mercedes-Benz
Mercedes-Benz is one of the world's most widely recognized brands. It stands for quality and luxury. Some people are surprised to learn that Mercedes-Benz manufactures some of its automobiles in Vance, Alabama. That's where Mercedes-Benz U.S. International (MBUSI) is located, and it's where the award winning M-Class SUV was born. The facility was created by a team of executives and workers who came from three countries—Germany, the United States, and Japan. Each country has its own approach to designing and building automobiles.

In Germany, engineers are highly trained experts who develop their skills by working as an apprentice to a *Meister* (a master in the profession). Workers accept the authority of the Meister and don't expect to be treated as equals to the Meister. Once they learn the skills they need, they expect to carry out their tasks without close supervision. This is a sign that they are respected and can be trusted to do a good job. Strong norms exist concerning the importance of producing automobiles of superior quality. In traditional U.S. automobile plants, managers control workers through division of labor and narrow spans of control. Henry's Ford's assembly line approach still dominates many production plants. At the Jeep plant in Ohio, relationships between managers and subordinates are relatively informal. People are quite direct in saying what they think. Americans tend to be driven to get things done, and they are more willing to begin production before working through every problem. In Japan, strong norms concerning the importance of quality are similar to those in Germany. However, quality is achieved using a system of team-based production and continuous improvement. Employees are generalists rather than specialists and it is important to reach consensus. At MBUSI, elements of all three cultures have been blended together. How did they do it?

The creation of MBUSI began with U.S. executives spending 18 months in Germany, where they worked with German engineers to design the plant. When the Vance plant was built, German engineers spent two years there helping to train the Americans. Following the Japanese model, multidisciplinary teams are used to manage the operation. Each team is autonomous and self-managing. They are held accountable for meeting quality standards, controlling costs, and meeting production schedules. Relationships between managers and their subordinates are egalitarian and open. Apparently the new hybrid organizational culture is a success. Demand for the M-Class SUV is stronger than expected, and customers seem to be delighted with it.

It is easy to see why geographic locations create organizational subcultures within global firms. But some people are surprised to learn that domestic firms also have regional subcultures. In the United States, many people in Midwestern Minneapolis behave differently than those in West Coast Los Angeles—that's readily apparent to anyone who visits these cities. In Switzerland, four regional subcultures can be found within the country—each is a unique blend of elements from the traditional Swiss culture and the cultures of neighboring France, Italy, and Germany. In China, there are at least three regions with distinct local cultures: one in the southeast, another in the northeast, and a third covering much of the central and western parts of the country. The subculture of the southeast region is the most individualistic, whereas the subculture of the central and western areas is the most collectivistic. The culture of the northeast region falls between these two extremes. Thus, a manager whose company operates at several locations in China needs to understand the subcultures that are created by these regional differences.[29]

Subcultures Created by Managers. Differences in the personalities and leadership styles of managers are another reason units in an organization have different subcultures. A recent survey of employees found that when fun happened at work, it usually was because lower level managers made fun happen. Employees clearly believe that in most organizations some units have more appealing cultures than others. What makes a unit's culture more positive for employees? According to the survey, positive cultures are created by managers who:

- recognize personal milestones, such as birthdays and employment anniversaries;
- hold public celebrations for professional achievements;
- sponsor picnics and parties; and
- listen to their employees and recognize the efforts they put into work.[30]

Subcultures Due to Workforce Demographics

During the past decade, many U.S. employers began to realize that workforce demographics are another reason why an organization may have several subcultures. **Workforce demographics** *describe employee characteristics such as ethnicity, age, and gender.* The fact that people with different demographic backgrounds live side by side doesn't mean that they share the same culture, however.

Ethnicity. In the United States, people from a variety of ethnic backgrounds are found in every region. Today, 1 in 10 workers in the United States is foreign born—the highest rate in 70 years. Millions of other workers are the children of recent immigrants. They were born in the United States and grew up in a family that was strongly influenced by the parents' home country culture. Many workers born in the United States still identify with the ethnic groups of their ancestors—even though their ancestors may have come to this country two, three, or several generations ago.

The dominant ethnic groups in the United States, as defined by the Census Bureau, are described in Table 18.1.[31] Note that each of the categories shown includes more specific geographic or ethnic groups that people may identify with more readily. For some people, ethnic origins may have a pervasive influence on their daily experiences, whereas for others their ethnic origins are much less salient than their "American" identity. Note also that the identity of many people is influenced by more than one ethnic group.

Census counts of people in the categories shown in Table 18.1 are, at best, rough estimates of the proportion of workers who identify with each ethnic group's culture. Although their consequences are difficult to quantify, ethnic subcultures can have a significant impact on an organization.

Darden is the parent company that owns the Olive Garden, Red Lobster, and Bahama Breeze restaurant chains. For many years, their headquarters buildings, located in Or-

Table 18.1 Ethnic Identities as Measured in the U.S. Census

Ethnic Category	Description	Percentage of Total Population
People choosing two or more ethnicities	Any combination of ethnic origins.	1.4
People choosing only one ethnicity		98.6
American Indian or Alaska Native	Origins in the original peoples of North, South, or Central America who maintain tribal affiliation and community attachment.	1.0
Asian	Origins in any of the original peoples of the Far East, Southeast Asia, or the Indian subcontinent, including Cambodia, China, India, Japan, Korea, Malaysia, Pakistan, the Philippines, Thailand, and Vietnam.	3.9
Black or African American	Origins in any of the black racial groups in Africa.	12.7
White		
Non-Hispanic	Origins in any of the original peoples of Europe, the Middle East, or North Africa.	68.9
Hispanic	Origins in Cuban, Puerto Rican, South American, Central American, or other Spanish culture, of white race.	12.0
Total Hispanic	Origins in Cuban, Puerto Rican, South American, Central American, or other Spanish culture, regardless of race.	13.0

Note: Respondents may identify themselves as belonging to more than one ethnic group.

lando, Florida, were decorated to celebrate the Christmas season. Managers thought the decorations were appropriate because they were secular and not religious in nature (e.g., Christmas trees and Santa, not a nativity scene.) Then some employees began to complain that the secular Christmas decorations failed to recognize the importance of other non-Christian holidays. And some Christians complained that the "Christ was being taken out of Christmas." This was a difficult situation for Darden. Should they stop celebrating holidays altogether, as one consultant recommended?

Should they try to celebrate all holidays that were important to their employees, as another consultant recommended? After surveying employees, Darden decided to celebrate the holidays that employees said they wanted to celebrate. In one recent year, they celebrated 12 holidays in the months of October through February. Employees are encouraged to celebrate their own religious and/or cultural heritage by putting up decorations for the holidays that they care about.[32]

Age. In a typical organization, employees of all ages can be found, from teenagers to people in their seventies. Employees within each generation tend to share experiences and values that are somewhat distinct from those of other generations. Different generational groups develop their own slang and they often develop symbols that have special meaning for them. Characteristics of four distinct generations are described in Table 18.2.[33] Of course, not all members of each generation are exactly alike. Also, people of different ages share many experiences and values. Nevertheless, age-based subcultures are found in many societies around the world.

Table 18.2   Generations Present in the U.S. Workforce

When They Were Born	Label Used	Characteristics
1945 or before	Traditionalists	Prize loyalty. Prefer top-down management approach. Information should be provided on a need-to-know basis.
1946–1964	Baby Boomers	Optimistic and idealistic. Achieve success by challenging authority and creating open lines of communication.
1965–1980	Generation Xers	More skeptical than other generations. Often distrust institutions and prize individualism. Value work–life balance.
1981 or after	Millennial	Approach work with realization that they will change employers many times and may also change the type of work they do.

Gender and Other Demographics. Differences in the way men and women are socialized and differences in the experiences they have at work are another source of organizational subcultures. Gender roles may seem to be more powerful in some ethnic communities than others, and they may be more powerful in some generations than others. Nevertheless, in many organizations, gender continues to be an important basis for the formation of subcultures. Other workforce demographics that can be the basis for organizational subcultures include marital status, family status, sexual orientation, and physical abilities. All of these characteristics can shape the experiences, values, and concerns of people. Demographic similarity often provides a basis for people to develop personal relationships and enjoy feelings of camaraderie. In short, people with similar demographic characteristics often develop their own subcultures, and these exist side by side with other subcultures within most organizations.

Implications of Organizational Subcultures

Managers have many different views about whether subcultures are "good" or "bad" for business. Sometimes organizational subcultures coexist peacefully within an overall organizational culture; at other times subcultures are a major source of continuing conflict.[34]

Benefits. Many managers believe that the presence of distinct subcultures in an organization can be beneficial and should be valued. Michael Critelli, chairman and CEO of Pitney Bowes, puts it this way: "There is no limit to what we can accomplish if we can crack the code of valuing diversity on a global basis as we move forward into the twenty-first century."[35] Disney CEO and Chairman Michael Eisner expresses a similar view: "We believe in diversity because the more diverse you are as an organization, the more diverse are the opinions that get expressed. That will make us more creative."[36] At Ford Motor Company, the rationale for valuing the perspectives present in different subcultures focuses on customers. According to Mary Ellen Heyde, director of Ford's lifestyle vehicles, "If you have a diverse workforce, then you know that the customer's point of view will always be represented." The design and marketing teams for Ford's Windstar minivan, which is bought mostly by women, included many women. Their involvement in the project accounts for features such as the "sleeping baby mode" for overhead lights.[37] At UPS, bilingual support centers have been set up in southern California to serve the area's many foreign-born entrepreneurs.

Disadvantages. The presence of subcultures sometimes creates problems for employees and employers. Consider what often occurs after one firm acquires another. Employees in the acquired firm may now be expected to give up the culture of their old company and adopt the culture of the company that acquired them. Suddenly, the old ways of doing things are unacceptable. Often, managers in the acquired firm feel that their level of status and influence has been reduced.

Like employees of an acquired firm, members of demographic minority groups often feel that their subculture is not valued as highly as the culture of the majority group. Consider the experience of Eula Adams. Adams was the first African American to become a partner at Touche (which is now Deloitte & Touche). That was in 1983. Adams began working at Touche 10 years earlier. There were about 800 partners at that time and none was African American. Remembering what it was like, he says, "The loneliness, especially in the early days, was the hardest. I lived in two worlds. I'd leave work and go home to one world, and then wake up and go back to work in that other world." Actually, the experiences of African Americans may not be much different today, given that there are still only about 10 African-American partners in the entire profession.[38] In general, research shows that employees who are part of a minority subculture often perceive that a glass ceiling exists, which limits their career opportunities.[39]

Despite the challenge of feeling that he didn't fit well in his company's culture, Adams has been very successful—recently, *Fortune* included him on its list of "The Most Powerful Black Executives in America." Other employees who experience a clash between the culture they work in and the one they live in outside of work decide to look for other employment. Clashes between ethnic cultures may be one reason why a recent survey conducted by the National Society of Black Engineers found that 71 percent of black engineers were considering leaving their companies. Surprisingly, even employees who work for companies that have been recognized as "America's Best Companies for

Minorities" often feel dominated and undervalued by members of the majority.[40] Worries about possible cultural clashes also play a role in the decisions gay and lesbian employees make about whether to be open about their sexual orientation.[41]

To reduce the negative consequences of clashes between subcultures, many organizations are in the process of transforming themselves into multicultural organizations. A **multicultural organization** *has a workforce representing the full mix of cultures found in the population at large, along with a commitment to utilize fully these human resources.* Multicultural organizations strive to permit many subcultures to coexist while ensuring that no one subculture dominates the others. That is, they strive to be *inclusive.* Next, we describe how U.S. managers are beginning to address the challenge of managing the diverse subcultures that often are present in organizations.

MANAGING CULTURAL DIVERSITY

Cultural diversity *encompasses the full mix of the cultures and subcultures to which members of the workforce belong.* Subcultures with which employees may identify include those described earlier in this chapter.

4. Describe several activities for successfully managing diversity.

The way managers think about diversity has evolved and changed over time. In the 1960s and 1970s, Equal Employment Opportunity (EEO) laws focused managers' attention on the task of eliminating race and sex discrimination in the workplace. In the 1980s, managers became more involved in taking proactive steps to increase the number of women and minority employees in their organizations. During the 1990s, managers began to understand the importance of creating a workplace that is great for everyone—regardless of their backgrounds.

Today, efforts to manage diversity effectively usually involve finding ways to manage people representing the wide variety of subcultures found in an organization, regardless of the basis for those subcultures—nationality, occupation, ethnicity, age, gender, and many other factors. Figure 18.4 shows the many aspects of diversity that are of concern to employers.[42]

The Competent Manager

"We have created a work environment that honors and values the many differences that employees bring to the workplace. . . . [Our] policy of inclusion allows us to take advantage of diverse perspectives, work as a team during difficult times, and develop breakthrough products and services."

Ned Barholt
CEO
Agilent

Figure 18.4   What Companies Cover in Diversity Initiatives

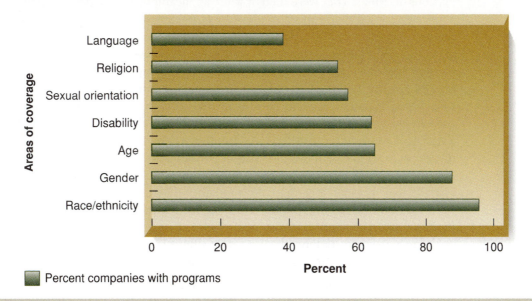

Percent companies with programs

Some experts believe that addressing such a broad variety of diversity issues may be detrimental to improving the treatment and career outcomes of ethnic minorities. Others believe that eventually the new, more inclusive approach to managing diversity is likely to pay off for members of all subcultures. The particular approach an organization takes to managing diversity depends partly on the goals it hopes to achieve.

Organizational Goals for Managing Cultural Diversity

We have already suggested that there are many reasons for managers to be concerned about managing diversity effectively. The three major goals that most organizations strive to achieve are complying with laws and regulations, creating a positive culture for employees, and creating economic value.

Legal Compliance. Complying with laws and regulations that prohibit discrimination, such as Title VII of the Civil Rights Act, is a necessary first step for any organization that seeks to manage diversity effectively. As we explained in Chapter 13, a variety of laws make it illegal for employers to discriminate against employees on the basis of personal characteristics that are unrelated to their jobs. The basic premise of such laws and regulations is that employment decisions should be based on job-related qualifications, not membership in a demographic group. Other regulations go further and state that employers should be proactive in their efforts to recruit, hire, and retain employees from demographic groups who traditionally have been underrepresented in their organizations. These regulations support the use of affirmative action policies and practices. Affirmative action regulations are built on the basic premise that organizations should actively recruit job applicants to build a workforce that reflects the demographics of the qualified labor force locally. In other words, they should strive to create a culturally diverse workforce. To monitor the success of their affirmative action programs, employers generally assess various employment numbers and ratios. These measures include female and minority hiring numbers, offer/acceptance ratios, turnover and retention rates, promotion patterns, downsizing decisions, and compensation levels.[43]

During the past three decades, affirmative action practices have become common and relatively well accepted in many organizations. But recently, they have become controversial. In 2003, the affirmative action practices built into the University of Michigan's student admissions procedures were challenged in a case heard by the U.S. Supreme Court. Like many employers, the University of Michigan argued that it was appropriate to take into account their desire for a culturally diverse student body when making admissions decisions. They were sued by white applicants who were denied admission—the applicants argued that it was illegal for the University of Michigan to take into account the ethnic background of applicants. Many employers supported the university's affirmative action practices. In fact, 30 prominent companies—including Microsoft, General Motors, Steelcase, and Bank One—publicly wrote in support of the university. In their brief, they explained their thinking: They argued that having a culturally diverse workforce is essential to business success because diversity "facilitates unique and creative approaches to problem solving" and makes it possible for their organizations to "appeal to a variety of consumers." Furthermore, employers need educated workers. If universities do not provide education to a diverse group of students today, then the future success of these businesses would be in jeopardy.[44] In deciding the case, the Supreme Court agreed with the logic presented by these 30 companies. Their ruling permits the University of Michigan to continue to strive to ensure that their student body is culturally diverse. At the same time, the Supreme Court made it clear that universities should not simply give points to non-white students. Each student's entire record should be considered in a wholistic approach when admissions decisions are made.

Creating a Positive Culture. A positive organizational culture is one in which everyone feels equally integrated into the larger organization. Members of majority and minority subcultures feel respected; everyone has an equal chance to express views and influence decisions; and everyone has similar access to both formal and informal networks within the organization. Some organizations that initially monitored their diversity numbers primarily because of concerns about legal compliance discovered that the numbers could also be used to gain insights into other problems. Addressing such problems promotes a positive culture.

At the accounting firm of Deloitte & Touche, employment numbers alerted the partners to a disturbing trend about a decade ago. Only 5 percent of the company's partners were women and the turnover rate for women throughout the firm was 30 percent. When Diana O'Brien left Deloitte & Touche to work elsewhere, she was just one of many women who did so. Subsequently, partners at Deloitte & Touche realized that they needed to change the company's culture. The changes they made were so successful that Diana O'Brien decided to return. "Before I left, I couldn't have a life and still do consulting. Now, enough has changed that I have been able to do that," she explained. One of the most significant changes has been the company's new flexible work arrangements. Today, employees can take advantage of compressed workweeks, flexible work arrangements, telecommuting, job sharing, and paid child-care leave. For Jeff McLane, the new policies made it possible to have a more balanced personal life, which included training to compete as an Olympic cyclist. To ensure that such arrangements don't hurt employee performance, managers are trained to manage flexibly.[45]

The most common methods used to assess organizational culture are employee surveys and focus groups. In addition to asking employees directly about the organization's culture, managers at companies such as Xerox, Levi Strauss, and Avon conduct cultural audits to evaluate the language used in organizational documents and advertising, the visible symbols that decorate public spaces, the types of awards given to employees, the types and quality of food available in the company cafeteria, policies regarding holidays and absences, and the types of social activity sponsored by the organization, among other items. Cultural audits often reveal that the organizational culture reflects the values and preferences of some subcultures while ignoring those of others. When such discrepancies are found, simple changes often can be made to create a more inclusive organizational culture.

Creating Economic Value. A third reason that managers are striving to foster diversity is because they believe that diversity will create greater economic value.[46] For Granite Broadcasting, which operates eight network-affiliated television stations, a diverse workforce helps ensure the company is in tune with its diverse viewer audience. With a diverse workforce and positive organizational culture in place, Cornwell and many other managers think that their companies will be able to

> **The Competent Manager**
>
> *"Our audience is growing more diverse, so the communities we serve benefit if our employees are racially and ethnically more diverse.*
>
> W. Don Cornwell
> CEO
> Granite Broadcasting,
>   New York, NY

- develop products and services for new markets,
- attract a broader range of customers,
- improve customer satisfaction and increase business from repeat customers, and
- reduce costs, including those associated with litigation.

To date, little research is available publicly to document the economic benefits of a diverse workforce and positive organizational culture.[47] Some managers use proprietary information to establish the economic benefits of diversity. Others simply believe that there is a link and don't require research evidence to support their view. One manager was convinced of the value of his company's diversity efforts when he and a team of his managers attended a meeting with one of the company's largest customers. Somewhat to his surprise, there wasn't a single white male on the other side of the table. When they expressed an interest in his company's diversity efforts, he was fortunate to be able to point to an excellent record, despite appearances. The CEO of another company with a less than stellar record was forced to recognize that the success of his business could depend on learning to manage diversity better. One of his most important distributors—a woman—recently criticized him about it at a meeting. And the manager of a mutual fund that owns millions of his company's shares—an African American—also chided him on the topic.

Undoubtedly, personal experiences with customers and clients have convinced some CEOs that managing diversity poorly is risky business. Multimillion-dollar legal penalties and the negative effects such penalties have on stock prices also grab the attention of CEOs. To settle a publicized discrimination lawsuit, Texaco paid $175 million. The cost of the settlement itself was substantial. But that cost paled in comparison to the nearly $1 billion decline in market value that occurred when the evidence against the company was reported by the news media. The most costly evidence was a tape recording in which a high-level executive was heard making racist remarks that were apparently accepted without comment by the other executives who were present. Texaco's share price later recovered, and management has since earned praise for its efforts to improve the company's organizational culture. But the cost of this episode to the company and its employees was enormous.[48]

The Process of Change

Organizations that succeed in managing diversity do so because senior managers are committed to achieving legal compliance, instituting an inclusive organizational culture, and using diversity to create economic value. As described in Chapter 12, considerable investments of time, money, and people are necessary to carry out successfully any type of large-scale organizational change.

Diagnosis. Before managers begin designing new approaches to managing diversity, they first need to be sure that they understand how current practices affect the amount and nature of diversity—both in the organization as a whole and within its smaller units. Traditional organizational practices tend to minimize cultural diversity in various ways. Recruiting practices emphasize finding candidates from "reliable" sources. Interviews screen out candidates who "don't fit." Socialization and training practices produce uniform ways of thinking and behaving. Attendance policies and pay practices standardize work schedules. Centralization often limits the amount of discretion that managers can exercise in addressing the special needs of employees. Many such practices were adopted by organizations for valid reasons. Standardization and centralization often evolve to increase efficiency and ensure the fair (equal) treatment of employees. Some types of homogeneity may be appropriate, or even essential, to effective operations and thus should be retained if justified after careful evaluation.

Once managers have analyzed their organization and agreed that they need to improve their approach to managing diversity, they can begin the process of planning for change. As described in Chapter 12, the planning process itself is the beginning of the change process. This is when a vision is formed and employees become involved in improving the organization.

Vision. Articulating and communicating a clear vision of how the future can be better is essential in developing a plan for change. Until leaders formulate a clear vision and persuade others to join them in being dedicated to that vision, they won't be able to generate the enthusiasm and resources needed for large-scale cultural change.

Most experts agree that the CEO is the key to articulating a vision of a new organizational culture that supports and builds on diversity. The CEO must be a tireless advocate and exemplar of the new culture. Otherwise, employees will not believe that change is important. In addition, the CEO may need to make a persuasive business case for changing the culture. The question to be answered is this: If the organization has been successful up to now, why does it need to change?

Involvement. For the plan to be effective, those who are affected must buy into it. The best way to ensure that they do so is through early involvement. The importance of involving employees should be obvious, but even experienced managers often forget to follow this principle. Xerox has a long record of enlightened diversity management. One of its earliest successes involved a caucus group for African-American employees. In fact, it was so successful that the company decided to create a caucus group for female employees. However, the first attempt to establish a women's caucus—in the mid-1970s—failed. One explanation for the failure was that the women's caucus was designed to duplicate the existing African-American caucus instead of being designed specifically to address the concerns of female employees. A few years later, female employees at Xerox began to establish caucus groups on their own. Eventually a dozen different women's caucuses emerged: Some are national, some are regional, and some are specific to one location; some are for minority women and others aren't; and some are for exempt employees and others are for nonexempt employees.

When General Motors initiated cultural change, one of the goals was to create a work environment in which all voices were heard. To explore what that might involve, GM created eight employee resource groups (ERGs) representing

- Asians,
- blacks,
- gays and lesbians,
- Hispanics,
- non-U.S. citizens working in the United States,
- people with disabilities,
- white males, and
- women.

According to Lorna Utley, director of diversity initiatives, "the whole purpose of the resource groups was to recommend specific steps that could enhance GM's implementation of management imperatives, things that are important to the success of our company from a cultural and organizational standpoint." Some 500 employees participated in these groups. They polled workers, investigated what other companies were doing, and drafted suggestions for senior management concerning how to remove barriers to productivity and improve the company's standing in the marketplace. This work took about a year. Then the groups began to present their suggestions to a strategy board, which decided which suggestions to adopt.[49]

Timing. Planned organizational change usually follows an evolutionary—not revolutionary—path. Realistic expectations about how quickly change will occur are important to the long-term success of change efforts. Usually, change occurs more slowly than expected. Xerox began changing its culture more than 30 years ago and continues to do so. Table 18.3 describes some of the many practices that were developed in order to improve the organization's approach to managing diversity.

Although meaningful changes in corporate cultures occur slowly, not all useful initiatives require decades to implement. At Texaco, for example, the promotion rates for African Americans doubled in two years after the CEO began to hold managers accountable for managing diversity. At GM, one policy change occurred in a matter of several weeks. A suggestion made by both the women's ERG and the gay and lesbian ERG was to revise the company's "escort" policy. The old policy provided travel expenses for a spouse to accompany an employee on certain types of business trips. The newly revised

Caucus Groups

- Employee-initiated and employee-funded caucus groups (based on gender, ethnicity, sexual orientation, disability, area of expertise) sponsor activities such as training workshops, conferences, and mentoring programs for their members.
- Caucus groups are allowed to use company facilities for meetings during nonworking hours; allowed to use company's internal electronic mail for communications; and routinely meet with senior managers to discuss their concerns and seek mutually acceptable solutions.

Management Resources Planning (MRP)

- MRP is a companywide formal succession planning process for identifying, developing, and tracking the flow of women and people of color through the company.
- The goal of MRP is to ensure upward mobility of women and minorities, and business unit leaders are responsible for the process.

Balanced Workforce Strategy

- Involves setting numerical targets that specify the percentages of white men, men of color, white women, and women of color to be hired and promoted into each major job category. Targets are based on labor market demographics.
- Incentive pay and promotions of managers are explicitly tied to their achievement of balanced workforce goals.

Work and Family Programs

- A corporate dependent care development fund provides financial grants for small-scale company and employee-initiated projects to improve work–family balance.
- Alternative work schedules include job sharing, flextime, and compressed workweeks.
- A variety of family friendly benefits are offered, including child-care and elder care resources and referral service, adoption assistance, and employee assistance programs.

Measurement

- Workforce demographics are tracked and monitored at all levels and within all units of the company.
- Annual employee surveys include questions that assess satisfaction with all aspects of work life, and results are analyzed to assess whether satisfaction differs by gender or ethnicity.

Community Outreach and Development

- To combat early gender and ethnic occupational stereotyping, science education days are offered in the community to stimulate interest in science and technology among all members of the future workforce.
- Partnerships with schools provide academic counseling, part-time employment, mentoring, and tutoring to encourage at-risk students to complete high school.

policy allows for expenses to be paid for anyone the employee wants to bring as his or her guest. Changing this policy required little more than a willingness to acknowledge employees' many different life situations.

The list of methods that organizations can use to manage cultural diversity is quite long and varied. Thus managers need to target specific efforts and set priorities for implementing them. When Coca-Cola settled a discrimination lawsuit in 1999, it agreed to pay $188 million and to change several of its management practices. Within three years, it established a uniform procedure for measuring individual job performance in order to minimize the effect of stereotypes and prejudices. Coke also created a new procedure for determining pay increases. Numerous studies have shown that women tend be paid less than men even when their education, experience, skills, performance, and job assignments are equivalent. By changing their procedures for setting pay rates to reduce the role of subjective judgments, organizations can quickly signal their intention to move toward becoming a multicultural organization.[50] The changes at Coca-Cola were a good start for creating change. On the other hand, some observers noted that the company could have done more. For example, Coca-Cola did not appoint any minority candidates to fill openings on its executive board. Doing so would have been another way to show that the company was serious about improving the work environment for minority employees.

For United Technologies, diversity management helps improve teamwork among employees. As described in the Teamwork Competency feature, practices that improve the way employees feel at work benefit everyone.[51]

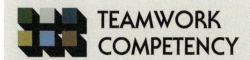

TEAMWORK COMPETENCY

United Technologies

United Technologies Corporation provides high-tech products and support to aerospace industries and to the building-systems industry. Headquartered in Hartford, Connecticut, with 153,000 employees worldwide, United Technologies is always competing to attract and retain the best talent available. It strives to be listed on the "Best Employer" lists published in business magazines and believes that managing diversity effectively is one way to get on those lists. Ossie Reid, director of diversity at United Technologies, says that diversity of many types is important to them. "Intellectual diversity is just as important as cultural diversity. People with varied educations and philoso-

phies bring different experiences to the table."

If team members feel comfortable drawing on their diverse backgrounds and teams are able to use their differences to solve problems, diversity can make the company more effective. The challenge for United Technologies is to ensure that employees from all backgrounds feel comfortable and committed to working for the company. "We work our people pretty hard, so they need to be in a place where they feel comfortable. Hartford is tough, especially for single people. It can be very cliquish," says Reid.

To maintain diversity within its workforce, United Technologies uses a variety of diversity management practices. During succession plan-

ning, a diversity manager participates to ensure that a diverse pool of employees is considered for career advancement. The company also provides performance appraisal training to help managers make judgments that accurately reflect each person's effort and contributions. It sponsors forums and symposia for women and minorities as well as employee mentoring networks. In the future, it plans to add diversity training modules to the company's emerging-leaders training program. For United Technologies, these investments are one approach to building a strong, positive organizational culture. "When we lose people because they aren't happy, it costs us a lot of money," Reid explains.

For most organizations, many options exist for improving how well diversity is managed. We cannot discuss all of these possible changes here. Instead, we describe just two of the most common approaches used by managers who are attempting to manage diversity more effectively. An organization's choice of specific efforts will reflect the nature of diversity that is important for the organization, the goals set, the actions of other organizations in the industry, and so on.

Diversity Training

Sending employees to diversity training sessions is perhaps the most common targeted action that organizations take when they initiate a diversity change program. Training programs vary greatly, but most attempt to provide basic information about cultural differences and similarities and sensitize participants to the powerful role that culture plays in determining their work behavior.

Awareness Training. Many of the diversity interventions offered by consultants and adopted by organizations during the 1990s focused on individual awareness training. **Awareness training** *is designed to provide accurate information about the many subcultures present in the organization.* A typical program is conducted over the course of one or two days. Activities may include information sharing intended to educate employees about differences between subcultures, educating employees about the negative consequences of stereotypes, and helping employees understand their own subculture's unique perspective.

Some organizations supplement formal training sessions with informal learning opportunities such as a Black History Month or a Gay and Lesbian Pride Week, using these times to focus on a group's history and cultural traditions. Ultimately, the goal of such change efforts is to eliminate unwanted employee behaviors and encourage behaviors that are consistent with a positive organizational culture.

Harassment Training. Another common type of training offered is harassment training. **Harassment training** *is aimed at ensuring that employees understand the meaning of harassment and the actions the company will take when someone complains of being harassed.* Employees should understand, for example, that some of the jokes they hear on television and radio may be unacceptable to repeat at work. Employees should also understand how to inform the company when they see harassment occur. Employees need to understand what the company's response will be if an employee engages in harassment. Many organizations terminate employees who create a negative atmosphere by engaging in harassment or other clearly inappropriate behavior.

Although research on the effectiveness of diversity training programs is scant, the general consensus is that training programs *alone* do little to create positive change. Learning about how men and women differ, or about differences among generational groups, may have some value, but understanding differences is not sufficient to improve the functioning of diverse work units. Employees must also understand how the mix of subcultures influences the way their work teams and departments function. And they need practical tools to use to ensure that the team functions well. Similarly, managers need to understand how diversity influences communication patterns, and they need practical tools to build and maintain effective communication. For these and other reasons, training entire teams and work units to manage and leverage their own diversity may prove more effective than training individuals about differences between subcultures.

Creating Family-Friendly Workplaces

To be competitive in the labor market, organizations need to survey their employees to find out their preferences. They should then consider offering a variety of options to meet employees' needs. In response to the influx of women with children and changing attitudes among men regarding child care, more and more employers are addressing employees' family needs. A recent survey of more than 10,000 firms employing 10 or more workers showed that 63 percent offered financial assistance, benefits, scheduling help, or services related to child care. Figure 18.5 shows the most common practices to creating a family-friendly workplace.[52]

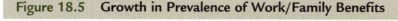

Figure 18.5   Growth in Prevalence of Work/Family Benefits

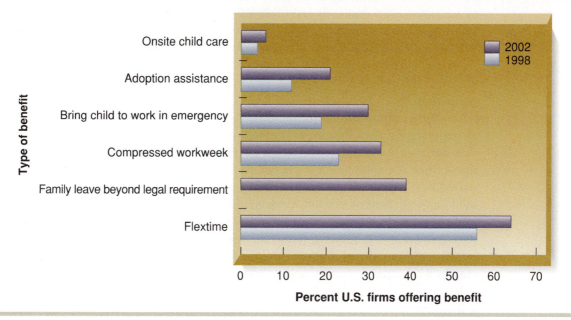

Some employers fear that childless employees may resent progressive policies to assist families. The formation of The Childfree Network—an advocacy group that serves as a voice for childless workers—is one indication that there is good reason to be prepared for some backlash from employees who feel they are not able to benefit from employers' investments in family-friendly workplaces. Research shows that employees without children are less positive about "family-friendly" practices, compared to employees with children. Nevertheless, most of the evidence indicates that any backlash that occurs tends to be limited.[53]

Even if some backlash occurs, the benefits and services associated with child-care initiatives may outweigh the disadvantages. A study of nine Western European countries found that parental leave-taking is associated with improved children's health and survival. In the countries studied, on average, eligible employees (men and women) used 32 weeks of parental leave benefits. Longer leaves significantly reduced deaths among infants and young children.[54] In the United States, the company's bottom line provides a sufficient rationale: At the groundbreaking ceremonies for its $8 million child-care center, Dick Parker, director of administrative services for Merck & Co., observed: "You don't provide child care just because you want to be a good guy. You do it for business reasons. Merck decided to build the center for three reasons: retention, recruitment, and productivity. Child care will become more and more of a recruitment issue in the future. If employees are worried about their child care services, that will affect their productivity and retention."[55] For the same reasons, many employers are finding ways to help workers who care for elderly relatives, also.

Holding Managers Accountable

When an organization offers a new product (good or service) in the marketplace, it almost always uses one or more numerical indicators to measure its success. How well the product does is important in determining managers' raises, bonuses, and promotions. When the development and sale of a product is successful, the people who contributed to that success often are recognized and rewarded. Many organizations apply these same principles to the introduction of diversity-related changes. Doing so seems to pay off.

Research shows that the success of diversity training initiatives is greater in organizations that evaluate the effectiveness of the training and in those that offer rewards to managers who make diversity-related improvements in their business units. At Dow Chemical, managers are encouraged to promote women at a rate at least equal to that of men. Hoechst Celanese sets numerical targets for its workforce based on its analysis of the available labor pool and ties managers' bonuses to their performance on diversity initiatives (e.g., training programs, mentoring, and developing employees for promotion).[56]

Not all top managers accept the idea of holding managers accountable by tying pay to achieving diversity objectives. Top managers at Colgate-Palmolive value diversity but they don't set numerical goals. Others worry that attempts to quantify results may backfire because things often get worse before they get better. After R. R. Donnelley & Sons started its cultural change efforts, black employment fell from 8 percent to 6 percent of the total. The small number of black employees, in turn, led the company to ask those who remained to attend multiple diversity training sessions to ensure that their views were represented. Employees found the training sessions to be stressful, and some resented having to attend multiple sessions, especially in light of the declining minority employment.[57]

Challenges

Any organizational change effort can run into unanticipated problems, and diversity programs are no exception. Cultural awareness training programs may backfire if they seem to reinforce stereotypes or highlight cultural differences that employees have tried to erase in order to fit into the company's culture. Special skill-building programs offered only to some subgroups also can feed negative stereotyping, or they may be viewed as giving the target group an unfair advantage. Employees assigned to work in markets that match their cultural backgrounds may view that as limiting rather than maximizing the contributions that they can make. Affirmative action programs may create a stigma for all members of groups targeted to benefit. As a result, even the best qualified people are presumed to have acquired their positions because of their demographic attributes rather than on the basis of merit. Networking or caucus groups may lead to increased segregation and fragmentation. Problems seem to arise in organizations when employees become focused on their cultural differences rather than on their common goals.

Ultimately, managing diversity successfully involves developing a strong organizational culture that values cultural differences and ensures that the talents of all employees are used to their fullest extent. Implementing the variety of changes that may be needed to manage diversity more effectively will take many years in most organizations. Observers familiar with the change process at Coca-Cola contend that the company is just getting started and that the benefits of their change efforts will not be fully realized for several more years.[58] During that time, many challenges will arise along the way. Among the most difficult challenges that companies face as they attempt to implement these changes are

■ managing the reactions of members of the dominant culture, who may feel that they have lost some of the power they had previously held and exercised;

- synthesizing the diversity of opinions from individuals and using them as the basis for reaching meaningful agreement on issues; and
- avoiding real and perceived tokenism and quota systems that can help the organization achieve its quantitative goals but can be destructive to developing a positive culture.[59]

Perhaps the biggest challenge to managers, however, is understanding that cultural diversity can have many organizational consequences. On the one hand, diversity can enhance a team's ability to solve problems creatively. On the other hand, the price of such creativity may be heightened conflict within the team. Similarly, changing the mix of men and women in a mostly male team or department toward a 50–50 split may improve the attitudes of the women involved while irritating the men. Managers shouldn't expect diversity-related initiatives to affect members of the organization in uniformly positive ways. They should be prepared to weigh carefully which costs they are willing to incur in order to achieve which gains.[60]

CHAPTER SUMMARY

The thoughts, feelings, motivations, and behaviors of employees reflect an organization's culture and subcultures. Subcultures in an organization may reflect the influence of cultures within societies, occupations, and various other social groupings. The greater the variety of subcultures in an organization, the more difficult it is to create a strong overarching organizational culture and the greater the need to actively manage cultural diversity.

1. Describe the core elements of a culture.
A culture is the unique pattern of shared assumptions, values, and norms that shape the socialization activities, language, symbols, narratives, and practices that unite members of a group and make them distinctive relative to nonmembers. Assumptions are the underlying thoughts and feelings that are taken for granted and believed to be true. Values are basic beliefs about a condition that has considerable importance and meaning to individuals and is stable over time. Socialization is a systematic process by which new members are brought into a culture and taught the norms for behavior. A symbol is anything visible that can be used to represent an abstract shared value or something having special meaning. Language is a shared system of vocal sounds, written signs, and/or gestures used to convey special meanings among members. Narratives are the unique stories, legends, and myths in a culture. Shared practices include taboos (forbidden behaviors) and rites and ceremonies (formal activities that generate strong feelings).

2. Compare and contrast four types of organizational culture.
Each organization's culture is unique. Nevertheless, four general types of organizational culture that are useful for comparing organizations are bureaucratic, clan, entrepreneurial, and market cultures. They are characterized by differences in formal control (ranging from stable to flexible) and focus of attention (ranging from internal to external).

3. Discuss several types of subcultures that may exist in organizations.
The cultural diversity of a workforce reflects the range of subcultures to which employees belong. When two organizations merge, the subcultures of the original firms may become subcultures within the new organization. Subcultures also reflect departmental and occupational differences. Subcultures that come about as a result of the demographic characteristics of employees include those based on age, gender, and ethnicity. In multicultural organizations, no one subculture dominates the others. The organizational culture is inclusive; it blends all the subcultures found within the organization.

4. Describe several activities for successfully managing diversity.
Concern about effectively managing workforce diversity reflects three types of organizational goals: complying with EEO laws and regulations, creating a positive organizational culture that makes work enjoyable for all employees, and improving organizational performance. Managing cultural diversity in order to achieve these objectives is a long-term process requiring substantial investments of time, money, and people. Organizations use many activities to manage diversity effectively. Diversity training and family-friendly practices are two popular approaches to creating a positive culture for a diverse workforce. An organization's approach to managing diversity is determined by its specific goals and objectives as well as by the subcultures present within the organization.

Awareness training
Bureaucratic culture
Ceremonies
Clan culture
Cultural diversity
Culture
Entrepreneurial culture
Harassment training
Language
Market culture

Multicultural organization
Narratives
Organizational subculture
Shared assumptions
Socialization
Strong culture
Symbol
Taboos
Value
Workforce demographics

QUESTIONS FOR DISCUSSION and COMPETENCY DEVELOPMENT

1. Describe the elements of GSD&M's culture. Does GSD&M have a strong culture? Defend your opinion.

2. Review Figure 18.2. In which type of organizational culture would you prefer to work? Why did you choose that particular culture?

3. Suppose MBNA acquired Commerce Bank. What challenges would the new CEO face in creating a strong culture for the new organization (MBNA Commerce)? Explain.

4. Choose two occupations with which you are familiar. Describe how the subcultures associated with these two occupations are similar or different. What would be the implications of these similarities and differences for a team with 50 percent of the members coming from each occupational group?

5. Do you agree that there are really different age-based subcultures for people who belong to the generational groupings shown in Table 18.2? Explain your opinion.

6. Suppose that you've been appointed to a task force to make suggestions for diversity initiatives at Xerox. Visit its home page at http://www.xerox.com to learn what the company is doing now. What would you add to its current efforts? Be sure to state the goals to be met by the initiatives you recommend adding.

7. Describe how the culture at your college or university influences your behavior.

8. What role does an organization's reward system play in maintaining its culture?

9. Why are organizational cultures and subcultures so difficult to change?

CASE FOR COMPETENCY DEVELOPMENT

BUILDING A NEW CULTURE AT THE CUNINGHAM GROUP

The Cuningham Group, an architectural firm in Minneapolis, Minnesota, decided to merge with Solberg + Lowe Architects, with offices in Los Angeles and Phoenix. The top management teams in both organizations thought that their cultures would meld easily. For the Cuningham Group, the goal of the merger was to expand geographically and to broaden its range of projects. Already well known for its educational and hotel buildings, the group's management wanted to begin doing design work for the entertainment industry. Partners Rick Solberg and Doug Lowe of Solberg + Lowe were well known for

their work in hotels and the entertainment industry, but economic conditions in the Los Angeles area meant that they needed to look for opportunities elsewhere. As is often the case, the managers at both firms discovered that, although analyzing whether a merger makes financial and strategic sense is easy, successfully merging two corporate cultures is much more difficult.

When Cuningham and his team visited the offices of Solberg + Lowe, they liked the look and feel of the work environment. The physical spaces reminded them of their own offices, and they could see that the principal partners still liked to be actively involved in project design. "I felt it would be easy for me to work there," recalled Cuningham. Solberg recalls feeling the same way when he visited Minneapolis. "I wanted to see live, vibrant contributors on the ownership side. I didn't want a bunch of dead initials on the door." What he and his partner saw led them to conclude, "This is where we'd want to be." Subsequent visits to each others' homes reinforced their beliefs that the two teams would work well together.

The honeymoon lasted less than a year. By then, the fundamental value differences between the two firms became more apparent. Although neither had a formal dress code, the Minnesotans often wore ties to work, whereas the staff in Los Angeles and Phoenix preferred knit shirts. The Minnesota group worked a full five-day week, but on Friday afternoons, they couldn't reach anyone in Phoenix or Los Angeles because those offices routinely closed at midday on Friday. "At first we wondered if they were just lazier than we were. But we just had to adjust," admits Cuningham.

Communication patterns within the firms also differed. The Cuningham Group didn't hold nearly as many meetings as Solberg + Lowe. And when they did meet, there was always a clear agenda. Solberg and Lowe admit that some of their partners' meetings were more like family fights than discussions between professionals. Solberg and Lowe's frankness with each other was beneficial, but the screaming shocked Cuningham's team, which Solberg described as using a "Minnesota-nice" style. There were even differences in how the two firms handled bill collections. The easy-going approach of Solberg + Lowe meant that they didn't press people whom they considered trustworthy for overdue payments. Cuningham disapproved: "If you don't pay your gas bill, they cut off your gas. It isn't mean or kind; it's just policy. And it has to be the same for everyone," he explained.

Five years after the merger, the two groups are working together well. A visit to the company's Web site makes it clear that employees in the company play well together, too. Uniting everyone is a common set of values that serve as the foundation of the firm's organizational culture. They describe some of these values as follows:

- ■ *Relationships:* Relationships should be open, forthright, and respectful.
- ■ *Spirit:* The firm shows respect for the environment and fosters the values and ideals of clients.
- ■ *People:* The firm is committed to having the best staff and the tools to support them.
- ■ *Balance:* The firm should offer people opportunities for personal as well as professional growth.
- ■ *Profitability:* Profitability fuels the growth of the organization and helps secure the future of its employees.

One way for Cuningham to continue its growth is to expand through another merger. This time, Solberg says that he would make even more effort to ensure that there is totally open communication with the other management team, as well as with the staff. "You can't hold anything back. Chances are, what you're concealing will be the problem. Better to find out today than after you've committed to the transaction."[61]

Questions for Discussion

1. How can Solberg determine whether the organizational culture of a potential acquisition partner is similar to Solberg + Lowe's? What steps should he take to assess the other firm's organizational culture?

2. Suppose that the acquisition partner looks favorable on most counts. However, Solberg realizes that after the acquisition, the new firm would have much more ethnic, gender, and age diversity than is present in his firm today. He is looking for advice about how to address the increased levels of workforce diversity in his new organization. What advice would you give him and why?

EXERCISE FOR COMPETENCY DEVELOPMENT

DIVERSITY KNOWLEDGE QUIZ

How informed are you about issues of workforce diversity? To get a sense of how well you are able to separate myth from fact, take the Diversity Knowledge quiz below.

Instructions: Indicate whether each of the following statements is true (by circling "T") or false (by circling "F"). Correct answers are given on page 540.

1. T F Joy and fear are feelings that can be accurately recognized from facial expressions, regardless of which cultures people are from.

2. T F A person who is older than 65 years and living in one of the world's developing regions (e.g., Southeast Asia, Africa, India) is three times more likely to be working than a person of that age living in a developed region (e.g., United States, Europe, Australia).

3. T F Worldwide, about 50 percent of women between the ages of 15 and 64 are in the labor force.

4. T F Most Americans with Japanese heritage come from families who have lived in the United States for two or three generations.

5. T F During the past decade, college graduation rates have been declining for men and increasing for women.

6. T F   Most people could count on their fingers the number of female and minority CEOs who head one of the 500 largest firms in the United States.

7. T F   In America's 10 largest cities, an average of one out of four persons is of Latino origin.

8. T F   Compared to other demographic groups, gay men tend to be better educated and hold higher paying jobs.

9. T F   Compared to other employees, people with disabilities have better safety records on the job.

10. T F   Mental speed begins to slow down slightly beginning at about age 30, but performance of many complex mental tasks continues to improve steadily as people age.

11. T F   As recently as 1970, interracial marriages were illegal in some parts of the United States.

12. T F   Almost all Fortune 500 firms indicate that they are implementing initiatives to manage diversity.

13. T F   The proportion of companies with at least one woman board director is greater among Fortune 500 companies than among companies ranked 501 through 1,000.

Scoring: Count the number of times you circled "T" for true. This is your total score. The highest score possible is 13—all of the statements are true.

Questions

1. Were you surprised by any of these statements of fact? This is a question you may wish to discuss with your classmates. Do some people seem to know more about diversity than others? If so, why do you think that might be?

2. If your score was less than 10, it indicates that you may not have accurate information about several aspects of cultural diversity. What are some implications of not having accurate knowledge about these facts? What could you do to improve your knowledge?

3. As a manager, why is it important for you to understand the subcultures associated with various demographic groups?

Chapter 1

1. *Adapted from* M. Williams. Penney to drop makeup. *Dallas Morning News*, January 31, 2003, p. 1D; A. McGill. How Allen Questrom saved J. C. Penney. *D Magazine*, April 2002, pp. 33–35; J. Collins. *Good to Great*. New York: Harpers Business, 2001; http://www.jcpenney.com (January 2003); M. Halkias. Penney moves to centralize function of 1,150 stores. *Dallas Morning News*, January 15, 2000, pp. 15D, 16D.

2. Our definition of competencies is *adapted from* the definition by M. W. McCall, Jr. *High Flyers: Developing the Next Generation of Leaders*. Boston: Harvard Business School Press, 1998; the Career Planning Competency Model developed by Bowling Green State University, as described in its Web site, http://www.bgsu.edu (January 2003).

3. The lists incorporate the competencies identified by others, including B. L. Davis. *Successful Manager's Handbook*. Minneapolis: Personnel Decisions, 1992; B. Howland. *The Prospector*. Greensboro, NC: Center for Creative Leadership, 1999; H. W. Goldstein, K. P. Yusko, and V. Nicolopoulos. Exploring black-white subgroup differences of managerial competencies. *Personnel Psychology*, 54, 2001, pp. 782–808.

4. G. Anders. The Carly chronicles. *Fast Company*, February 2003, pp. 66–73.

5. Personal conversation with L. A. Dimpfel, vice president, Worldwide Olympic Technology Systems, IBM, Dallas, TX, January 2003.

6. S. Holmes, D. Bennett, K. Carlisle, and C. Dawson. Starbucks. *Business Week*, September 9, 2002, pp. 100–110.

7. *Adapted from* L. Goldman. Greased lightning. *Forbes*, October 28, 2002, pp. 247–250; http://www.sonicdrivein.com.

8. G. Colvin. How to be a great CEO. *Fortune*, May 24, 1999, pp. 104–126.

9. I. F. Kesner. The coach who got poached. *Harvard Business Review*, 80(3), 2002, pp. 31–39; J. R. Katzenbach and J. Santamaria. Firing up the front line. *Harvard Business Review*, 77(3), 1999, pp. 107–115.

10. M. Kripalani. Wired villages. *Business Week*, October 14, 2002, p. 116.

11. Q. N. Huy. Emotional balancing of organizational continuity and radical change: The contribution of middle managers. *Administrative Science Quarterly*, 47, 2002, pp. 31–69.

12. Personal conversation with Audrey Van Drew, regional sales manager, Alcatel, Dallas, TX, January 2003.

13. T. S. Bateman, H. O'Neill, and A. Kenworthy-U'Ren. A hierarchical taxonomy of top managers' goals. *Journal of Applied Psychology*, 87, 2002, pp. 1134–1148.

14. http://www.interface.com (January 2003).

15. A. M. Francesco and B. A. Gold. *International Organizational Behavior*. Upper Saddle River, NJ: Prentice Hall, 1998, p. 48.

16. J. P. Briscoe and D. T. Hall. Grooming and picking: Leaders using competency frameworks: Do they work? *Organizational Dynamics*, Autumn 1999, pp. 37–52; B. L. Kedia and A. Mukherji. Global managers: Developing a mindset for global competitiveness. *Journal of World Business*, 34, 1999, pp. 230–251.

17. J. T. Li, A. S. Tsui, and E. Weldon. *Management and Organizations in the Chinese Context*. New York: Macmillan, 2000; J. P. Walsh, E. Wang, and K. R. Xin. Same bed, different dreams: Working relationships in Sino American joint ventures.

Journal of World Business, 34, 1999, pp. 69–93.

18. Personal conversation with Rachel Cheeks, Manager, PepsiCo, Dallas, TX, January 2003.

19. *Adapted from* article titled Edwards Jones tops *Fortune* list of 100 best companies to work for; company holds position for second year in a row, as does No. 2, Container Store. *Business Wire*, January 6, 2003, pp. 2078ff; http://www.containerstore.com (January 2003).

20. M. Buckingham and C. Coffman. *First, Break all the Rules*. New York: Simon and Schuster, 1999.

21. P. Lencioni. *The Five Dysfunctions of a Team*. San Francisco, CA: Jossey-Bass, 2002; C. E. Nicholls, H. W. Lane, and M.B. Brechu. Taking self-managed teams to Mexico. *Academy of Management Executive*, 13(3), 1999, pp. 15–25; L. L. Thompson. *Making the Team: A Guide for Managers*. Upper Saddle River, NJ: Prentice Hall, 2000.

22. *Adapted from* C. Fishman. Whole Foods is all teams. *Fast Company*, April 1996, pp. 103–106; http://www.wholefoods.com (January 2003).

23. http://www.penguin.com (January 2003).

24. I. Harpaz, B. Honing, and P. Coetsier. A cross-cultural longitudinal analysis of the meaning of work and the socialization process of career starters. *Journal of World Business*, 37, 2002, pp. 230–244.

25. A. Joshi, G. Labianca, and P. M. Caliguri. Getting along long distance: Understanding conflict in a multinational team through network analysis. *Journal of World Business*, 37, 2002, pp. 277–284; G. K. Stalh, E. L. Miller, and R. L. Tung. Towards a boundaryless career: A closer look at the expatriate career concept and perceived implications of an

international assignment. *Journal of World Business*, 37, 2002, pp. 216–227.

26. *Adapted from* K. Brooker. The Un-CEO. *Fortune*, September 16, 2002, pp. 89–96; http://www.proctergamble.com.

27. http://www.visa.com (January 2003); M. Waldrop. The trillion-dollar vision of Dee Hock. *Fast Company*, October/November 1996, 75–86.

28. S. W. Wellington. *Women of Color in Corporate Management: Opportunities and Barriers*. New York: Catalyst, 1999.

29. J. Slocum, C. Ragan, and A. Casey. On death and dying: The corporate leadership capacity of CEOs. *Organizational Dynamics*, 30, 2002, pp. 269–281.

Chapter 2

1. *Adapted from* http://www.ups.com; http://www.hoovers.com; K. H. Hammonds. Handle with care: How UPS handles packages starts with how it handles people. Here are the five lessons on the art of delivering for your people. *Fast Company*, August 2002, pp. 102–107; S. Marta. Carrying the load. *Dallas Morning News*, December 19, 2002, pp. D1, D4.

2. M. Weber. *The Theory of Social and Economic Organization*, trans. by M. A. Henderson and T. Parsons. New York: Free Press, 1947.

3. *Adapted from* D. McGray. Please stay on the line. *Fast Company*, October 2002, p. 48; B. B. Read. Attracting and keeping your valued virtual servants—Call center work is often stressful and thankless. *Call Center*, April 1, 2002, pp. 52–56; T. Rutkowski. Call centers measure up. *Insurance Networking*, October, 2002, pp. 24–27.

4. Interview with Audrey Van Drew, regional sales manager, Alcatel, December 2002, Dallas, TX.

5. F. W. Taylor. *Scientific Management*. New York: Harper & Row, 1947.

6. M. M. Davis, N. J. Aquilano, and R. B. Chase. *Fundamentals of Operations Management*, 4th ed. Boston: Irwin McGraw-Hill, 2003.

7. M. M. Davis et al., p. 16.

8. M. C. Bolino, W. H. Turnley, and J. M. Bloodgood. Citizenship behavior and the creation of social capital in organizations. *Academy of Management Review*, 27, 2002, pp. 505–522.

9. H. Fayol. *General and Industrial Management*. London: Pitman & Sons, 1949.

10. F. Luthans. Positive organizational behavior: Developing and managing psychological strengths. *Academy of Management Executive*, 16, 2002, pp. 57–75.

11. M. P. Follett. *Prophet of Management*. Boston: Harvard Business School Press, 1995.

12. J. Reed and R. Cunningham. *Team Member General Information Guidebook*. Austin, TX: Whole Foods Market, 1998.

13. C. Barnard. *The Functions of the Executive*. Cambridge, MA: Harvard University Press, 1938.

14. E. Mayo. *The Social Problems of an Industrial Civilization*. Boston: Harvard Business School, 1945.

15. L. Thompson. *Making the Team*. Upper Saddle River, NJ: Prentice Hall, 2000.

16. B. L. Kirkman and B. Rosen. Powering up teams. *Organizational Dynamics*, Winter 2000, pp. 67–79.

17. *Adapted from* C. McLaughlin. A strong foundation. *Training*, 38(3), 2001, pp. 80ff; interview with B. Ferguson, managing director, TDIndustries, Dallas, TX, December 2002.

18. N. M. Ashkanasy and C. S. Davis. Emotion in the workplace: The new challenge for managers. *Academy of Management Executive*, 16, 2002, pp. 76–86.

19. M. M. Davis et al., pp. 4–18.

20. *Adapted from* address by T. Kennedy. Baldrige tools for process management. Kisco Senior Living, Carlsbad, CA, August 2000; J. Carbone. Solectron prepares for the upturn. *Purchasing*, October 24, 2002, pp. 31–34.

21. C. Ranganathan and V. Sethi. Rationality in strategic information technology decisions: The impact of shared domain knowledge and IT unit structure. *Decision Sciences*, 33(1), 2002, pp. 59–86.

22. S. Postrel. Islands of shared knowledge: Specialization and mutual understanding in problem-solving teams. *Organization Science*, 13(3), 2002, pp. 303–320.

23. J. R. Hollenback, H. Moon, B. J. West, D. R. Ilgen, L. Sheppard, C. O. L. H. Porter, and J. A. Wagner, III. Structural contingency theory and individual differences: Internal person–team fit. *Journal of Applied Psychology*, 87, 2002, pp. 599–607; G. P. Castrogiovanni. Organization task environments: Have they changed fundamentally over time? *Journal of Management*, 28(2), 2002, pp. 129–150.

24. A. E. Mill. Total quality management and the salient patient. *Business Ethics Quarterly*, 12(4), 2002, pp. 481–505; N. P. Repenning and J. D. Sterman. Capability traps and self-confirming attribution errors in the dynamics of improvement. *Administrative Science Quarterly*, 47, 2002, pp. 265–296.

25. M. Walton. *The Deming Method*. New York: Dodd Mead, 1986; J. Spigener. What would Deming say? *Quality Progress*, 34(3), 2002, pp. 61–65.

26. T. E. Vollmann, W. L. Berry, and D. C. Wybark. *Manufacturing Planning and Control*. Burr Ridge, IL: Irwin, 1997.

27. J. Bowen and R. C. Ford. Managing service organizations: Does having a "thing" make a difference? *Journal of Management*, 28(3), 2002, pp. 447–469.

28. A. Haasen. M-Class: The making of the new Daimler-Benz. *Organiza-*

tional Dynamics, Spring 1998, pp. 74–78.

29. L. L. Berry. The Soul of Service. New York: Free Press, 1999; N. Gans. Customer loyalty and supplier quality competition. Management Science, 48(2), 2002, pp. 207–222.

30. S. Nambisan. Designing virtual customer environments for new product development: Toward a theory. Academy of Management Review, 27, 2002, pp. 392–413.

31. Adapted from G. Bylinsky. They're setting lofty standards in quality control, preventive maintenance, and automation. Fortune, September 2, 2002, pp. 171ff.

32. Adapted from R. Gibson. Starbucks chairman 2: Seizing opportunity in Japan. FWN, November 15, 2002, p. 100831; V. Vishwanath and D. Harding. The Starbucks effect. Harvard Business Review, 78(2), 2000, pp. 17–18; http://www.starbucks.com (February 2003).

33. Adapted from A. J. Dubrin. Essentials of Management. Cincinnati, OH: South-Western, 1997.

Chapter 3

1. Adapted from interviews with J. Birch, senior vice president, Operations, Central Division, Taco Bell, Dallas, TX, January 2003; P. Scheibmeir, manager, Sales and Marketing, Pizza Hut, Dallas, TX, January 2003; R. Blanchette, vice president, Northeast, Carslon Companies, Dallas, TX, December 2002; A. Veiga. Burger warfare hurting. Dallas Morning News, December 25, 2002, p. 3D; M. Wells. Happier meals. Forbes, January 20, 2003, pp. 77–78.

2. P. S. Adler and S. Kwon. Social capital: Prospects for a new concept. Academy of Management Review, 27, 2002, pp. 17–40.

3. W. A. McEachern. Economics: A Contemporary Introduction, 5th ed. Cincinnati, OH: South-Western, 2000, p. 2.

4. Adapted from C. Meyer. What's the matter? Business 2.0, March 2000, pp. 193–196; M. Sawney. Making new markets. Business 2.0, March 2000, pp. 202–211; D. F. Spulber. Clock wise. Business 2.0, March 2000, pp. 212–215; D. Tapscott. Minds over matter. Business 2.0, March 2000, pp. 220–229.

5. R. A. Pitts and D. Lei. Strategic Management: Building and Sustaining Competitive Advantage. Cincinnati, OH: South-Western, 2003, pp. 307–347.

6. M. Sawney, pp. 197–201.

7. D. Lei and J. W. Slocum, Jr. Organization designs to renew competitive advantage. Organizational Dynamics, 31, 2002, pp. 1–18.

8. S. A. Mohrman, D. Finegold, and J. A. Klein. Designing the knowledge enterprise. Organizational Dynamics, 31, 2002, pp. 134–150; R. Lubit. Tacit knowledge and knowledge management. Organizational Dynamics, 29, 2001, pp. 164–178.

9. Calgary sheds new light on environmental stewardship: Launch of environSmart streetlights retrofit project. Canadian Corporate News, March 27, 2002; http://www.gov. calgary.ab.ca/roads/streetlight (December 2002).

10. G. J. Castrogiovanni. Organization task environments: Have they changed? Journal of Management, 28, 2002, pp. 129–150.

11. L. V. Ryan and M. Schneider. The antecedents of institutional investor activism. Academy of Management Review, 27, 2002, pp. 544–573.

12. M. DiNatale and S. Boraa. The labor force experience of women from "Generation X." Monthly Labor Review, March 2002, pp. 3–15; H. N. Fullerton, Jr., and M. Toossi. Labor force projections to 2010: Steady growth and changing composition. Monthly Labor Review, December 2001, pp. 21–38.

13. S. Mohrman. Designing work for knowledge-based competition. In S. Jackson, M. Hitt, and A. DeNisi (Eds.). Managing Knowledge for Sustained Competitive Advantage: Designing Strategies for Effective Human Resource Management. San Francisco: Jossey-Bass, 2003, pp. 94–126.

14. B. Rajagopalan, B. Peterson, and S. Watson. The rise of free agency: Is it inevitable? Organizational Dynamics, 32(1), 2003, pp. 93–104.

15. R. C. Barnett and D. T. Hall. How to use reduced hours to win the war for talent. Organizational Dynamics, 29, 2001, pp. 192–210; M. K. Duffy, D. C. Ganster, and M. Pagon. Social undermining in the workplace. Academy of Management Journal, 45, 2002, pp. 331–351.

16. G. Hofstede. Cultures and Organizations: Software of the Mind. New York: McGraw-Hill, 2000, p. 5.

17. G. Hofstede. Culture's Consequences: International Differences in Work-Related Values. London: Sage, 1980; F. Trompenaars and C. Hampden-Turner. Riding the Waves of Culture. New York: McGraw-Hill, 1998.

18. Used with permission from P. Dorfman. Cultural Values Questionnaire. Las Cruces: New Mexico State University, 2000.

19. G. Hofstede. Culture's Consequences: Comparing Values, Behaviors Institutions and Organizations Across Cultures, 2nd ed. London: Sage, 2001; R. Hallowell, D. Bowen, and C. Knoop. Four Seasons goes to Paris. Academy of Management Executive, 16(4), 2002, pp. 7–24; M. Door. Cultural Study of France (unpublished paper). Dallas, TX: Southern Methodist University, 2003; B. McSweeney. Hofstede's model of national cultural differences and their consequence: A triumph of faith. Human Relations, 55, 2002, pp. 89–119.

20. M. Javidan and R. J. House. Leadership and cultures around the world: Findings from GLOBE. Journal of World Business, 37, 2002, pp. 1–89; M. Voronov and J. A. Singer. The myth of individualism-collectivism: A critical review. Journal

of *Social Psychology*, 42(4), 2002, pp. 461–481.

21. M. E. Porter. *Competitive Strategy: Techniques for Analyzing Industries and Competitiveness.* New York: Free Press, 1980; D. C. Hambrick and J. W. Frederickson. Are you sure you have a strategy? *Academy of Management Executive*, 15, 2001, pp. 48–59; R. A. Burgelman. Strategy as vector and the inertia of coevolutionary lock-in. *Administrative Science Quarterly*, 47, 2002, pp. 325–357.

22. Interview with J. Birch, senior vice president, Operations, Taco Bell, Dallas, TX, December 2002.

23. Interview with B. Mike, director of communications, Yum Brands Inc., Dallas, TX, January 2003.

24. M. Seo and W. E. D. Creed. Institutional contradictions, praxis, and institutional change: A dialectical perspective. *Academy of Management Review*, 27, 2002, pp. 222–247.

25. D. L. Coutu. Negotiating with a net. *Harvard Business Review*, 80(10), 2002, pp. 49–54.

26. M. Bennedsen and S. Feldmann. Lobbying legislatures. *Journal of Political Economy*, 110, 2002, pp. 919–937.

27. B. R. Koka and John E. Prescott. Strategic alliances as social capital: A multidimensional view. *Strategic Management Journal*, 23, 2002, pp. 795–817; L. A. Isabella. Managing an alliance is nothing like business as usual. *Organizational Dynamics*, 31, 2002, pp. 47–59.

28. P. Kenis and D. Knoke. How organizational field networks shape interorganizational tie-format. *Academy of Management Review*, 27, 2002, pp. 275–294.

29. W. E. Hopkins and S. A. Hopkins. Effects of cultural recomposition on group interaction processes. *Academy of Management Review*, 27, 2002, pp. 541–553.

30. *Adapted from* http://www.aarp.org, and http://www.aarp.org/ontheissues/issueAARPVote.html (December 2002).

31. L. Aiman-Smith and S. G. Green. Implementing new manufacturing technology: The related effects of technology characteristics and user learning activities. *Academy of Management Journal*, 45, 2002, pp. 421–430; R. D. Klassen and D. C. Whybark. The impact of environmental technologies on manufacturing performance. *Academy of Management Journal*, 42, 1999, pp. 599–615.

32. H. J. Watson, B. H. Wixom, and D. L. Goodhue. The effects of technology-enabled business strategy at First American Corporation. *Organizational Dynamics*, 31, 2002, pp. 313–323.

33. *Adapted from* P. Siekman. Jeep builds a new kind of plant. *Fortune*, November 11, 2002, pp. T166A-T168J.

34. *Adapted from* R. A. Pitts and D. Lei. *Strategic Management: Building and Sustaining Competitive Advantage,* 3rd ed. Cincinnati, OH: South-Western, 2003, pp. 179–180.

35. See http://www.internationalcargosystems.com.

36. *Adapted from* http://www.hoovers.com; http://www.galoob.com; http://www.natoonline.org; interviews with Terrell Falk, vice president, Sales and Marketing, Cinemark Theaters, Dallas, TX, March 2003; Mariann Grosso, manager, NATO, Los Angeles, January 2003; G. Verter and A. M. McGahan. *Coming Soon: A Theater Near You.* Boston, MA: Harvard Business School, 1998, Case Number 9-797-011.

Chapter 4

1. *Adapted from* B. Saporito. Can Wal-Mart get any bigger? *Time*, January 13, 2003, pp. 38–43; B. Rahman. Wal-Mart tightens hold on Seiyu. *Financial Times*, January 15, 2003, p. 27; interview with Jody Ewing, replenishment manager, Wal-Mart, Dallas, TX, January 2003.

2. K. Moore and A. Rugman. Does globalization wear Mickey Mouse ears? *Across the Board*, January/February 2003, pp. 11–12.

3. D. Fonda. Innocents abroad. *Time*, November 25, 2002, pp. A17ff; S. Werner and L. E. Brouthers. How international is management? *Journal of International Business Studies*, 33, 2002, pp. 583–592.

4. R. S. Bhagat, B. L. Kedia, P. D. Harveston, and H. Triandia. Cultural variations in crossborder transfer of organizational knowledge: An integrative framework. *Academy of Management Review,* 27, 2002, pp. 204–222; M. Javidan and R. J. House. Leadership and cultures around the world: Findings from GLOBE. *Journal of World Business*, 37, 2002, pp. 1–89; D. A. Griffith. The role of communication competencies in internal business relationship development. *Journal of World Business*, 37, 2002, pp. 256–265.

5. C. Nakata and K. Sivakumar. Instituting the marketing concept in a multinational setting: The role of national culture. *Journal of the Academy of Marketing Science*, 29, 2001, pp. 20–28.

6. J. M. Mezias. Identifying liabilities of foreignness and strategies to minimize their effect: A case of labor lawsuit judgments in the United States. *Strategic Management Journal*, 23, 2002, pp. 229–245.

7. V. Pothukuchi, F. Damanpour, J. Choi, and S. H. Park. National and organizational culture differences in international joint ventures. *Journal of International Business Studies*, 2002, 33, pp. 243–253; G. Apfelthaler, H. J. Muller, and R. R. Rehder. Corporate global cultures as a competitive advantage: Learning from Germany and Japan in Alabama and Austria. *Journal of World Business*, 37, 2002, pp. 108–119.

8. R. M. Peterson, C. C. Dibrell, and T. L. Pett. Long vs. short-term performance perspectives of Western Europe, Japanese and U.S. countries: Where do they lie? *Journal of World Business*, 37, 2002, pp. 245–256.

9. N. J. Adler. *International Dimensions of Organizational Behavior*, 4th ed. Cincinnati, OH: South-Western, 2002.

10. J. B. Cullen. *Multinational Management: A Strategic Approach*, 2nd ed. Cincinnati, OH: South-Western, 2002, pp. 68–97; G. Gordon and T. Williams. *Doing Business in Mexico: A Practical Guide*. New York: Best Business Books, Hawthorne Press, 2002.

11. Cullen, p. 553.

12. R. Ghemawat. Distance still matters. *Harvard Business Review*, 79(8), 2001, pp. 137–146.

13. *Adapted from* R. J. Mockler. *Multinational Strategic Management*. New York: International Business Press, Hawthorne Press, 2002, pp. 276–298; N. J. Adler. *International Dimensions of Organizational Behavior*, 3rd ed. Cincinnati, OH: South-Western, 1997, pp. 209–211.

14. J. Nesteruk. Conceptions of the corporation and the prospects of sustainable peace. *Vanderbilt Journal of Transnational Law*, 35, 2002, pp. 437–455; C. J. Waller, T. Verdier, and R. Gina. Corruption: Top down or bottom up? *Economic Inquiry*, 40(4), 2002, pp. 688–704.

15. A more detailed description of the CPI can be found at http://www.transparency.org/cpi/index.html#cpi; also see J. M. Oetzel, R. A. Bettis, and M. Zenner. Country risk measures: How risky are they? *Journal of World Business*, 36, 2001, pp. 128–145.

16. N. King. Trade imbalance: Why Uncle Sam wrote a big check to a sparkler maker. *Wall Street Journal*, December 5, 2002, pp. A1ff.

17. Coke and small farmers lobby against sugar producers. *Asia Pacific Intelligence Wire*, November 14, 2002; D. Salierno. Bribery gauged worldwide. *Internal Auditor*, 59(4), 2002, pp. 14–16; Adler, *International Dimensions*, 4th ed.; B. W. Husted. Culture and international anti-corruption agreements in Latin America. *Journal of Business Ethics*, 37(4), 2002, pp. 413–423.

18. L. O. Omolo. UNHCR milking refugees. *New African*, April 2001, pp. 10–11.

19. M. A. Geo-JaJa, and G. L. Mangum. The Foreign Corrupt Practices Act's consequences for U.S. trade. *Journal of Business Ethics*, 24(3), 2000, pp. 245–256.

20. Gifts and gratuities abounded in the last days of HIH. *Asia Africa Intelligence Wire*, August 7, 2002; http://www.ethics.org (January 2003).

21. *Adapted from* R. Calori, T. Atamer, and P. Nunes. *The Dynamics of International Competition*. London: Sage Publications, 2000, pp. 121–126.

22. http://www.wto.org/english/news (January 2003).

23. http://www.usmcoc.org/n6.html (January 2003).

24. 31 *maquiladora* plants close in Yucatan. *Internet Securities*, December 9, 2002, p. 1008343; Taking stock of the North American Free Trade Agreement. *AgExporter*, 14(8), 2002, pp. 4–7; E. S. Kras. *Management in two cultures: Bridging the gap between U.S. and Mexican Managers*. Yarmouth, ME: Intercultural Press, 1995.

25. *Adapted from* H. W. Lane, M. B. Brechu, and D. T. A. Wesley. Mabe's president Luis Berrondo Avalos on teams and industry competitiveness. *Academy of Management Executive*, 13(3), 1999, pp. 8–10, and http://www.mabe.com.mx (January 2003); also see N. Athanassiou, W. F. Crittenden, L. M. Kelly, and P. Marquez. Founder centrality effects on the Mexican family top management's group. Firm culture, strategic vision and goals, and firm performance. *Journal of World Business*, 37, 2002, pp. 139–150.

26. http://europa.eu.int/comm/eurostat (January 2003).

27. Ibid.

28. W. P. Wan and R. E. Hoskisson. Home country environments, corporation diversification strategies: Theory and evidence. *Academy of Management Journal*, 46, 2003, pp. 27–45.

29. Interview with M. Bohn, manager, Quality and Business Systems, Celanese Chemical Corporation, Dallas, TX, January 2003; also see S. M. Toh and A. S. DeNisi. A model of the impact of expatriate human resources practices on host country national: A social identity perspective. *Academy of Management Review*, 28, 2003, in press.

30. http://www.countertrade.org/faqs.htm (January 2003); D. West. Countertrade. *Business Credit*, 104(4), 2002, pp. 48–52.

31. R. Culpan. *Global Business Alliances: Theory and Practice*. Westport, CT: Quorum Books, 2002, pp. 91–93.

32. http://www.newhorizons.com (January 2003).

33. H. Chen and T. Chen. Governance structure in strategic alliances: Transaction cost versus resource-based perspective. *Journal of World Business*, 38, 2003, pp. 1–14.

34. I. Berdrow and H. W. Lane. International joint ventures: Creating value through successful knowledge management. *Journal of World Business*, 38, 2003, pp. 15–30; S. Zahra and A. P. Nielsen. Sources of capabilities, integration and technology commercialization. *Strategic Management Journal*, 23(6), 2002, pp. 377–399.

35. Adler, *International Dimension*, 4th ed.

36. *Adapted from* http://www.icipaints.com (January 2003).

37. D. Lei and J. W. Slocum, Jr. Organization designs to renew competitive advantage. *Organizational Dynamics*, 31, 2002, pp. 1–18; J. K. Sebenius. The hidden challenge of cross-border negotiations. *Harvard Business Review*, 80(3), 2002, pp. 76–89.

38. *Adapted from* http://www.elcompanies.com/htm (January 2003).

Chapter 5

1. *Adapted from* Carolyn Minerich, Carmin Industries: SBA small business winner. http//:appl.sba.gov/sbsuccess/2002/ (November 4, 2002); Carmin Industries. http//:www.waterjet.net (November 4, 2002).

2. *Adapted from* A. Abrams. *The Successful Business Plan: Secrets & Strategies*. Palo Alto, CA: Running 'R' Media, 2000, p. 2.

3. U1: Jake Burton. *Fast Company*, April 2000, p. 122; J. B. Carpenter, How we got started. http://www.fortune.com/sitelets/innovators/burton.html (November 1, 2002).

4. M. Hofman. The razor's edge. *Inc.*, March 2000, pp. 86–87; HeadBlade Company, LLC. http://www.headblade.com (November 4, 2002).

5. *Adapted from* M. Kwak. People person. *INC 500*, October 15, 2002, pp. 104–105.

6. Letter from TOG's president. http:www.tog-usa.com (November 6, 2002).

7. D. L. Sexton and H. Landstrom (Eds.). *Handbook of Entrepreneurship*. Malden, MA: Blackwell, 2000.

8. T. W. Zimmerer and N. W. Scarborough. *Essentials of Entrepreneurship and Small Business Management*, 3rd ed. Upper Saddle River, NJ: Pearson Education, 2002.

9. National Business Incubation Association. What defines a business incubator? http://www.nbia.org (November 6, 2002).

10. *Adapted from* University of North Carolina at Chapel Hill. Incubator characteristics. http://www.planning.unc.edu/courses (November 6, 2002).

11. About Kohler Co. http://www.kohlers.com/corp (November 6, 2002).

12. A. J. Sherman. *Parting Company*. Washington, DC: Kiplinger Washington Editors, 1999.

13. D. P. Moore and E. H. Buttner. *Women Entrepreneurs: Moving Beyond the Glass Ceiling*. Thousand Oaks, CA: Sage, 1997.

14. R. G. McGrath and I. MacMillan. *The Entrepreneurial Mindset*. Boston: Harvard Business School Press, 2000; B. A. Baron and G. D. Markham. Beyond social capital: How social skills can enhance entrepreneurs' success. *Academy of Management Executive*, 14(1), 2000, pp. 106–116.

15. D. C. McClelland. Characteristics of successful entrepreneurs. *Journal of Creative Behavior*, 21, 1987, pp. 219–233; O. C. Hansemark. Predictive validity of TAT and CMPS on the entrepreneurial activity "start of a new business": A longitudinal study. *Journal of Managerial Psychology*, 15, 2000, pp. 634–654.

16. C. Ghosh. The comeback queen. *Forbes*, September 20, 1999, pp. 86–87. Radio One, Inc. Hoover's Online. http://cobrands.hoovers.com (November 8, 2002).

17. H. Page. Like father, like son? Entrepreneurial history repeats itself. *Entrepreneur*, 20, 1997, pp. 45–53.

18. *Adapted from* Adrian Lugo: SBA small business 2002 state winner. http://appl.sba.gov/sbsuccess/2002 (November 4, 2002); LUGO Construction Inc. http://lugoconst.com (November 8, 2002).

19. *Adapted from* Joseph Sanda: SBA small business 2002 state winner. http://app1.sba.gov/sbsuccess/2002 (November 4, 2002); Astute Solutions. http://www.astutesolutions.com (November 8, 2002).

20. *Adapted from* Daniel Driesenga: SBA small business 2002 state winner. http://appl.sba.gov/sbsuccess/2002 (November 4, 2002); Driesenga & Associates Inc. http:www.driesenga.com (November 8, 2002).

21. Ibid.

22. A. Baron and G. D. Markham. Beyond social capital: How social skills can enhance entrepreneurs' success. *Academy of Management Executive*, 14, 2000, pp. 106–115.

23. *Adapted from* J. Finegan. Pipe dreams. *Inc.*, August 1994, pp. 64–72.

24. G. J. Castrogiovanni. Pre-startup planning and the survival of new small businesses: Theoretical linkages. *Journal of Management*, 22, 1996, pp. 801–822.

25. *Adapted from* W. A. Sohlman. How to write a great business plan. *Harvard Business Review*, July–August 1997, p. 106.

26. Our company: Barnes & Noble. http://www.barnesandnobleinc.com/company (December 21, 2002).

27. *Adapted from* S. Venkataraman. Ten principles of entrepreneurial creation. *Batten Briefings* (newsletter of the Batten Institute, Darden Business School, University of Virginia), Autumn 2002, pp. 1, 6, 7.

28. P. J. Adelman and A. M. Marks. *Entrepreneurial Finance: Finance for Small Business*, 2nd ed. Upper Saddle River, NJ: Prentice Hall, 2001.

29. N. M. Carter, M. Williams, and P. D. Reynolds. Discontinuance among new firms in retail: The influence of initial resources, strategy, and gender. *Journal of Business Venturing*, 12, 1997, pp. 125–145.

30. B. Zider. How venture capital works. *Harvard Business Review*, November–December 1998, pp. 131–139; H. Riquelme and J. Walson. Do venture capitalists' implicit theories on new business success/failure have empirical validity? *International Small Business Journal*, 20, 2002, pp. 395–421.

31. N. Brodsky and B. Burlingham. My life as an angel. *Inc.*, July 1997, pp. 43–48.

32. H. J. Sapienza and M. A. Korsgaard. Procedural justice in entrepreneur-investor relations. *Academy of Management Journal*, 39, 1996, pp. 544–574; D. M. Cable and S. Shane. A prisoner's dilemma approach to entrepreneur-venture capitalist relationships. *Academy of Management Review*, 22, 1997, pp. 142–176.

33. T. S. Manolova, C. G. Brush, L. F. Edelman, and P. G. Greene.

Internationalization of small firms: Personal factors revisited. *International Small Business Journal*, 20, 2002, pp. 9–31.

34. B. M. Oviatt and P. Phillips McDougall. Global start-ups: Entrepreneurs on a worldwide stage. *Academy of Management Executive*, 9, 1995, pp. 30–79.

35. T. W. Zimmerer and N. M. Scarborough. *Essentials of Entrepreneurship and Small Business Management*, 3rd ed. Upper Saddle River, NJ: Prentice Hall, 2002, p. 19.

36. M. Coulter. *Entrepreneurship in Action*. Upper Saddle River, NJ: Prentice Hall, 2001.

37. M. Selz. Caught in the crossfire. *Wall Street Journal*, May 22, 1997, p. R15.

38. C. Hayes. Business dynamos: Women business achievers. *Black Enterprise*, August 1998, pp. 58–79; K. Greenberg. The pacesetter: ACT*1 Personnel Services. *Los Angeles Business Journal*, September 23, 2002, p. 3. For more information on ACT*1 Personnel Services, go to http://www.act-1.com (December 23, 2002).

39. *Adapted from* L. Cowan. The board of directors. *Wall Street Journal*, October 28, 2002, p. R6; Ready Pac Produce. http://www.readypacproduce.com/about (December 23, 2002).

40. G. Hamel. *Leading the Revolution*. Boston: Harvard Business School Press, 2000.

41. G. Pinchott III. *Intrapreneurship*. New York: Harper & Row, 1985.

42. For more information on Lou Dobbs, go to http://www.cnn.com/CNN/anchors_reporters (December 24, 2002).

43. M. Buckingham and C. Coffman. *First, Break All the Rules: What the World's Great Managers Do Differently*. New York: Simon & Schuster, 1999.

44. M. E. McGill and J. W. Slocum, Jr. *The Smarter Organization: How to Adapt to Meet Marketplace Needs*. New York: John Wiley & Sons, 1994.

45. S. Venkataraman, pp. 1, 6, 7.

46. Kink BMX: SBA young entrepreneur of the year winner. http://app1.sba.gov/sbsuccess/2002 (November 14, 2002); Kink Bike Co. news. http://www.kinkbmx.com/news.html (November 4, 2002).

Chapter 6

1. *Adapted from* Nortel Networks. *Code of Business Conduct.* http://www.nortelnetworks.com (March 10, 2003).

2. Ibid.

3. W. W. George. Restoring governance to our corporations: Crisis in the corporate world. *Vital Speeches of the Day*, 68, 2002, pp. 791–796.

4. Ibid.

5. Business for Social Responsibility. *Business Ethics*. BSR White Paper. http://www.bsr.org (September 25, 2002); A. J. Vogl. Does it pay to be good! *Across the Board*, January/February 2003, pp. 16–23.

6. L. L. Nash. *Good Intentions Aside: A Manager's Guide to Ethical Problems*. Boston: Harvard Business School Press, 1993.

7. W. W. George, pp. 793–794.

8. *Adapted from* S. E. Jackson and R. S. Schuler. *Managing Human Resources: A Partnership Perspective*, 8th ed. Cincinnati, OH: South-Western, 2002. Used with permission.

9. *Adapted from Employment Law Briefs*. Washington, DC: Schmeltzer, Aptaker, and Shepard, November 2002, pp. 1–4.

10. F. Navran. Are your employees cheating to keep up? *Workforce*, August 1997, pp. 58–61; J. Krohe, Jr. Ethics are nice, but business is business. *Across the Board*, April 1997, pp. 16–22.

11. Ethics Resource Center. http://www.ethic.org (March 2003).

12. *Adapted from* F. Navran. Seven steps for changing the ethical culture of an organization. http://www.ethics.org/resources (March 2003); J. Joseph. *Integrating Ethics and Compli-ance Programs*. Washington, DC: Ethics Resource Center, 2001; J. Brown. Setting the stage for modeling ethical behavior. http://www.ethics.org/resources (March 2003).

13. *Adapted from* Nortel Networks. *Conflicts of Interest.* http://www.nortelnetworks.com (March 10, 2003). For a discussion of cross-cultural ethics, see C. J. Robertson and W. F. Crittenden. Mapping moral philosophies: Strategic implications for multinational firms. *Strategic Management Journal*, 24, 2003, pp. 385–392.

14. L. Kohlberg. *Psychology of Moral Development: The Nature and Validity of Moral Stages: Essays on Moral Development Series*. Glenview, IL: Harper-Collins, 1984; G. D. Boxterand and C. A. Rarick. Education and moral development of managers: Kohlberg's stages of moral development and integrative education. *Journal of Business Ethics*, 6, 1987, pp. 243–248; also see M. Kaptein. The diamond of managerial integrity. *European Management Journal*, 21, 2003, pp. 99–108.

15. J. P. Near and M. P. Miceli. Effective whistle-blowing. *Academy of Management Review*, 20, 1995, pp. 679–708; M. J. Gundlach, S. C. Douglas, and M. J. Martinko. The decision to blow the whistle: A social information processing framework. *Academy of Management Review*, 28, 2003, pp. 107–123.

16. L. M. Franze. The whistleblower provisions of the Sarbanes-Oxley Act of 2002. *Insights: The Corporate and Securities Law Advisor*, December 2002, pp. 12–21.

17. R. A. Johnson. *Whistleblowing: When It Works—and Why*. Boulder, CO: Lynne Rienner Publishers, 2001.

18. *Adapted from* P. Dwyer and D. Carney. The year of the whistleblower. *Business Week*, December 16, 2002, pp. 107–110.

19. *Adapted from* C. Haddad and A. Barrett. A whistle-blower rocks an industry. *Business Week*, June 24, 2002, pp. 126–130.

20. *Source:* Marshall Sashkin. Used with permission.

21. M. Schminke, M. L. Ambrose, and T. W. Noel. The effect of ethical frameworks on perceptions of organizational justice. *Academy of Management Journal*, 40, 1997, pp. 1198–1207; J. S. Mill. *Utilitarianism.* Indianapolis: Bobs-Merrill, 1957 (originally published 1863).

22. M. A. Friedman. Friedman doctrine: The social responsibility of business is to increase its profits. *New York Times Magazine*, September 13, 1970, pp. 32ff.

23. J. Q. Wilson. Adam Smith on business ethics. *California Management Review*, Fall 1989, pp. 59–72.

24. S. M. Puffer and D. J. McCarthy. Finding the common ground in Russian and American business ethics. *California Management Review*, Winter 1995, pp. 29–46.

25. J. D. Aram. *Presumed Superior: Individualism and American Business.* Englewood Cliffs, NJ: Prentice Hall, 1993.

26. L. E. Lomasky. *Persons, Rights, and the Moral Community.* New York: Oxford University Press, 1997.

27. M. Gowen, S. Ibarreche, and C. Lackey. Doing the right things in Mexico. *Academy of Management Executive*, 10, 1996, pp. 74–81.

28. E. Alderman and C. Kenne. *The Right to Privacy.* New York: Random House, 1997.

29. *Adapted from Notice of Privacy Policies.* Bloomington, IL: State Farm Insurance, 2003.

30. P. Jenkins. *Beyond Tolerance: Child Pornography Online.* New York: New York University Press, 2001.

31. J. E. Roemer. *Theories of Distributive Justice.* Cambridge, MA: Harvard University Press, 1998.

32. B. Spence. Welcoming address. 2002 National Association of Female Executives Conference. http://www.nafe.com (March 2003); also see C. Goldin. *Understanding the Gender Gap: An Economic History of American Women.* New York:

Oxford University Press, 1990; R. J. Burke and D. L. Nelson (Eds.). *Advancing Women's Careers.* Malden, MA: Blackwell, 2002.

33. S. Prasso and L. Lavelle. CEO pay: Pain, but still plenty of gain. *Business Week*, February 24, 2003, pp. 16–20.

34. B. P. Niehoff and R. H. Moorman. Justice as a mediator of the relationship between methods of monitoring and organizational citizenship behavior. *Academy of Management Journal*, 36, 1993, pp. 527–556.

35. P. Feuille and D. R. Chachere. Looking fair or being fair. Remedial voice procedures in nonunion workplaces. *Journal of Management*, 21, 1995, pp. 27–42.

36. A. Carroll and A. K. Buchholtz. *Business and Society: Ethics and Stakeholder Management.* Cincinnati, OH: South-Western, 2003.

37. S. A. Waddock, C. Bodwell, and S. B. Graves. Responsibility: The new business imperative. *Academy of Management Executive*, 16, 2002, pp. 132–148.

38. T. M. Jones, A. C. Wicks, and R. E. Frieman. Stakeholder theory: The state of the art. In N. E. Bowie (Ed.) *The Blackwell Guide to Business Ethics*. Malden, MA: Blackwell, 2002, pp. 19–37.

39. Nortel Networks. *Commitments to Stakeholders.* http://www.nortelnetworks.com (March 2003).

40. W. M. Lafferty and J. R. Meadowcroft (Eds.). *Implementing Sustainable Development Strategies and Initiatives in High Consumption Societies.* New York: Cambridge University Press, 2001.

41. Norm Thompson, Inc. *Our Commitment to Sustainability.* http://www.normthompson.com (March 2003).

42. Ibid.

43. C. A. Raiborn, B. E. Joyner, and J. W. Logan. ISO 14000 and the bottom line. *Quality Progress*, November 1999, pp. 89–93. To learn more about the ISO 14000 standards, go

to International Organization for Standardization. http://www.iso.ch (March 2003).

44. J. E. Post, L. E. Preston, and S. Sachs. Managing the extended enterprise: The new stakeholder view. *California Management Review*, 45(1), 2002, pp. 6–28; D. A. Rondinelli and T. London. How corporations and environmental groups cooperate: Assessing cross-sector alliances and collaborations. *Academy of Management Executive*, 17(1), 2003, pp. 61–76.

45. M. Treacy and F. Wiersema. *The Discipline of Market Leaders: Choose Your Customers, Narrow Your Focus, Dominate Your Market.* Reading, MA: Addison-Wesley, 1997.

46. J. T. Mahoney, A. S. Huff, and J. O. Huff. Toward a new social contract theory in organization science. *Journal of Management Inquiry*, 3, 1994, pp. 153–168.

47. V. Rath. The Collins Companies environmental excellence awards. *Business Ethics*, November/December 2001, pp. 10–11. For a description of the many sustainability practices of the Collins Companies, go to http://www.collinswood.com (March 2003).

48. Nortel Networks. *Code of Business Conduct.* http://www.nortelnetworks.com (March 2003).

49. General Motors. *Corporate Responsibility and Sustainability Report.* http://gm.com/company/gmability (March 2003).

50. Ibid.

51. C. C. Verschoor. Should ethical principles apply to all? *Strategic Finance*, January 2003, pp. 18, 22. This case was prepared by Curtis C. Verschoor, School of Accountancy and MIS, DePaul University. Used with permission.

52. *Scenario 1:* James R. Harris. *The Harris Survey,* Auburn University; *scenario 2:* B. Z. Posner and W. H. Schmidt. Ethics in American companies: A managerial perspective. *Journal of Business Ethics*, 6, 1987, pp. 383–391; *scenario 3:* D. J.

Fritzsche and H. Becker. Linking management behavior to ethical philosophy: An empirical investigation. *Academy of Management Journal*, 27, 1984, pp. 172–180.

Chapter 7

1. Our credo. http://www.jnj.com (April 2003); see also A. Barrett. Staying on top. *Business Week*, May 5, 2003, pp. 60–68.

2. Letter to shareholders. In *Johnson & Johnson 2002 Annual Report*. http://www.jnj.com/2002 Annual Report (April 2003).

3. S. Kaplan and E. D. Beinhocker. The real value of strategic planning. *MIT Sloan Management Review*, Winter 2003, pp. 71–76; T. Leahy. Strategic planning meets business performance. *Business Finance*, February 2003, pp. 21–26.

4. Strategic planning at Johnson & Johnson. http://www.investor. jnj.com (April 2003).

5. M. A. Hitt, R. D. Ireland, and R. E. Hoskisson. *Strategic Management: Competitiveness and Globalization*, 5th ed. Cincinnati: South-Western, 2003.

6. M. D. Watkins and M. H. Bazerman. Predictable surprises: The disasters you should have seen coming. *Harvard Business Review*, March 2003, pp. 72–80; C.W. Roney. Planning for strategic contingencies. *Business Horizons*, 46(2), 2003, pp. 35–42.

7. *Adapted from* C. Vitello and J. Kuhn. Business continuity planning: Partner with your bank to ensure disaster readiness. *AFP Exchange*, September/October 2002, pp. 156–160; S. Craig and P. Beckett. What will Wall Street do on red alert? *Wall Street Journal*, February 27, 2003, pp. C1, C3.

8. M. Lisack and J. Roos. Be coherent, not visionary. *Long Range Planning*, 34(1), 2001, pp. 53–70.

9. Vision and mission statements are from the Web sites for Lowe's, http://www.lowes.com (April 2003); Intel, http://www.intel.com (April 2003); and Dell Computer, http://www.dell.com (April 2003).

10. *Johnson and Johnson 2002 Annual Report*. http://www.jnj.com (April 2003).

11. D. O. Faulkner and A. Campbell (Eds.). *Oxford Handbook of Strategy*. New York: Oxford University Press, 2003.

12. N. Argyres and A. M. McGahan. An interview with Michael Porter. *Academy of Management Executive*, 16(2), 2002, pp. 43–52.

13. *Adapted from* M. Dell. *Direct from Dell: Strategies That Revolutionized Industry*. New York: HarperBusiness, 1999; Michael Dell's keynote address. 2003 CES International Conference, January 9, 2003. Available at http://www.dell.com (April 2003); K. Jones. The Dell way. *Business 2.0*, February 2003, pp. 60–66.

14. Lowe's Form 10-Q. Submitted to Securities and Exchange Commission, November 1, 2002. Available at http://www.lowes.com (April 2003).

15. R. Sidel, S. Hensley, and D. P. Hamilton. Leading the news: Johnson & Johnson is in talks to buy Scios for $2 billion. *Wall Street Journal*, February 7, 2003, pp. A3, A5.

16. D. Henry. Mergers: Why most big deals don't pay off. *Business Week*, October 14, 2002, pp. 60–70; see also W. P. Wan and R. E. Hoskisson. Home country environments, corporate diversification strategies, and firm performance. *Academy of Management Journal*, 46(1), 2003, pp. 27–45.

17. Dynergy exits communication business. Dynergy press release, March 31, 2003. http://www.dynergy.com (April 2003); see also L. Dranikoff, T. Koller, and A. Schneider. Divestiture: Strategy's missing link. *Harvard Business Review*, May 2002, pp. 74–85.

18. M. Ligos. Clicks and misses. *Sales & Marketing*, June 2000, pp. 68–76; Retail brief: Toys 'R' Us. *Wall Street Journal*, March 25, 2003, p. D.7.

19. D. Fisher. Pulled in a new direction. *Forbes*, June 12, 2002, pp. 102–112.

20. K. H. Hammonds. How Google grows. *Fast Company*, April 2003, pp.

74–81; Google Inc. Company overview. http://www.google.com (April 2003).

21. CEMEX: About us. http://www. cemex.com (April 2003); D. Lindquist. From cement to services. *Chief Executive*, November 2002, pp. 48–50.

22. *Johnson and Johnson 2003 Annual Report*. http://www.jnj.com (April 2003).

23. Conglomerates. *Hoover's Online*. http://www.hoovers.com (April 2003); see also M. A. Hitt, J. S. Harrison, and R. D. Ireland. *Mergers and Acquisitions: A Guide to Creating Value for Stakeholders*. New York: Oxford University Press, 2001.

24. GE Business Directory. http://www.ge.com (April 2003).

25. Jeff Immelt on corporate governance. http://www.ge.com/en/ (April 2003).

26. *General Electric 2002 Annual Report*. http://www.ge.com (April 2003).

27. S. Tallman and K. Fladmoe-Lindquist. Internationalization, globalization, and capability-based strategy. *California Management Review*, 45(1), 2002, pp. 116–136.

28. S. Thurm. Leading the news: Cisco to buy home-networking leader. *Wall Street Journal*, March 21, 2003, pp. A3, A5.

29. Baxter international purchase. *Wall Street Journal*, March 25, 2003, p. B.4.

30. C. Edwards. The new HP: How's it doing? *Business Week*, December 23, 2002, pp. 52–54.

31. Hewlett-Packard: About us. http://www.hp.com (April 2003).

32. *Johnson & Johnson–Merck Consumer Pharmaceuticals Co.* http://www.hoovers.com (April 2003); see also J. J. Reuer (Ed.). *Strategic Alliances: Theory and Evidence*. New York: Oxford University Press, 2002.

33. Cadbury Schweppes completes acquisition of Adams. Cadbury Schweppes press release.

March 31, 2003. http://www.cadburyschweppes.com (April 2003); D. Ball, Adams to bring Cadbury debt as well as revenue. *Wall Street Journal*, December 18, 2002, pp. B8, B10.

34. *Berkshire Hathaway 2002 Annual Report*. http://www.berkshirehathaway.com (April 2003).

35. R. E. Hoskisson, M. A. Hitt, and R. D. Ireland. *Competing for Advantage*. Mason, OH: South-Western, 2004.

36. C. A. DeKluyer and J. A. Pearce II. *Strategy: A View from the Top*. Upper Saddle River, NJ: Prentice Hall, 2002.

37. About Lowe's. http://www.lowes.com (April 2003); see also B. A. Gutek, M. Groth, and B. Cherry. Achieving service success through relationships and enhanced encounters. *Academy of Management Executive*, 16(4), 2002, pp. 132–144.

38. S. E. Jackson and R. S. Schuler. *Managing Human Resources through Strategic Partnerships*. Mason OH: South-Western, 2002.

39. Lowe's careers. http://www.lowes.com (April 2003).

40. *American Express 2002 Annual Report*. http://www.americanexpress.com (April 2003).

41. J. Collins. *Good to Great: Why Some Companies Make the Leap . . . and Others Don't*. Glenview, IL: HarperCollins, 2002.

42. About Citigroup. http://www.citigroup.com (April 2003).

43. A. S. Horowitz. Extreme outsourcing: Does it work? *Computerworld*, May 10, 1999, pp. 50–51.

44. R. A. Pitts and D. Lei. *Strategic Management: Building and Establishing Competitive Advantage*. Mason, OH: South-Western, 2003.

45. T. W. Porter and S. C. Harper. Tactical implementation: The devil is in the details. *Business Horizons*, January–February 2003, pp. 53–60.

46. *Adapted from* H. J. Watson, B. H. Wixom, and D. L. Goodhue. The effects of technology-enabled business strategy at First American Corporation. *Organizational Dynamics*, 31, 2002, pp. 313–323.

47. M. E. Porter. *Competitive Advantage: Creating and Sustaining Superior Performance*, 2nd ed. New York: Free Press, 1998; M. E. Porter. *Michael E. Porter on Competition*. Boston: Harvard Business School Press, 1998.

48. D. Dexter. Bentley Beijing: Chariots on fire. *Business Week*, March 24, 2003, p. 66.

49. About E*Trade. http://www.etrade.com (April 2003).

50. L. Margonelli. How Ikea designs its sexy price tags. *Business 2.0*, October 2002, pp. 106–112; K. Kling and I. Goteman. IKEA CEO Anders Day on international growth and IKEA's unique corporate culture and brand identity. *Academy of Management Executive*, 17(1), 2003, pp. 31–37.

51. Ibid., pp. 106–112.

52. W. C. Kim and R. Mauborgne. Charting your company's future. *Harvard Business Review*, June 2002, pp. 76–83; D. Rosenblum, D. Tomlinson, and L. Scott. Bottom-feeding for blockbuster business. *Harvard Business Review*, March 2003, pp. 52–61.

53. *Adapted from* Andrew B. Stephens. *A Strategy Bred from Success: Grupo Bimbo*. Unpublished paper. Southern Methodist University, Dallas, TX, May 2003. Used with permission.

54. *Adapted from* Business description: HDI. http://www.multexinvestor.com (April 2003); Profile: Harley-Davidson, Inc. http://www.biz.yahoo.com (April 2003); *Harley-Davidson 2002 Annual Report*. http://www.harley-davidson.com (April 2003); J. Teresko. Fueled by innovation. *Industry Week*, December 2002, pp. 52–57.

Chapter 8

1. *Adapted from* G. T. Doran and J. Gunn. Decision making in high-tech firms: Perspectives of three executives. *Business Horizons*, November–December 2002, pp. 7–16.

2. J. G. Koomey. *Turning Numbers into Knowledge: Mastering the Art of Problem Solving*. Oakland, CA: Analytics Press, 2003.

3. G. T. Doran and J. Gunn, p. 13.

4. G. H. Anthes. Riding herd on risk. *Computerworld*, July 8, 2002, pp. 24–25.

5. E. F. Harrison. *The Managerial Decision-Making Process*, 5th ed. Boston: Houghton Mifflin, 1999.

6. *Adapted from* T. Mucha. The payoff for trying harder. *Business 2.0*, July 2002, pp. 84–86; About Avis. http://www.avis.com (May 2003).

7. L. Meulbroek. The promise and challenge of integrated risk management. *Risk Management and Insurance Review*, Spring 2002, pp. 55–66.

8. C. Dahle. Risky business. *Fast Company*, July–August 1999, pp. 70–72.

9. *Adapted from* Form 10-K for Intel Corporation. Filed with U.S. Securities and Exchange Commission on March 11, 2003; http://www.sec.gov/edgar.

10. I. I. Mitroff and M. C. Alpaslan. Preparing for evil. *Harvard Business Review*, April 2003, pp. 109–115.

11. *Adapted from* F. Warner. Finbarr O'Neill is not a car guy. *Fast Company*, November 2002, pp. 84–88; S. Freeman. Consumer Reports sees quality gains for GM, Hyundai. *Wall Street Journal*, November 8, 2002, p. B2; S. Freeman. Hyundai seeks big upgrade in its image. *Wall Street Journal*, March 19, 2002, p. B2.

12. R. Bohn. Stop fighting fires. *Harvard Business Review*, April 2000, pp. 83–91.

13. D. Miller, Q. Hope, R. Eisenstat, N. Foote, and J. Galbraith. The problem of solutions: Balancing clients and capabilities. *Business Horizons*, March–April 2002, pp. 3–12.

14. D. L. Coutu. Psychologist Karl E. Weick: Sense and reliability. *Harvard Business Review*, April 2003, pp. 84–91.

15. R. Hallowell, D. E. Bowen, and C. I. Knoop. Four seasons goes to

Paris. *Academy of Management Executive*, 16(4), 2002, pp. 7–24.

16. J. Goldenberg, R. Horowitz, A. Levav, and D. Mazursky. Finding your innovation sweet spot. *Harvard Business Review*, March 2003, pp. 120–129.

17. Ibid., pp. 120–129.

18. M. B. Chrissis, M. Conrad, and S. Shrum. *CMMI: Guidelines for Process Integration and Product Improvement.* Reading, MA: Addison-Wesley, 2003.

19. B. Dale and H. Bunney. *Total Quality Management Blueprint.* Malden, MA: Blackwell, 1999.

20. *Adapted from* G. H. Anthes. When five 9s aren't enough. *Computerworld*, October 8, 2001, pp. 48–49. About Visa. http://www.visa.com (May 23, 2003); J. Vijayan. 35 years of IT leadership: Securing the data. *Computerworld*, September 30, 2002, pp. 46–48.

21. L. V. Shavinina (Ed.). *The International Handbook of Innovation.* New York: Pergamon, 2003.

22. *Adapted from* G. Hamel. Innovation now. *Fast Company*, December 2002, pp. 115–123.

23. *Adapted from* A. Raskin. Physician, sell thyself. *Business 2.0*, May 2003, pp. 109–113.

24. The AmeriScan vision and mission. http://www.ameriscan.org (May 22, 2003).

25. R. M. Dawes and R. Hastie. *Rational Choice in an Uncertain World: The Psychology of Judgment and Decision Making.* Thousand Oaks, CA: Sage Publications, 2001.

26. J. Baron. *Thinking and Deciding*, 3rd ed. New York: Cambridge University Press, 2001.

27. M. Ray and R. Myers. *Creativity in Business.* Garden City, NY: Doubleday, 1986, pp. 94–96.

28. *Adapted from* T. Peterson. Getting real about real time. *Computerworld*, April 21, 2003, p. 36; About Maxtor. http://www.maxtor.com (May 24, 2003).

29. *Adapted from* C. D. Charitou and C. C. Markides. Responses to disruptive strategic innovation. *MIT Sloan Management Review*, Winter 2003, pp. 55–63; About Edward Jones. http://www.edwardjones.com (May 24, 2003).

30. T. Skinner, *Beyond the Summit: Setting and Surpassing Extraordinary Business Goals.* New York: Viking, 2003.

31. D. P. Baron. *Business and Its Environment,* 4th ed. Upper Saddle River, NJ: Prentice Hall, 2002.

32. C. R. Schoenberger. The greenhouse effect. *Forbes*, February 3, 2003, pp. 54–60.

33. G. T. Doran and J. Gunn, p. 9.

34. *Adapted from* R. C. Ford, C. P. Heaton, and S. W. Brown. Delivering excellent service: Lessons from the best firms. *California Management Review*, Fall 2001, pp. 39–56.

35. *Adapted from* A. DeMeyer, C. H. Lock, and M. T. Rich. Managing project uncertainty: From variation to chaos. *MIT Sloan Management Review*, Winter 2002, pp. 60–67.

36. *Adapted from* G. T. Doran and J. Gunn, p. 11.

37. G. T. Doran and J. Gunn, p. 13.

38. *Adapted from* C. Dahle. A steelmaker's heart of gold. *Fast Company*, June 2003, pp. 46–48; Dofasco's corporate profile. http://www.dofasco.ca (May 25, 2003); M. Rola. Dofasco retools to create communities of practice. *Computing Canada*, April 11, 2003, pp. 6–7.

39. E. Bonableau. Don't trust your gut. *Harvard Business Review*, May 2003, pp. 116–123.

40. H. A. Simon. *Administrative Behavior: A Study of Decision-Making Processes in Administrative Organizations*, 4th ed. New York: Free Press, 1997; A. Rubinstein. *Modeling Bounded Rationality.* Cambridge, MA: MIT Press, 1998.

41. T. D. Gilovich, D. W. Griffin, and D. Kahneman (Eds.). *Heuristics and Biases: The Psychology of Intuitive Judgment.* New York: Cambridge University Press, 2002.

42. G. Klein and K. E. Weick. Decisions: Making the right ones, learning from the wrong ones. *Across the Board*, June 2000, pp. 16–22.

43. G. T. Doran and J. Gunn, p. 9.

44. E. H. Foreman. How additional information can lead to inferior decisions—A paradox. *Decision Line*, July 1993, p. 3.

45. L. W. Busenitz. Entrepreneurial risk and strategic decision making: It's a matter of perspective. *Journal of Applied Behavioral Science*, 35, 1999, pp. 325–340.

46. M. Harvey and M. Novicevic. The trials and tribulations of addressing global organizational ignorance. *European Management Journal*, 17, 1999, pp. 431–443.

47. J. M. Roach. Simon says: Decision making is a "satisficing" experience. *Management Review*, January 1979, pp. 8–9.

48. P. M. Todd and G. Gigerenzer. Bounding rationality to the world. *Journal of Economic Psychology*, 24, 2003, pp. 143–165.

49. J. Frooman. Stakeholder influence strategies. *Academy of Management Review*, 24, 1999, pp. 191–205; J. Pfeffer. *Managing with Power: Politics and Influence in Organizations.* Boston: Harvard Business School Press, 1992.

50. E. B. Smith. Fluor settles whistleblower suit for $8.4 million. *Knight-Ridder/Tribune News*, June 23, 1997, p. 623B.

51. D. A. Buchanan, R. Badham, and D. Buchanan. *Power, Politics, and Organizational Change: Winning the Turf War.* Thousand Oaks, CA: Corvin Press, 1999.

52. J. Pfeffer. *New Directions for Organization Theory.* New York: Oxford University Press, 1997.

53. *Adapted from* E. Torbinson. The deal that kept American Airlines flying. *Bryan-College Station Eagle*, April 28, 2003, p. A2; W. Zellner. What was Don Carty thinking. *Business Week*, May 5, 2003, p. 32; W. Zellner and M. France. How American

execs covered the bases with Chapter 11 possible, they protected their pensions. *Business Week*, April 28, 2003, pp. 40–41; S. McCartney. At American, 48 hours of drama help airline avert bankruptcy. *Wall Street Journal*, April 28, 2003, pp. A1, A5.

54. *Adapted from* E. H. Neilsen and M. V. Hayagreeva Rao, "The Strategy-Legitimacy Nexus: A Thick Description," *Academy of Management Review*, 12, 1987, pp. 523–533; S. A. Hershon and L. B. Barnes. *A Meeting of the Board of Directors of the Henry Manufacturing Company* (Case 9-475-031). Boston: Intercollegiate Case Clearing House, 1979.

55. *Adapted from* G. J. Duran and E. E. Gomar. Living ethics: Meeting challenges in decision making. In *The 1997 Annual: Volume 1, Training*. San Francisco: Jossey-Bass/Pfeiffer, 1997, pp. 127–138.

56. *Adapted from* J. G. Lamkin. Ethics in action: Aligning decisions with organizational values. In *1998 Annual: Volume 2, Consulting*. San Francisco: Jossey-Bass/Pfeiffer, 1998, pp. 75–80.

57. *Adapted from* R. Roskin. Coping with ambiguity. In J. W. Peiffer and L. D. Goodstein (Eds.). *The 1982 Annual for Facilitators, Trainers, and Consultants*. San Diego: University Associates, 1982, pp. 108–116.

Chapter 9

1. *Adapted from* M. Zetlin. Putting communities to work. *Computerworld*, June 3, 2002, p. 40; Schlumberger's knowledge management hub. http://www.slb.com/hub (June 1, 2003); About SchlumbergerSema. http://www.schlumbergersema.com/about (June 1, 2003).

2. R. A. Noe, J. A. Colquitt, M. J. Simmering, and S. A. Alvarez. Knowledge management: Developing intellectual and social capital. In S. E. Jackson, M. A. Hitt, and A. S. DeNisi (Eds.). *Knowledge Management: Knowledge for Sustaining Competitive Advantage*. San Francisco: Jossey-Bass, 2003, pp. 209–242.

3. K. Mertins, P. Heisig, and J. Vorbeck (Eds.). *Knowledge Management: Concepts and Best Practices,* 2nd ed. New York: Springer Verlag, 2003.

4. T. H. Davenport, R. J. Thomas, and S. Cantrell. The mysterious art and science of knowledge-worker performance. *MIT Sloan Management Review*, Fall 2002, pp. 23–30.

5. J. Kluge, W. Stein, and T. Licht. *Knowledge Unplugged: The McKinsey & Company Global Survey on Knowledge Management*. Basingstoke, Hampshire, UK: Palgrave Macmillan, 2002.

6. W. C. Rappleye, Jr. Knowledge management: A force whose time has come. *Across the Board*, June 2000, special section–unpaginated; M. Easterby-Smith and M. Lyles (Eds.). *The Blackwell Handbook of Organizational Learning and Knowledge Management*. Cambridge, MA: Blackwell Publishing, 2004.

7. B. Buchel and S. Raub. Building knowledge-creating value networks. *European Management Journal,* 20(6), 2002, pp. 587–596.

8. M. Zetlin. Putting Communities to work. *Computerworld*, June 3, 2002, p. 40; About Clerica. http://www.clerica.com/e/about (June 2, 2003).

9. P. Gralla. Web services in action. *Computerworld*, May 19, 2003, pp. 36–39.

10. D. B. Fogel and C. J. Robinson (Eds.). *Computational Intelligence: The Experts Speak*. New York: John Wiley & Sons, 2003.

11. E. Turban and J. E. Aronson. *Decision Support Systems and Intelligent Systems*, 6th ed. Upper Saddle River, NJ: Prentice-Hall, 2001.

12. G. MacSweeney. Insurance visionaries: The innovation advantage. *Insurance and Technology*, March 1999, pp. 51–52; *Lincoln National Corporation 2002 Annual Report to Shareholders*, 2003, http://www.lfg.com (June 27, 2003).

13. G. Von Krogh, K. Ichijo, and I. Nonaka. *Enabling Knowledge Creation: How to Unlock the Mystery of Tacit Knowledge and Release the Power of Inno-vation*. New York: Oxford University Press, 2000.

14. Schlumberger's knowledge management hub. http://www.schlumbergersema.com/about (June 1, 2003).

15. Strategic technologies for 2020. http://www.battelle.org/forecasts (June 3, 2003).

16. J. E. Hanke, A. G. Reitsch, and D. W. Wichern. *Business Forecasting*, 7th ed. Upper Saddle River, NJ: Prentice-Hall, 2001.

17. *Adapted from* J. Huber. Trend track: Experts tell you how to spot tomorrow's hottest trends. *Business Startups*, January 1995, pp. 49–51; C. Russell. *Demographics of the U.S.: Trends and Projections*. Ithaca, NY: New Strategist Publications, 2001.

18. C. E. Sahakian. *The Delphi Method*. Skokie, IL: Corporate Partnering Institute, 1997.

19. G. Rowe and G. Wright. The Delphi technique as a forecasting tool: Issues and analysis. *International Journal of Forecasting*, 15(4), 1999, pp. 353–375.

20. *Adapted from* S. J. Adams. Projecting the next decade in safety management. *Professional Safety*, October 2001, pp. 26–29; C. W. Holsappe and K. D. Joshi. Knowledge manipulation activities: Results of a Delphi study. *Information & Management*, 39(6), 2002, pp. 477–490.

21. *Adapted from* D. Bertsche, C. Crawford, and S. E. Macadam. Is simulation better than experience? *The Mackenzie Quarterly*, 1996, 1, pp. 15–22.

22. Crystal Ball boasts ExperCorp's new venture planning for recreation markets. http://www.crystalball.com (June 27, 2003).

23. J. A. Ogilvy. *Creating Better Features: Scenario Planning as a Tool for a Better Tomorrow*. New York: Oxford University Press, 2002.

24. L. Fahey. Competitor scenarios. *Strategy & Leadership*, 31(1), 2003, pp. 32–44.

25. G. Ringland, K. Todd, and P. Schwartz. *Scenario Planning: Managing for the Future.* Somerset, NJ: John Wiley & Sons, 1998; H. Courtney. Decision-driven scenarios for assessing four levels of uncertainty. *Strategy & Leadership*, 31(1), 2003, pp. 14–22.

26. *Adapted from* S. Alden. Thinking ahead. *Credit Union Management*, July 2002, pp. 24–26.

27. Ibid, pp. 24–26; About Citizens-First Credit Union. http://www.citizensfirst.com (June 3, 2003).

28. This section draws on A. G. Robinson and S. Stern. *Corporate Creativity: How Innovation and Improvement Actually Happen.* San Francisco: Berrett-Koehler, 1997; J. Mauzy and R. A. Harriman. *Creativity, Inc.: Building an Inventive Organization.* Boston: Harvard Business School Press, 2003.

29. P. Israel. *Edison: A Life of Invention.* New York: John Wiley & Sons, 1999.

30. A. F. Osborn. *Applied Imagination*, 3rd ed. New York: Scribner's, 1963.

31. P. B. Paulus and Huei-Chang Yang. Idea generation in groups. A basis for creativity in organizations. *Organizational Behavior and Human Decision Processes*, 82(1), 2000, pp. 76–87.

32. A. F. Osborn, pp. 229–290.

33. A. F. Osborn, pp. 155–158.

34. A. F. Osborn, p. 156.

35. *Adapted from* A. F. Osborn, pp. 166–196.

36. G. Bachman. Brainstorming deluxe. *Training & Development*, January 2000, pp. 15–17; F. Hurt. Beyond brainstorming. *Successful Meetings*, June 2000, pp. 81–82.

37. *Adapted from* R. I. Sutton and T. A. Kelly. Creativity doesn't require isolation. Why product designers bring visitors "backstage." *California Management Review*, Fall 1997, pp. 75–91; J. Myerson. *IDEO: Masters of Innovation.* New York: Neues Publishing, 2001; T. Kelley, J. Littman, and T. Peters. *The Art of Innovation: Lessons in Creativity from IDEO, America's Leading Design Firm.* New York: Doubleday, 2001; About IDEO. http://www.ideo.com (June 4, 2003).

38. S. D. Williams. Self-esteem and the self-censorship of creative ideas. *Personnel Review*, 31(4), 2002, pp. 495–303.

39. J. M. Hender, D. L. Dean, T. L. Rodgers, and J. F. Nunamaker, Jr. An examination of the impact of stimuli type and GSS structure on creativity: Brainstorming versus non-brainstorming techniques in GSS environment. *Journal of Management Information Systems*, 18(4), 2002, pp. 59–85.

40. A. R. Dennis et al. Structuring time and task in electronic brainstorming. *MIS Quarterly*, 23(1), 1999, pp. 95–108.

41. B. Dale and H. Bunney. *Total Quality Blueprint.* Malden, MA: Blackwell, 1999, pp. 1–36.

42. R. Reider. *Benchmarking Strategies: A Tool for Profit Improvement.* New York: John Wiley & Sons, 2000.

43. M. T. Czarnecki. *Managing by Measuring: How to Improve Your Organization's Performance Through Effective Benchmarking.* New York: AMACOM, 1999.

44. To learn more about these issues, visit the home page for the American Productivity and Quality Center. http://www.apqc.org (June 4, 2003).

45. K. N. Dervitsiotis. Benchmarking and business paradigm shifts. *Total Quality Management*, 11(4/6), 2000, pp. S641–S647.

46. W. E. Deming. *The New Economics for Industry, Government, and Education.* Cambridge, MA: Center for Advanced Engineering Study, Massachusetts Institute of Technology, 1993; G. R. Russell. The Deming cycle extended to software development. *Production and Inventory Management Journal*, 39(3), 1998, pp. 32–37.

47. *Adapted and modified from* G. Langley, K. Nolan, and T. Nolan. The foundation of improvement. Presented at the Sixth Annual International Deming's User's Group Conference, Cincinnati, OH, August 1992; J. W. Dean, Jr., and J. R. Evans. *Total Quality: Management, Organization, and Strategy.* St. Paul, MN: West, 1994, pp. 81–82.

48. R. S. Kaplan and D. P. Norton. *The Balanced Scorecard: Translating Strategy into Action.* Boston: Harvard Business School Press, 1996.

49. R. S. Kaplan and D. P. Norton. *The Strategy-Focused Organization: How Balanced Scorecard Companies Thrive in the New Business Environment.* Boston: Harvard Business School Publishing, 2000.

50. R. W. Beatty, M. A. Huselid, and C. E. Schneier. New HR in metrics: Scoring on the business scorecard. *Organizational Dynamics*, 32(2), 2003, pp. 107–121.

51. *Adapted from* G. H. Anthes. Balanced scorecard. *Computerworld*, February 17, 2003, p. 34; *Southwest Airlines 2002 Annual Report.* Dallas: Southwest Airlines, 2003.

52. G. Kenny. Strategy: Balanced scorecard—Why it isn't working. *New Zealand Management*, March 5, 2003, pp. 32–34; M. W. Meyer. *Rethinking Performance Measurement: Beyond the Balanced Scorecard.* New York: Cambridge University Press, 2003.

53. *Adapted from* M. Tolan. The art of the possible: Potential for dramatic energy mix shift. IVEC/2003. http://www.accenture.com (June 6, 2003); R. King. Mary Tolan's modest proposal. *Business 2.0*, June 2003, pp. 116–122.

54. L. P. Martin. Inventory of barriers to creative thought and innovation action. Reprinted from J. William Pfeiffer (Ed.). *The 1990 Annual: Developing Human Resources.* San Diego: University Associates, 1990, pp. 138–141. Used with permission.

Chapter 10

1. *Adapted from* J. Creswell. Scandal hits—now what. *Fortune*, July 7,

2003, pp. 127–130; Waste Management, Inc. *Hoover's Online*. http://www.hoovers.com (July 7, 2003); N.A. Martin. Cleaning up the mess. *Barron's*, June 24, 2002, pp. 20–21; M. Fickes. A $12 billion start-up. *Waste Age*, January 2002, pp. 28–35.

2. V. Govindarajan and R. Newton. *Management Control Systems*. Columbus, OH: McGraw-Hill/Irwin, 2001.

3. R. Simmons. *Levers of Control: How Managers Use Innovative Control Systems to Drive Strategic Renewal*. Boston: Harvard University Press, 1995.

4. U.S. Environmental Protection Agency. *Draft Report on the Environment*, 2003. http://www.epa.gov (July 8, 2003).

5. *Adapted from* McDonald's statement on corporate social responsibility. http://www.mcdonalds.com (July 8, 2003).

6. *Adapted from* N. Desmond. The CEO dashboard. *Business 2.0*, August 2002, p. 34; Siebel's employee relationship management software. http://www.siebel.com (July 9, 2003); M. Veserka. Plugged in: Enterprise disintegration. *Barron's*, May 26, 2003, pp. T2–T3.

7. J. Creswell, p. 130.

8. J. Graham. Cypress melds into one. *EBN*, December 17, 2001, pp. PG30–31.

9. T. Lowe and J. L. Machin. *New Perspectives on Managerial Control*. New York: Macmillan, 1987.

10. G. T. Hult, B. D. Keillor, and R. Hightower. Value product attributes in an emerging market: A comparison between French and Malaysian consumers. *Journal of World Business*, 35, 2000, pp. 206–220.

11. R. W. Brislin and E. S. Kim. Cultural diversity in people's understanding and uses of time. *Applied Psychology: An International Review*, 52, 2003, pp. 363–382; S. S. Standifird and R. S. Marshall. The transaction cost advantage of guanxi-based business practices. *Journal of World Business*, 35, 2000, pp. 21–42.

12. *Adapted from* L. M. Sixel. True path to safety is likely not lined with big prizes. *Houston Chronicle*, May 23, 2003, pp. 1C, 4C.

13. J. Hulbert, L. Pitt, and M. Ewing. Defections, discourse, and devotion: Some propositions on customer desertion, dialogue and loyalty. *Journal of General Management*, 28(3), 2003, pp. 43–52.

14. *Adapted from* R. Johnston and S. Mehra. Best-practice complaint management. *Academy of Management Executive*, 16(4), 2002, pp. 145–154.

15. J. S. Rosenbloom (Ed.). *The Handbook of Employee Benefits*, 5th ed. New York: McGraw-Hill, 2001.

16. Business brief—Ford Motor Co.: Profit sharing is planned for 95,000 hourly workers. *Wall Street Journal*, January 20, 2003, p. B8.

17. 45th Annual survey of profit sharing and 401(k) plans. *Pension Benefits*, December 2002, pp. 1–3.

18. S. D. Pugh, J. Dietz, J. W. Wiley, and S. M. Brooks. Driving service effectiveness through employee-customer linkages. *Academy of Management Executive*, 16(4), 2002, pp. 73–84; M. Davidow. Organizational responses to customer complaints: What works and what doesn't. *Journal of Service Research*, 5(3), 2003, pp. 225–250.

19. I. Morgan and J. Rao. Aligning service strategy through super-measure management. *Academy of Management Executive*, 16(4), 2002, pp. 121–131.

20. Personal communication with Carl Sewell, president, Sewell Lexus, Dallas, TX, July 2003.

21. P. B. Miller and P. R. Bahnson. *Quality Financial Reporting*. New York: McGraw-Hill, 2002.

22. K. G. Palepu, P. M. Healy, and V. L. Bernard. *Business Analysis & Valuation, Text and Cases*, 3rd. ed. Mason, OH: South-Western, 2004.

23. C. P. Stickney and R. L. Weil. *Financial Accounting*, 10th ed. Mason, OH: South-Western, 2003.

24. S. S. Rao. ABCs of cost control. *Inc. Tech*, 2, 1997, pp. 79–81.

25. G. Cokins. *Activity-Based Cost Management: An Executive's Guide*. New York: John Wiley, 2002.

26. *Adapted from* S. J. Baxendale and V. Dornbusch. Activity-based costing for a hospice. *Strategic Finance*, Spring 2000, pp. 65–70.

27. G. Cokins, pp. 68–70.

28. D. R. Anderson, D. J. Sweeney, and T. A. Williams. *Quantitative Methods for Business*, 9th ed. Mason, OH: South-Western, 2004.

29. T. Aeppel. Working without workers. *Wall Street Journal*, November 19, 2002, p. B1; Air Products and Chemicals, Inc. http://www.airproducts.com (July 9, 2003).

30. D. Grimshaw, F. Cooke, I. Grugulis, and S. Vincent. New technology and changing organizational forms: Implications for managerial controls and skills. *New Technology, Work, and Employment*, 17(3), 2002, pp. 186–203.

31. R. A. Monks and N. Mineow (Eds.). *Corporate Governance*, 2nd ed. Malden, MA: Blackwell Publishing, 2002.

32. Corporate governance glossary. http://www.corp-gov.org (July 9, 2003).

33. Ibid.

34. W. J. Salmon and J. Conger (Eds.). *Harvard Business Review on Corporate Governance*. Boston: Harvard Business School Press, 2000.

35. C. M. Daily, D. R. Dalton, and A. A. Cannella, Jr. Corporate governance: Decades of dialogue and data. *Academy of Management Review*, 28(3), 2003, pp. 371–382.

36. C. Sundaramurthy and M. Lewis. Control and collaboration: Paradoxes of governance. *Academy of Management Review*, 28(3), 2003, pp. 397–415.

37. A. J. Hillman and T. Dalzeil. Board of directors and firm performance. Integrating agency and resource dependence perspectives.

Academy of Management Review, 28(3), 2003, pp. 383–396.

38. American Corporate Counsel Association. Understanding the Sarbanes-Oxley Act. *Business Week*, special section, March 31, 2003, unpaginated.

39. Sarbanes-Oxley Act of 2002. http://www.findlaw.com (July 10, 2003).

40. Ibid.

41. *Adapted from* TIAA-CREF policy statement on corporate governance. http://www.tiaa-cref.org (July 10, 2003); J. Sonnenfeld. What makes boards great. *Harvard Business Review*, September 2002, pp. 106–113; W. Shen. The dynamics of CEO-board relationship: An evolutionary perspective. *Academy of Management Review*, 28(3), 2003, pp. 466–476.

42. *Adapted from* Newell Rubbermaid Inc. corporate governance guidelines. http://www.newellrubbermaid.com (July 10, 2003).

43. M. Fickes, pp. 28–35.

44. Jeff Immelt on corporate governance. http://www.ge.com (July 11, 2003).

45. *Adapted from* L. R. Jaunch et al. *The Management Experience: Cases, Exercises and Readings*, 4th ed. Chicago: Dryden, 1986, pp. 254–255.

Chapter 11

1. *Adapted from* http://www.hoovers.com (May 2003), search under "Home Depot"; J. Revell. Can Home Depot gets its groove back? *Fortune*, January 21, 2003, pp. 110–111; A do-it-yourself-disaster. *The Economist (US)*, January 11, 2003, pp. 34–35.

2. S. Nambisan. Designing virtual customer environments for new product development: Toward a theory. *Academy of Management Review*, 27, 2002, pp. 392–413; C. R. James. Designing learning organizations. *Organizational Dynamics*, 32(1), 2003, pp. 46–61.

3. R. A. Pitts and D. Lei. *Strategic Management: Building and Sustaining Competitive Advantage*. Cincinnati, OH: Thomson Learning, 2003, p. 399.

4. P. Lawrence and J. Lorsch. *Organization and Environment*. Homewood, IL: Richard D. Irwin, 1969.

5. G. M. Spreitzer and A. K. Mishra. To stay or to go: Survivor turnover following an organizational downsizing. *Journal of Organizational Behavior*, 23, 2003, pp. 707–730.

6. J. R. Galbraith. *Designing Organizations*. San Francisco: Jossey-Bass, 2002.

7. P. Thompson and D. McHugh. *Work Organizations*. London: Global Publishing, 2003.

8. W. R. Scott. *Organizations: Rational, Natural and Open Systems,* 5th ed. Upper Saddle River, NJ: Prentice Hall, 2003.

9. C. Holmes. Fighting the urge to fight fires. *Harvard Business Review*, November–December 1999, pp. 30–31.

10. *Adapted from* E. Iankova and J. Katz. Strategies for political risk mediation by international firms in transition economies: The case of Bulgaria. *Journal of World Business*, 38, 2003, pp. 182–203.

11. B. Adbul-Jalbar, J. Gutierrez, J. Puerto, and J. Sicilia. Policies for inventory/distribution systems: The effect of centralization vs. decentralization. *International Journal of Production Economics*, January 11, 2003, pp. 281–294.

12. A. F. Alkhafji. *Strategic Management*. New York: Haworth Press, 2003.

13. *Adapted from* http://www.harley-davidson.com (May 2003); http://www.hoovers.com (May 2003), search under "Harley-Davidson."

14. D. Nadler and M. I. Tushman. *Competing by Design: The Power of Organizational Architecture*. New York: Oxford University Press, 1997.

15. J. R. Galbraith. Organizing to deliver solutions. *Organizational Dynamics*, 31, 2002, pp. 194–206.

16. Pitts and Lei, pp. 375–376.

17. *Adapted from* http://www.starbucks.com (May 2003); http://www.hoovers.com (May 2003), search under "Starbucks."

18. K. T. Dirks and D. L. Ferrin. The role of trust in organizational settings. *Organization Science*, 12, 2001, pp. 450–469.

19. Z. Rahman and S. K. Bhattachryya. Virtual organization: A stratagem. *Singapore Management Review*, 24(2), 2002, pp. 29–46.

20. T. J. Newton. Creating the new ecological order? Elias and actor-network theory. *Academy of Management Review*, 27, 2002, pp. 523–540.

21. Pitts and Lei, pp. 401–403.

22. G. Van Ness and K. Van Ness. *Being There without Going There*. New York: Aspatore, 2003; H. W. Chesbrough and D. J. Teece. Organizing for innovation: When is virtual, virtuous? *Harvard Business Review*, August 2002, pp. 127–134.

23. *Adapted from* http://www.hoovers.com (May 2003), search under "DreamWorks"; http://www.artesia.com/pr/dreamworks.html (May 2003); http://www.dvdtoons.com (May 2003).

24. T. Burns and G. M. Stalker. *The Management of Innovation*. London: Tavistock, 1961, pp. 119–122.

25. *Adapted from* http://www.hoovers.com (May 2003), search under "Flextronics International Ltd."; Flextronics: Few rules, fast responses. *Business Week*, October 23, 2000, pp. 148ff; S. Moore. Flextronics bulks up sales. *Modern Plastics*, September 2001, pp. 49ff.

26. J. D. Thompson. *Organizations in Action*. New York: McGraw-Hill, 1967, pp. 51–67.

27. K. E. Weick and K. M. Sutcliffe. *Managing the Unexpected*. San Francisco: Jossey-Bass, 2001.

28. *Adapted from* G. Walker and R. Kerin. *Kinko's* (unpublished case study). Dallas, TX: Cox School of Business, May 2003; http://www.kinkos.com/about_us/history/

history.php (May 2003); http://www.hoovers.com (May 2003), search under "Kinkos"; http://www.kinkos.com/pr/pr_otct162001.php (May 2003).

29. Used by permission by Professor Robert T. Keller, College of Business Administration, University of Houston, Houston, TX, May 2003.

Chapter 12

1. *Adapted from* C. Sulter. On the road again. *Fast Company*, January 2002, p. 58.

2. G. J. Young, M. P. Charns, and S. M. Shorttell. TQM manager and network effects on the adoption of innovative management practices: A study of TQM in a public hospital system. *Strategic Management Journal*, 22, 2001, pp. 935–951.

3. J. P. Kotter and D. S. Cohen. *The Heart of Change*. Boston: Harvard Business School Press, 2002; M. Beer and N. Nohria. *Breaking the Code of Change*. Boston: Harvard Business School Press, 2000; R. A. Johnson. Antecedents and outcomes of corporate refocusing. *Journal of Management*, 22, 1996, pp. 439–483.

4. N. A. Wishart, J. J. Elam, and D. Robey. Redrawing the portrait of a learning organization: Inside Knight-Ridder, Inc. *Academy of Management Executive*, 10, 1996, pp. 7–20.

5. K. Lewin. *Field Theory in Social Science*. New York: Harper & Row, 1951; C. Hendry. Understanding and creating organizational change through learning theory. *Human Relations*, 49, 1996, pp. 621–641.

6. This and other stage models are reviewed in A. A. Armenakis and A. G. Bedeian. Organizational change: A review of theory and research in the 1990s. *Journal of Management*, 25, 1999, pp. 293–315.

7. R. C. Wood and G. Hamel. The World Bank's Innovation Market. *Harvard Business Review*, November, 2002, pp. 104–112.

8. J. E. Dutton, S. J. Ashford, R. M. O'Neill, and K. A. Lawrence. Moves that matter: Issue selling and organizational change. *Academy of Management Journal*, 44, 2001, pp. 716–736.

9. D. E. Myers. *Tempered Radicals: How People Use Difference to Inspire Change at Work*. Boston: Harvard Business School Press, 2001; D. E. Meyers. Radical change, the quiet way. *Harvard Business Review*, October, 2001, pp. 92–104.

10. Turning an industry inside out: A conversation with Robert Redford. *Harvard Business Review*, May 2002, pp. 57–62.

11. For a description of the turn-around at IBM UK, see R. Balgobin and N. Pandit. Stages in the turn-around process: The case of IBM UK. *European Management Journal*, 19, 2001, pp. 301–316.

12. D. Ulrich, S. Kerr, and R. Ashkenas. *The GE Work-out*. New York: McGraw-Hill, 2002.

13. D. Leonhardt. Weak outlook leads to shake-up at Procter & Gamble. *New York Times*, June 9, 2000, pp. C1, C5.

14. T. A. Judge, C. J. Thorensen, V. Pucik, and T. M. Welbourne. Managerial coping with organizational change: A dispositional perspective. *Journal of Applied Psychology*, 84, 1999, pp. 107–122.

15. W. W. Burke. *Organizational Change: Theory and Practice*. Thousand Oaks, CA: Sage, 2002; M. S. Poole, A. H. Van de Ven, K. Dooley, and M. E. Holmes. *Organizational Change Processes*. Oxford, UK: Oxford University Press, 2000.

16. S. B. Bacharach, P. Bamberger, and W. J. Sonnenstuhl. The organizational transformation process: The micropolitics of dissonance reduction and the alignment of logics of action. *Administrative Science Quarterly*, 41, 1996, pp. 477–506.

17. J. Waclawski and A. H. Church. *Organization Development: A Data-Driven Approach to Organization Change*. San Francisco: Jossey-Bass, 2002.

18. A. Muoio. The change-agent blues. *Fast Company*, May 2000, pp. 44–45.

19. S. Fox and Y. Amichai-Hamburger. The power of emotional appeals in promoting organizational change programs. *Academy of Management Executive*, 15(4), 2001, pp. 84–95. For more details about the role of top management in communicating during organizational change, see Delta Consulting Group. *Strategic Communication: A Key to Implementing Change*. New York: Delta Consulting Group, 1999.

20. D. M. Rousseau and S. A. Tijoriwala. What's a good reason to change? Motivated reasoning and social accounts in promoting organizational change. *Journal of Applied Psychology*, 84, 1999, pp. 514–528.

21. L. Herscovitch and J. P. Meyer. Commitment to organizational change: Extension of a three-component model. *Journal of Applied Psychology*, 87, 2002, pp. 474–487.

22. *Adapted from* S. E. Jackson and R. S. Schuler. *Managing Human Resources through Strategic Partnerships*. Mason, OH: South-Western, 2003.

23. T. D. Ludwig and E. S. Geller. Assigned versus participative goal setting and response generalization: Managing injury control among professional pizza deliverers. *Journal of Applied Psychology*, 82, 1997, pp. 253–261.

24. P. Prasad and A. Prasad. Stretching the iron cage: The constitution and implications of routine workplace resistance. *Organization Science*, 11, 2000, pp. 387–403; R. Maurer. *Beyond the Wall of Resistance*. Austin, TX: Bard Books, 1996.

25. R. Kegan and L. L. Lahey. The real reason people won't change. *Harvard Business Review*, November, 2001, pp. 84–93.

26. T. Petzinger, Jr. Georg Bauer put burden of downsizing into employees' hands. *Wall Street Journal*, May 10, 1996, p. B1.

27. J. Clarke, C. Ellett, J. Bateman, and J. Rugutt. Faculty receptivity/resistance to change, personal and organizational efficacy, decision deprivation and effectiveness in

research universities. Paper presented at the Twenty-First Annual Meeting of the Association for the Study of Higher Education, Memphis, TN, 1996.

28. P. Strebel. Why do employees resist change? *Harvard Business Review*, May–June 1996, pp. 86–106.

29. M. McHugh. The stress factor: Another item for the change management agenda? *Journal of Organizational Change Management*, 10, 1997, pp. 345–362.

30. T. Petzinger, Jr., p. B1.

31. R. McKnight, J. Doel, and K. Christine. One Prudential Exchange: The insurance giant's business literacy and alignment platform. *Human Resource Management Journal*, 40, 2001, pp. 241–247.

32. J. Dean, P. Brandes, and R. Dharwadkar. Organizational cynicism. *Academy of Management Review*, 23, 1998, pp. 341–352; A. E. Reichers, J. P. Wanous, and J. T. Austin. Understanding and managing cynicism about organizational change. *Academy of Management Executive*, 11, 1997, p. 48.

33. C. Axtell, T. Wall, C. Stride, K. Pepper, C. Clegg, P. Gardner, and R. Bolden. Familiarity breeds content: The impact of exposure to change on employee openness and well-being. *Journal of Occupational and Organizational Psychology*, 2002, 75, pp. 207–213.

34. J. E. Mathieu and D. M. Zajkac. A review and meta-analysis of the antecedents, correlates, and consequences of organizational commitment. *Psychological Bulletin*, 108, 1990, pp. 171–194; J. F. R. E. Allen, M. A. Lucero, and K. L. Van Norman. An examination of the individual's decision to participate in an employee involvement program. *Group & Organization Management*, 22, 1997, pp. 117–143; see also L. Hirschorn. Campaigning for change. *Harvard Business Review*, June, 2002, pp. 98–104.

35. C. L. Bernick. When your culture needs a makeover. *Harvard Business Review*, June 2001, pp. 53–64.

36. For a detailed review of the effectiveness of various change programs, see B. A. Macy and H. Izumi. Organizational change, design, and work innovation: A meta-analysis of 131 North American field studies—1961–1991. In R. W. Woodman and W. A. Pasmore (Eds.). *Research in Organizational Change and Development*, volume 7. Greenwich, CT: JAI Press, 1993, pp. 235–313.

37. C. Hymowitz. Task of managing changes in workplace takes a careful hand. *Wall Street Journal*, July 1, 1997, p. B1.

38. V. B. Wayman and S. Werner. The impact of workforce reductions on financial performance: A longitudinal perspective. *Journal of Management*, 26, 2000, pp. 341–363.

39. W. F. Cascio. Strategies for responsible restructuring. *Academy of Management Executive*, 16(3), pp. 80–91; W. F. Cascio. Financial consequences of employment-change decisions in major U. S. corporations. *Academy of Management Journal*, 40, 1997, pp. 1175–1189.

40. E. Brynjolfsson, A. A. Renshaw, and M. V. Alstyne. The matrix of change. *Sloan Management Review*, Winter 1997, pp. 37–54; M. Hammer and J. Champy. *Reengineering the Corporation*. New York: Harper-Collins, 1993; M. Hammer. *Beyond Reengineering: How the Process-Centered Organization Is Changing Our Lives.* New York: HarperBusiness, 1996; J. Champy. *Reengineering Management: The Mandate for New Leadership.* New York: HarperBusiness, 1996.

41. J. Guaspari. Dispatch from the front: A shining example. *Across the Board*, May/June 2002, pp. 67–68.

42. J. Waclawski and A. H. Church (Eds.). *Organization Development: A Data-Driven Approach to Organizational Change.* San Francisco: Jossey-Bass, 2002; H. K. Sinangil and F. Avallone. Organizational development and change. In N. Anderson, D. S. Ones,

H. K. Sinangil and C. Viswesvaran (Eds.). *Handbook of Industrial, Organizational and Work Psychology*, Vol. 2. Thousand Oaks, CA: Sage, pp. 332–344; D. P. Bate., R. Khan, and A. Pye. Toward a culturally sensitive approach to organization structuring: Where organization design meets organization development. *Organization Science*, 11, 2000, pp. 197–211; T. T. Baldwin, C. Danielson, and W. Wiggenhorn. The evolution of learning strategies in organizations: From employee development to business redefinition. *Academy of Management Executive*, 11(4), 1997, pp. 47–58.

43. J. Waclawski and S. G. Rogelberg. Interviews and focus groups: Quintessential organizational development techniques. In J. Waclawski and A. H. Church (Eds.). *Organization Development: A Data-Driven Approach to Organizational Change.* San Francisco: Jossey-Bass, 2002, pp. 103–126

44. A. I. Kraut. *Organizational Surveys: Tools for Assessment and Change.* San Francisco: Jossey-Bass, 1996.

45. S. V. Falletta and W. Combs. Surveys as a tool for organization development and change. In J. Waclawski and A. H. Church (Eds.). *Organization Development: A Data-Driven Approach to Organizational Change.* San Francisco: Jossey-Bass, 2002, pp. 78–102.

46. M. A. West. Sparkling fountains or stagnant ponds: An integrative model of creativity and innovation implementation in work groups. *Applied Psychology: An International Review*, 51, 2001, pp. 355–424; C. K. W. D. Dreu and M. A. West. Minority dissent and team innovation: The importance of participation in decision-making. *Journal of Applied Psychology*, 86, 2001, pp. 1191–1201.

47. J. Reingold and M. Stepanek. Why the productivity revolution will spread. *Business Week*, February 14, 2000, pp. 112–118.

48. S. F. Gale. For ERP success, create a culture change. *Workforce*, September 2002, pp. 80–83.

49. For a thorough discussion of this topic, see L. V. Shavinina. *The International Handbook of Innovation*. Oxford, UK: Elsevier Science.

50. Associated Press. Kodak's hometown feels little security. *Dallas Morning News*, November 13, 1997, p. 4D.

51. F. Warner. In a word, Toyota drives for innovation. *Fast Company*, August 2002, pp. 36–38.

52. *Adapted from* S. E. Jackson and R. S. Schuler. *Managing Human Resources through Strategic Partnerships*. Mason, OH: South-Western, 2003.

53. S. V. Brull. Gateway's big gamble. *Business Week E.Biz*, June 5, 2000, pp. EB26–36.

54. A. C. Edmondson. The local and variegated nature of learning in organizations: A group-level perspective. *Organization Science*, 13, 2002, pp. 128–146; A. Hargadon and R. I. Sutton. Building an innovation factory. *Harvard Business Review*, May–June 2000, pp. 157–166; see also S. E. Jackson, M. A. Hitt, and A. S. DeNisi, *Managing Knowledge for Sustained Competitive Advantage*. San Francisco: Jossey-Bass, 2003.

55. B. Sugarman. A learning-based approach to organizational change: Some results and guidelines. *Organizational Dynamics*, 30(1), 2001, pp. 62–76; P. Senge, A. Kleiner, C. Roberts, R. Ross, G. Rotin, and B. Smith. *The Dance of Change*. New York: Doubleday, 1999; E. C. Nevis, A. J. DiBella, and J. M. Gould. Understanding organizations as learning systems. *Sloan Management Review*, Winter 1995, 73–85; P. Senge, *The Fifth Discipline: The Art and Practice of the Learning Organization*. New York: Doubleday, 1990.

56. Y.-T. Cheng and A. H. Van de Ven. Learning the innovation journey: Order out of chaos. *Organization Science*, 7, 1996, pp. 593–614.

57. J.-L. Denis, L. Lamothe, and A. Langley. The dynamics of collective leadership and strategic change in pluralistic organizations. *Academy of Management Journal*, 44, 2001, pp. 809–837.

58. P. B. Sunoo. Nantucket Nectars' recipe for participation. *Workforce*, May 1998, pp. 25–26.

59. T. Maxon. Southwest to go "ticketless" on all routes January 31. *Dallas Morning News*, January 11, 1995, p. 1D.

60. For suggestions about how to encourage people to share their knowledge, see K. Husted and S. Michailova. Diagnosing and fighting knowledge-sharing hostility. *Organizational Dynamics*, 31(1), 2002, pp. 60–73; see also M. Baer and M. Frese. Innovation is not enough: Climates for initiative and psychological safety, process innovations and firm performance. *Journal of Organizational Behavior*, 2003, 24, pp. 45–68.

61. C. Kim and R. Mauborgne. Fair process: Managing in the knowledge economy. *Harvard Business Review*, July–August, 1997, pp. 65–75; R. Pascale, M. Millimann, and L. Gioja. Changing the way we change. *Harvard Business Review*, November–December 1997, pp. 127–139.

62. J. P. MacDuffie. The road to "Root Cause": Shop-floor problem-solving at three auto assembly plants. *Management Science*, 43, 1997, pp. 479–502.

63. N. A. Wishart et al.; see also C. Gilbert and J. L. Bower. Disruptive change: When trying harder is part of the problem. *Harvard Business Review*, May, 2002, pp. 94–104.

64. D. Lei, J. W. Slocum, Jr., and R. A. Pitts. Building cooperative advantage: Managing strategic alliances to promote organizational learning. *Journal of World Business*, 32(3), 1997, pp. 203–223; R. C. Hill and D. Hellriegel. Critical contingencies in joint venture management: Some lessons from managers. *Organization Science*, 5, 1994, pp. 594–607.

65. J. B. Goes and S. H. Park. Interorganizational links and innovation: The case of hospital services. *Academy of Management Journal*, 40, 1997, pp. 673–696.

66. J. D. Wolpert. Breaking out of the innovation box. *The Innovative Enterprise*, August, 2002, pp. 77–83; R. M. Grant. Prospering in dynamically-competitive environments: Organizational capability as knowledge integration. *Organization Science*, 7, 1996, pp. 357–411; J. P. Liebeskind, A. L. Oliver, L. Zucker, and M. Brewer. Social networks, learning, and flexibility: Sourcing scientific knowledge in new biotechnology firms. *Organization Science*, 7, 1996, pp. 428–443.

67. See L. B. Cardinal. Technological innovation in the pharmaceutical industry: The use of organizational control in managing research and development. *Organization Science*, 12, 2001, pp. 19–36.

68. J. S. Brown and P. Duguid. Capturing knowledge without killing it. *Harvard Business Review*, May–June 2000, pp. 73–80.

69. B. Cross, A. Parker, L. Prusak, and S. P. Borgatti. Knowing what we know: Supporting knowledge creation and sharing in social networks. *Organizational Dynamics*, 30, 2001, pp. 100–120.

70. G. Anders. *Perfect Enough: Carly Fiorina and the Reinvention of Hewlett-Packard*. New York: Portfolio/Penguin Putnam, 2003; A. Lashinsky. Now for the hard part. *Fortune*, November 18, 2002, pp. 95–106; P. Sellers. True grit. *Fortune*, October 14, 2002, pp. 101–105; C. Fiorina, Speech at Hewlett-Packard Shareholders Meeting, February 29, 2000 (accessed at http://www.hp.com on September 24, 2000); Q. Hardy. All Carly all the time. *Forbes*, December 13, 1999, pp. 138–144.

Chapter 13

1. C. M. Solomon. HR's push for productivity. *Workforce*, August 2002, pp. 28–33; A. Wheat. The 100 best companies to work for. *Fortune*, January 20, 2003, pp. 127–152; C. O'Reilly and J. Pfeffer. *Hidden*

Value: How Great Companies Achieve Extraordinary Results with Ordinary People. Boston: Harvard Business School Press, 2000, pp. 49–77.

2. *Human Capital ROI Study: Creating Shareholder Value through People.* Deloitte and Touche, 2002.

3. G. S. Hansen and B. Wernerfelt. Determinants of firm performance: Relative importance of economic and organizational factors. *Strategic Journal of Management,* 1989, pp. 399–411.

4. M. Buckingham and C. Coffman. *First Break All the Rules.* New York: Simon and Schuster, 1999; L. Grant. Happy workers, happy returns. *Fortune,* January 12, 1998, p. 81; G. E. Fryzell and J. Wang. The Fortune Corporation "reputation" index: Reputation for what? *Journal of Management,* 20, 1994, pp. 1–14; M. J. Schmit and S. P. Allscheid. Employee attitudes and customer satisfaction: Making the theoretical and empirical connections. *Personnel Psychology,* 48, 1995, pp. 521–536; C. A. Lengnick-Hall. Customer contributions to quality: A different view of the customer-oriented firm. *Academy of Management Review,* 21, 1996, pp. 791–824; and P. S. Goodman, M. Fichman, F. J. Lerch, and P. R. Snyder. Customer–firm relationships, involvement, and customer satisfaction. *Academy of Management Journal,* 38, 1995, pp. 1310–1324.

5. C. M. Solomon.

6. C. Handy. A better capitalism. *Across the Board,* April 1998, pp. 16–22.

7. T. M. Welbourne and A. O. Andrews. Predicting the performance of initial public offerings: Should human resource management be in the equation? *Academy of Management Journal,* 39, 1996, pp. 891–919.

8. P. J. Kiger. Succession planning keeps Wellpoint competitive. *Workforce,* April 2002, pp. 50–54.

9. M. A. Konovsky. Understanding procedural justice and its impact on business organizations. *Journal of Management,* 26, 2000, pp. 489–511;

J. Greenberg. Looking fair vs. being fair: Managing impressions of organizational justice. In B. M. Staw and L. L. Cummings (Eds.). *Research in Organizational Behavior,* Vol. 12, Greenwich, CT: JAI Press, 1990, pp. 111–157.

10. J. C. Morrow, P. C. Morrow, and E. J. Mullen. Intraorganizational mobility and work-related attitudes. *Journal of Organizational Behavior* 17, 1996, pp. 363–374.

11. Number of EEO lawsuits appears to be "leveling off." *HR Magazine,* June 2000, p. 27; S. Siwolop. Recourse or retribution? Employers are taking on disgruntled workers in court. *New York Times,* June 7, 2000, pp. C1, C6.

12. E. D. Demby. Weighing your options. *HR Magazine,* November 2002, pp. 44–49.

13. J. Collison and C. Frangos. *Aligning HR with Organizational Strategy Survey.* Alexandria, VA: Society for Human Resource Management, 2002.

14. J. Useem. From heroes to goats and back again: How corporate leaders lost our trust. *Fortune,* November 18, 2002, pp. 40–48; L. Lawrence. Microsoft "permatemp" settlement seen as warning to employers. *HR News,* February 2001, p. 8; C. von Hippel, S. L. Mangum, D. B. Greenberger, R. L. Heneman, and J. D. Skoglind. Temporary employment: Can organizations and employees both win? *Academy of Management Executive,* 11, 1997, pp. 93–104.

15. A. Bernstein. Too many workers? Not for long. *Business Week,* May 2002, pp. 126–130.

16. E. Zimmerman. Why deep layoffs hurt long-term recovery. *Workforce,* November 2001, pp. 48–53; P. Cappelli. A market-driven approach to retaining talent. *Harvard Business Review,* January–February 2001, pp. 103–111.

17. E. E. Lawler III and G. E. Ledford, Jr. New approaches to organizing: Competencies and the decline

of the bureaucratic model. In C. L. Cooper and S. E. Jackson (Eds.). *Creating Tomorrow's Organizations: Handbook for Future Research in Organizations.* Chichester, England: John Wiley & Sons, 1997, pp. 231–249.

18. J. S. Shippmann, R. A. Ash, and associates. The practice of competency modeling. *Personnel Psychology,* 53, 2000, pp. 703–740.

19. J. S. MacNeil. Hey, look us over. *Growth,* October 2002, p. 146.

20. For a comprehensive review, see J. A. Breaugh and M. Starke. Research on employee recruitment: So many studies, so many remaining questions. *Journal of Management,* 26, 2000, pp. 405–434.

21. S. Hays. Hiring on the Web. *Workforce,* August 1999, pp. 76–84; B. Leonard. Online and overwhelmed. *HR Magazine,* August 2000, pp. 37–42; B. Parus. The sky's the limit in online recruiting. *Workspan,* January 2001, pp. 54–56; P. Cappelli. Making the most of online recruiting. *Harvard Business Review,* March 2001, pp. 139–146.

22. S. F. Gale. Three companies cut turnover with tests. *Workforce,* April 2002, pp. 66–69.

23. For suggestions about how to avoid such problems, see I. Kotlyar. If recruitment means building trust, where does technology fit in? *Canadian HR Reporter,* October 7, 2002, pp. 21–24.

24. A. Van Vianen. Person–organization fit: The match between newcomers' and recruiters' preferences for organizational cultures. *Personnel Psychology,* 53, 2000, pp. 113–149; T. A. Judge and D. M. Cable. Applicant personality, organizational culture, and organizational attraction. *Personnel Psychology,* 50, 1997, pp. 359–394; R. W. Griffeth, P. W. Hom, L. S. Fink, and D. J. Cohen. Comparative tests of multiple models of recruiting sources effects. *Journal of Management,* 23, 1997, pp. 19–36.

25. For more details, see J. F. Kehoe (Ed.). *Managing Selection in Changing*

Organizations. San Francisco: Jossey-Bass, 2000; C. J. Collins and C. K. Stevens. The relationships between early recruitment-related activities and application decisions of new labor-market entrants: A brand equity approach to recruitment. *Journal of Applied Psychology,* 2002, 27, pp. 1121–1133.

26. A. M. Ryan and R. E. Ployhart. Applicants' perceptions of selection procedures and decisions: A critical review and agenda for the future. *Journal of Management,* 26, 2000, pp. 565–606.

27. S. Caudron. Who are you really hiring? *Workforce,* November 2002, pp. 28–32.

28. C. Daniels. To hire a lumber expert, click here. *Fortune,* April 3, 2000, pp. 267–270.

29. R. A. Posthuma, F. P. Morgeson, and M. A. Campion. Beyond employment interview validity: A comprehensive narrative review of recent research and trends over time. *Personnel Psychology,* 55, 2002, 1–81.

30. J. Merritt. Improv at the interview. *Business Week,* February 3, 2003, p. 63.

31. S. L. Rynes, K. G. Brown, and A. E. Colbert. Seven misconceptions about human resource practices: Research findings versus practitioner beliefs. *Academy of Management Executive,* 16 (3), 2002, pp. 92–103; F. L. Schmidt and J. E. Hunter. The validity and utility of selection methods in personnel psychology: Practical and theoretical implications of 85 years of research findings. *Psychological Bulletin,* 124, 1998, pp. 252–274.

32. A. Tziner, S. Ronen, and D. A. Hacohen. A four-year study of an assessment center in a financial corporation. *Journal of Organizational Behavior,* 14, 1993, pp. 225–237.

33. P. Carbonara. Hire for attitude. Train for skill. *Fast Company,* April–May 1996, pp. 64–71.

34. H. Cooper-Thomas and N. Anderson. Newcomer adjustment: The relationship between organizational socialization tactics, informa-tion acquisition and attitudes. *Journal of Occupational and Organizational Psychology,* 75, 2002, pp. 423–437.

35. C. Lachnit. Hire right: Do it the Ritz way. *Workforce,* April 2002, p. 16.

36. S. J. Marks. E-Mergency measures. *Human Resource Executive,* November 2002, pp. 80–86; R. Balu. KPMG faces the Internet test. *Fast Company,* March 2000, pp. 50–52.

37. M. Moravec, O. J. Johannessen, and T. A. Hjelmas. Thumbs up for self-managed teams. *Management Review,* July–August 1997, pp. 234–241; S. E. Prokesch. Unleashing the power of learning: An interview with British Petroleum's John Browne. *Harvard Business Review,* September–October 1997, pp. 127–133; M. Moravec, O. J. Johannessen, and T. A. Hjelmas. We have seen the future and it is self-managed. *PM Network,* September 1997, pp. 20–22.

38. See C. O. Trevor. Interactions among actual ease-of-movement determinants and job satisfaction in the determination of voluntary turnover. *Academy of Management Journal,* 44, 2001, pp. 621–638.

39. R. V. Gerbman. Corporate universities 101. *HR Magazine,* February 2000, pp. 101–106.

40. F. Warner. Inside Intel's mentoring movement. *Fast Company,* April 2002, pp. 116–120.

41. B. Filipczak. The executive coach: Helper or healer. *Training,* March 1998, pp. 30–36.

42. S. R. Davis, J. H. Lucas, and D. R. Marcotte. GM links better leaders to better business. *Workforce,* April 1998, pp. 62–68; see also D. Cole. Even executives can use help from the sidelines. *New York Times,* October 29, 2002, p. B5.

43. For a review, see R. D. Arvey and K. R. Murphy, Performance evaluation in work settings. *Annual Review Psychology,* 49, 1998, pp. 141–168.

44. For an excellent discussion of how performance standards can affect employees' satisfaction and motivation, see P. Bobko and A. Colella. Employee reactions to performance standards: A review and research propositions. *Personnel Psychology,* 47, 1994, pp. 1–29.

45. A. G. Walker and J. W. Smither. A five-year study of upward feedback: What managers do with their results matters. *Personnel Psychology,* 52, 1999, pp. 393–423.

46. See J. W. Smither (Ed.). *Performance Appraisal: State of the Art in Practice.* San Francisco: Jossey-Bass, 1998.

47. D. Grote. Forced ranking: Behind the scenes. *Across the Board.* November/December 2002, pp. 40–45.

48. D. B. Neary. Creating a company-wide, on-line performance management system: A case study at TRW, Inc. *Human Resource Management Journal,* 41, 2002, pp. 491–498.

49. T. J. Maurer, J. K. Palmer, and D. K. Ashe. Diaries, checklists, evaluations, and contrast effects in measurement of behavior. *Journal of Applied Psychology,* 78, 1993, pp. 226–231.

50. N. M. A. Hauensstein. Training raters to increase accuracy of appraisals and the usefulness of feedback. In J. W. Smither (Ed.). *Performance Appraisal: State of the Art in Practice.* San Francisco: Jossey-Bass, 1998, pp. 404–442.

51. W. W. Tornow and M. London (Eds.). *Maximizing the Value of 360-Degree Feedback.* Greensboro, NC: Center for Creative Leadership, 1999.

52. R. F. Martell and M. R. Borg. A comparison of the behavioral rating accuracy of groups and individuals. *Journal of Applied Psychology,* 78, 1993, pp. 43–50.

53. A. Farnham. How to nurture creative sparks. *Fortune,* January 10, 1994, p. 98.

54. Society for Human Resource Management. Workers redefine what leads to job satisfaction, poll shows. *HR News,* January 2003, p. 5.

55. A. E. Barber and R. D. Bretz, Jr. Compensation, attraction and retention. In S. L. Rynes and B. Gerhart (Eds.). *Compensation in Organizations: Current Research and Practice.* San Francisco: Jossey-Bass, 2000.

56. R. Batt. Managing customer services: Human resource practices, quit rates, and sales growth. *Academy of Management Journal,* 45, 2002, pp. 587–597; J. Davis and C. Harris. Retaining your hot skills employees— use dollars and sense. *ACA Journal,* First Quarter 2000, pp. 47–56; C. O. Trevor, B. Gerhart, and J. W. Boudreau. Voluntary turnover and job performance: Curvilinearity and the moderating influences of salary growth on promotions. *Journal of Applied Psychology,* 82, 1997, pp. 44–61.

57. For example, see A. J. S. Colvin, R. Batt, and H. C. Katz. How high performance human resource practices and workforce unionization affect managerial pay. *Personnel Psychology,* 54, 2001, pp. 903–934.

58. R. L. Heneman, G. E. Ledford, Jr., and M. T. Gresham. The changing nature of work and its effects on compensation design and delivery. In S. L. Rynes and B. Gerhart (Eds.). *Compensation in Organizations: Current Research and Practice.* San Francisco: Jossey-Bass, 2000.

59. S. E. Jackson and R. S. Schuler. *Managing Human Resources through Strategic Partnerships.* Mason, OH: South-Western, 2003. Used with permission.

60. D. Brady. Rethinking the rat race. *Business Week,* August 26, 2002, pp. 142–143.

61. Society for Human Resource Management. Work–life balance. *Workplace Visions,* 4, 2002, pp. 1–8.

62. For recent discussions of these, see N. R. Lockwood. Different familial studies needed to reflect work–family changes. *HR News,* January 2003, p. 7, 12; K. E. Pearlson and C. S. Saunders. There's no place like home: Managing telecommuting paradoxes. *Academy of Management Executive,* 15, 2001, pp. 117–127;

D. Denlin. California dreamin'. *The Star-Ledger,* October 7, 2002, p. 25; B. Brandth and K. Erin. Reflexive fathers: Negotiating parental leave and working life. *Gender, Work and Organization,* 9, 2002, pp. 186–203; W. R. Nord, S. Fox, A. Phoenis, and K. Viano. Real-world reactions to work-life balance programs: Lessons for effective implementation. *Organization Dynamics,* 30(3), pp. 223–238.

Chapter 14

1. J. Mackintosh. How BMW put the Mini back on track. *Financial Times,* March 19, 2003, p. 14.

2. T. A. Judge, C. J. Thorensen, J. E. Bono, and G. K. Patton. The job satisfaction-job performance relationship: A qualitative and quantitative review. *Psychological Bulletin,* 127(3), 2001, pp. 376–407.

3. J. K. Harter, F. L. Schmidt, and T. L. Hayes. Business-unit-level relationship between employee satisfaction, employee engagement, and business outcomes: A meta-analysis. *Journal of Applied Psychology,* 87(2), 2002, pp. 268–279.

4. B. Buckingham and C. Coffman. *First, Break All the Rules.* New York: Simon & Schuster, 1999.

5. W. W. George. Medtronic's Chairman William George on how mission-driven companies create long-term shareholder value. *Academy of Management Executive,* 15(4), 2001, pp. 39–47.

6. E. A. Locke. Motivation, cognition, and action: An analysis of studies of task goals and knowledge. *Applied Psychology: An International Review,* 49, 2000, pp. 408–429; E. A. Locke. Toward a theory of task motivation and incentives. *Organizational Behavior and Human Performance,* 3, 1968, pp. 157–189; E. A. Locke and G. P. Latham. *A Theory of Goal Setting and Task Performance.* Upper Saddle River, NJ: Prentice Hall, 1990.

7. P. J. Kiger. How performance management reversed NCCI's fortunes. *Workforce,* May 2002, pp. 48–51.

8. G. P. Latham and G. H. Seijts. The effects of proximal and distal goals on performance on a moderately complex task. *Journal of Organizational Behavior,* 20, 1999, pp. 421–429; see also P. M. Gollwitzer. Implementation intentions: Strong effects of simple plans. *American Psychologist,* 54, 1999, pp. 493–503.

9. A. D. Stajkovic and F. Luthans. Self-efficacy and work-related performance: A meta-analysis. *Psychological Bulletin,* 124, 1998, pp. 240–261.

10. N. W. Van Yperen and O. Janssen. Fatigued and dissatisfied or fatigued but satisfied: Goal orientations and responses to high job demands. *Academy of Management Journal,* 45, 2002, pp. 1161–1171.

11. S. Caudron. How HR drives profits. *Workforce,* December 2001, pp. 26–31.

12. E. A. Locke and G. P. Latham. Building a Practically Useful Theory of Goal Setting and Task Motivation: *A 35-Year Odyssey. American Psychologist,* 2002, 57(9), pp. 705–717.

13. J. E. Sawyer, W. R. Latham, R. D. Pritchard, and W. R. Bennett, Jr. Analysis of work group productivity in an applied setting: Application of a time series panel design. *Personnel Psychology,* 52, 1999, pp. 927–967; D. VandeWalle, G. N. Challagalla, S. Ganeson, and S. P. Brown. An Integrated Model of Feedback-Seeking Behavior: Disposition, Context, and Cognition. *Journal of Applied Psychology,* 85, 2000, pp. 996–1003.

14. For an example of how using feedback can improve workplace safety, see D. Zohar. Modifying supervisory practices to improve subunit safety: A leadership-based intervention model. *Journal of Applied Psychology,* 2002, 87, pp. 156–163.

15. J. Wegge. Procrastination in group goal setting: Some novel findings and a comprehensive model as a new ending to an old story. *Applied Psychology: An International Review,* 49,

2000, pp. 498–516; A. M. O'Leary-Kelly, J. J. Martocchio, and D. D. Fink. A review of the influence of group goals on group performance. *Academy of Management Journal*, 37, 1994, pp. 1285–1301.

16. C. Garvey. Steer teams with the right pay. *HR Magazine,* May 2002, pp. 71–78.

17. B. F. Skinner. *Contingencies of Reinforcement.* New York: Appleton-Century-Crofts, 1969; B. F. Skinner. *Beyond Freedom and Dignity.* New York: Bantam, 1971; B. F. Skinner. *About Behaviorism.* New York: Knopf, 1974.

18. A. D. Stajkovic and F. Luthans. Differential effects of incentive motivators on work performance. *Academy of Management Journal*, 4(3), 2001, pp. 580–590.

19. F. Luthans and A. D. Stajkovic. Reinforce for performance: The need to go beyond pay and even rewards. *Academy of Management Executive*, 12(2), 1999, pp. 49–57; A. D. Stajkovic and F. Luthans. A meta-analysis of the effects of organizational behavior modification on task performance, 1975–1995. *Academy of Management Journal*, 40, 1997, pp. 1122–1149.

20. S. E. Markham, K. D. Scott and G. H. McKee. Recognizing good attendance: A longitudinal, quasi-experimental field study. *Personnel Psychology*, 55, 2002, pp. 639–660.

21. P. A. Rivera. A cure for sick leave abuse? *The Dallas Morning News*, 2003, March 4, p. 3D.

22. J. Macht. Pulp addiction. *Inc. Technology*, 1, 1997, pp. 43–46.

23. S. E. Seibert, J. M. Crant, and M. L. Kraimer. Proactive personality and career success. *Journal of Applied Psychology*, 84, 1999, pp. 416–427.

24. A. Bandura and E. A. Locke. Negative self-efficacy and goal effects revisited. *Journal of Applied Psychology,* 88, 2003, pp. 87–99.

25. S. Bates. Top pay for best performance. *HR Magazine*, January 2003, pp. 32–36.

26. W. Van Erde and H. Thierry. Vroom's expectancy models and work-related criteria: A meta-analysis. *Journal of Applied Psychology*, 81, 1996, pp. 575–586.

27. T. J. Maurer. Career-relevant learning and development, worker age, and beliefs about self-efficacy for development. *Journal of Management*, 27, 2001, pp. 123–140.

28. S. Bates. Murky corporate goals can undermine recovery. *HR Magazine*, November 2002, p. 14.

29. J. M. Brett and L. K. Stroh. Working 61 plus hours a week: Why do managers do it? *Journal of Applied Psychology*, 88, 2003, pp. 67–78.

30. T. R. Zenger and C. R. Marshall. Determinants of incentive intensity in group-based rewards. *Academy of Management Journal*, 43(2), 2000, pp. 149–163.

31. T. Shanker. New incentives for pilots of remote plane. *New York Times,* October 17, 2002, p. A22.

32. S. F. Gale. Incentives and the art of changing behavior. *Workforce*, November 2002, pp. 80–82.

33. G. P. Latham. The importance of understanding and changing employee outcome expectancies for gaining commitment to an organizational goal. *Personnel Psychology*, 54, 2001, pp. 707–716.

34. For more about how employees weigh the costs and benefits of unethical behavior, see M. J. Gundlach, S. C. Douglas, and M. J. Martinko. The decision to blow the whistle: A social information processing framework. *Academy of Management Review*, 2003, 28, pp. 107–123.

35. *Source:* J. R. Hackman and G. R. Oldham. *Work Redesign.* Reading, MA: Addison-Wesley, 1980, p. 83. Reprinted with permission. See also N. G. Dodd and D. C. Ganster. The interactive effects of variety, autonomy, and feedback on attitudes and performance. *Journal of Organizational Behavior*, 17, 1996, pp. 329–347.

36. P. W. Mulvey, G. E. Ledford, and P. V. LeBlanc. Rewards of work:

How they drive performance, retention and satisfaction. *WorldatWork Journal*, Third Quarter 2000, pp. 6–28.

37. R. Forrester. Empowerment: Rejuvenating a potent idea. *Academy of Management Executive*, 14(3), 2000, pp. 67–77; see also S. Caudron. How HR drives profits. *Workforce*, December 2001, pp. 26–31.

38. R. W. Renn and R. J. Vandenberg. The critical psychological states: An underrepresented component in job characteristics model research. *Journal of Management*, 21, 1995, pp. 279–303; S. P. Brown and T. W. Leigh. A new look at psychological climate and its relationship to job involvement, effort, and performance. *Journal of Applied Psychology*, 81, 1996, pp. 358–368.

39. R. A. Roe, I. L. Zinovieva, E. Dienes, and L. A. T. Horn. A comparison of work motivation in Bulgaria, Hungary, and the Netherlands: Test of a model. *Applied Psychology: An International Review*, 49(4), 2000, pp. 658–687.

40. B. P. Sunoo. Blending a successful workforce. *Workforce*, March 2000, pp. 44–48.

41. F. Herzberg, B. Mausner, and B. Snyderman. *The Motivation to Work.* New York: John Wiley & Sons, 1959; see also F. Herzberg. One more time: How do you motivate employees? *Harvard Business Review,* January 2003, pp. 87–96.

42. J. Wiscombe. Rewards get results. *Workforce*, April 2002, pp. 42–48.

43. C. L. Jurkiewicz and T. K. Massey, Jr. What motivates municipal employees: A comparison study of supervisor and non-supervisory employees. *Public Personnel Management*, 26, 1997, pp. 367–376.

44. J. Wiscombe. Rewards get results. *Workforce*, April 2002, pp. 42–48.

45. J. S. Adams. Toward an understanding of equity. *Journal of Abnormal and Social Psychology*, 67, 1963, pp. 422–436.

46. A. S. Tsui, J. L. Pearce, L. W. Porter, and A. M. Tripoli. Alternative approaches to the employee–organization relationship: Does investment in employees pay off? *Academy of Management Journal*, 40, 1997, pp. 1089–1121.

47. H. Baum. Care for the little guy. *Harvard Business Review*, January 2003, p. 45.

48. For a recent study of how laid-off executives react to their re-employment situation, see D. C. Feldman, C. R. Leana, and M. C. Bolino. Underemployment and relative deprivation among re-employed executives. *Journal of Occupational and Organizational Psychology*, 75, 2002, pp. 453–471.

49. J. D. Shaw, N. Gupta, and J. E. Delery. Pay dispersion and workforce performance: Moderating effects of incentives and interdependence. *Strategic Management Journal*, 23, 2002, pp. 491–512; S. J. Wayne, L. M. Shore, W. H. Bommer, and L. E. Tetrick. The role of fair treatment and rewards in perceptions of organizational support and leader-member exchange. *Journal of Applied Psychology*, 87, 2002, pp. 590–598.

50. See R. Kanfer and P. L. Ackerman. Individual differences in work motivation: Further explorations of a trait framework. *Applied Psychology: An International Review*, 49, 2000, pp. 470–482; K. R. Murphy (Ed.). *Individual Differences and Behavior in Organizations*. San Francisco: Jossey-Bass, 1996.

51. A. H. Maslow. *Motivation and Personality*, 2nd ed. New York: Harper & Row, 1970; see also D. H. Shapiro, Jr., C. E. Schwartz, and J. A. Astin. Controlling ourselves, controlling our world. Psychology's role in understanding positive and negative consequences of seeking and gaining control. *American Psychologist*, 51, 1996, pp. 1213–1230; for a recent discussion of self-actualization, see S. A. Haslam, R. A. Eggins, and K. J. Reynolds. The ASPIRe model : Actualizing social and personal identity resources to enhance organizational

outcomes. *Journal of Occupational and Organizational Psychology*, 77, 2003, pp. 83–113.

52. U1: Richard Branson. *Fast Company*, August 2000, p. 78.

53. A. Bourdain. Management by fire: A conversation with Chef Anthony Bourdain. *Harvard Business Review*, July 2002, pp. 57–61.

54. C. P. Alderfer. *Existence, Relatedness and Growth: Human Needs in Organizational Settings*. New York: Free Press, 1972.

55. For a discussion of this and other common pitfalls, see S. Kerr. An academy classic: On the folly of rewarding A, while hoping for B. *Academy of Management Executive*, 9, 1995, pp. 7–16.

56. A. N. Kluger and A. DeNisi. The effects of feedback interventions on performance: A historical review, a meta-analysis, and a preliminary feedback intervention theory. *Psychological Bulletin*, 119, 1996, pp. 254–284.

57. W. G. Bennis and R. J. Thomas. *Geeks and Geezers: How Era, Values and Defining Moments Shape Leaders*. Boston: Harvard Business School Press, 2002.

Chapter 15

1. Q. Hardy. All Carly all the time. *Forbes*, December 13, 1999, pp. 138–144; C. Fiorina, Speech at Hewlett-Packard Shareholders Meeting, February 29, 2000; retrieved September 24, 2000, from http://www.hp.com; P. Burrows. Carly's last stand? *Business Week*, December 24, 2001, pp. 63–71; P. Sellers. True grit. *Fortune*, October 14, 2002, pp. 101–110; A. Lashinsky. Now for the hard part. *Fortune*, November 18, 2002, pp. 95–106; G. Anders. *Perfect Enough: Carly Fiorina and the Reinvention of Hewlett-Packard*. New York: Portfolio, 2003.

2. D. L. Daft. *The Leadership Experience*. Mason, Ohio: South-Western, 2002. For more detailed discussions of leadership, see also D. N. Den Hartog and P. L. Koopman. Leader-

ship in organizations. In N. Anderson, D. S. Ones, H. K. Sinangil, and C. Viswesvaran (Eds.), *Handbook of Industrial, Work, and Organizational Psychology*, Vol. 2. Thousand Oaks, CA: Sage, 2001, pp. 166–187; P. G. Northouse. *Leadership: Theory and Practice*. Thousand Oaks, CA: Sage, 2001.

3. G. Anders, *Perfect Enough*.

4. T. Carvell. Your staff hates you. *Fortune*, September 28, 1998, pp. 200–206.

5. J. O. Whitney, T. Parker, and S. Noble. *Power Plays: Shakespeare's Lessons in Leadership and Management*. Old Tappan, NJ: Simon & Schuster, 2000; B. Lee and S. R. Covey. *The Power Principle: Influence with Honor*. New York: Fireside, 1998.

6. B. Fryer. Leading through tough times: An interview with Novell's Eric Schmidt. *Harvard Business Review*, May 2001, pp. 117–123.

7. Executive sweet: Andrea Jung Asian American Wonder Woman. Retrieved April 15, 2003, from http://www.goalsea.com/WW/Jungandrea/jungandrea.html.

8. T. A. Judge, R. Ilies, J. E. Bono, and M. W. Gerhardt. Personality and leadership: A qualitative and quantitative review. *Journal of Applied Psychology*, 87, 2002, pp. 765–780.

9. For a history of work on emotional intelligence, see C. Cherniss. Emotional intelligence: What it is and why it matters. Retrieved from *The Consortium for Research on Emotional Intelligence*, http://www.eiconsortium.org (April 2003).

10. Q. Nguyen Huy. Emotional capability, emotional intelligence and radical change. *Academy of Management Review*, 24, 1999, pp. 325–345; D. Goleman, R. Boyatzis, and A. McKee. Primal leadership: The hidden driver of great performance. *Harvard Business Review*, December 2001, pp. 42–51; C.-S. Wong and K. S. Law. The effects of leader and follower emotional intelligence on performance and attitude. *The Leadership Quarterly*, 13, 2002, pp. 243–274.

11. R. J. Sternberg and V. Vroom. The person versus the situation in leadership. *The Leadership Quarterly,* 13, 2002, pp. 301–323.

12. D. McGregor. The human side of enterprise. *Management Review,* 46(11), 1957, pp. 22–28, reprinted in *Reflections: The SOL Journal,* Fall 2000, pp. 6–14; G. Heil, D. C. Stephens, D. McGregor, and W. G. Bennis. *Douglas McGregor, Revisited: Managing the Human Side of the Enterprise.* New York: John Wiley & Sons, 2000.

13. H. Seifter and P. Economy. *Leadership Ensemble: Lessons in Collaborative Management from the World's Only Conductorless Orchestra.* New York: Henry Holt and Company, 2001; B. Jepson. The Orpheus mystic (and myths). *New York Times,* October 6, 2002, pp. AR32; 38; History of Orpheus. http://www. orpheusnyc.com/about/history.htm (April 2003).

14. R. R. Blake and J. S. Mouton. *The Managerial Grid.* Houston: Gulf, 1985; C. T. Lewis and S. M. Jobs. Conflict management: The essence of leadership. *Journal of Leadership Studies,* November 1993, pp. 47–60.

15. A. G. Robertson and C. L. Walt. The leader within. *Outlook,* June 1999, pp. 19–23.

16. R. F. Littrell. Desirable leadership behaviors of multi-cultural managers in China. *Journal of Management Development,* 21, 2002, pp. 5–74.

17. G. A. Yukl. *Leadership in Organizations,* 4th ed. Upper Saddle River, NJ: Prentice Hall, 1997.

18. L. D. Shaeffer. The leadership journey. *Harvard Business Review,* October 2002, pp. 42–47; quote appears on p. 43.

19. P. Hersey. *The Management of Organizational Behavior: Leading Human Resources,* 8th ed. Escondido, CA: Center for Leadership Studies, 2001.

20. *Source:* P. Hersey. *The Management of Organizational Behavior: Leading Human Resources.* © 2001 Center for Leadership Studies. Used with permission.

21. K. Brooker. It took a lady to save Avon. *Fortune,* October 15, 2001, pp. 203–208; P. Sellers. True grit. *Fortune,* October 14, 2002, pp. 101–110; Business Week Staff. The best (& worst) managers of the year. *Business Week,* January 13, 2003, pp. 8–11; see also Executive sweet: Andrea Jung.

22. W. E. Norris and R. P. Vecchio. Situational leadership theory: A replication. *Group & Organization Management,* 17, 1992, pp. 331–343.

23. *Adapted from* V. H. Vroom. Leadership and the decision-making process. *Organizational Dynamics,* Spring 2000, pp. 82–94.

24. V. H. Vroom. Leadership and the decision-making process. *Organizational Dynamics,* Spring 2000, pp. 82–94. Used with permission.

25. *Adapted from* V. H. Vroom. Leadership and the decision-making process.

26. K. R. Xin and L. H. Pelled. Supervisor–subordinate conflict and perceptions of leadership behavior: A field study. *The Leadership Quarterly,* 14, 2003, pp. 25–40.

27. *Adapted from* B. L. Kirkman and B. Rosen. Powering up teams. *Organizational Dynamics,* Winter 2000, pp. 48–66.

28. C. P. Egri and S. Herman. Leadership in the North American environmental sector: Values, leadership styles, and contexts of environmental leaders and their organizations. *Academy of Management Journal,* 43, 2000, pp. 571–604; F. J. Yammarino, W. D. Spangler, and A. J. Dubinsky. Transformational and contingent reward leadership: Individual dyad and group levels of analysis. *Leadership Quarterly,* 9, 1998, pp. 27–54

29. J. R. McColl-Kennedy and R. D. Anderson. Impact of leadership style and emotions on subordinate performance. *The Leadership Quarterly,* 13, 2002, pp. 545–559.

30. B. M. Bass, D. J. Jung, B. J. Avolio, and Y. Berson. Predicting unit performance by assessing transformational and transactional lead-

ership. *Journal of Applied Psychology,* 88, 2003, pp. 207–218; K. T. Durks and D. L. Ferrin. Trust in leadership: Meta-analytic findings and implications for research and practice. *Journal of Applied Psychology,* 87, 2002, pp. 611–628.

31. *Adapted from* H. H. Friedman, M. Lingbert, and K. Giladi. Transformational leadership: Instituting revolutionary change in accounting. *National Public Accountant,* May 2000, pp. 8–11; B. J. Avolio. *Full Leadership Development: Building the Vital Forces in Organizations.* Thousand Oaks, CA: Sage, 1999; B. J. Avolio and B. M. Bass (Eds.), *Developing Potential across a Full Range of Leadership.* Mahwah, NJ: Erlbaum Associates, 2002.

32. P. LaBarre. Hospitals are about healing; This one is about changing lives. *Fast Company,* May 2002, pp. 64–78.

33. S. E. Ante. The new Blue. *Business Week,* March 17, 2003, pp. 80–88; S. E. Ante and I. Sager. IBM's new boss. *Business Week,* February 11, 2002. Retrieved April 25, 2003, from www.businessweek.com/ magazine/content/02_06/ b3769001.htm.

34. M. A. Berman. Sweating the soft stuff. *Across the Board,* January 1998, pp. 39–43.

35. A. J. Alessandra and T. Allissandra. *Charisma: Seven Keys to Developing the Magnetism That Leads to Success.* New York: Warner Books, 2000; D. De Cremer and D. van Knippenberg. How do leaders promote cooperation? The effects of charisma and procedural fairness. *Journal of Applied Psychology,* 87, 2002, pp. 858–866.

36. Anonymous. Face value: The acceptable face of capitalism? *The Economist,* December 14, 2002, p. 61.

37. B. L. Kirkman and B. Rosen. Powering up teams. *Organizational Dynamics,* Winter 2000, pp. 48–66; N. Turner, J. Barling, O. Epitropaki, V. Butcher, and C. Milner. Transformational leadership and moral

reasoning. *Journal of Applied Psychology,* 87, 2002, pp. 304–311.

38. T. Dvir, D. Eden, B. J. Avolio, and B. Shamir. Impact of transformational leadership on follower development and performance: A field experiment. *Journal of Applied Psychology,* 45, 2002, pp. 735–744.

39. B. M. Bass. Ethics, character, and authentic transformational leadership behavior. *Leadership Quarterly,* 10, 1999, pp. 187–217; C. E. Johnson. *Meeting the ethical challenges of leadership. Casting light or shadow.* Thousand Oaks, CA: Sage, 2002.

40. R. Kark, B. Shamir, and G. Chen. The two faces of transformational leadership: Empowerment and dependency. *Journal of Applied Psychology,* 88, 2003, pp. 246–255; J. J. Sosik and L. E. Megerian. Understanding leader emotional intelligence and performance: The role of self–other agreement on transformational leadership perceptions. *Group & Organization Management,* 24, 1999, pp. 367–390.

41. S. Caudron. Where have all the leaders gone? *Workforce,* December 2002, pp. 29–32; see also W. C. Byham, A. B. Smith, and M. J. Paese. *Grow Your Own Leaders: How to Identify, Develop, and Retain Leadership Talent.* New Jersey: Prentice Hall, 2002.

42. R. Silzer (Ed.). *The 21st Century Executive: Innovative Practices for Building Leadership at the Top.* San Francisco: Jossey-Bass, 2002.

43. H. Row. Is management for me? That is the question. *Fast Company.* February–March 1998, pp. 50–52; see also J. B. Briscoe and D. T. Hall. Grooming and picking leaders using competency frameworks: Do they work? *Organizational Dynamics,* Autumn 1999, pp. 37–52; F. Hesselbein, L. Tiger, R. Gilmartin, F. Smith, C. Tragge-Lakra, and A. Zelznik. Breakthrough leadership. *Harvard Business Review,* December 2001, pp. 54–66.

44. G. P. Hollenbeck. Coaching executive: Individual leader develop-

ment. In R. Silzer (Ed.). *The 21st Century Executive: Innovative Practices for Building Leadership at the Top.* San Francisco: Jossey-Bass, 2002, pp. 137–167.

45. M. Conlin. CEO coaches. *Business Week,* November 11, 2002, pp. 98–104.

46. J. A. Conger and B. Benjamin. *Building Leaders: How Successful Companies Develop the Next Generation.* San Francisco: Jossey-Bass, 1999; M. C. Higgins and K. E. Kram. Reconceptualizing mentoring at work: A developmental network perspective. *Academy of Management Review,* 26, 2001, pp. 264–288.

47. M. Whigham-Desir. Leadership has its rewards. *Black Enterprise,* September 1999, pp. 73–85; American Express Company. http://hoovers.com (October 12, 2000); G. Bell. *In the Black: A History of African Americans on Wall Street.* New York: John Wiley & Sons, 2002; J. A. Bynre and H. Timmons. Tough times for a new CEO. *Business Week,* October 29, 2001. Retrieved April 25, 2003, from http://www.businessweek.com/magazine/content/01_44/b3755001.htm.

48. N. S. Schutte, J. M. Malouf, L. E. Hall, D. J. Haggerty, J. T. Cooper, C. J. Golden, and L. Dornheim. Development and validation of a measures of emotional intelligence. *Personality and Individual Differences,* 25, 1998, pp. 167–177.

Chapter 16

1. *Adapted from* L. Tischler. Bank of (Middle) America. *Fast Company,* March 2003, pp. 104–109; J. Moules. Tellers as marketing tools. *The Banker,* 152(10), 2002, pp. 160–161.

2. J. T. Wood. *Communication in Our Lives.* New York: Wadsworth, 1997.

3. J. Penrose, R. W. Rasberry, and R. Myers. *Advanced Business Communications.* Cincinnati: South-Western, 2001.

4. J. T. Hazer and J. R. Jacobson. Effects of screener self-monitoring

on the relationships among applicant positive self-presentation, objective credentials, and employability ratings. *Journal of Management,* 29, 2003, pp. 119–138; J. A. Breaugh and M. Starke. Research on employee recruitment: So many studies, so many remaining questions. *Journal of Management,* 26, 2000, pp. 405–434.

5. Personal communication with J. Sudduth, vice president, Southwest Bank, Houston, TX, March 2003.

6. D. M. Smith. *Women at Work: Leadership for the Next Century.* Upper Saddle River, NJ: Prentice Hall, 2002, pp. 26–32.

7. V. Manusov and A. R. Trees. "Are you kidding me?" The role of nonverbal cues. *Journal of Communication,* 52, 2002, pp. 640–657.

8. K. M. Hiemstra. Shake my hand: Making the right first impression in business with nonverbal communications. *Business and Communication Quarterly,* 62(4), 1999, pp. 71–74; A. M. Ryan and R. E. Ployhart. Applicants' perceptions of selection procedures and decisions: A critical review and agenda for the future. *Journal of Management,* 26, 2000, pp. 565–606.

9. S. E. Jones and C. D. LeBaron. Research of the relationship between verbal and nonverbal communications. *Journal of Communication,* 52, 2002, pp. 499–523.

10. *Adapted from* J. W. Gibson and R. M. Hodgetts. *Organizational Communication: A Managerial Perspective.* Orlando: Academic Press, 1986, p. 99.

11. Based on E. Hall. *Understanding Cultural Differences.* Yarmouth, ME: Intercultural Press, 1989; M. Munter. *Guide to Managerial Communication,* 6th ed. Upper Saddle River, NJ: Prentice Hall, 2002; Workplace potpourri: Strict etiquette in Japanese firms lives on. *Manpower Argus,* August 1996, p. 11.

12. F. Becker and F. Steele. *Work-place by Design: Mapping the*

High-Performance Workscape. San Francisco: Jossey-Bass, 1995.

13. *Adapted from* I. Ross. Good ch'i helps businesses prosper: Feng Shui practitioners hail ancient Chinese practice as savior to workplace balance. *Northern Ontario Business,* 22(11), pp. 15–16; K. R. Carter. *Move Your Stuff, Change Your Life: How to Use Feng Shui to Get Love, Money and Happiness.* New York: Fireside Books, 2000; K. Lagatree. *Feng Shui at Work: Arranging Your Workspace to Achieve Peak Performance.* New York: Villard Books, 1998.

14. H. Aguinis and C. A. Henle. Effects of nonverbal behavior on perceptions of female employee's power base. *Journal of Social Psychology,* 141, 2001, pp. 537–548.

15. J. R. Carlson and R. W. Zmud. Channel exposition theory and the experiential nature of media richness perceptions. *Academy of Management Journal,* 42, 1999, pp. 153–170.

16. L. M. Hitt and F. X. Fries. Do customers utilize electronic distribution channels? *Management Science,* 48, 2002, pp. 732–749.

17. A. Dragoon. The amazing traveling show. *CIO,* November 1, 2002, pp. 96–101.

18. J. S. Lubin. Dear boss: I'd rather not tell you my name, but. . . . *Wall Street Journal,* June 18, 1997, p. B1.

19. L. Gratton and S. Ghosal. Improving the quality of conversations. *Organizational Dynamics,* 31, 2002, pp. 209–223.

20. S. W. Wellington. *Women of Color in Corporate Management: Opportunities and Barriers.* New York: Catalyst, 1999, pp. 78–80.

21. *Adapted from* D. A. Whetten and K. S. Cameron. *Developing Management Skills.* Reading, MA: Addison-Wesley, 1998, pp. 36–37. Used with permission.

22. D. VandeWalle. A goal orientation model of feedback-seeking behavior. *Human Resource Management,* in press.

23. M. A. Fournier, D. S. Moskowitz, and D. C. Zuroff. Social rank strategies in hierarchical relationships. *Journal of Personality and Social Psychology,* 83, 2002, pp. 425–434.

24. D. Butcher and M. Clarke. Organizational politics. *Organizational Dynamics,* 31, 2002, pp. 35–46.

25. R. Moxley. *Leadership and Spirit.* San Francisco: Jossey-Bass, 1999.

26. *Adapted from* M. R. Solomon and E. W. Stuart. *Marketing,* 2nd ed. Upper Saddle River, NJ: Prentice Hall, 2000, pp. 95–102.

27. A. Joshi, G. Labianca, and P. M. Caliguri. Getting along long distance: Understanding conflict in a multinational team through network analysis. *Journal of World Business,* 37, 2002, pp. 277–285; D. Griffith. The role of communication competencies in international business relationship development. *Journal of World Business,* 37, 2002, pp. 256–265.

28. M. S. Thompson and M. S. Feldman. Electronic mail and organizational communication: Does saying "Hi" really matter? *Organization Science,* 9, 1998, pp. 685–698; J. Yaukey. E-mail out of control for many: Take steps to ease load. *Wall Street Journal,* May 8, 2001, p. F1.

29. C. M. Solomon. Communicating in a global environment. *Workforce,* November 1999, p. 54.

30. These guidelines are abridged from *Ten Commandments for Good Communications.* New York: American Management Association, 1955.

31. D. Charters. Electronic monitoring and privacy issues in business marketing. *Journal of Business Ethics,* 35, 2002, pp. 243–255.

32. Computer Ethics Institute. Ten Commandments of Computer Ethics. http://www.cpsr.org/program/ethics/ (March 2003).

33. *Adapted from* K. D. Kelsey. Computer ethics: An overview of the issues. *Ethics: Easier Said Than Done,* December 15, 1991, pp. 30–33;

T. E. Webber. Does anything go? *Wall Street Journal,* December 8, 1997, pp. R29–31.

34. D. Charters. Electronic monitoring and privacy issues in business-marketing: The ethics of the DoubleClick experience. *Journal of Business Ethics,* 35, 2002, pp. 243–255; C. J. Sykes. *The End of Privacy.* New York: St. Martin's Press, 2000.

35. *Adapted from* L. L. Berry. Clueing in customers. *Harvard Business Review,* February 2003, pp. 100–107; L. Berry. Communicating without words. *Healthcare Design,* September 2002, pp. 15–18; S. H. Haeckel, L. P. Carbone, and L. L. Berry. How to lead the customer experience. *Marketing Management,* January–February 2003, pp. 18–23.

36. *Adapted from* J. S. Osland, D. A. Kolb, and I. M. Rubin. *Organizational Behavior: An Experiential Approach,* 7th ed. Upper Saddle River, NJ: Prentice Hall, 2001, pp. 150–151. Used with permission; J. I. Castican and M. A. Schmeidler. Communication climate inventory. In J. W. Pfeiffer and L. D. Goodstein (Eds.), *The 1984 Annual: Developing Human Resources.* Copyright © 1984 by Pfeiffer and Company, San Diego, CA. Used with permission.

Chapter 17

1. *Adapted from* G. Anders. Roche's new scientific method. *Fast Company,* January 2002, pp. 60–67.

2. E. J. Lawler and B. Markovsky (Eds.). *Social Psychology of Groups: A Reader.* Greenwich, CT: JAI Press, 1995.

3. C. R. Emery and L. D. Fredenall. The effect of teams on firm profitability and customer satisfaction. *Journal of Service Research,* 4, 2002, pp. 217–229.

4. C. Joinson. Teams at work. *HR Magazine,* May 1999, pp. 30–36.

5. N. Steckler and N. Fondas. Building team leader effectiveness: A diag-

nostic tool. *Organizational Dynamics,* Winter 1995, pp. 20–35.

6. R. J. Grossman. Office vs. open space. *HR Magazine,* September 2002, pp. 36–40.

7. *The Hay Report: Compensation and Benefits Strategies for 1997 and Beyond.* New York: Hay Group, 1997.

8. H. Axel. Teaming in the global arena. *Across the Board*, February 1997, p. 56; G. M. Parker, K. B. Clark, and S. C. Wheelwright. *The Product Development Challenge: Competing Through Speed, Quality, and Creativity.* Boston: Harvard Business School Press, 1995; S. A. Mohrman and A. M. Mohrman, Jr. *Designing and Leading Team-Based Organizations: A Workbook for Organizational Self-design.* San Francisco: Jossey-Bass, 1997.

9. P. B. Paulus. Groups, teams and creativity: The creative potential of idea-generating groups. *Applied Psychology: An International Review*, 49, 2000, pp. 237–262; M. A. West and G. Hirst. Cooperation and teamwork for innovation. In M. A. West, D. Tjosvold, and K. G. Smith (Eds.), *International Handbook of Organizational Teamwork and Cooperative Working.* Chichester, UK: John Wiley & Sons, 2003, pp. 297–319.

10. C. Fishman. Engines of democracy. *Fast Company*, October 1999, pp. 175–202.

11. J. S. Brown. Research that reinvents the corporation. *Harvard Business Review,* August 2002, pp. 105–114.

12. C. Joinson.

13. B. Nagler. Recasting employees into teams. *Workforce*, January 1998, pp. 101–106.

14. R. L. Cross, A. Yan, and M. R. Louis. Boundary activities in "boundaryless" organizations: A case study of a transformation to a team-based structure. *Human Relations*, 56, 2000, pp. 841–859.

15. For several excellent articles describing the work of multinational multidisciplinary teams, see the entire issue of the *Journal of World Business,* Vol. 31, 2003.

16. C. Fishman.

17. B. L. Kirkman and B. Rosen. Powering up teams. *Organizational Dynamics*, Winter 2000, pp. 48–66.

18. *Adapted from* S. E. Jackson, K. E. May, and K. Whitney. Understanding the dynamics of diversity in decision making teams. In R. A. Guzzo, E. Salas, and Associates (Eds.), *Team Effectiveness and Decision Making in Organizations.* San Francisco: Jossey-Bass, 1995, pp. 204–261; see also J. R. Hackman. *Leading Teams: Setting the Stage for Great Performances.* Boston: Harvard Business School, 2002; S. Holland, K. Gaston, and J. Gomes. Critical success factors for cross-functional teamwork in new product development. *International Journal of Management Reviews*, 2, 2000, pp. 231–259.

19. B. D. Janz, J. A. Colquitt, and R. A. Noe. Knowledge worker team effectiveness: The role of autonomy, interdependence, team development, and contextual support variables. *Personnel Psychology*, 50, 1997, pp. 877–904; G. L. Stewart and M. R. Barrick. Team structure and performance: Assessing the mediating role of intrateam process and the moderating role of task type. *Academy of Management Journal*, 43, 2000, pp. 146–163. For extensive descriptions of research relevant to each of the four components, see M. A. West (Ed.), *Handbook of Work Group Psychology.* Chichester, UK: Wiley, 1996.

20. M. Hoegl and H. G. Gemuenden. Teamwork quality and the success of innovative projects: A theoretical concept and empirical evidence. *Organization Science*, 12, 2001, pp. 435–449; S. W. Lester, B. M. Meglina, and M. A. Korsgaard. The antecedents and consequences of group potency: A longitudinal investigation of newly formed work groups. *Academy of Management Journal*, 45, 2002, 352–368.

21. Copyright © South-Western College Publishing. All rights reserved.

The items listed here are based on a version of this survey that appears in South-Western's *Team Handbook,* 1996.

22. K. T. Dirks. The effects of interpersonal trust on work group performance. *Journal of Applied Psychology*, 84, 1999, pp. 445–555; A. Edmondson. Psychological safety and learning behavior in work teams. *Administrative Science Quarterly*, 44, 1999, pp. 350–383; T. L. Simons and R. S. Peterson. Task conflict and relationship conflict in top management teams: The pivotal role of intragroup trust. *Journal of Applied Psychology*, 85, 2000, pp. 102–111.

23. Adapted and modified from B. W. Tuckman and M. A. C. Jensen. Stages of small-group development revisited. *Group and Organization Studies*, 2, 1977, pp. 419–442; B. W. Tuckman. Developmental sequence in small groups. *Psychological Bulletin*, 63, 1965, pp. 384–389; C. J. G. Gersick. Marking time: Predictable transitions in task groups. *Academy of Management Journal*, 32, 1989, pp. 274–309; A. Chang, P. Bordia, and J. Duck. Punctuated equilibrium and linear progression: Toward a new understanding of group development. *Academy of Management Journal*, 46, 2003, pp. 106–117.

24. K. A. Jehn and E. A. Mannix. The dynamic nature of conflict: A longitudinal study of intragroup conflict and group performance. *Academy of Management Journal*, 44, 2001, pp. 238–251; M. A. Marks, J. E. Mathieu, and S. J. Zaccaro. A temporally based framework and taxonomy of team processes. *Academy of Management Review*, 26, 2001, pp. 356–375.

25. R. S. Dooley and G. E. Fryzell. Attaining decision quality and commitment from dissent: The moderating effects of loyalty and competence in strategic decision-making teams. *Academy of Management Journal*, 42, 1999, pp. 389–402.

26. M. J. Waller, M. E. Zellmer-Bruhn, and R. C. Giambatista.

Watching the clock: Group pacing behavior under dynamic deadlines. *Academy of Management Journal, 45,* 2002, pp. 1046–1055.

27. M. J. Stevens and M. A. Campion. The knowledge, skill, and ability requirements for teamwork: Implications for human resource management. *Journal of Management,* 20, 1994, pp. 503–530; A. M. O'Leary-Kelly, J. J. Martocchio, and D. D. Frink. A review of the influence of group goals on group performance. *Academy of Management Journal,* 37, 1994, pp. 1285–1301.

28. For a more detailed discussion, see M. A. West. The human team: Basic motivations and innovations. In N. Anderson, D. S. Ones, H. K. Sinangil, and C. Viswesvaran (Eds.), *Handbook of Industrial, Work, and Organizational Psychology,* Vol. 2. London: Sage, 2001, pp. 270–288; M. A. Korsgaard, S. E. Brodt, and H. J. Sapienza. Trust, identity, and attachment: Promoting individuals' cooperation in groups. In M. A. West, D. Tjosvold, and K. G. Smith (Eds.), *International Handbook of Organizational Teamwork and Cooperative Working.* Chichester, UK: John Wiley & Sons, 2003, pp. 113–130.

29. J. W. Bishop and E. D. Scott. An examination of organizational and team commitment in a self-directed team environment. *Journal of Applied Psychology,* 85, 2000, pp. 439–450.

30. S. F. Gale. No sacred cows, small or large. *Workforce,* February 2003, pp. 60–62.

31. A. Zander. *Making Groups Effective,* 2nd ed. San Francisco: Jossey-Bass, 1994.

32. B. Mullen, T. Anthony, E. Salas, and J. E. Driskell. Group cohesiveness and quality of decision making: An integration of tests of the groupthink hypothesis. *Small Group Research,* 25, 1994, pp. 189–204; S. M. Miranda. Avoidance of groupthink: Meeting management using group support systems. *Small Group Research,* 25, 1994, pp. 105–136.

33. K. M. Eisenhardt, J. L. Kahwajy, and L. J. Bourgeois III. Conflict and strategic choice: How top management teams disagree. *California Management Review,* 39, 1997, pp. 42–62.

34. Hay Group. *Top Teams: Why Some Work and Some Don't.* Philadelphia, PA: Hay Group, 2001.

35. G. Imperator. Their specialty? Teamwork. *Fast Company,* January–February 2000, pp. 54–56.

36. For a discussion of how managers and team members handle disciplinary problems, see R. C. Liden, S. J. Wayne, T. A. Judge, R. T. Sparrowe, M. L. Kraimer, and T. M. Franz. Management of poor performance: A comparison of manager, group member and group disciplinary decisions. *Journal of Applied Psychology,* 84, 2000, pp. 835–851.

37. S. Adams and L. Kydoniefs. Making teams work: Bureau of Labor Statistics learns what works and what doesn't. *Quality Progress,* January 2000, pp. 43–48; R. Ginnett. The essentials of leading a high-performance team. *Leadership in Action,* 18(6), 1999, pp. 1–5; P. E. Tesluk and J. E. Mathieu. Overcoming roadblocks to effectiveness: Incorporating management of performance barriers into models of work group effectiveness. *Journal of Applied Psychology,* 84, 1999, pp. 200–217; V. U. Druskat and D. C. Kayes. The antecedents of team competence: Toward a fine-grained model of self-managing team effectiveness. *Research on Managing Groups and Teams,* 2, 1999, pp. 221–231.

38. R. Wageman. How leaders foster self-managing team effectiveness: Design choices versus hands-on coaching. *Organization Science,* 12, 2001, pp. 557–577.

39. D. C. Ganster and D. J. Dwyer. The effects of understaffing on individual and group performance in professional and trade occupations. *Journal of Management,* 21, 1995, pp. 175–190.

40. A. P. Hare. Group size. *American Behavioral Scientist,* 24, 1981, pp. 695–708; G. G. Rutte. Social loafing in teams. In M. A. West, D. Tjosvold, and K. G. Smith (Eds.), *International Handbook of Organizational Teamwork and Cooperative Working.* Chichester, UK: John Wiley & Sons, 2003, pp. 361–378.

41. E. Sundstrom, K. P. DeMeuse, and D. Futrell. Work teams: Applications and effectiveness. *American Psychologist,* 45, 1990, pp. 120–133; K. G. Smith and Associates. Top management team demography and process: The role of social integration and communication. *Administrative Science Quarterly,* 39, 1994, pp. 412–438.

42. B. L. Kirkman, B. Rosen, C. B. Gibson, P. E. Tesluk, and S. O. McPherson. Five challenges to virtual team success: Lessons from Sabre, Inc. *Academy of Management Executive,* 16(3), 2002, pp. 67–79; for more suggestions about leading virtual teams, see the entire issue of *Organizational Dynamics,* 31(4), 2003, which is devoted to this topic.

43. W. R. Pape. Group insurance: Virtual teams can quickly gather knowledge even from far-flung staff. *Inc. Tech,* No. 2, 1997, pp. 29–31. An interesting study showing how computer-mediated group decision making differs from face-to-face influence is P. L. McLeod, R. S. Baron, M. W. Marti, and K. Yoon. The eyes have it: Minority influence in face-to-face and computer-mediated group discussion. *Journal of Applied Psychology,* 82, 1997, pp. 706–718. Also see D. Armstrong and P. Cole. Managing distances and differences in geographically distributed work groups. In S. E. Jackson and M. N. Ruderman (Eds.), *Diversity in Work Teams: Research Paradigms for a Changing Workplace.* Washington, DC: American Psychological Association, 1996, pp. 187–215.

44. C. M. Solomon. Managing virtual teams. *Workforce,* June 2001, pp. 60–65; A. M. Townsend, S. M.

DeMarie, and A. R. Hendrickson. Virtual teams: Technology and the workplace of the future. *Academy of Management Executive,* 12(3), 1998, pp. 17–29; S. Jarvenpaa and D. E. Leidner. Communication and trust in global virtual teams. *Organization Science,* 10, 1999, pp. 791–815.

45. B. L. Kirkman and D. I. Shapiro. The impact of cultural values on job satisfaction and organizational commitment in self-managing work teams: The mediating role of employee resistance. *Academy of Management Journal,* 44, 2001, pp. 557–569.

46. For a comparison of the United States and several European countries, see J. B. Leslie and E. Van Velsor. *A Cross-National Comparison of Effective Leadership and Teamwork: Toward a Global Workforce.* Greensboro, NC: Center for Creative Leadership, 1998; see also C. B. Gibson and M. E. Zellmer-Bruhn. Metaphors and meaning: An intercultural analysis of the concept of teamwork. *Administrative Science Quarterly,* 46, 2001, pp. 274–303; P. C. Earley and C. B. Gibson. *Multinational Work Teams: A New Perspective.* Mahwah, NJ: Lawrence Erlbaum, 2002.

47. G. A. Neuman and J. Wright. Team effectiveness: Beyond skills and cognitive ability. *Journal of Applied Psychology,* 84, 1999, pp. 376–389; S. Taggar. Individual creativity and group ability to utilize creative resources: A multilevel model. *Academy of Management Journal,* 45, 2002, pp. 315–330.

48. J. Martin. Mercedes: Made in Alabama. *Fortune,* July 7, 1997, pp. 150–158; B. L. Kirkman, C. B. Gibson, and D. L. Shapiro. "Exporting" teams: Enhancing the implementation and effectiveness of work teams in global affiliates. *Organizational Dynamics,* 30(1), 2001, pp. 12–29.

49. A. Edmondson, R. Bohmer, and G. Pisano. Speeding up team learning. *Harvard Business Review,* October 2001, pp. 125–132.

50. H. W. Lane, M. B. Brechu, and D. T. A. Wesley. Mabe's President Luis Berrondo Avalos on teams and industry competitiveness. *Academy of Management Executive,* 13(3), 1999, pp. 9–11.

51. E. Salas, C. A. Bowers, and E. Eden. *Improving Teamwork in Organizations: Applications of Resource Management and Training.* Englewood Cliffs, NJ: Lawrence Erlbaum, 2001; M. A. Marks, M. J. Sabella, C. S. Burke, and S. J. Zaccaro. The impact of cross-training on team effectiveness. *Journal of Applied Psychology,* 87, 2002, pp. 3–13.

52. S. M. Gully, K. A. Incalcaterra, A. Joshi, and J. M. Beaubien. A meta-analysis of team efficacy, potency, and performance: Interdependence and level of analysis as moderators of observed relationships. *Journal of Applied Psychology,* 87, 2002, pp. 819–832.

53. J. W. Dean, Jr., and M. P. Sharfman. Does decision process matter? A study of strategic decision making effectiveness. *Academy of Management Journal,* 39, 1996, pp. 368–396; C. K. W. De Dreu and M. A. West. Minority dissent and team innovation: The importance of participation in decision making. *Journal of Applied Psychology,* 86, 2001, pp. 1191–2000; L. Thompson. Improving the creativity of organizational work groups. *Academy of Management Executive,* 17, 2003, pp. 96–111.

54. S. S. K. Lam and J. Schaubroeck. Improving group decisions by better pooling information: A comparative advantage of group decision support systems. *Journal of Applied Psychology,* 85, 2000, pp. 565–573; for more about the challenges faced by virtual teams, see F. Agarwal. Teamwork in the netcentric organization. In M. A. West, D. Tjosvold, and K. G. Smith (Eds.), *International Handbook of Organizational Teamwork and Cooperative Working.* Chichester, UK: John Wiley & Sons, 2003, pp. 443–462.

55. H. Campbell. Adventures in teamland: Experiential training makes the lesson fun. *Personnel Journal,* May 1996, pp. 56–62; D. Knight, C. C. Durham, and E. A. Locke. The relationship of team goals, incentives, and efficacy to strategic risk, tactical implementation, and performance. *Academy of Management Journal,* 44, 2001, pp. 326–338.

56. J. McAdams and E. J. Hawk. Making group incentives work. *WorldatWork,* Third Quarter 2000, pp. 28–39; G. Parker, J. McAdams, and D. Zielinski. *Rewarding Teams: Lessons from the Trenches.* San Francisco: Jossey-Bass, 2000.

57. C. Fishman.

Chapter 18

1. *Adapted from* J. M. Higgins and C. McAllaster. Want innovation? Then use cultural artifacts that support it. *Organizational Dynamics,* 31(1), 2002, pp. 74–84.

2. H. M. Trice and J. M. Beyer. *Cultures of Work Organizations.* Upper Saddle River, NJ: Prentice-Hall, 1992; N. M. Ashkanasy and C. R. A. Jackson. Organizational culture and climate. In N. Anderson, D. S. Ones, H. K. Sinangil, and C. Viswesvaran (Eds.), *Handbook of Industrial, Work, and Organizational Psychology,* Vol. 2. London: Sage, 2001, pp. 398–415.

3. G. Colvin. The changing art of becoming unbeatable. *Fortune,* November 24, 1997, pp. 299–300.

4. The culture wars (An interview with Allan Kennedy). *Inc.,* 20th Anniversary Issue, 1999, pp. 107–108.

5. R. Suskind. Humor has returned to Southwest Airlines after 9/11 hiatus. *Wall Street Journal,* January 18, 2002, pp. A1, A8.

6. G. B. Voss, D. M. Cable, and Z. G. Voss. Linking organizational values to relationships with external constituencies. A study of nonprofit professional theatres. *Organizational Science,* 11, 2000, pp. 330–347.

7. N. J. Allen and J. P. Meyer. Organizational socialization tactics: A longitudinal analysis of links to

newcomers' commitment and role orientation. *Academy of Management Journal*, 33, 1990, pp. 847–858.

8. P. Hemp. My week as a room-service waiter at the Ritz. *Harvard Business Review,* June 2002, pp. 50–62.

9. C. Lachnit. Cheesy corporate cheers. *Workforce,* October 2002, p. 19.

10. B. Burlingham. What's your culture worth? *Inc.*, September 2001, p. 133; B. Burlingham. *A Stake in the Outcome.* New York: Doubleday, 2002.

11. H. M. Trice and J. M. Beyer. *The Culture of Work Organizations.*

12. C. Salter. Customer service. *Fast Company*, May, 2002, pp. 80–91.

13. H. M. Trice and J. M. Beyer. *The Culture of Work Organizations.*

14. A. R. Jassawalla and H. C. Sashittal. Cultures that support product-innovation processes. *Academy of Management Executive,* 16(3), 2002, pp. 42–54.

15. H. M. Trice and J. M. Beyer. Cultural leadership in organizations. *Organization Science*, 2, 1991, pp. 149–169.

16. S. F. Gale. *Workforce.* February 2003, p. 61.

17. *Adapted from* R. Hooijberg and F. Petrock. On cultural change: Using the competing values framework to help leaders execute a transformational strategy. *Human Resource Management*, 32, 1993, pp. 29–50; R. E. Quinn. *Beyond Rational Management: Mastering the Paradoxes and Competing Demands of High Performance.* San Francisco: Jossey-Bass, 1988.

18. S. G. Harris and K. W. Mossholder. The affective implications of perceived congruence with culture dimensions during organizational transformation. *Journal of Management,* 22, 1996, pp. 527–547.

19. D. A. Morand. The role of behavioral formality and informality in the enactment of bureaucratic versus organic organizations. *Academy of Management Review,* 20, 1995, pp. 831–872.

20. R. Denison and A. K. Mishra. Toward a theory of organizational culture and effectiveness. *Organization Science*, 6, 1995, pp. 204–222.

21. E. H. Schein. What is culture? In P. J. Frost, L. F. Moore, M. R. Louis, C. C. Lundberg, and J. Martin (Eds.), *Reframing Organizational Culture.* Newbury Park, CA: Sage, 1991, pp. 243–253.

22. J. B. Sorensen. The strength of corporate culture and the reliability of firm performance. *Administrative Science Quarterly,* 47, 2002, pp. 70–91; B. Schneider, A. N. Salvaggio, and M. Subirats. Climate strength: A new direction for climate research. *Journal of Applied Psychology,* 87, 2002, pp. 220–229.

23. N. Varchaver. Who's the king of Delaware? *Fortune,* May 13, 2002, pp. 125–130.

24. M. J. Mandel. The new economy: It works in America. Will it go global? *Business Week*, January 31, 2000, pp. 73–77; P. Giles. The importance of HR in making your merger work. *Workspan*, August 2000, pp. 16–20; M. L. Marks and P. E. Mirvis. Making mergers and acquisitions work: Strategic and psychological preparation. *Academy of Management Executive,* 15(2), 2001, pp. 80–94; S. E. Jackson, M. A. Hitt, and A. S. DeNisi (Eds.), *Managing Knowledge for Sustained Competitive Advantage.* San Francisco: Jossey-Bass, 2003.

25. *The Role of Human Capital in M&A: A White Paper Based on Opinions of 132 Senior Executives Worldwide.* London: Towers Perrin, 2002.

26. J. P. van Oudenhove and K. I. van der Zee. Successful international cooperation: The influence of cultural similarity, strategic differences, and international experience. *Applied Psychology: An International Review,* 51, 2002, pp. 633–653.

27. L. Saari and M. Erez. Cross-cultural diversity and employee attitudes. Paper presented at the annual conference of the Society for Industrial and Organizational Psychology, Toronto, April 2002.

28. G. Apfelthaler, H. J. Muller, and R. R. Rehder. Corporate global culture as a competitive advantage: Learning from Germany and Japan in Alabama and Austria? *Journal of World Business*, 37, 2002, pp. 108–118.

29. D. A. Ralston, Y. Kai-Cheng, X. Wang, R. H. Terpstra, and H. Wei. The cosmopolitan Chinese manager: Findings of a study on managerial values across the six regions of China. *Journal of International Management,* 2, 1996, pp. 79–109.

30. B. McConnell. Fun at work good for business, HR pros say in survey. *HR News,* January 2003, p. 18.

31. L. Clemetson. Hispanics now largest minority, census shows. *New York Times,* January 22, 2003, pp. A1, A17; S. Greenhouse. Foreign workers at highest level in seven decades. *New York Times*, September 4, 2000, pp. A1, A12.

32. V. Liberman. Tough issues. *Across the Board,* May/June 2002, pp. 22–29.

33. L. C. Lancaster and D. Stillman. *When Generations Collide.* New York: Harper Business, 2002; T. Gutner. A balancing act for Gen X women. *Business Week,* January 21, 2002, p. 82; W. G. Bennis and R. J. Thomas. *Geeks and Geezers: How Era, Values and Defining Moments Shape Leaders.* Boston: Harvard Business School Press, 2002.

34. H. M. Trice and J. M. Beyer. *The Culture of Work Organizations,* pp. 175–253; R. Goffee and G. Jones. What holds the modern company together? *Harvard Business Review,* November–December 1996, pp. 133–148.

35. Pitney Bowes Web page, http://www.pitneybowes.com (June 5, 2000).

36. S. Wetlaufer. Common sense and conflict: An interview with Disney's Michael Eisner. *Harvard Business Review*, January–February 2000, pp. 113–124.

37. U1: Mary Ellen Heyde. *Fast Company*, April 2000, p. 112.

38. C. Daniels. The most powerful black executives in America. *Fortune,* July 22, 2002, pp. 60–80.

39. S. Foley, D. L. Kidder, and G. N. Powell. The perceived glass ceiling and just perceptions: An investigation of Hispanic law associates. *Journal of Management,* 28, 2002, pp. 471–496.

40. S. H. Mehta. What minorities really want. *Fortune*, July 10, 2000, pp. 181–186; E. LaBlanc, L. Vanderkam, and K. Vella-Zarb. America's best 50 companies for minorities. *Fortune*, July 10, 2000, pp. 190–200.

41. K. H. Griffeth and M. R. Hebl. The disclosure dilemma for gay men and lesbians: "Coming out" at work. *Journal of Applied Psychology*, 87, 2002, pp. 191–199.

42. L. Grensing-Pophal. Reaching for diversity. *HR Magazine*, May 2002, pp. 53–56.

43. A study of how the design of affirmative action policies affect reactions to them is reported in D. A. Kravita and S. L. Klineberg. Reactions to two versions of affirmative action among whites, blacks, and Hispanics. *Journal of Applied Psychology*, 85, 2000, pp. 597–611.

44. R. O. Crockett. Memo to the Supreme Court: "Diversity is good for business." *Business Week*, January 27, 2003, pp. 96; L. Greenhouse. Justices look for nuance in race-preference case. *New York Times,* April 2, 2003, pp. A1, A15.

45. K. Townsend. Female partners double thanks to gender initiative. *Financial Times*, May 8, 2000, p. 35.

46. G. Robinson and K. Dechant. Building a business case for diversity. *Academy of Management Executive,* 11(3), 1997, pp. 21–31.

47. T. Kochan, K. Bezrukova, R. Ely, E. S. Jackson, A. Joshi, K. Jehn, J. Leonard, D. Levine, and D. Thomas. The effects of diversity on business performance: Report of the diversity research network. *Human Resource Management Journal,* 42, 2003, pp. 3–22.

48. K. Labich. No more crud at Texaco. *Fortune*, September 6, 1999, pp. 205–212; Rooting out racism. *Business Week*, January 10, 2000, pp. 66–67.

49. J. Cook. Taking the diversity tour. *Human Resources Executive*, May 16, 2000, pp. 80–83; K. Bradsher. Big carmakers extend benefits to gay couples. *New York Times*, June 9, 2000, pp. B1, C12.

50. C. J. Whalen. Closing the pay gap. *Business Week,* August 28, 2000, p. 38.

51. S. F. Gale. Diversity as a recruitment strategy. *Workforce*, February 2002, pp. 68–69.

52. Work–life balance. *Workplace Visions*, No. 4, 2002, p. 3. Based on results of the 2002 Benefits Survey, Society for Human Resource Management.

53. A. Hayashi. Mommy-track backlash. *Harvard Business Review,* March, 1997, pp. 3–42; J. Rothauser, J. A. Gonzalez, N. E. Clarke, and L. L. O'Dell. Family-friendly backlash—fact or fiction? The case of organizations' on-site child care centers. *Personnel Psychology*, 51, 1998, pp. 685–706.

54. Parental leave: Healthier kids. *Business Week,* January 18, 1999, p. 30.

55. C. M. Loder. Merck and Co. breaks new ground for employee child care centers. *Star Ledger,* May 1999, p. 12.

56. L. Himelstein and S. A. Forest. Breaking through. *Business Week*, February 17, 1997, pp. 64–70.

57. A. Markels. A diversity program can prove divisive. *Wall Street Journal*, January 30, 1997, pp. B1, B5.

58. S. Day. Anti-bias task force gives Coca-Cola good marks, but says challenges remain. *New York Times*, September 26, 2002, p. C3

59. J. R. W. Joplin and C. S. Daus. Challenges of leading a diverse workforce. *Academy of Management Executive*, 11(3), 1997, pp. 32–47; J. E. Slaughter, E. F. Sinar, and P. D. Bachiochi. Black applicants' reactions to affirmative action plans: Effects of plan content and previous experience with discrimination. *Journal of Applied Psychology*, 87, 2002, pp. 333–344.

60. S. E. Jackson and A. Joshi. Research on domestic and international diversity in organizations: A merger that works. In N. Anderson, D. S. Ones, H. K. Sinangil, and C. Viswesvaran (Eds.), *Handbook of Work and Organizational Psychology*. Thousand Oaks, CA: Sage, 2001, pp. 206–231.

61. C. Caggiano. Merge now, pay later. *Inc.*, April 2000, pp. 86–96; http://www.cuningham.com/profile/offculture.html (May 15, 2003).

Note: The *n* in selected entries designates a reference. The page number with the R– prefix indicates the page where the note can be found in its entirety. The number following the *n.* is the appropriate footnote number. The number in parentheses indicates the page on which the note reference appears.

Power, 228
Power distance: defined, 78; illustrated, 104
Practices, as element of culture, 517
Pregnancy Discrimination Act, 358
Preparation stage, 248–49
Preventive controls, 267
Principle of affordable loss, 139
Principle of selectivity, 273
Privacy Act, 161
Privatization, 100
Probability, 210
Problem-solving work team, 484–85
Problem types, of decisions, 213–14
Procedural justice, 164
Process innovation, 342
Process view, activity-based costing, 283
Product design, 307–8
Product development strategy, 197
Product differentiation, 82
Productive controversy, 496
Profit center, 118
Profit-sharing plans, 278
Protectionism, 107
Proxemics, 453
Proxy statement, 287
Punishment, 392

Qualitative techniques, 53–54
Quality: defined, 56; dimensions, illustrated, 58; fostering, 252–58; importance of, 58–60, illustrated, 59
Quality circle, 485
Quality viewpoint: of management, 56–61; quality control process of, 56–58
Quota, 108

Radical change: defined, 325; illustrated, 325
Radical innovators, 218
Ratio analysis, 280
Rational decision, 219
Rational–legal authority, 41
Rational model: decision making, 219–26; defined, 219; illustrated, 220
Rationality, 41
Reactive change, 326
Readiness, 427
Real-time enterprise, 220
Receiver, 451–52
Reciprocal interdependence, 317
Reciprocity principle, 111
Recognition, 403–4; illustrated, 404
Recruitment, 364–65
Reengineering, 337
Reference checks, 366
Reinforcement theory: defined, 390; illustrated, 391
Related-business firm, 186
Related diversification, 190
Relationship behavior, 427
Reliable process, 195–96
Representation, 87
Research and development budget, 282
Resistance, anticipating, and reducing, 332–34
Resource allocation, 183
Resource commitment, 115
Responsibility, 302

Restructuring, 336
Results, controlling and diagnosing, 198–99
Résumés, 365–66
Return on investment (ROI), 280
Rewards, 419, 504–5; illustrated, 505; offering, 390–94
Risk, 210–11; defined, 210; illustrated, 212
Routine decisions, 215–16
Rules, 39

Sales budget, 281
Sarbanes-Oxley Act, 153, 157, 187, 287, 292, 293
Satisfaction, 384–86; defined, 384; illustrated, 385
Satisfaction–progression hypothesis, 409
Satisficing, 228
Scapegoating, 229
Scenarios, 246–48; competitor, 246–47; defined, 246; illustrated, 247
Scientific management, 44–46
Security needs, 408
Selection, 365–67
Selective perception, 462
Selective perception bias, 226
Self-actualization needs, 408
Self-assessment inventory, 28–33
Self-awareness, of leaders, 421–22; defined, 421; illustrated, 421
Self-control, leaders, 422; defined, 422; illustrated, 421
Self-management competency, 24–25, 134; defined, 24; illustrated, 26
Self-managing work team, 486–87; defined, 486; illustrated, 487, 502
Selling style, 429
Semantics, 465
Sender, 449–51
Sequential interdependence, 317
Shared assumptions, 512
Shared purposes, 419
Sigma, 56
Simulation, 245–46; defined, 245; illustrated, 245
Single-business firm, 186
Situational interview, 366
Situational Leadership® Model, 427–30; defined, 427; illustrated, 428
Skill variety, 400
Skunkworks, 144
Small-business owners, 128–29
Social audit: defined, 170; illustrated, 170
Social awareness, leaders, 422; defined, 422; illustrated, 421
Social change, 101
Social performance, evaluating, 169–71
Social responsibility, stakeholder, 165–71
Social skill, defined, 422; illustrated, 421
Social value, of human resources, 356–57
Socialization: defined, 87, 514; element of culture, 514
Solution types, of decisions, 214–15
Source of advantage, 199
Space, 453
Span of control, 301–2
Specialization, 300

Stakeholder control, 268
Stakeholder social responsibility, 165–71
Stakeholders, 165–67; defined, 165; illustrated, 166; pressures of, 167, illustrated, 168; primary, 165; secondary, 165
Standards, 273
Statistical process control, 56
Status, 463
Stereotyping, 463
Storming stage, of work team development, 493
Strategic action competency, 20–22, 132–33; defined, 20; illustrated, 22
Strategic business unit (SBU), 188
Strategic goals, 270–71
Strategic levels, 187–93; illustrated, 188
Strategic planning, 179–83; defined, 179; illustrated, 184; preparation, 197
Strategic questions, 183–85
Strategic target, 199
Strategy: alliance, 117–18, 189; backward integration, 189; business-level, 191–92; concentric diversification, 190; corporate-level, 187–91; cost leadership, 200–1; customer-focused, learning organizations, 346; defined, 182; developing, 196–97; differentiation, 200; exporting, 115–16; finance, 192; focused cost leadership, 201; focused differentiation, 200; forward integration, 189; franchising, 116–17; functional-level, 192–93; global, 118–20; horizontal integration, 189; international business, 114–20, illustrated, 115; licensing, 116; market development, 197; market penetration, 196; marketing, 192; multidomestic, 118; operations, 192; planning, 176–205; product development, 197; technology's role, 89–90; upstream, 189
Strengths, diagnosing, 195–96; illustrated, 197
Strong culture, 519
Subculture. See Organizational subculture.
Subjective probability, 211
Subsidy, 108
Substitute goods and services, 82
Suppliers, 83–84
Survey feedback, 338
Sustainable development, 167
Symbol: defined, 514–15; as element of culture, 514
System: closed, 52; concepts, 51–52; defined, 51; integration through, 314–16; mechanistic, 314; open, 52; organic, 314; types, 52–53
Systems analysis, 51
Systems viewpoint, of management, 51–54; assessing, 54; defined, 51; illustrated, 52; qualitative techniques used in, 53–54

Taboos, 517
Tacit knowledge, 239
Tactical planning, 183; defined, 183; illustrated, 184; preparation for, 198
Tariff, 107
Task behavior, 427

Task force, 485
Task identity, 400
Task significance, 400
Team building, 339
Team design, 497–99
Team member selection, 501
Team proximity, 498
Team training, 368–69, 501–4; illustrated, 504
Teams. *See* Work teams.
Teamwork competency, 18–20, 134; defined, 18; illustrated, 21
Technical innovation, 341–42; defined, 341; illustrated, 343
Technical proficiency attribute, of entrepreneurs, 132
Technological change, 335–36
Technological forces, 89–92
Technological interdependence: defined, 316; illustrated, 316
Technology: defined, 55; enabling, 239; information, 335; integration through, 316–17; role in distribution, 91–92; role in manufacturing, 90–91; role in strategy, 89–90
Telling style, 428
Tempered radicals: defined, 326; illustrated, 326
Territory, 453; illustrated, 454
Tests, 366–67; cognitive ability, 366; performance, 367; personality, 366
Theory X, 423–24, 425, 426, 440; defined, 423; illustrated, 423
Theory Y, 423–24, 425, 426, 440; defined, 424; illustrated, 423
Threats, diagnosing, 194–95
360-degree appraisal, 374
Time-and-motion study, 44

Time-driven model, illustrated, 432
Time orientation, 101–2
Time to market, 484
Title VII of the Civil Rights Act, 528; defined, 357
Top managers, 13–14
Total quality management, 56, 324, 326; defined, 56
TQM team, 485
Trade associations, 100
Trademarks, 111, 116
Traditional authority, 39
Traditional viewpoint, management, 36–47; administrative management, 46; bureaucratic management, 39–44; defined, 38; illustrated, 38, 46; scientific management, 44–46
Training, 367–71; awareness, 534; basic skills, 368; career development, 369; coaching, 370–71, 440; defined, 367; e-learning, 368; mentoring, 369–70, 440; orientation, 367–68; team, 368–69, 501–4
Transformation processes, 52
Transformational leaders, 434–38; defined, 434; illustrated, 435
Transparency principle, 111
Truth in Lending Act, 85
Two-factor theory, 402–4; defined, 402; illustrated, 402

Uncertainty, 211–13; defined, 211; illustrated, 212
Uncertainty avoidance, 78
Unity of command principle, 46
Unrelated-business firm, 186
Upstream strategy, 189
Upward channels, 458
Utilitarian approach, 158, 160

Valence, 396
Value: defined, 75, 513; as element of culture, 513–14; systems, 102–4
Value system, 76
Venture capitalists, 139
Verification stage, of creative process, 249
Vertical design, 301–5
Video Privacy Protection Act, 161
Virtual organization, 310
Virtual work team: defined, 498; illustrated, 500
Vision: articulating and communicating, 330–31; defined, 181; developing, 193–94
Visionary leaders, 434–36
Vroom–Jago Leadership Model, 430–34; defined, 430; illustrated, 432

Weaknesses, diagnosing, 195–96; illustrated, 197
"What if" questions, 246; illustrated, 247
Whistleblowers, 153, 156; defined, 156; and Sarbanes-Oxley Act, 288
Work motivation, 382–415
Work teams, 480–84; causes for poor performance, 497–5; culture, 499–501; defined, 480; feelings, 494–95; framework for effectiveness, 488–89; functional, 485–86; managing, 478–509; multidisciplinary, 486; problem-solving, 484–85; self-managing, 486–87; stages of development, 493–94; terms, illustrated, 481; types, 484–87; virtual, 498, 500; why organizations use, 483–84
Worker Adjustment and Retraining Notification Act, 358
Workforce demographics, 523–26; age, 525, illustrated, 525; defined, 523; ethnicity, 523–25, illustrated, 524; gender, 525–26